376 Decorative Allover Patterns

from Historic Tilework and Textiles

Charles Cahier and Arthur Martin

DOVER PUBLICATIONS, INC.
New York

Published in Canada by General Publishing Company, Ltd.,
30 Lesmill Road, Don Mills, Toronto, Ontario.
Published in the United Kingdom by Constable and Company, Ltd.,
10 Orange Street, London WC2H 7EG.

376 Decorative Allover Patterns from Historic Tilework and Textiles, first published by Dover Publications, Inc., in 1989, contains all the plates from *Suite aux mélanges d'archéologie . . . ,* originally published in two portfolios by A. Morel, Paris, 1868. For details, see the Publisher's Note (based partially on the original French "Préface"), specially written for the present edition.

DOVER *Pictorial Archive* SERIES

Manufactured in the United States of America
Dover Publications, Inc.
31 East 2nd Street
Mineola, N.Y. 11501

Library of Congress Cataloging-in-Publication Data

Cahier, Charles, 1807–1882.
[Carrelages et tissus]
376 decorative allover patterns from historic tilework and textiles / Charles Cahier and Arthur Martin.
p. cm. — (Dover pictorial archive series)
"Contains all the plates from Suite aux Mélanges d'archéologie . . . [Première série: Carrelages et tissus], originally published in two portfolios by A. Morel, Paris, 1868"—T.p. verso.
ISBN 0-486-26146-8
1. Repetitive patterns (Decorative arts) 2. Tiles, Medieval. 3. Tiles, Renaissance. 4. Textile fabrics, Medieval. 5. Textile fabrics, Renaissance. I. Martin, Arthur, 1801–1856. II. Title. III. Title: Three hundred seventy-six decorative allover patterns from historic tilework and textiles. IV. Series.
NK1570.C34 1989
745.4′42—dc20 89-36970
CIP

Publisher's Note

THE QUALITY OF DESIGN in crafted and manufactured products of all types—and in the packaging and advertising of those products—was a primary concern of the great industrial nations in the nineteenth century. Rivalry between France and England for design leadership in Europe was increased by each of the great world's fairs held periodically in London and Paris, beginning with the Crystal Palace Exhibition of 1851. Numerous publications were devoted to visual examples of design masterpieces—often drawing upon all periods of history, since the era was eclectic, making creative use of material from many times and places. The present volume contains all the illustrations from just such a set of portfolios, but a set that is particularly rare and unusual.

The two authors were French Jesuit priests. From its inception in the sixteenth century, the Society of Jesus has had an important educational mission. In the case of Fathers Cahier and Martin, this took the form of art-historical investigations of motifs and patterns from Christian lands, chiefly of the medieval period. The older man, Arthur-Marie Martin, born in 1801, was a gifted amateur artist from childhood. Charles Cahier, born in 1807, shared Martin's antiquarian interests and became a steady coworker. From 1841 to 1844 they issued the plates and commentary for the *Monographie des vitraux de St-Etienne* [or *de la cathédrale*] *de Bourges* (Monograph on the Stained Glass Windows of St-Etienne [the Cathedral] of Bourges), a publication partly funded by their clerical order. Between 1847 and 1856, Cahier and Martin were responsible for four installments of an ongoing project they called *Mélanges d'archéologie, d'histoire et de littérature* (Miscellany of Archaeology, History and Literature). In the latter year, shortly after receiving the Cross of the Legion of Honor for his services to his country (he had also designed actual art projects, including church buildings), Martin died.

Father Martin left behind him not only numerous drawings on paper to be worked up into further publications, but also over 800 drawings that he had made directly on woodblocks, all ready for engraving and subsequent printing. At least half of these blocks contained drawings of tile and textile designs. In 1868, Cahier issued a work in two portfolios based on a selection of these blocks. It was titled *Suite aux mélanges d'archéologie rédigés ou recueillis par les auteurs des Vitraux de Bourges (les PP. Ch. Cahier et Arth. Martin de la Compagnie de Jésus) publiée par le survivant / Première série.—Carrelages et tissus* (Continuation of the "Miscellany of Archaeology" Written or Compiled by the Authors of the "Stained Glass Windows of Bourges" [Fathers C. Cahier and A. Martin of the Society of

Jesus], Published by the Survivor / First Series: Tiles and Textiles). (No further "series" of this "continuation" seem ever to have been published, although Cahier lived until 1882.)

It is this *Suite aux mélanges* from which the illustrations in this Dover volume are reproduced. The original French publication consisted of 250 numbered plates on separate sheets, 125 in each of the two portfolios. Three of the sheets were double-size and folded in two. Of these, one has been slightly reduced for the present volume (the one on Dover page 220) and two have been reproduced without reduction on two Dover pages apiece (Dover pages 213/214 and 221/222). Thus, there are 252 Dover pages of illustrations.

In his foreword to the original publication, Father Cahier pointed out that the patterns came from medieval and Renaissance objects made not only in northern Europe (France, England and Germany) but also in Spain (hence the strong Moorish geometric style evident in many examples). Aside from patterns of wall and floor tiles, which comprise the heart of the book, there are also patterns from textiles, including garments, tapestries and other wall hangings. A number of these textile patterns are based not only on extant examples but also on depictions in paintings of the fifteenth and sixteenth centuries. Cahier refrained from identifying the sources of the various patterns, feeling that only Martin's prodigious memory could have done justice to the documentation. Thus, there were *never* any captions.

The plates proceed, generally, from simpler linear patterns to more complex ones; those that incorporate figural material are reserved for the latter part of the work. The noticeable joins between design elements in many of the tile patterns were left that way on purpose, so that the reader could isolate the elements and emulate the manner of creating the allover patterns. For similar reasons, some of the patterns are shown not completely squared off around the edges. Wherever a corner of a pattern is missing, there was no evidence for its actual appearance, and Cahier decided not to invent a corner purely out of his imagination. For not more than half a dozen patterns out of the 376 included in his publication, he intuitively joined together elements that cannot be proved to have been originally joined.

This impressive monument of scrupulous scholarship, friendship and faith is now made available once more for the same purpose that underlay its first publication: to provide fascinating visual material for practicing artists, designers and craftspeople.

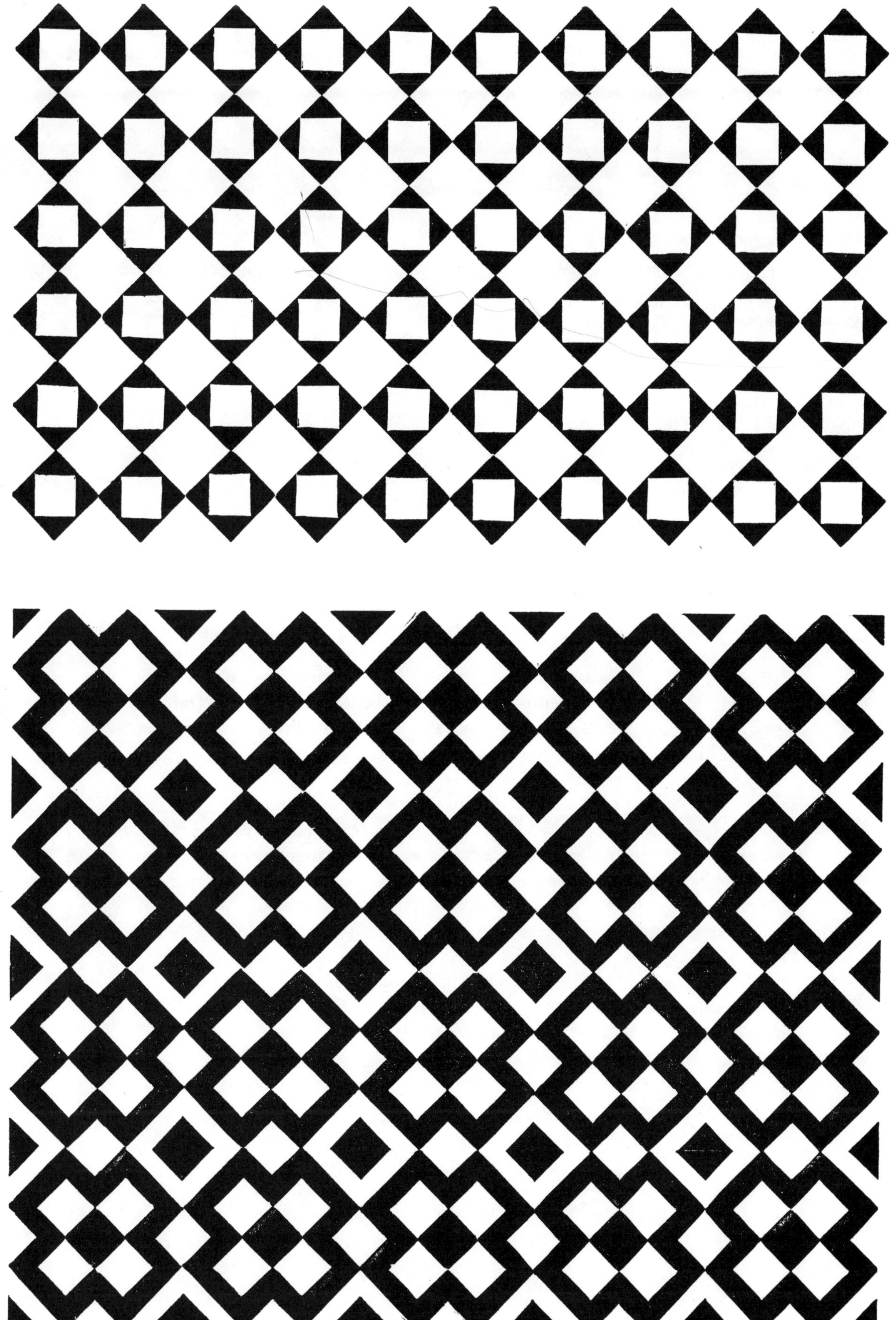

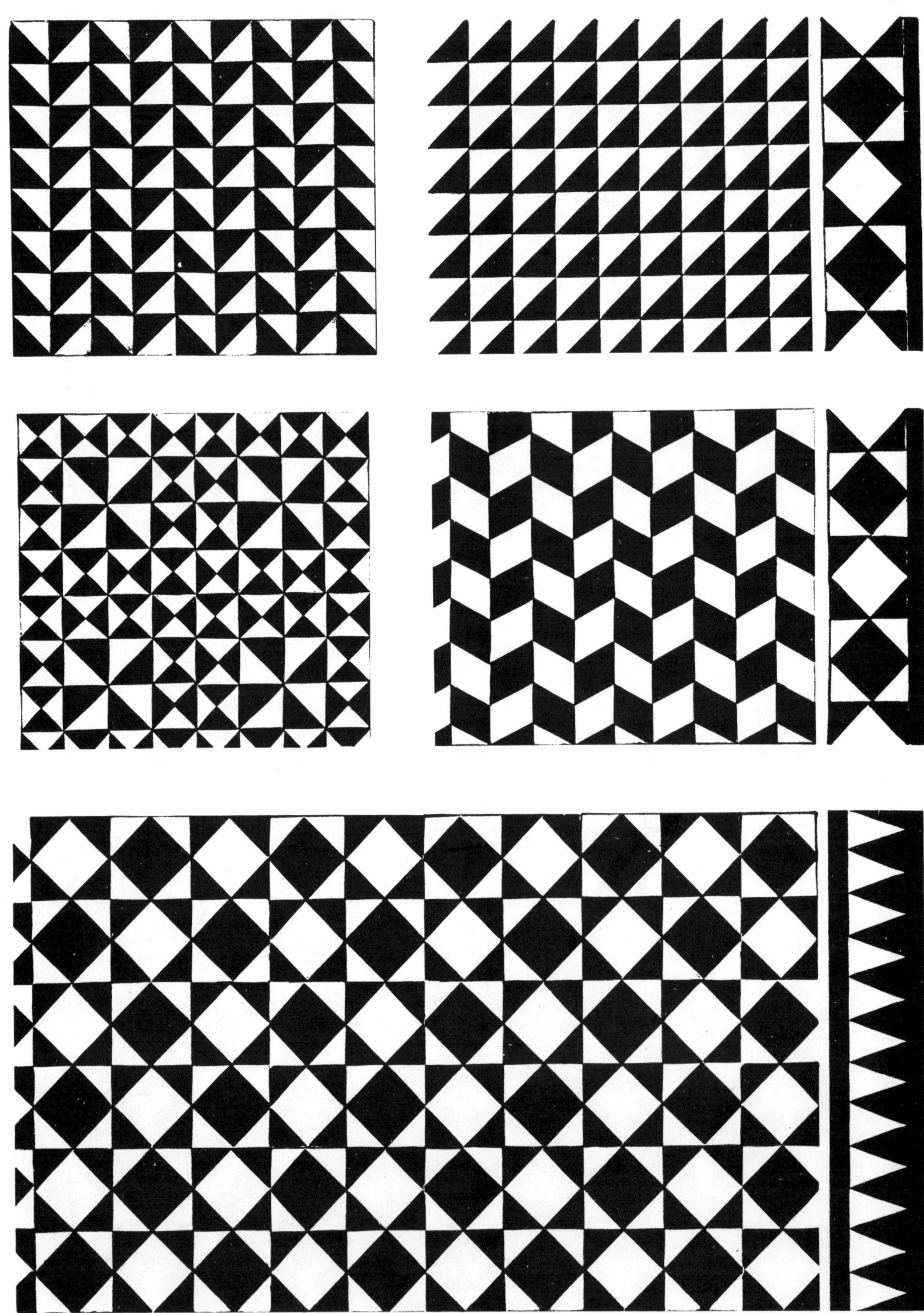

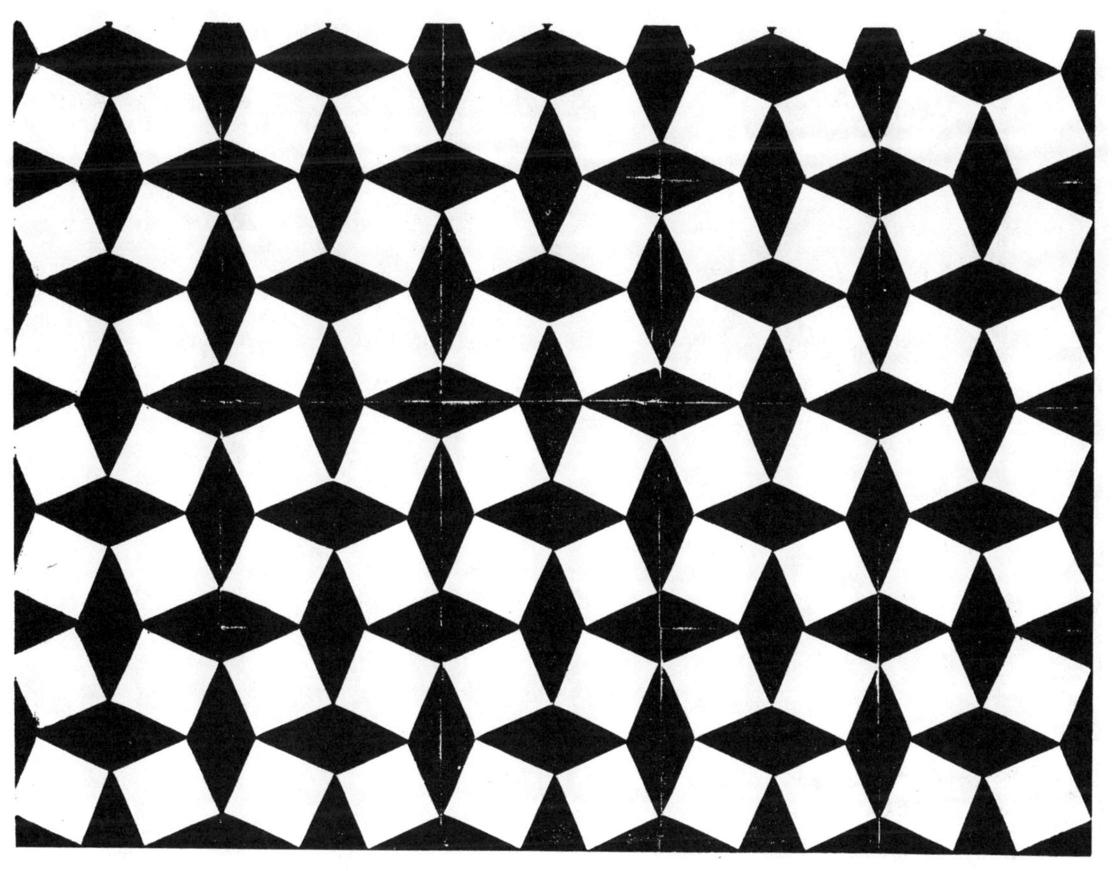

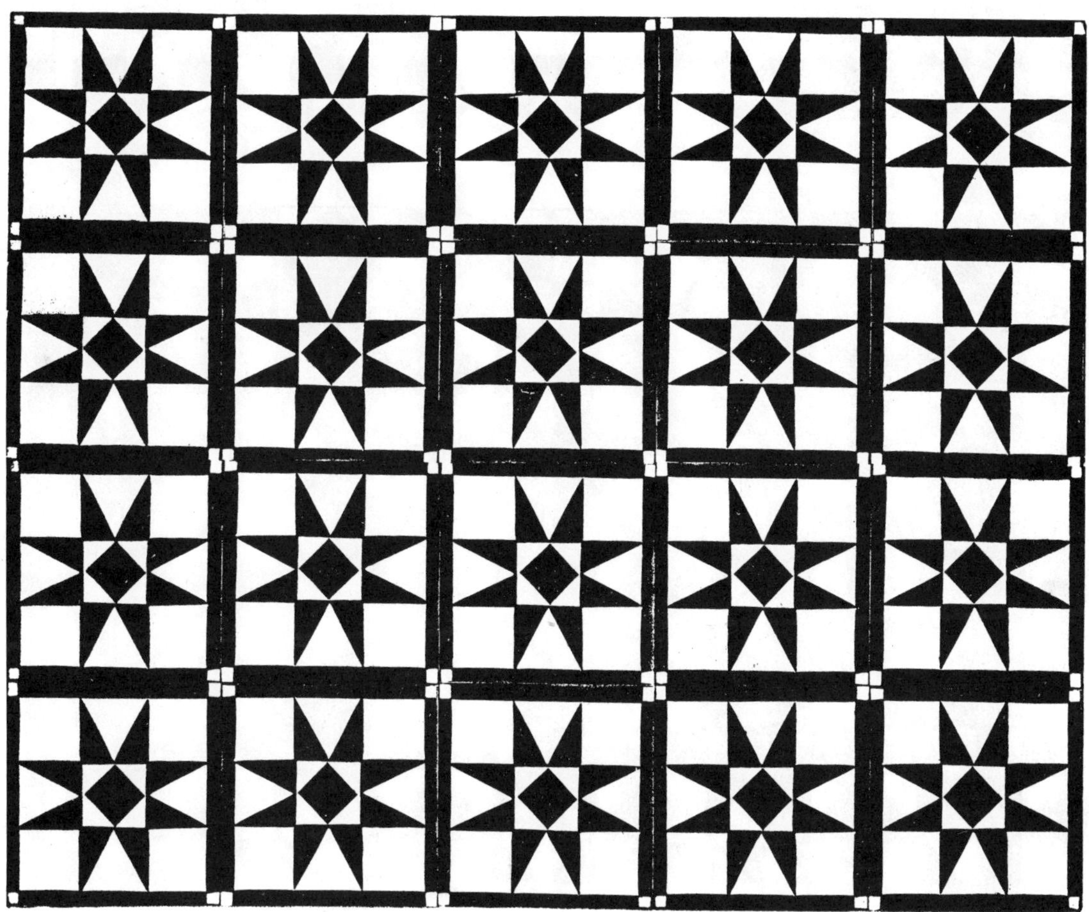

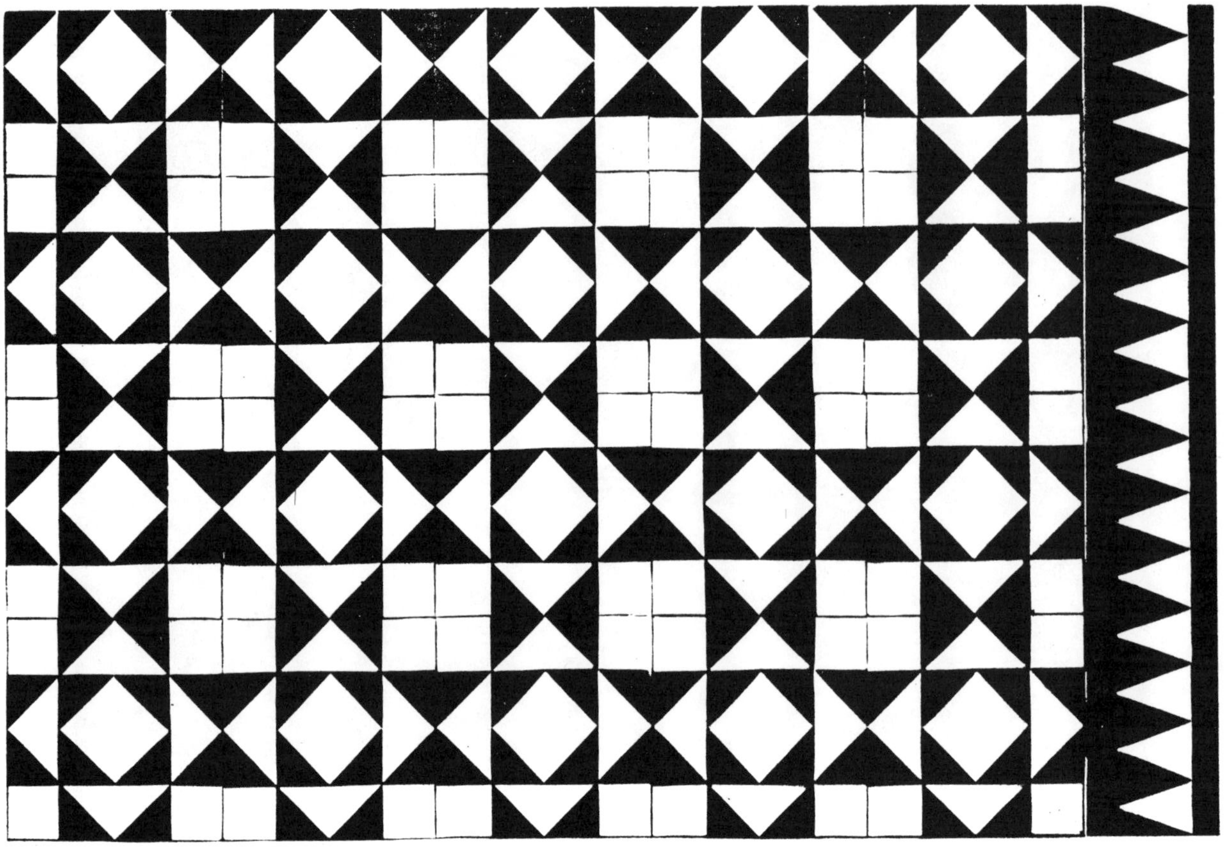

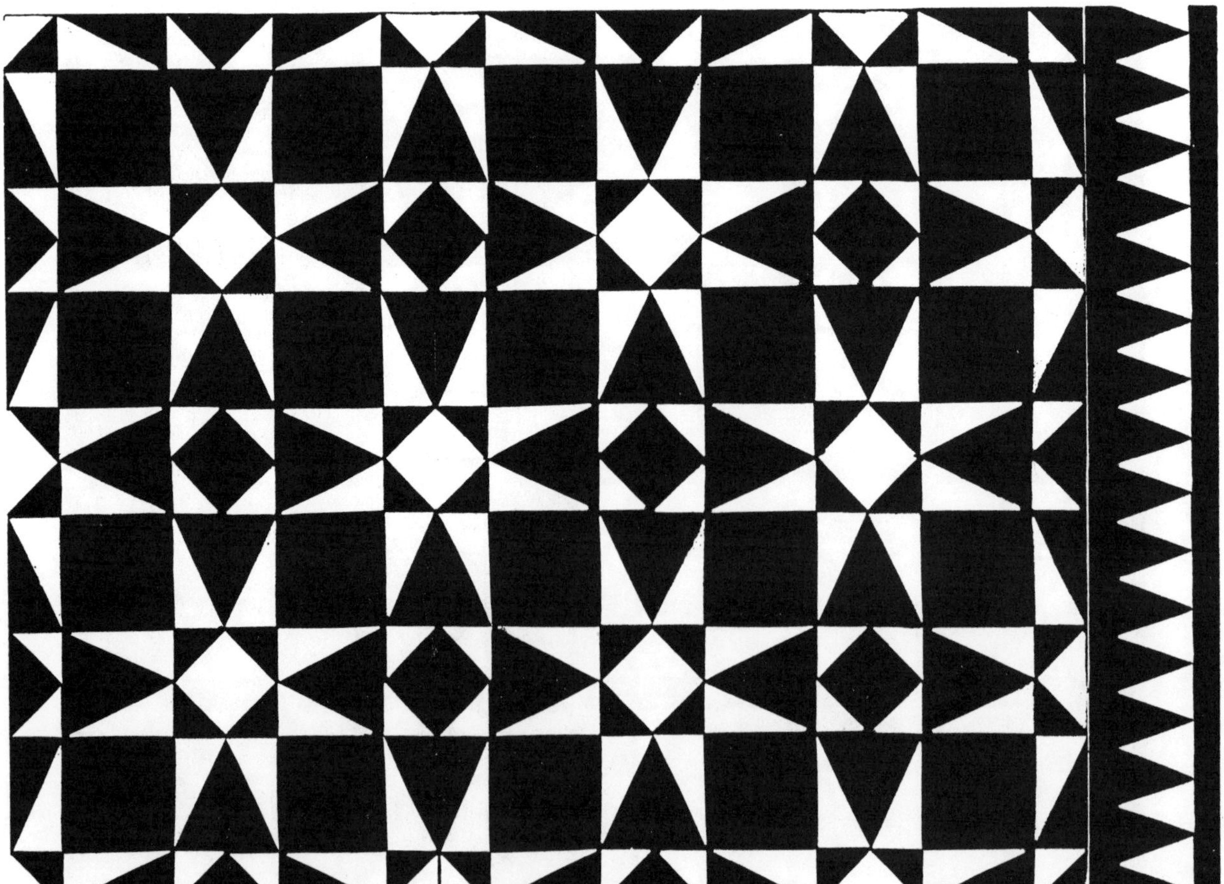

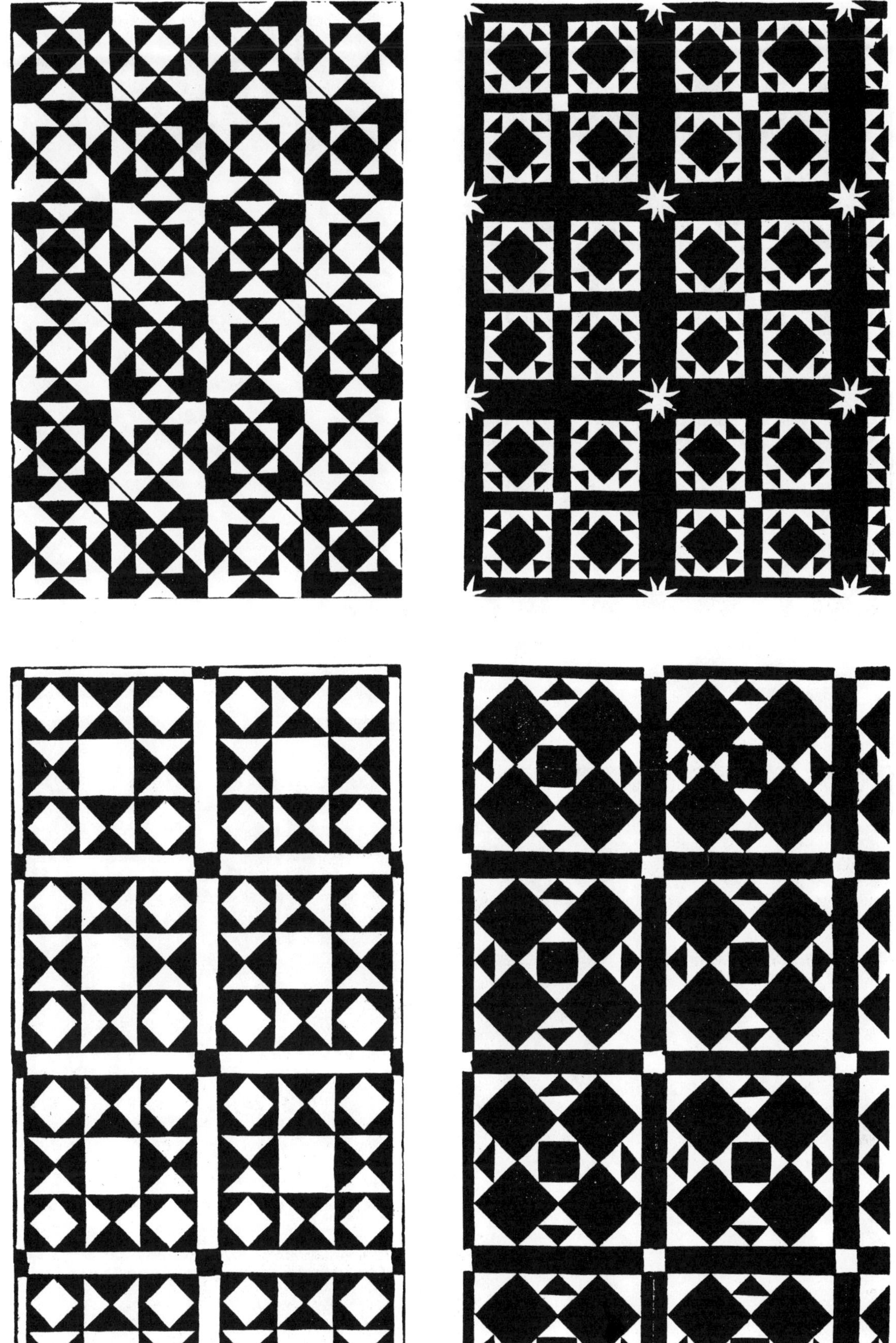

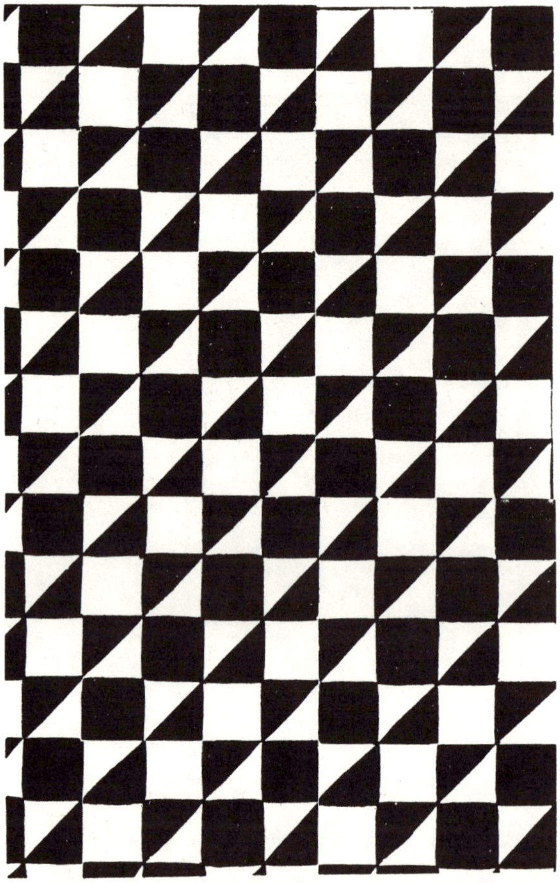

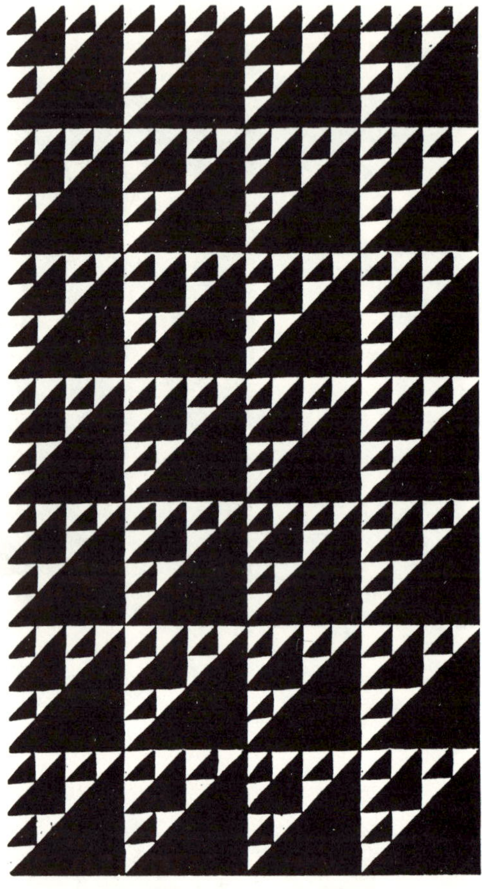

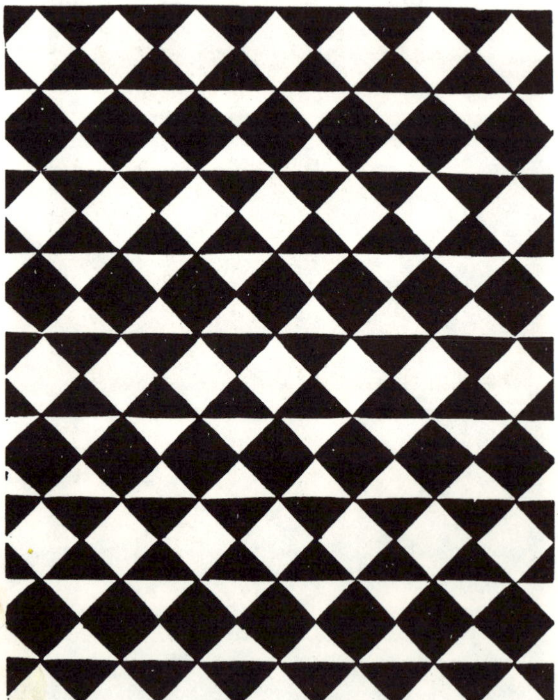

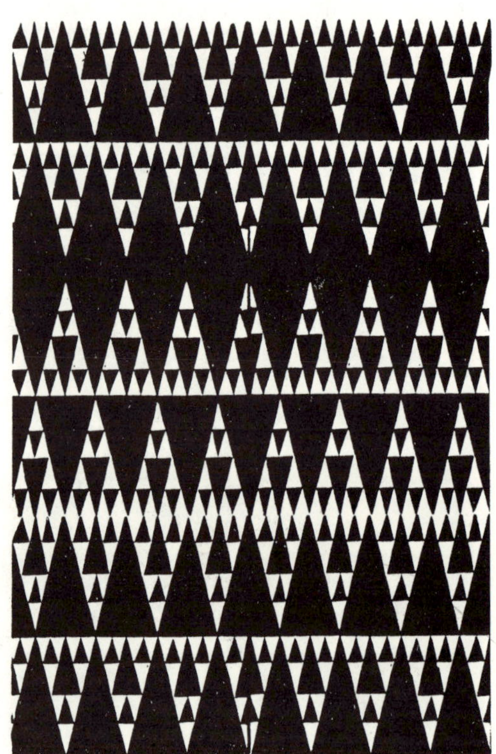

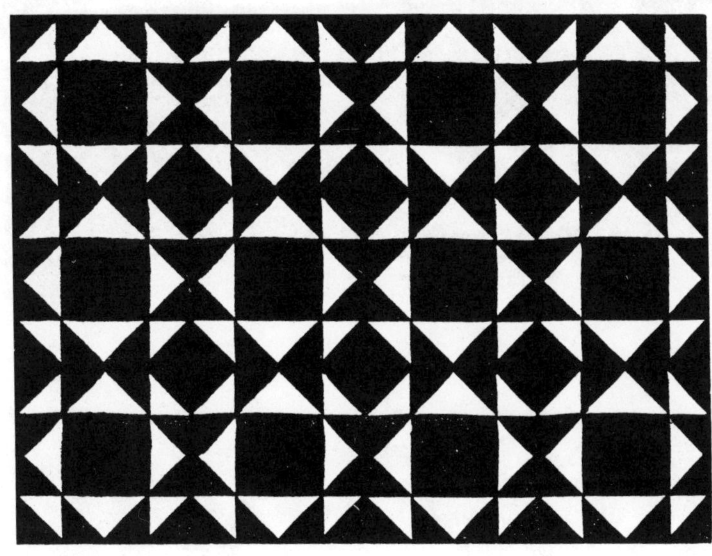

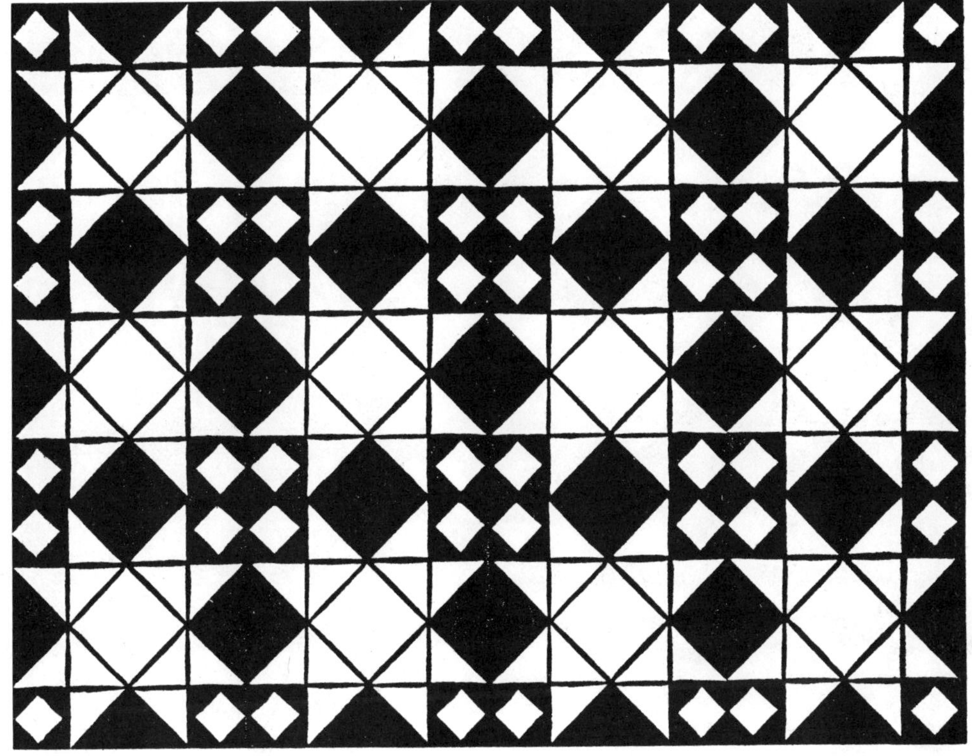

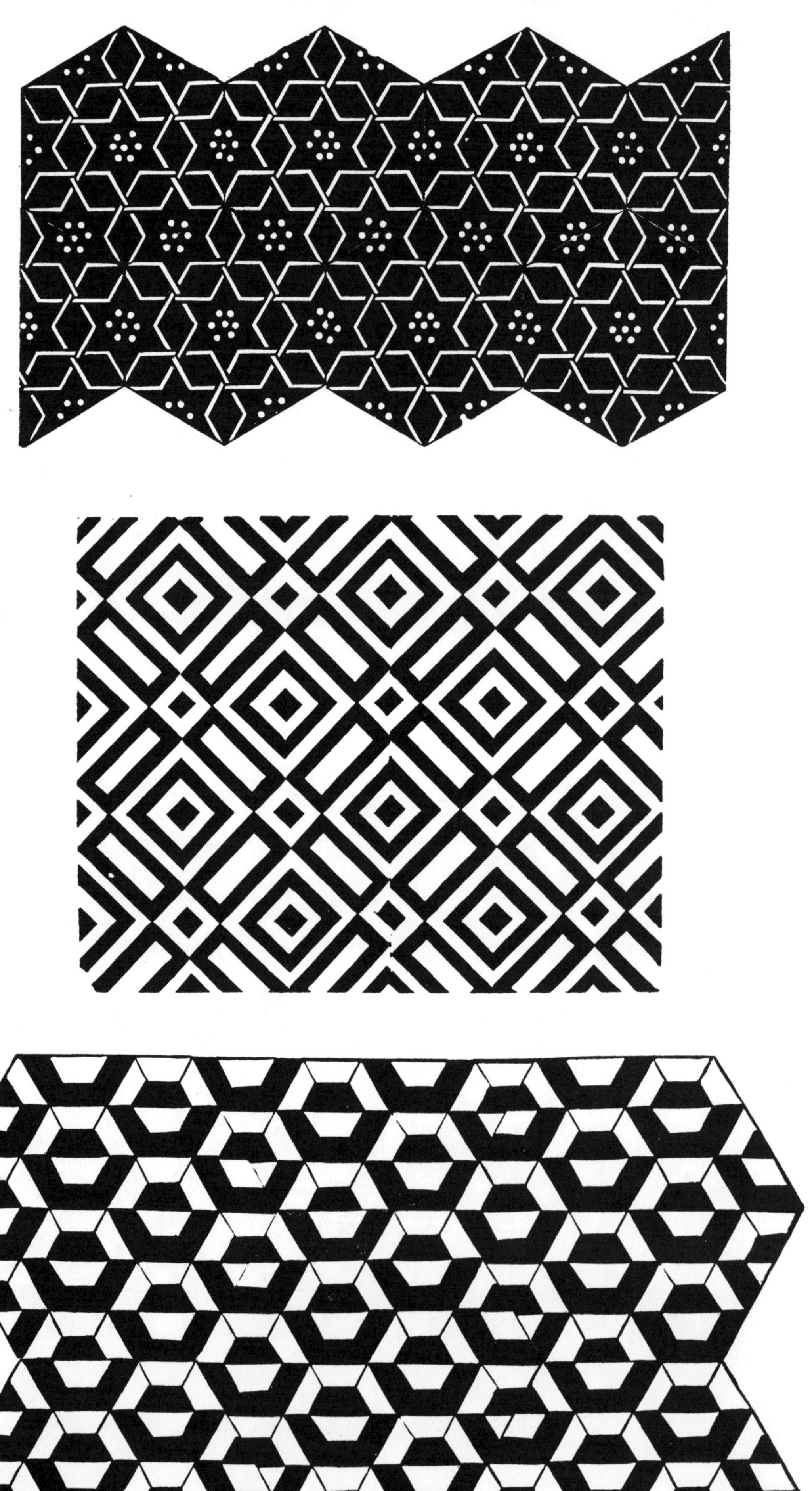

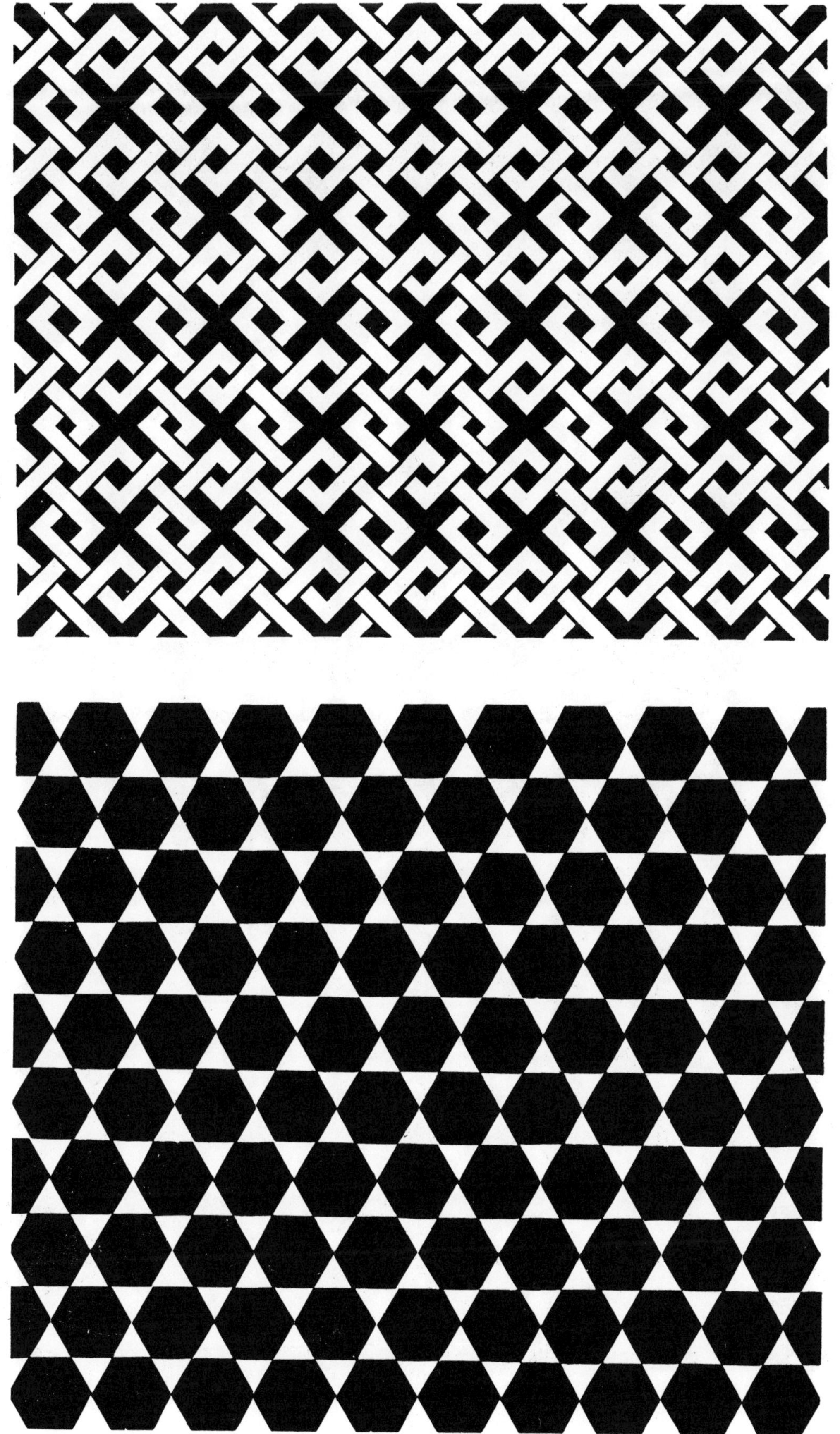

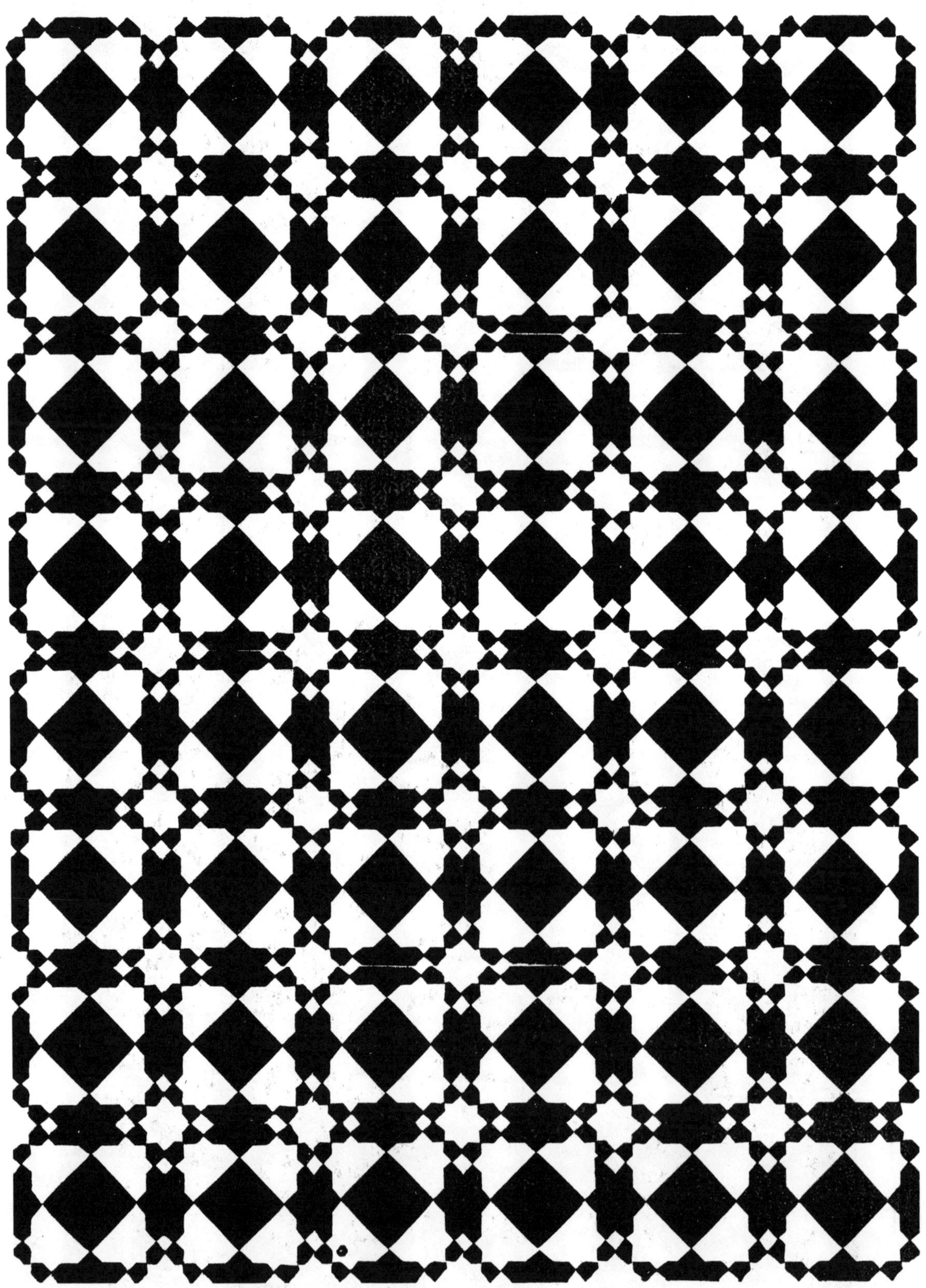

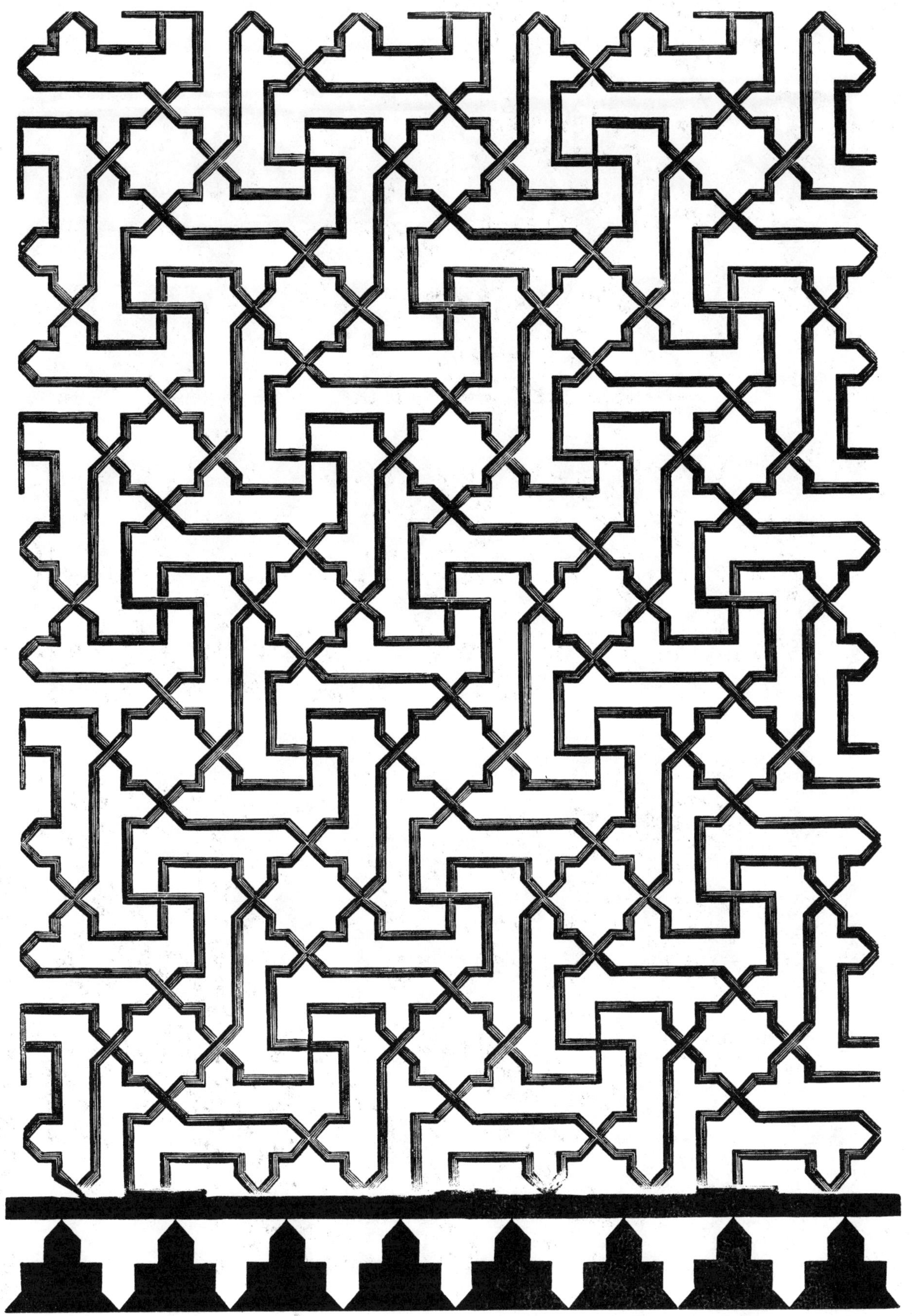

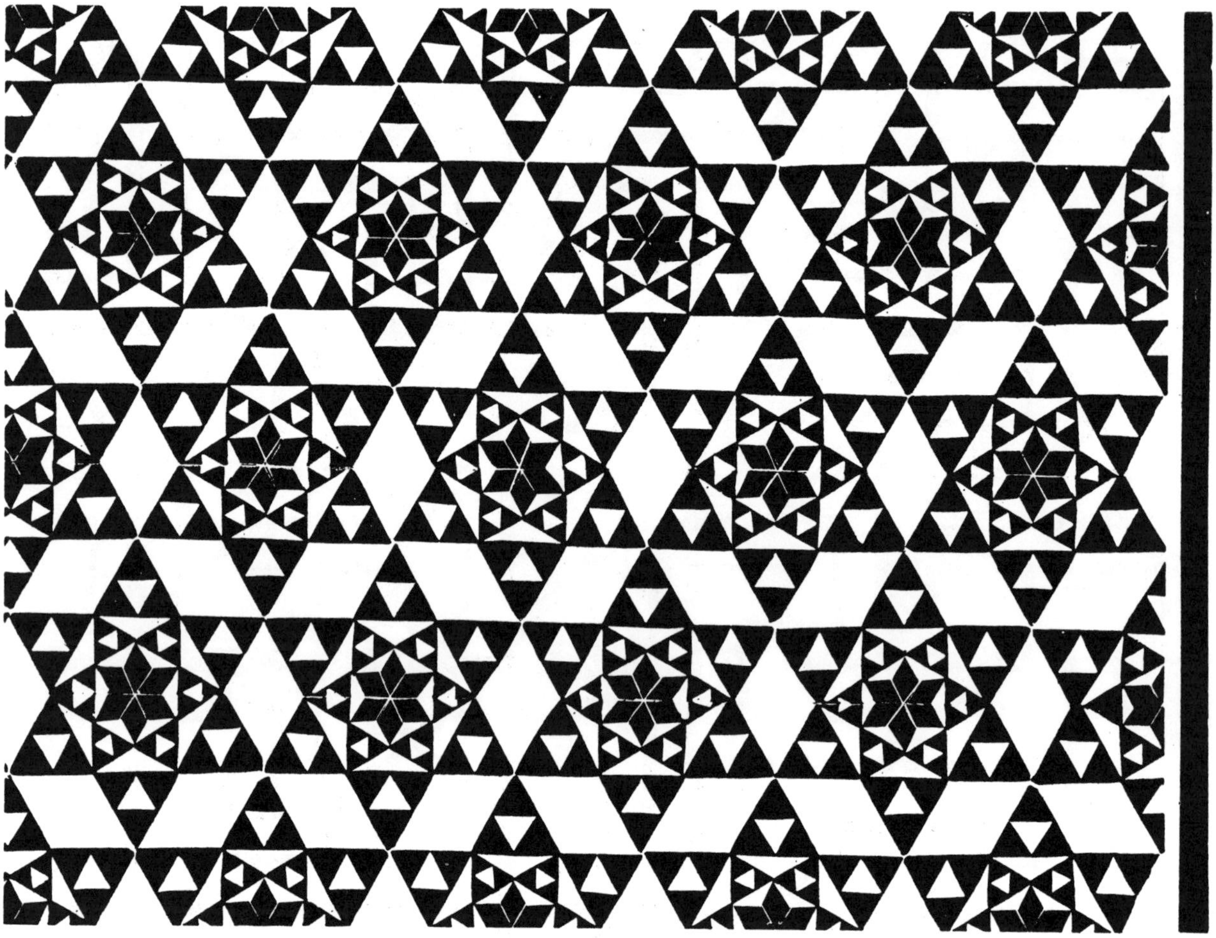

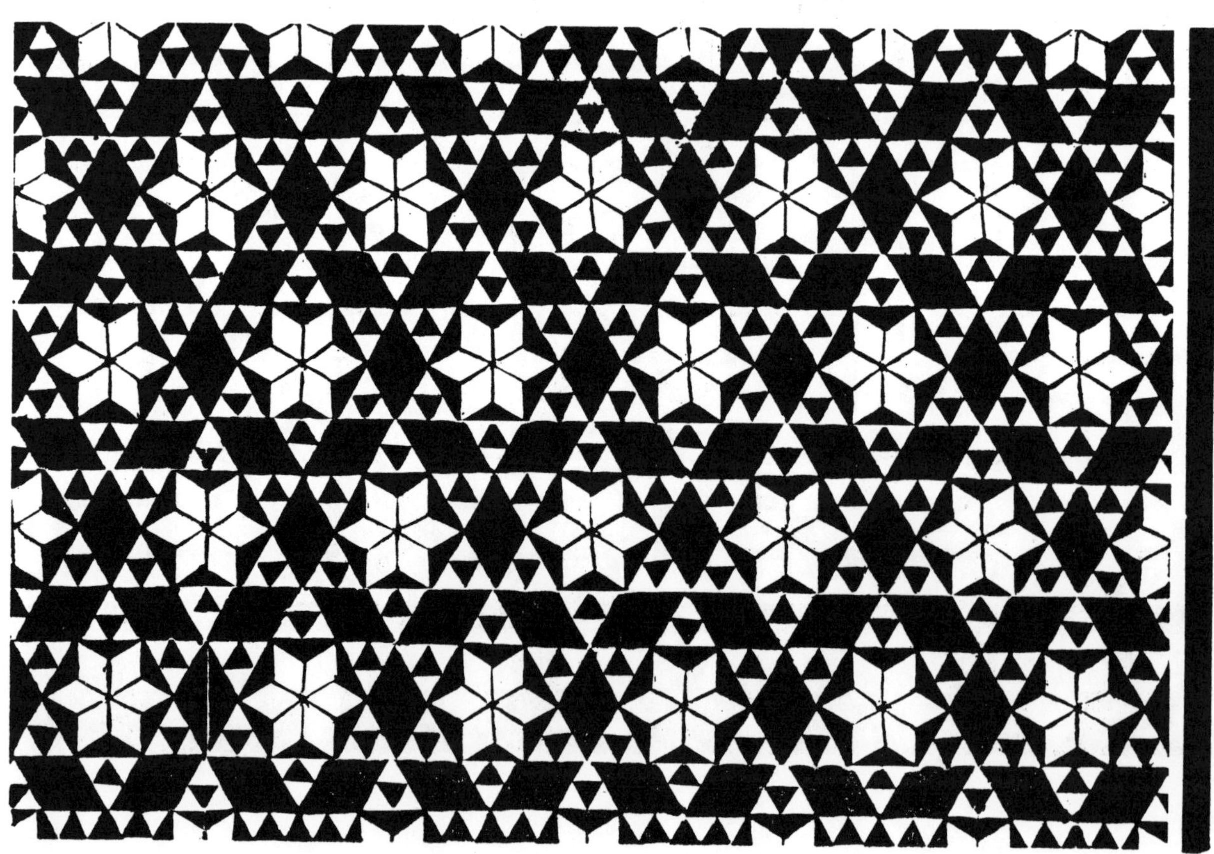

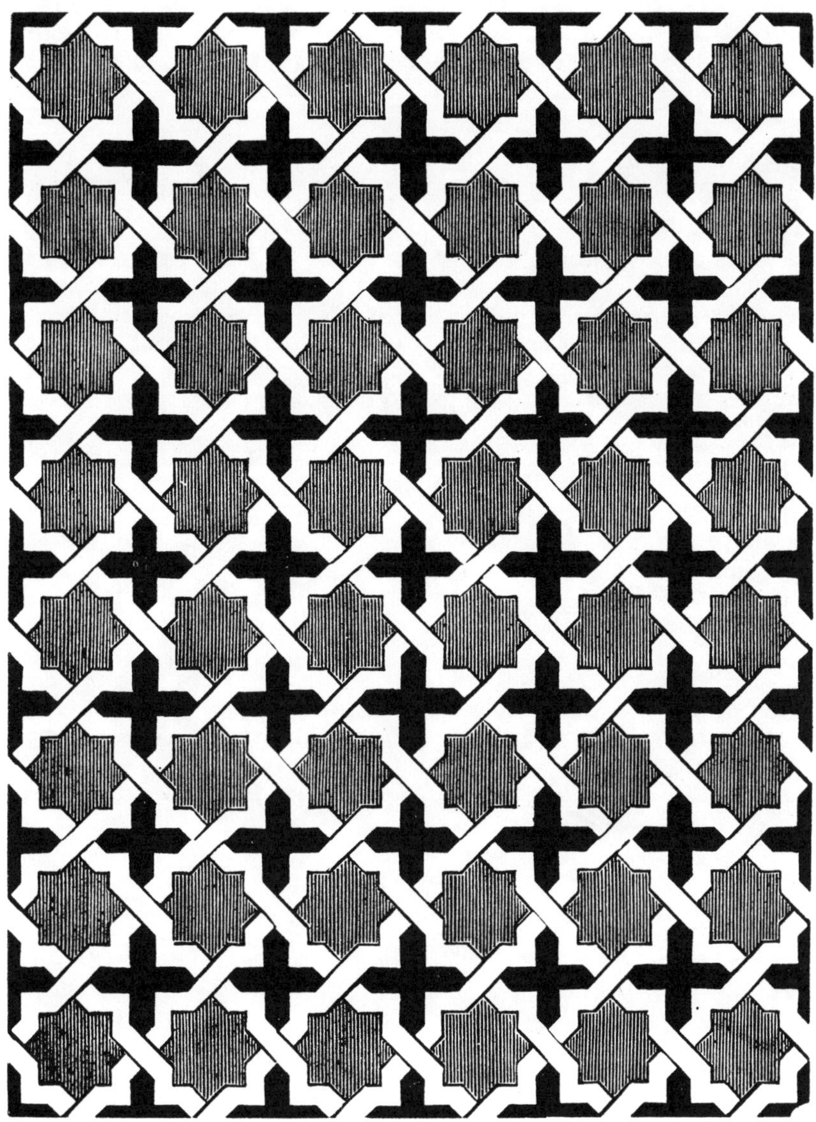

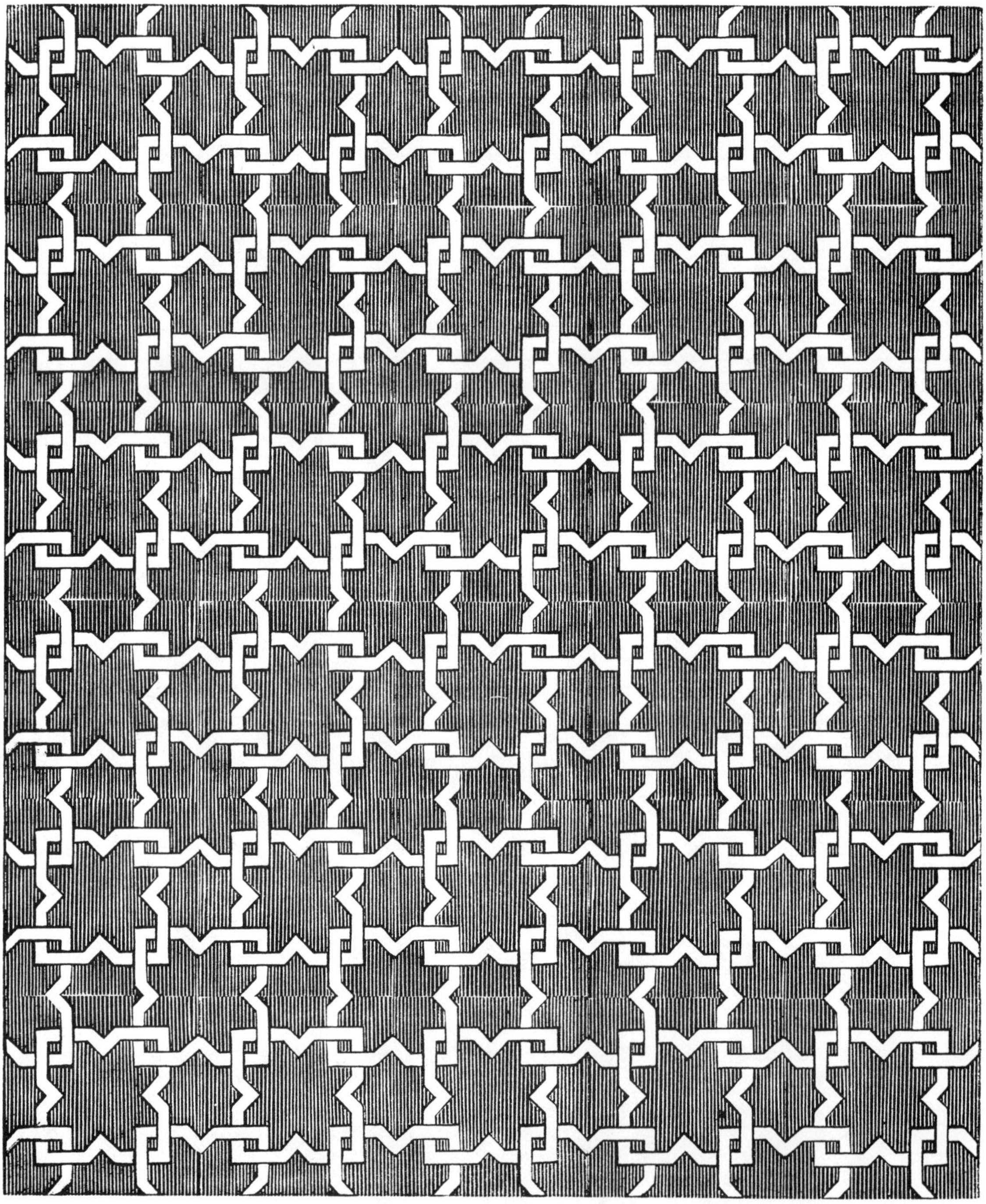

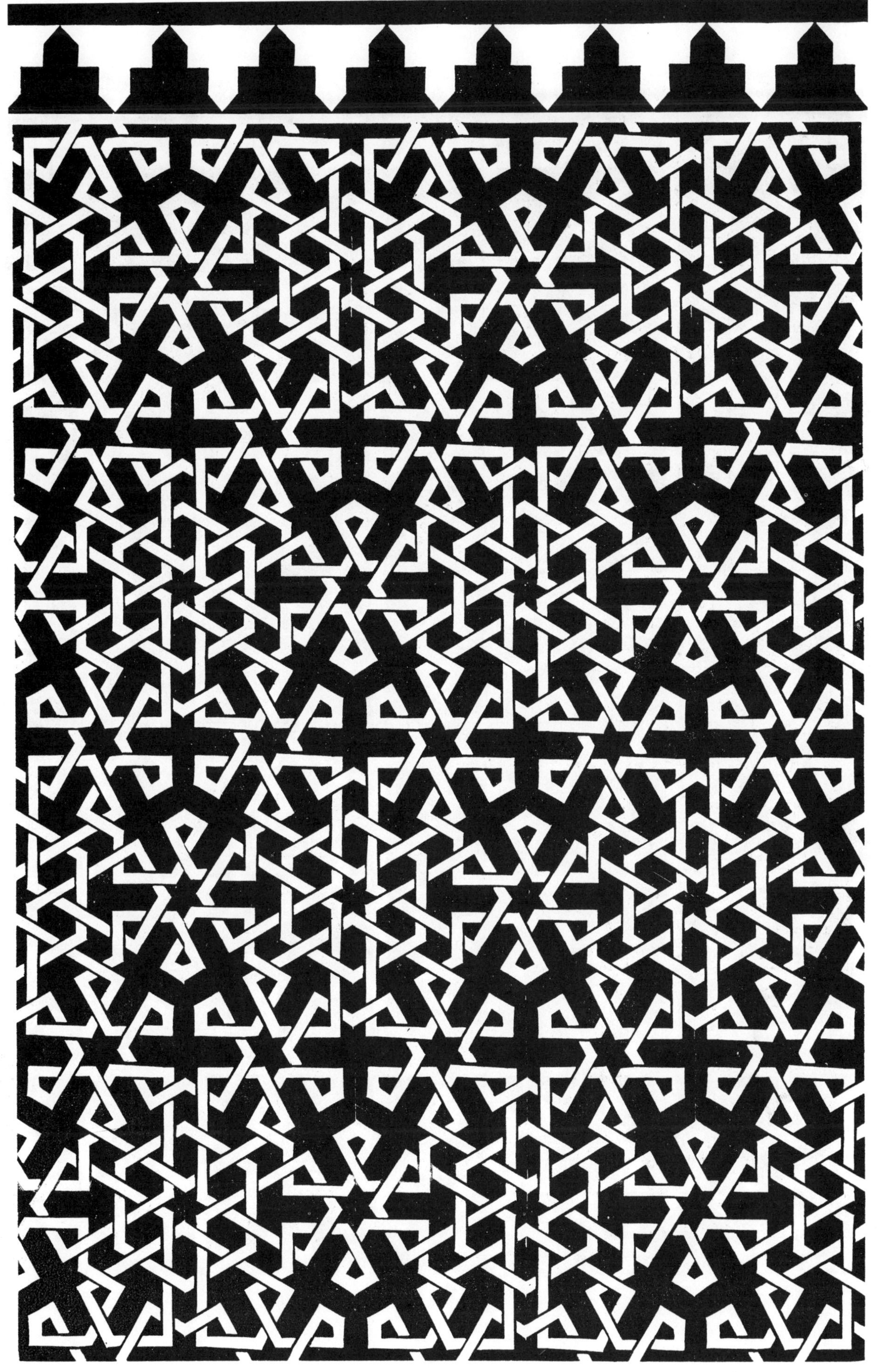

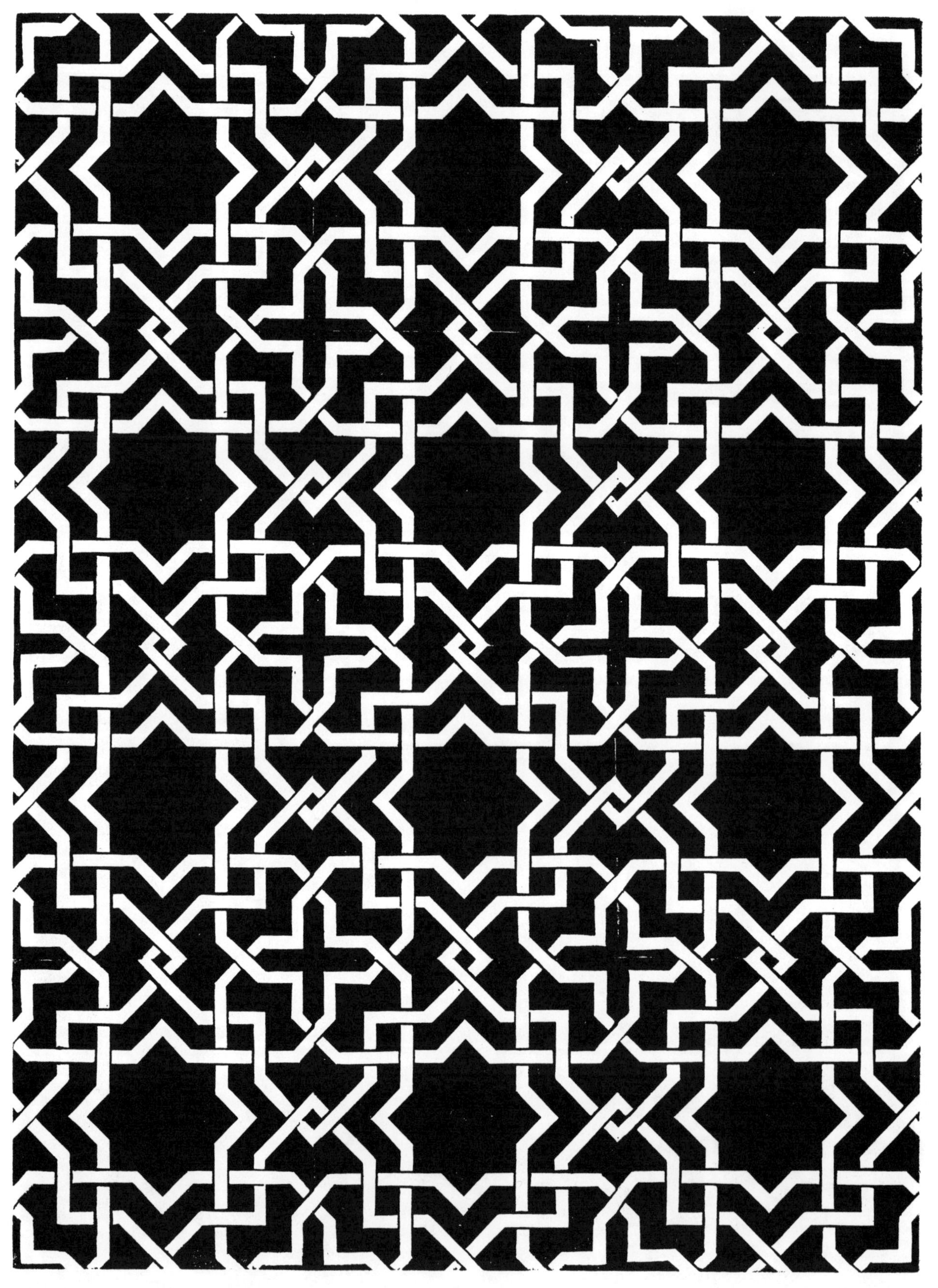

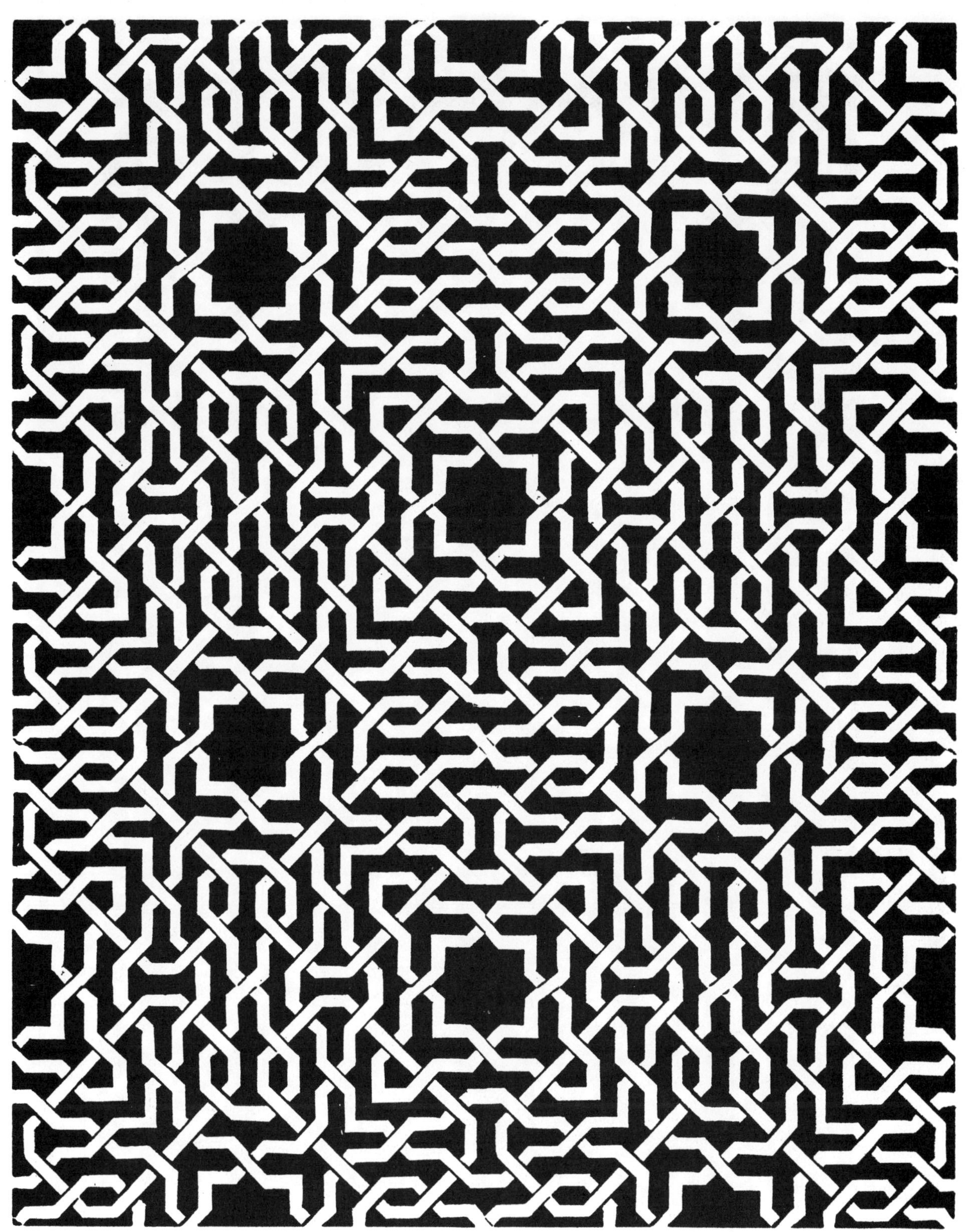

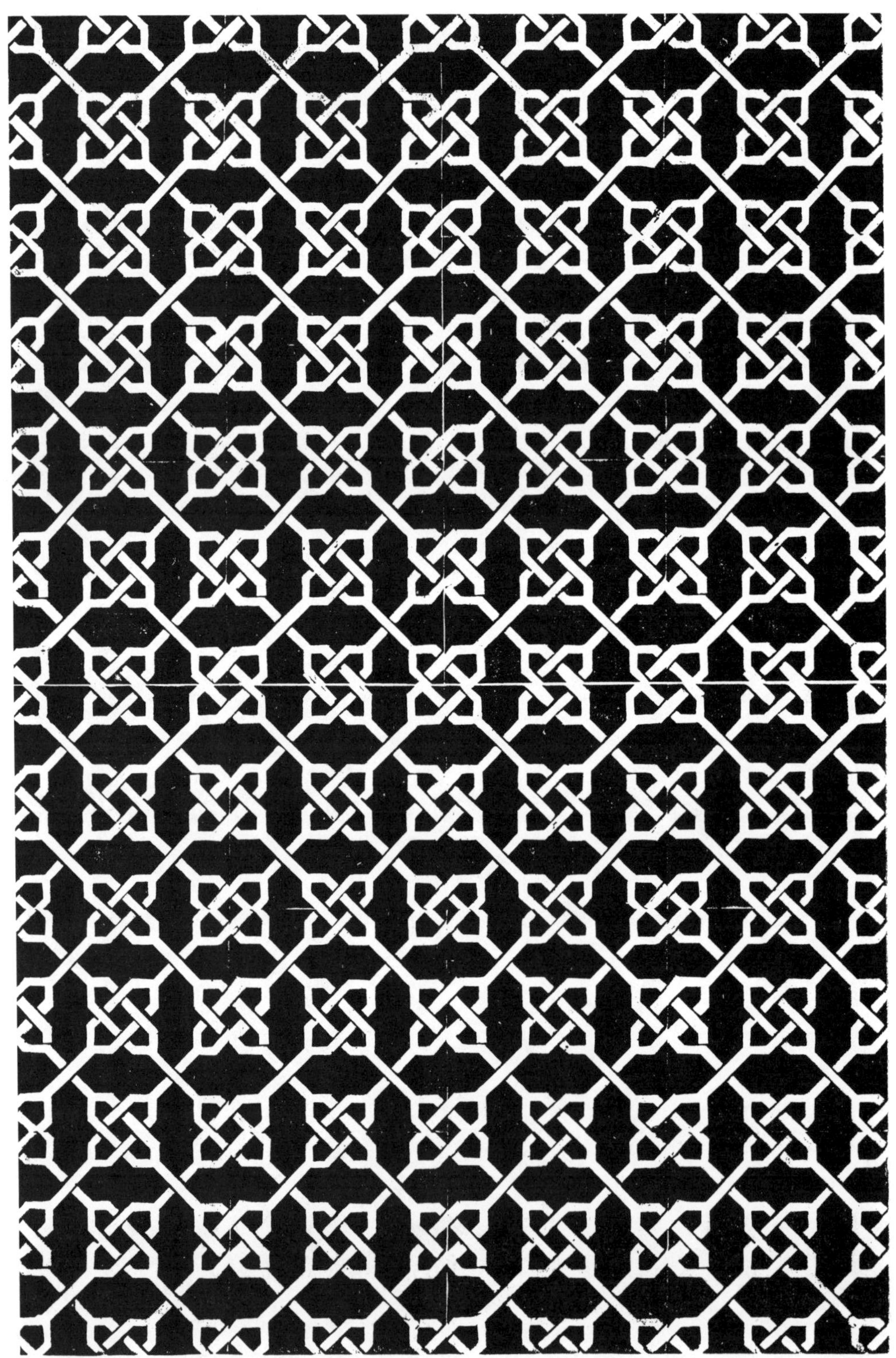

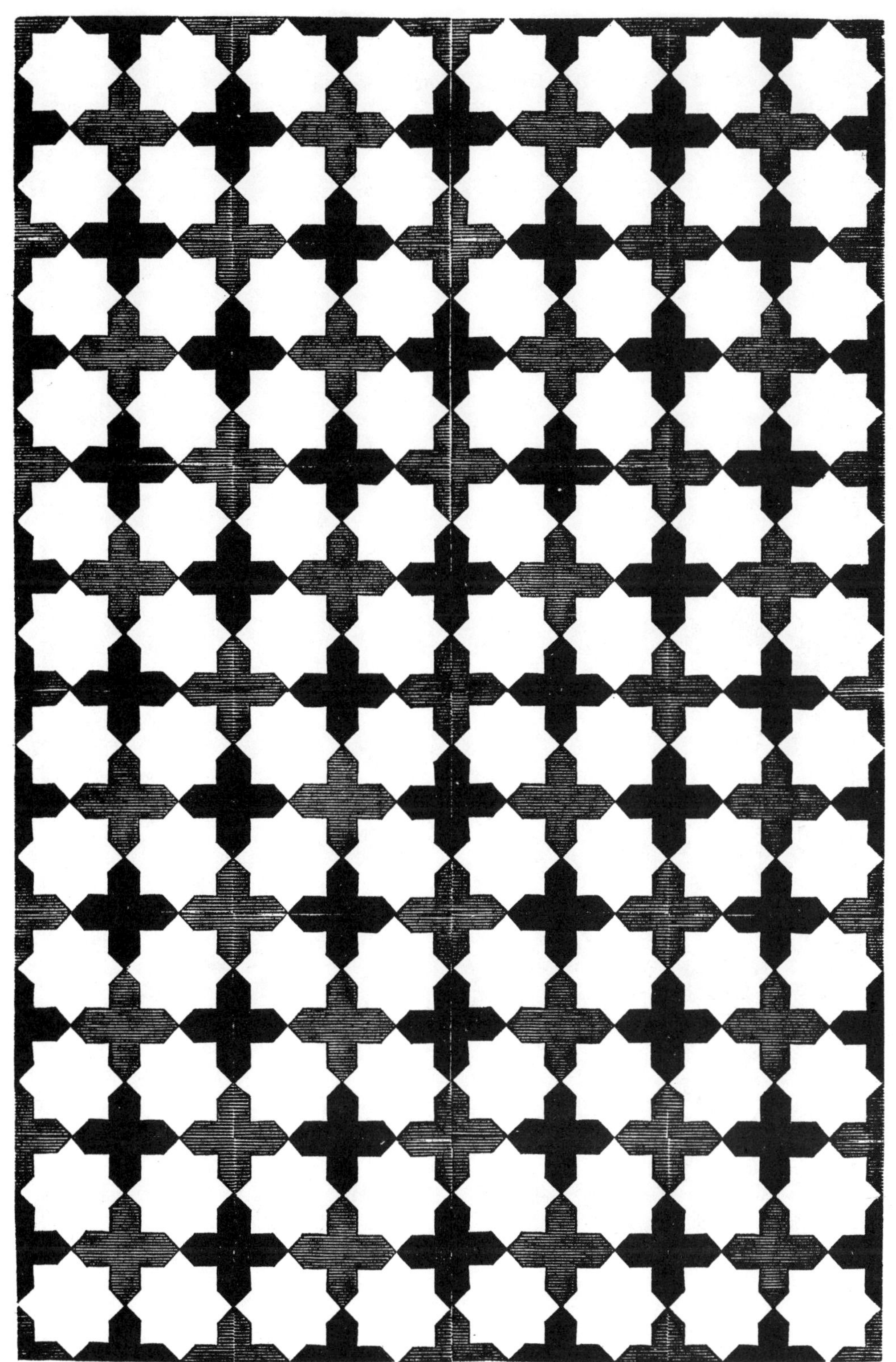

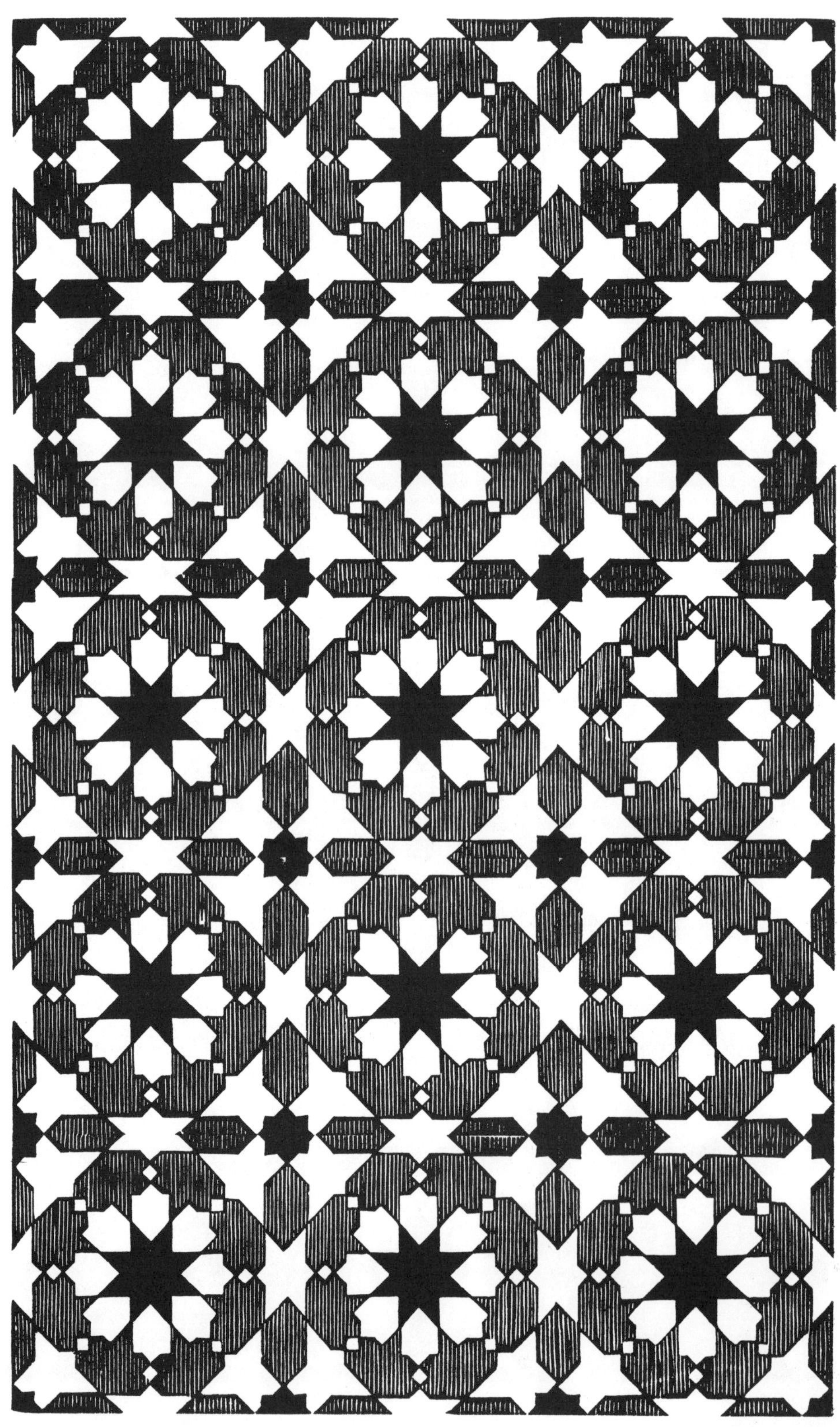

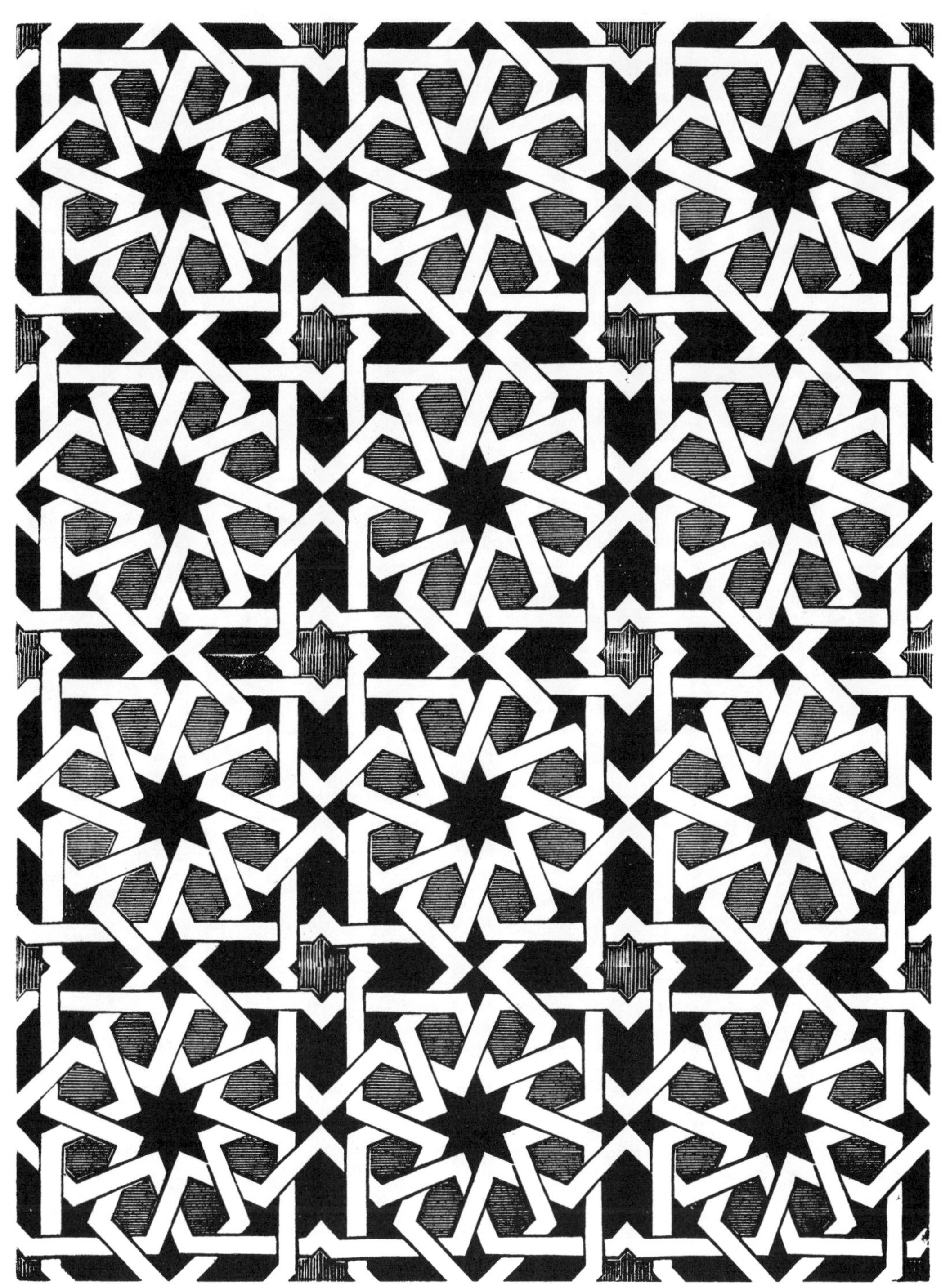

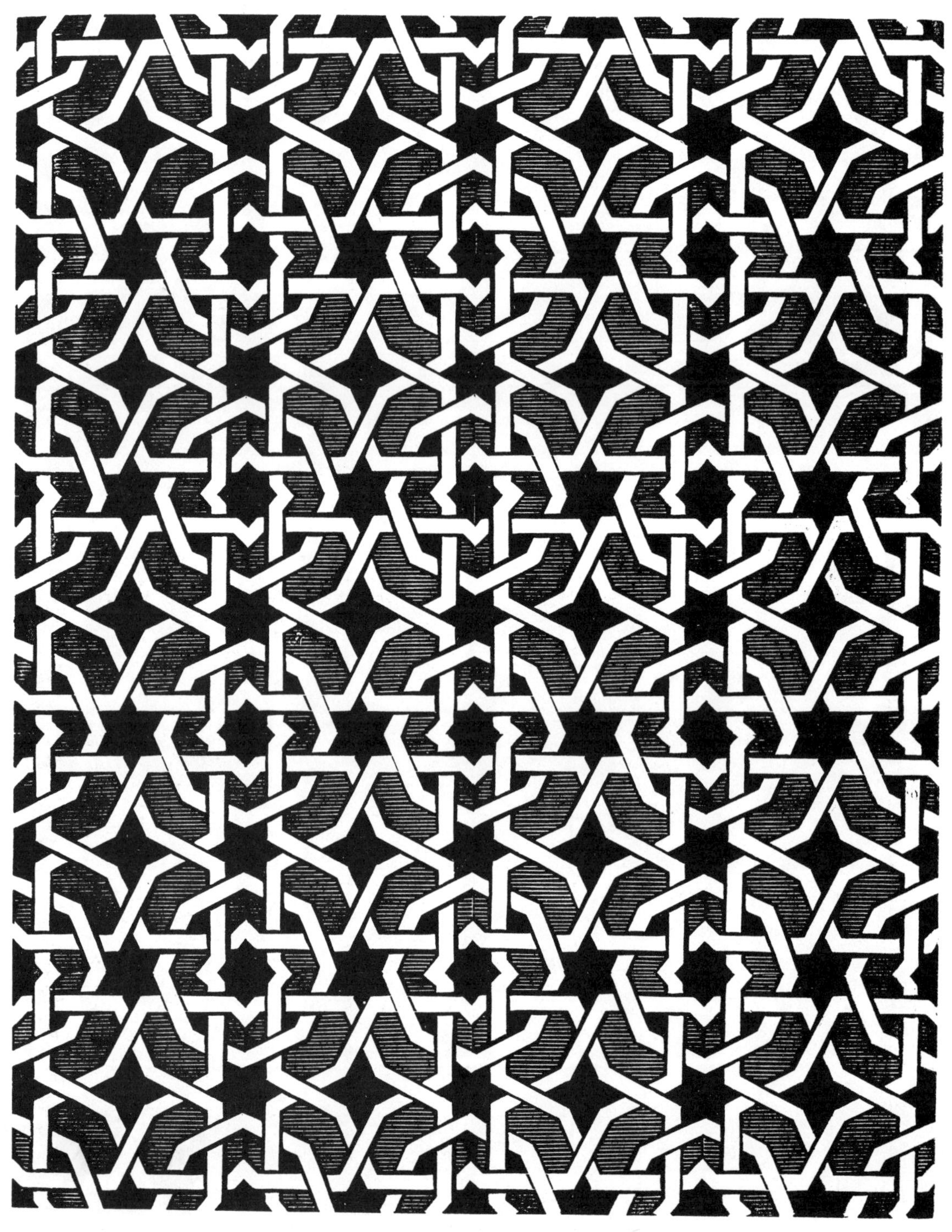

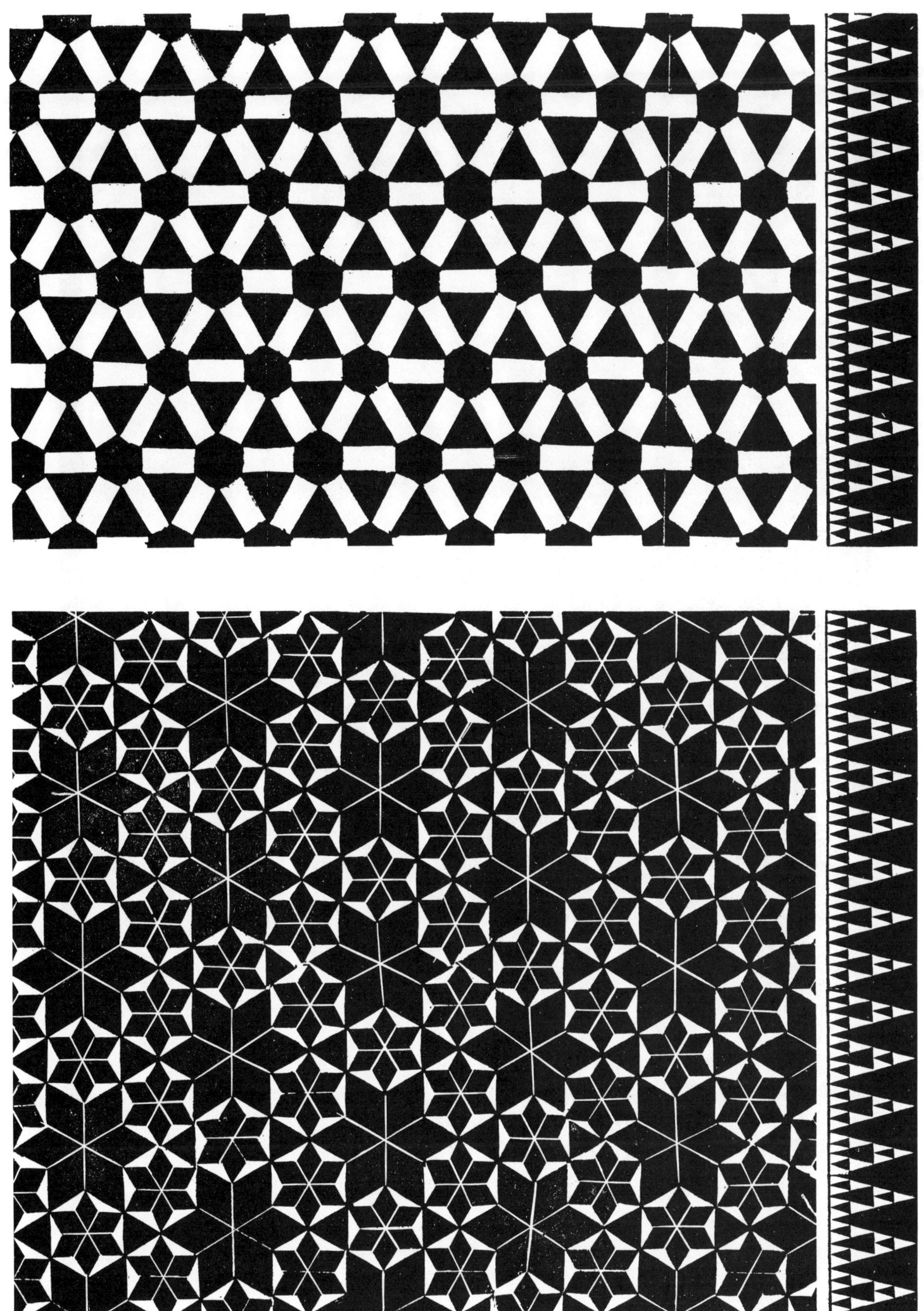

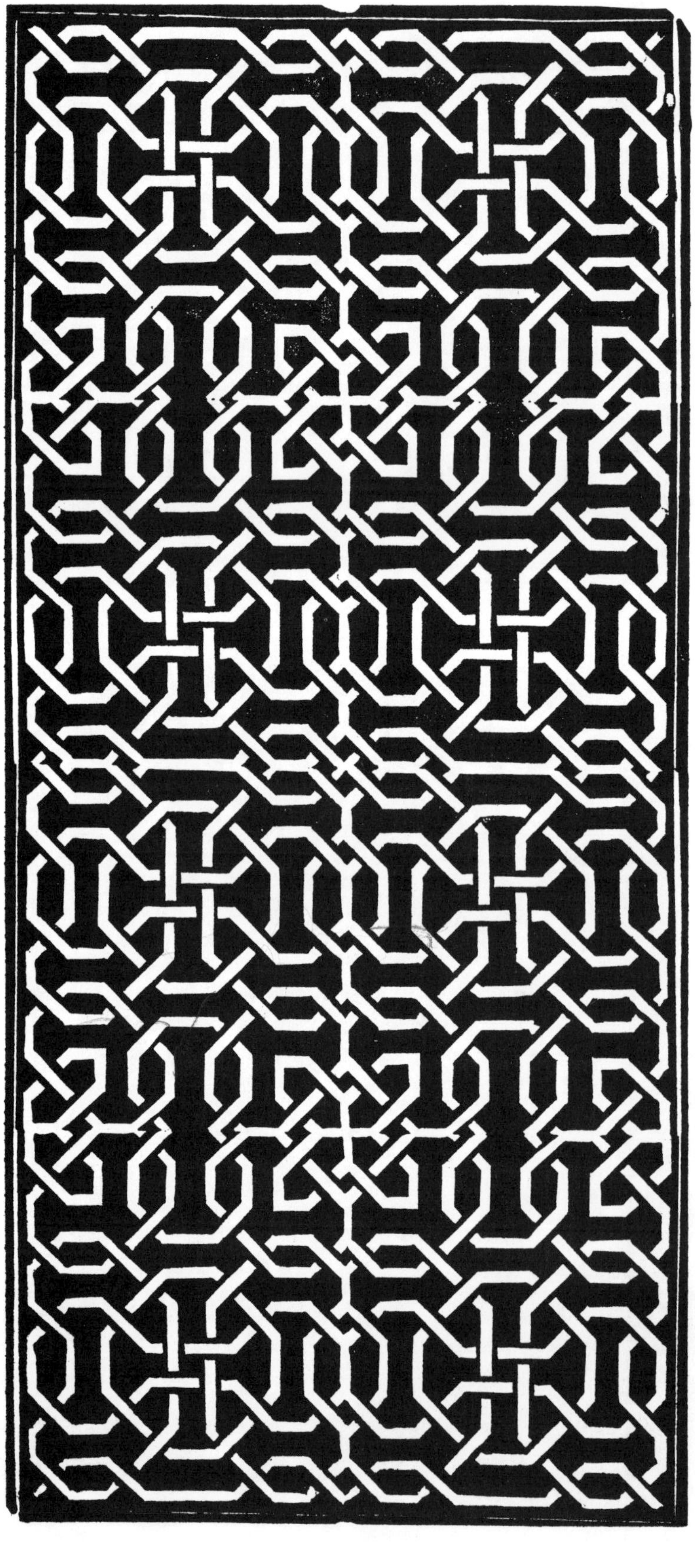

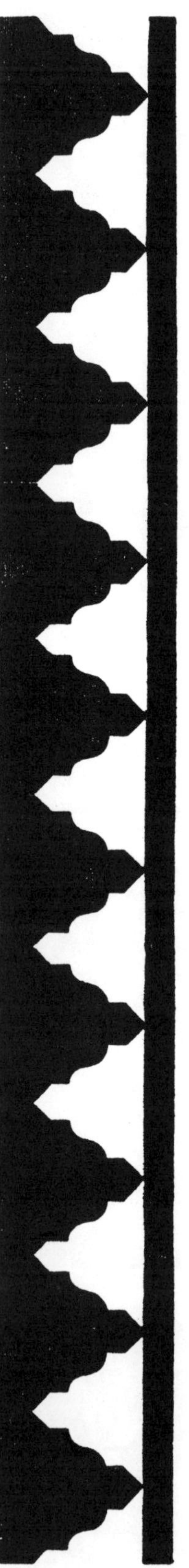

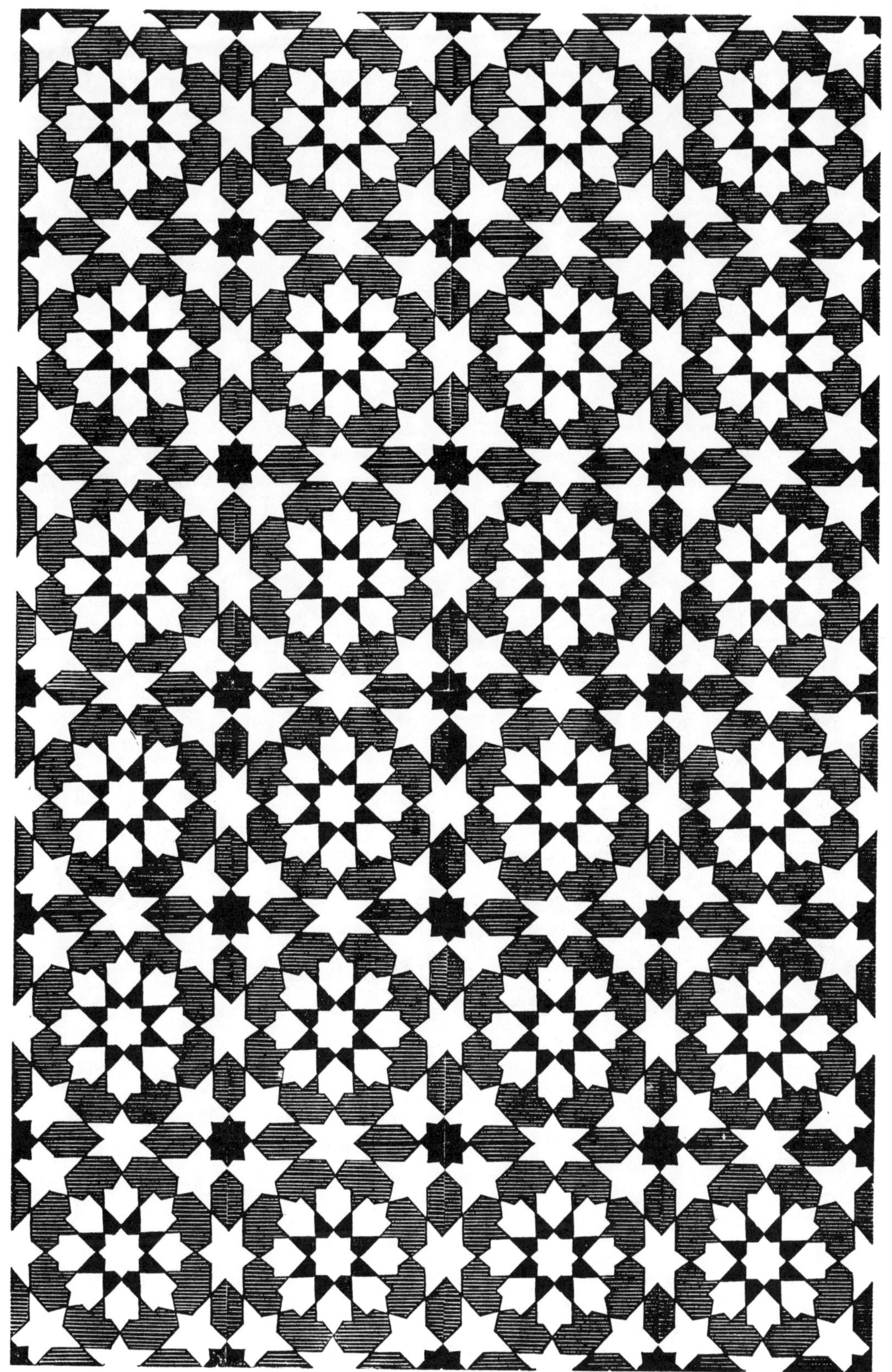

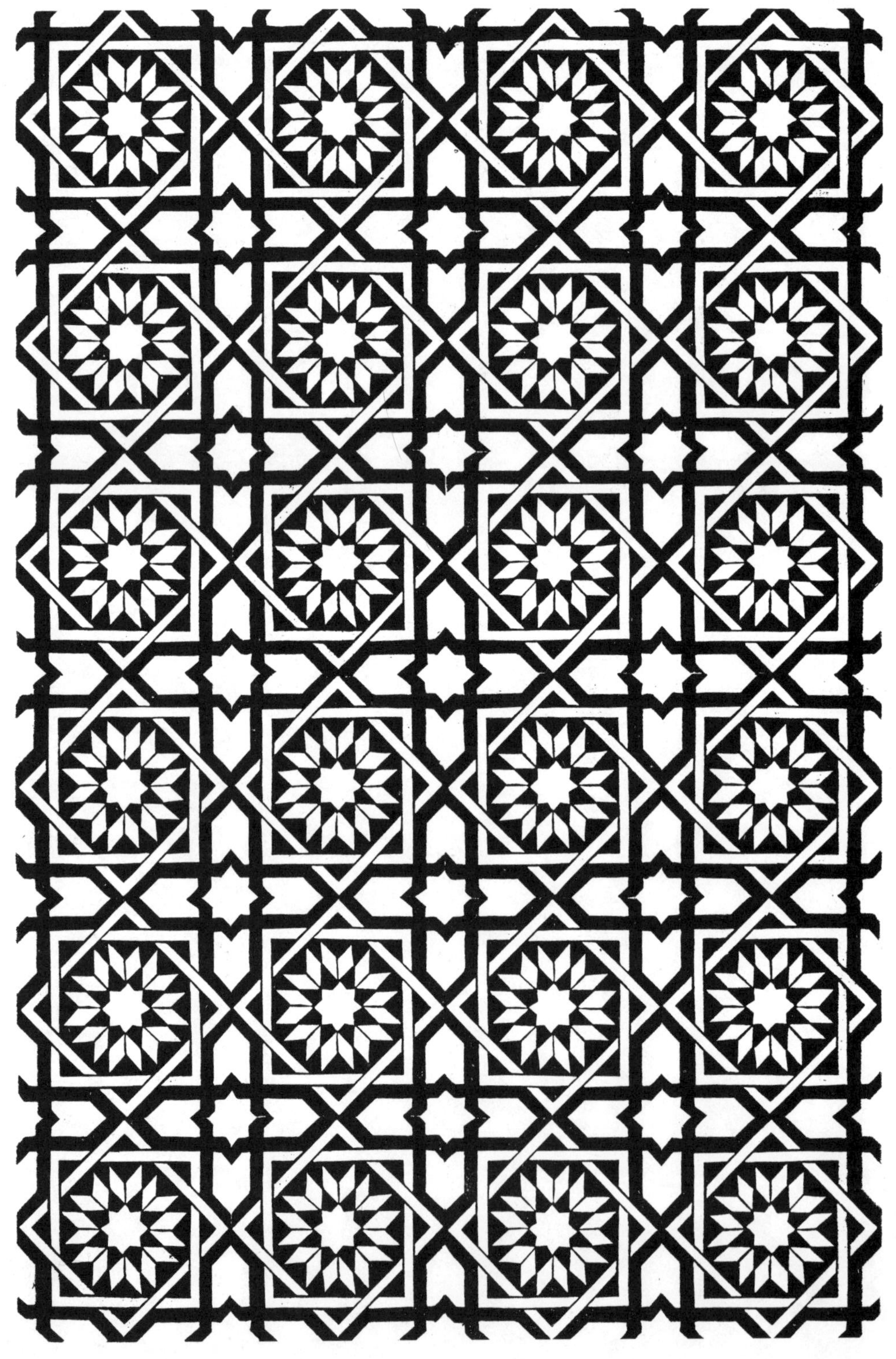

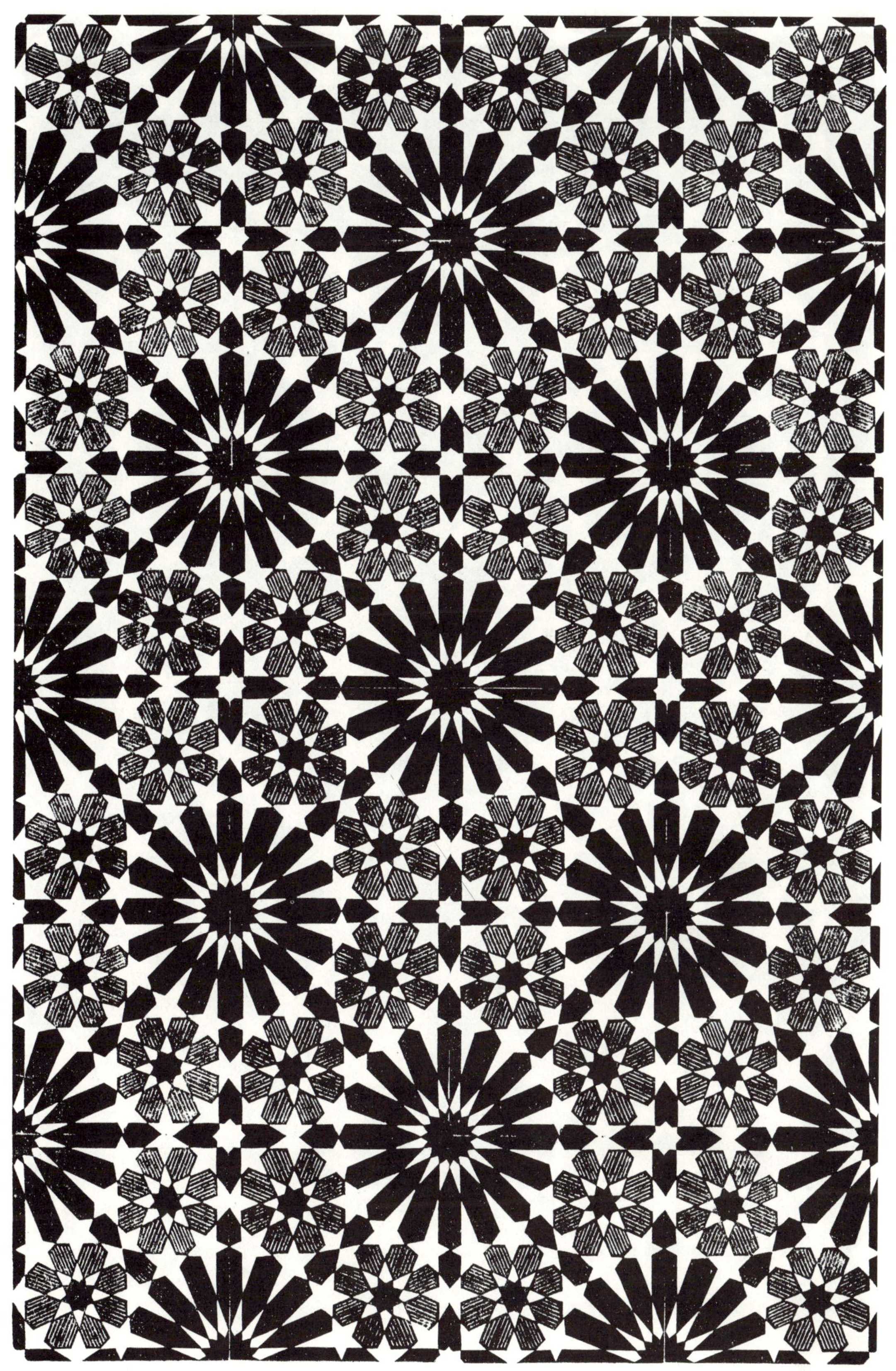

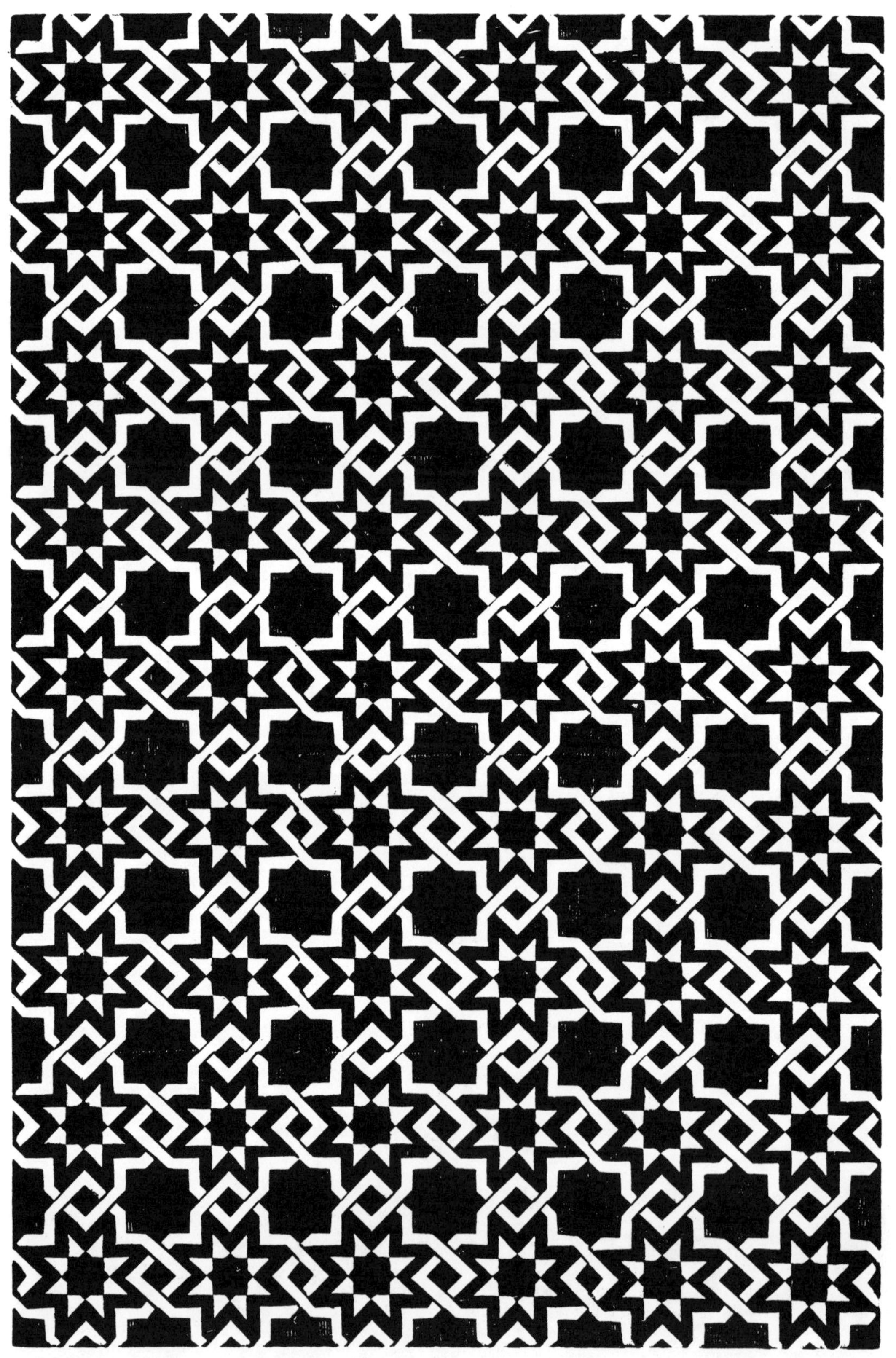

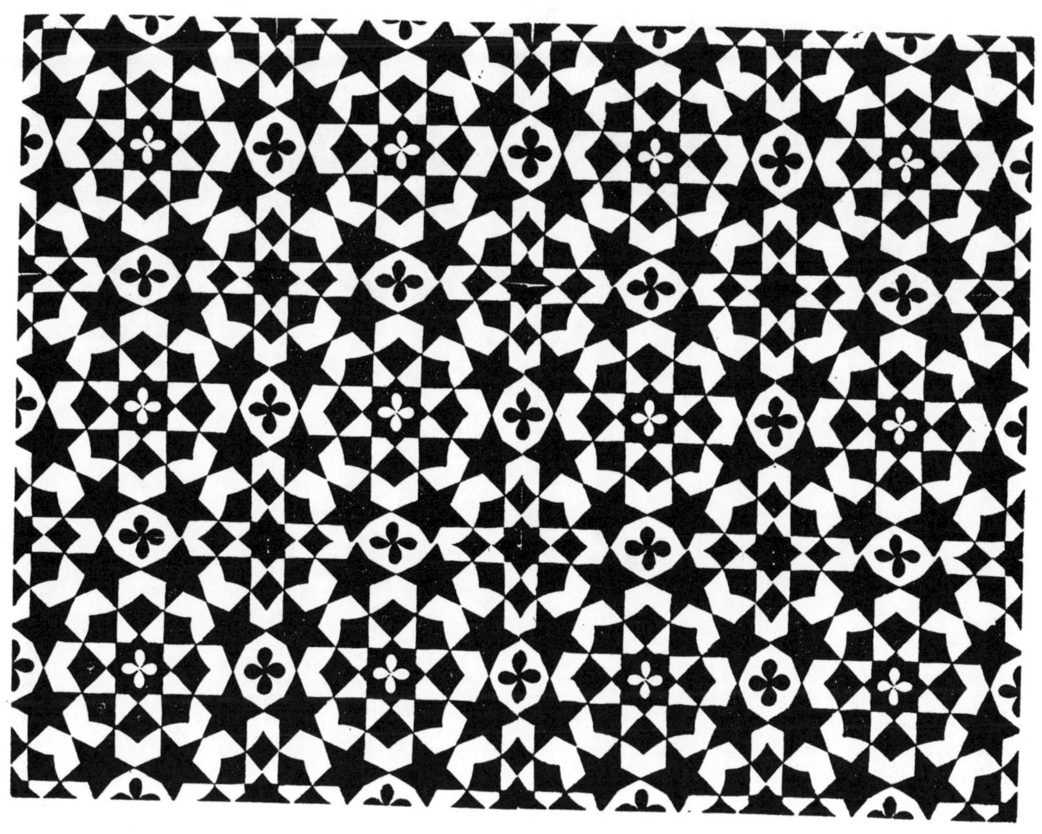

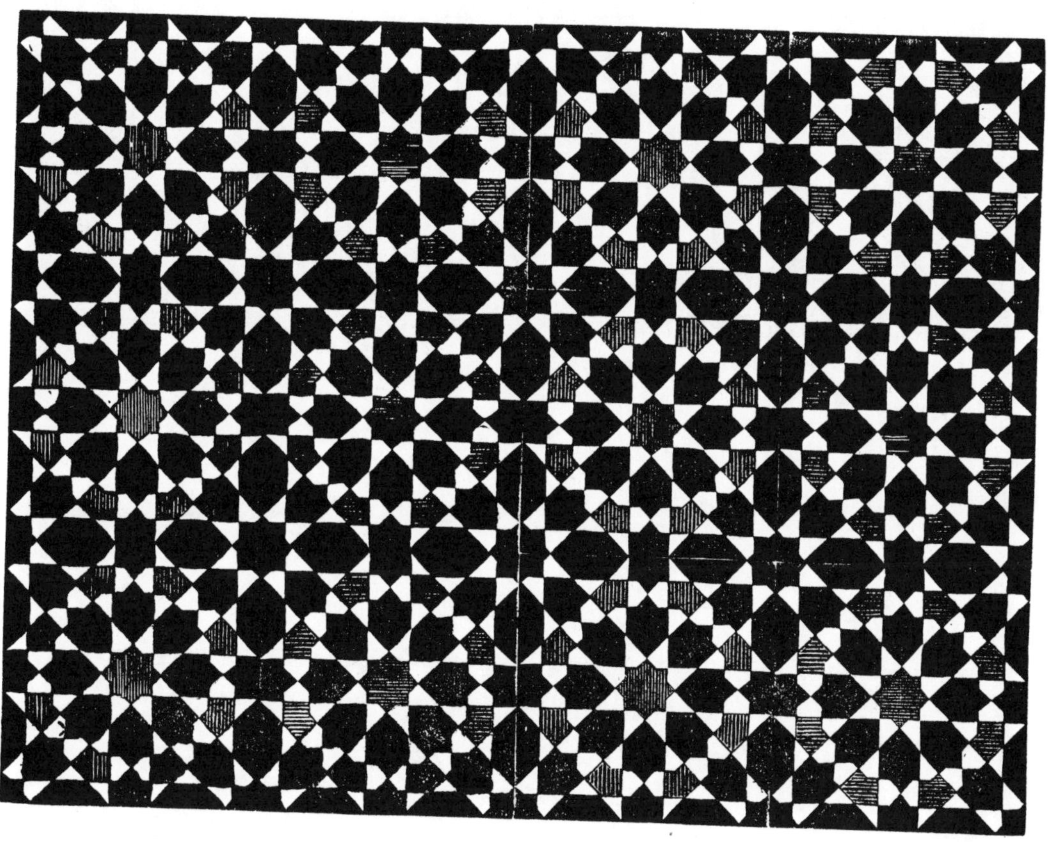

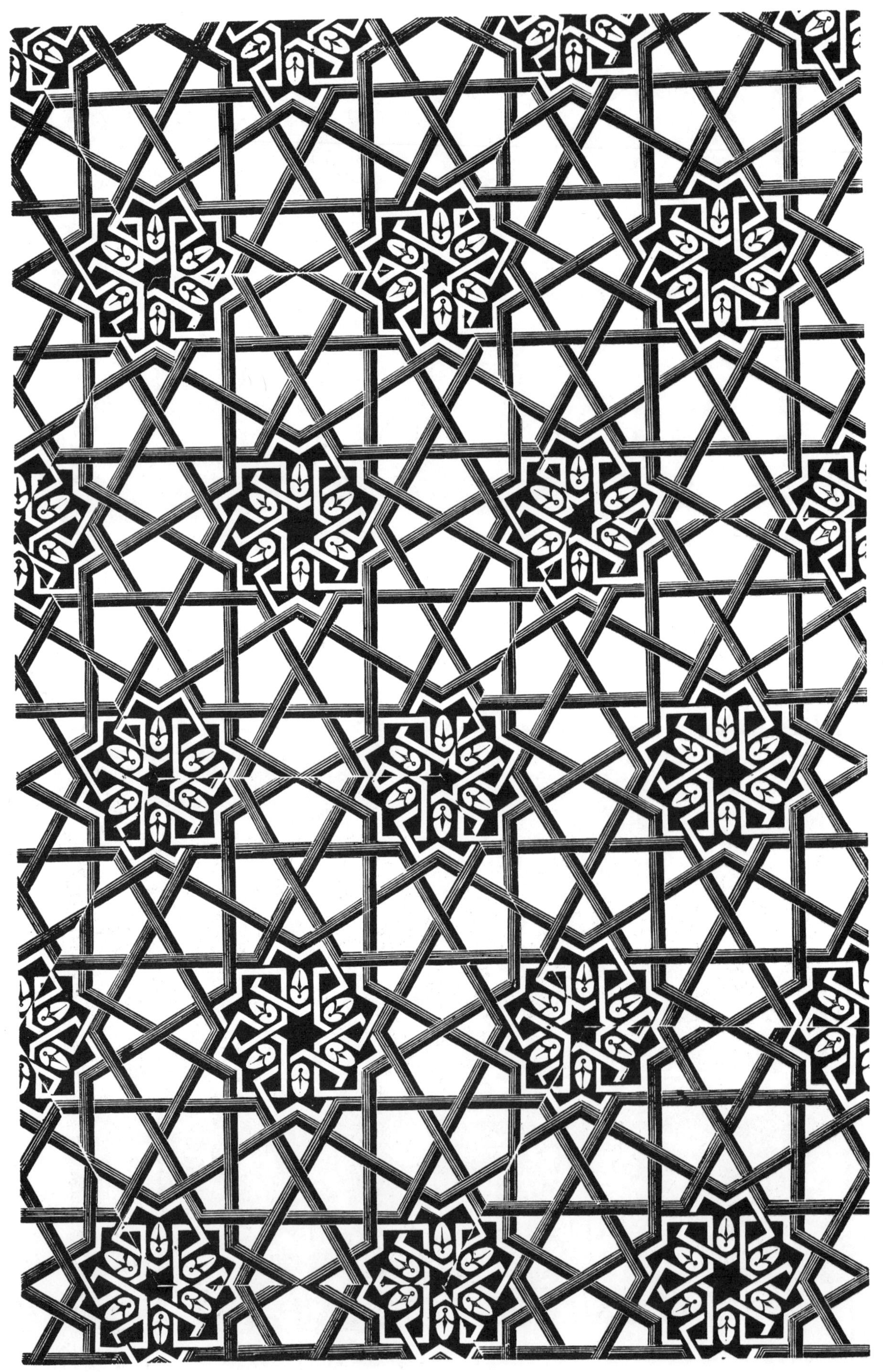

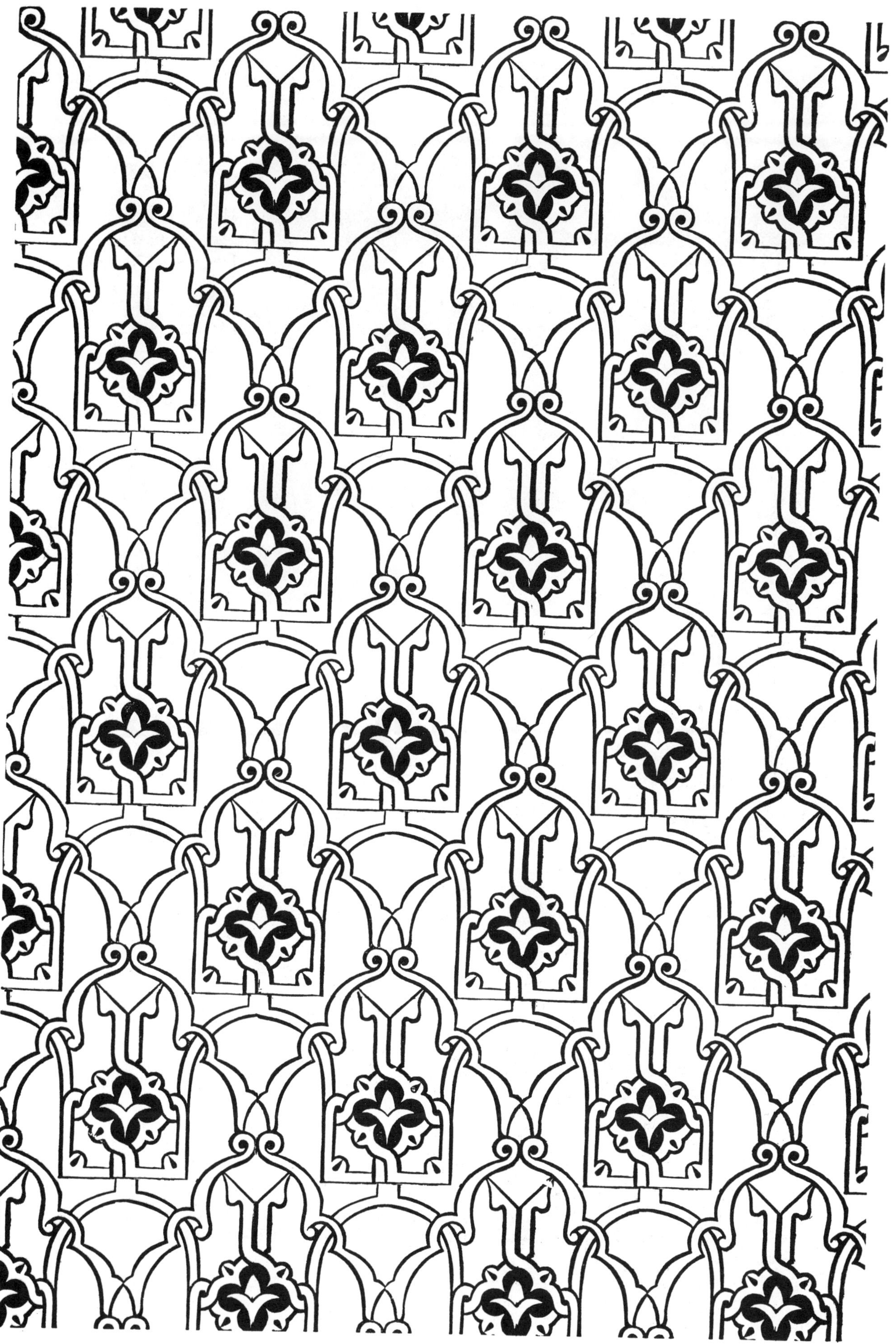

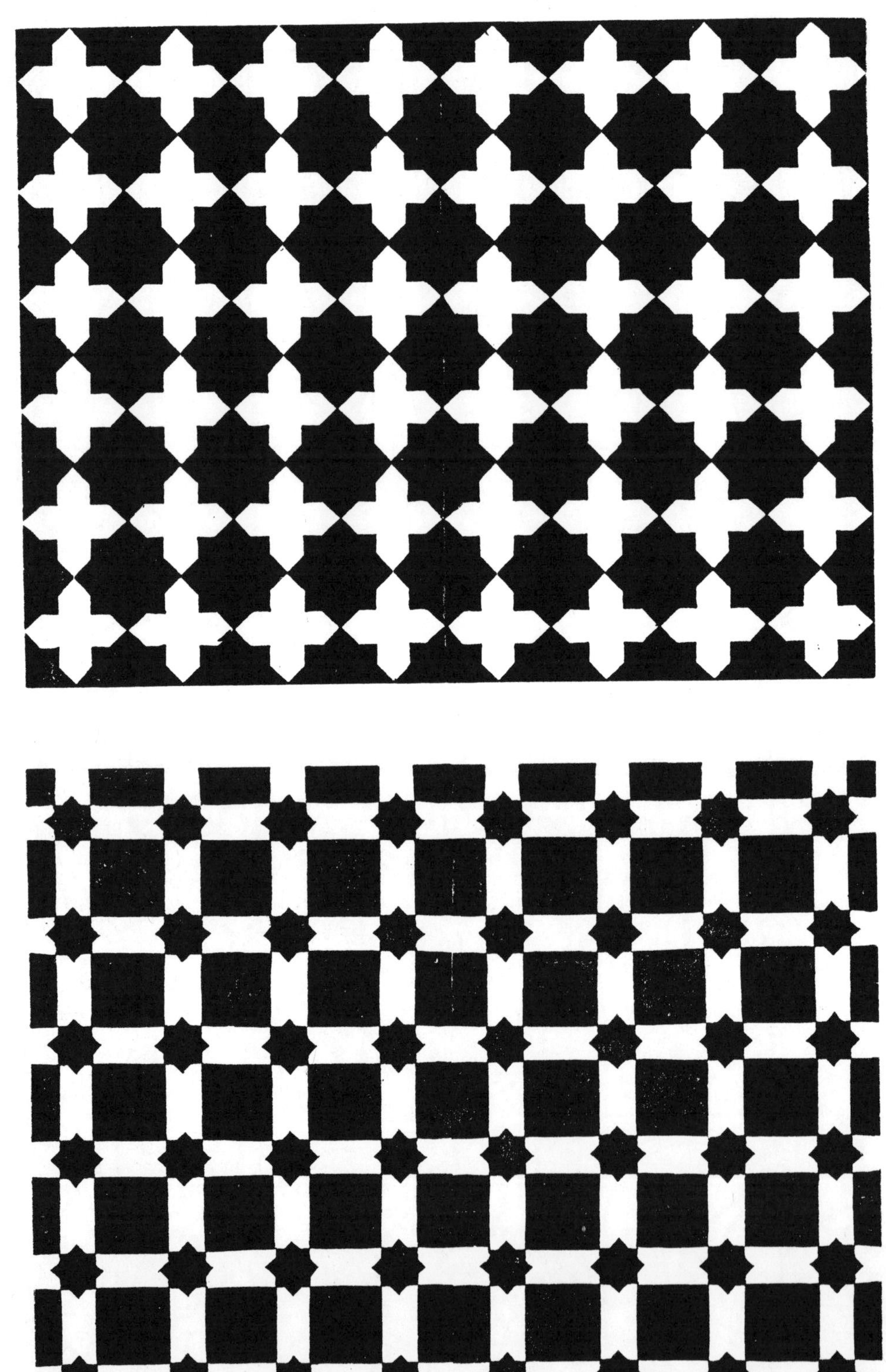

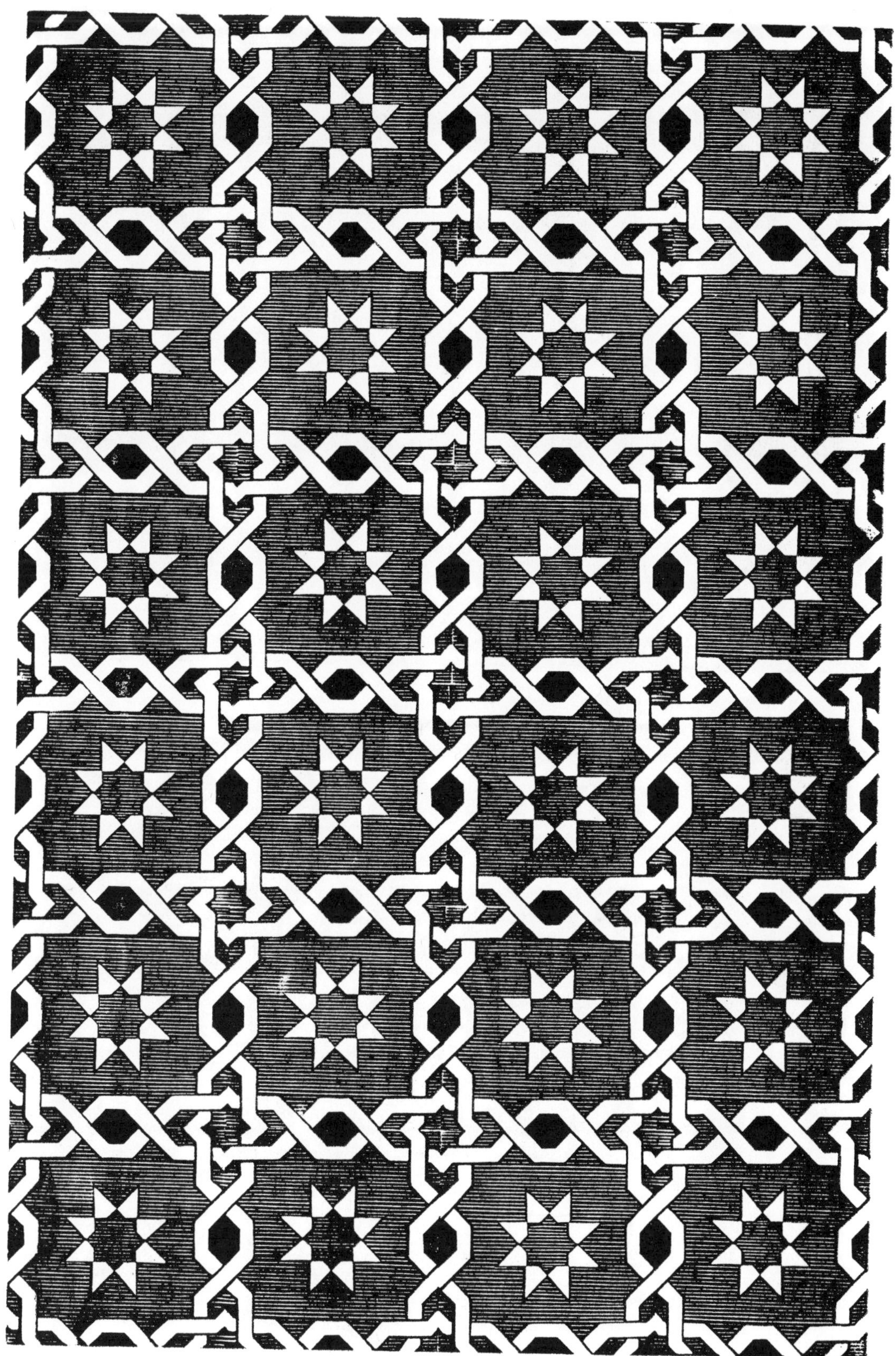

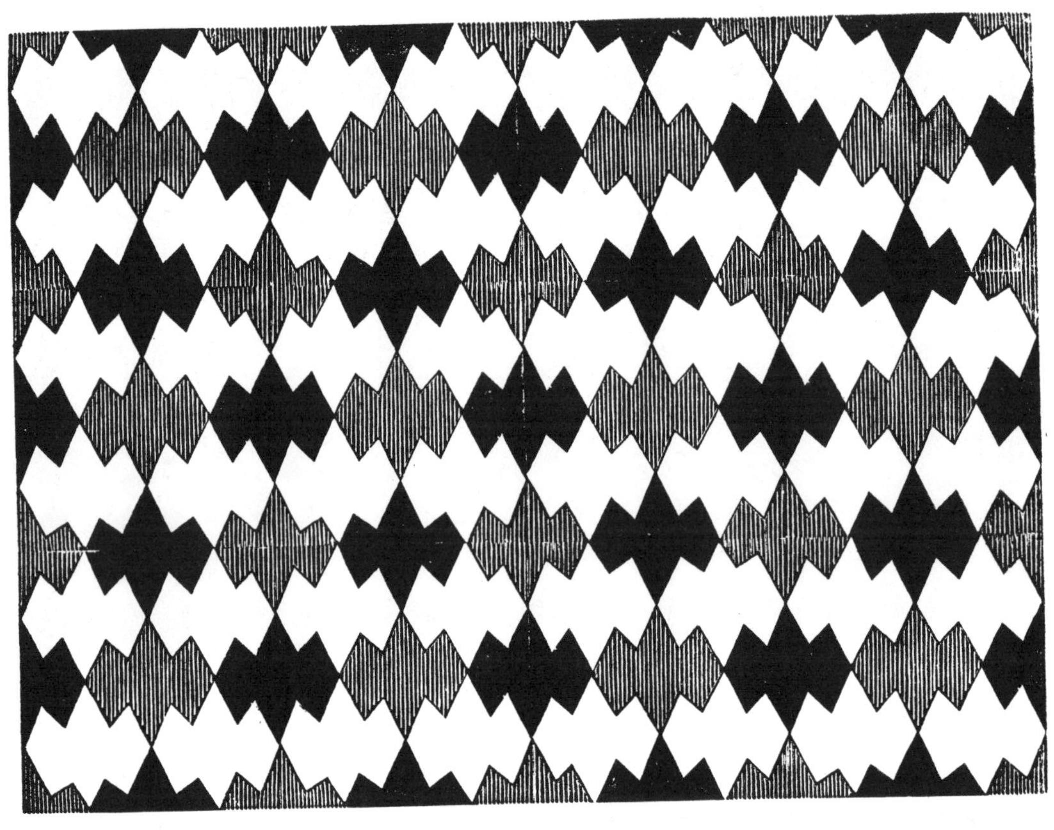

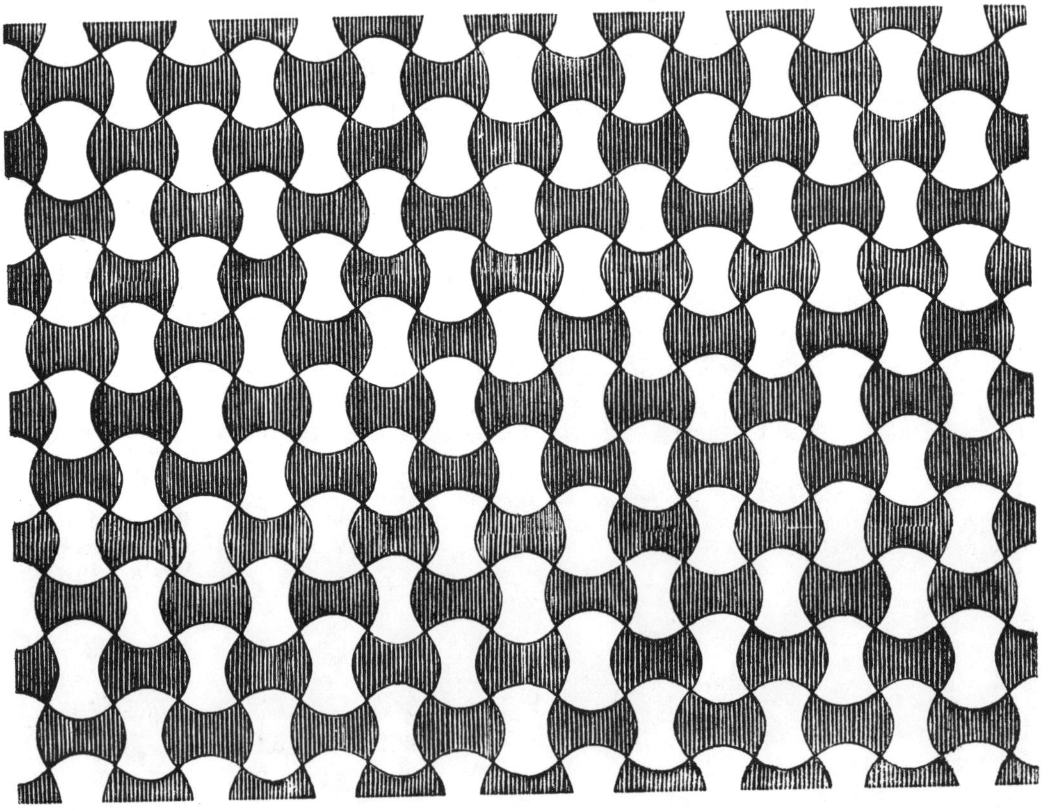

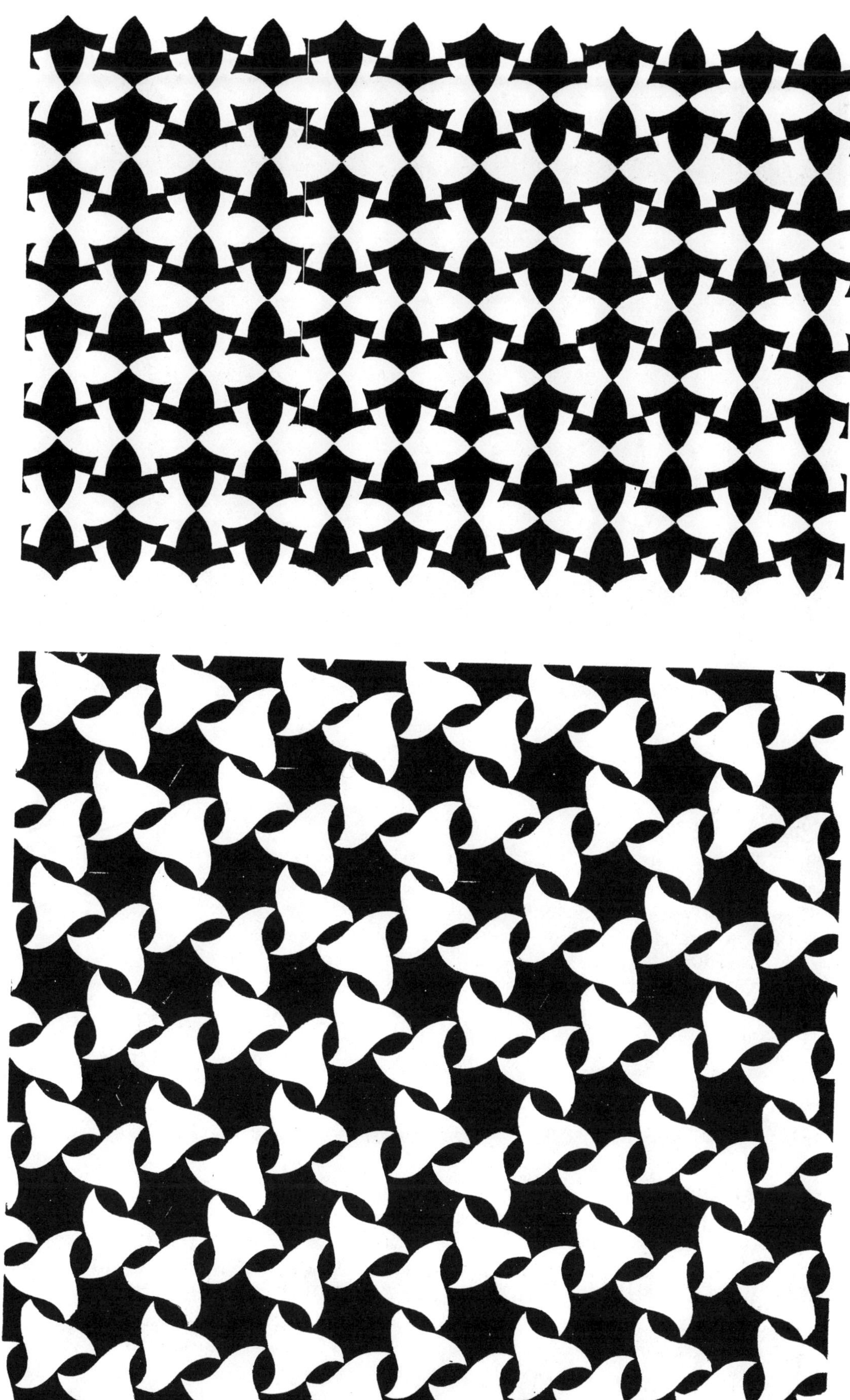

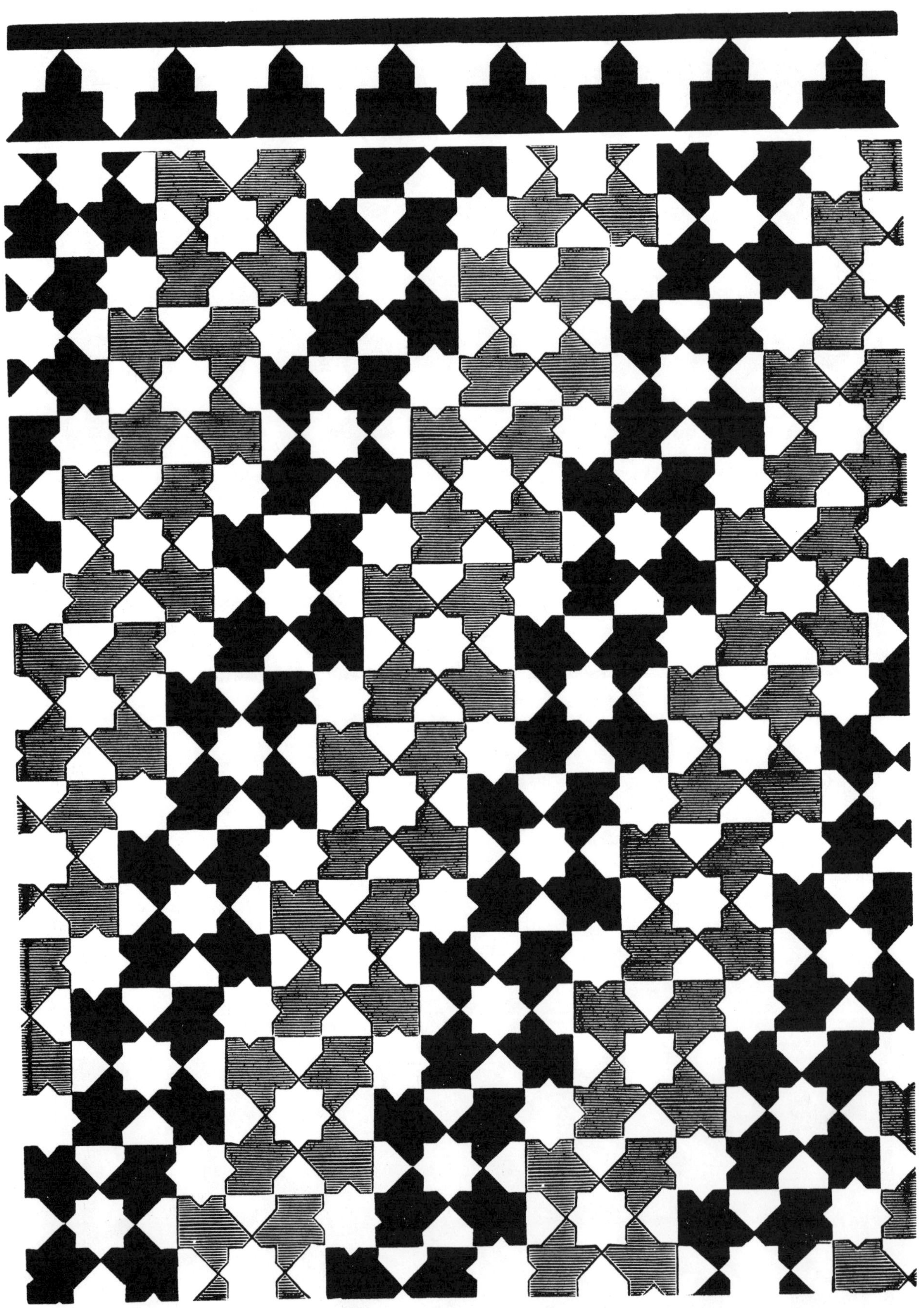

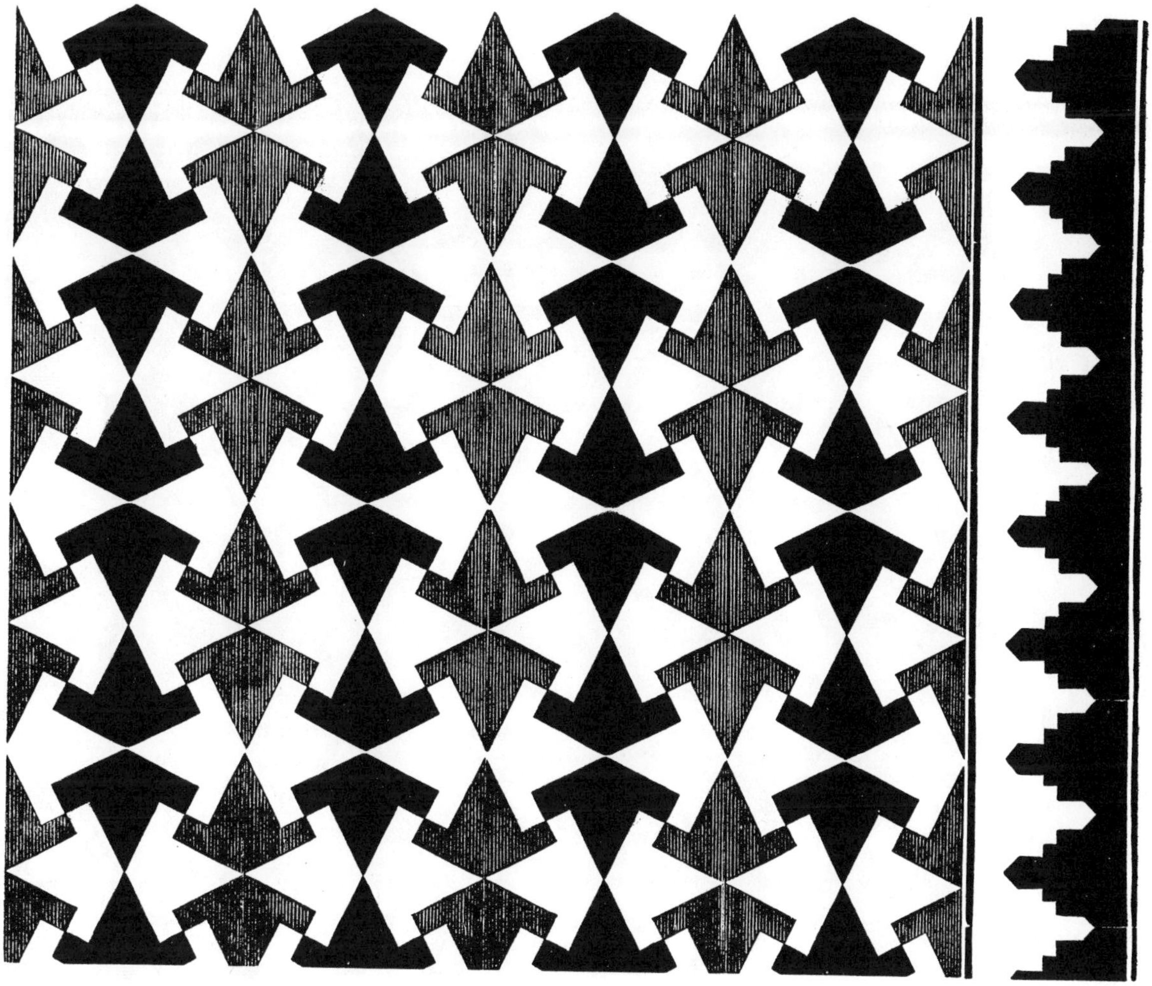

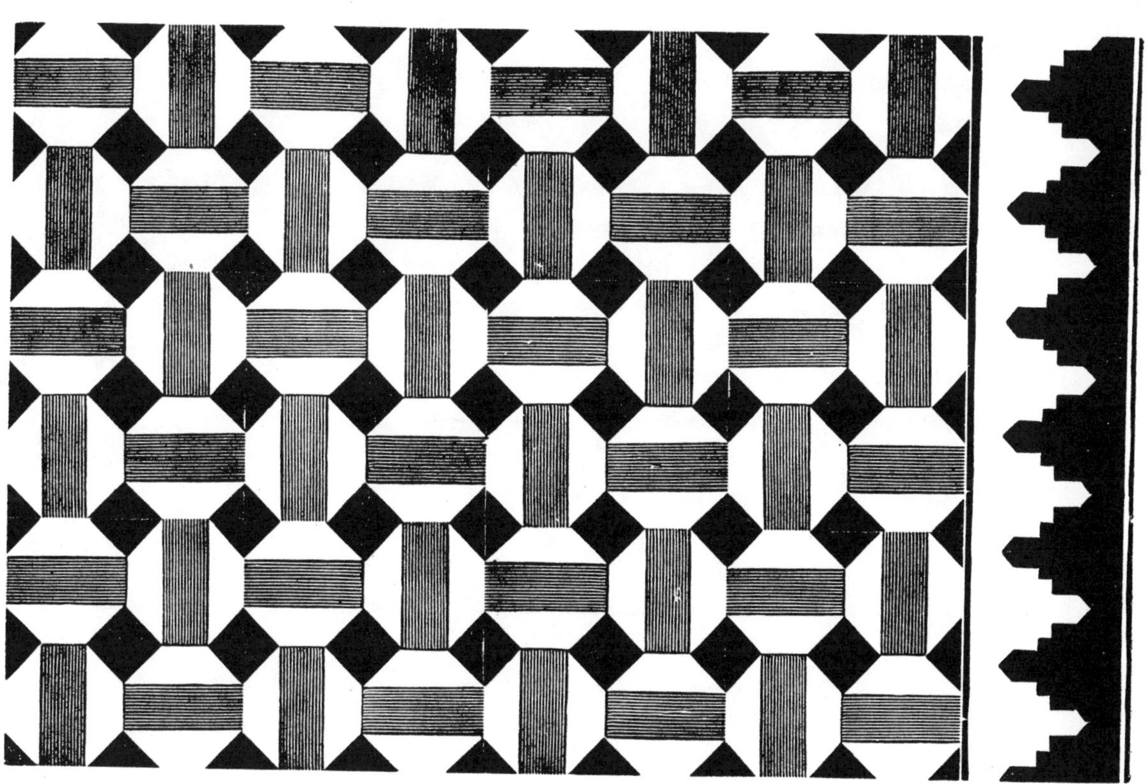

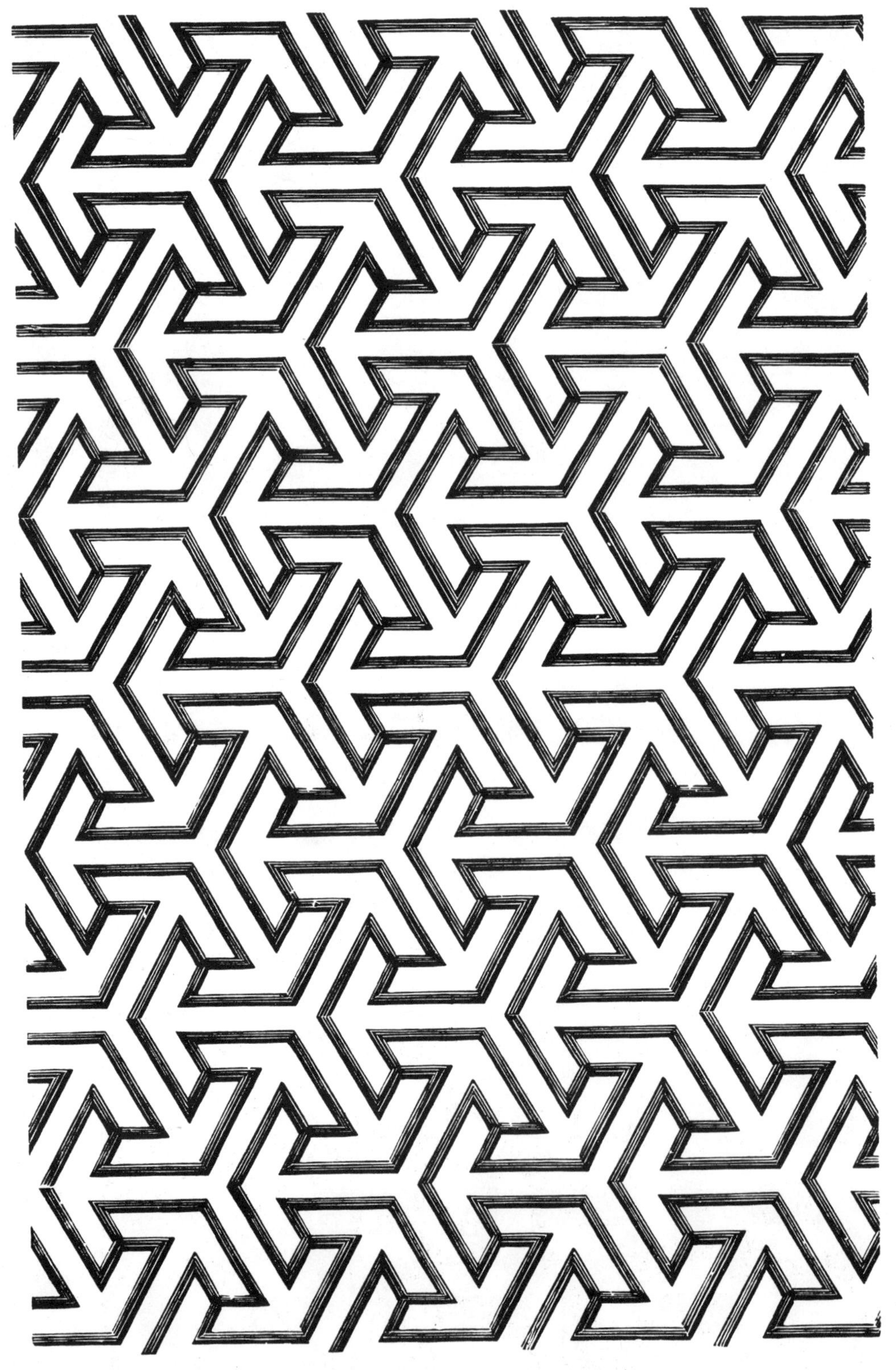

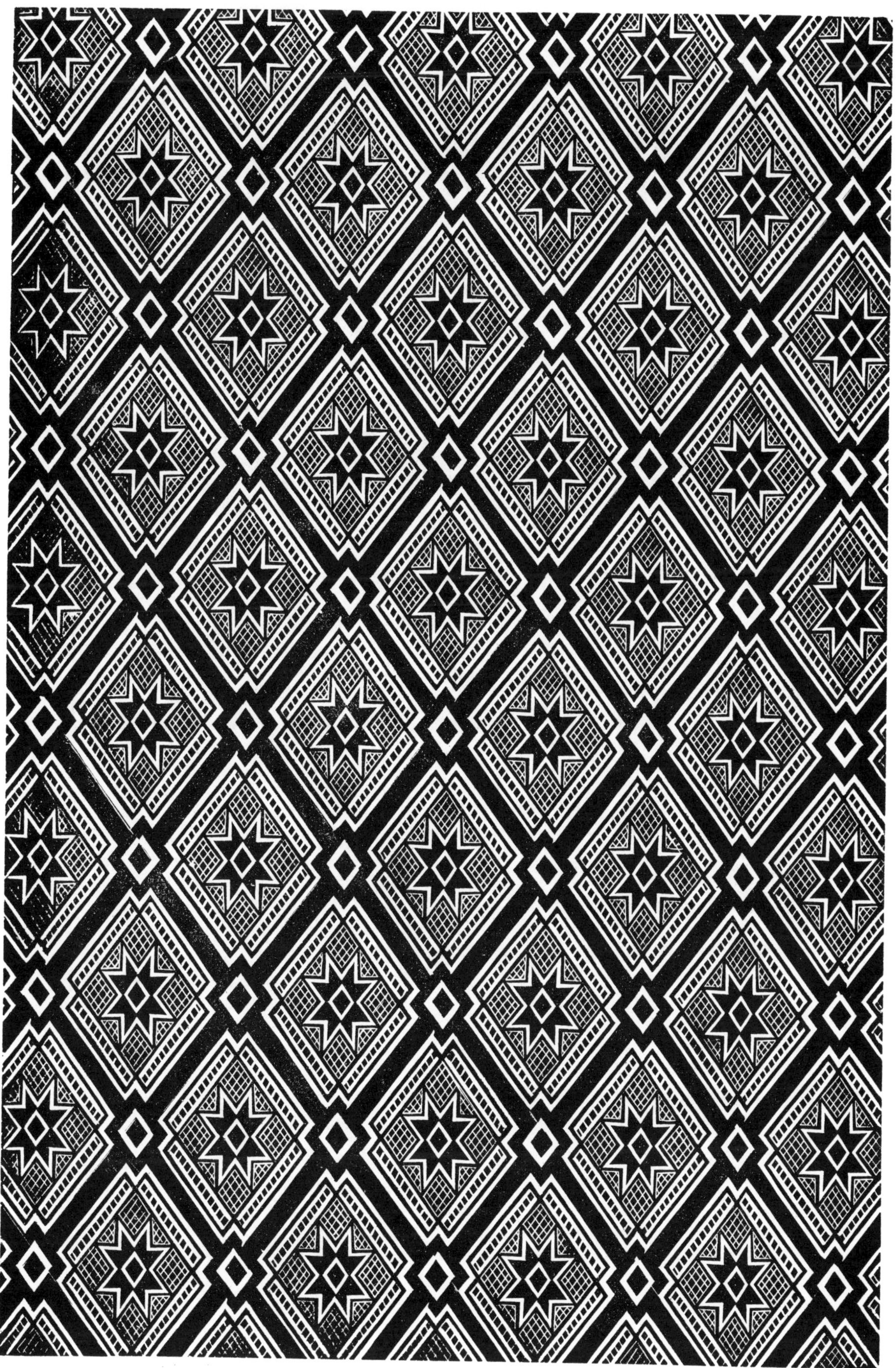

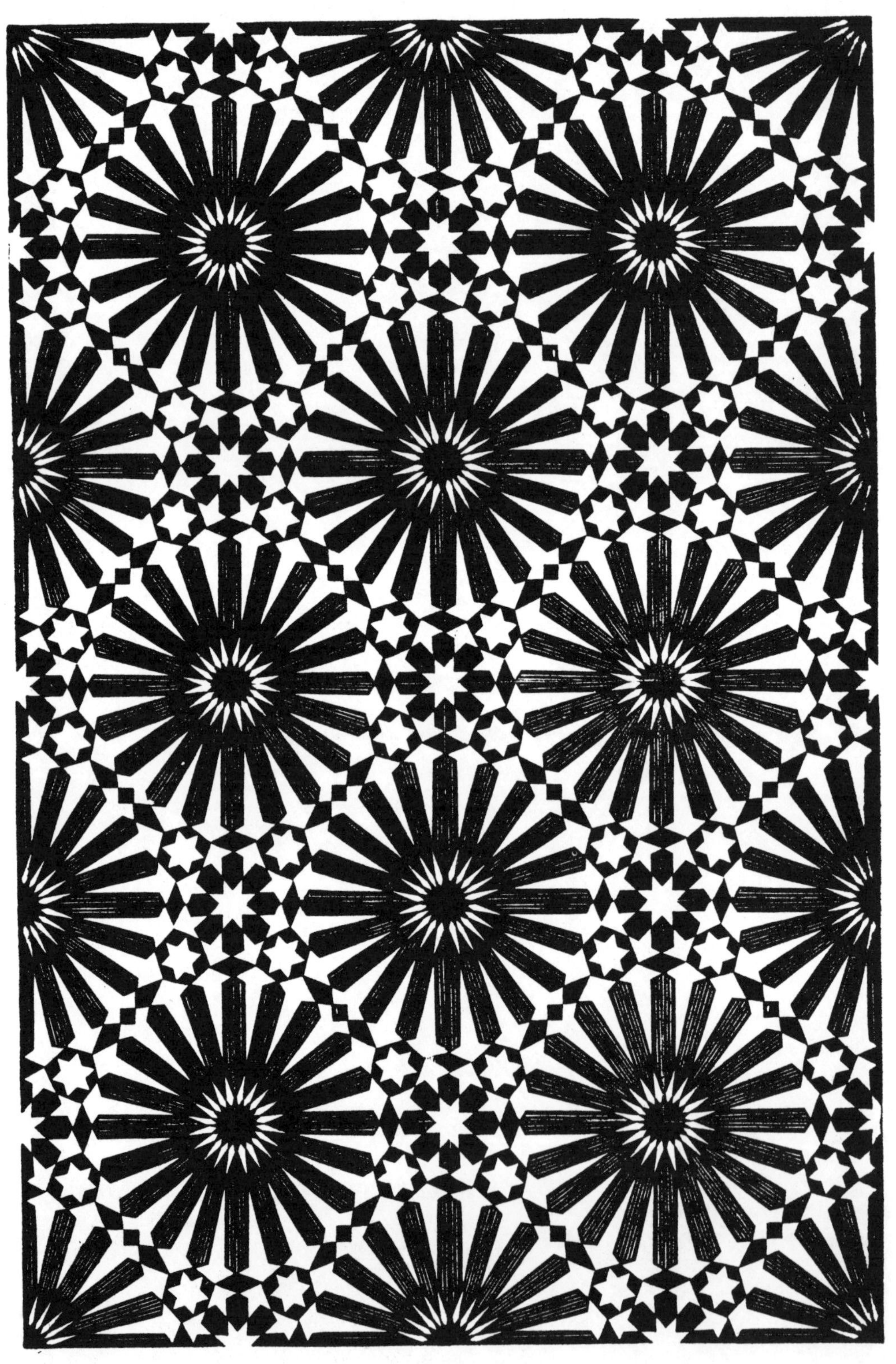

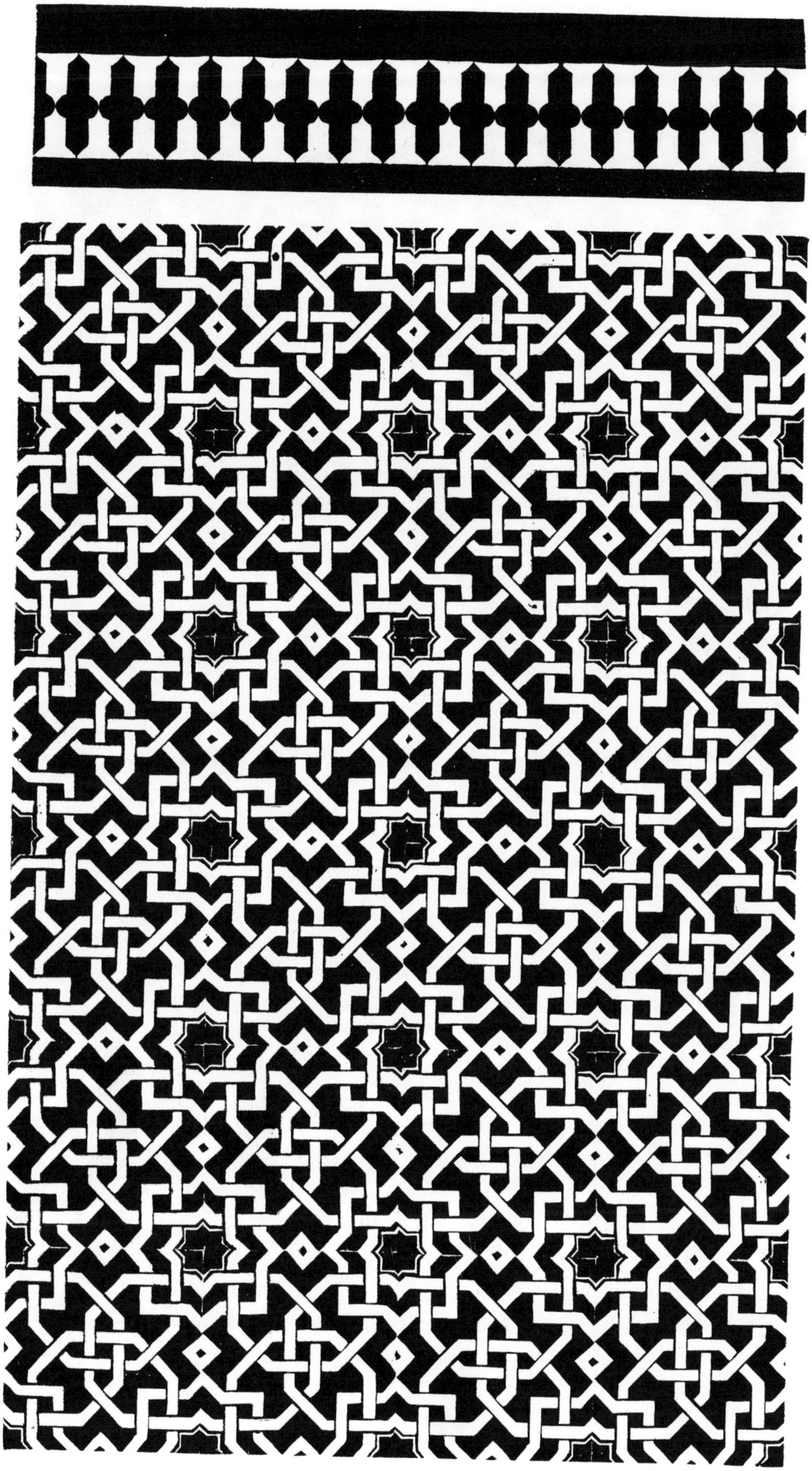

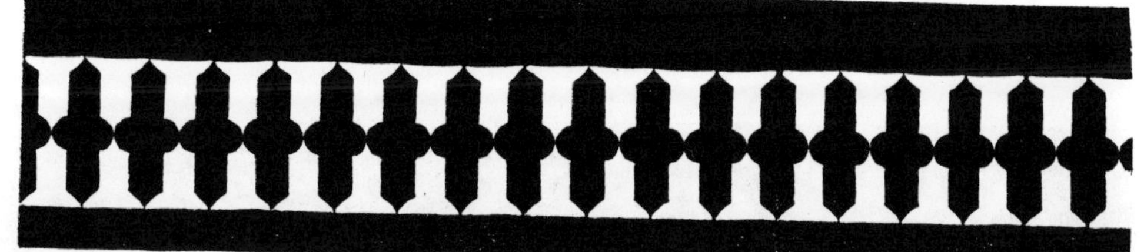

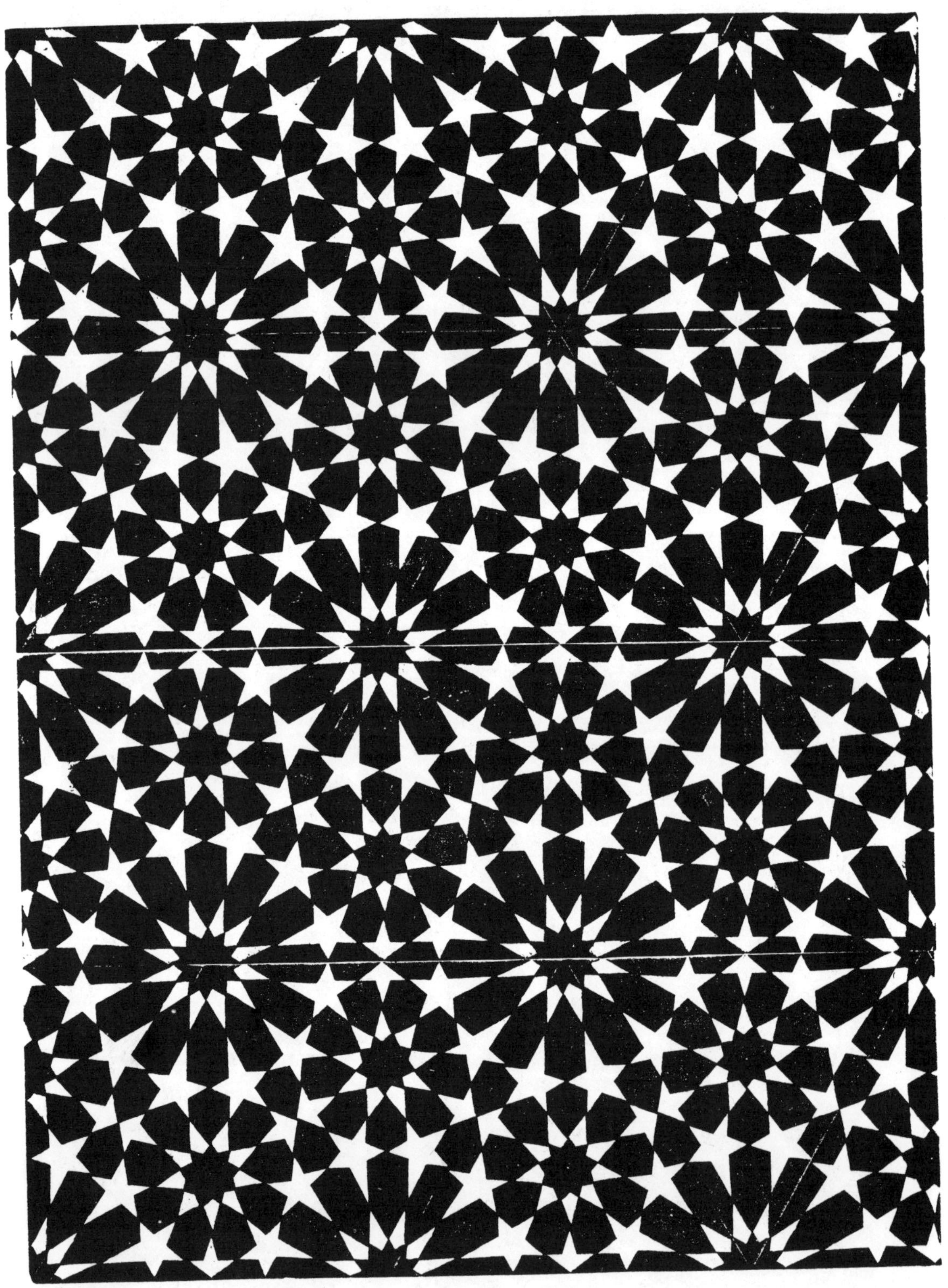

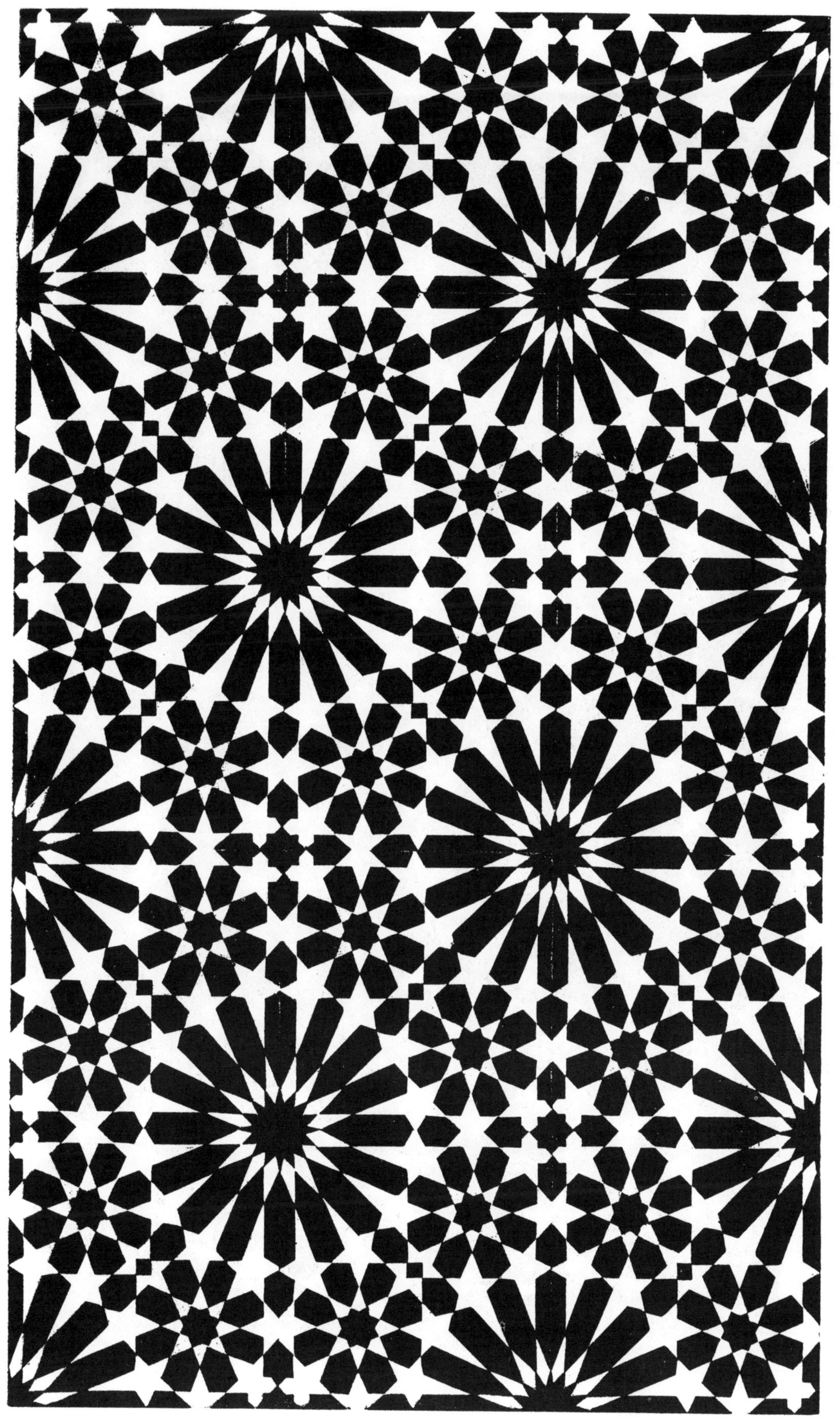

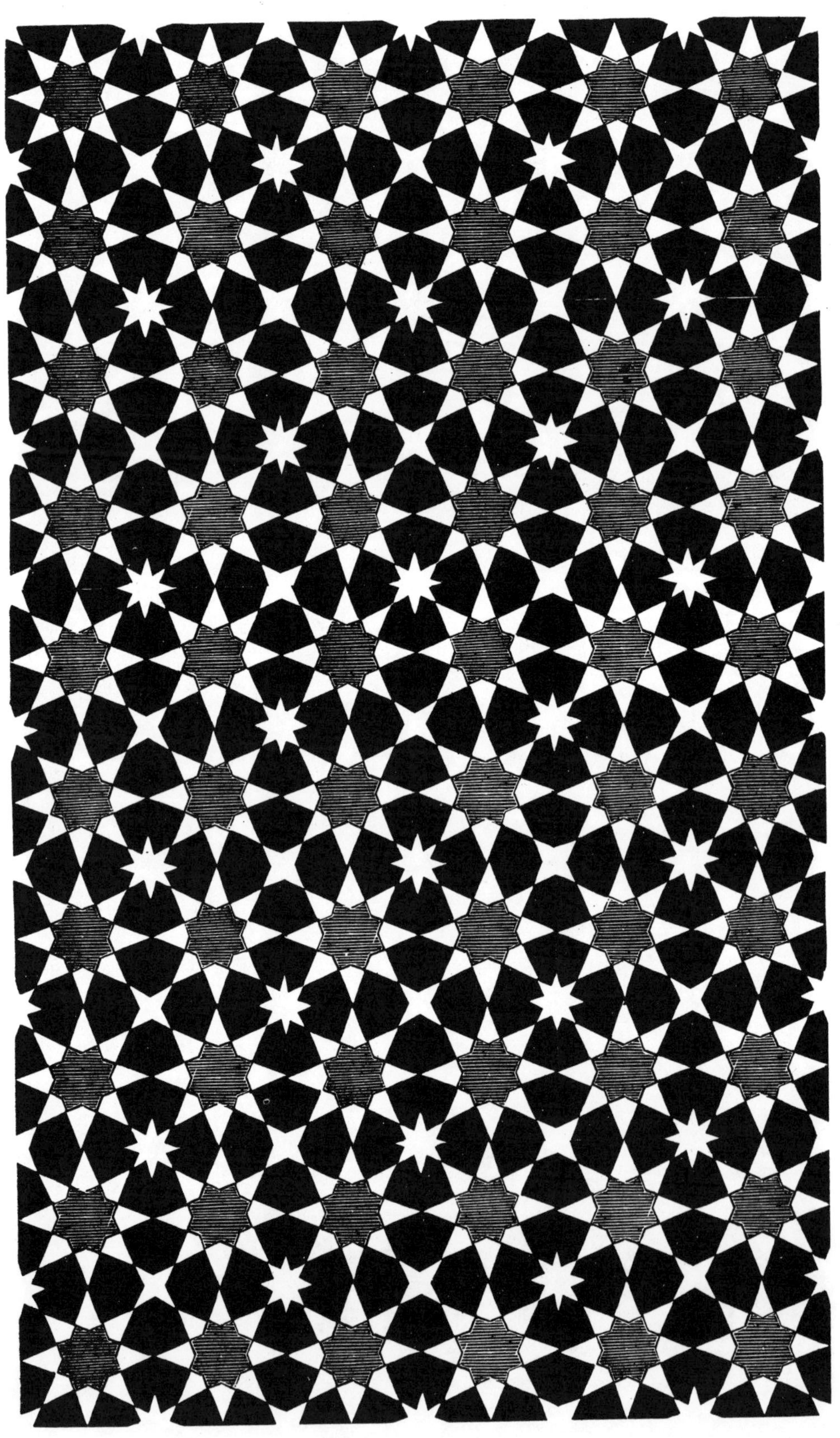

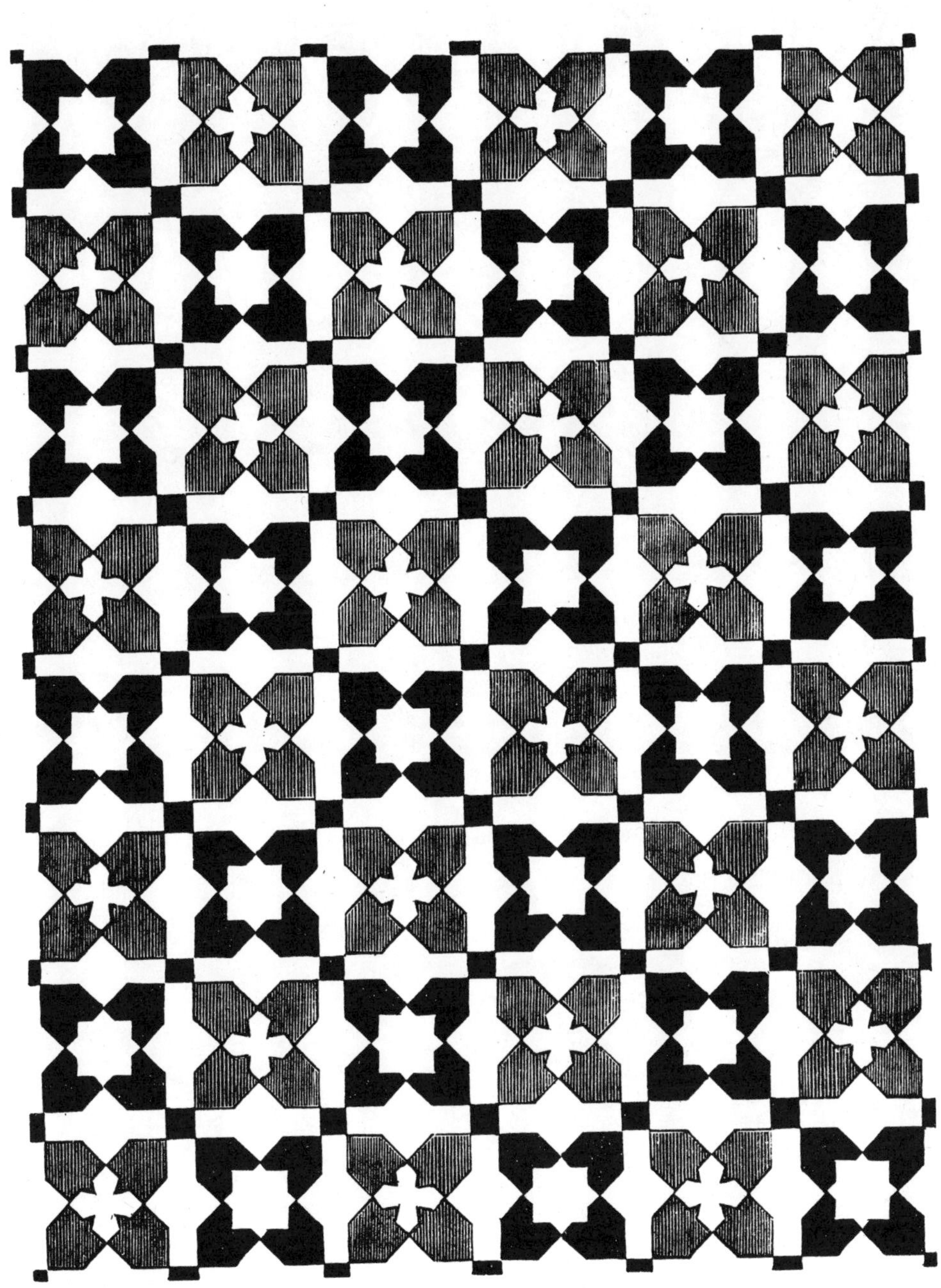

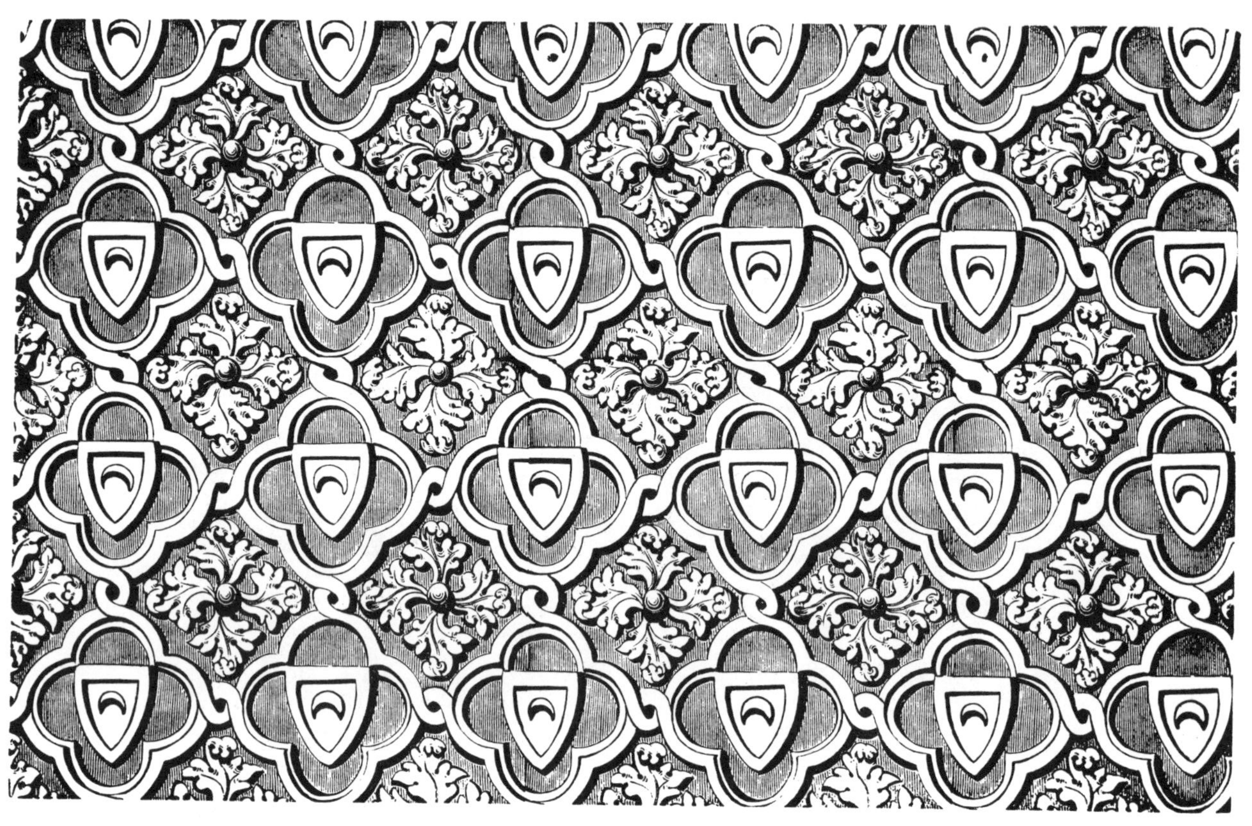

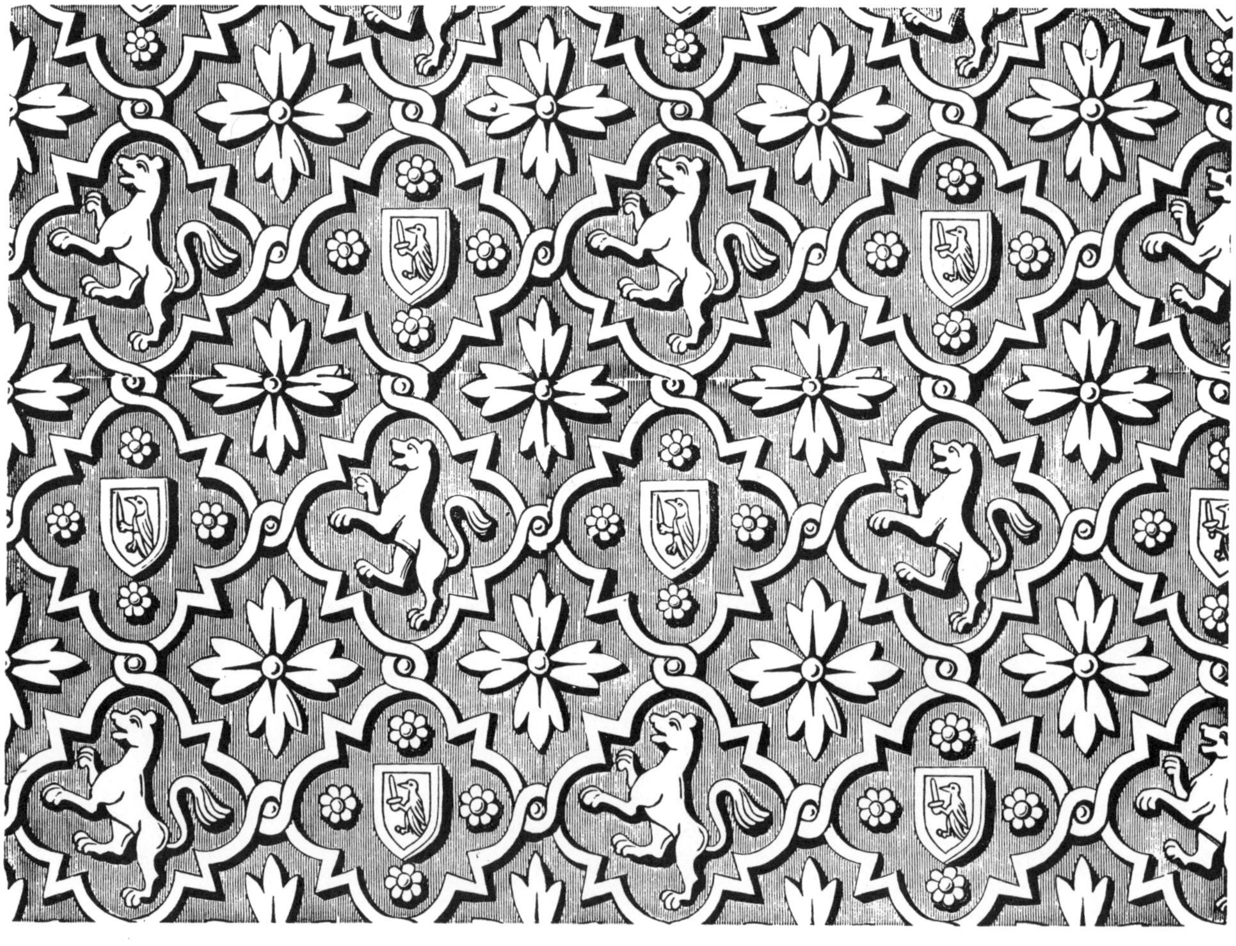

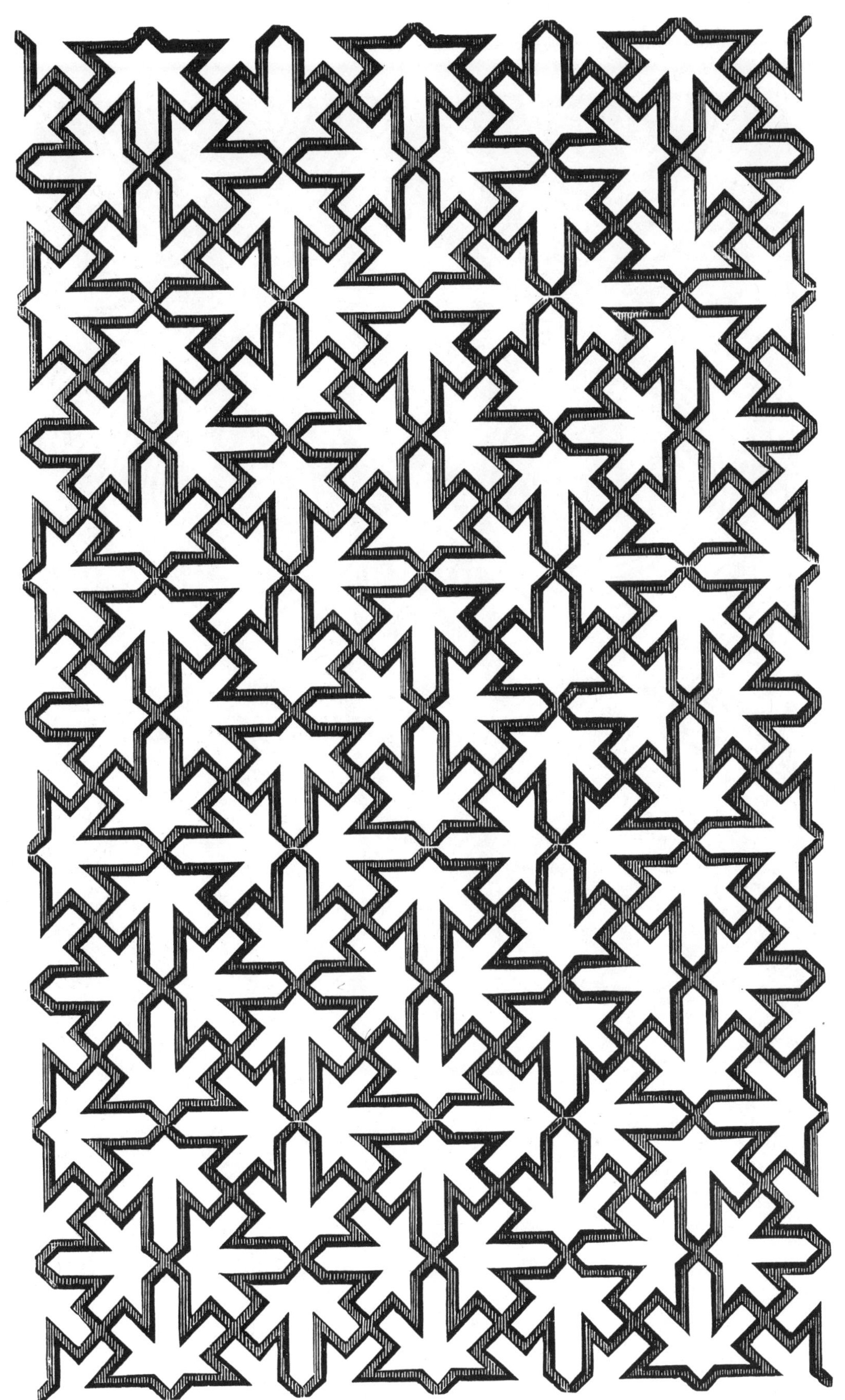

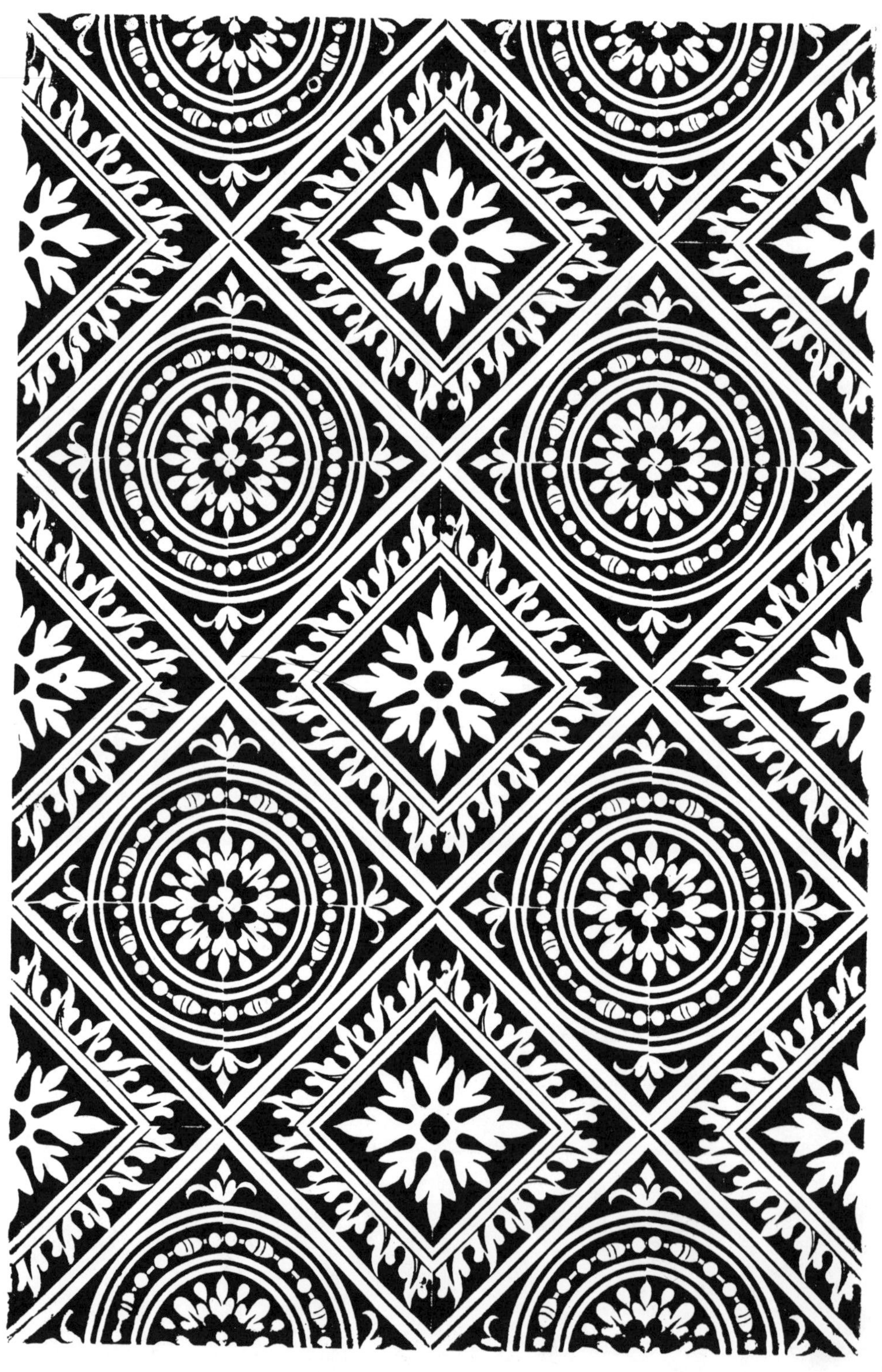

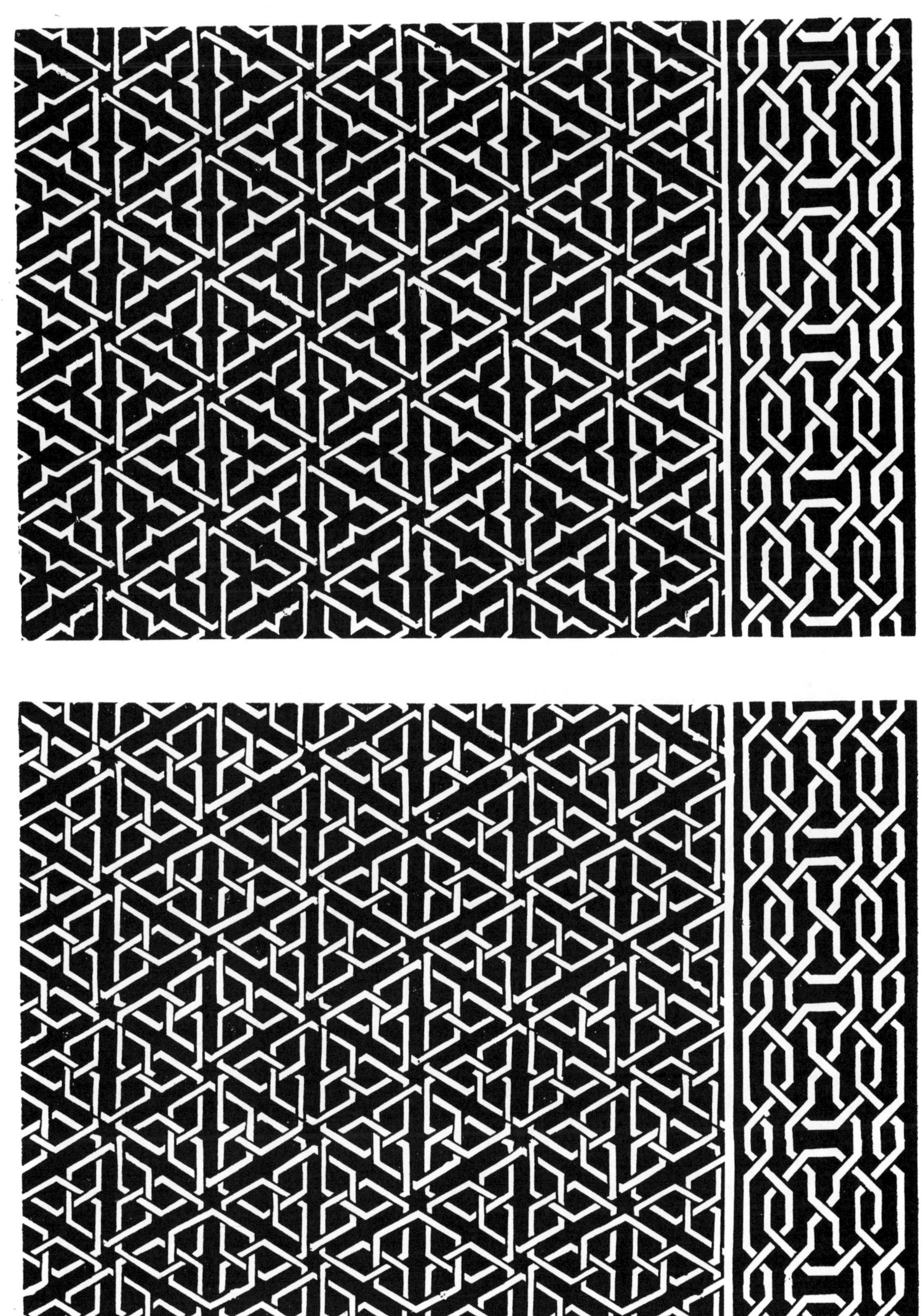

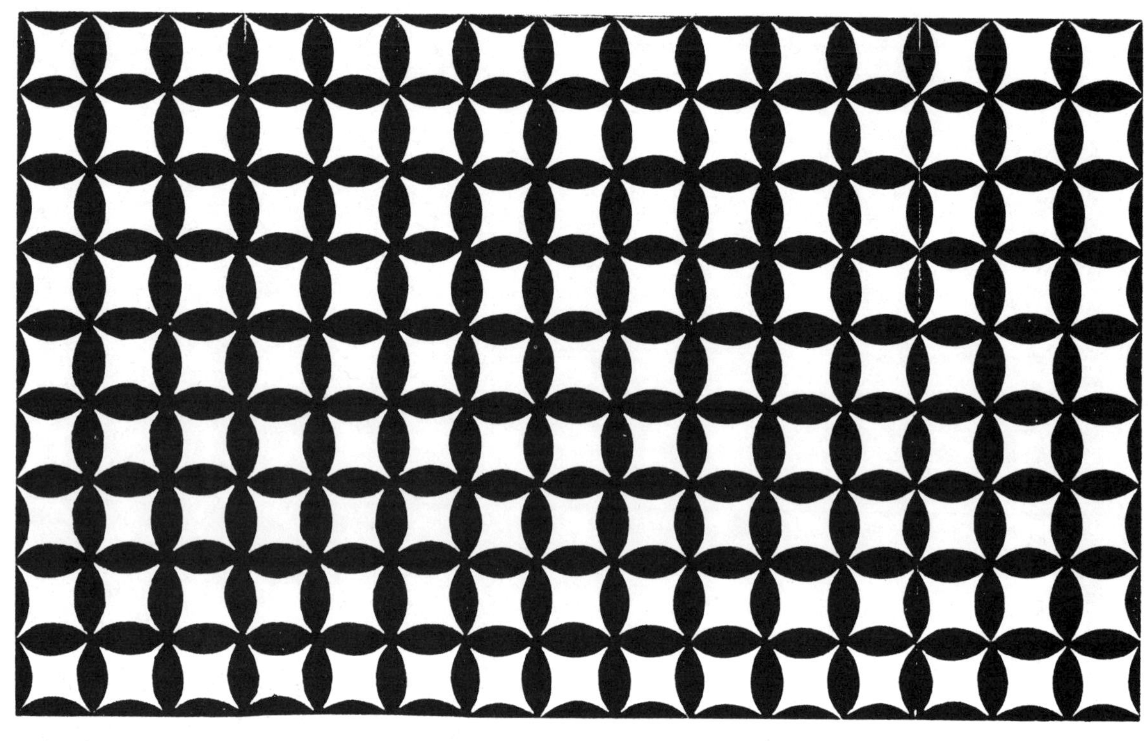

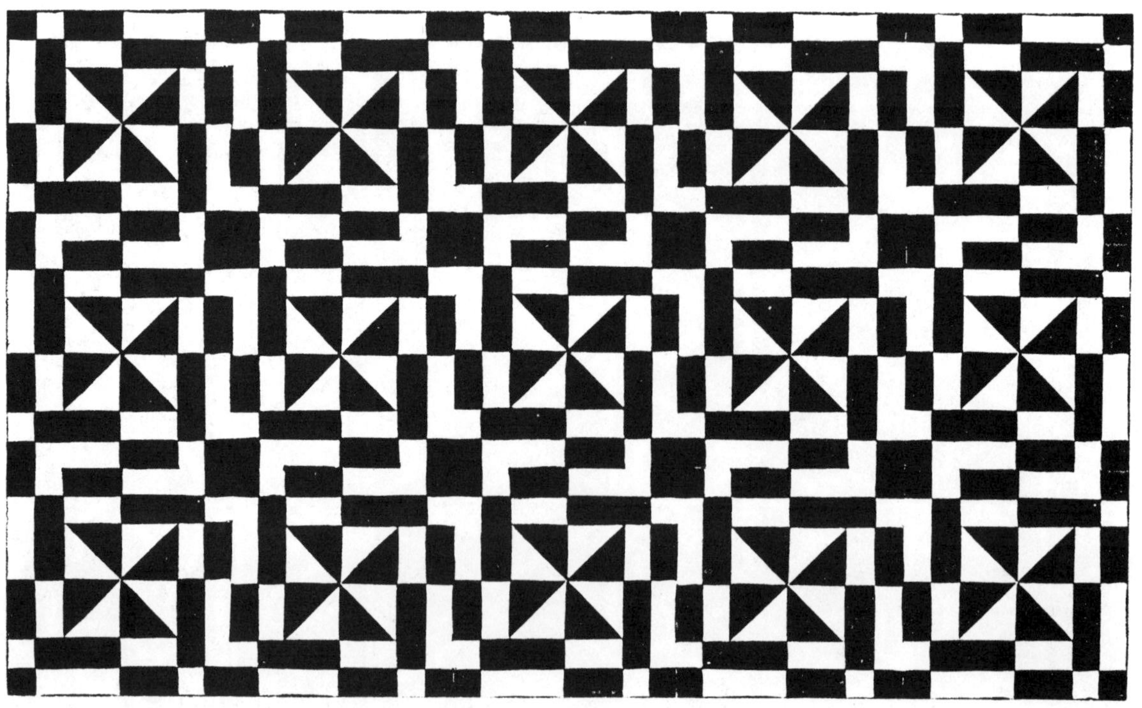

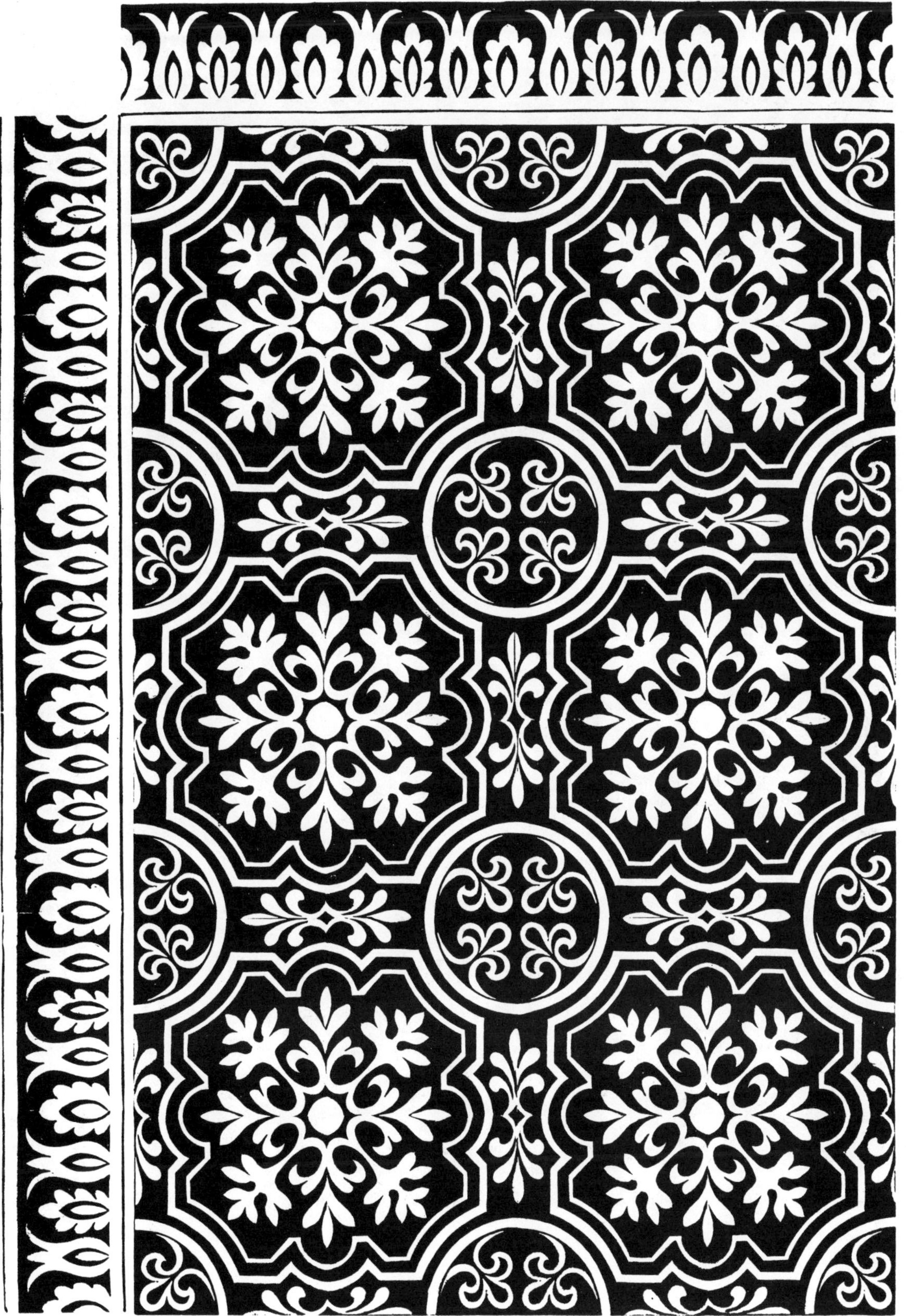

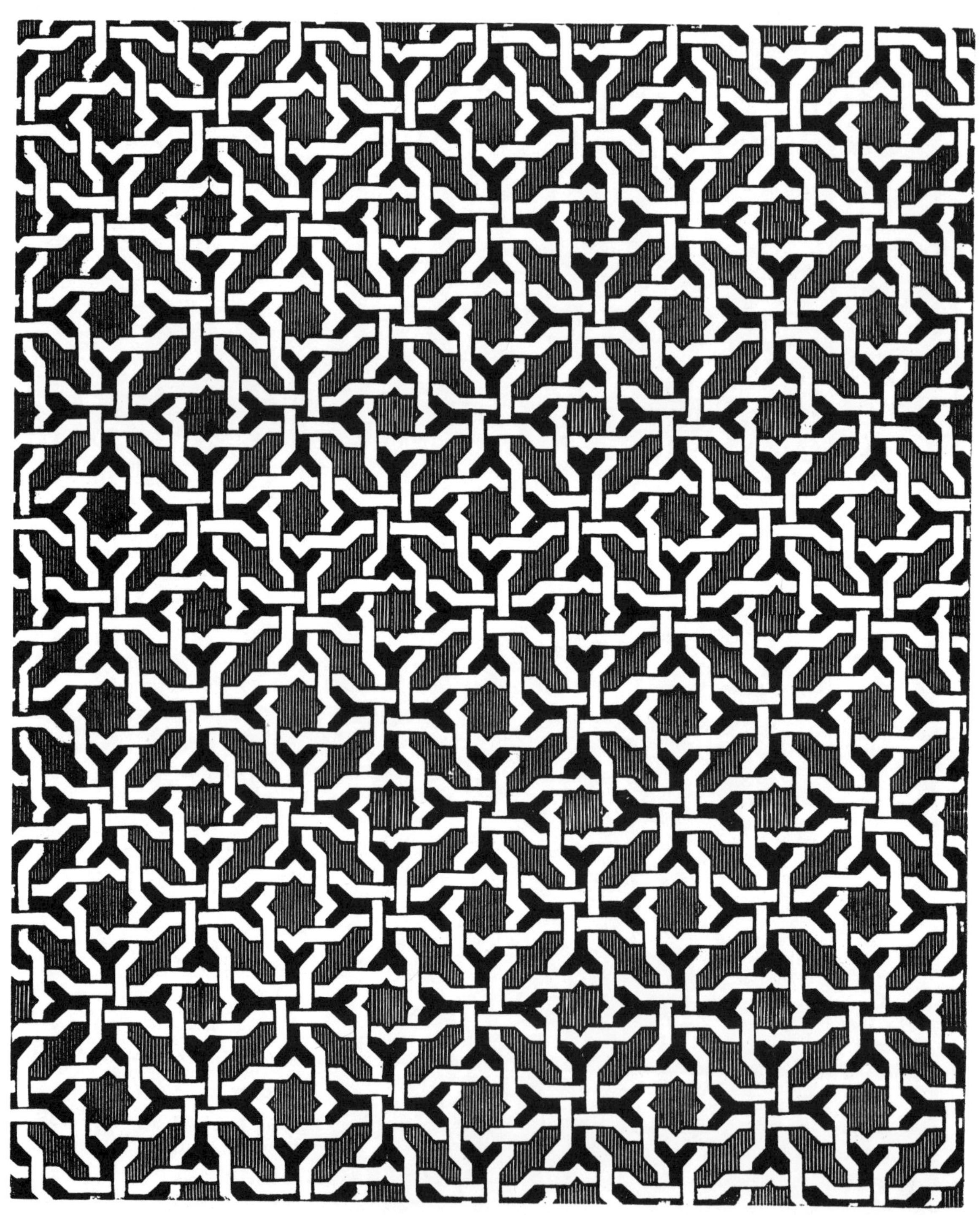

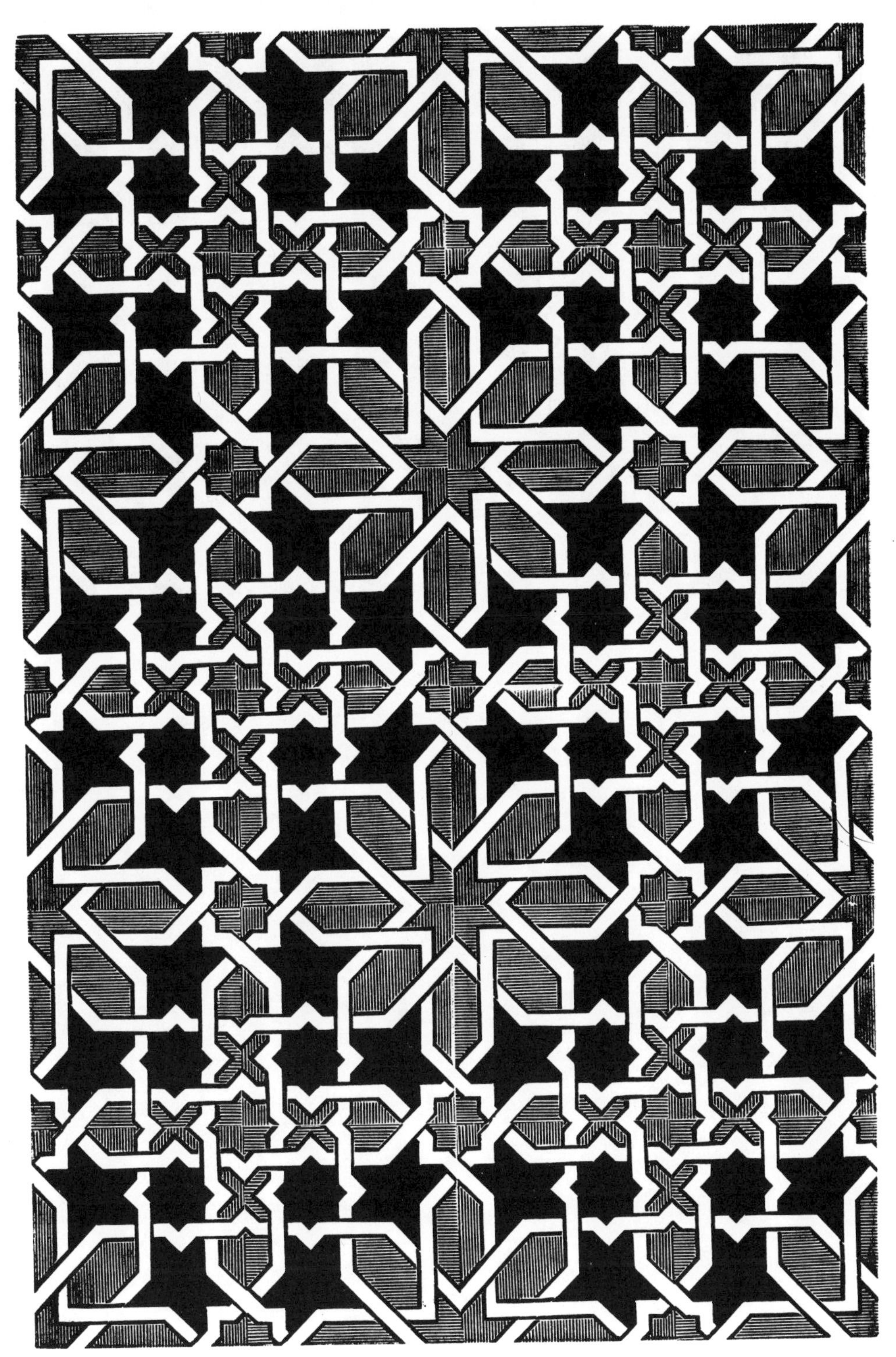

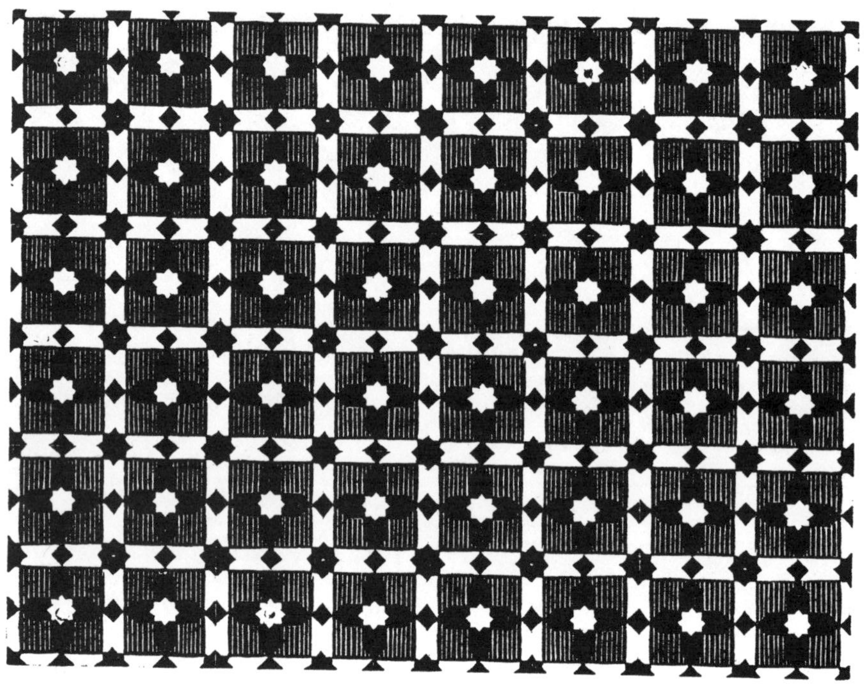

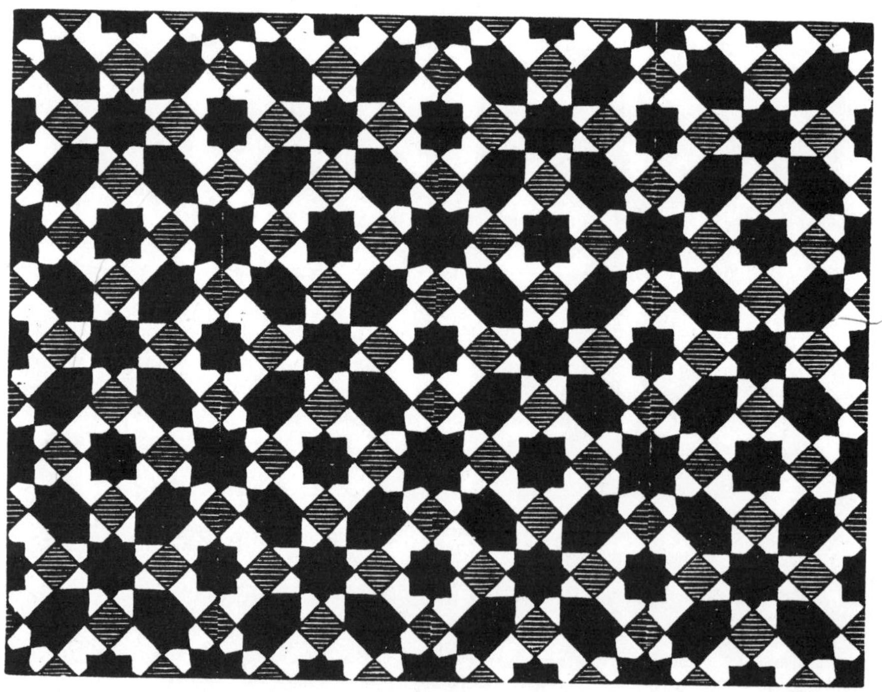

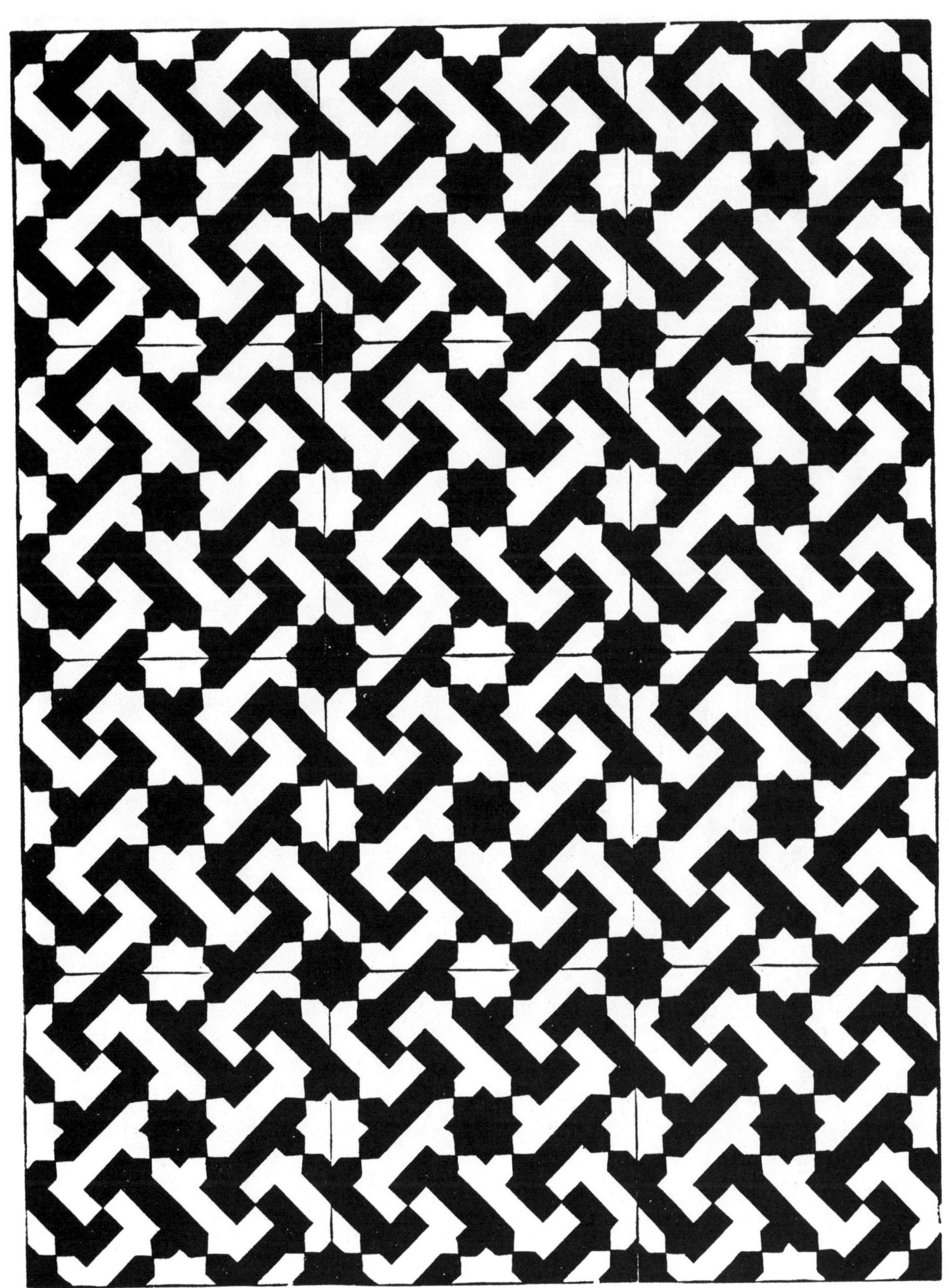

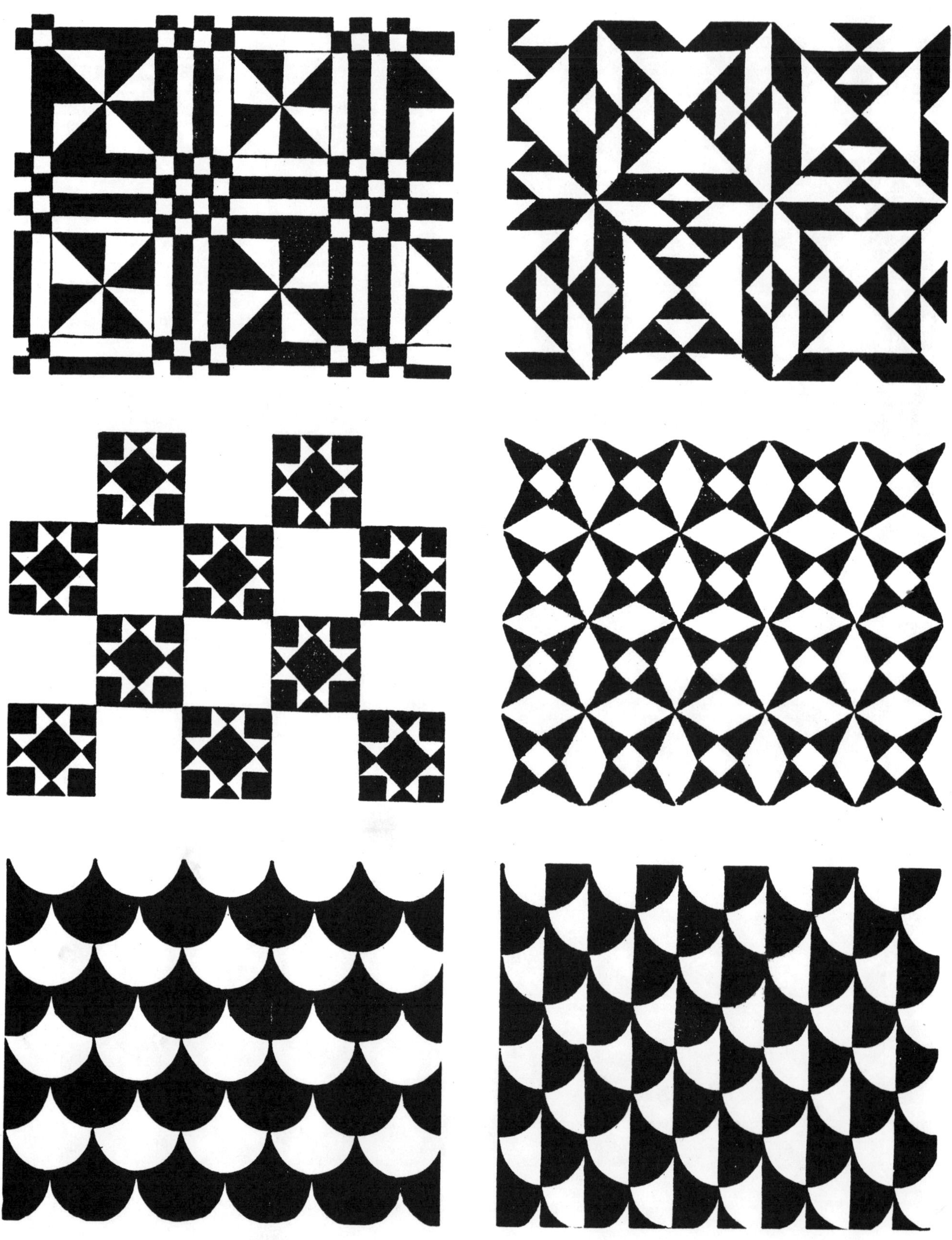

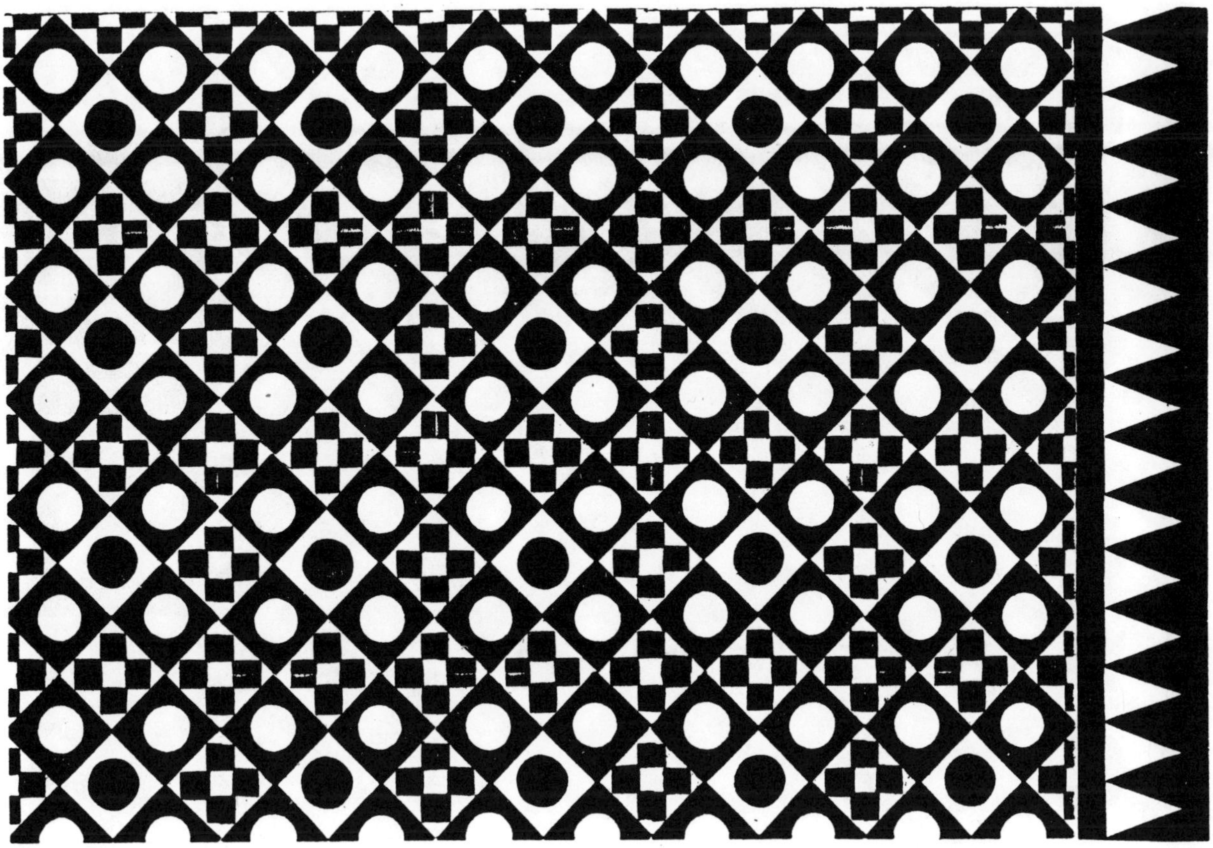

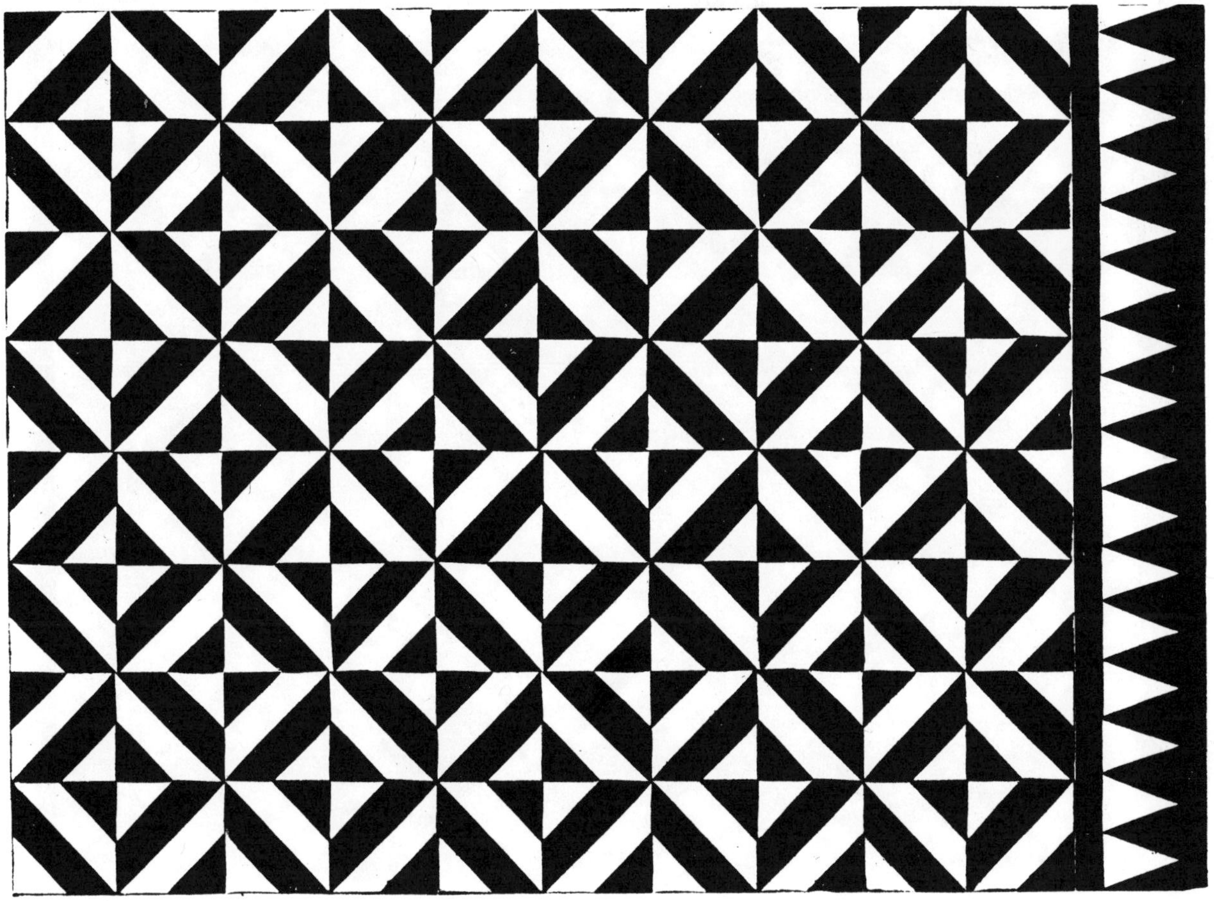

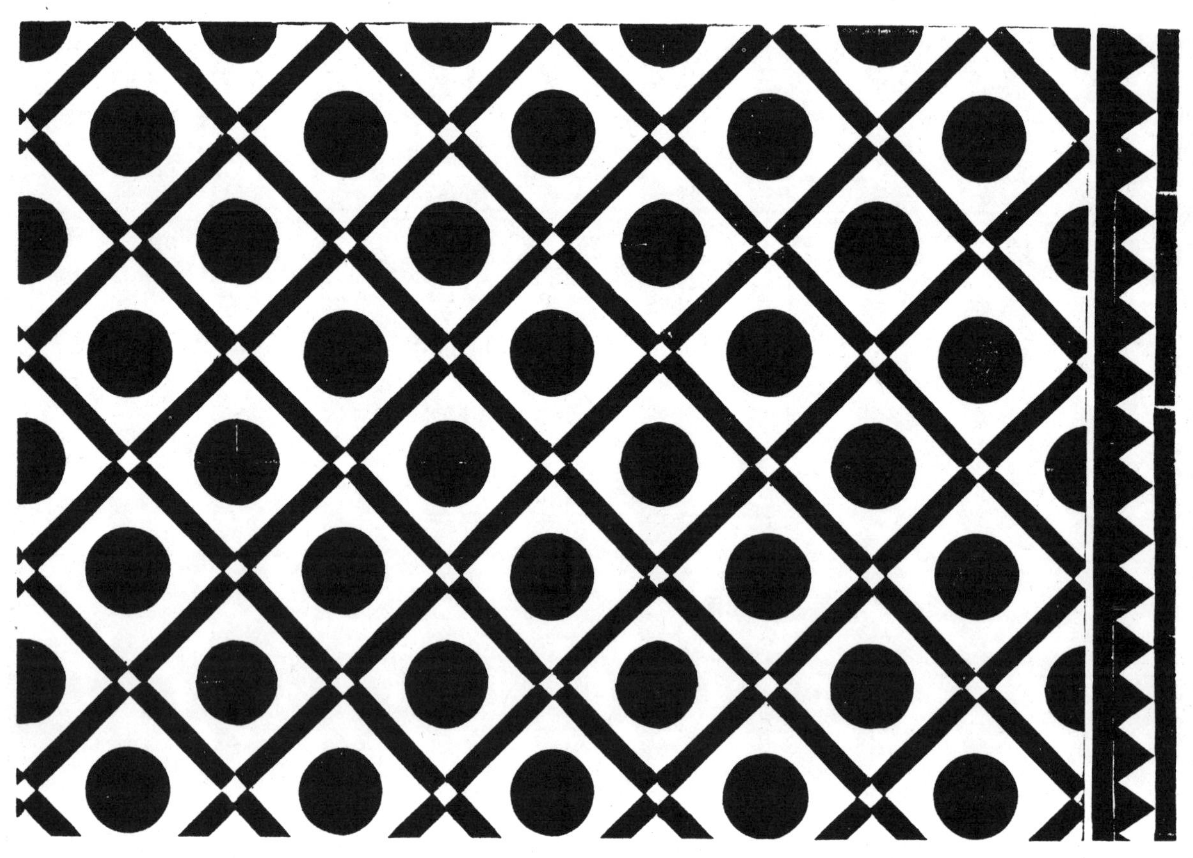

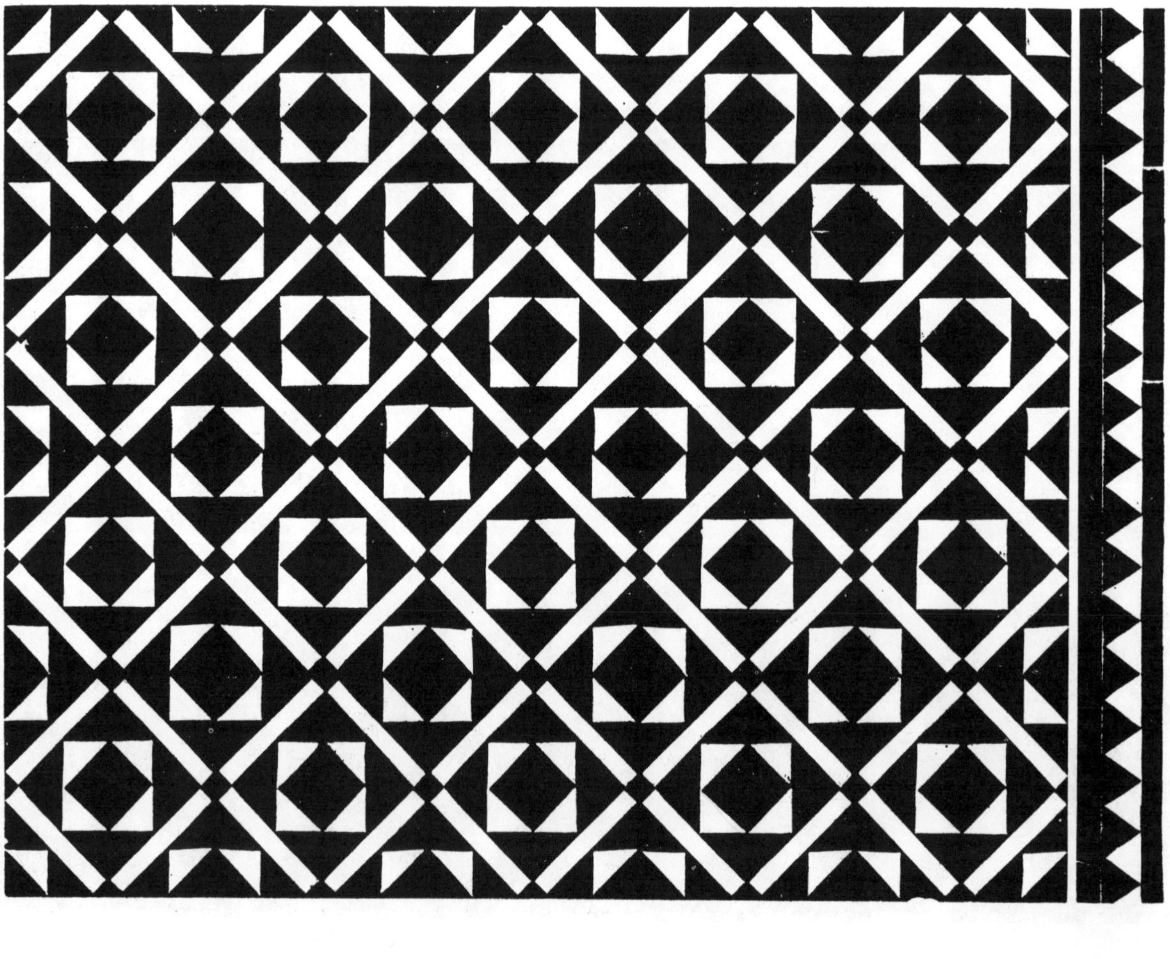

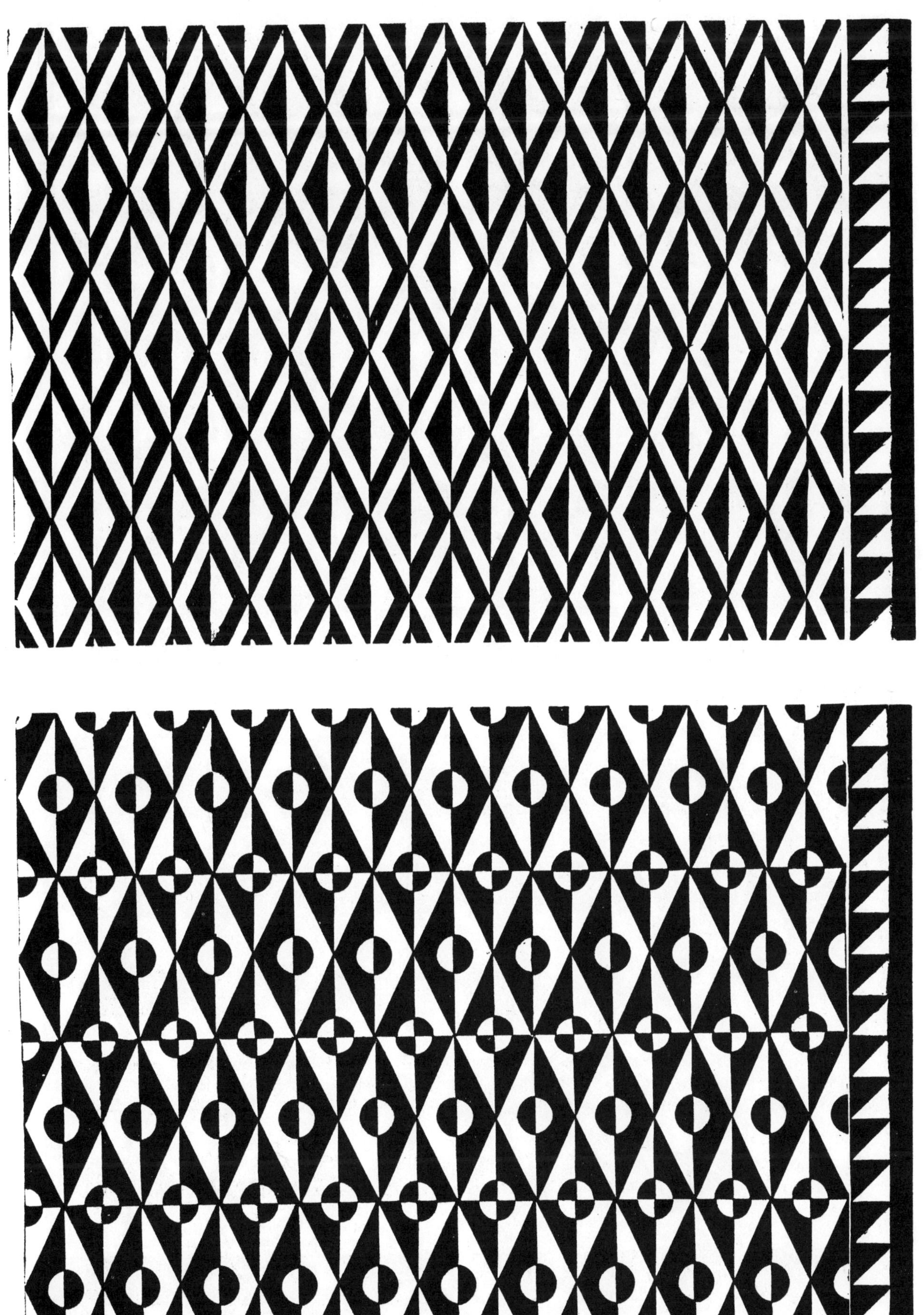

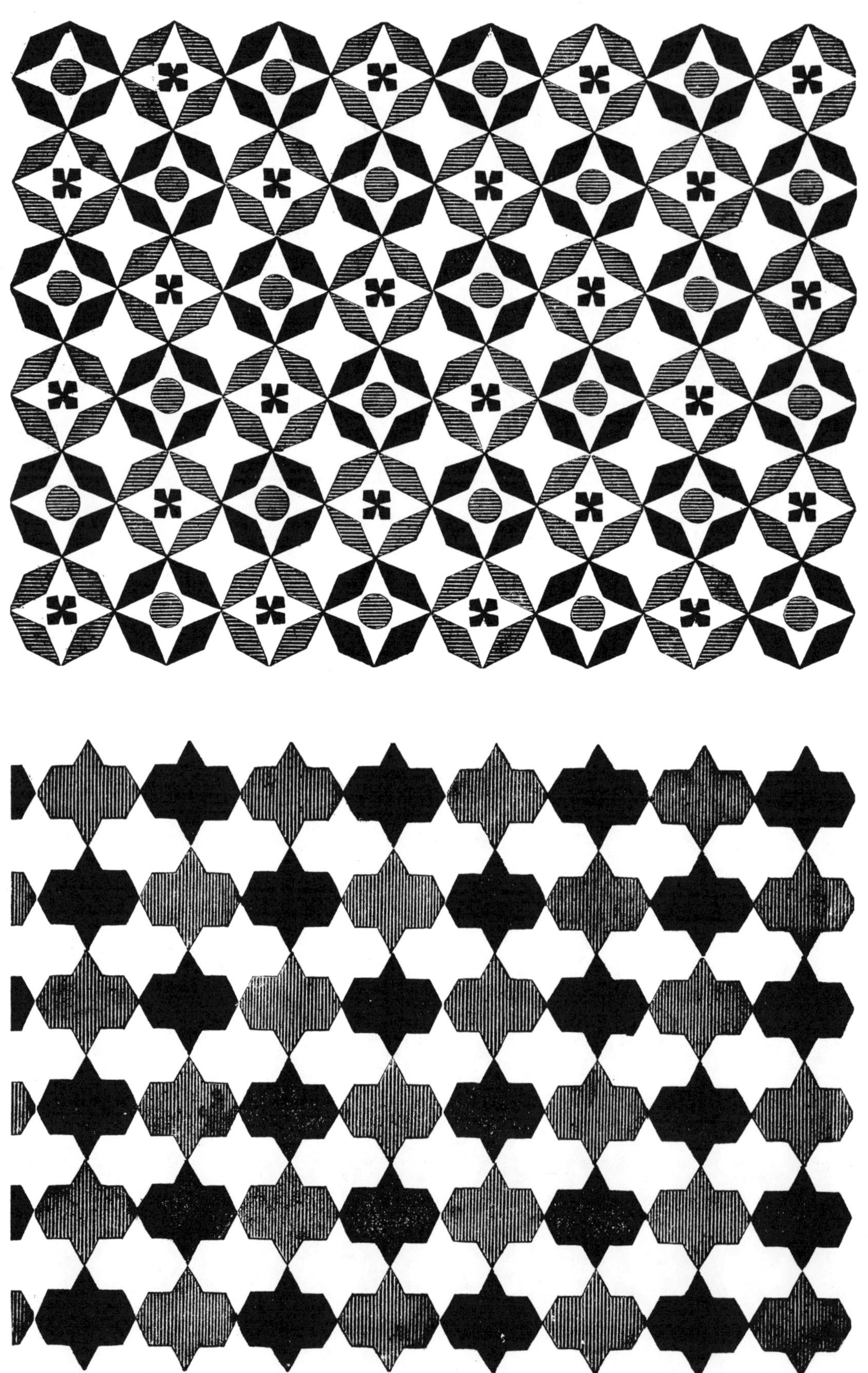

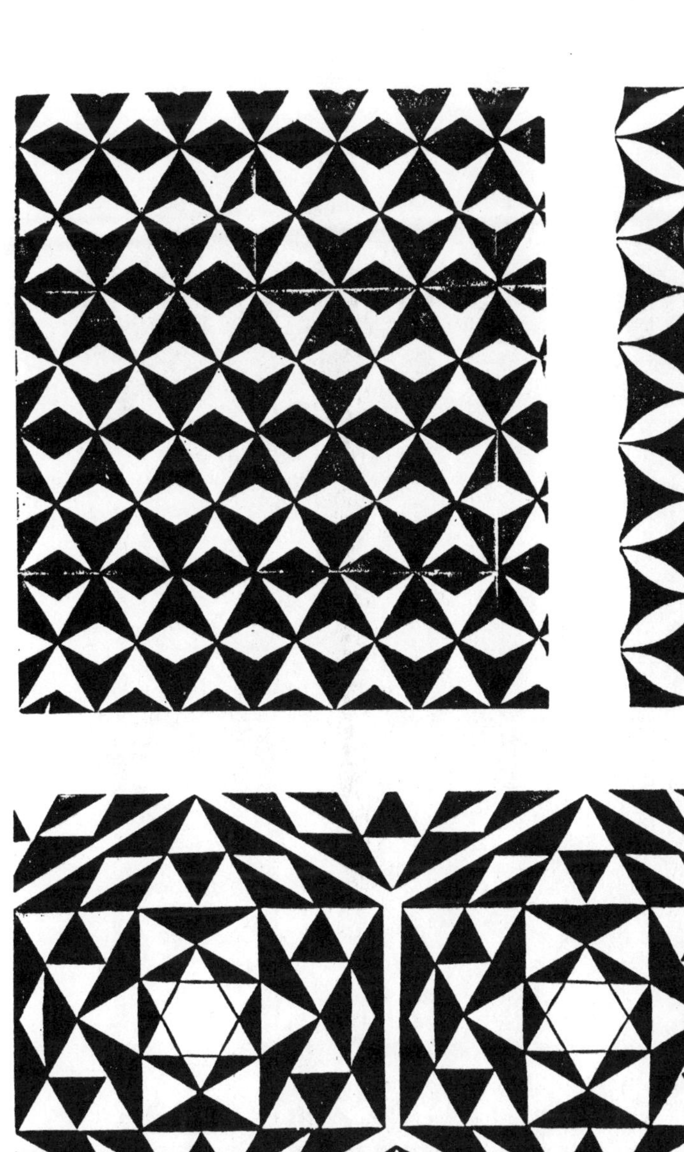

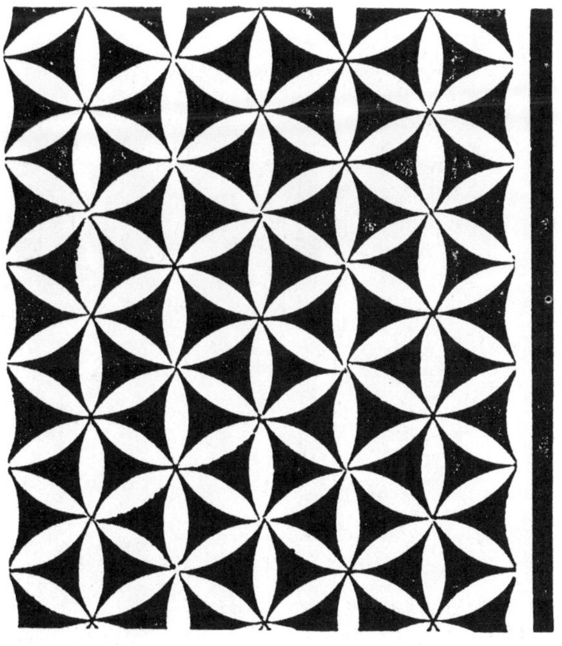

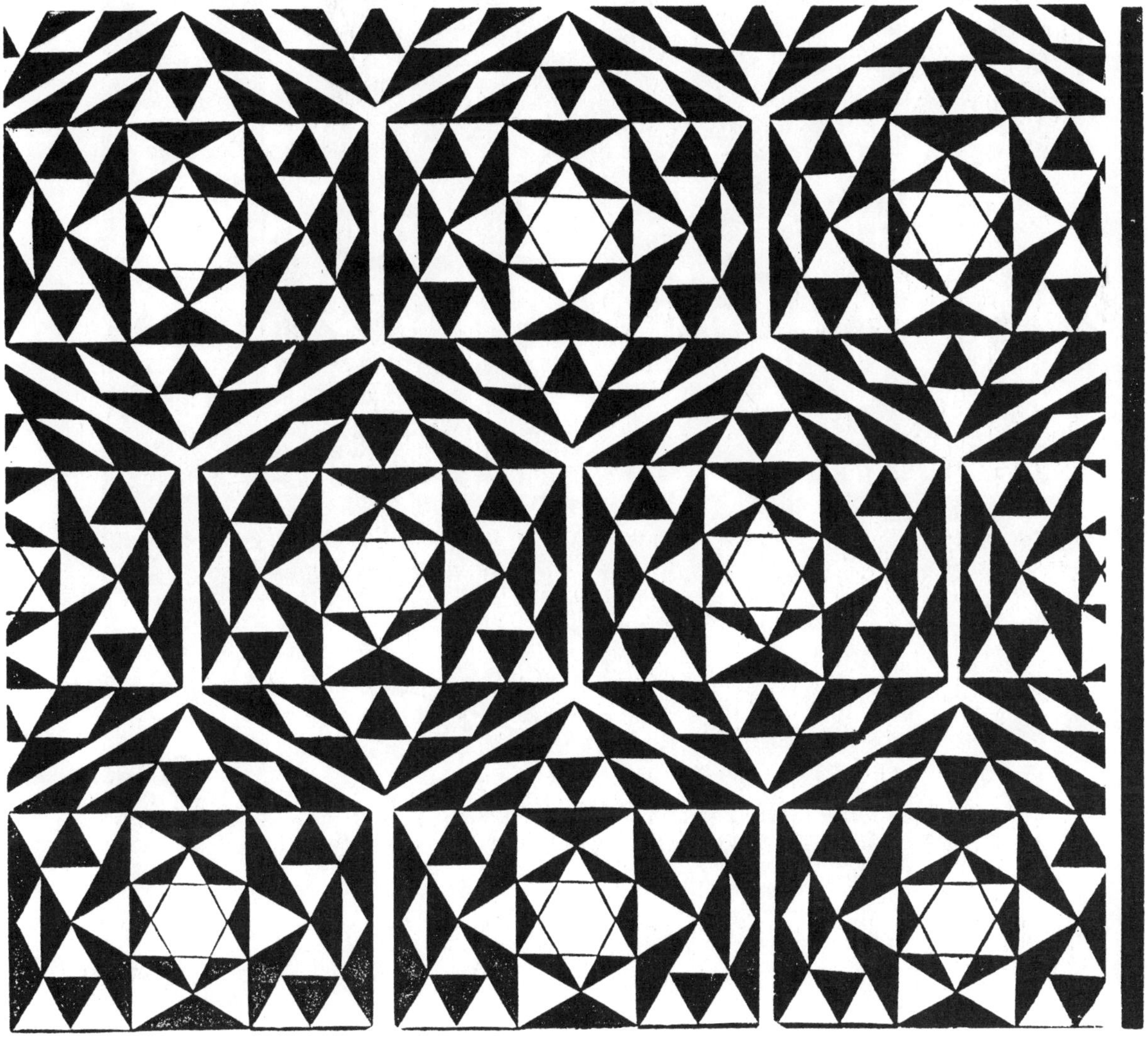

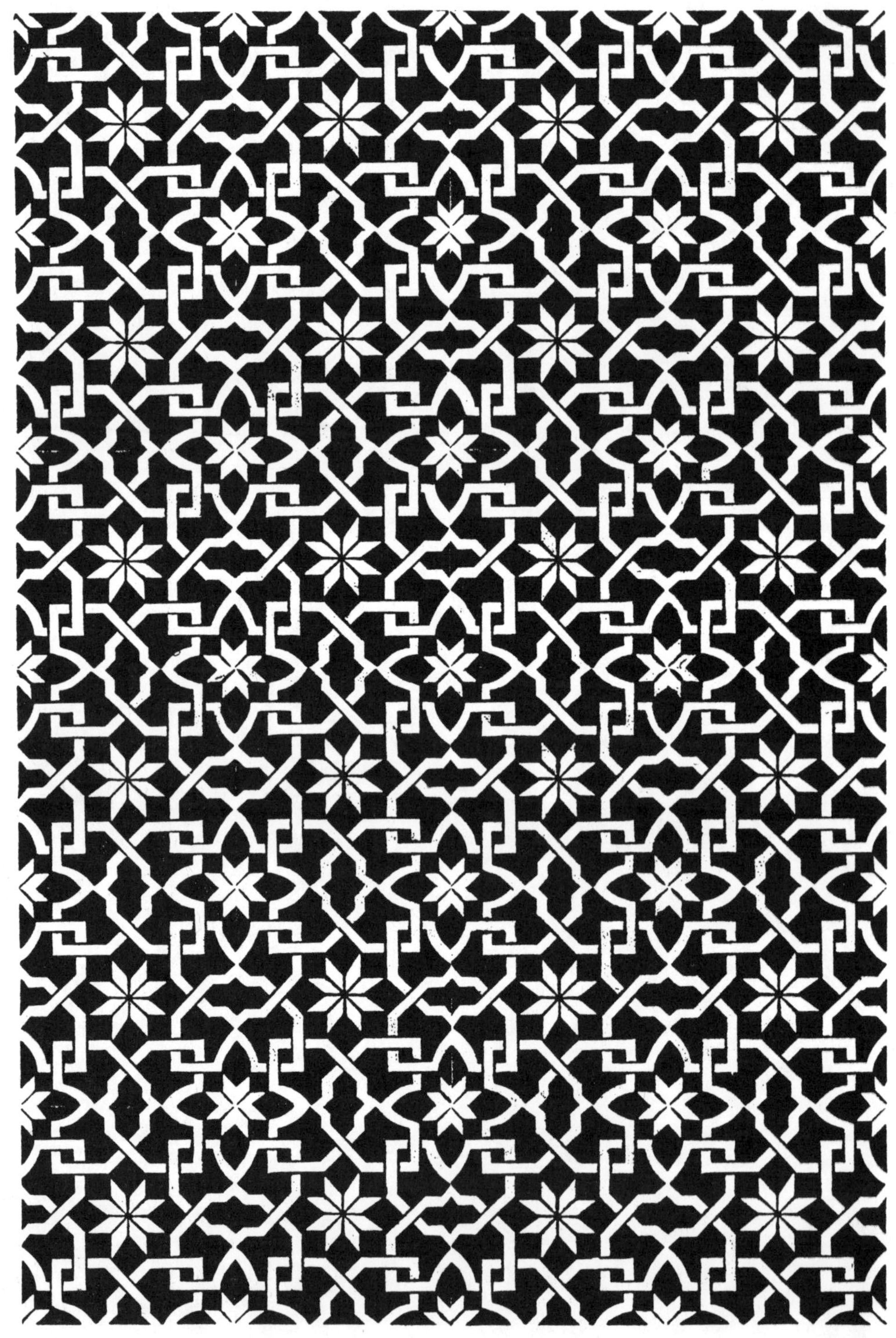

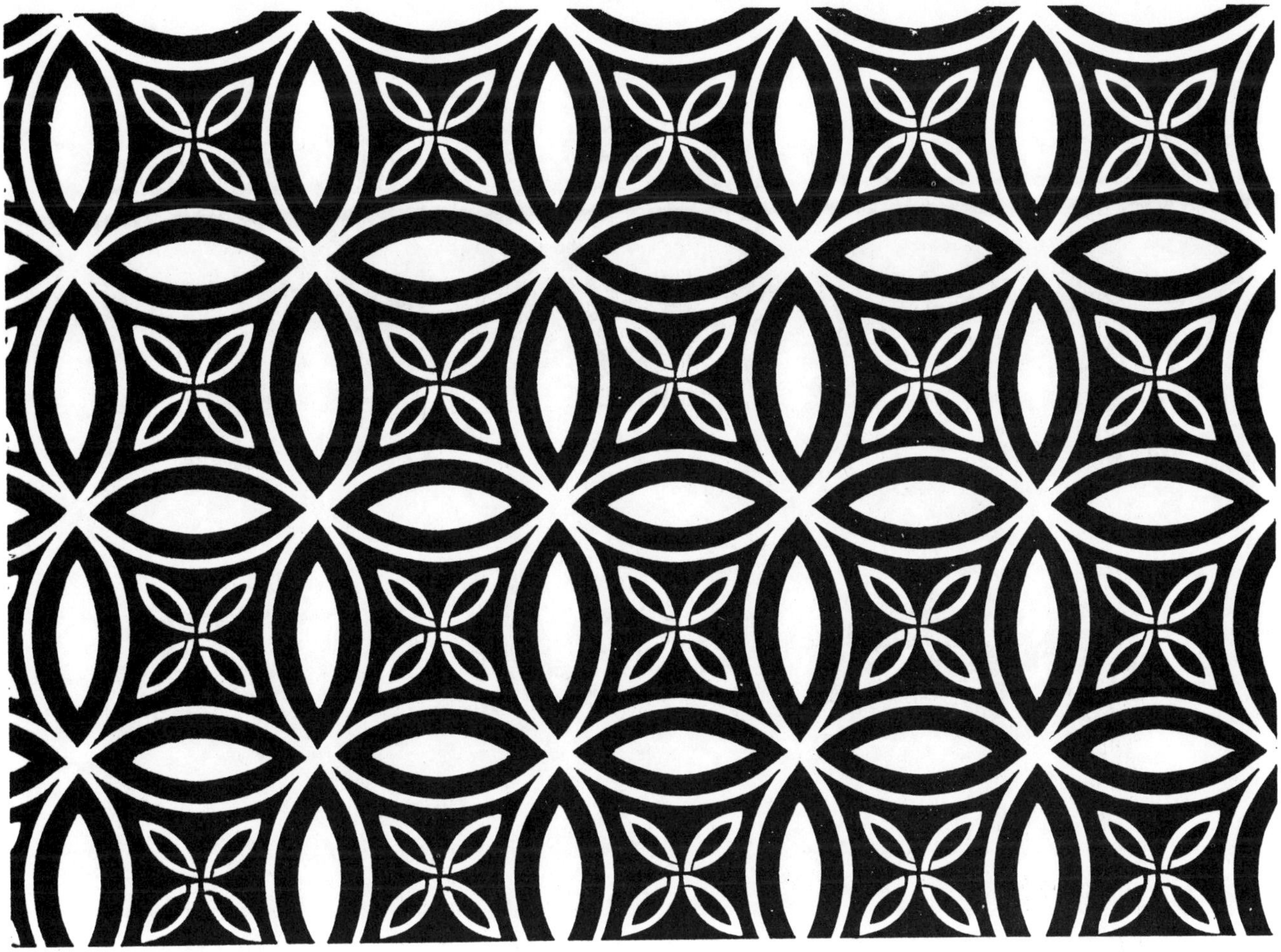

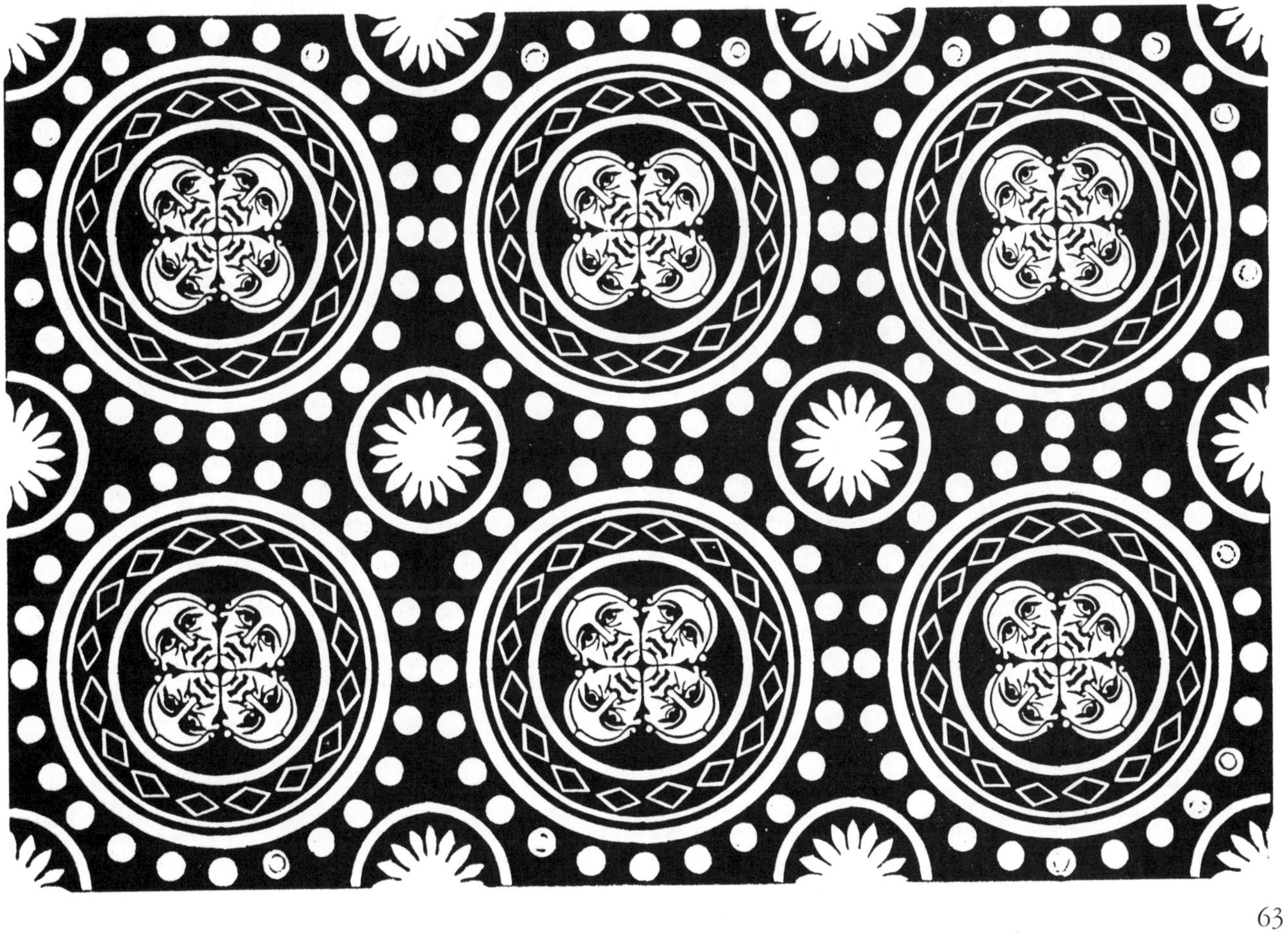

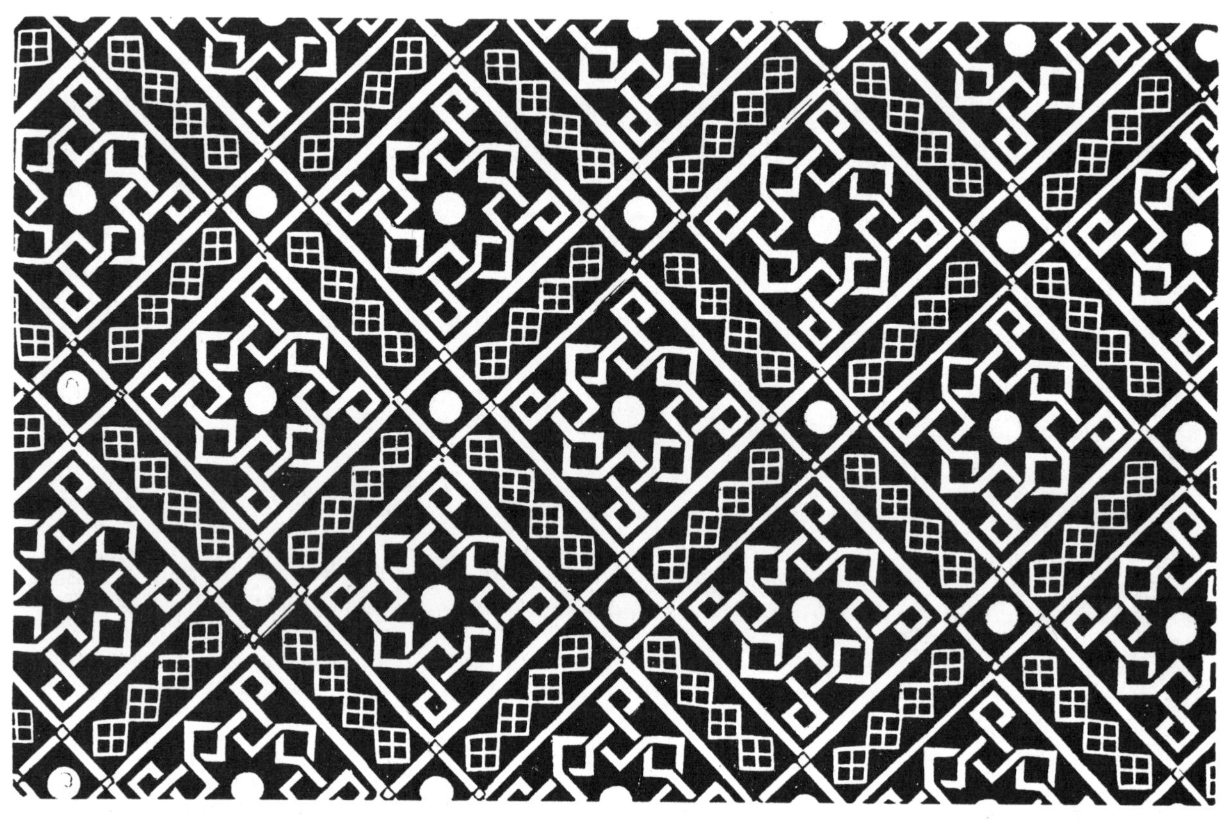

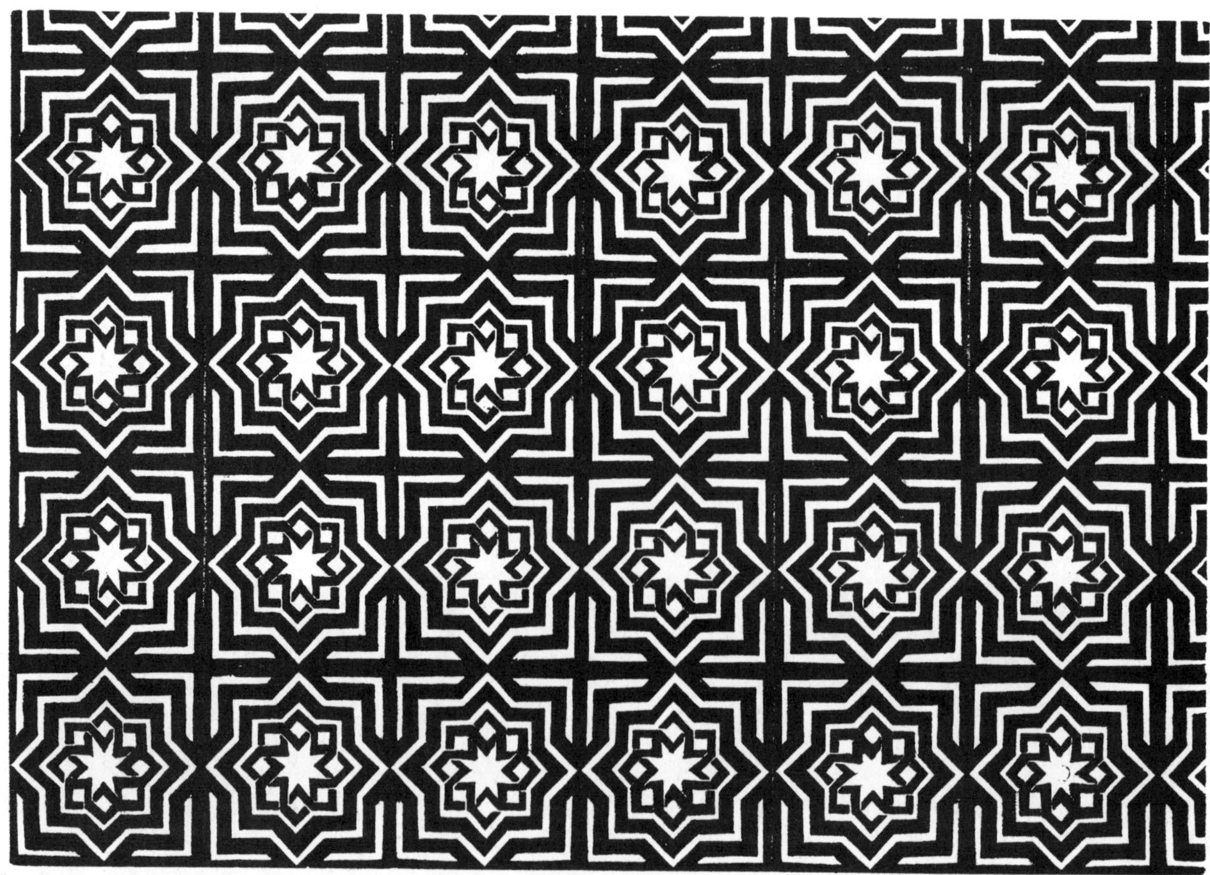

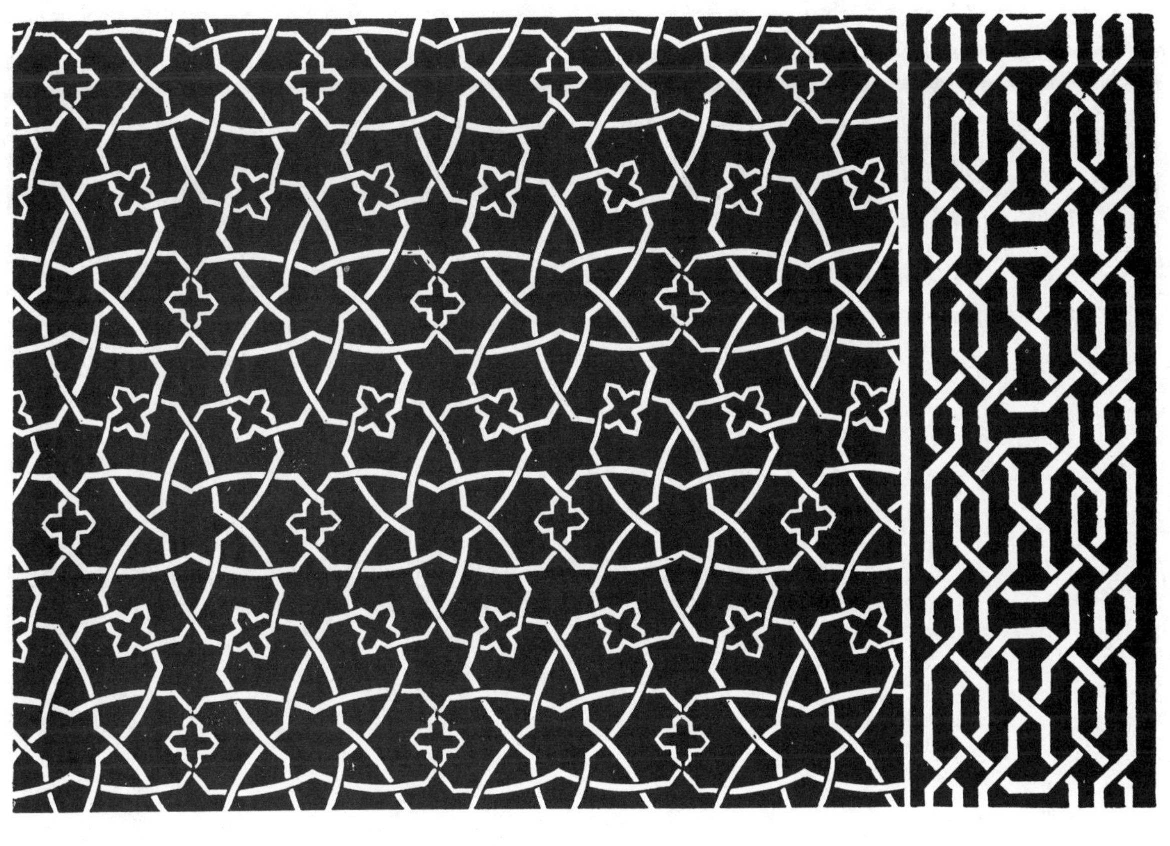

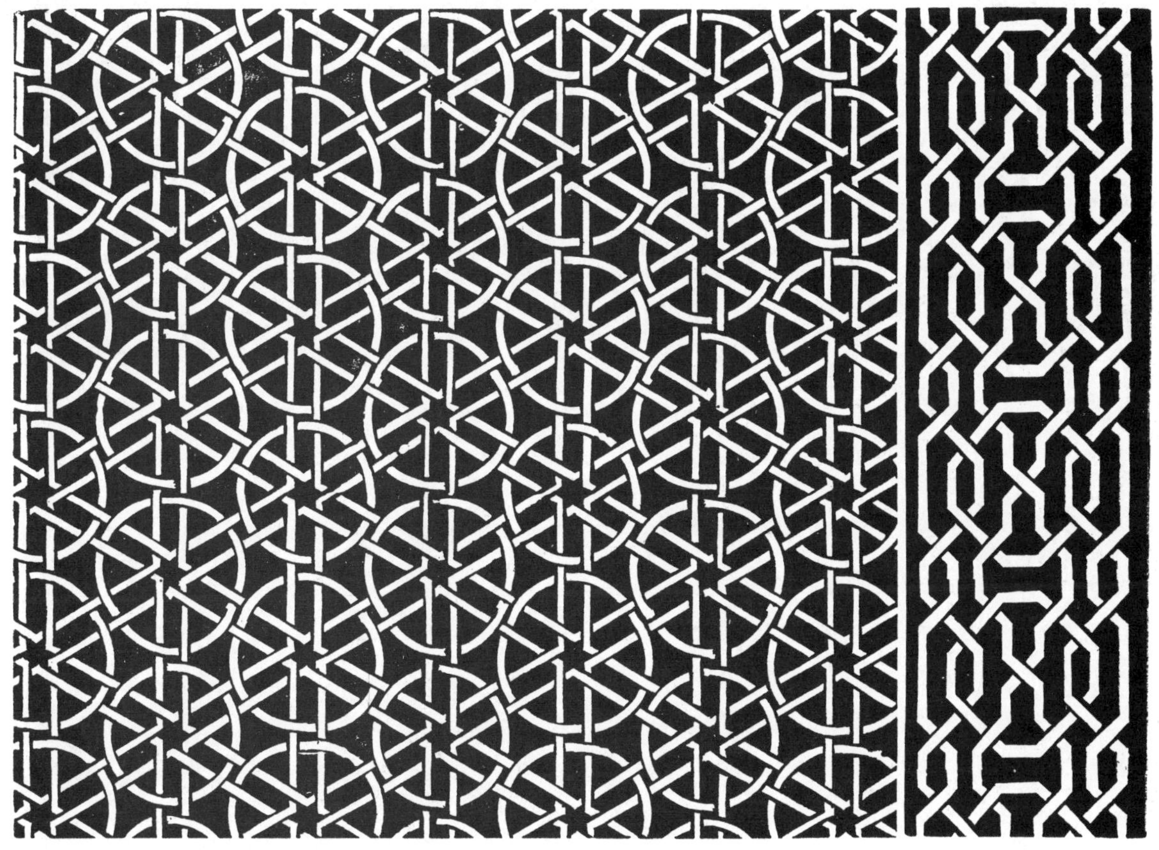

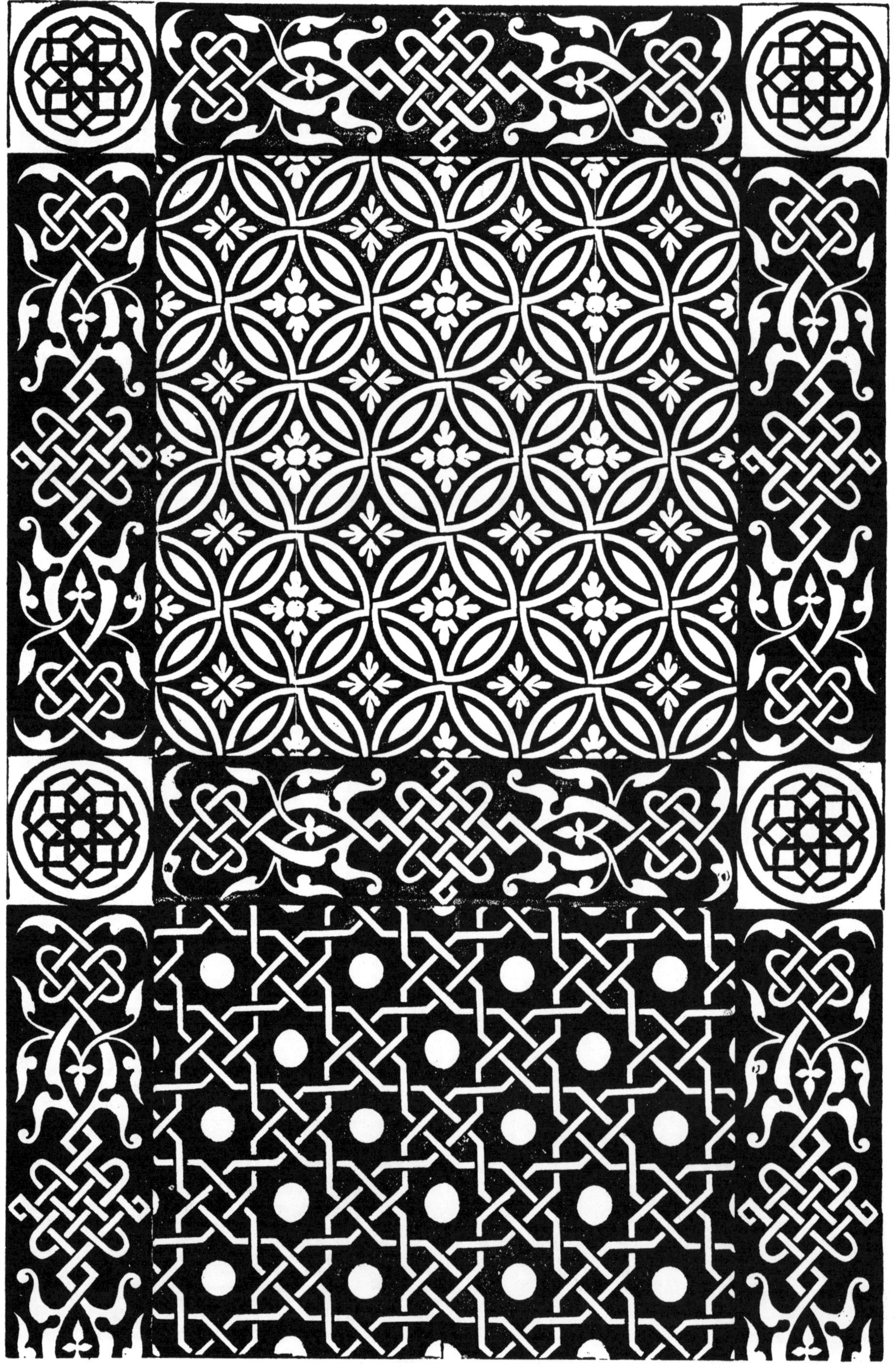

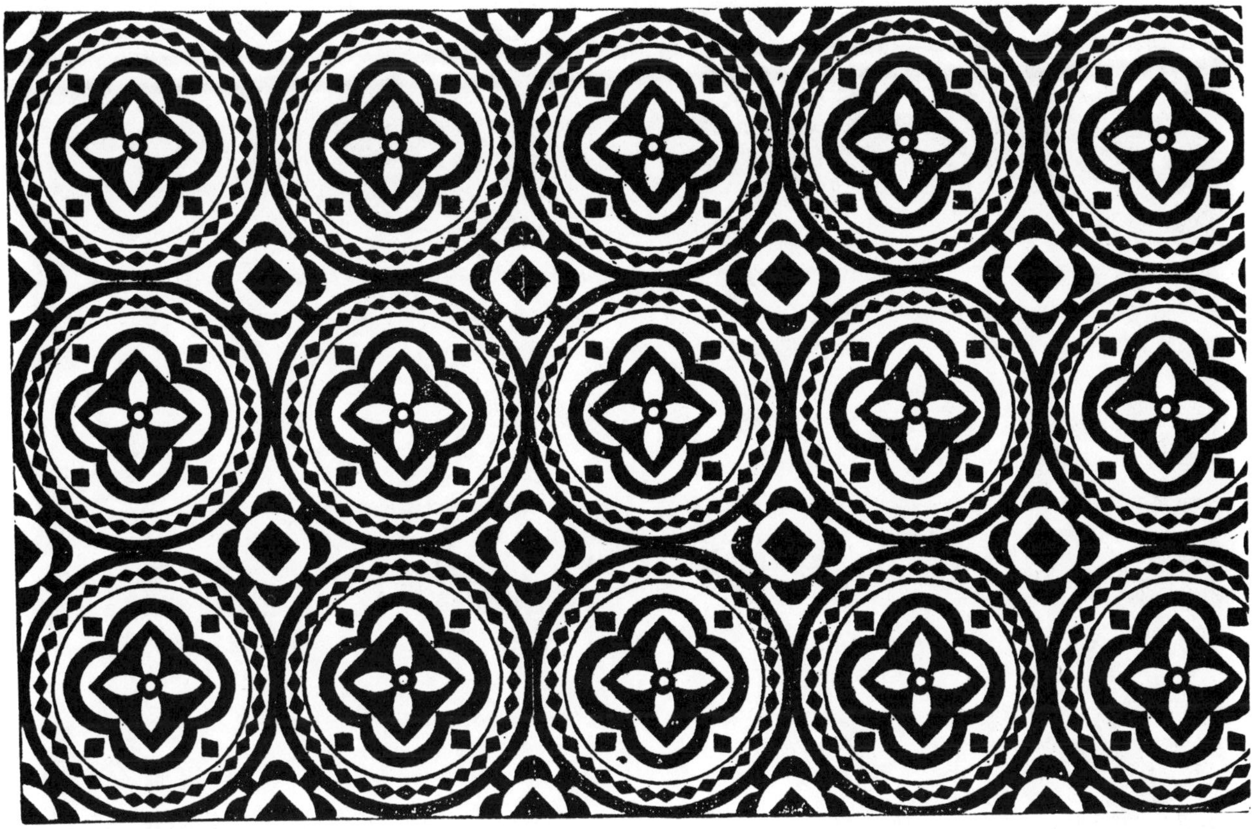

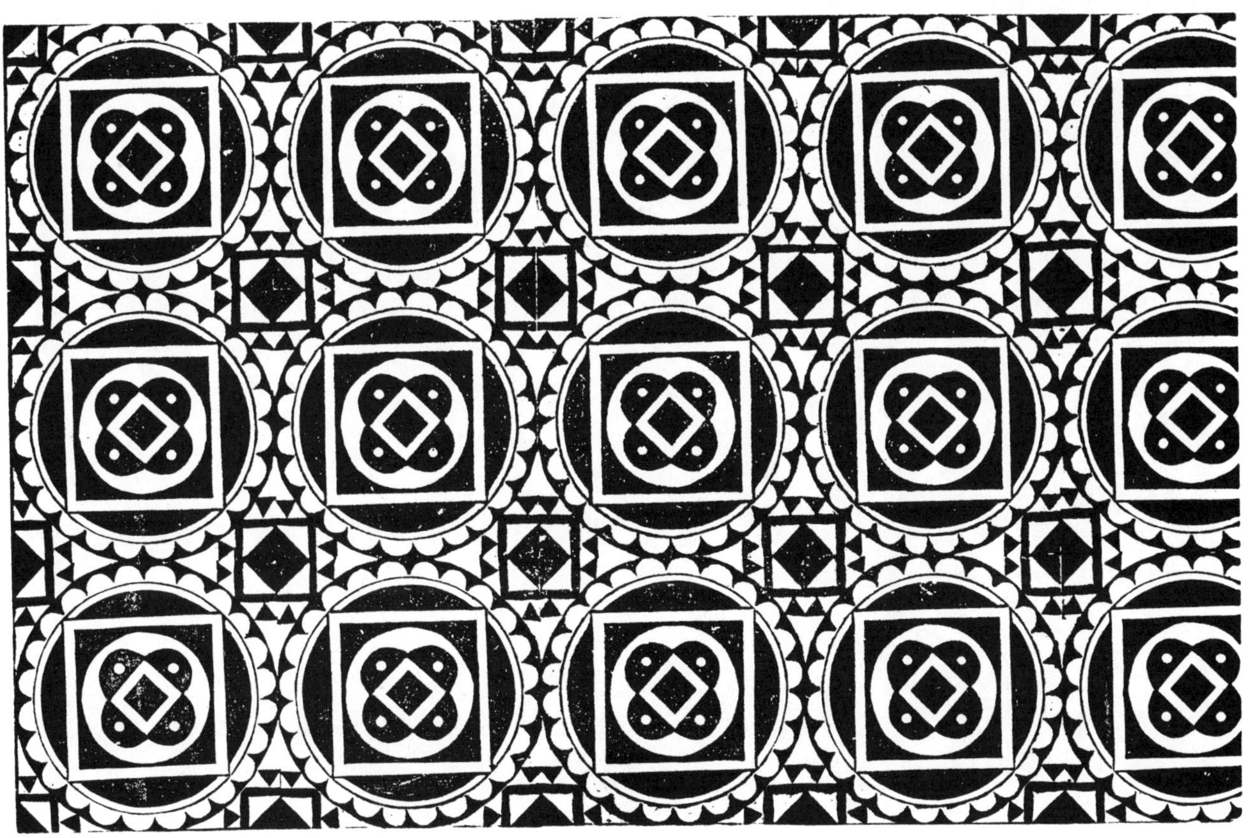

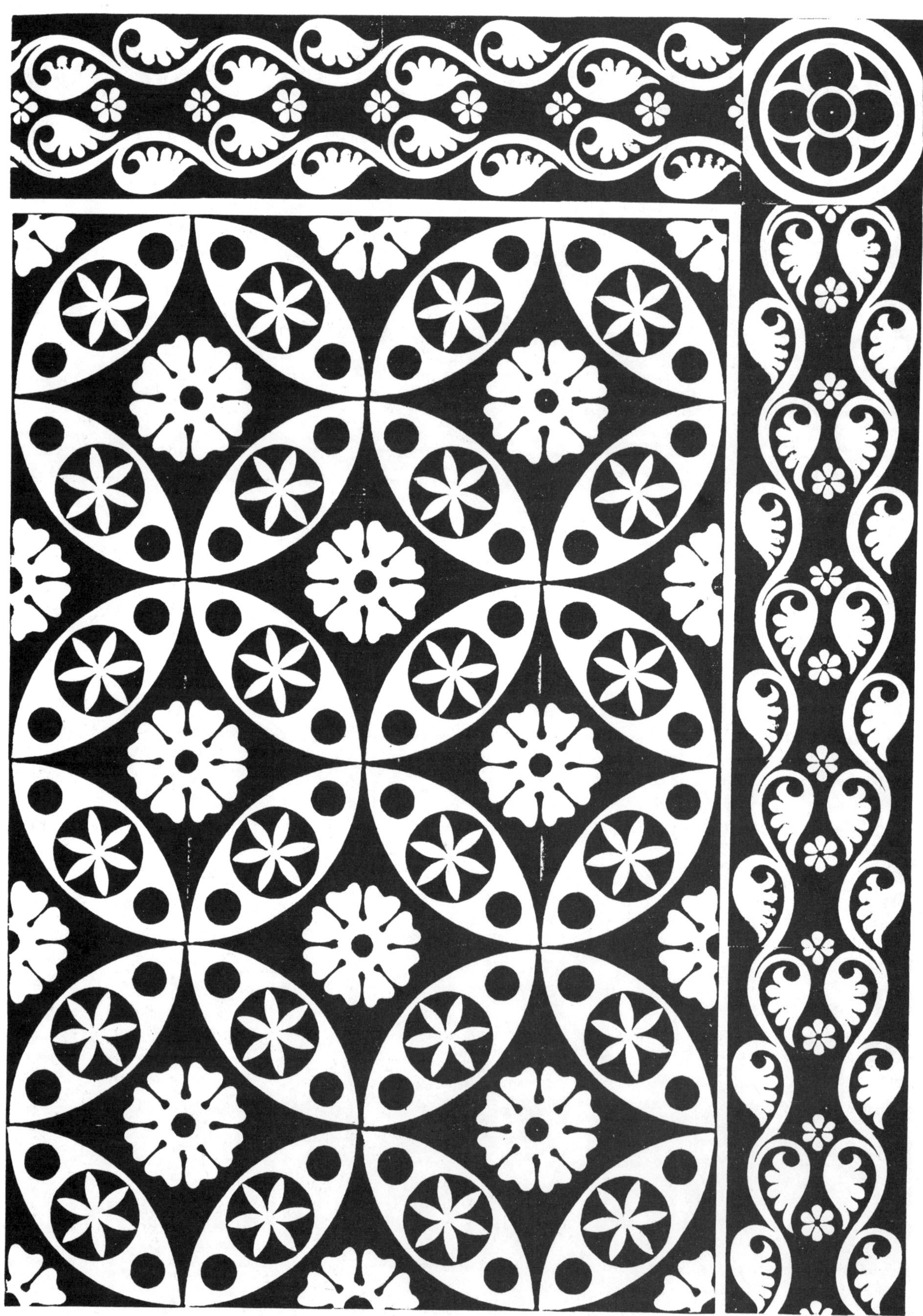

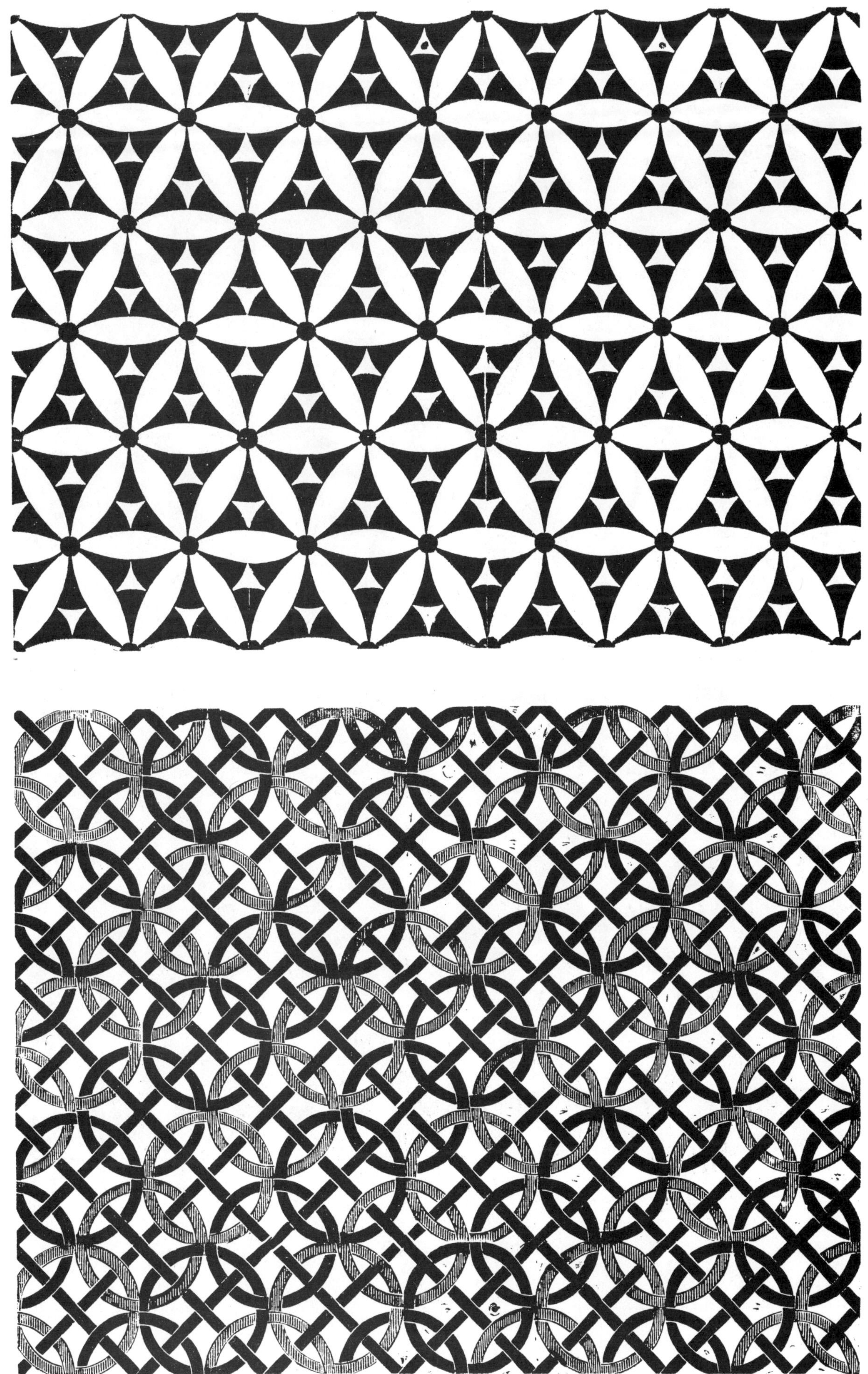

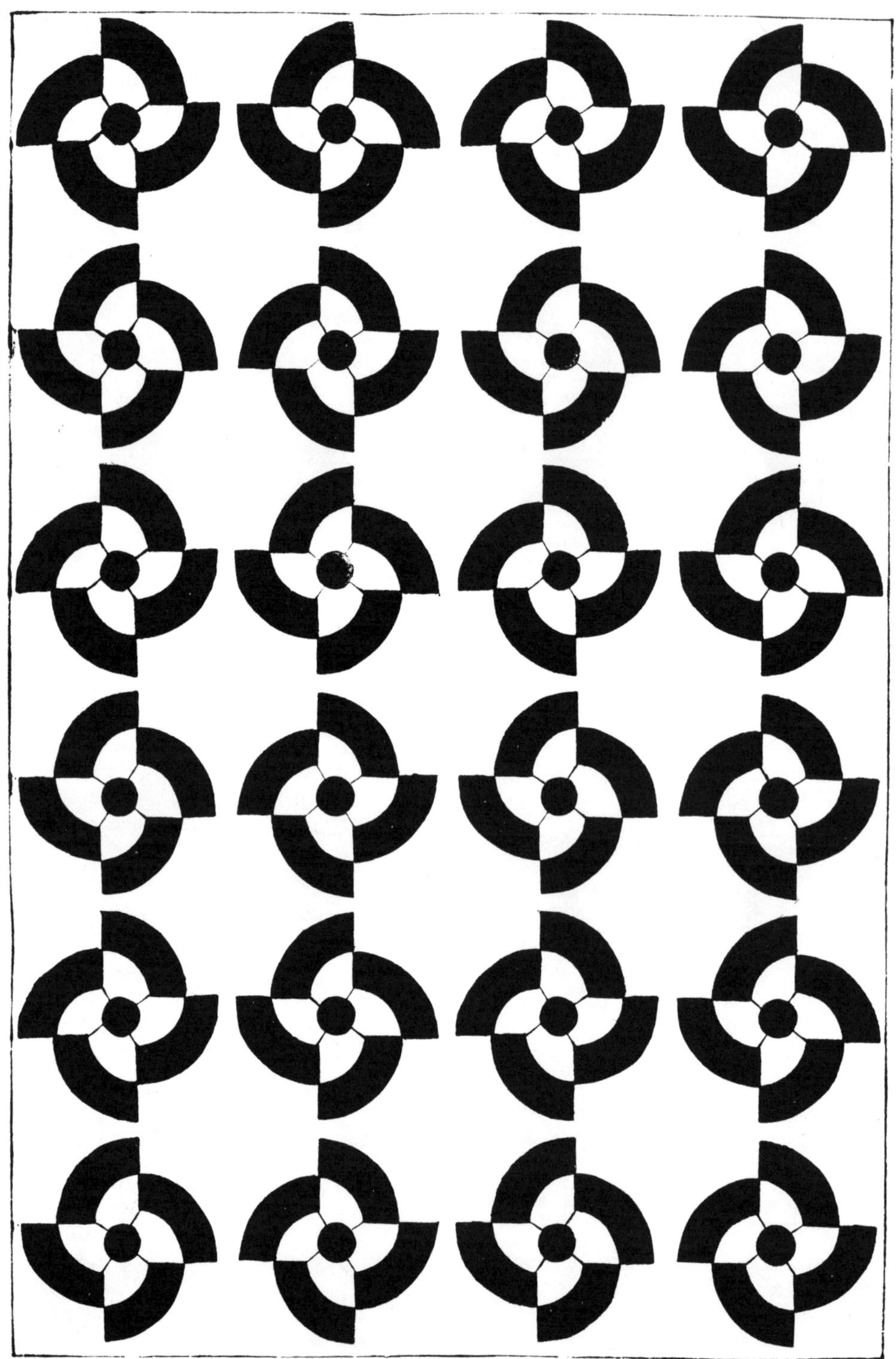

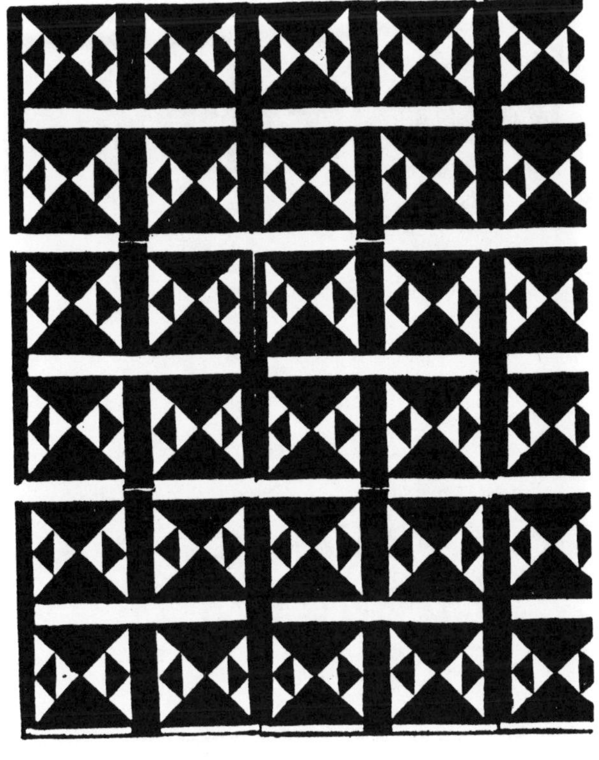

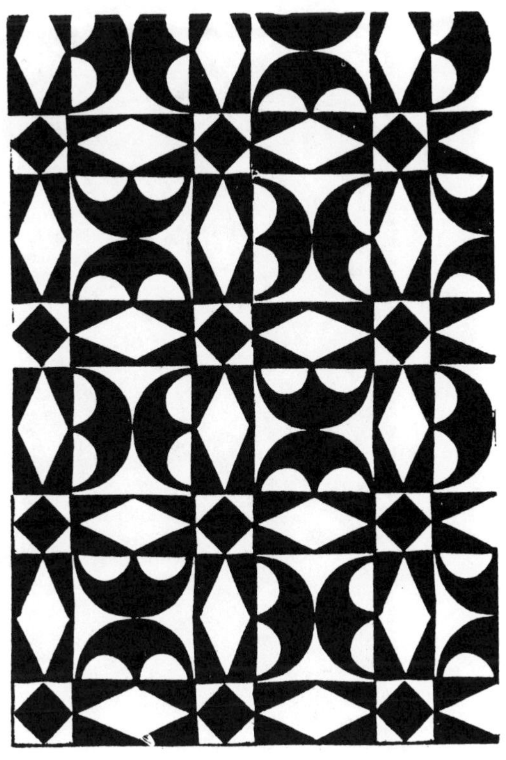

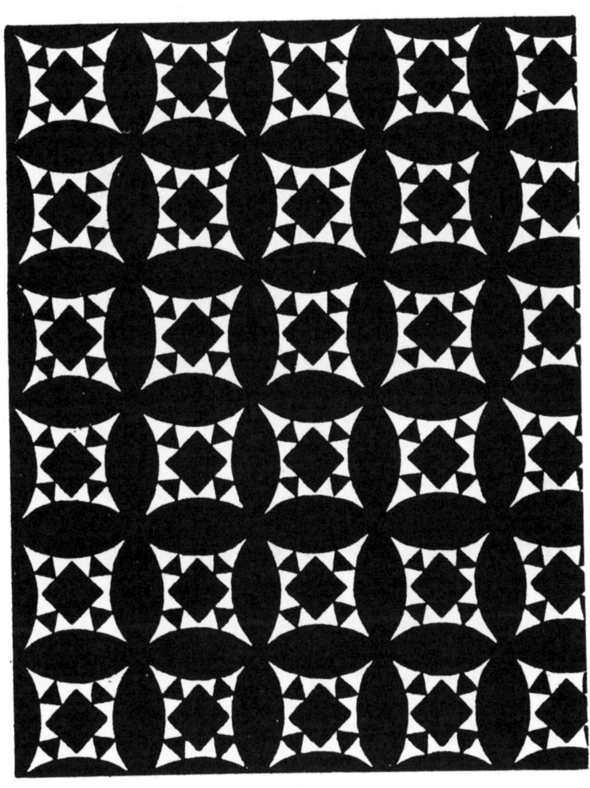

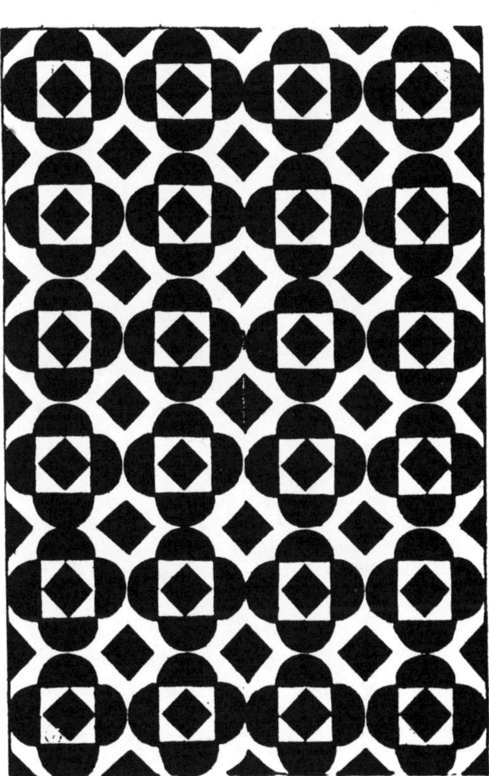

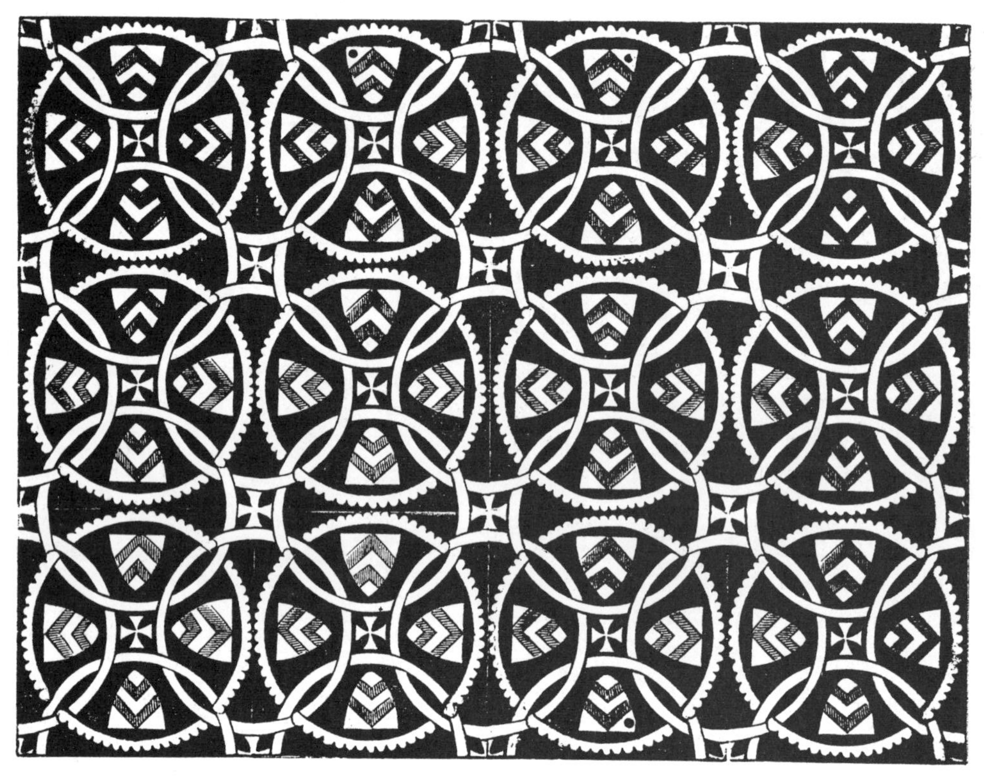

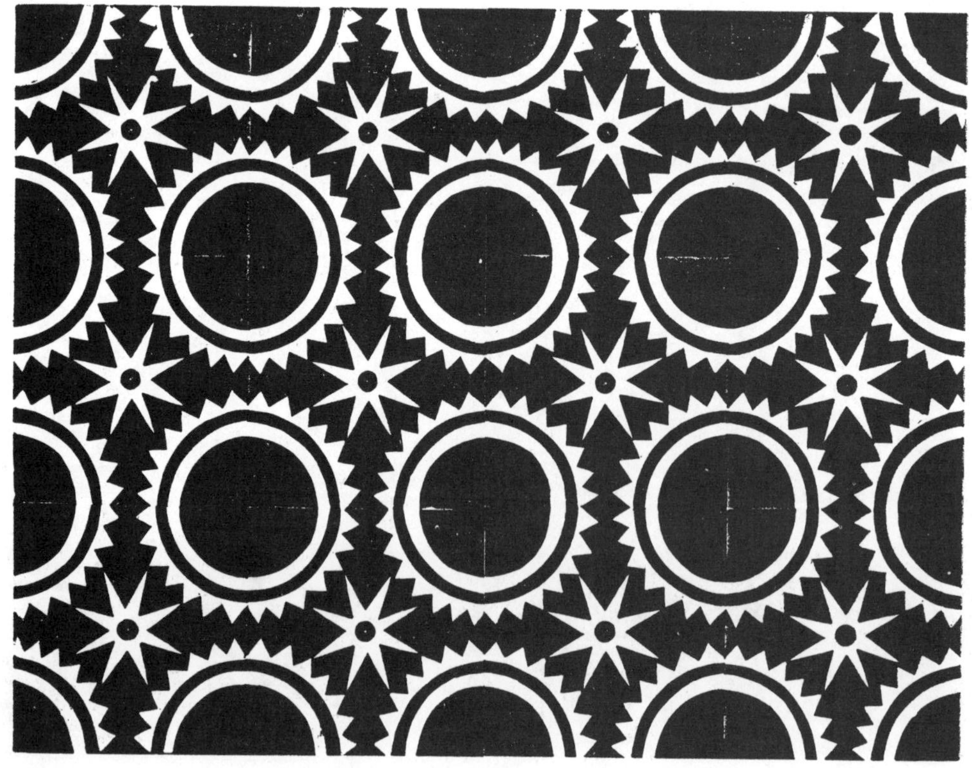

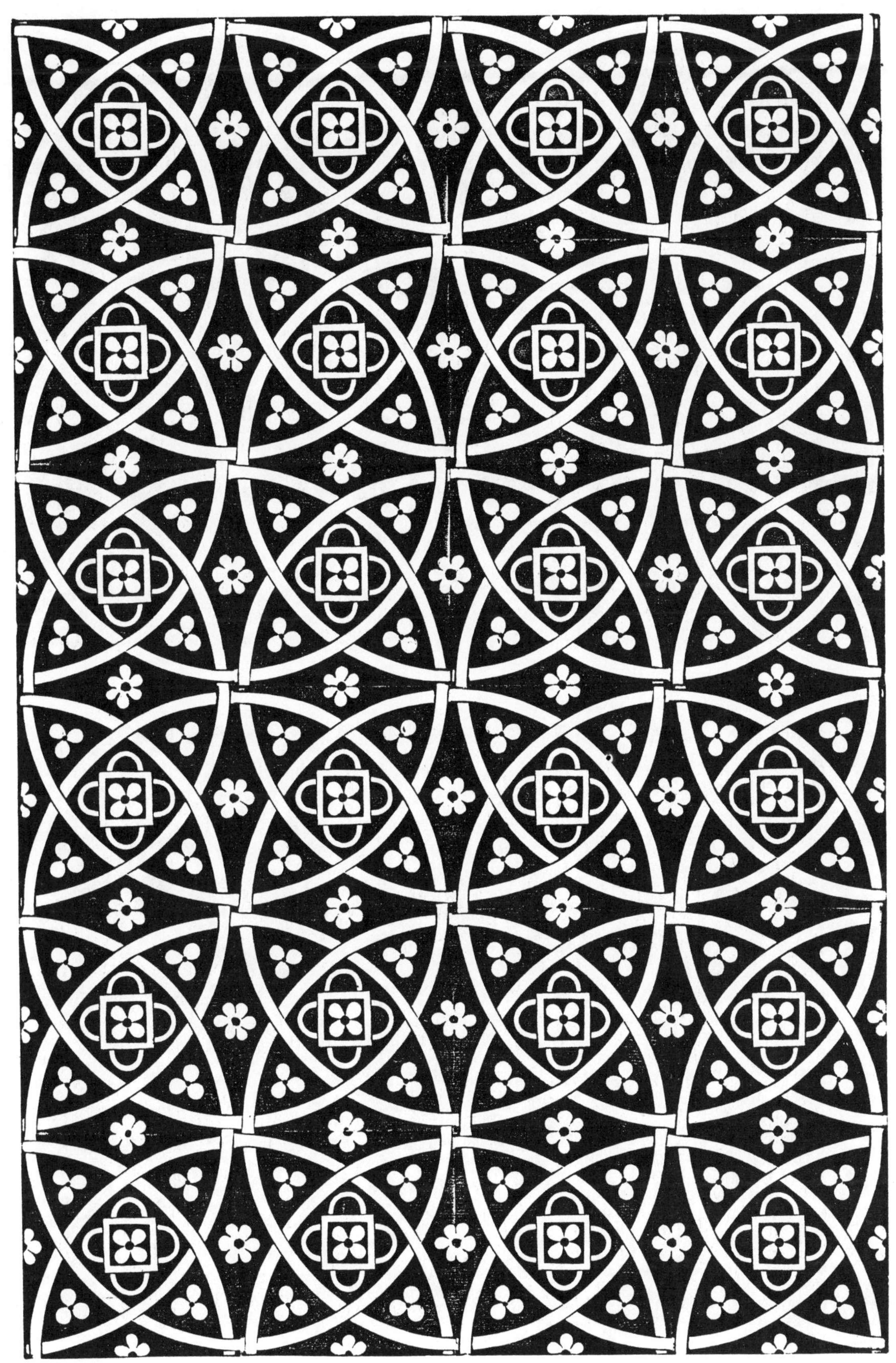

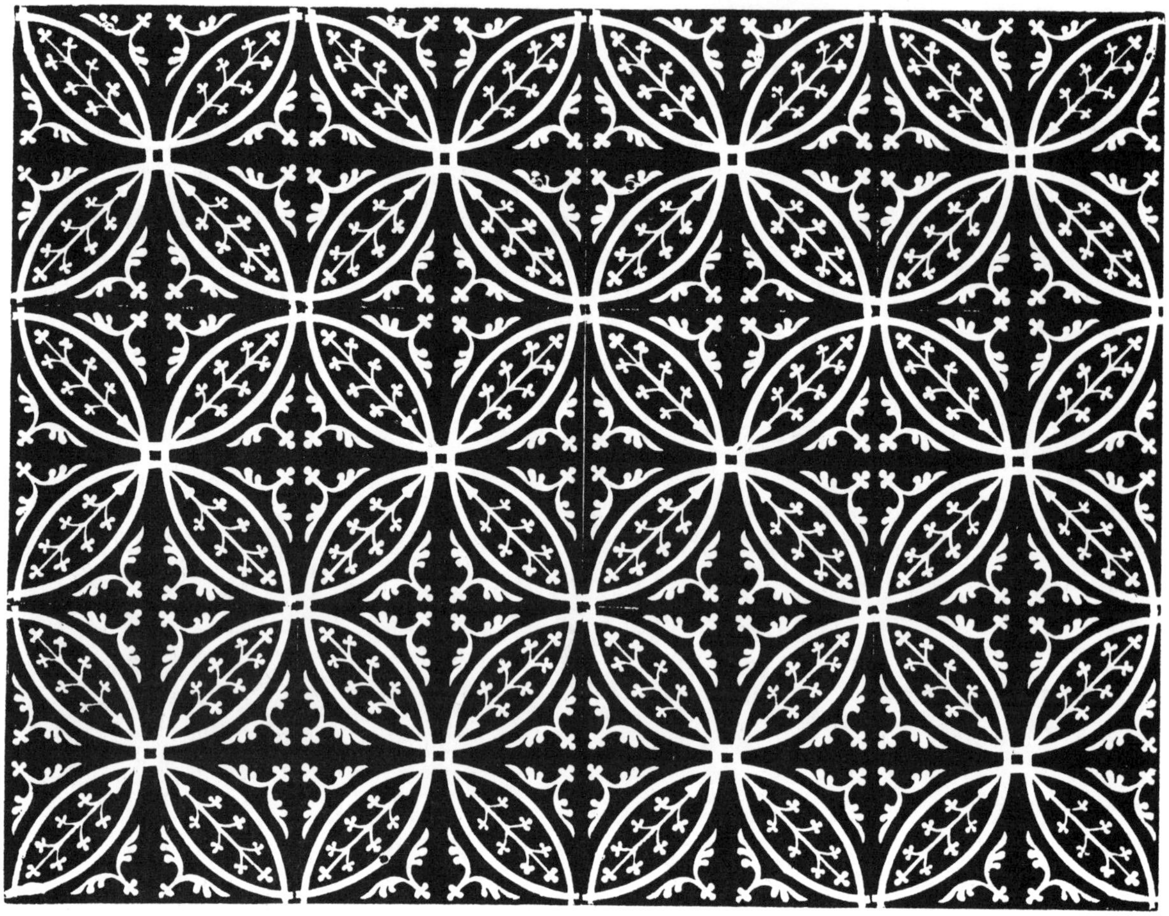

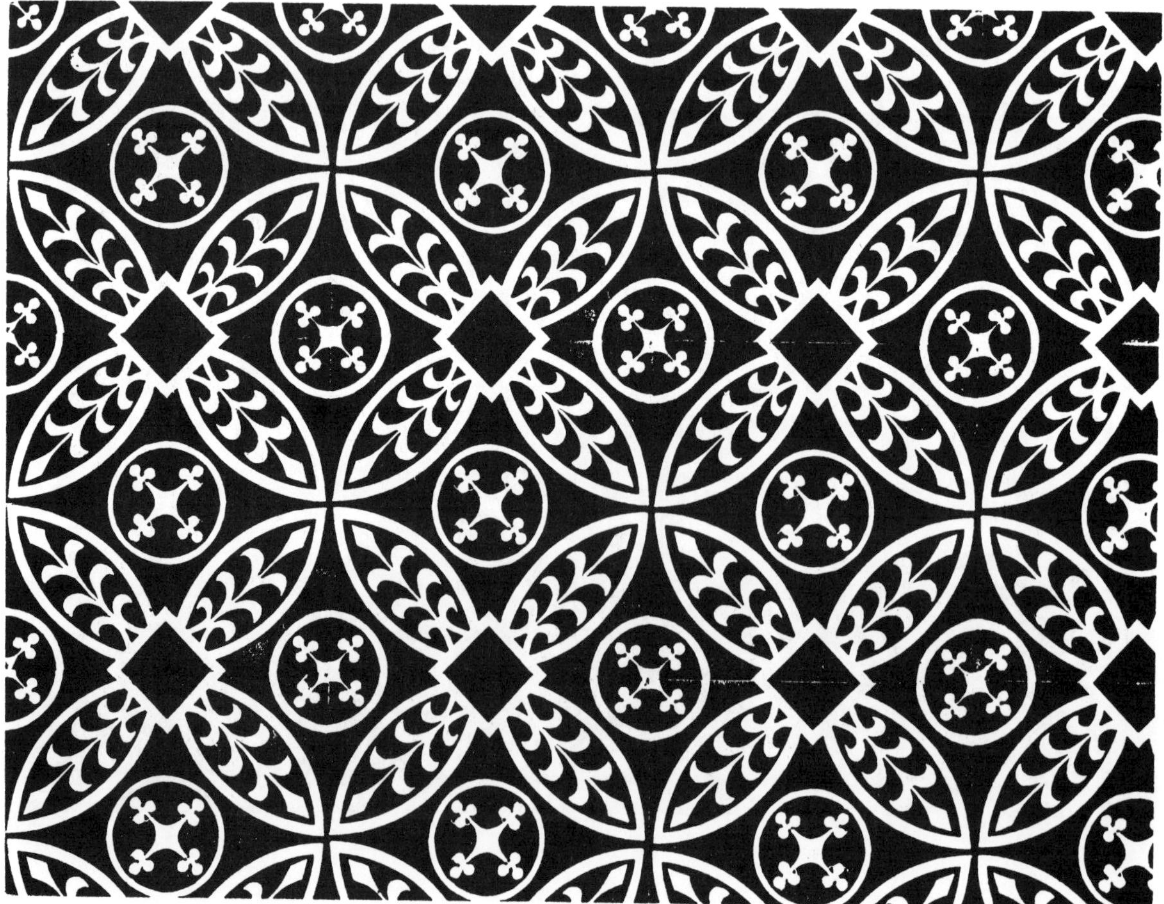

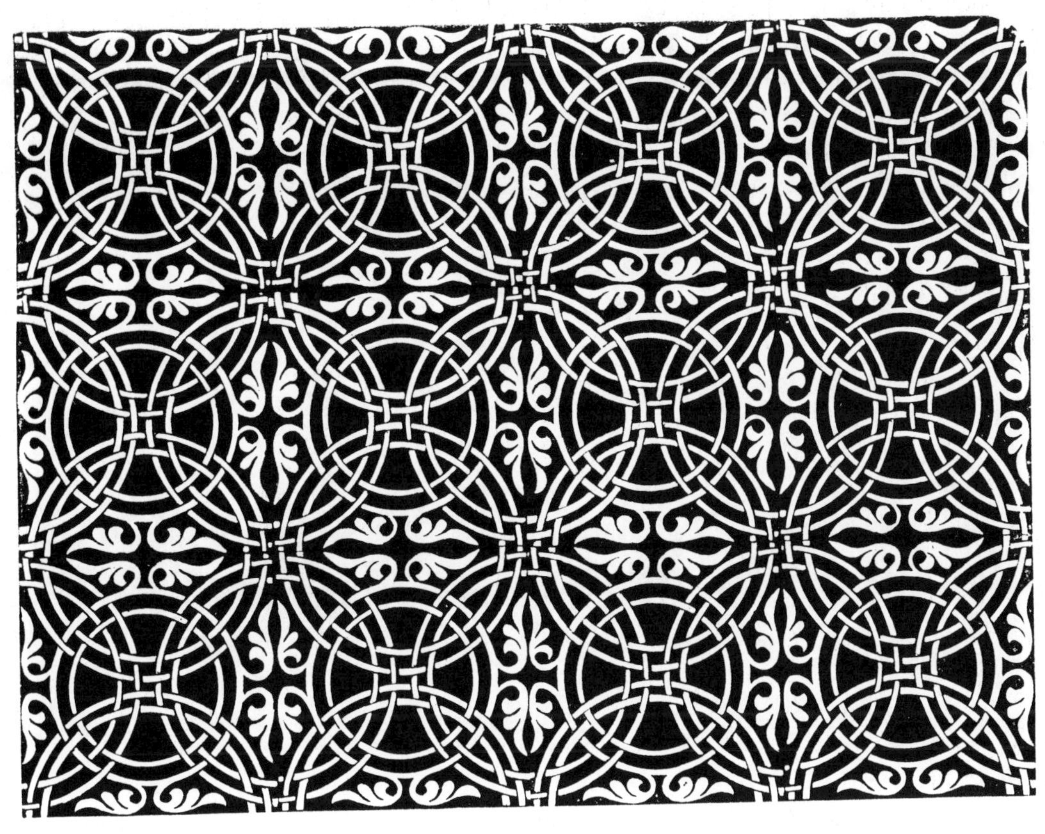

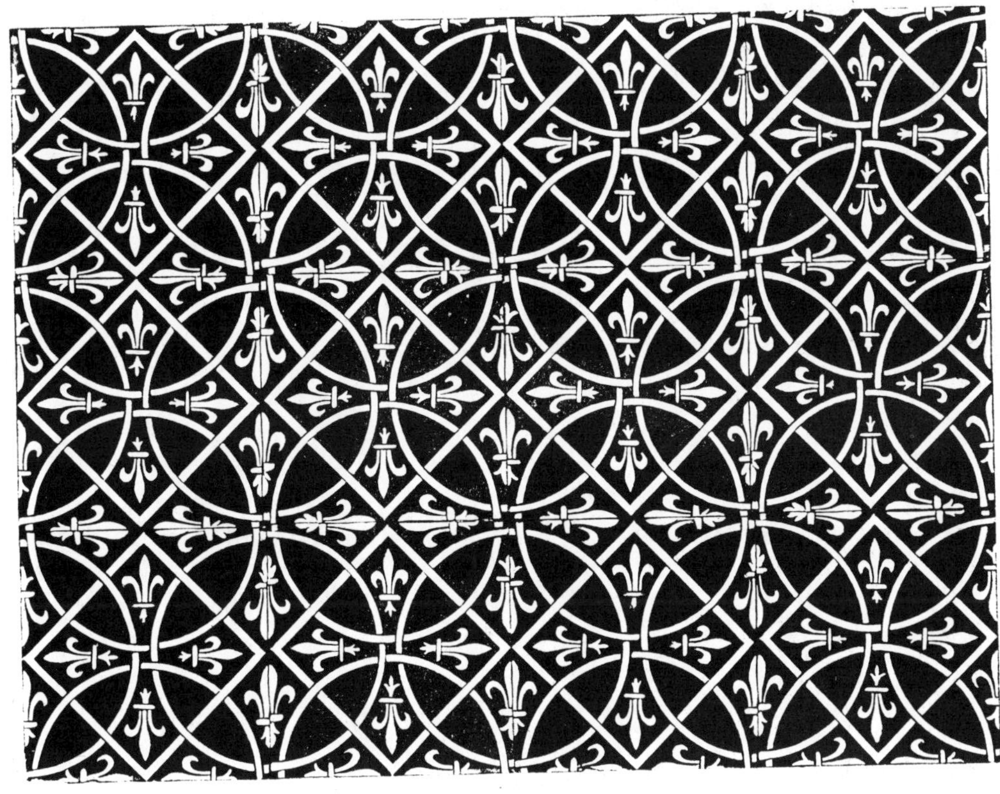

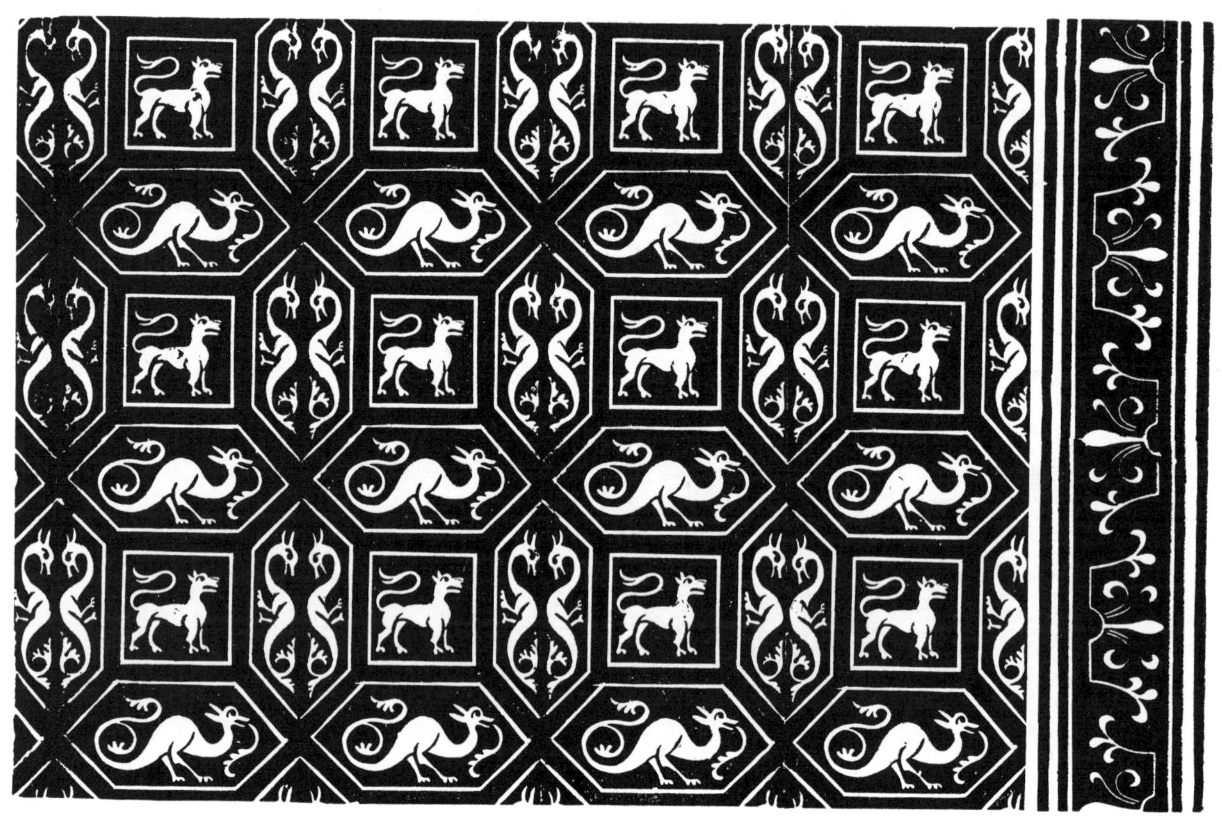

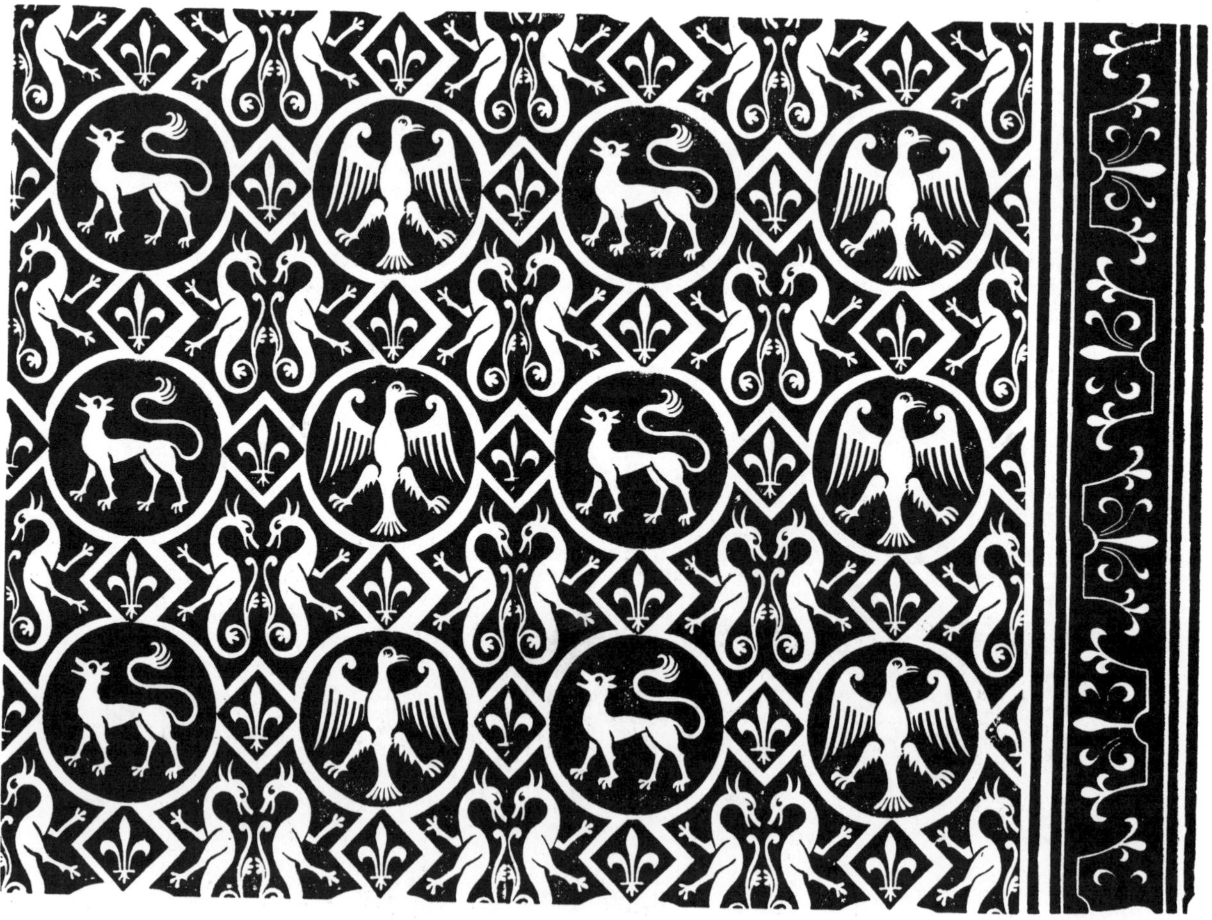

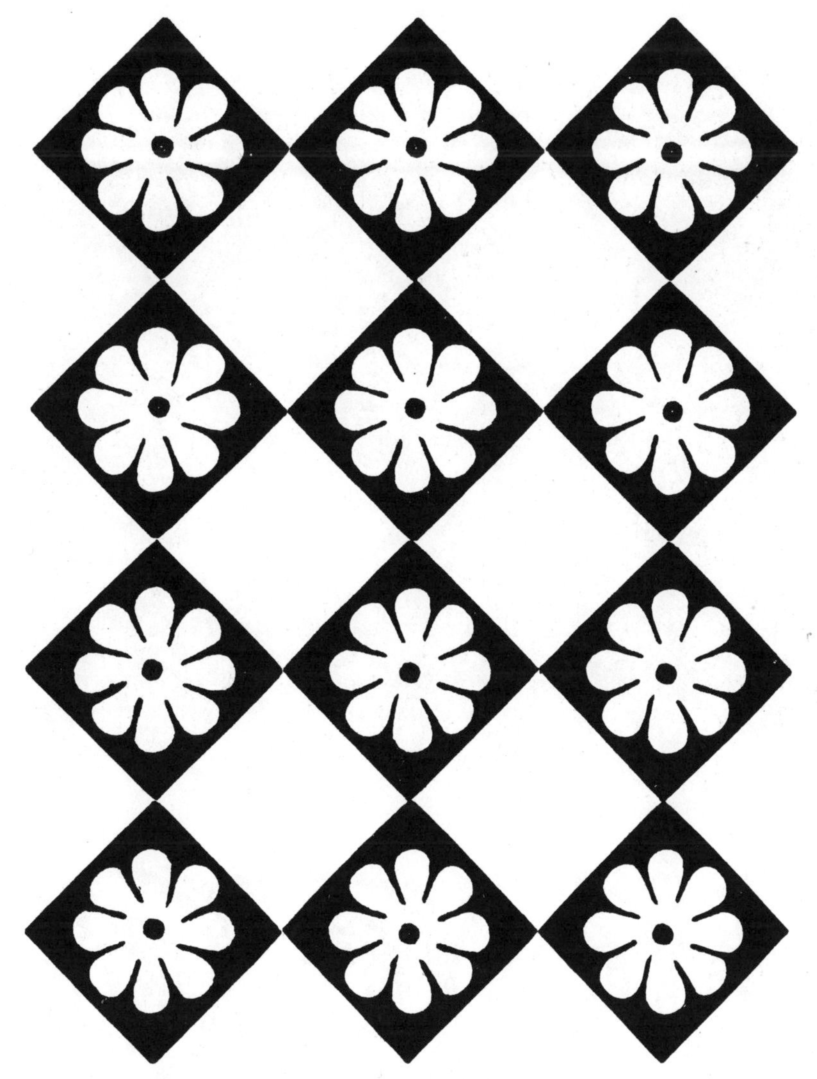

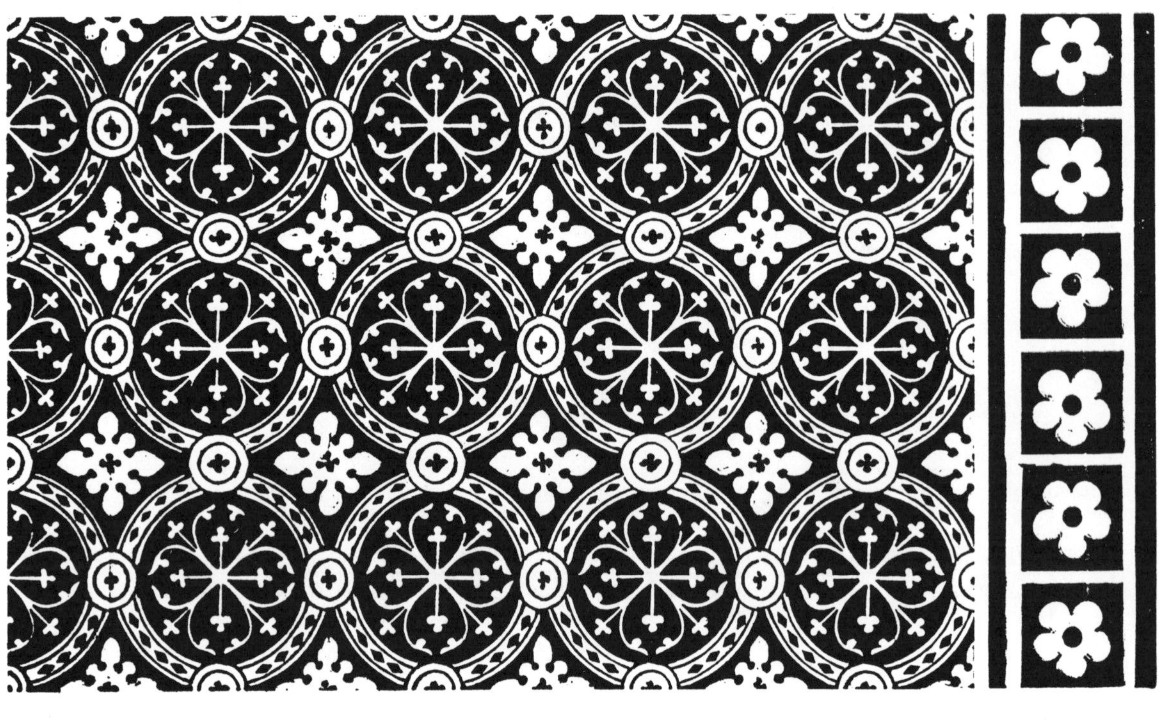

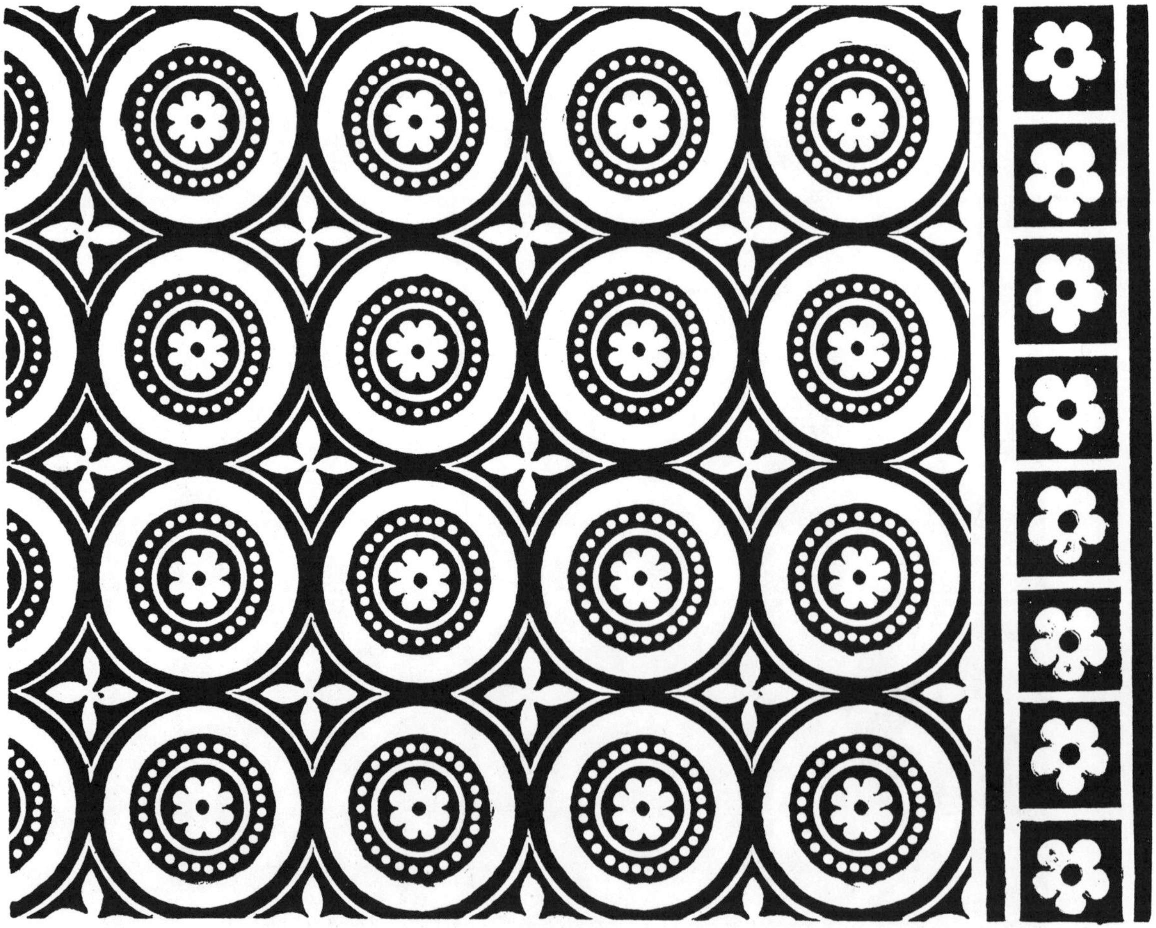

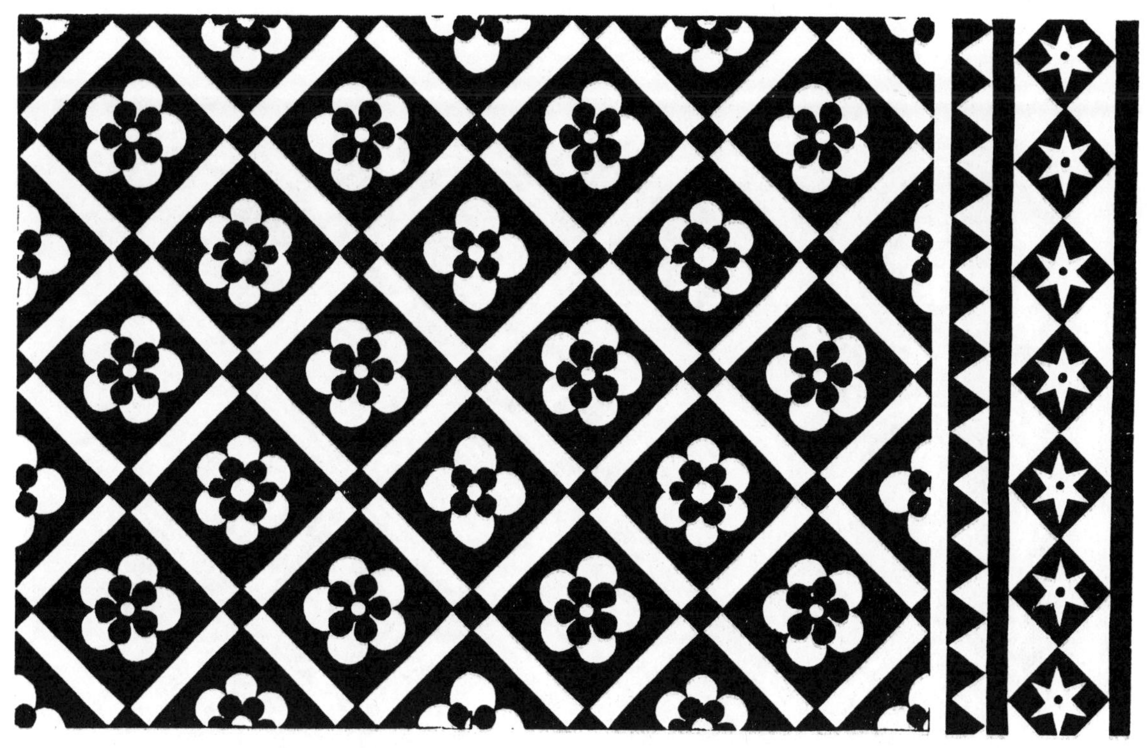

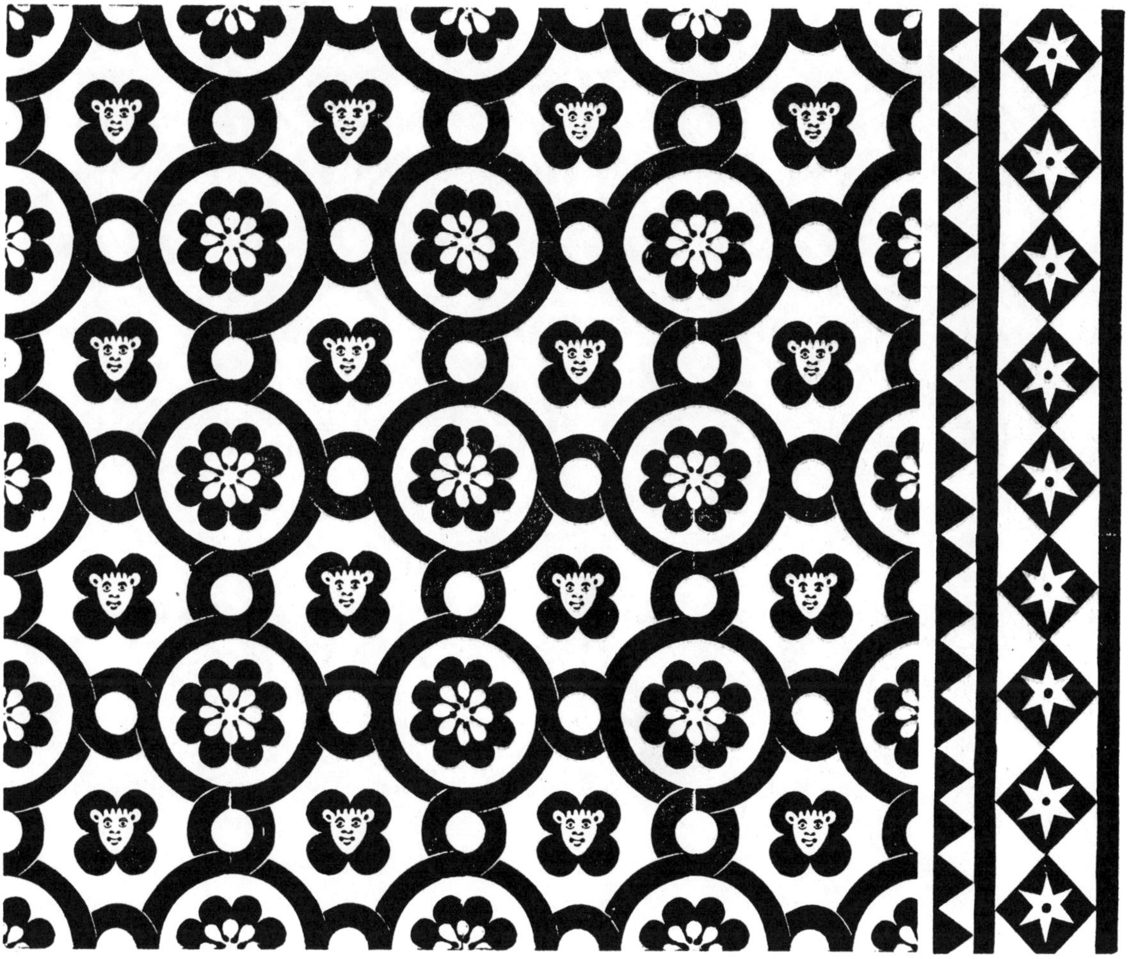

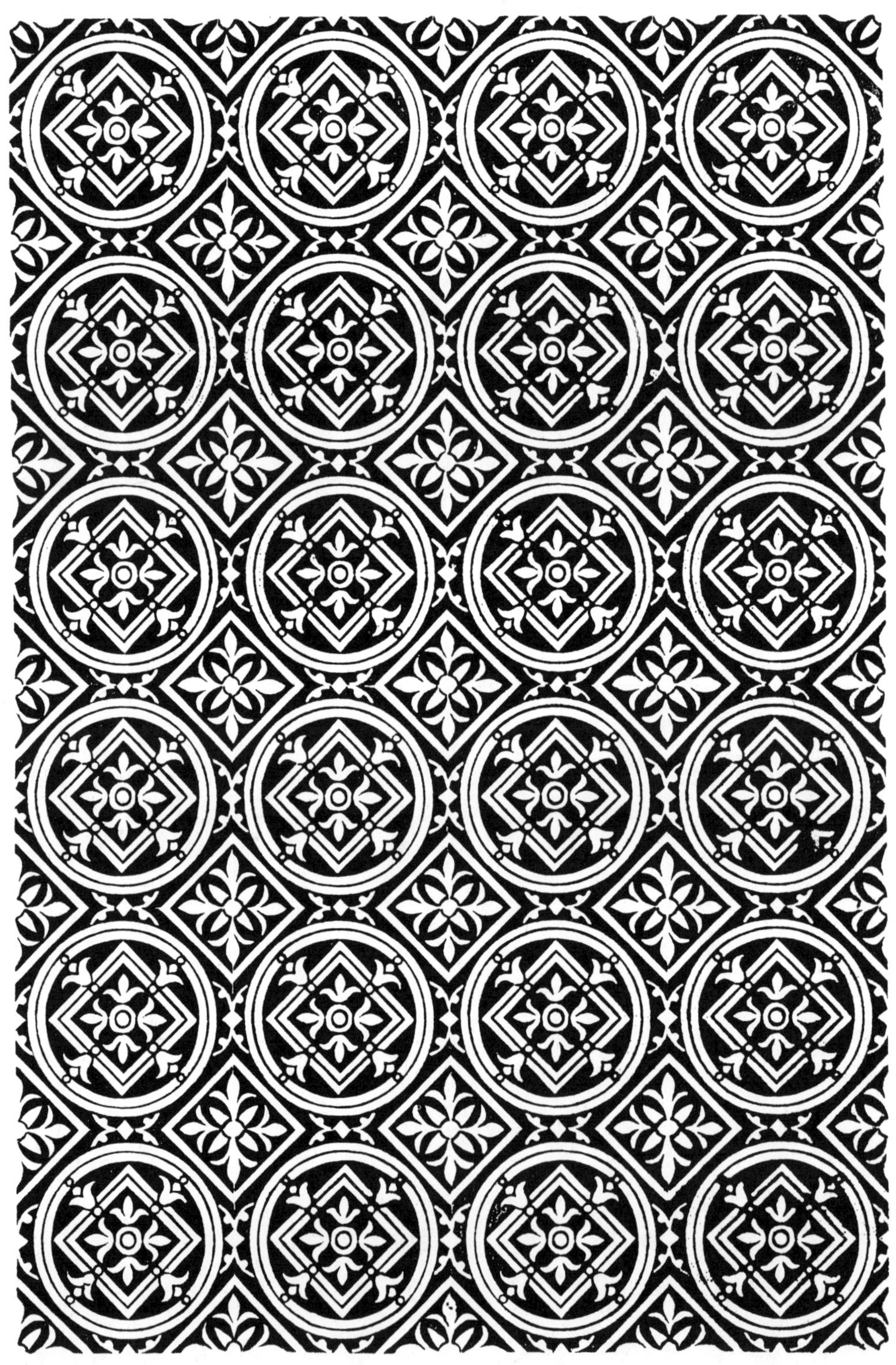

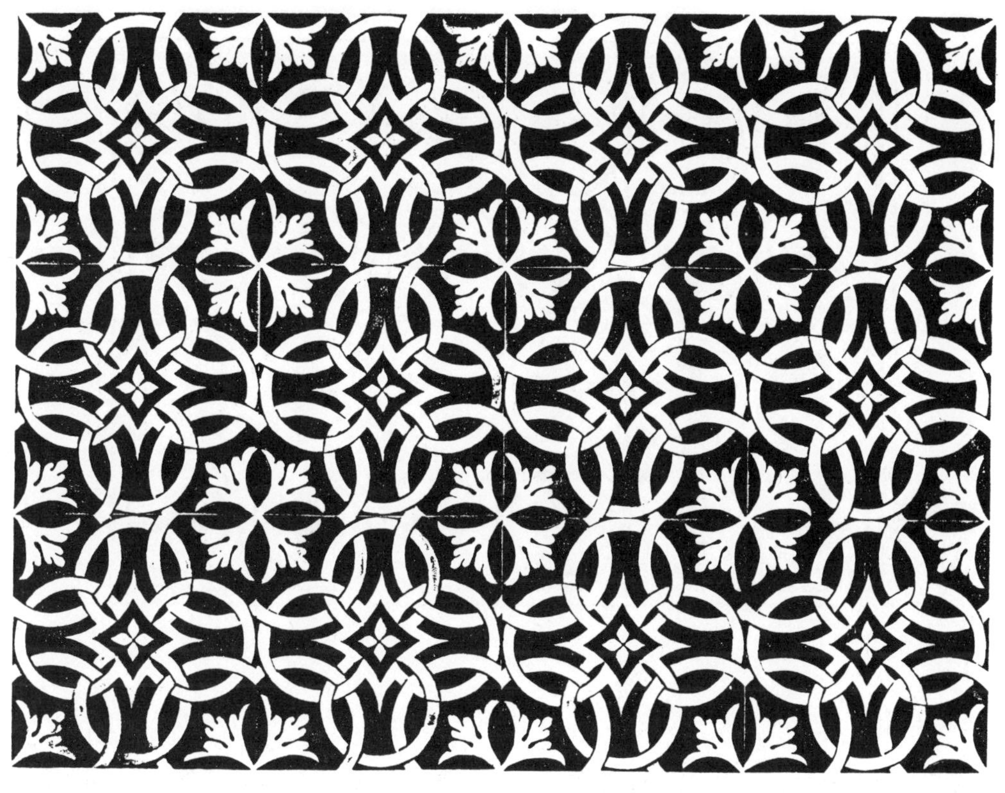

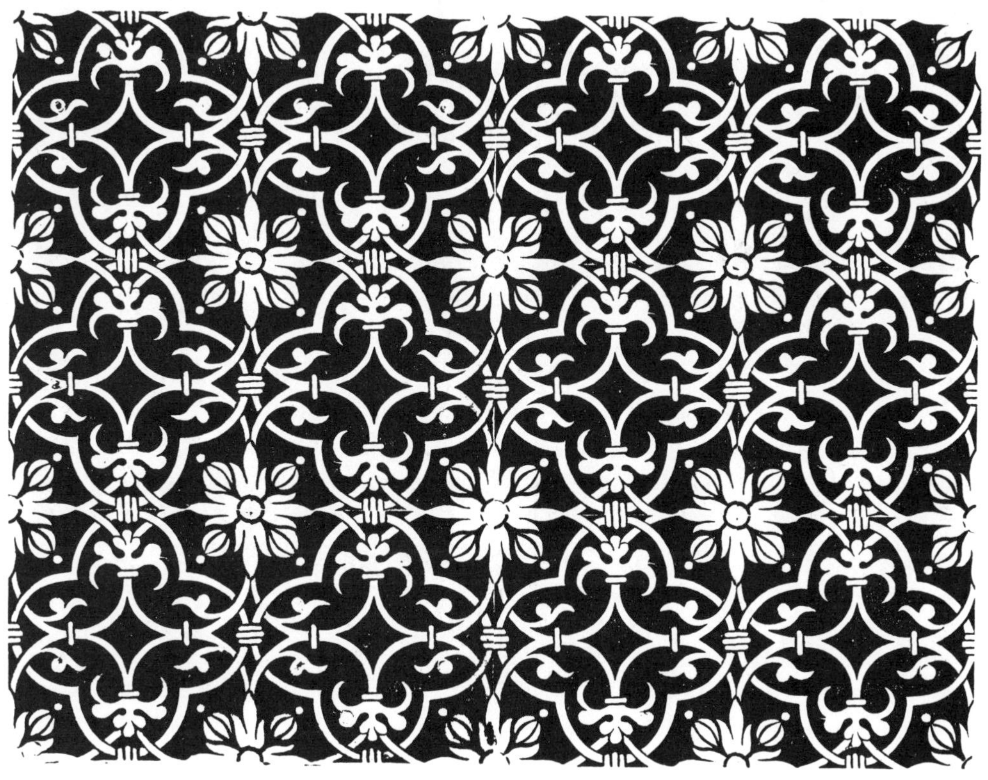

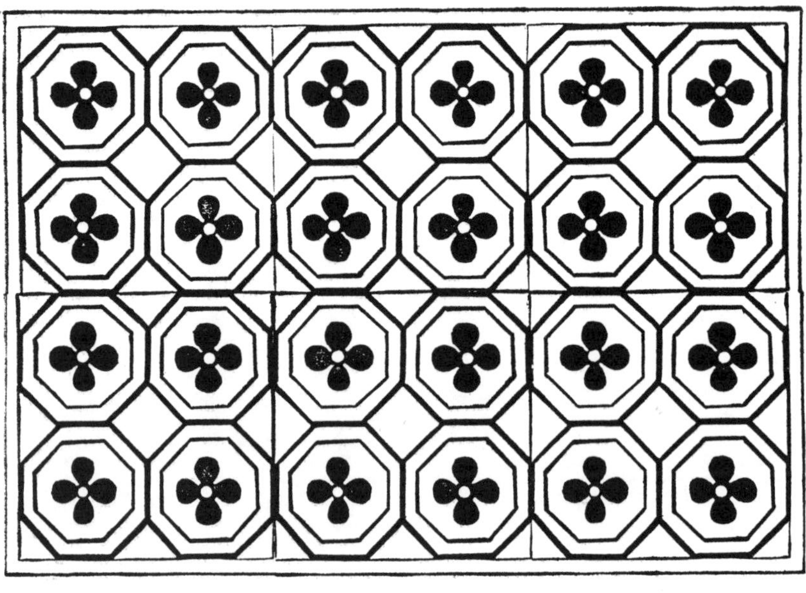

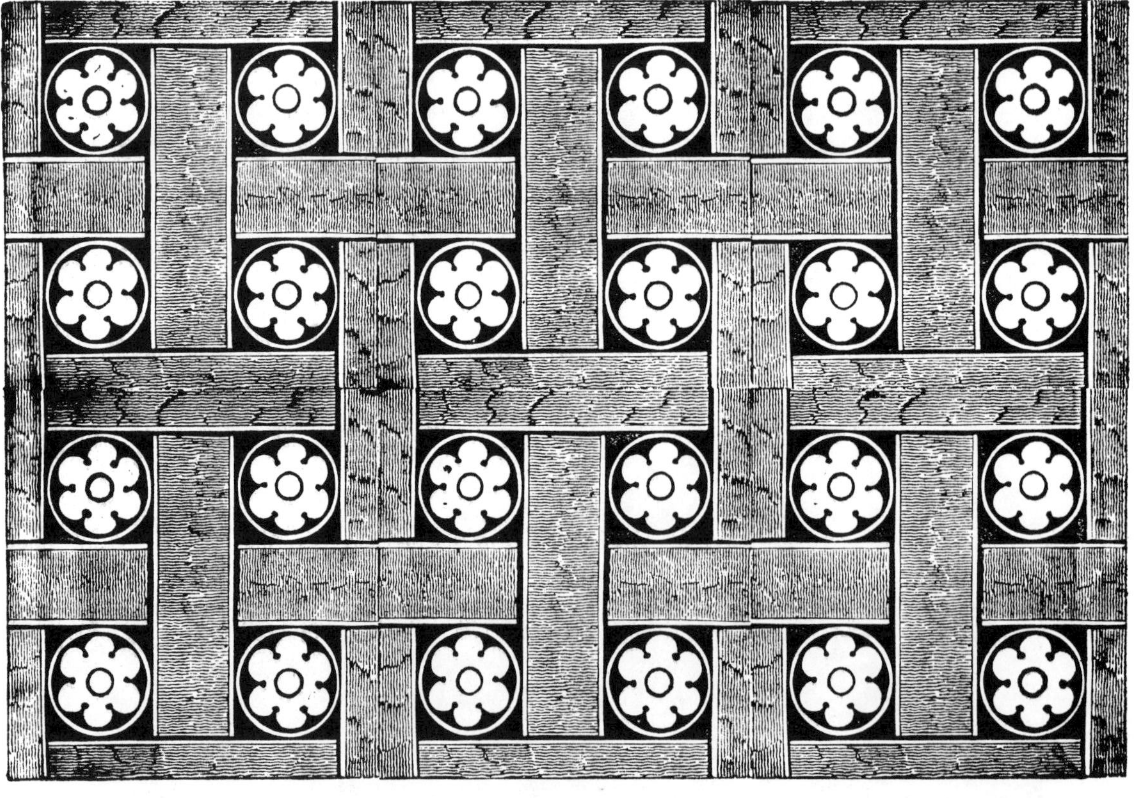

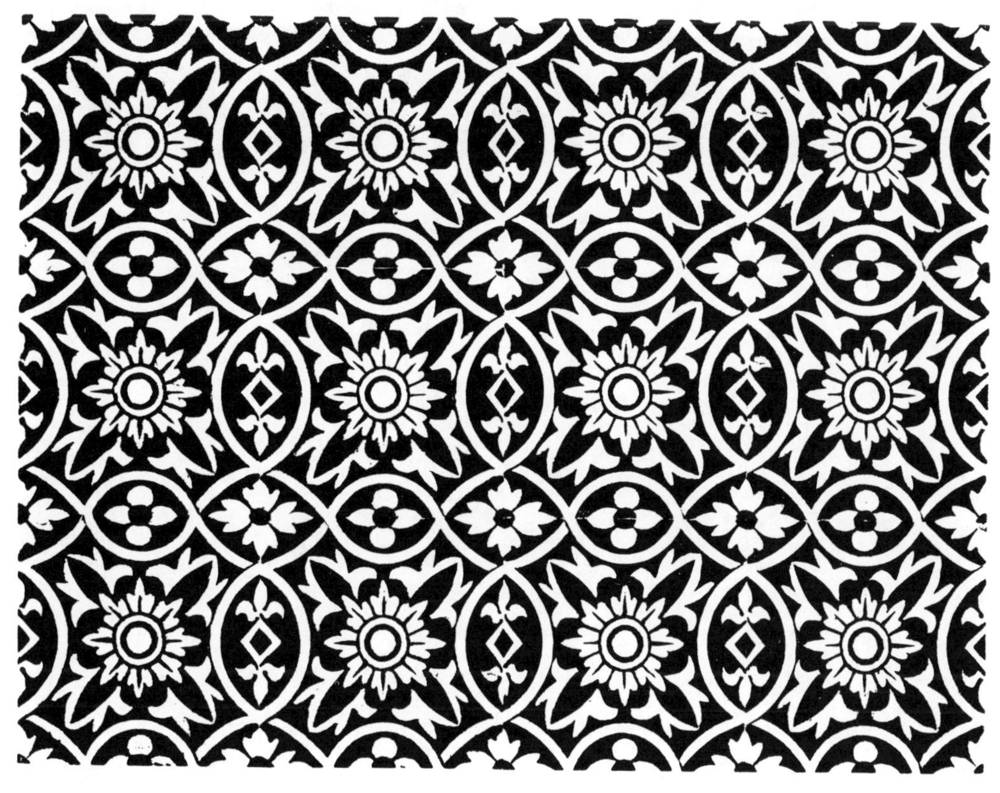

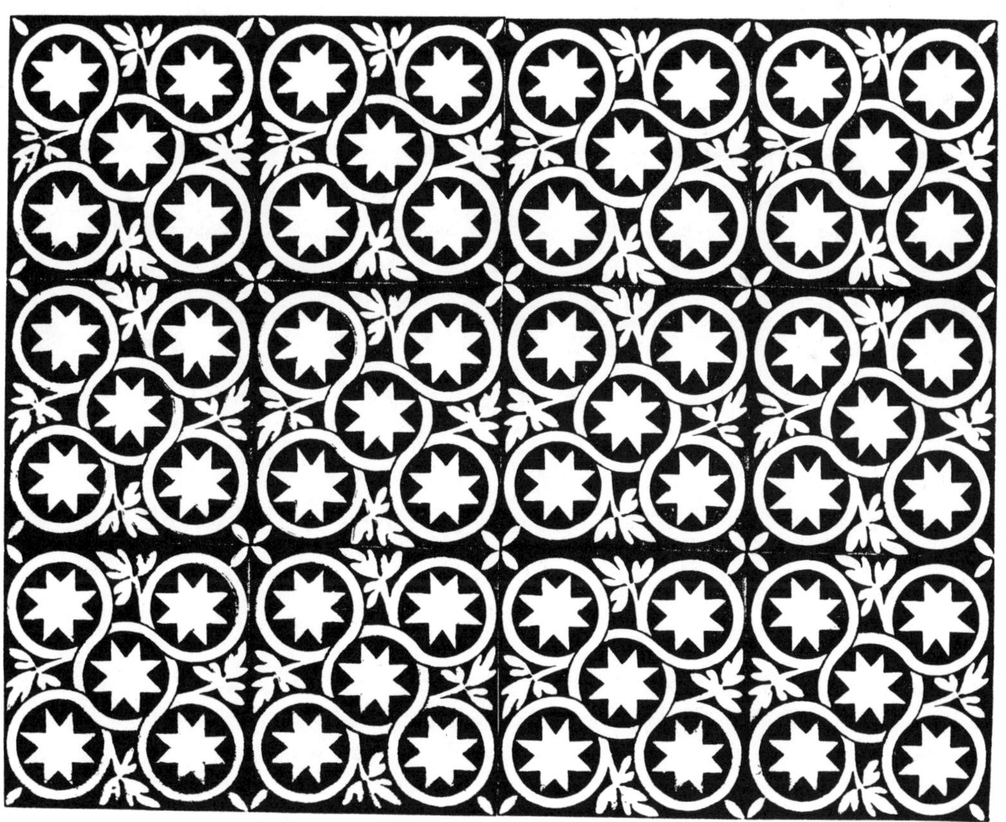

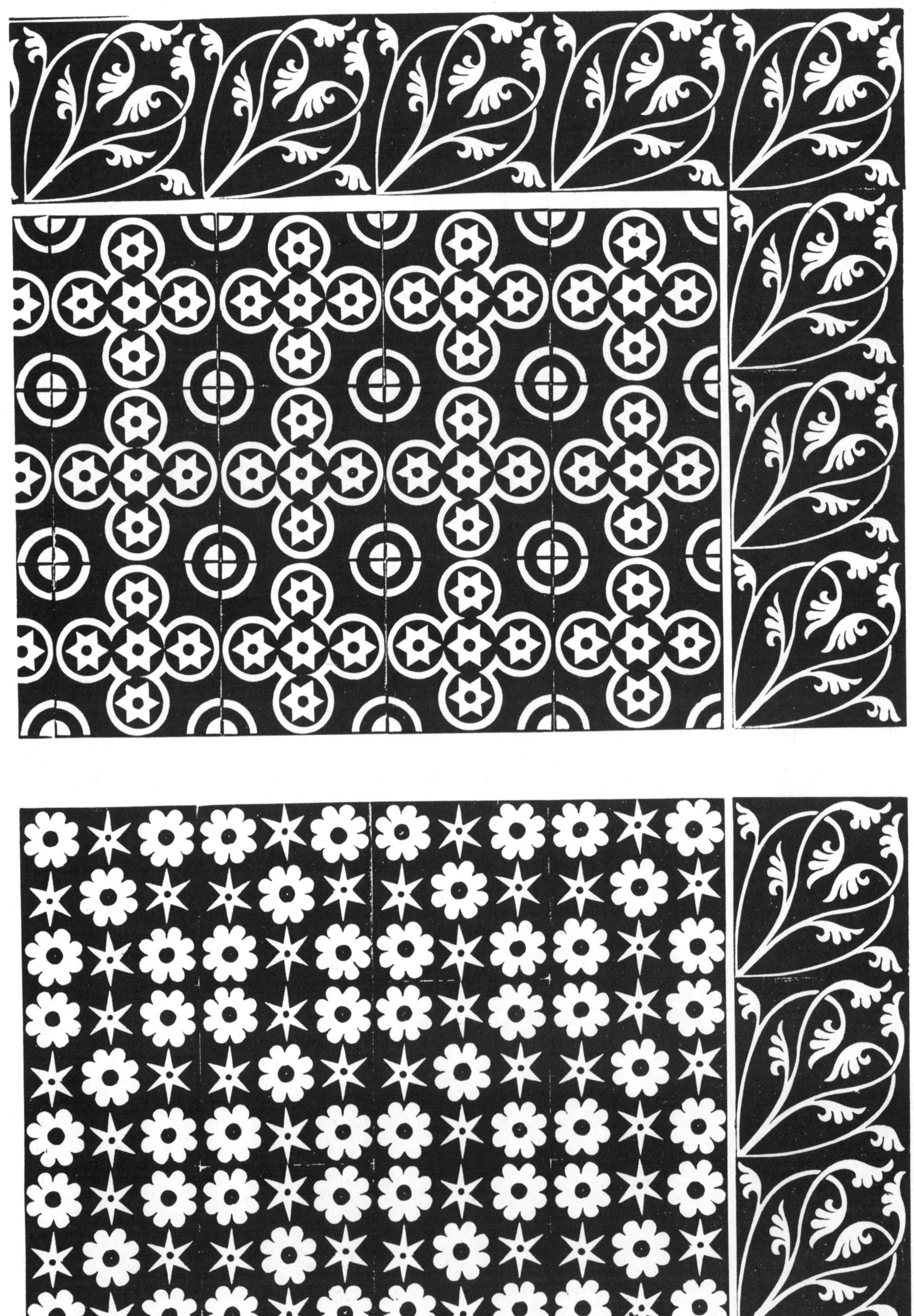

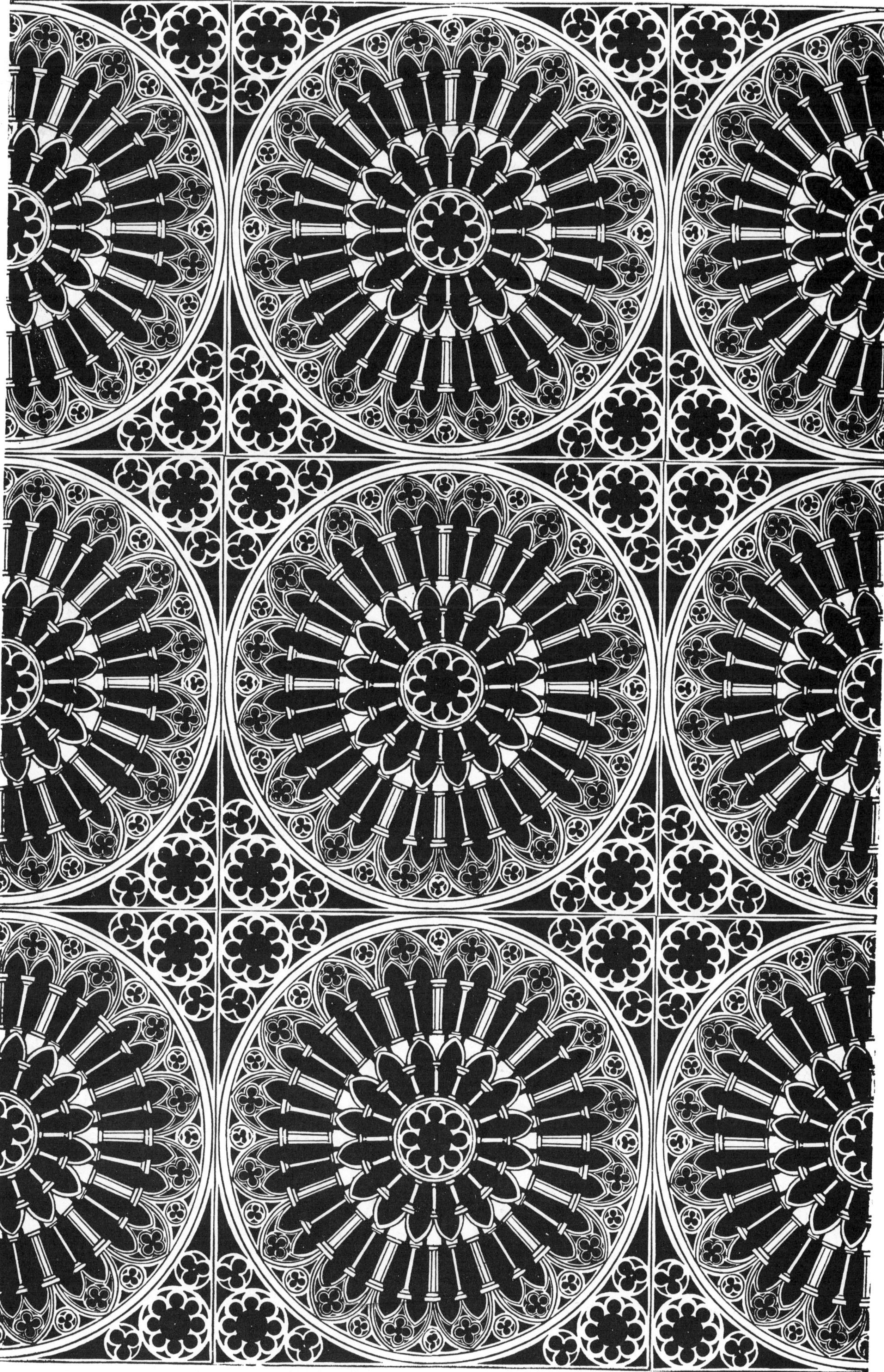

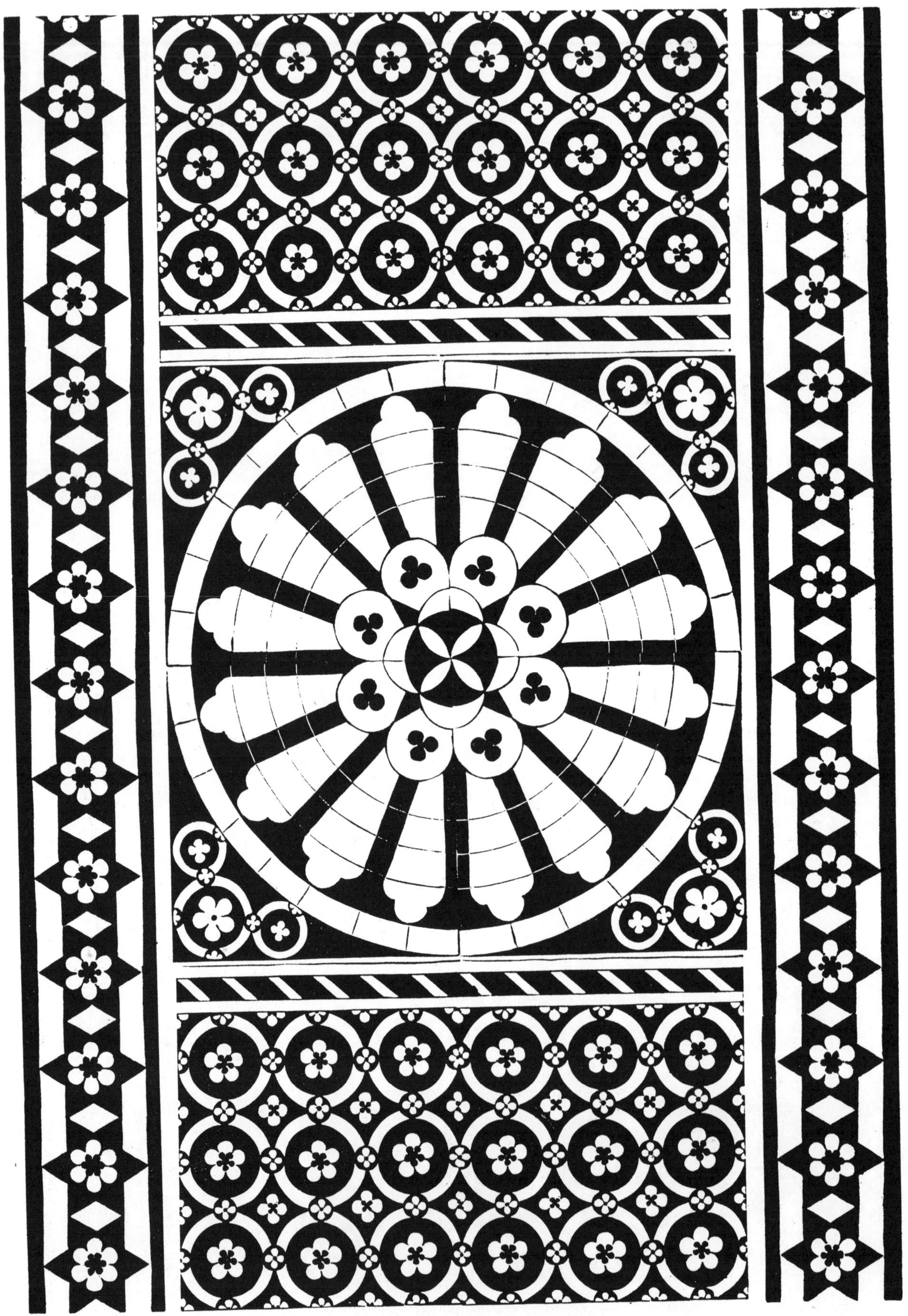

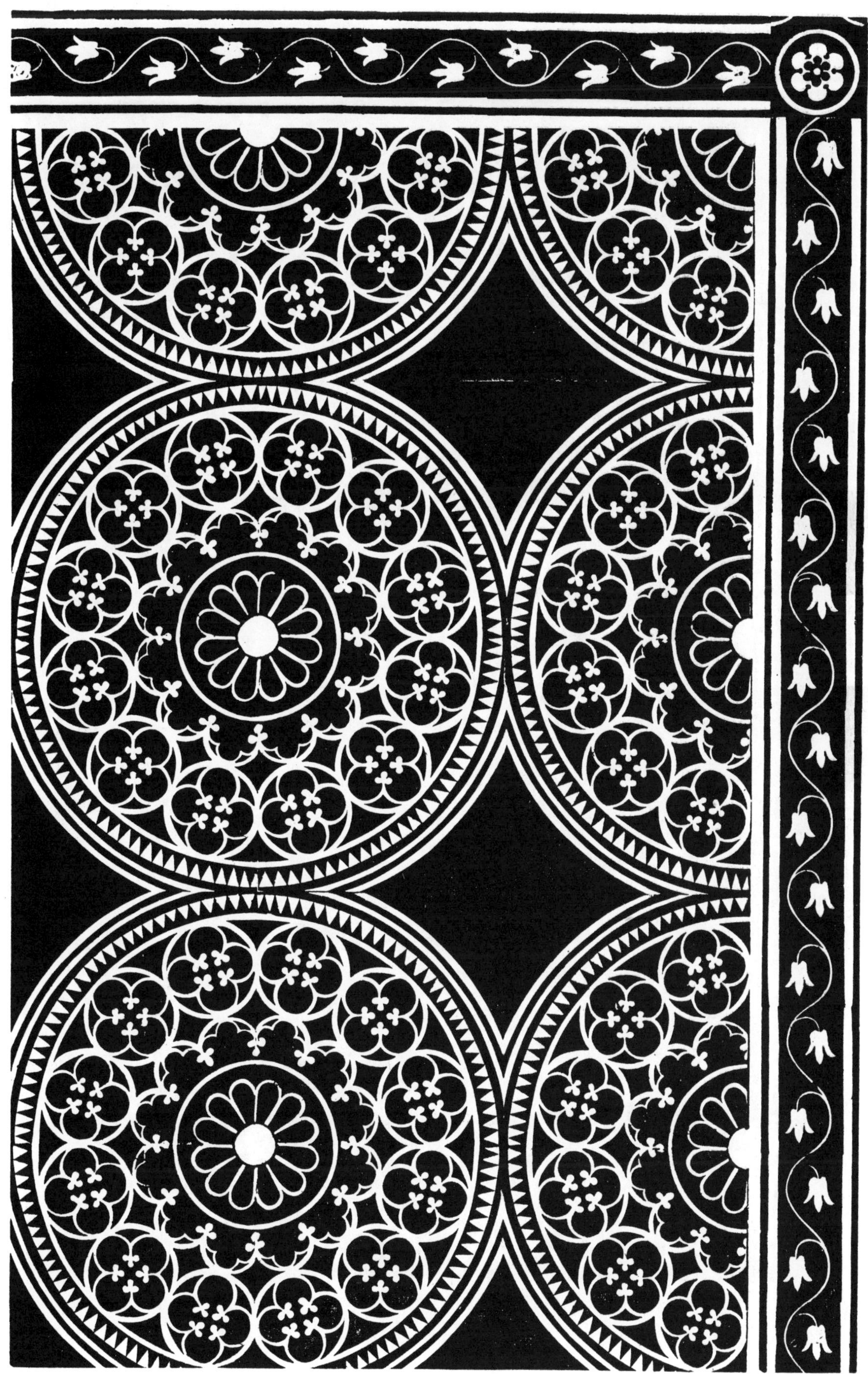

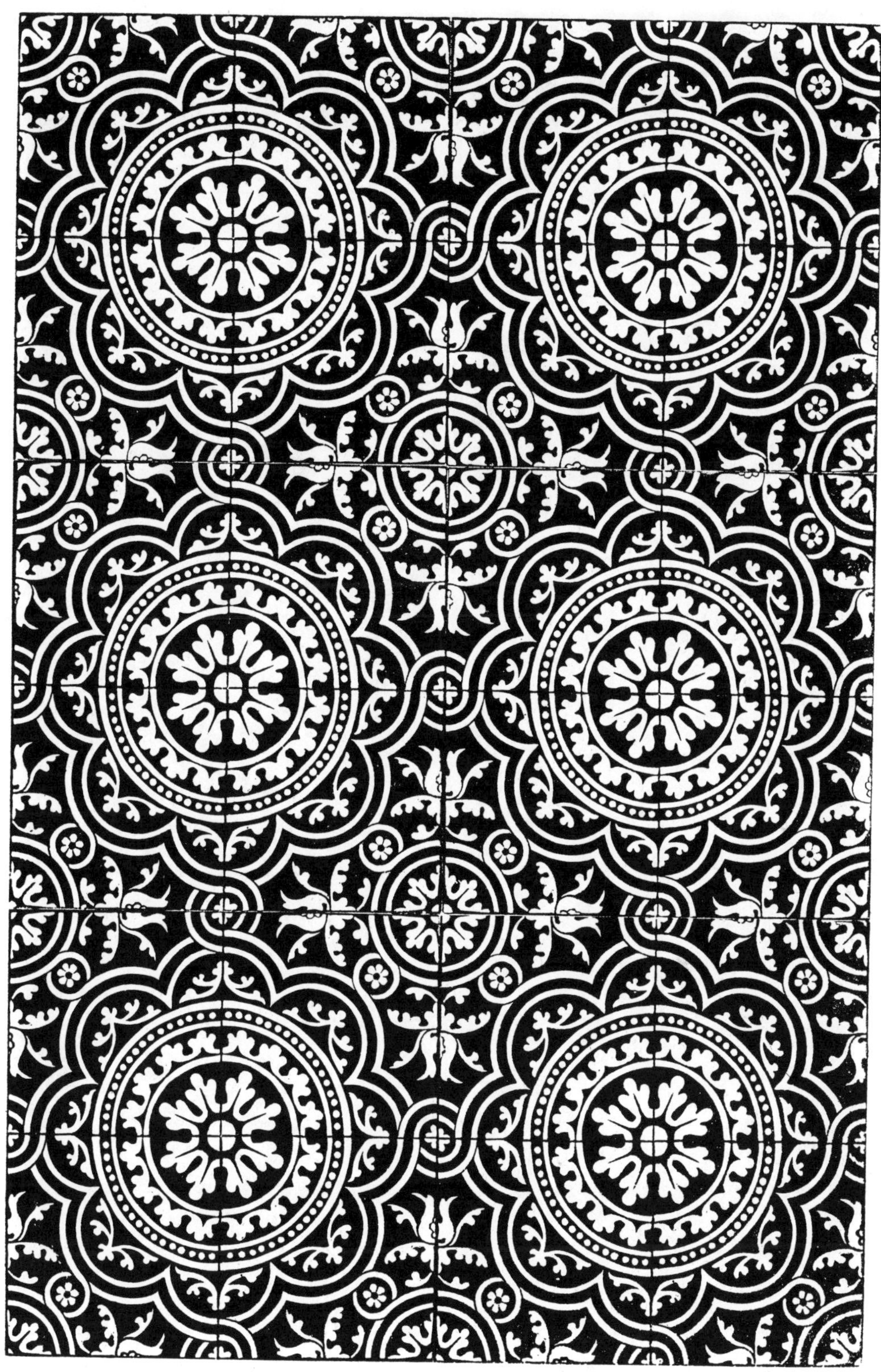

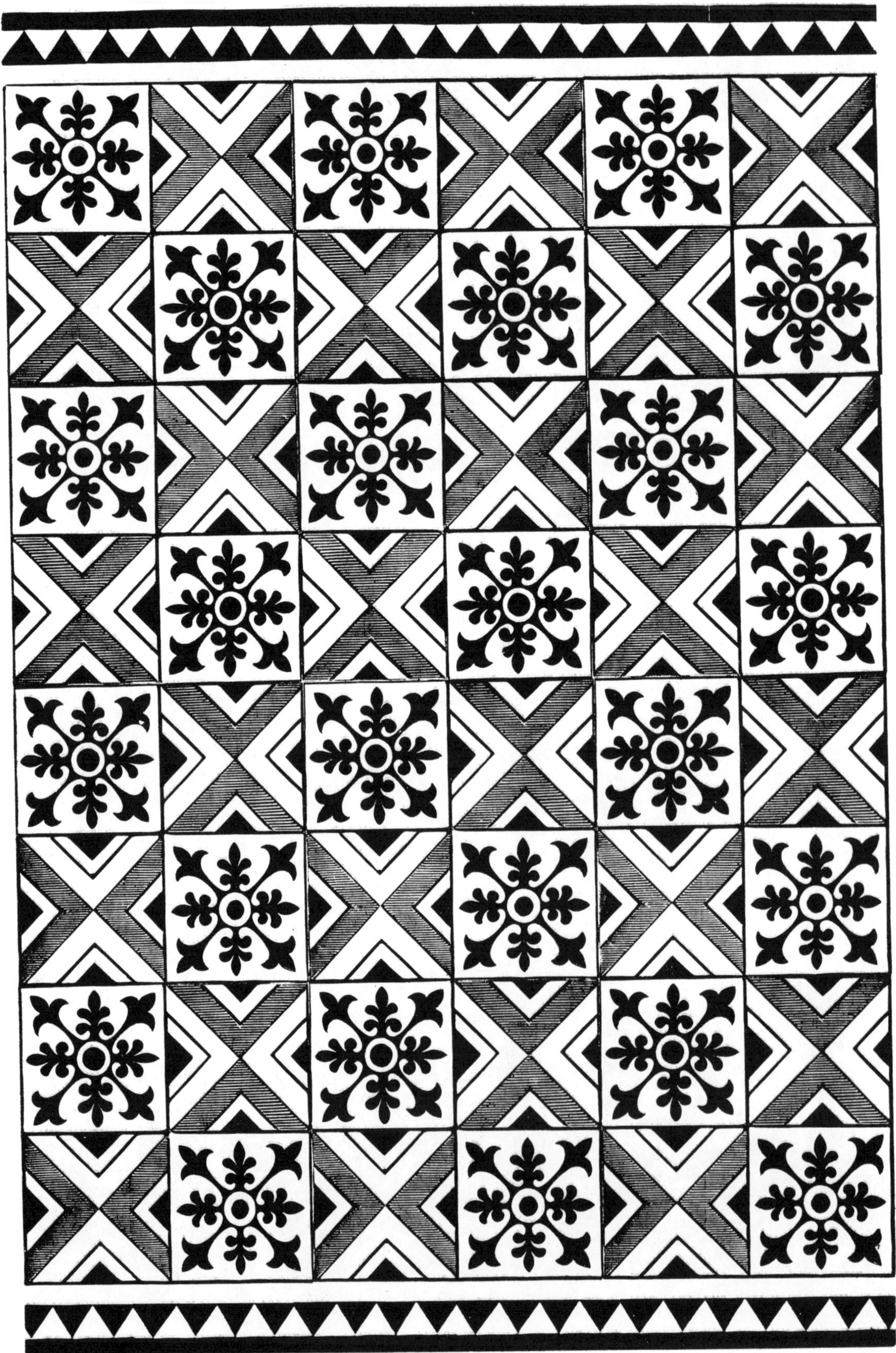

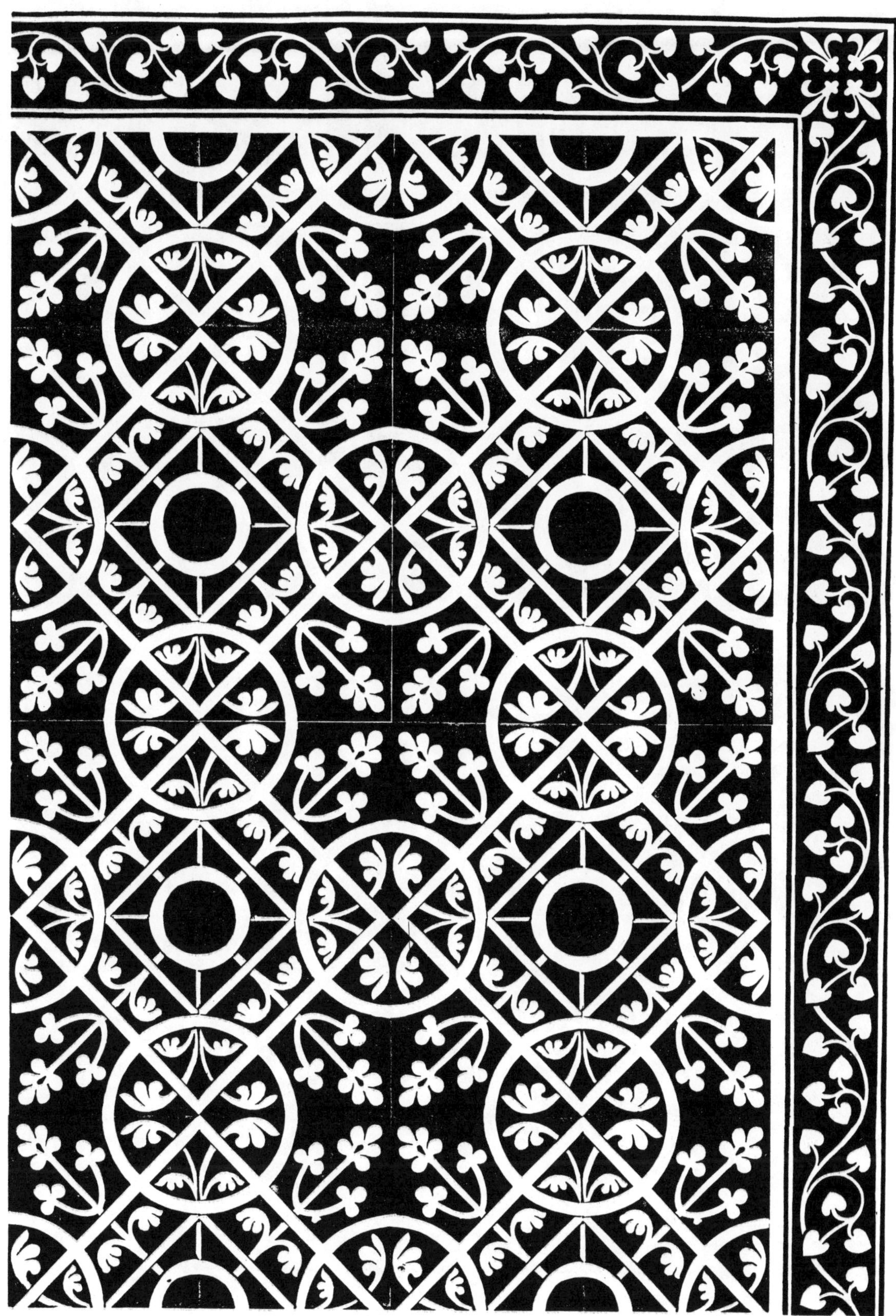

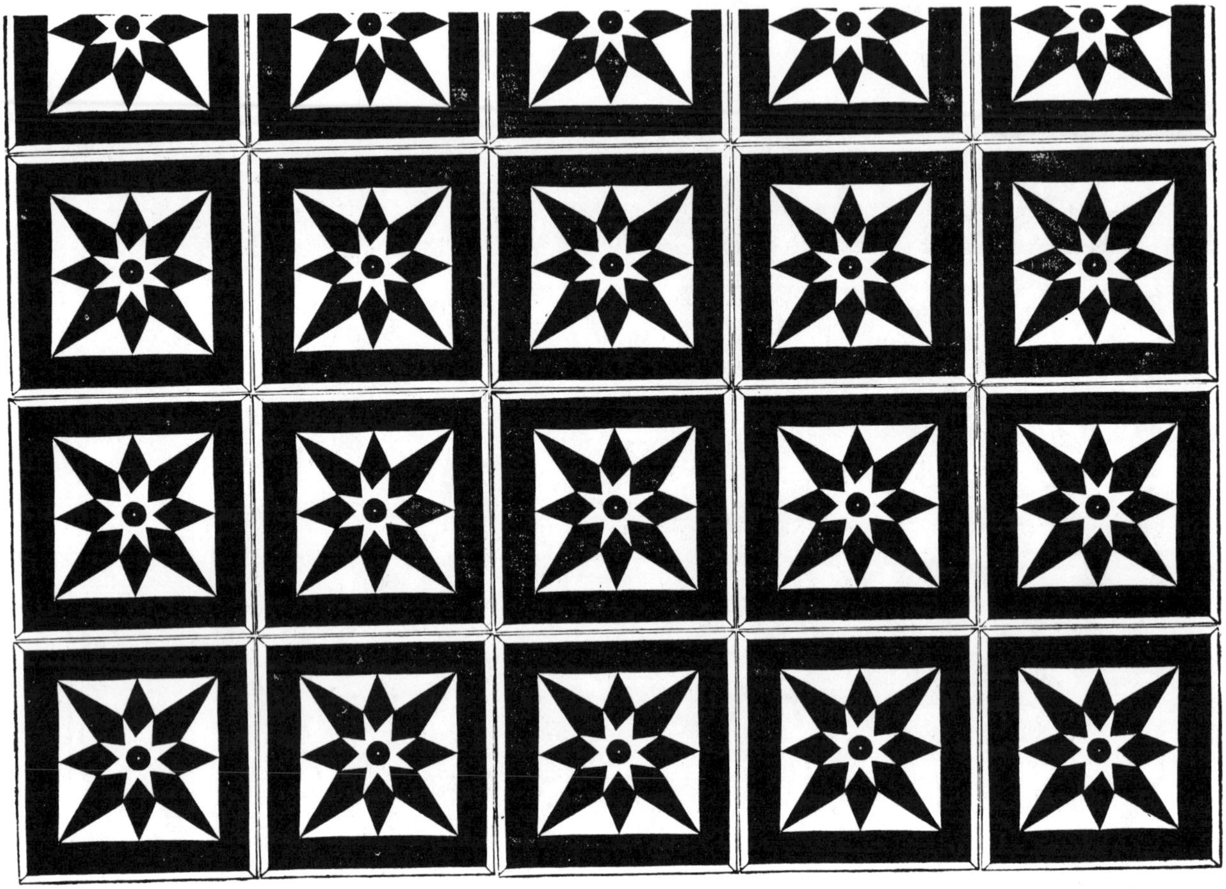

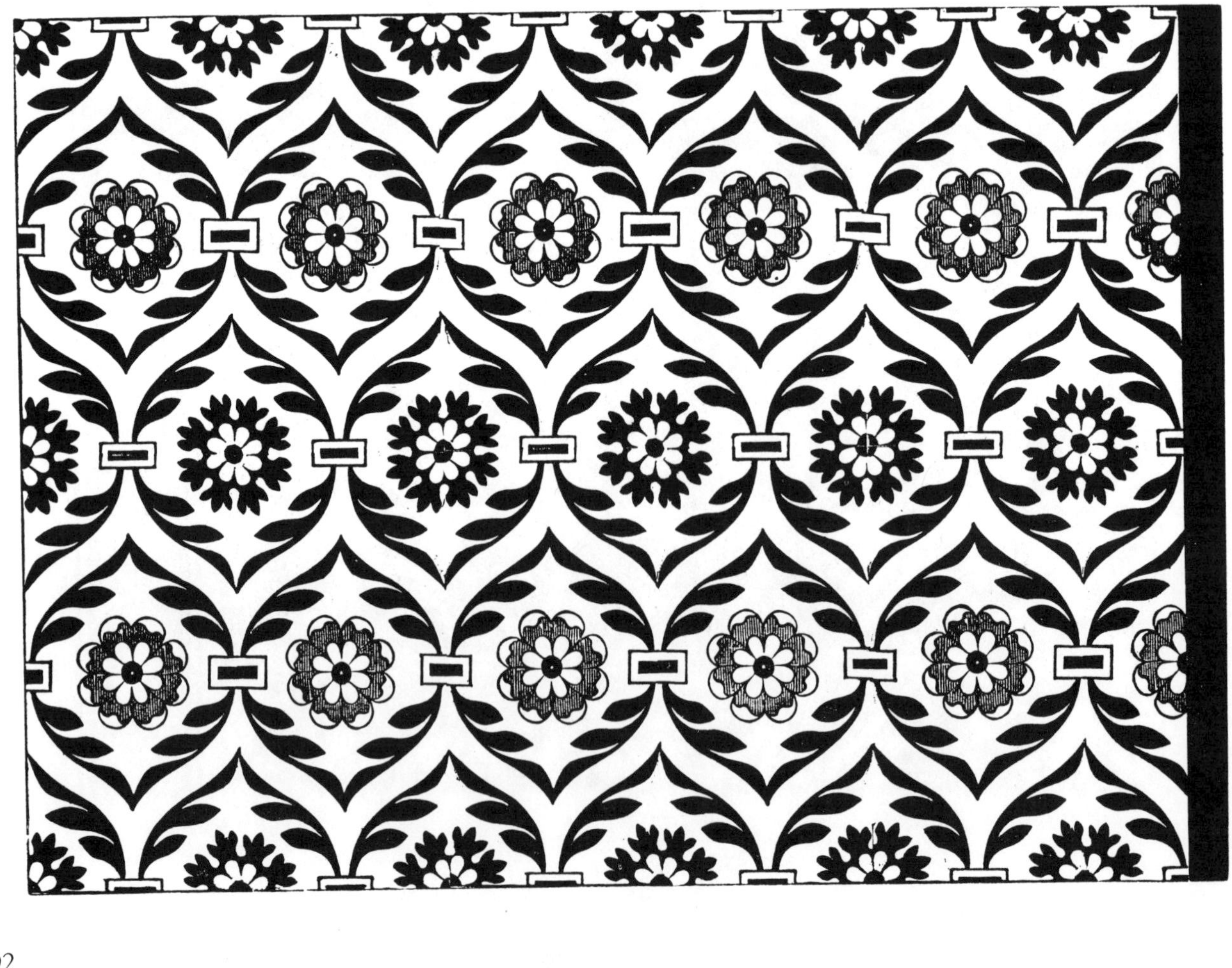

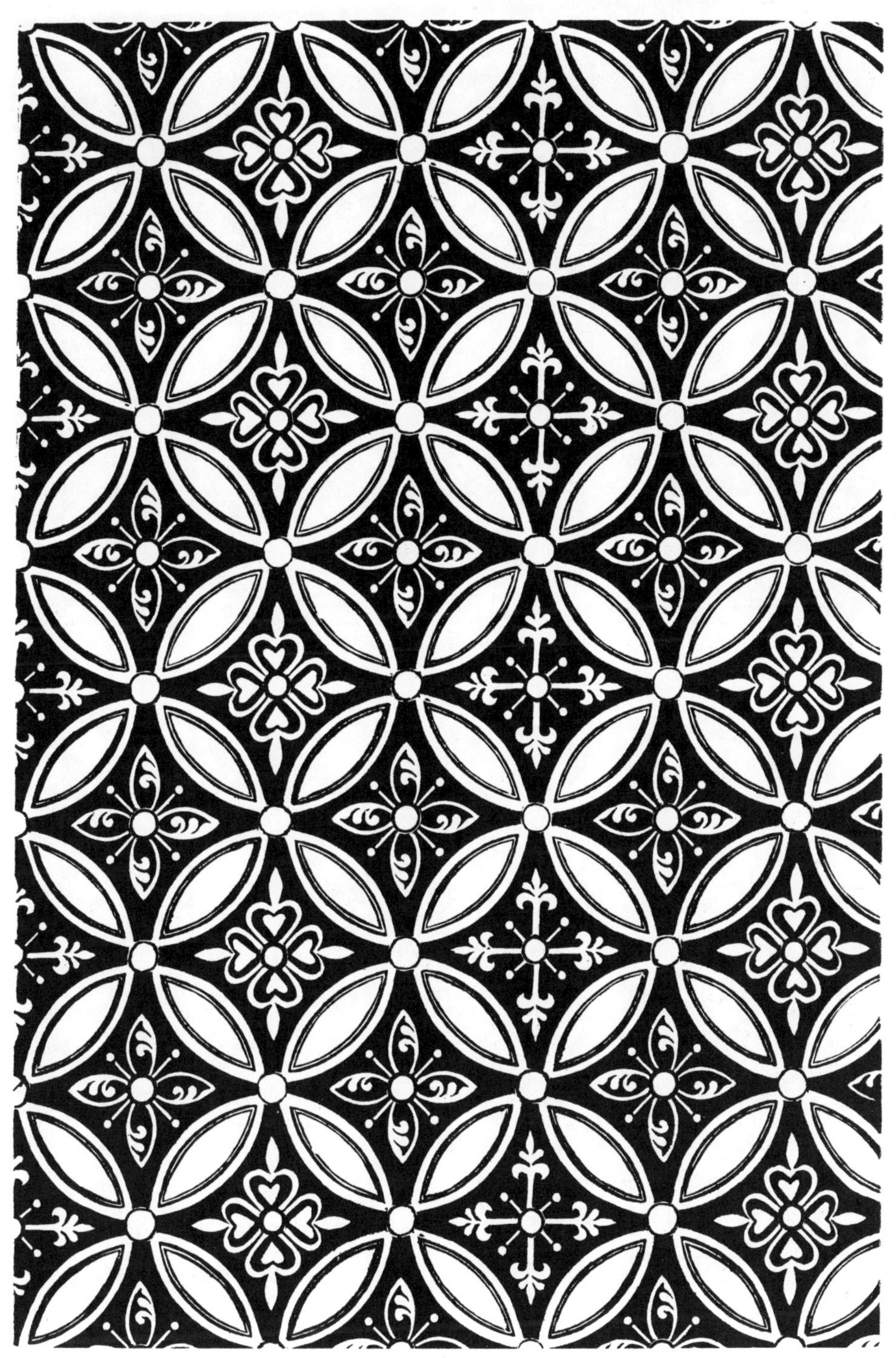

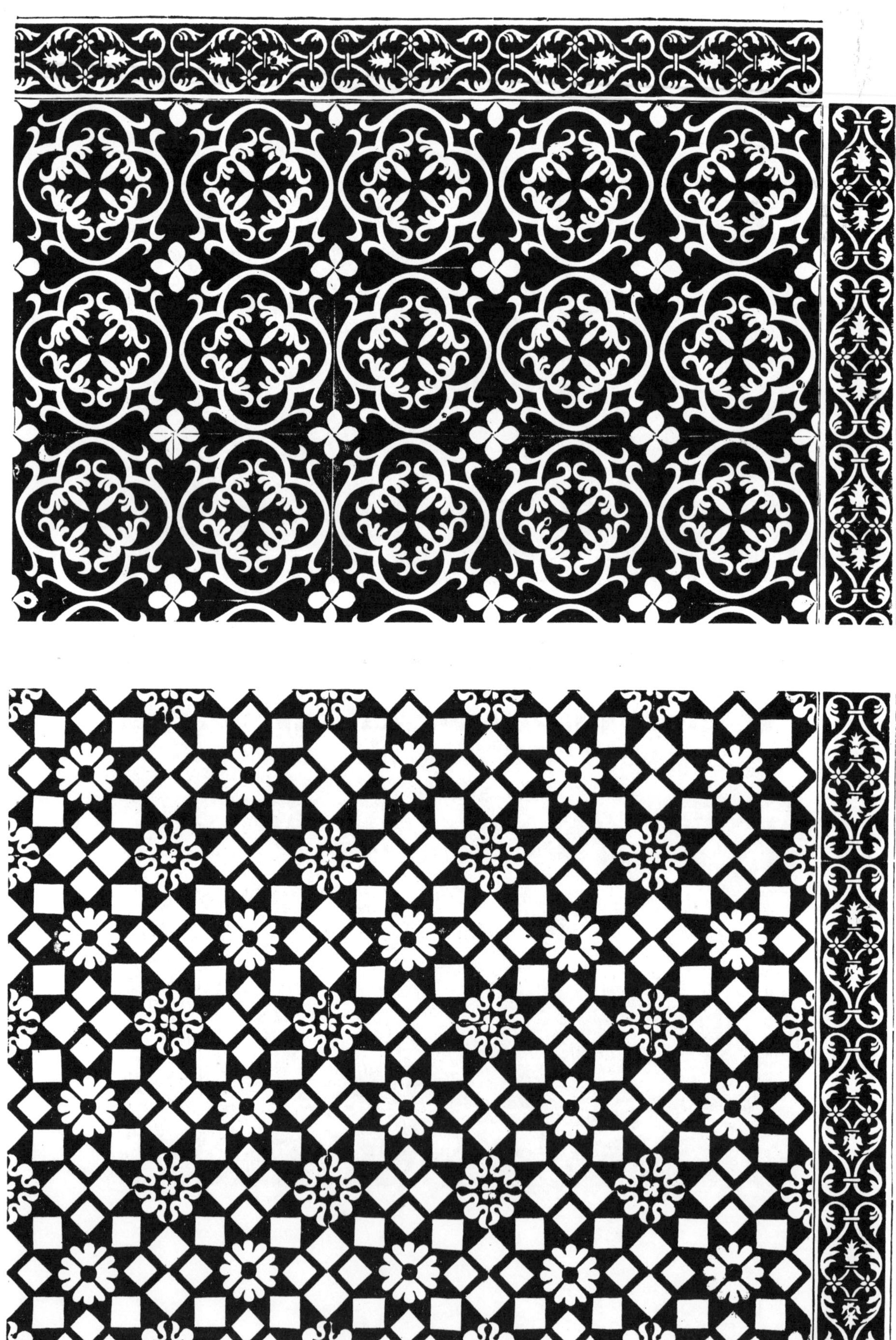

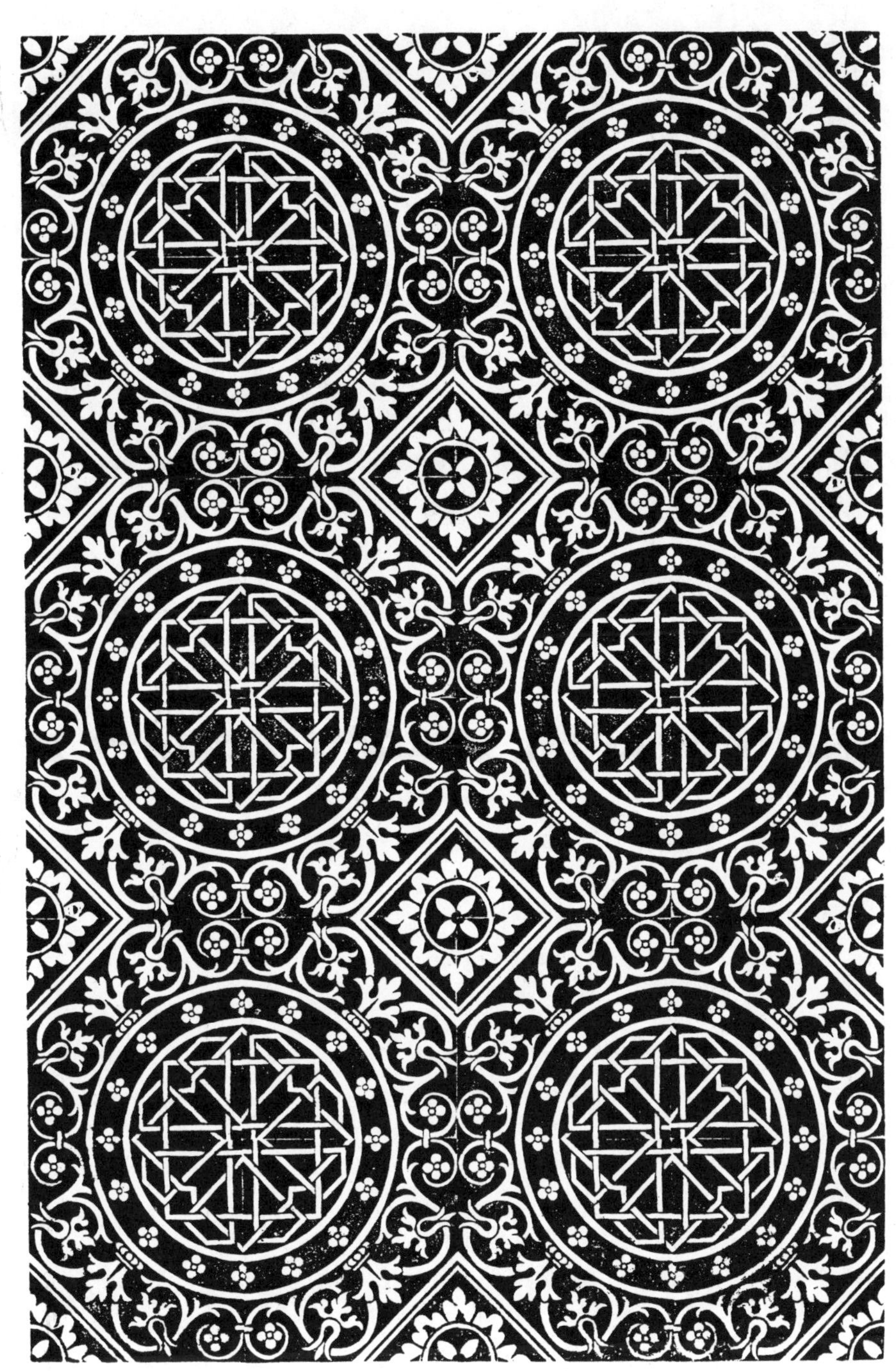

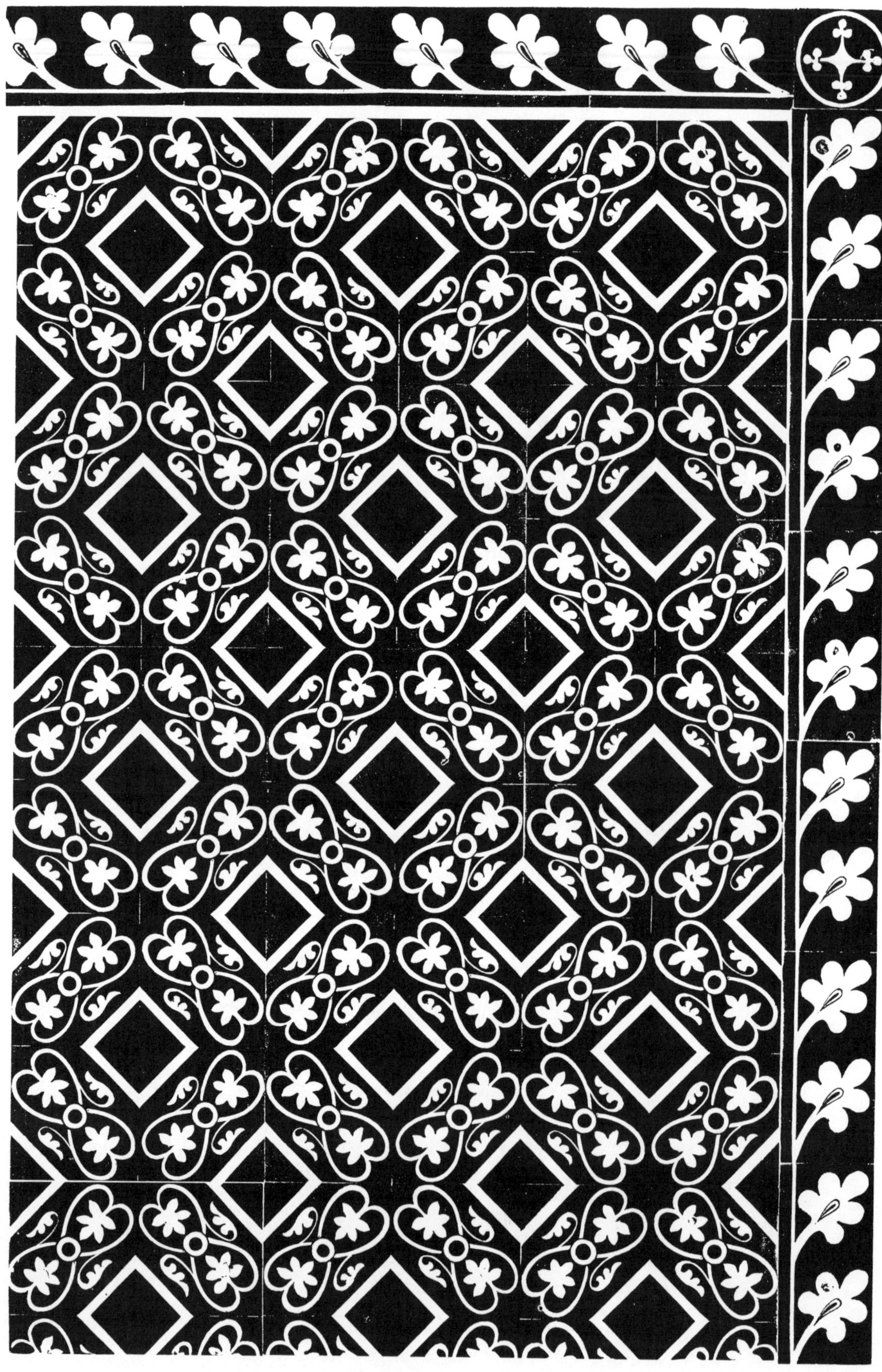

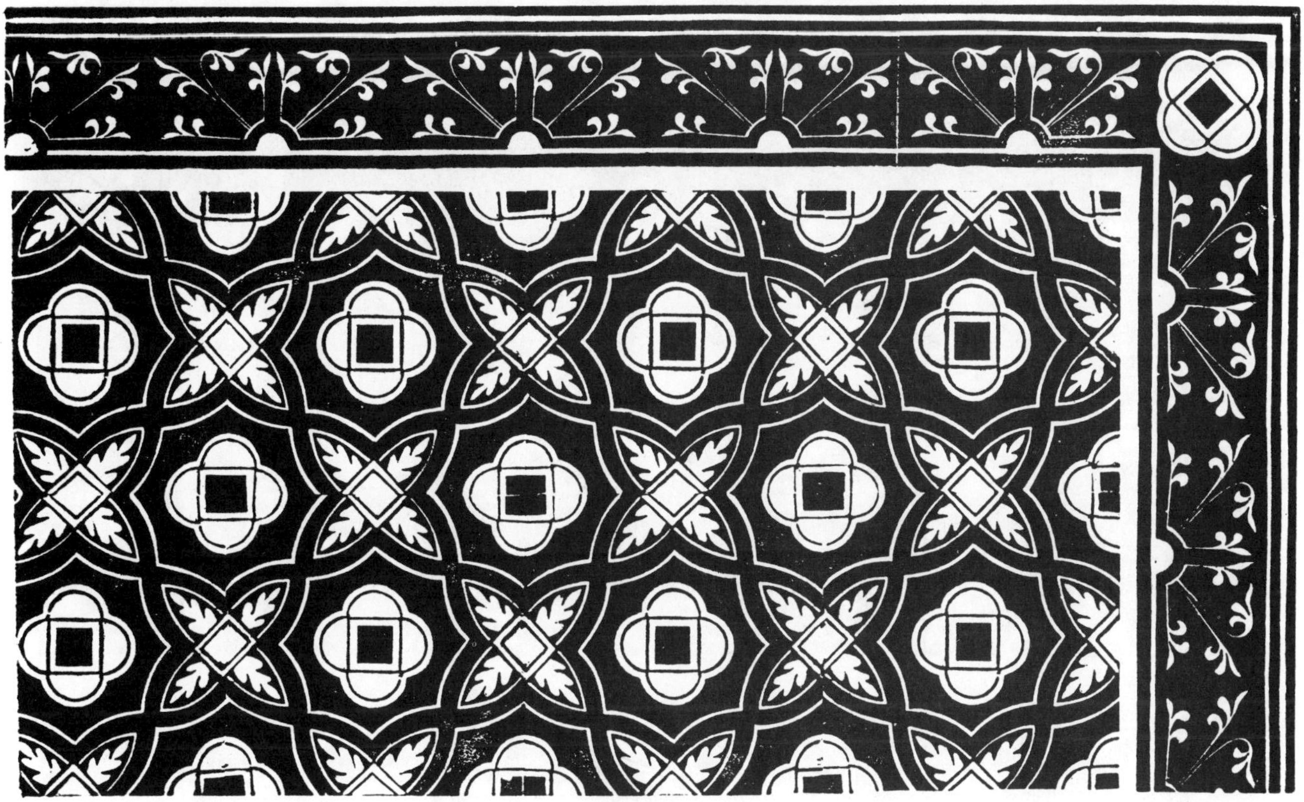

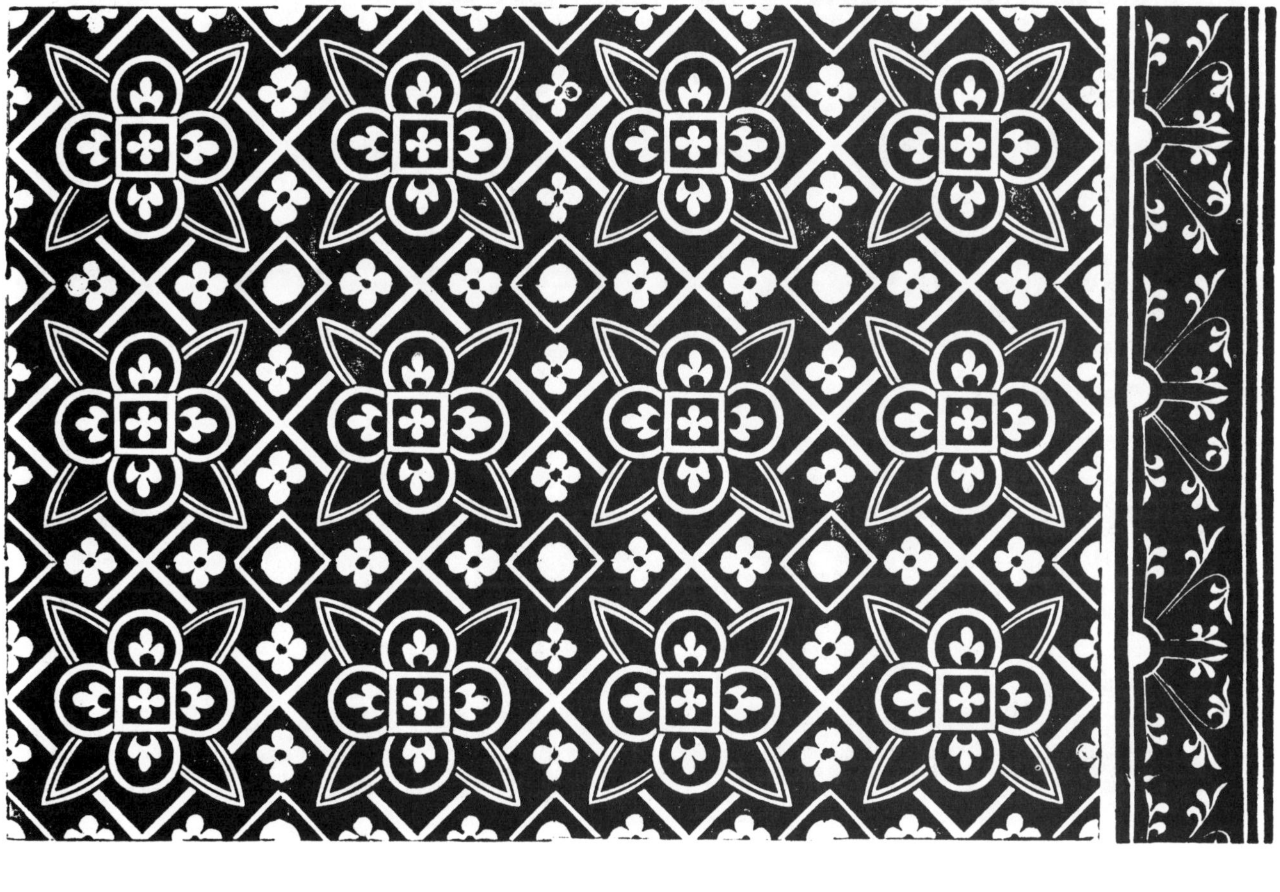

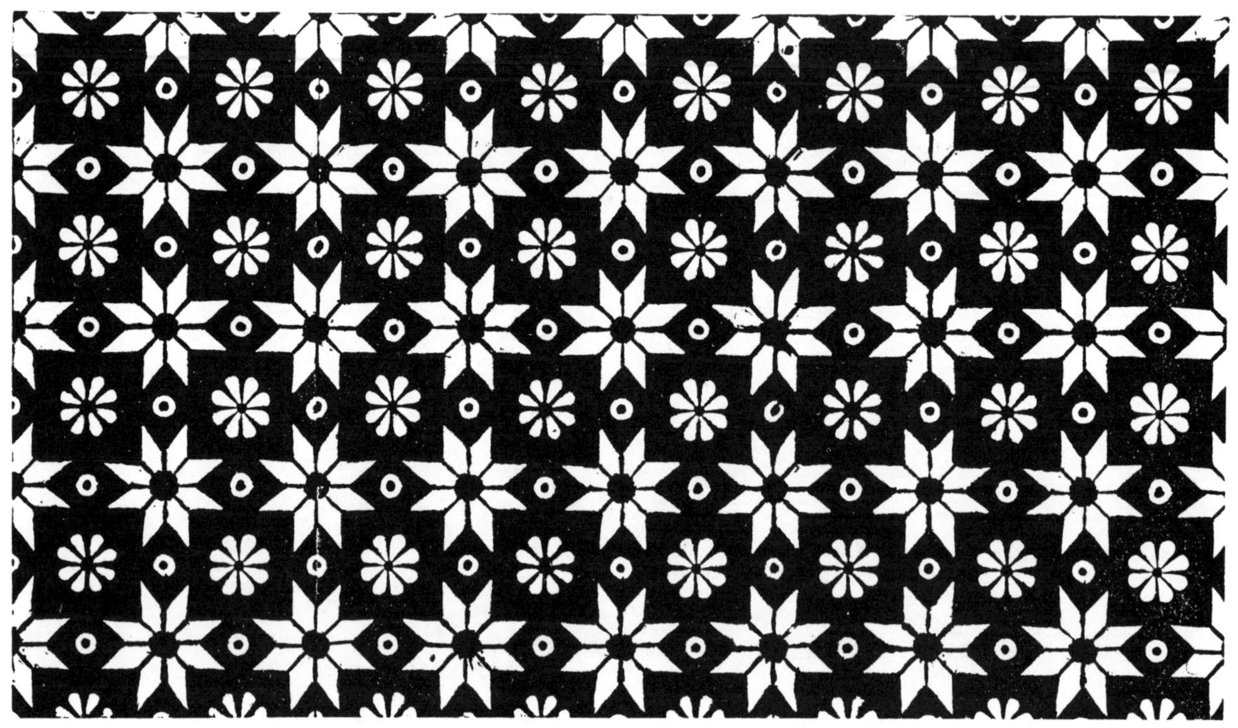

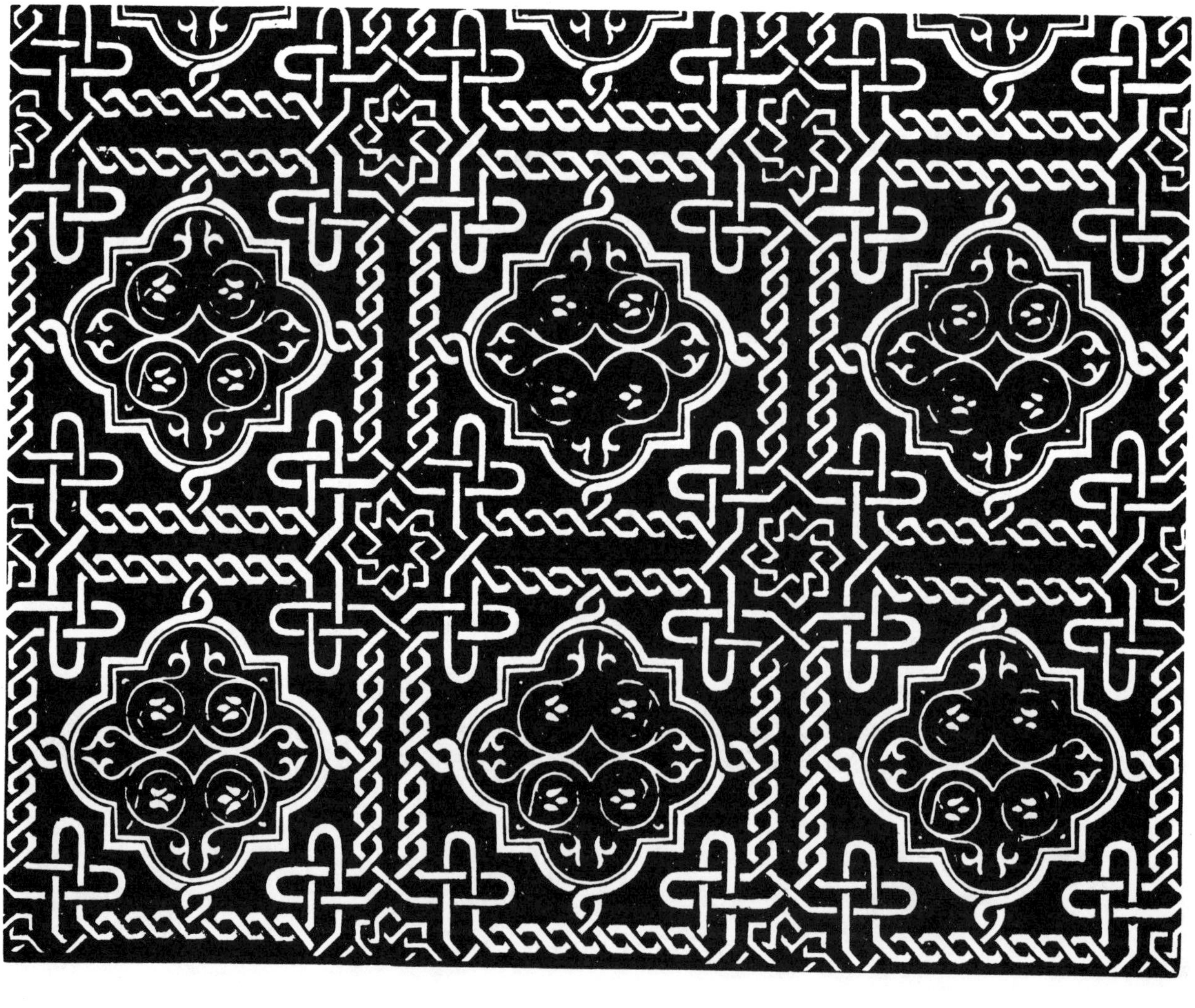

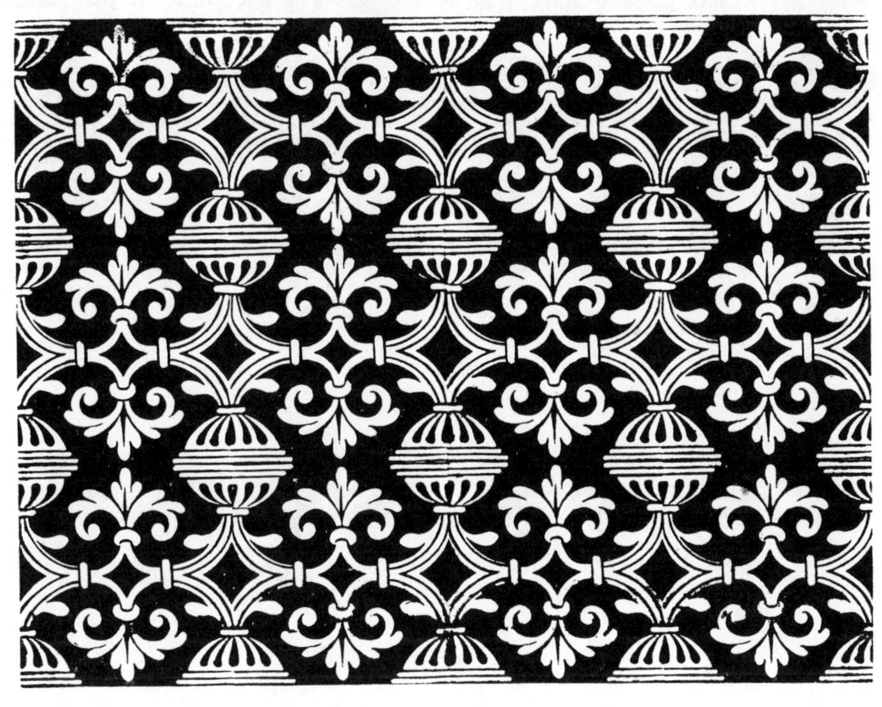

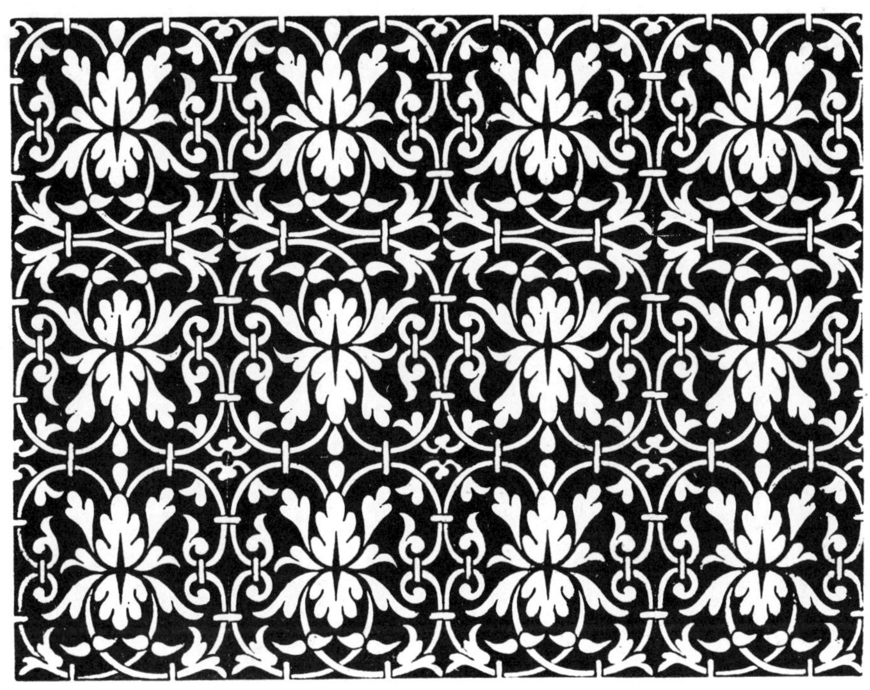

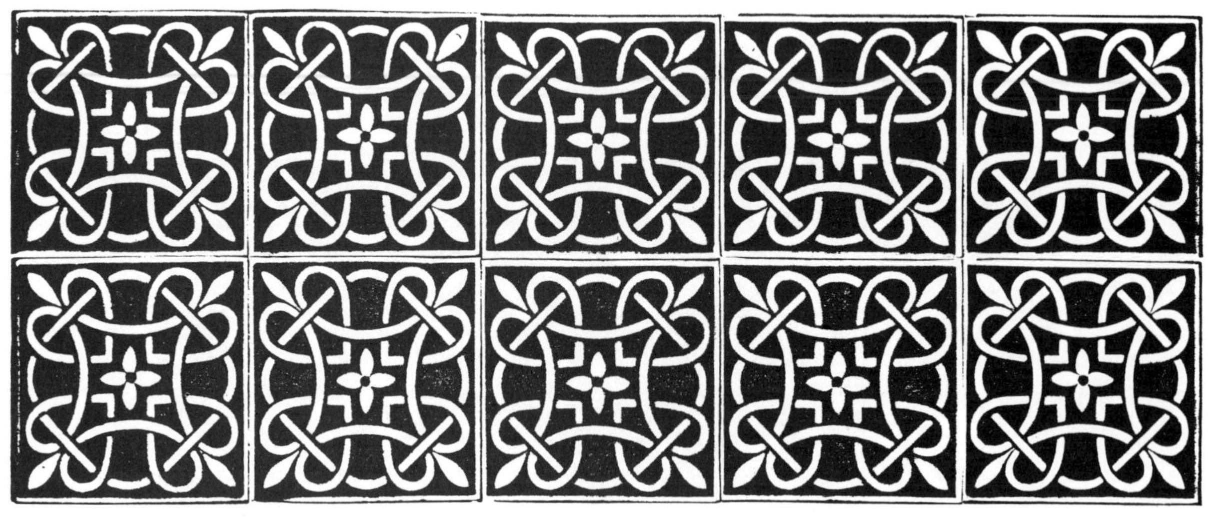

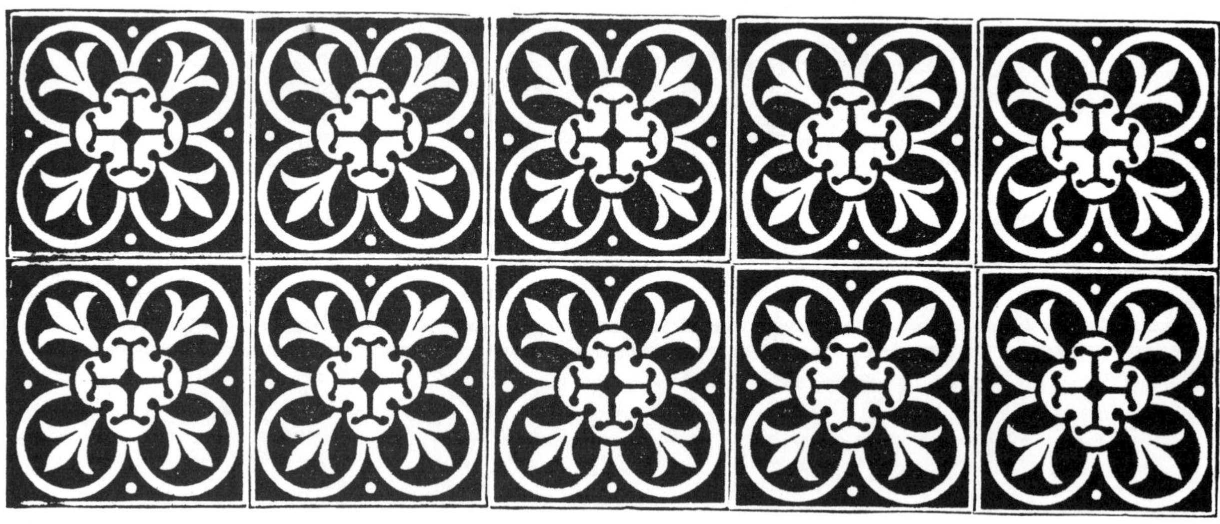

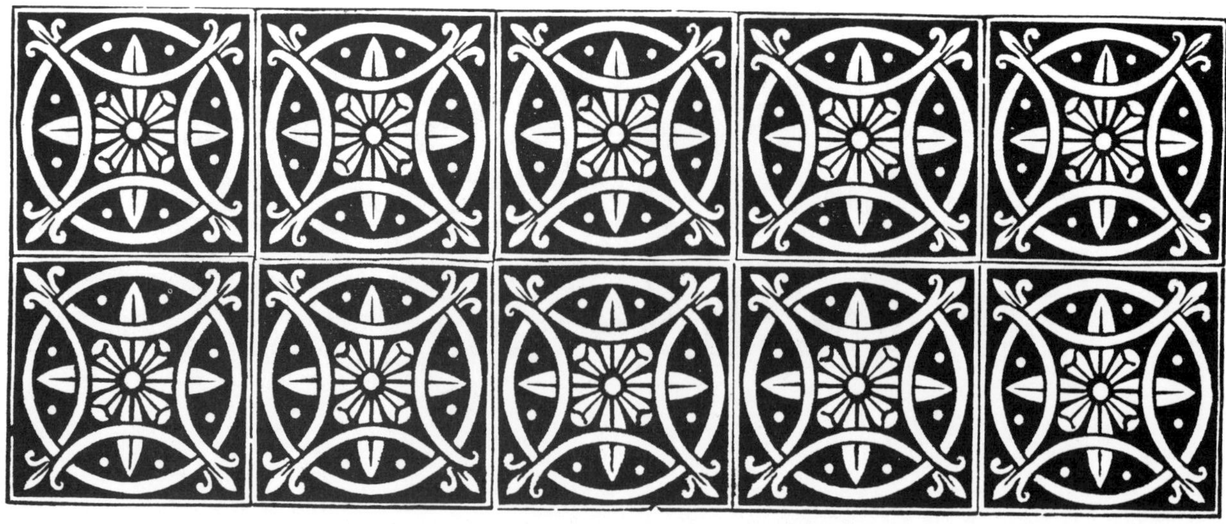

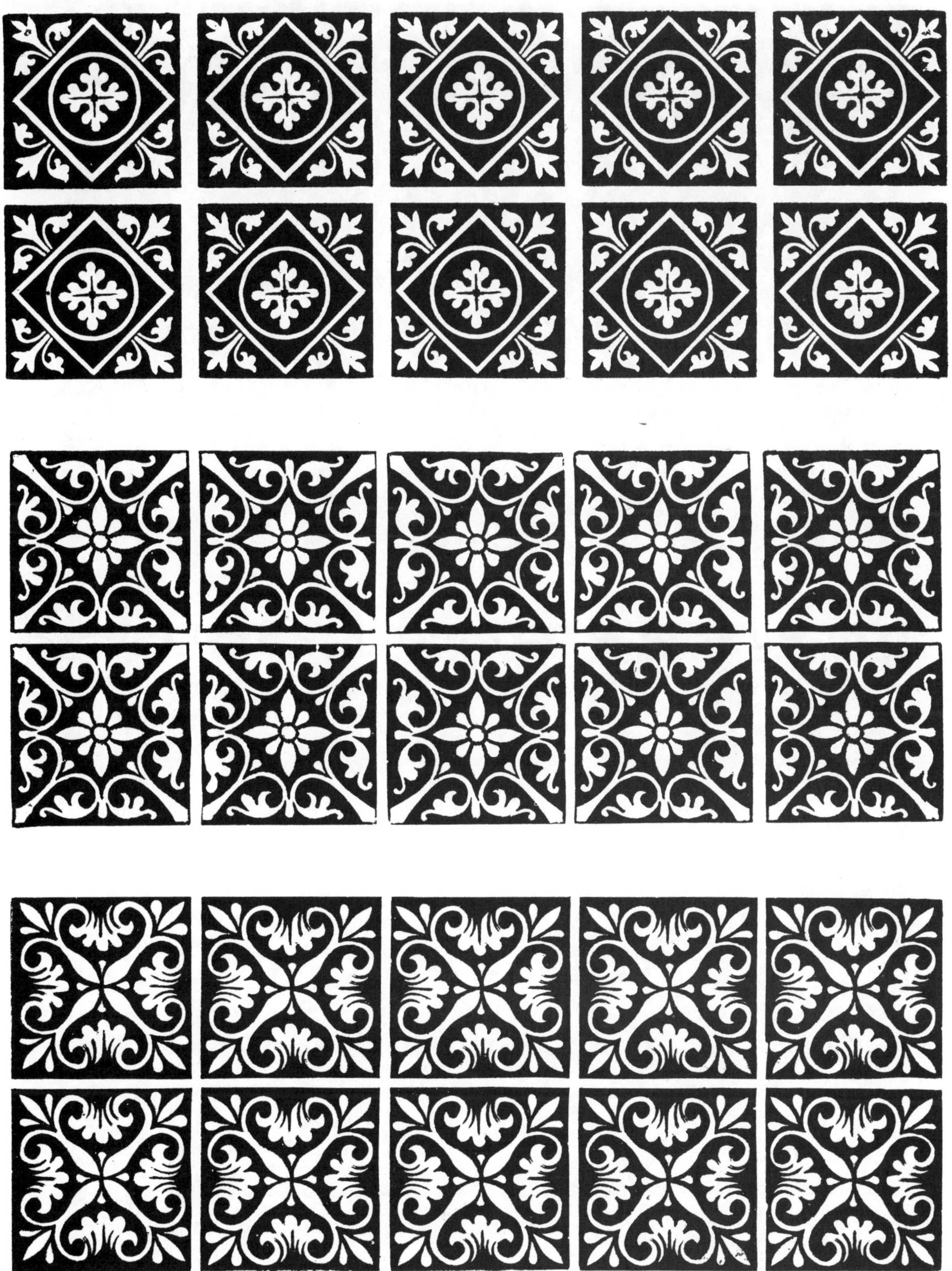

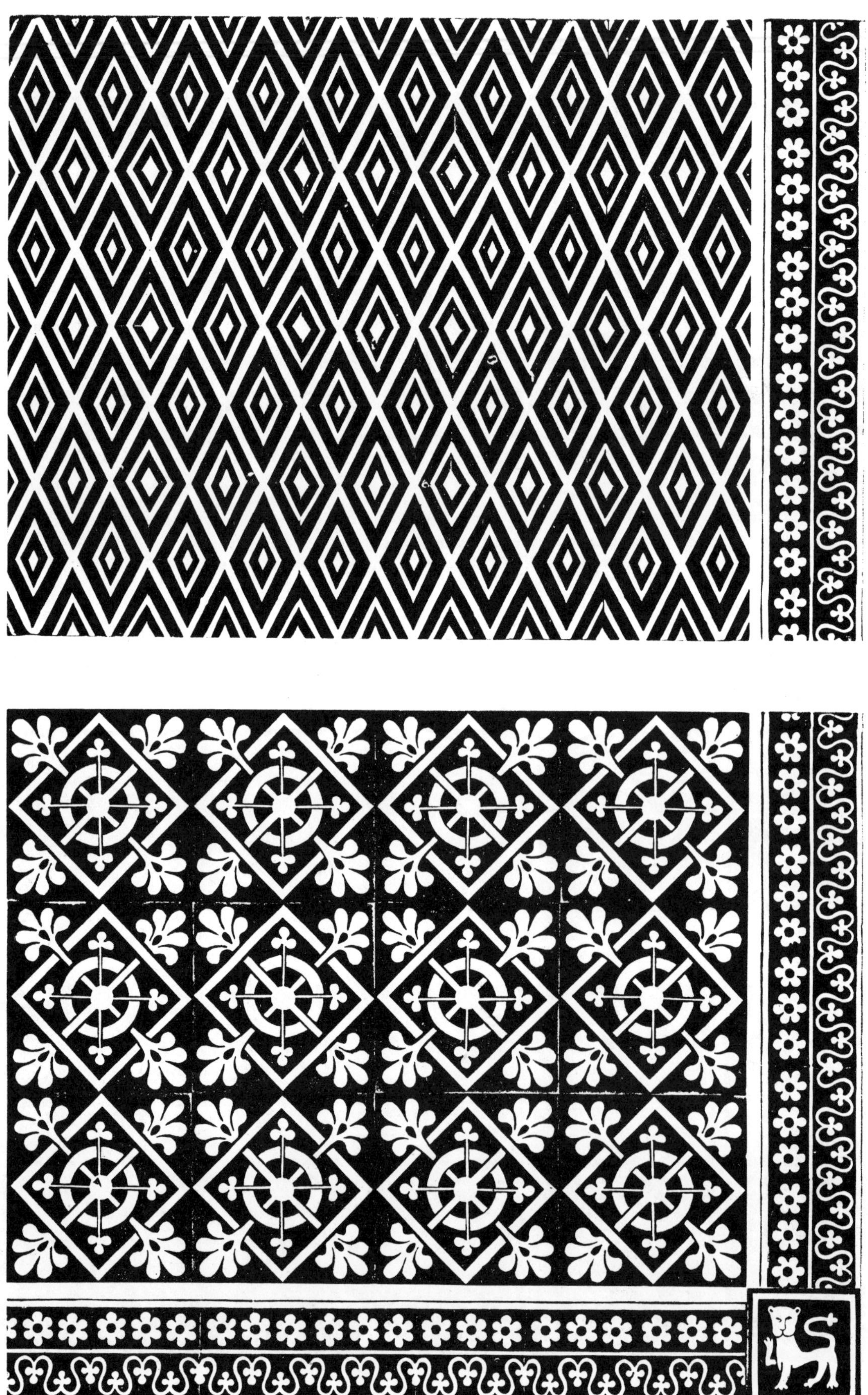

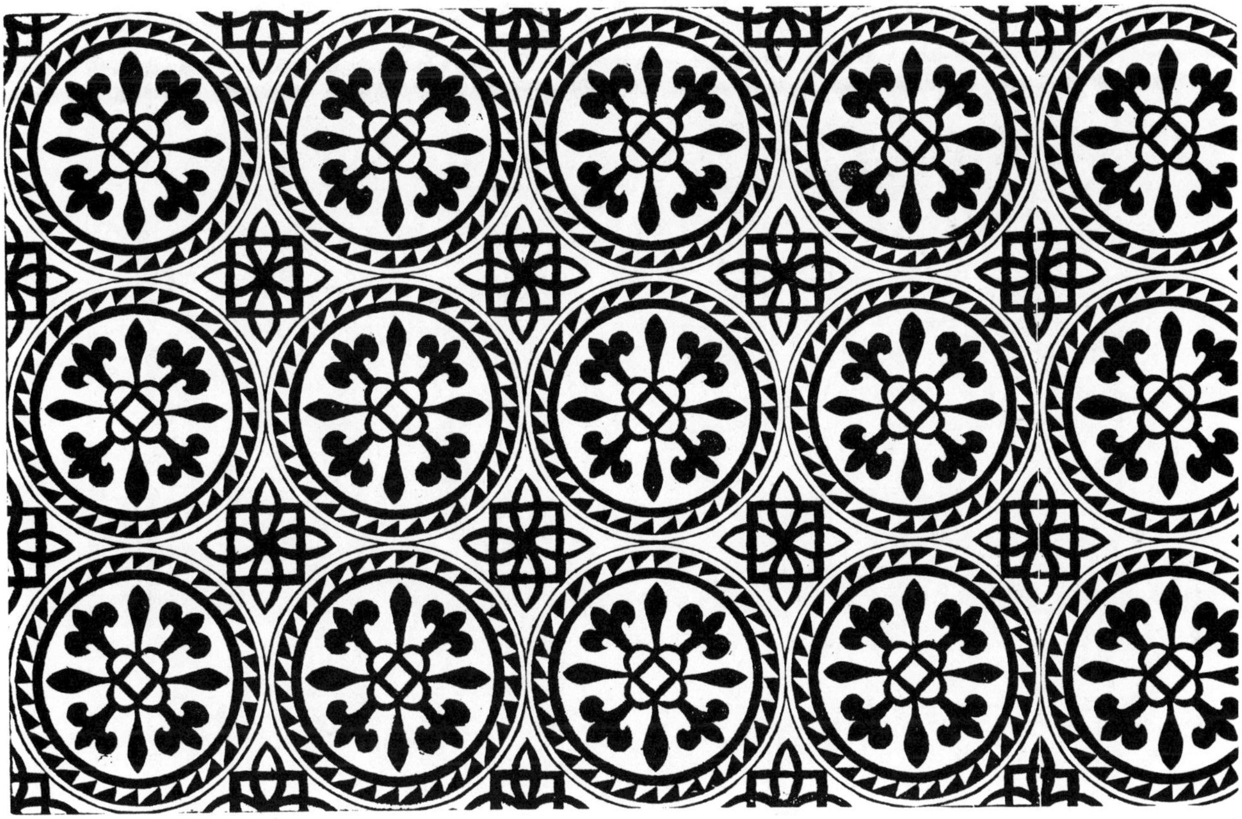

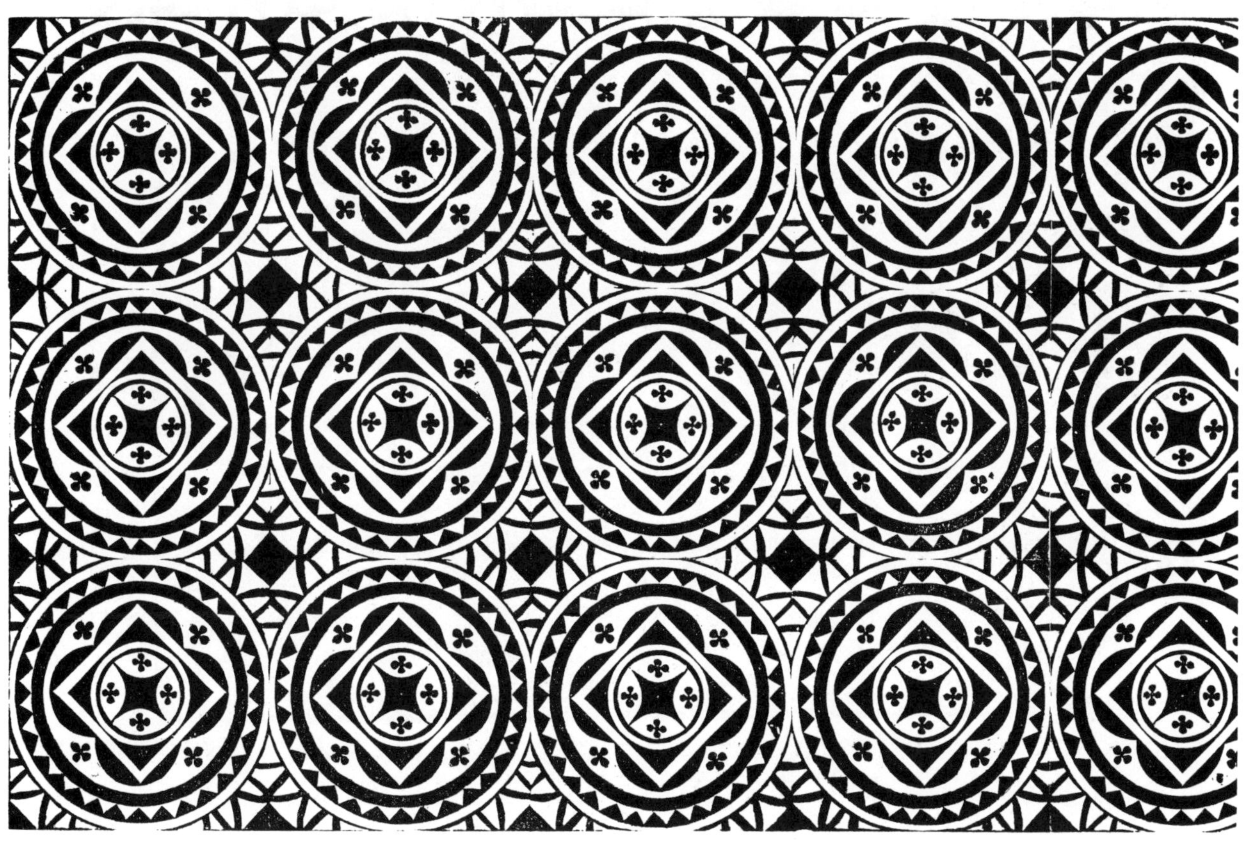

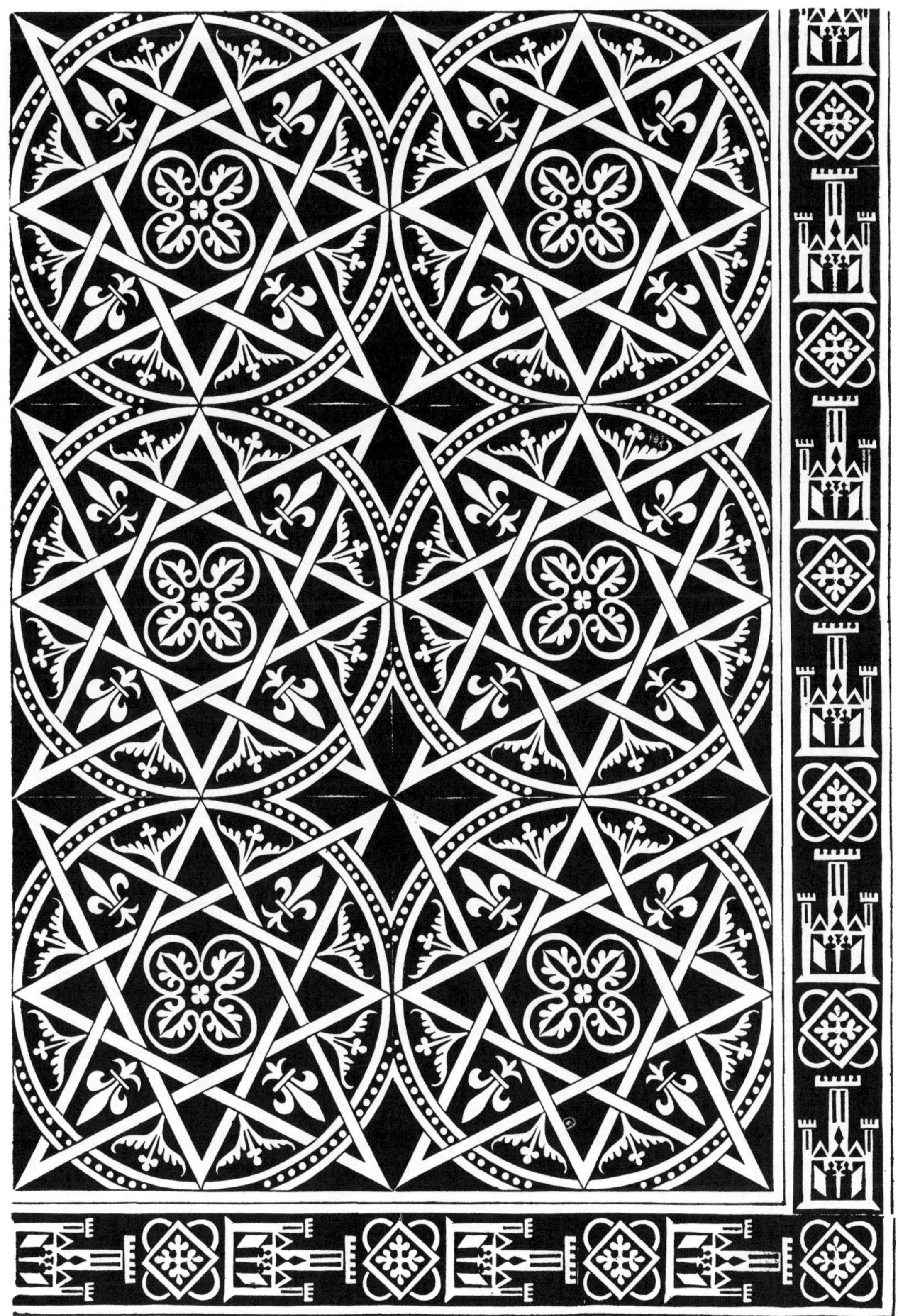

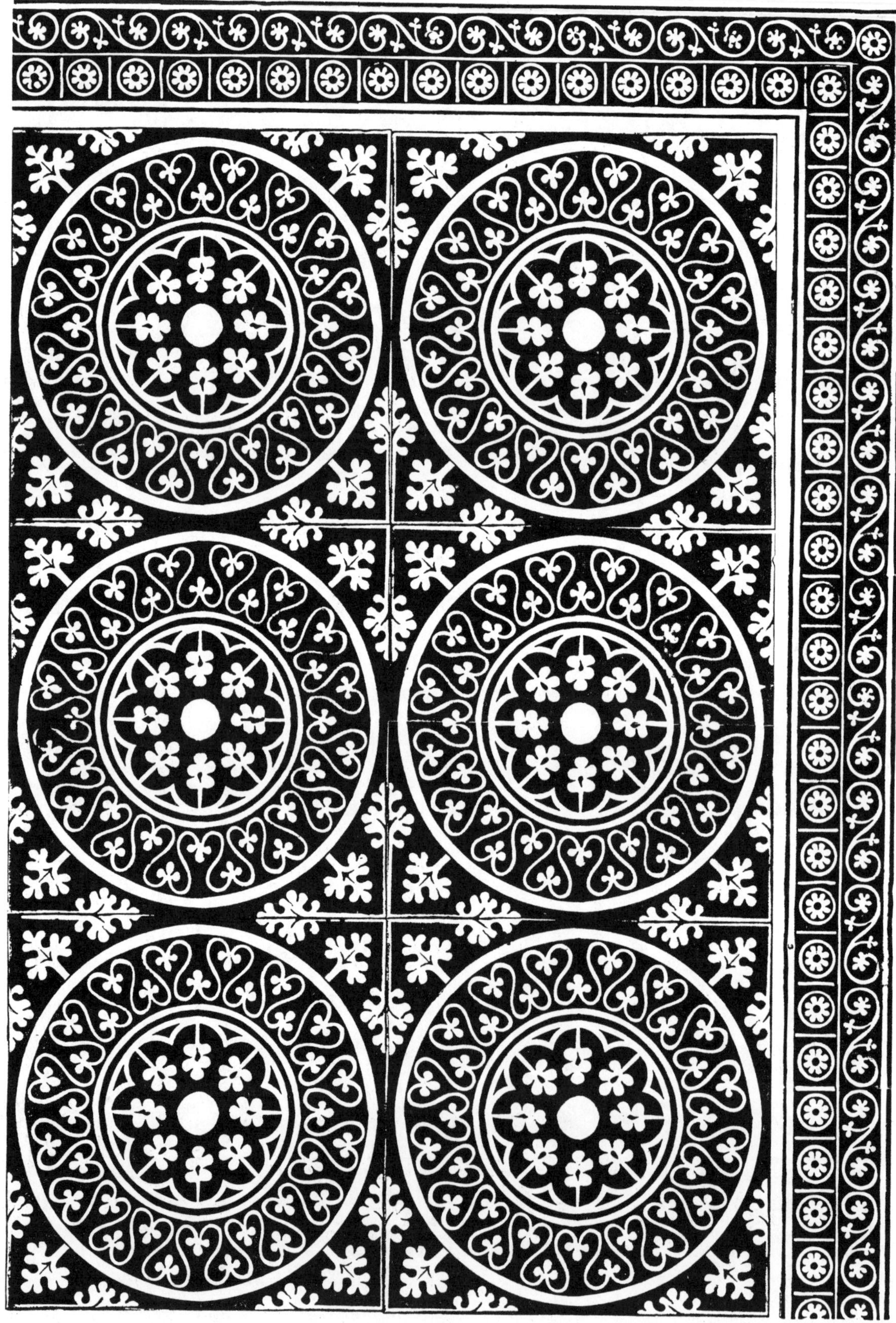

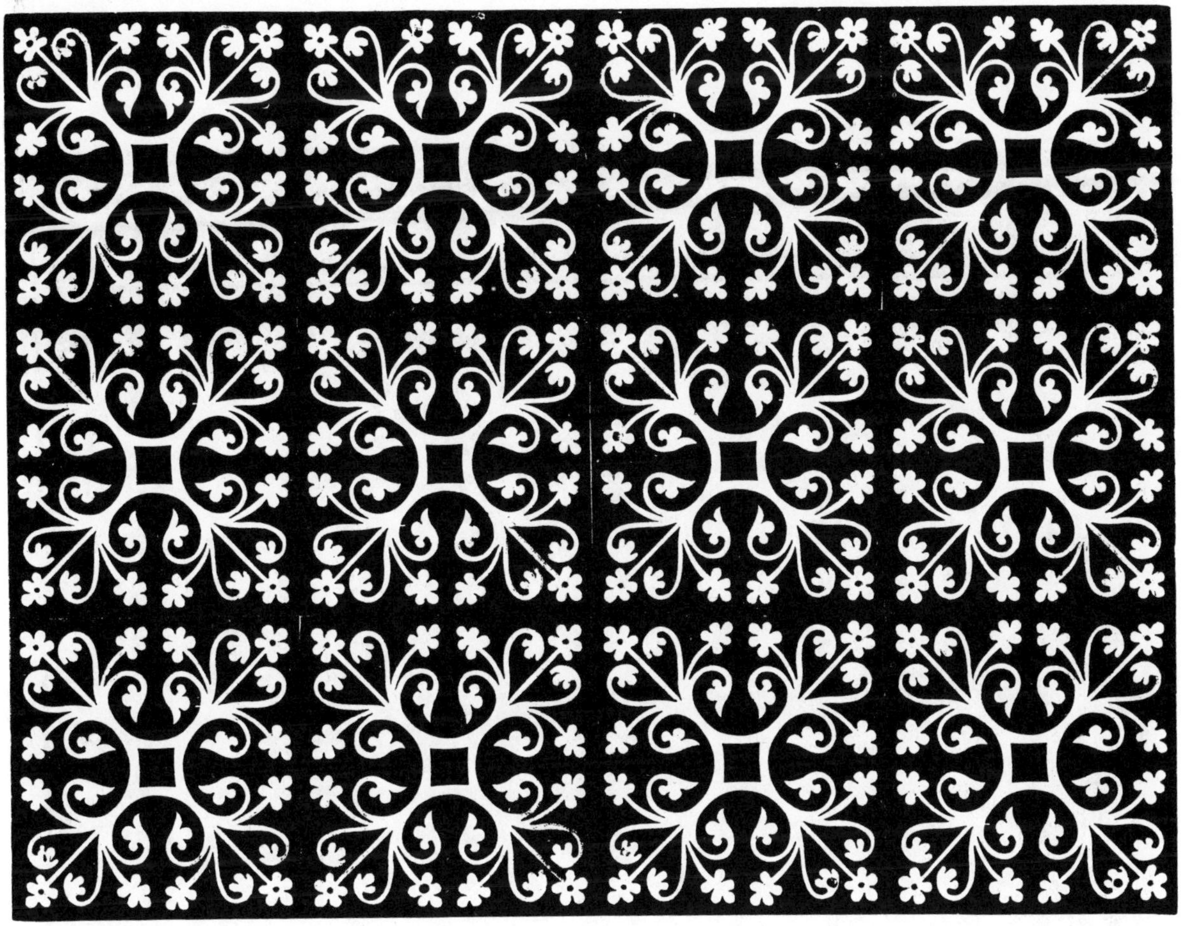

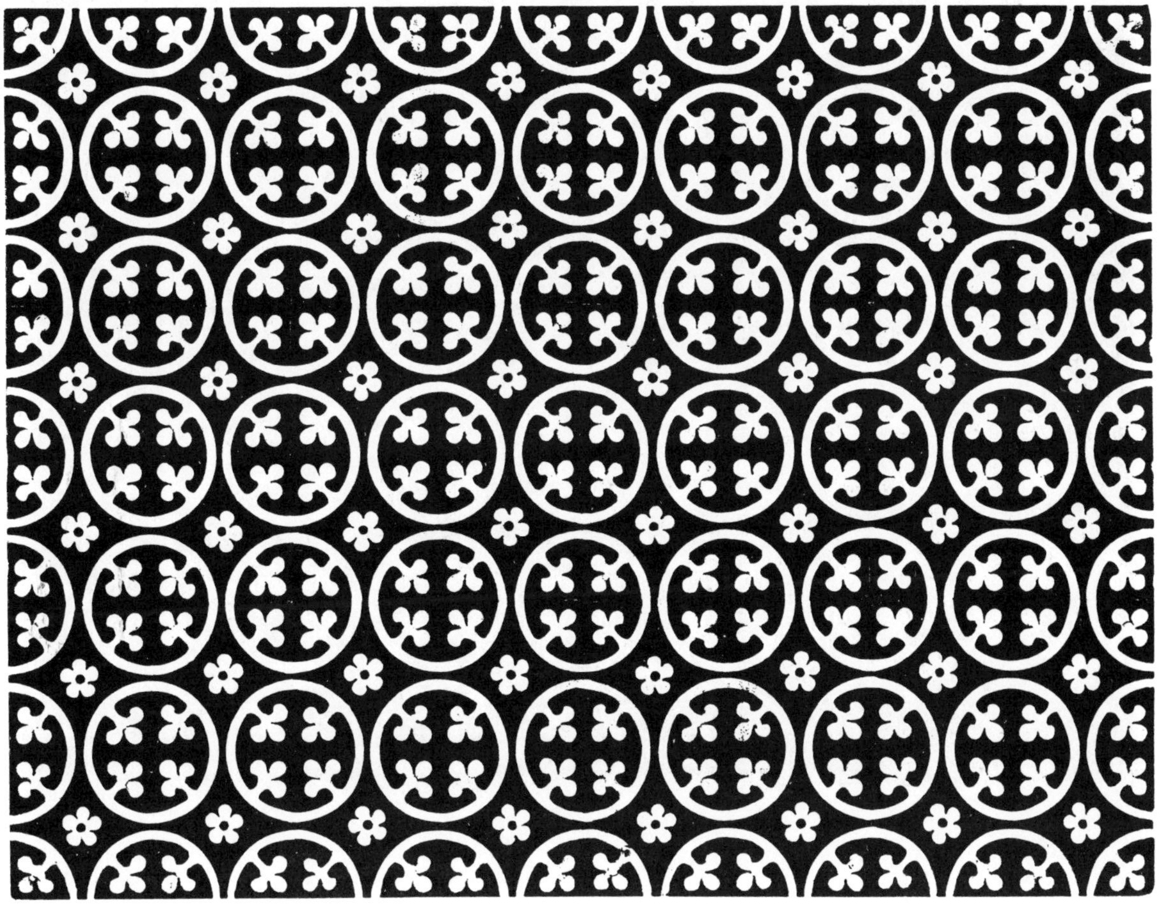

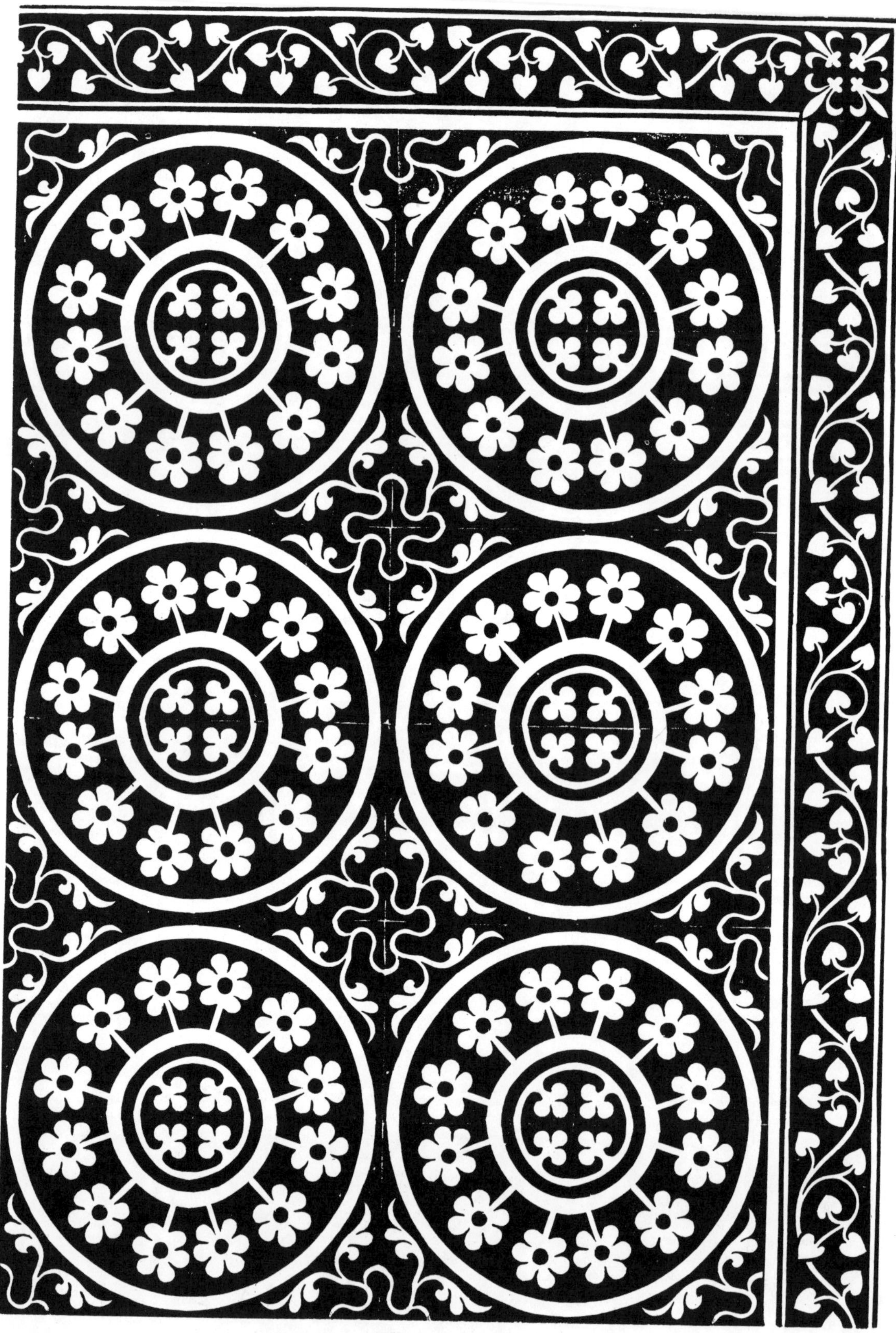

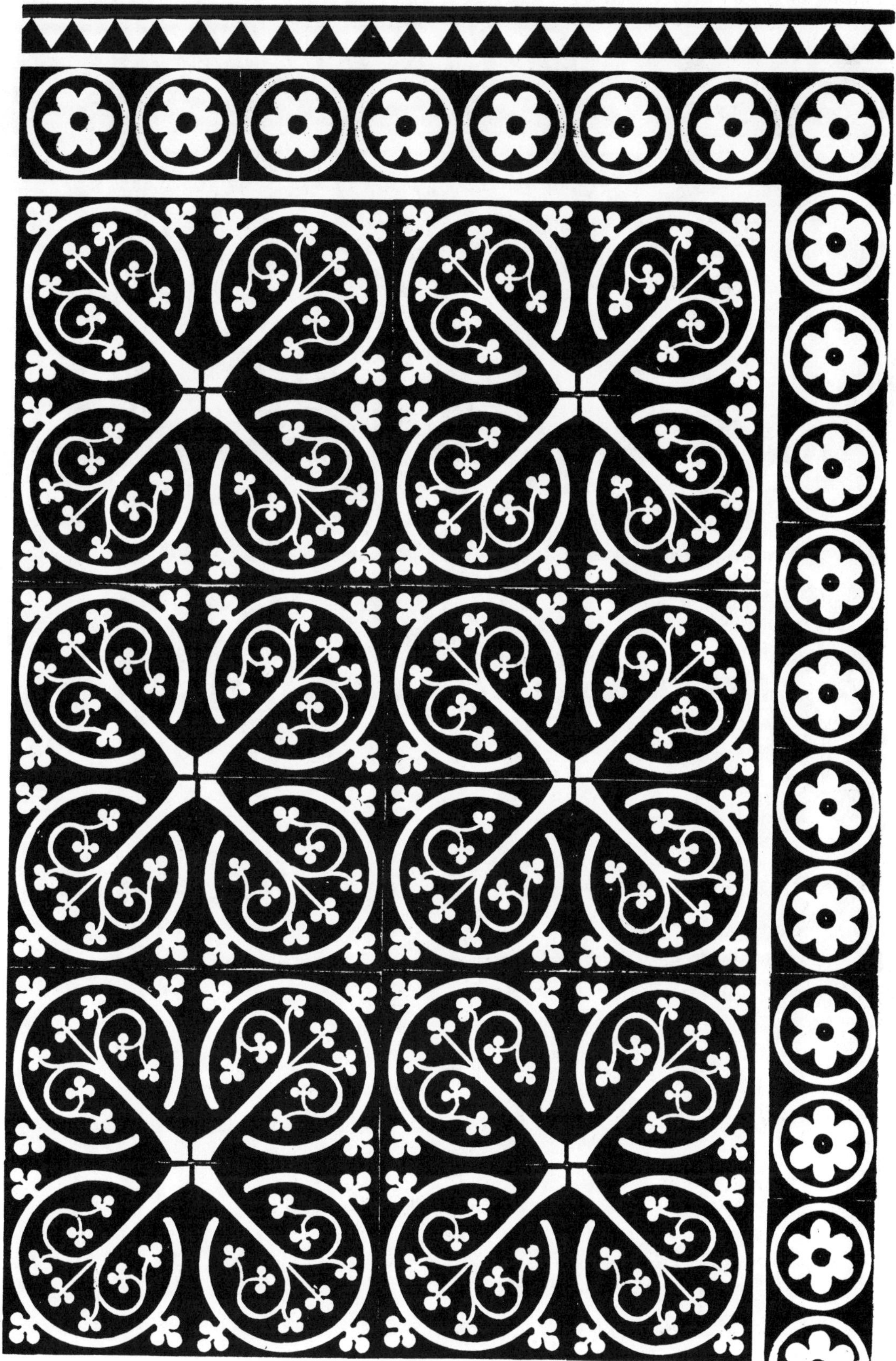

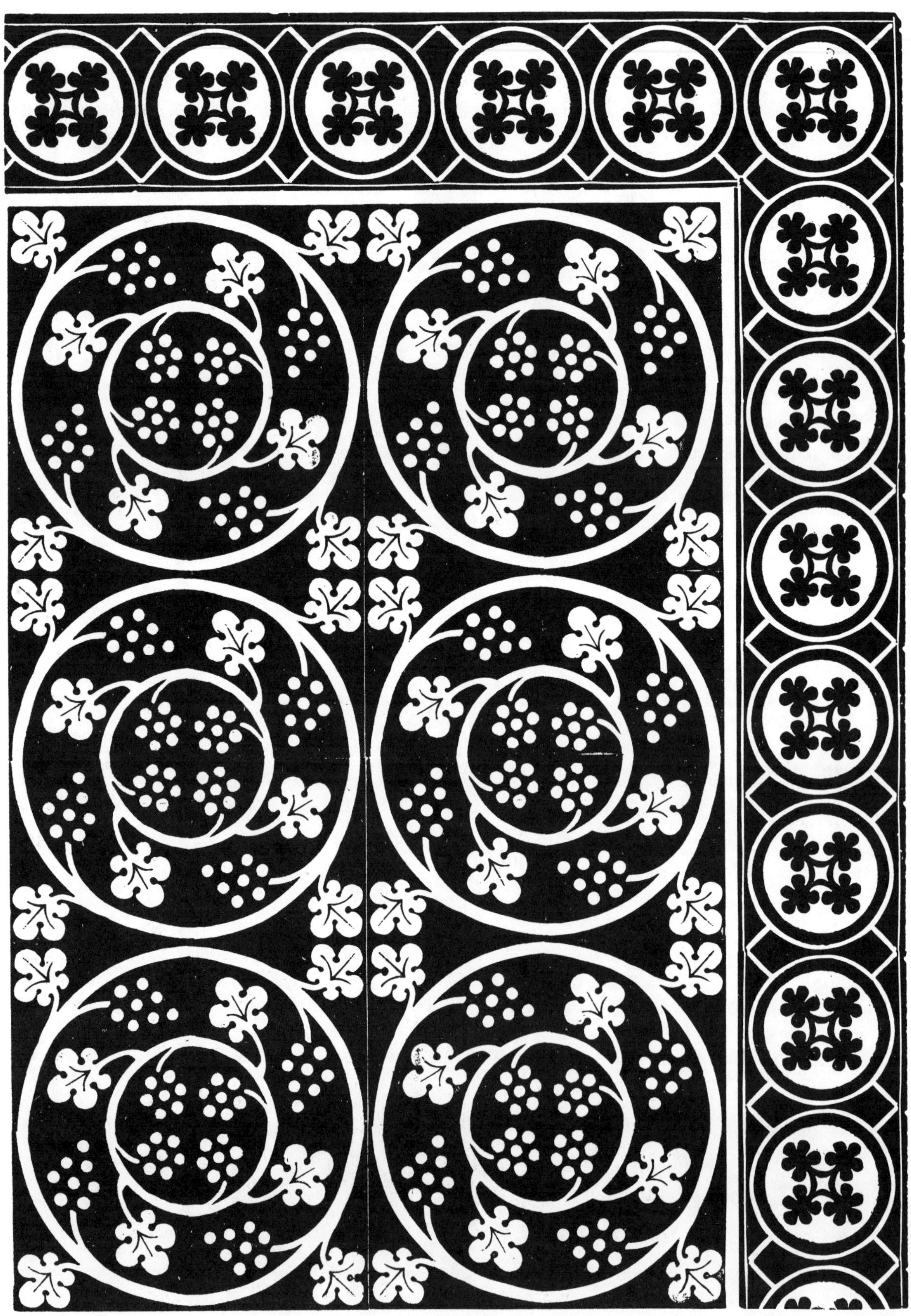

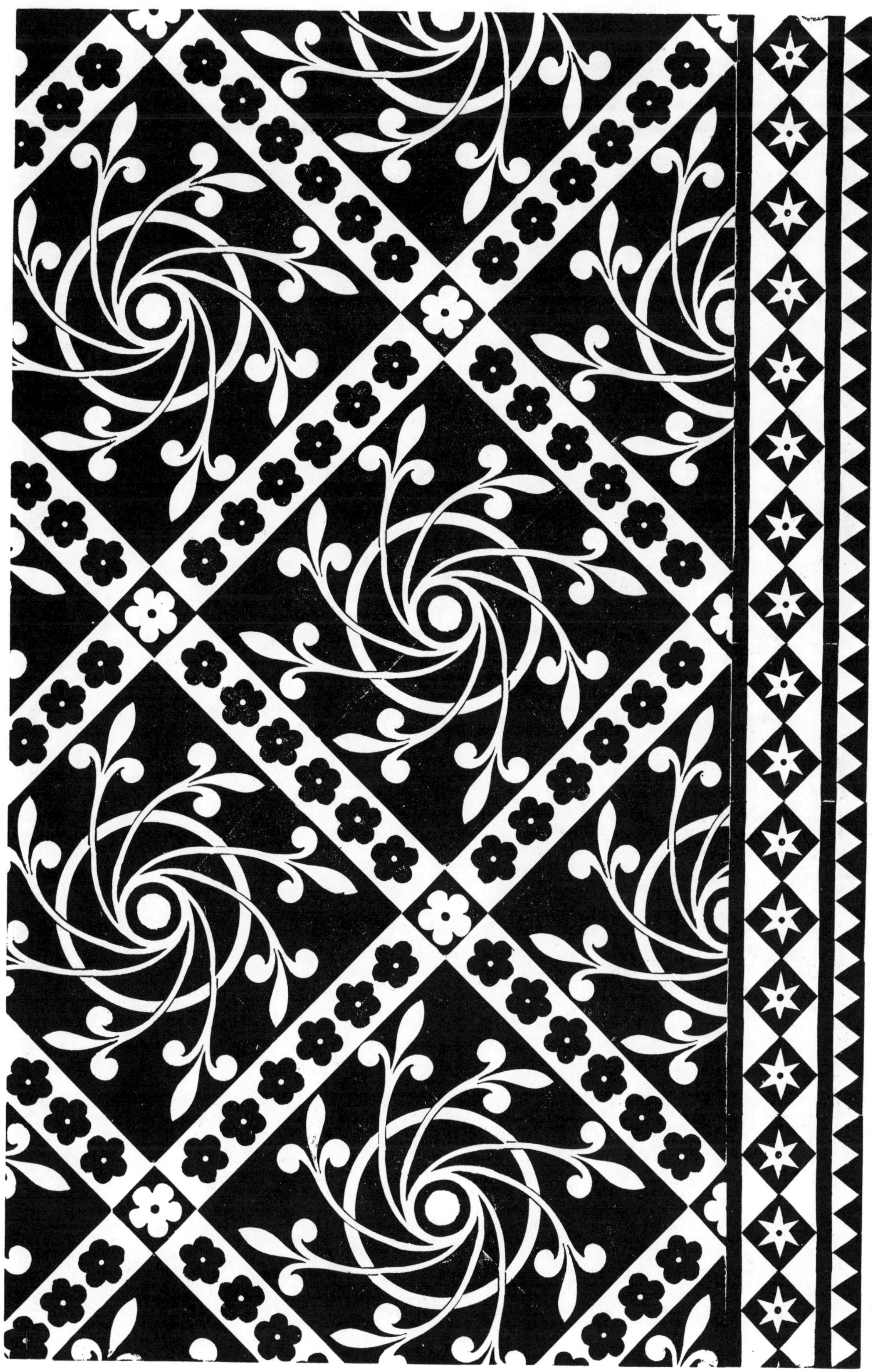

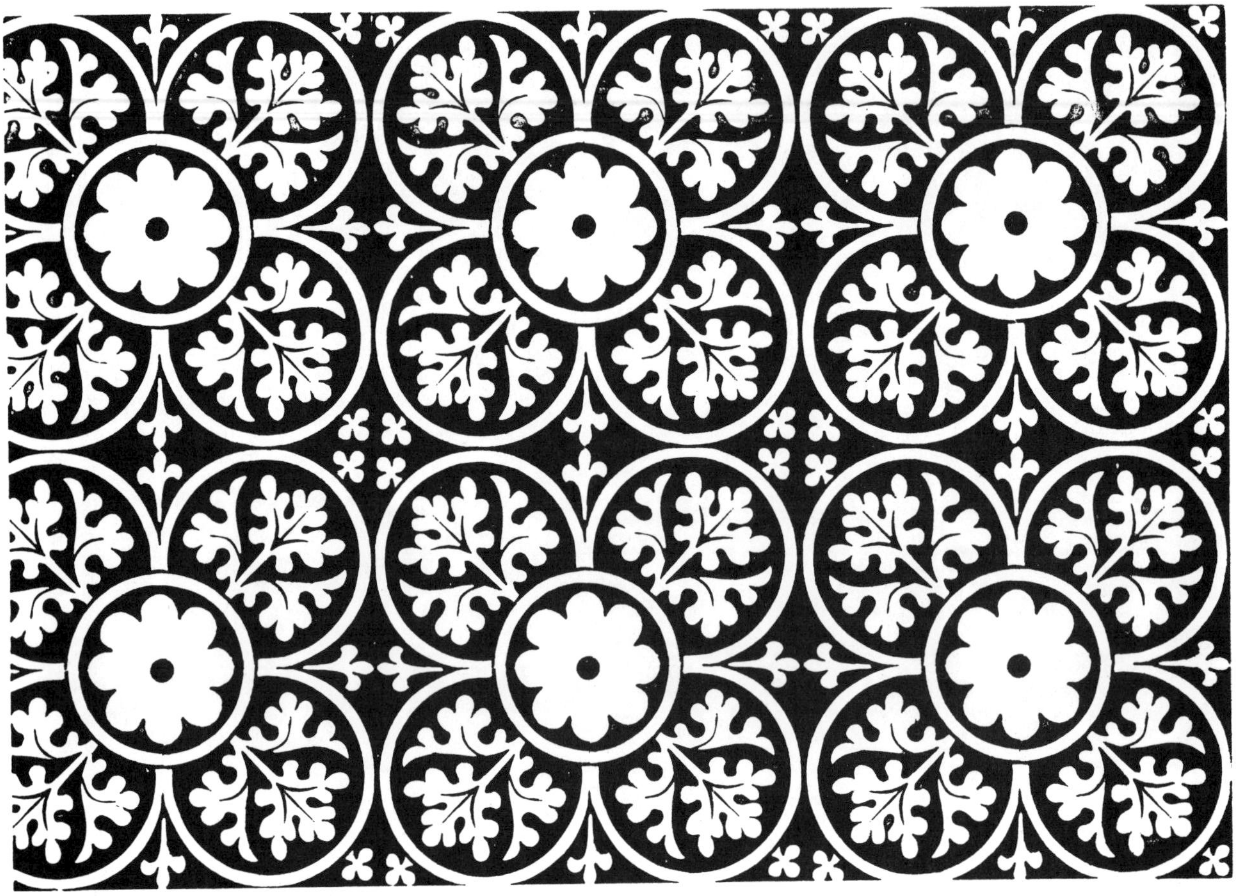

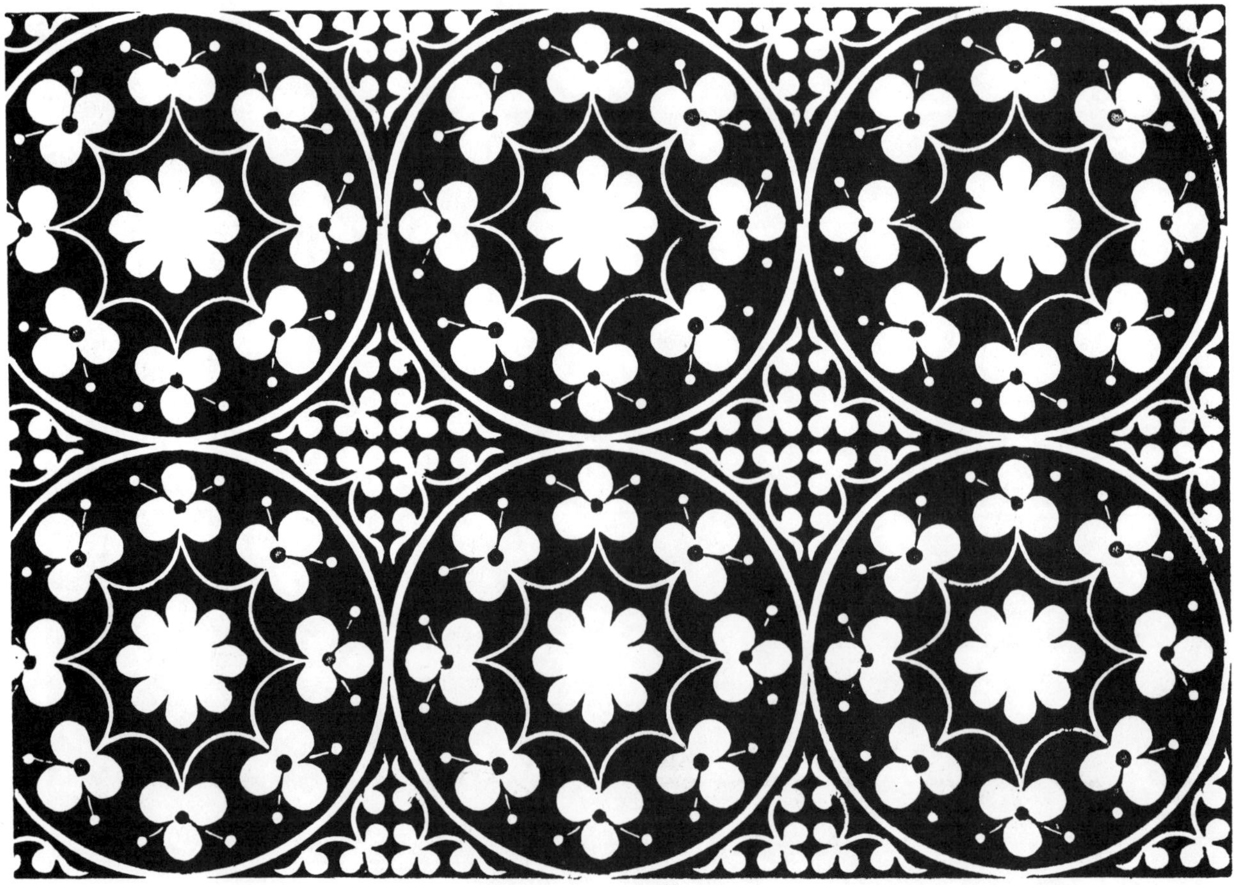

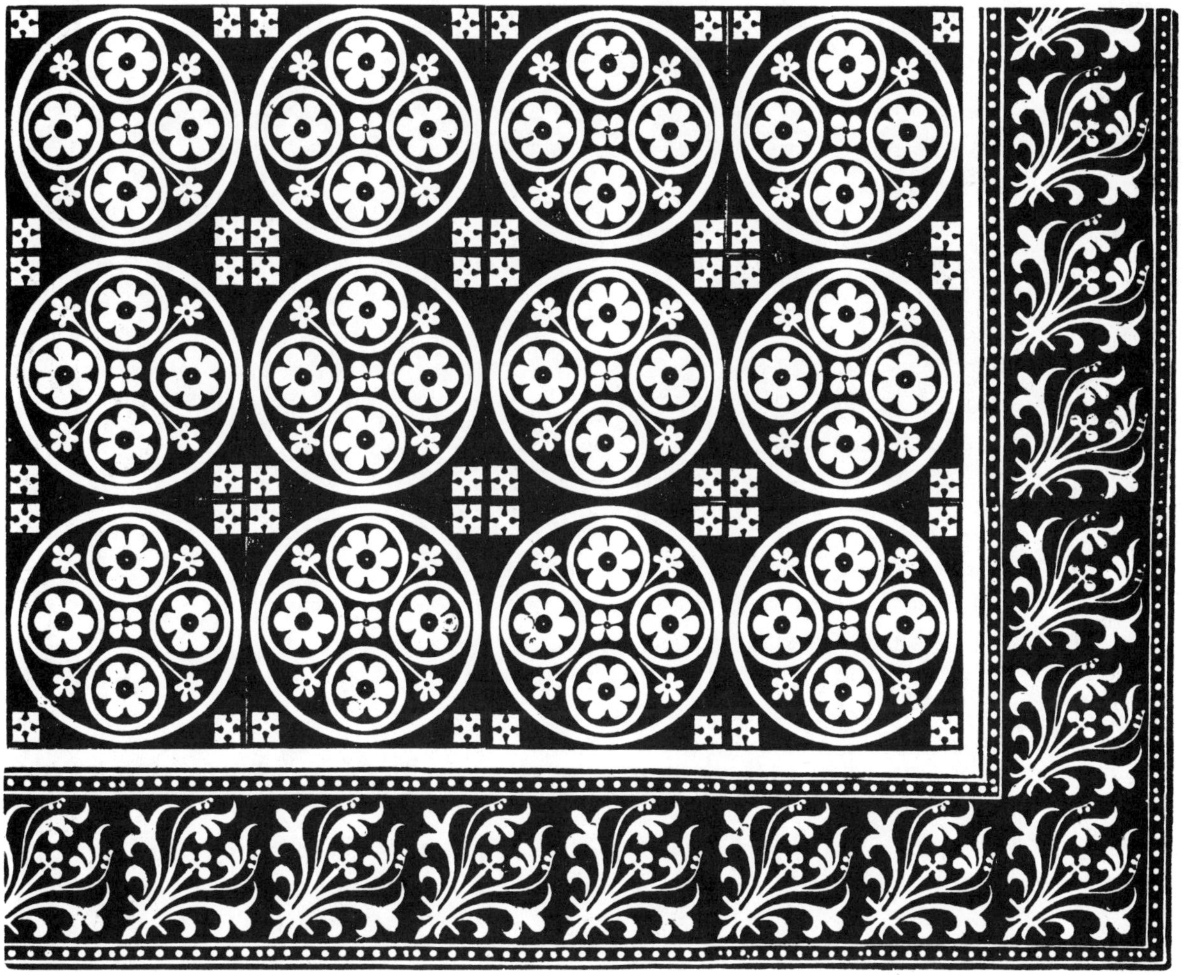

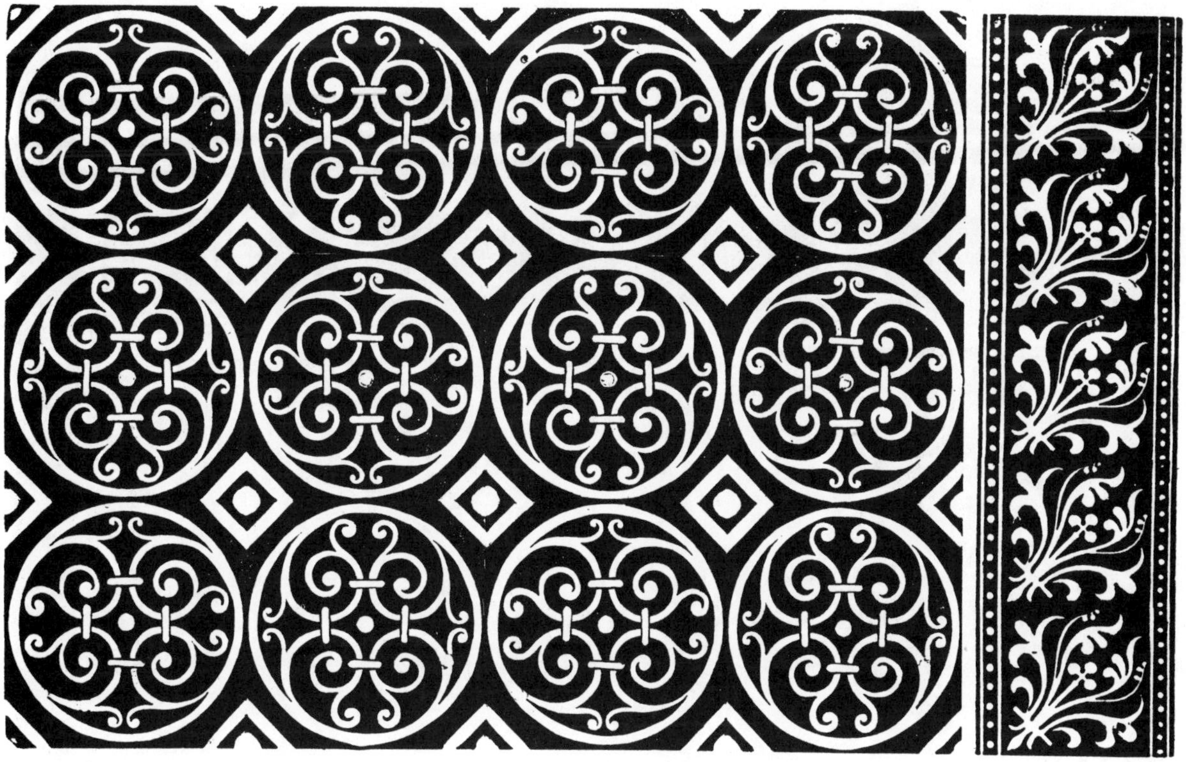

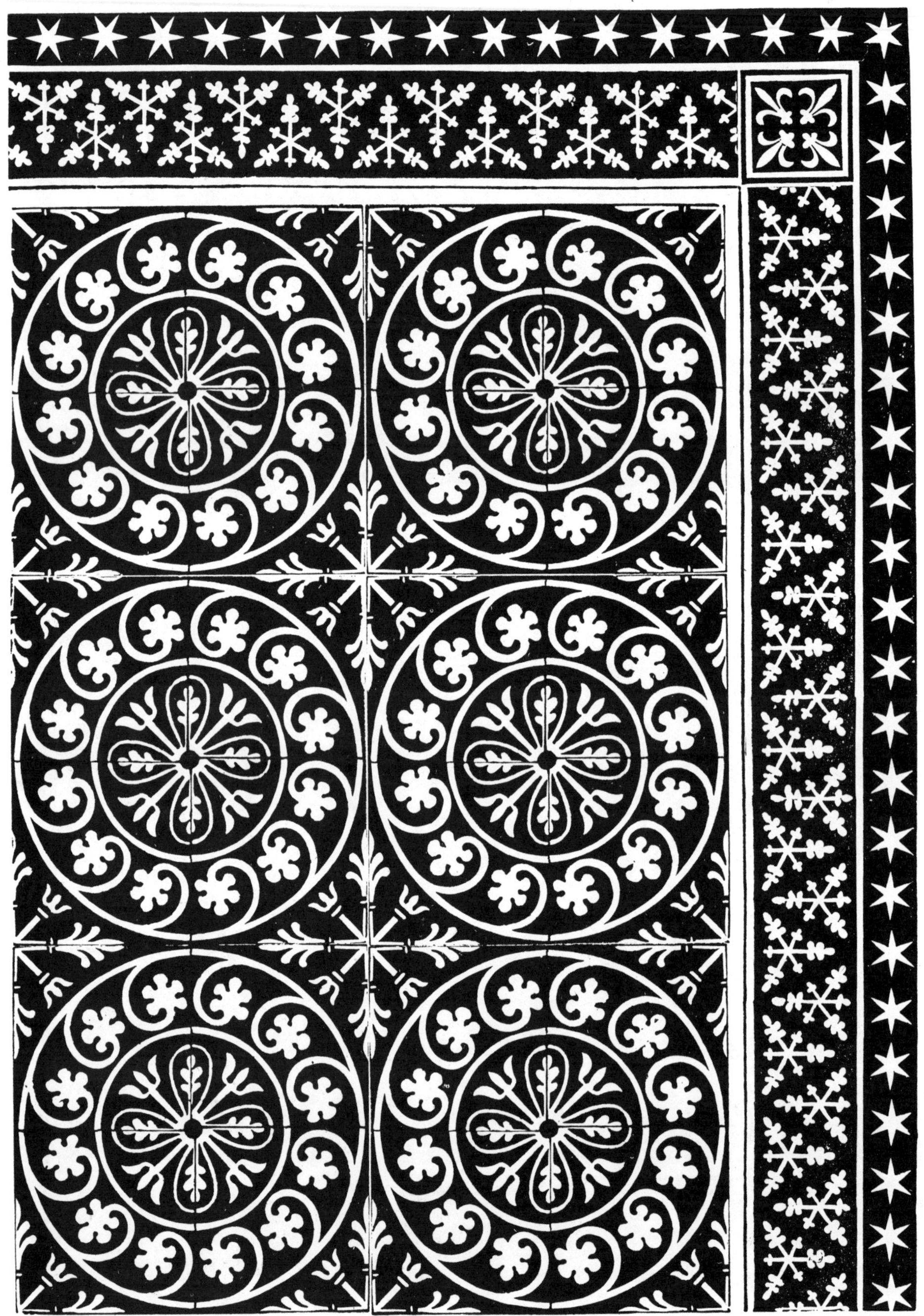

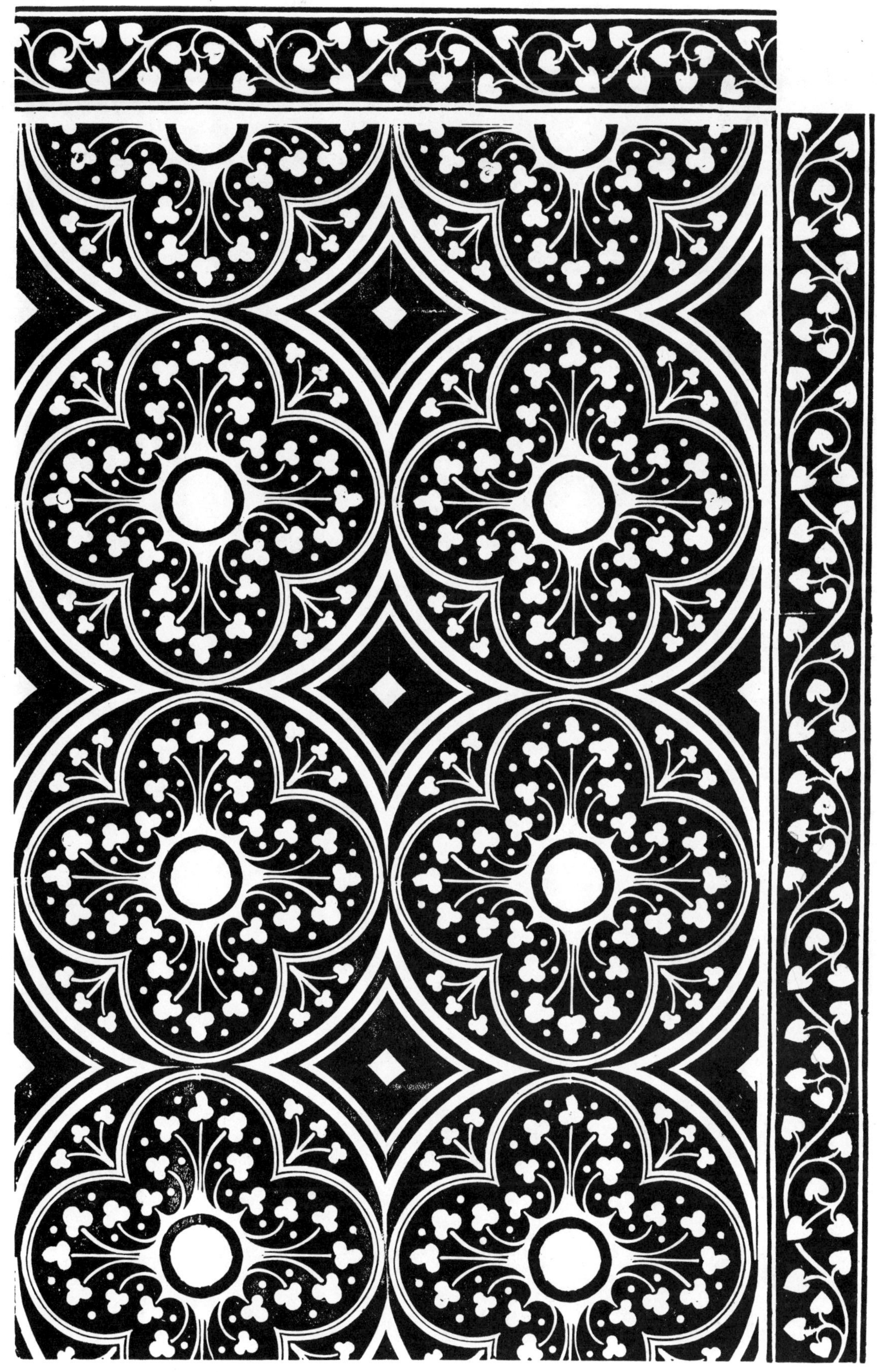

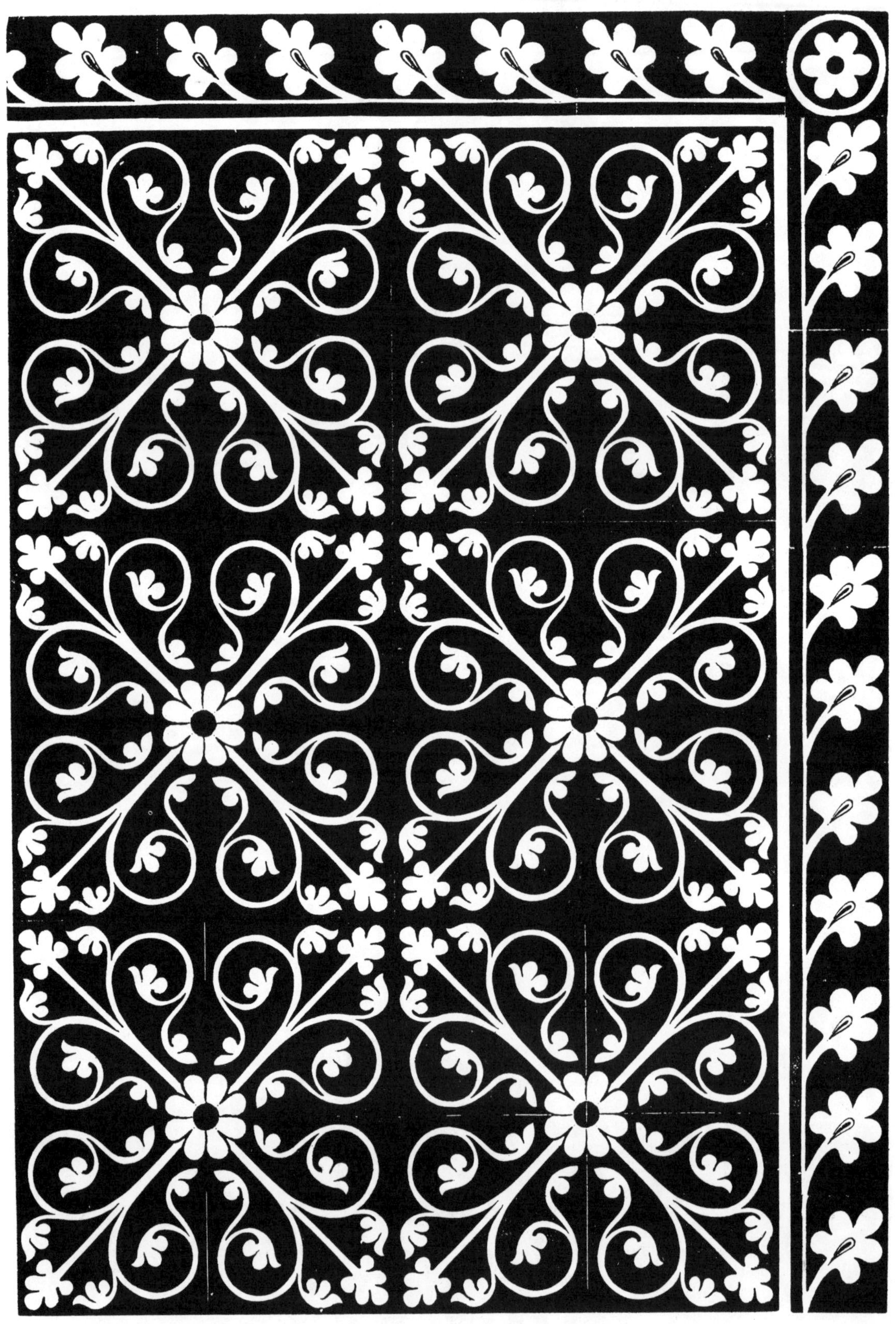

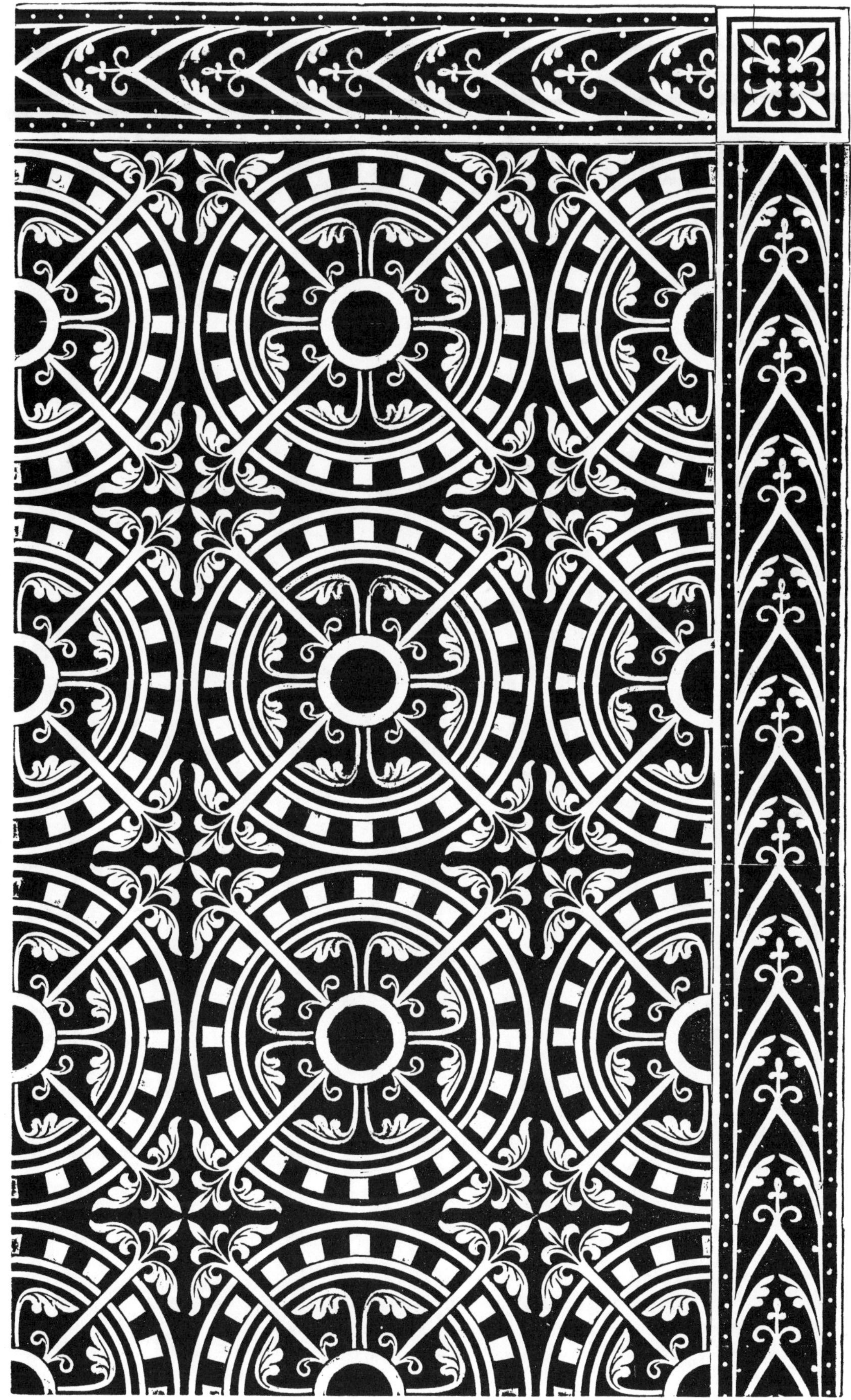

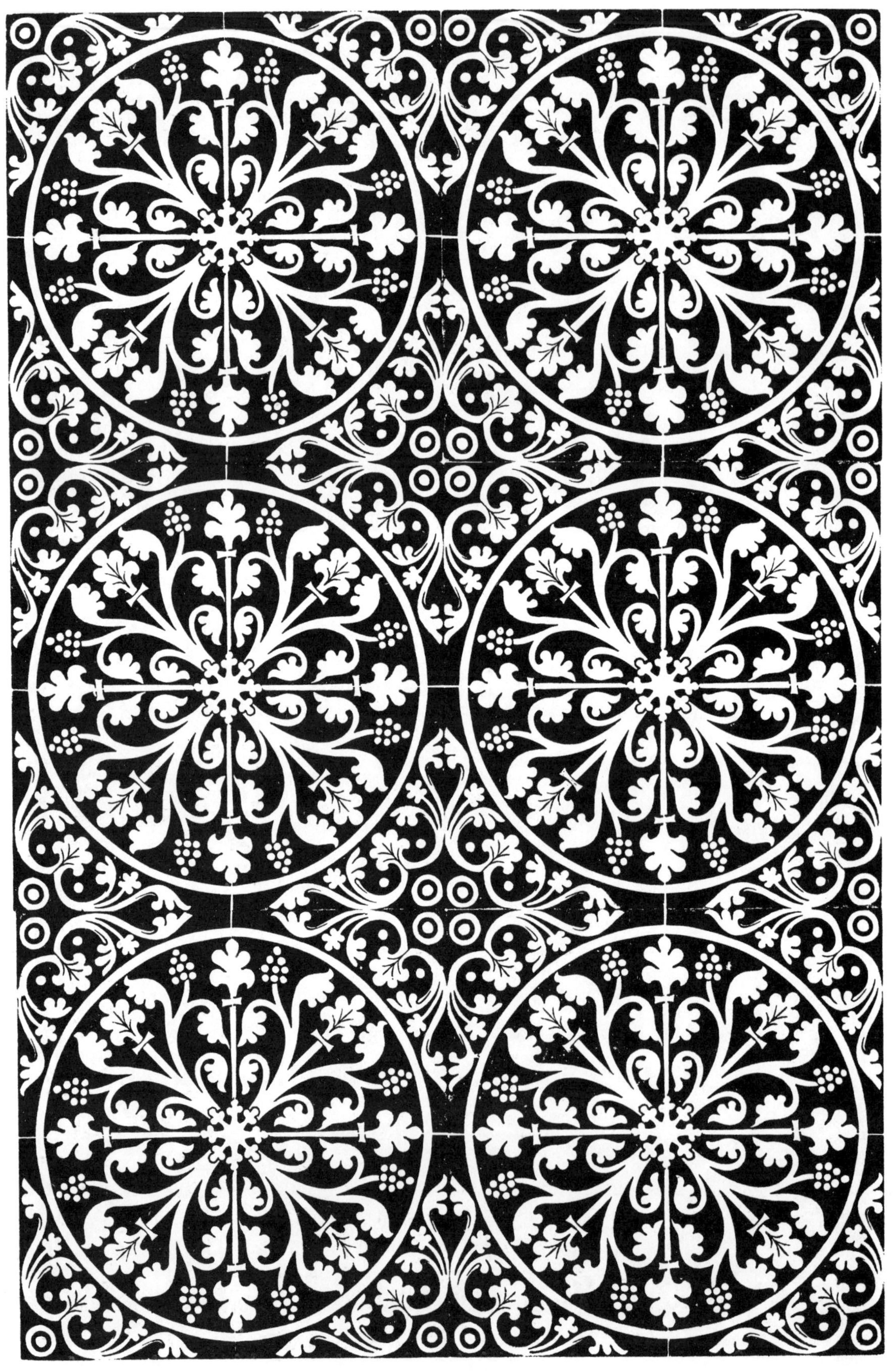

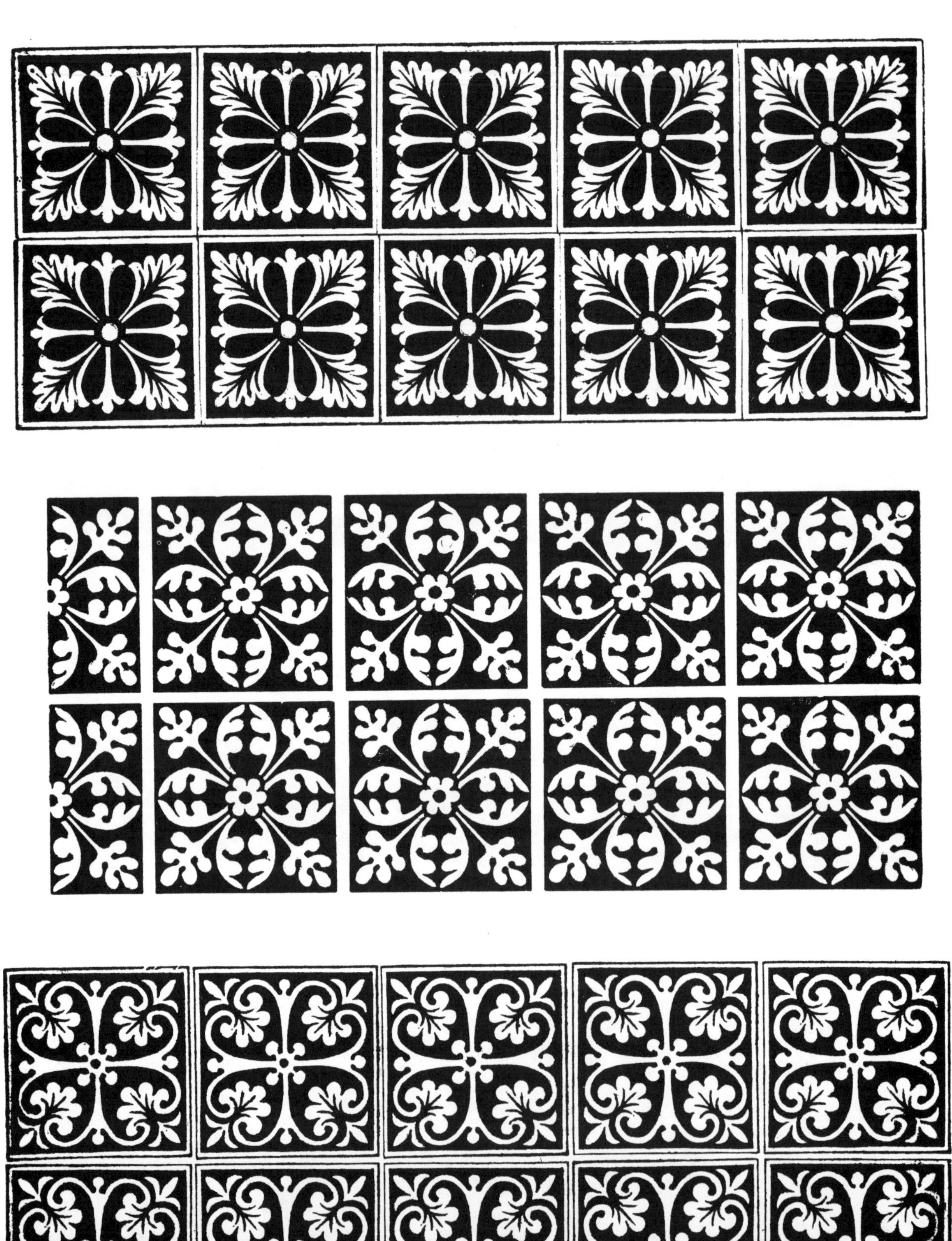

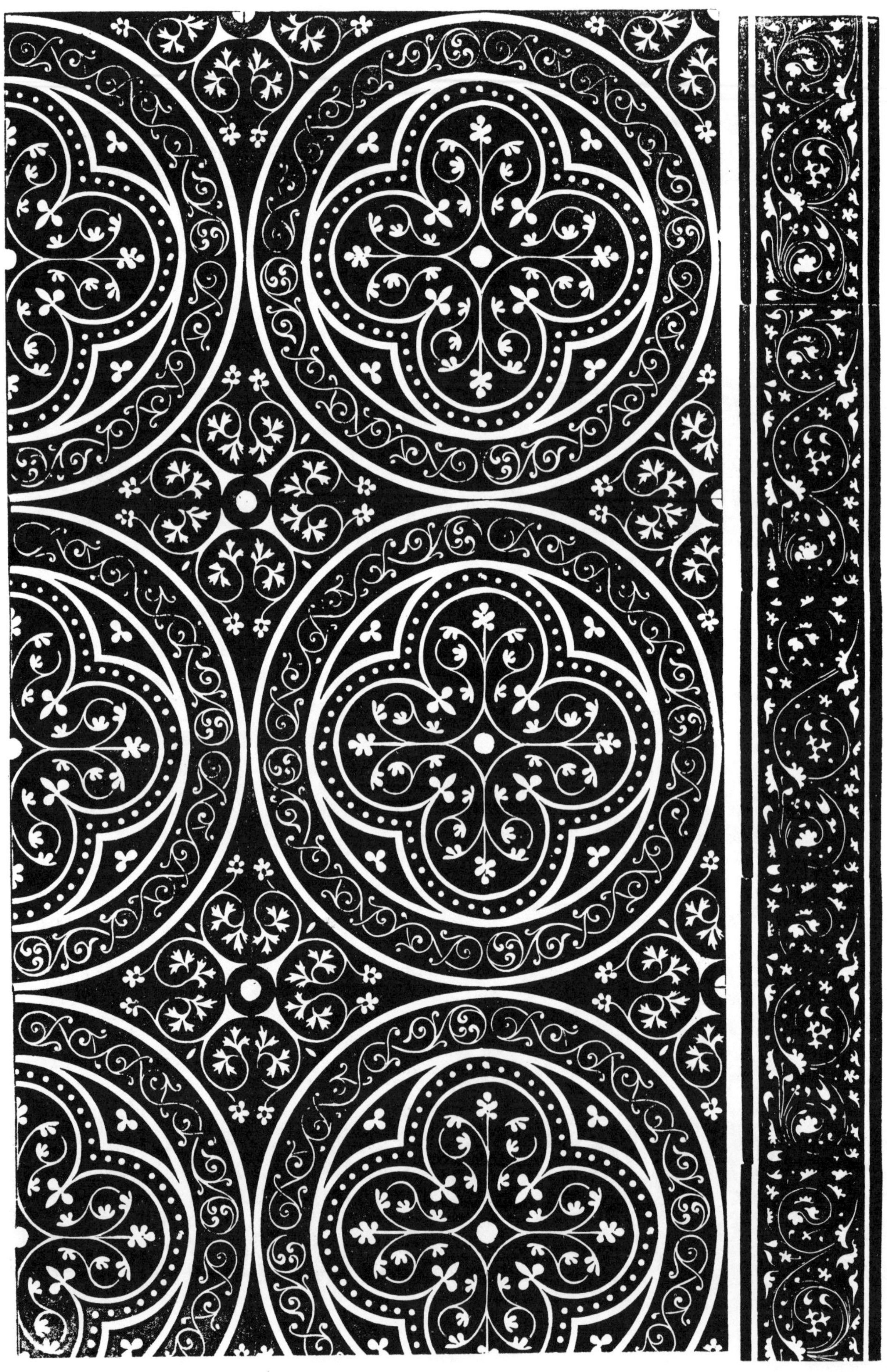

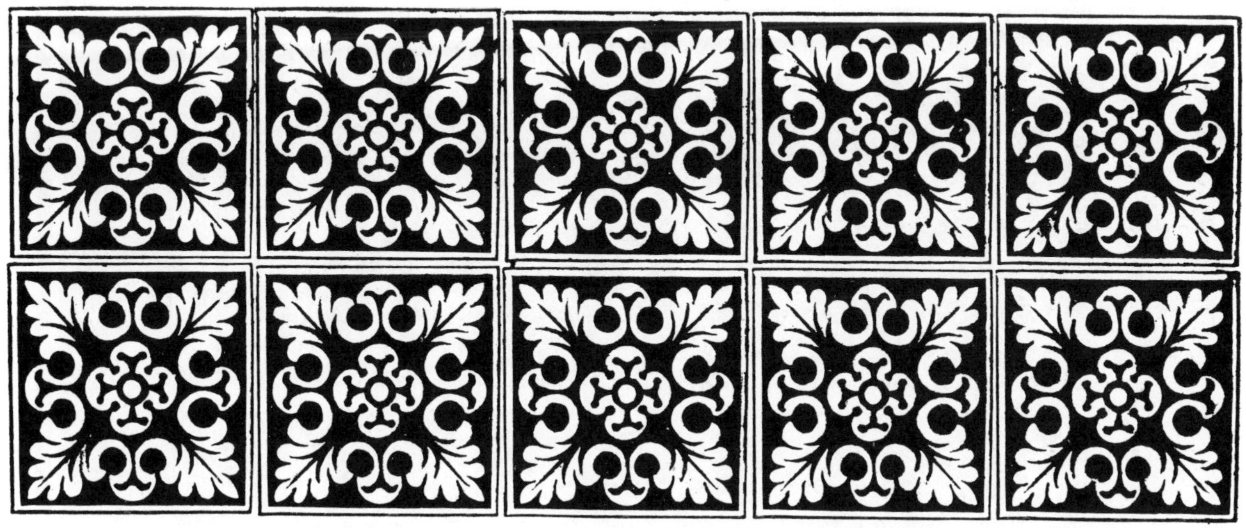

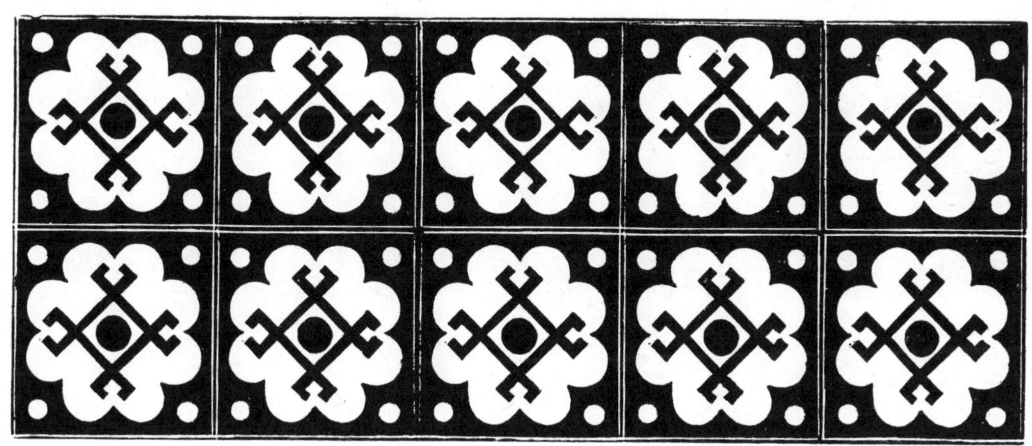

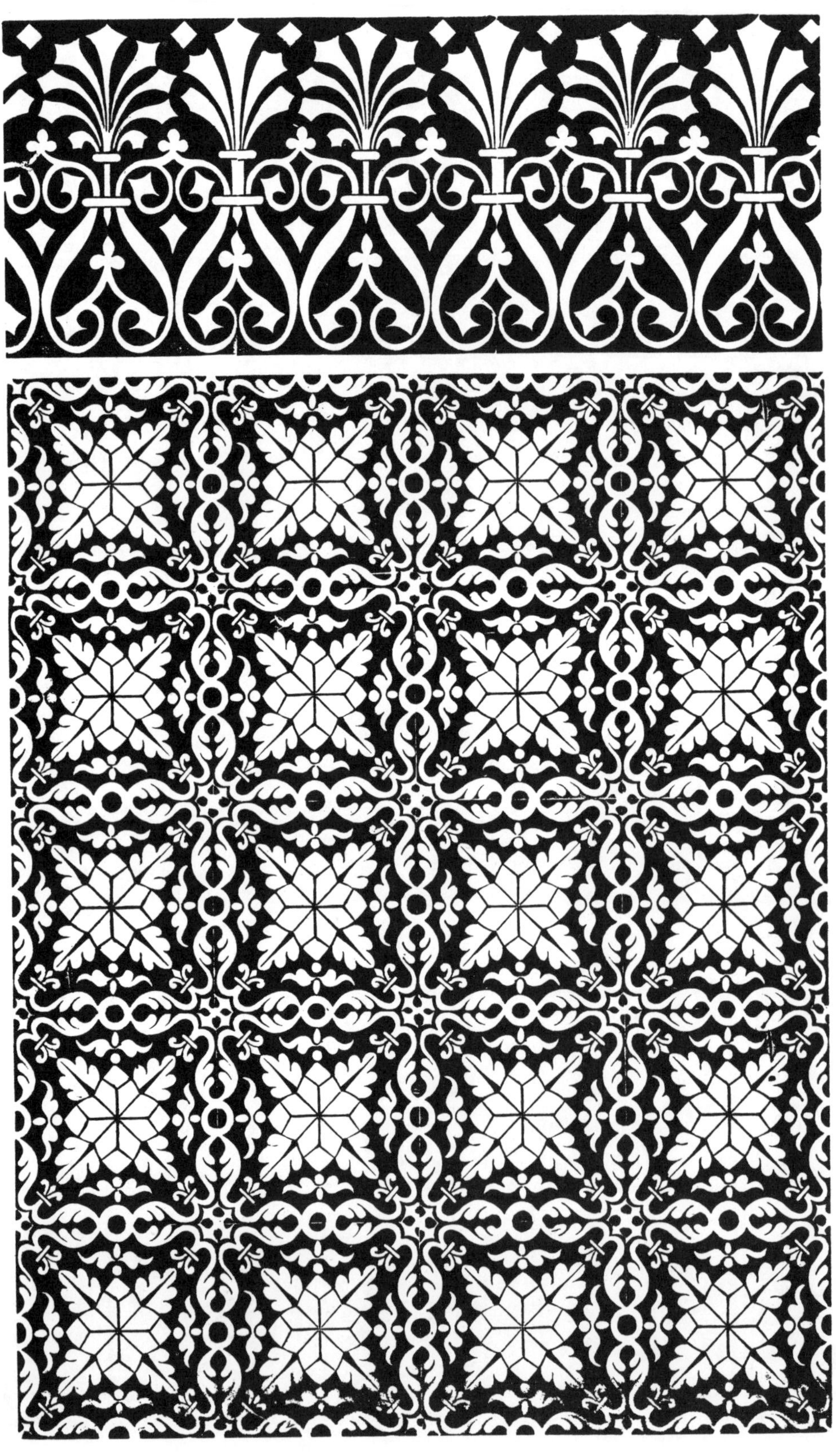

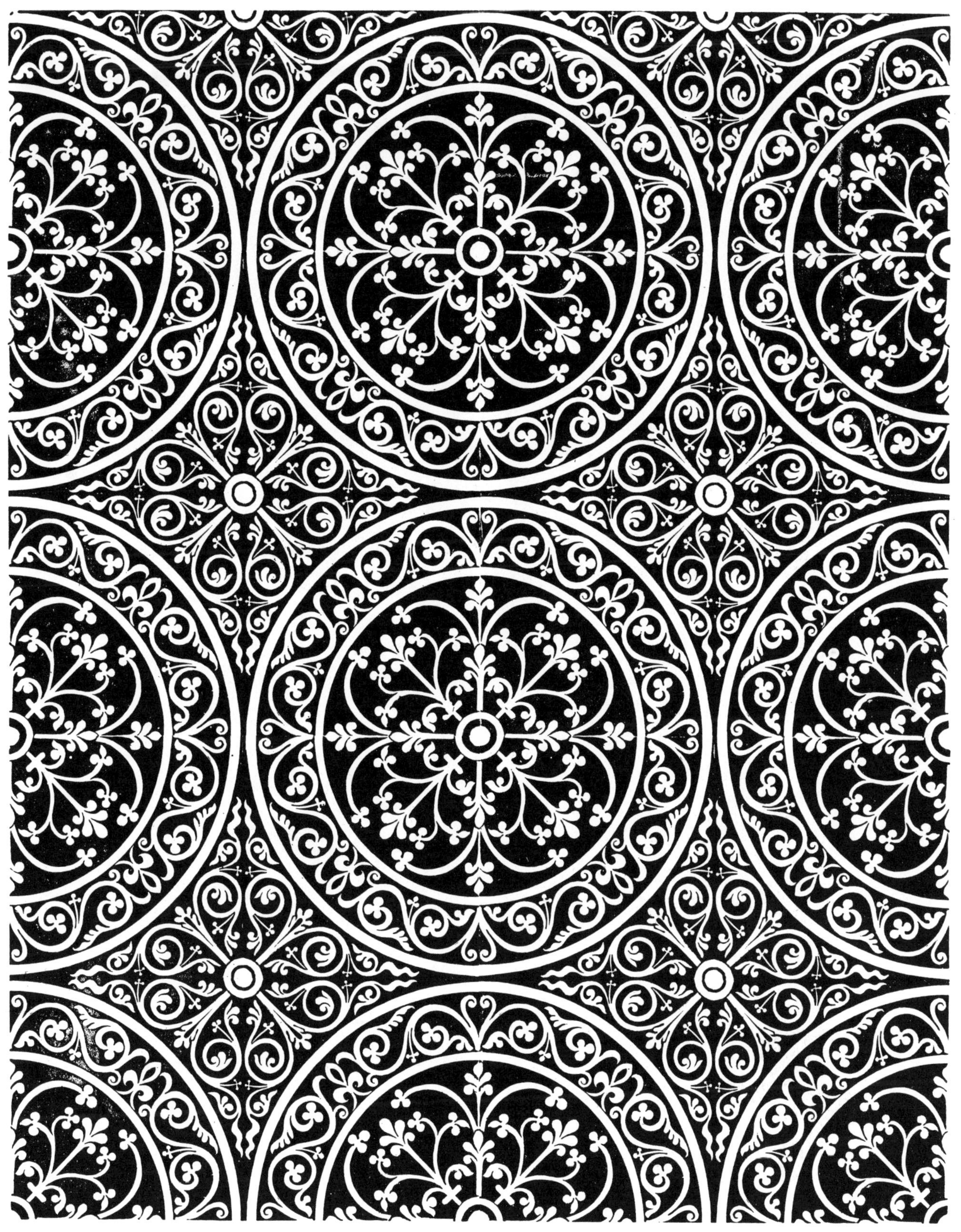

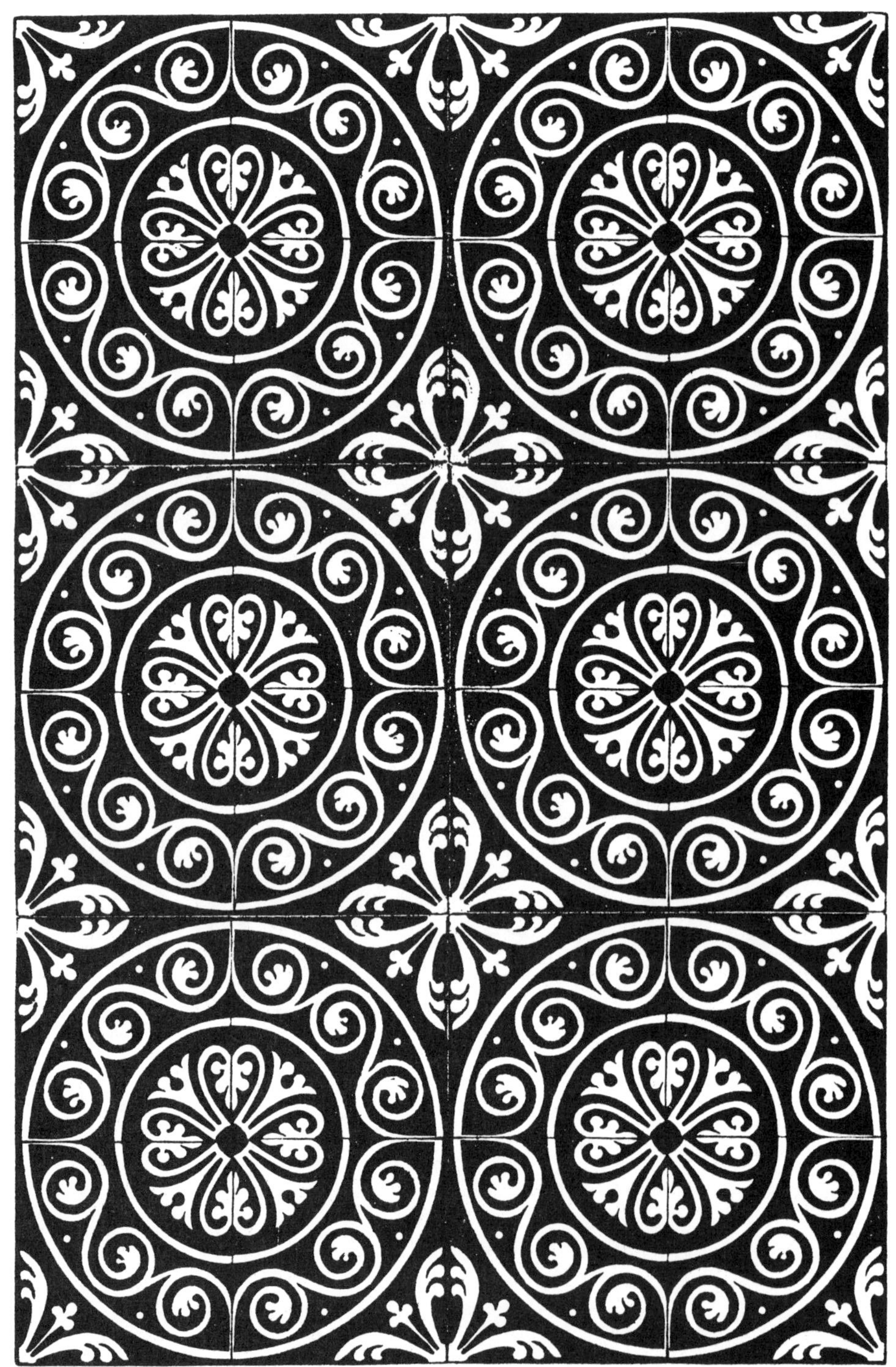

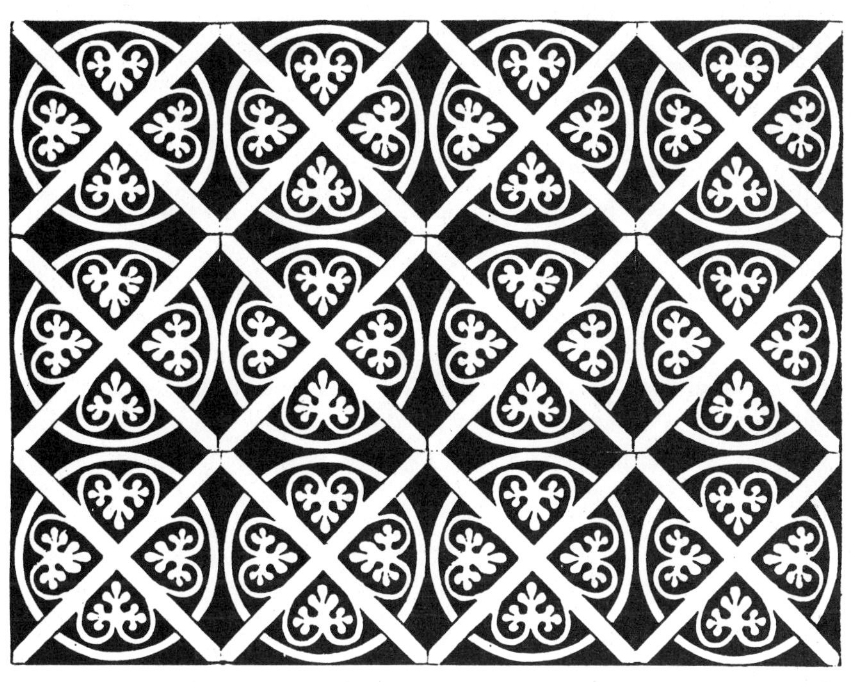

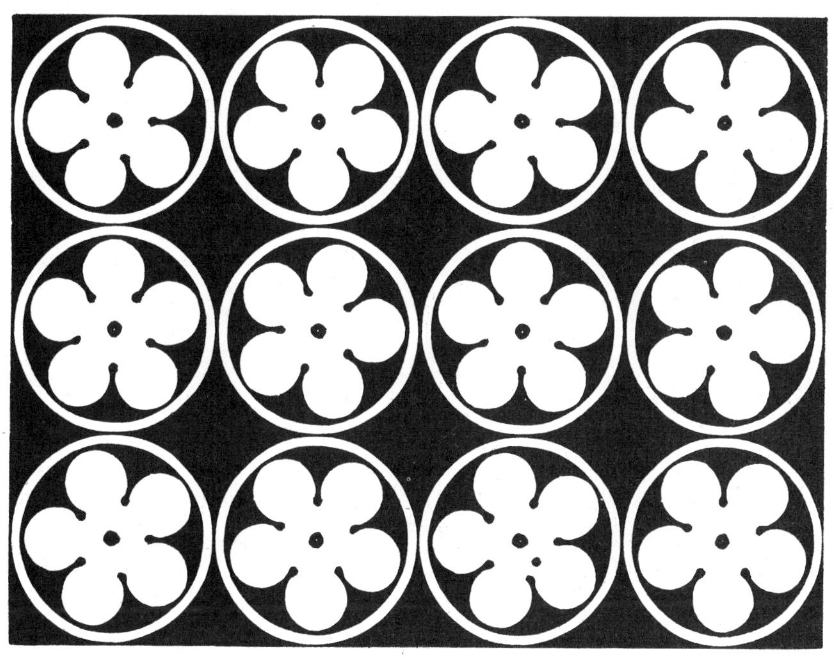

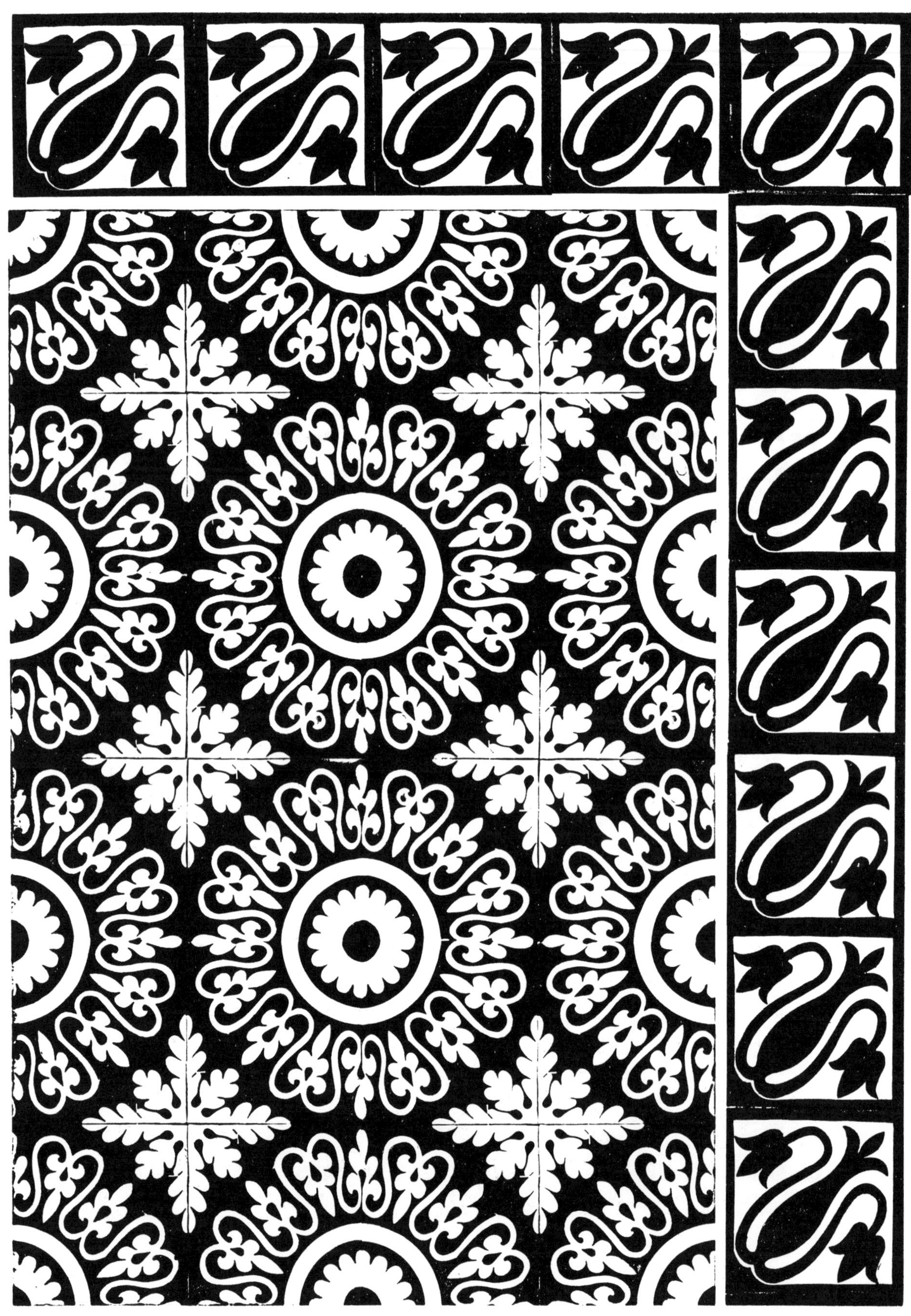

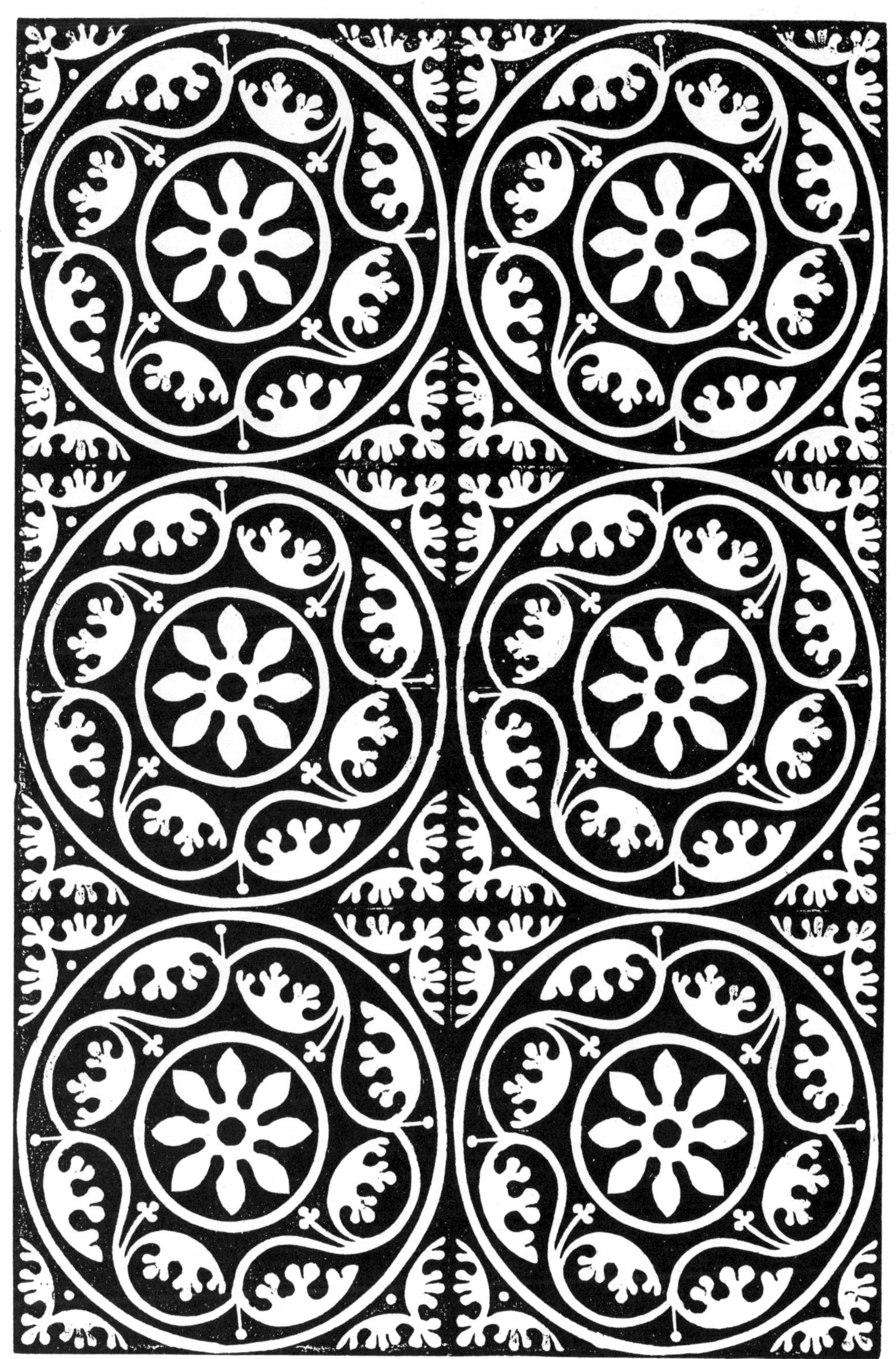

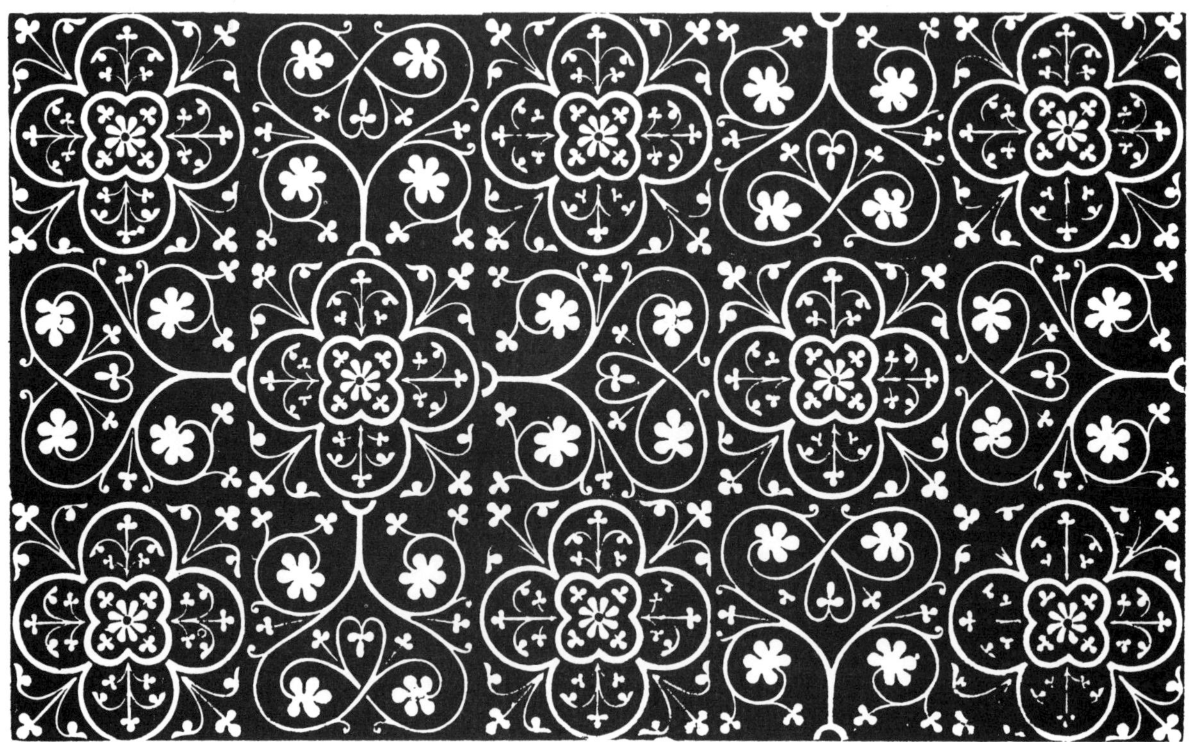

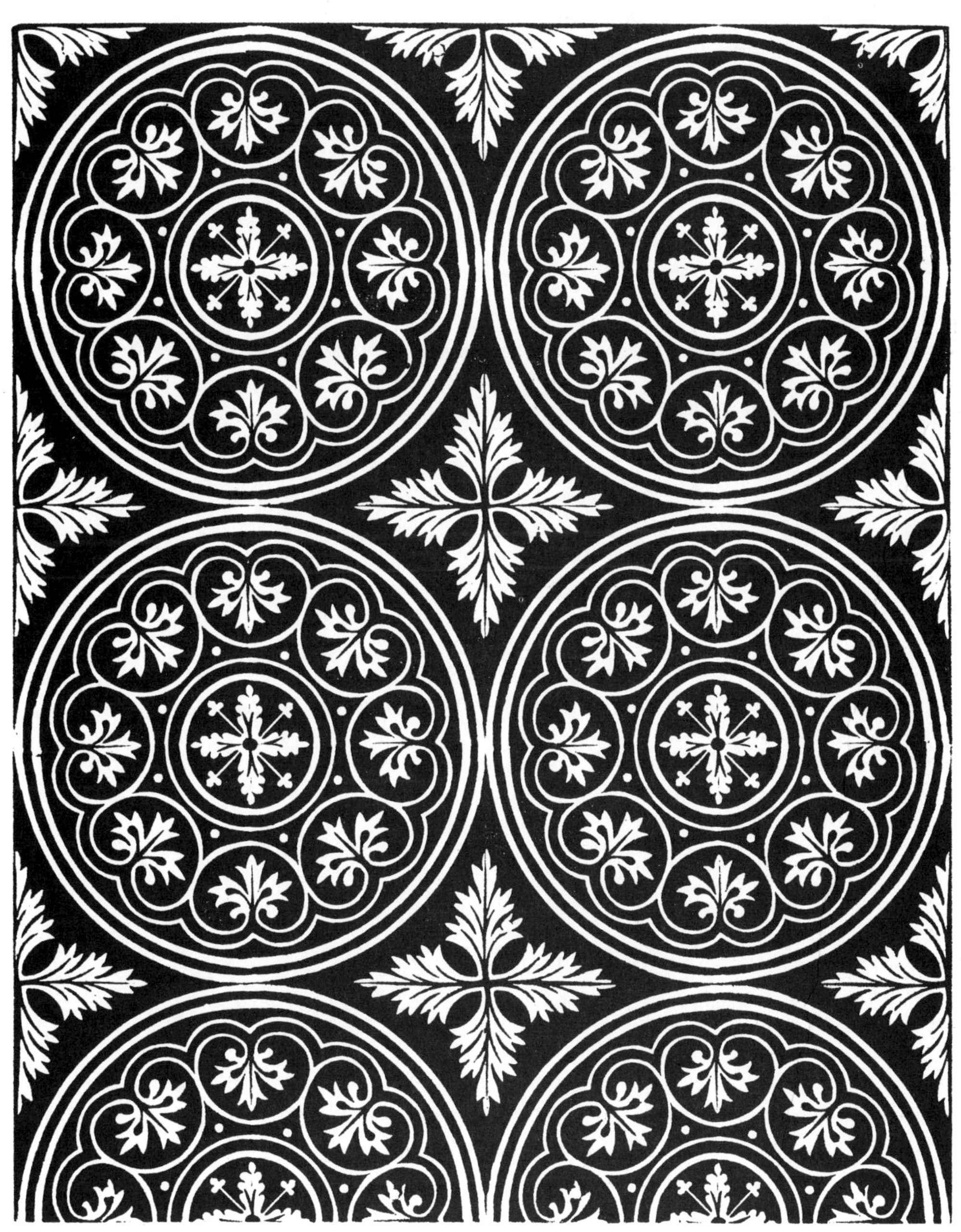

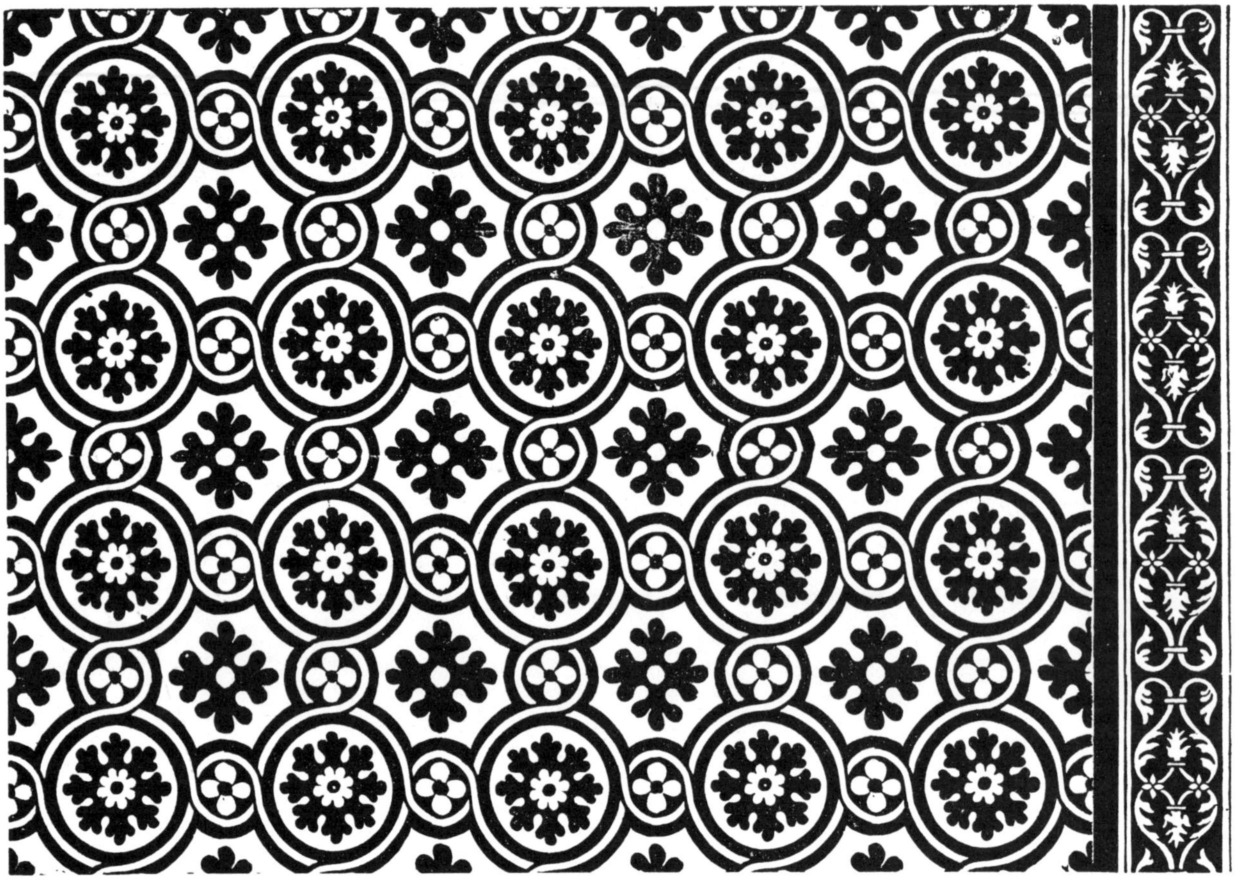

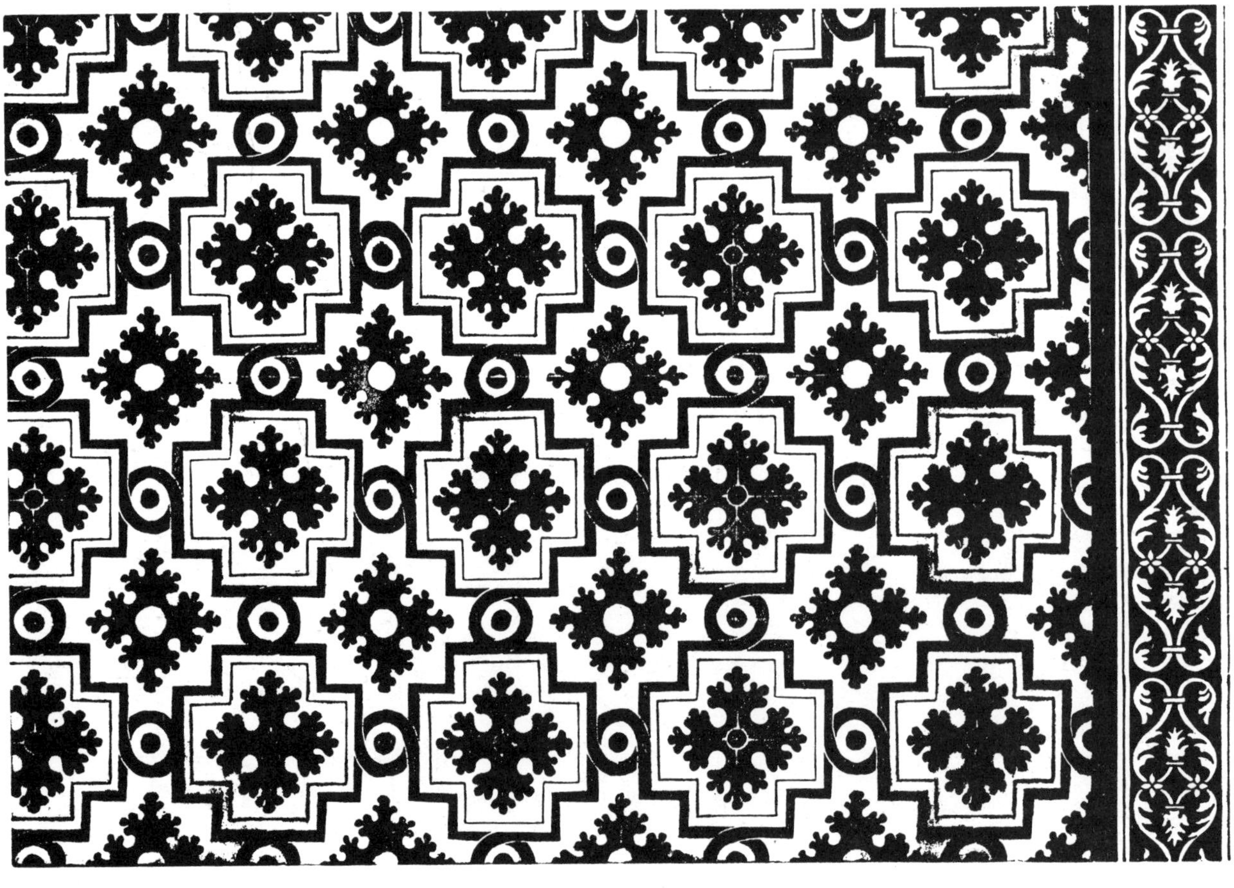

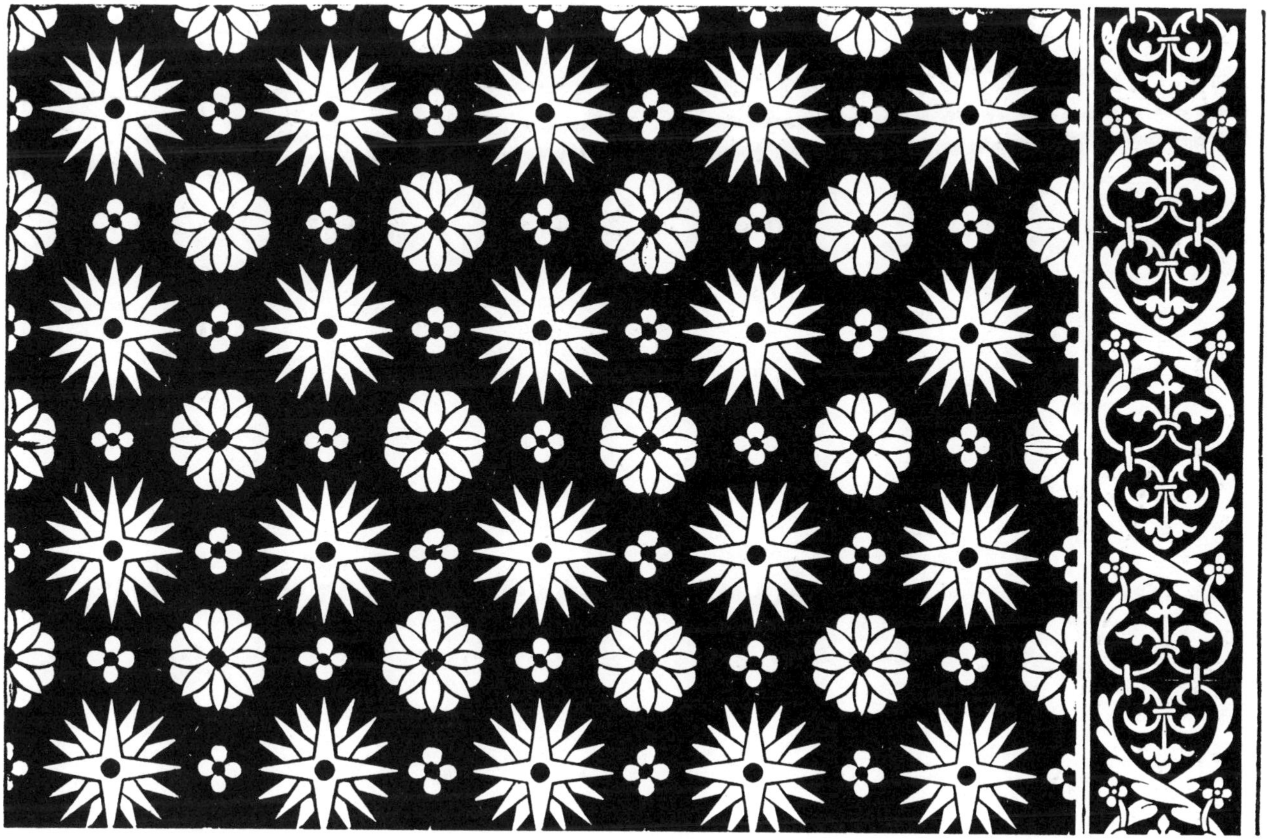

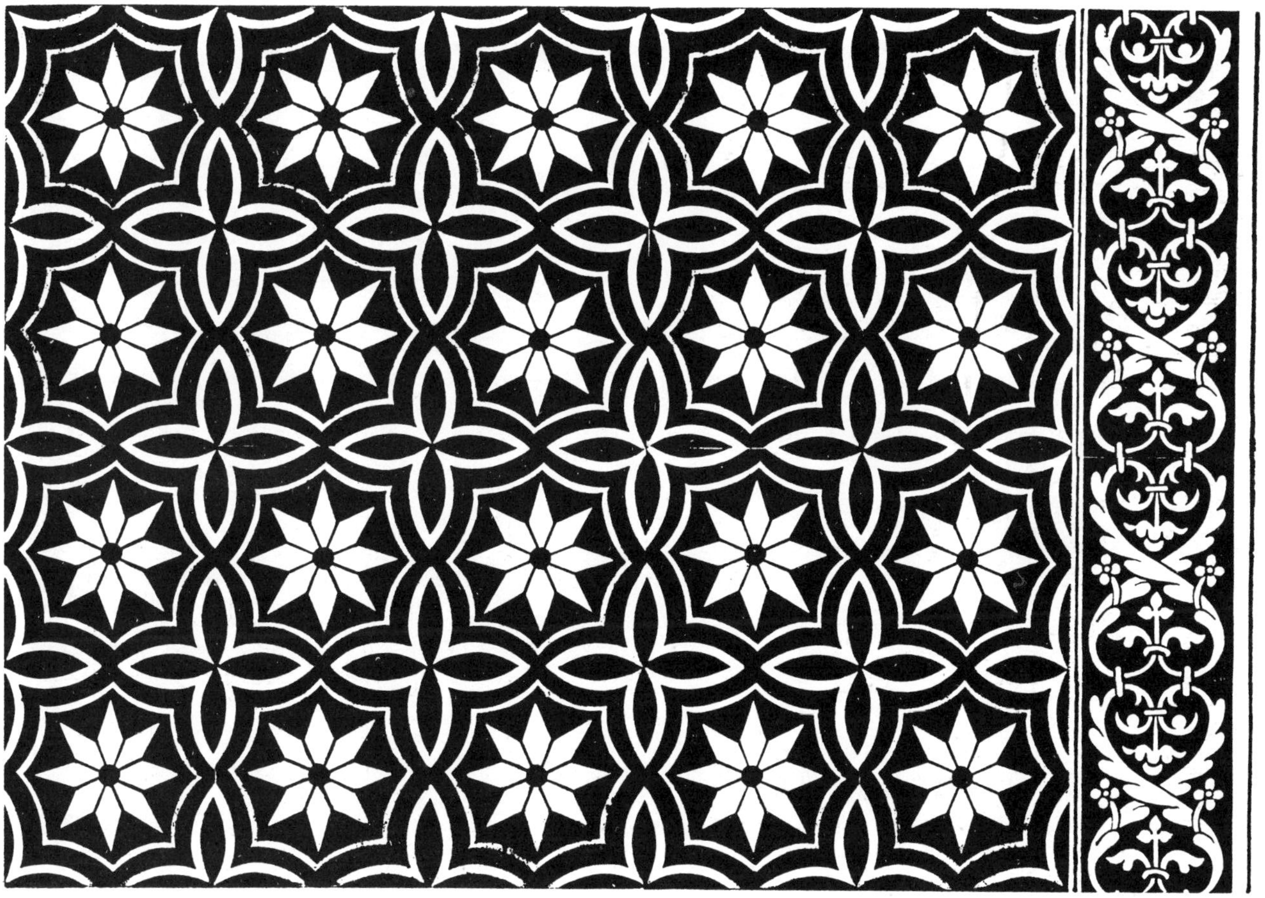

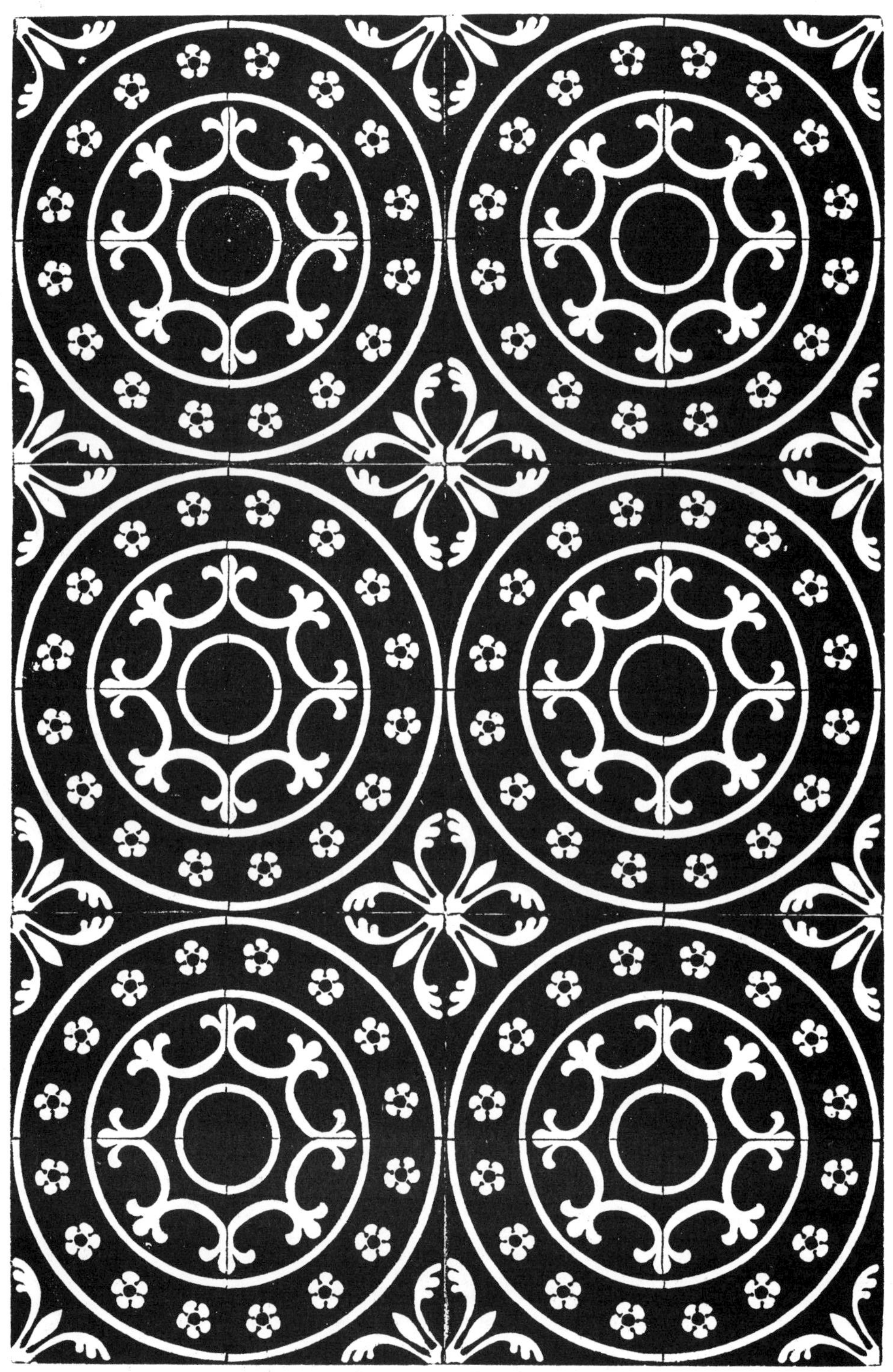

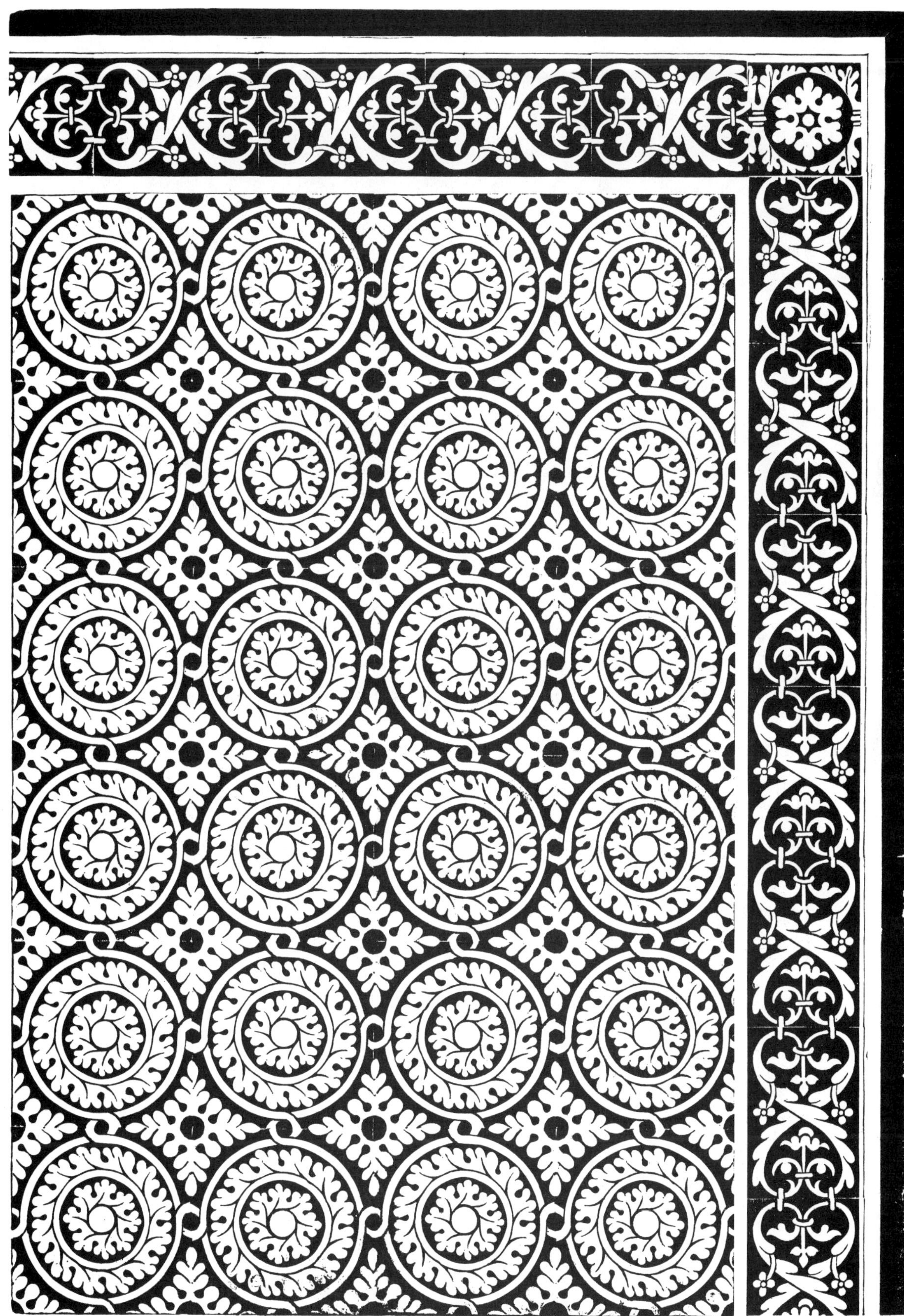

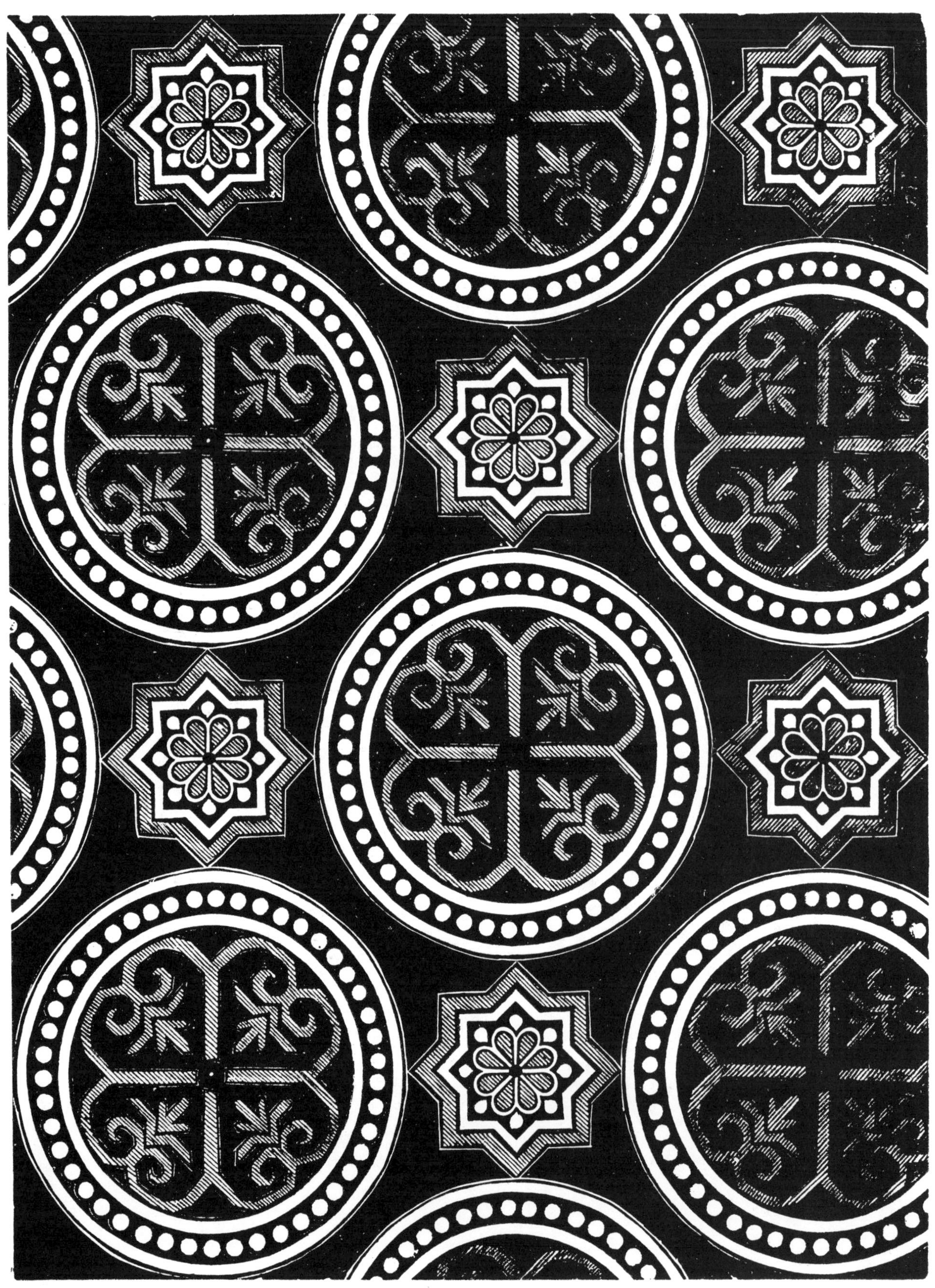

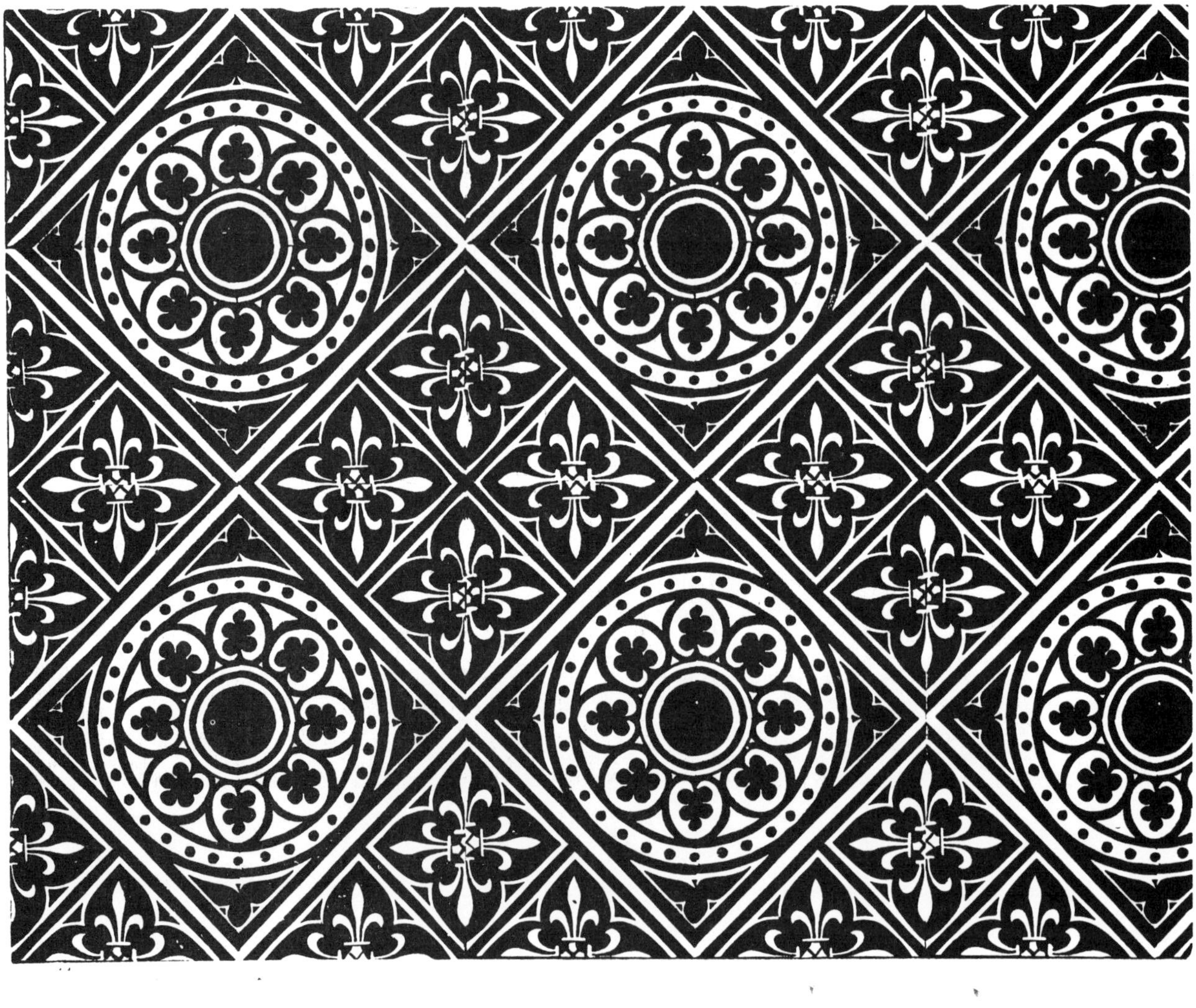

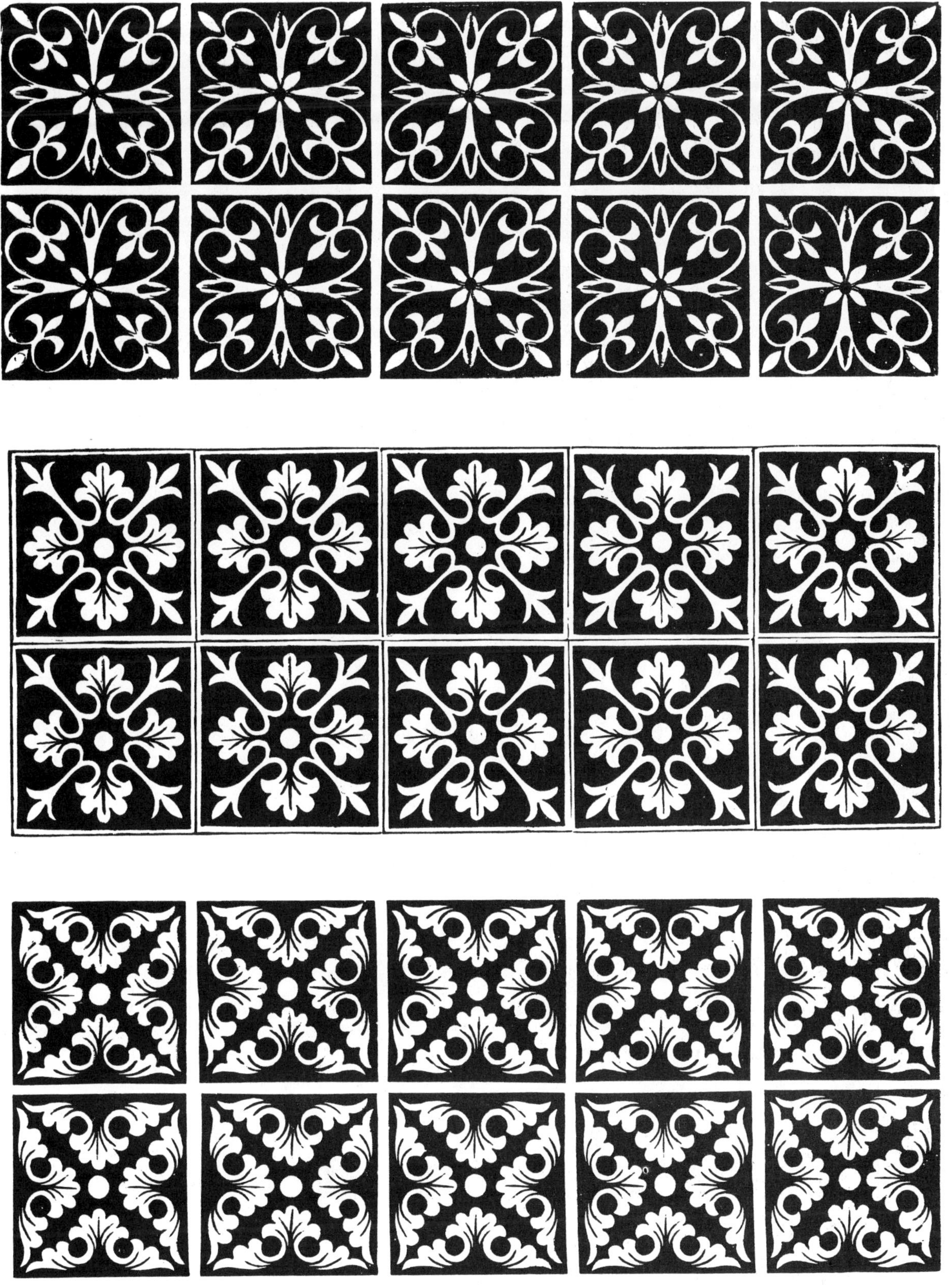

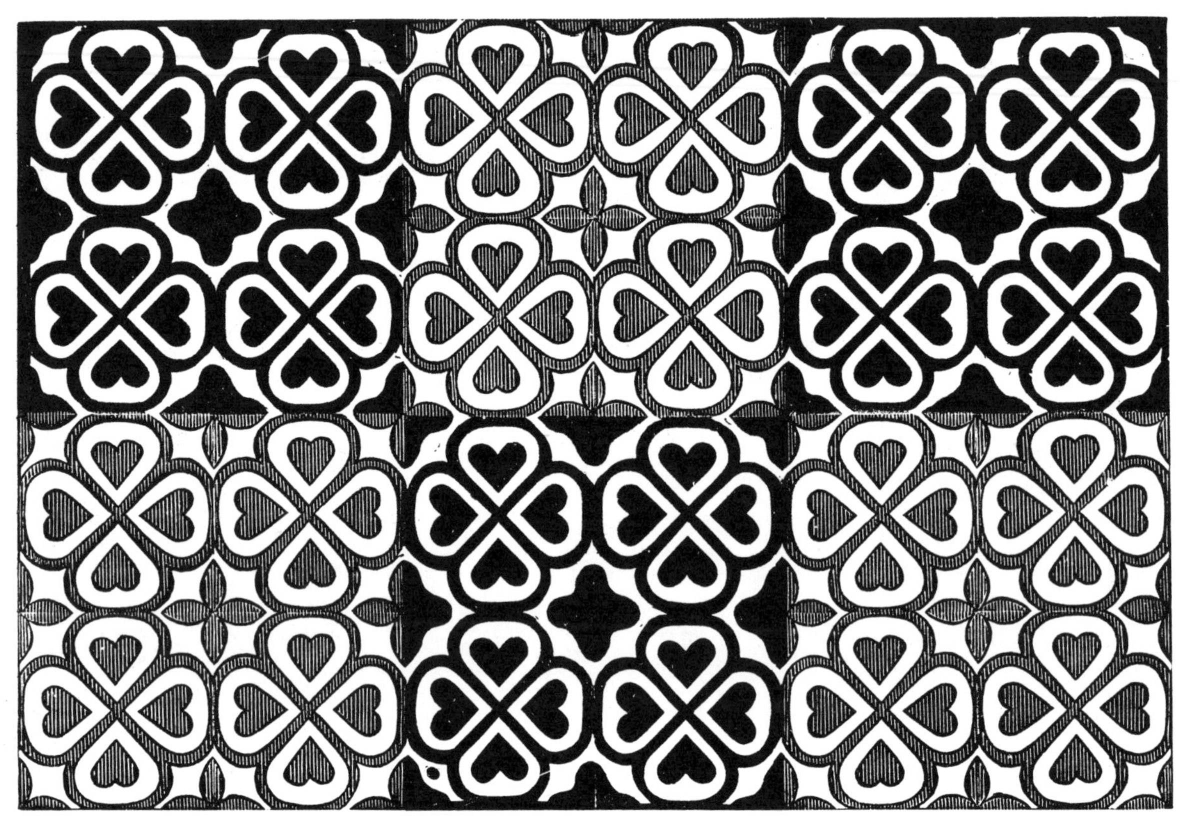

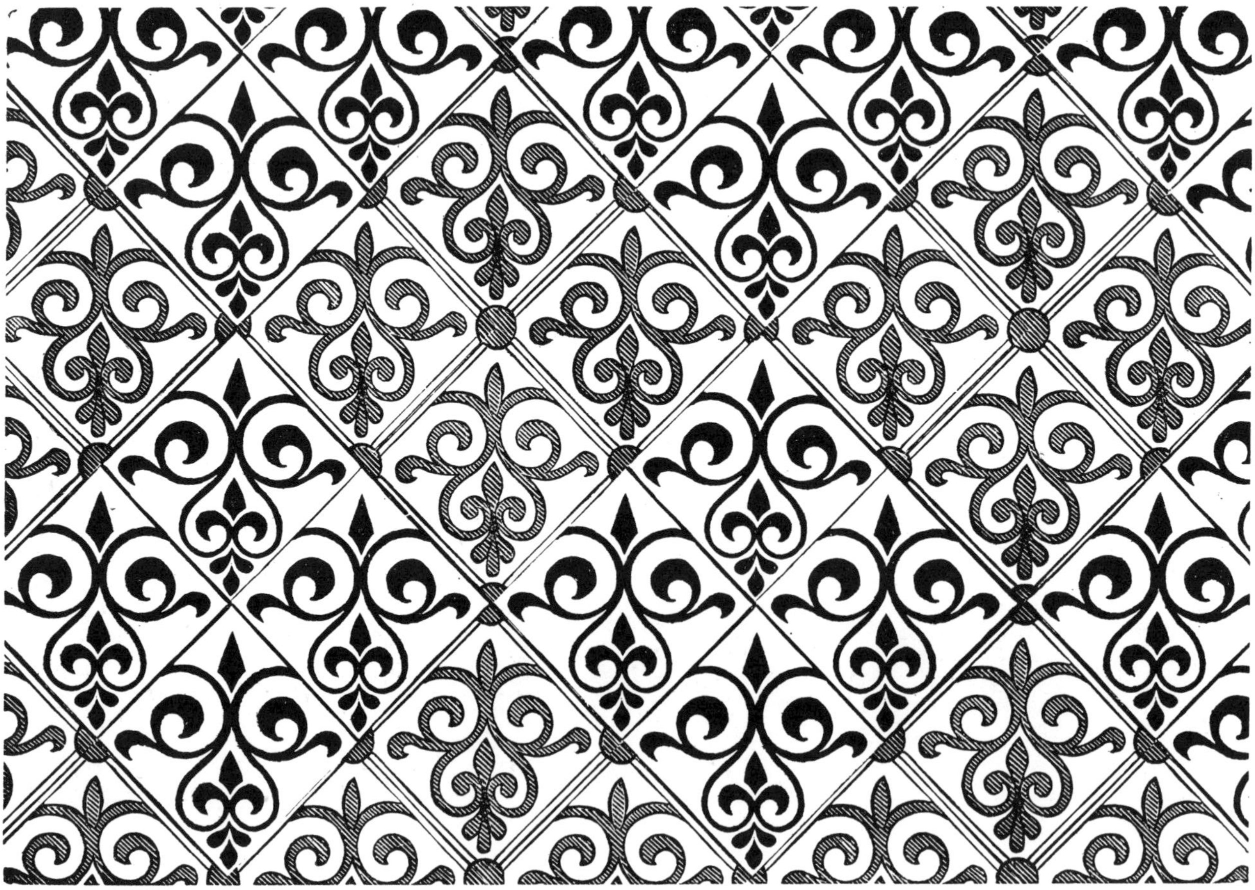

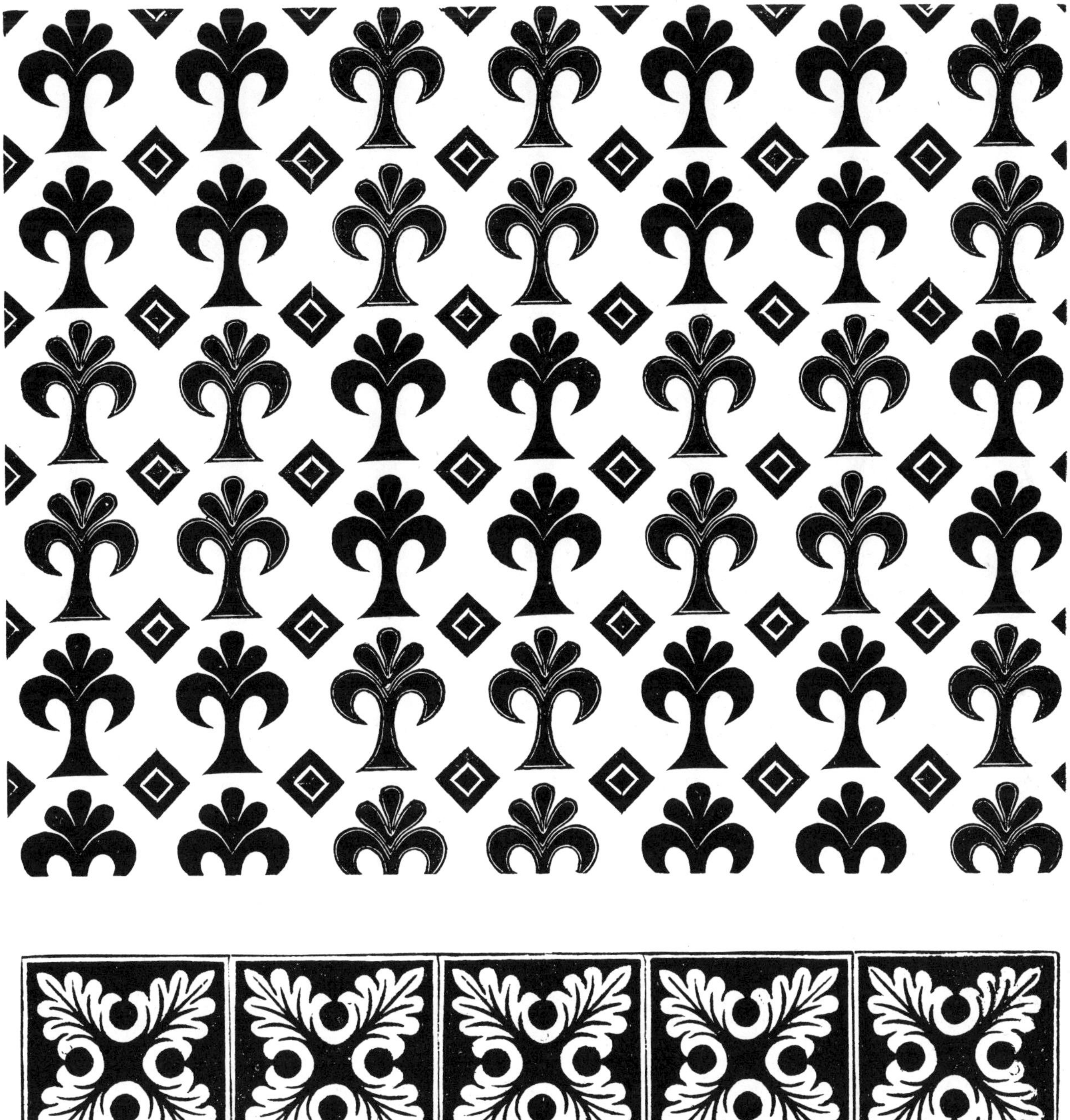

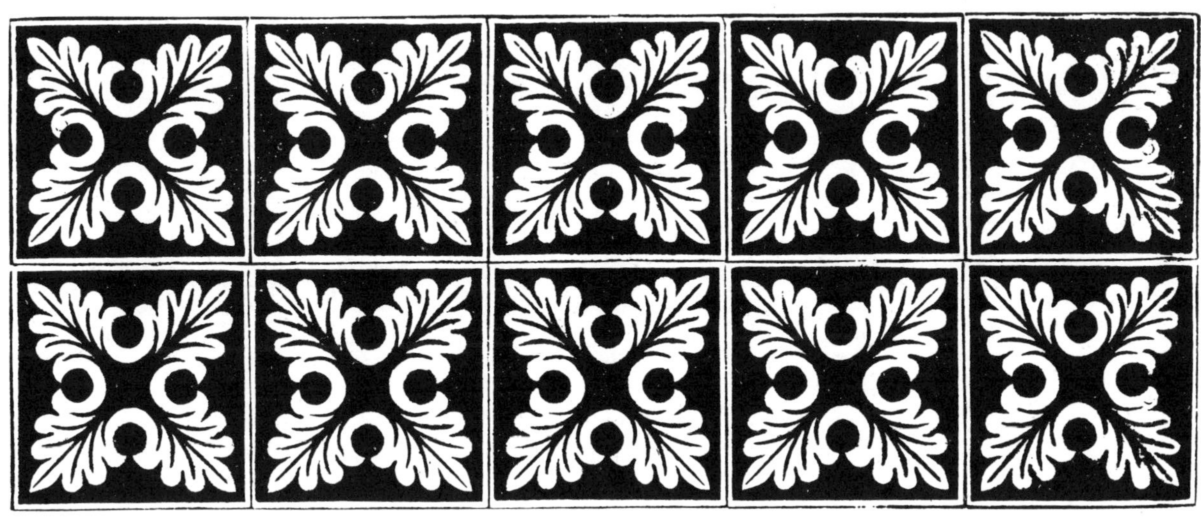

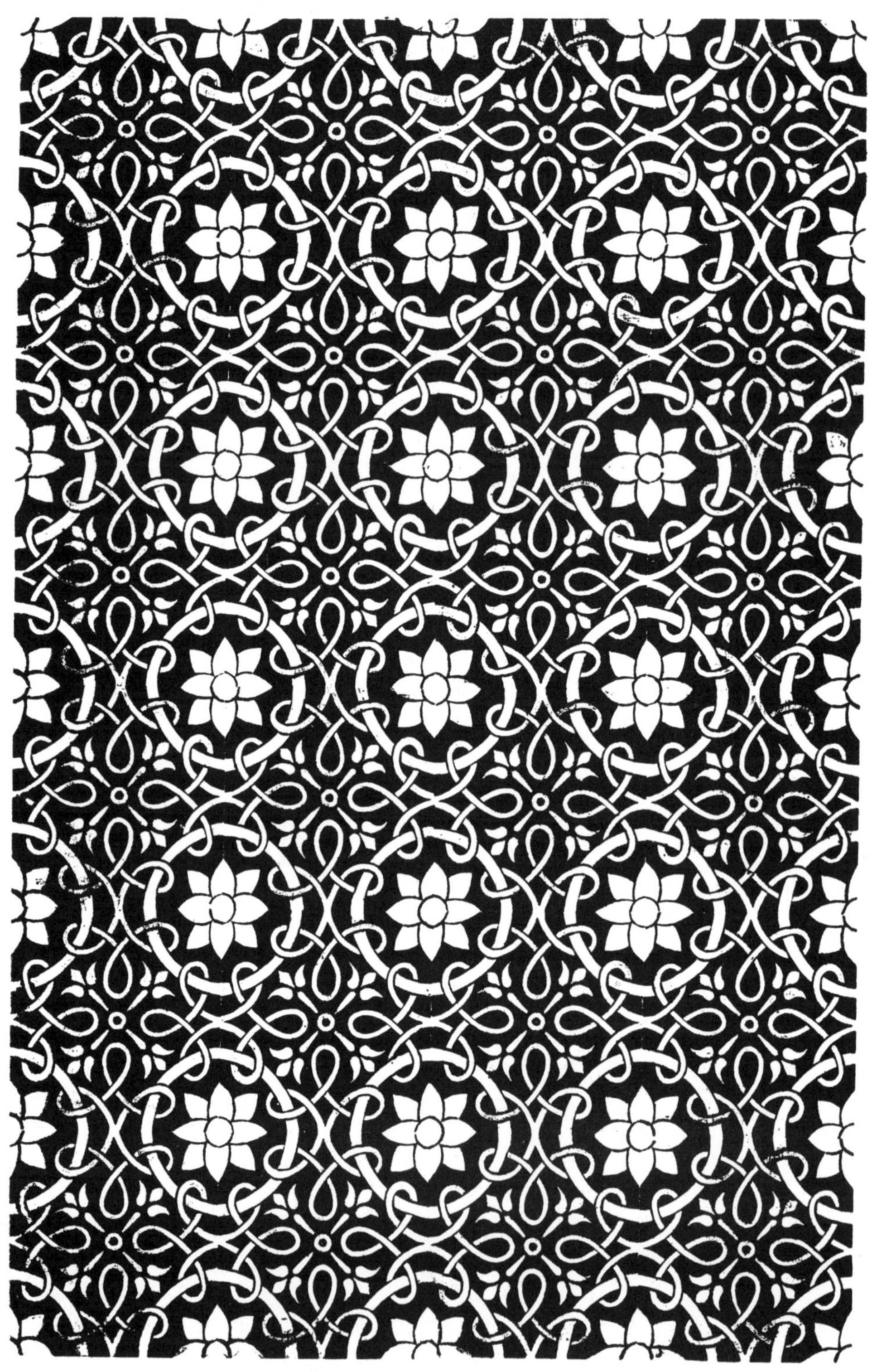

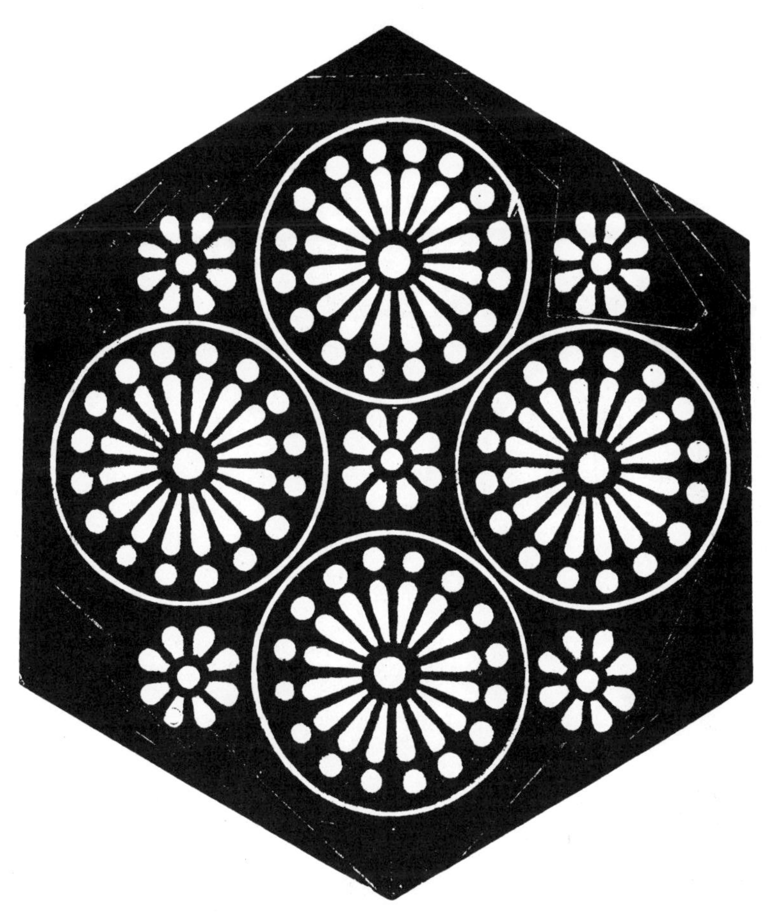

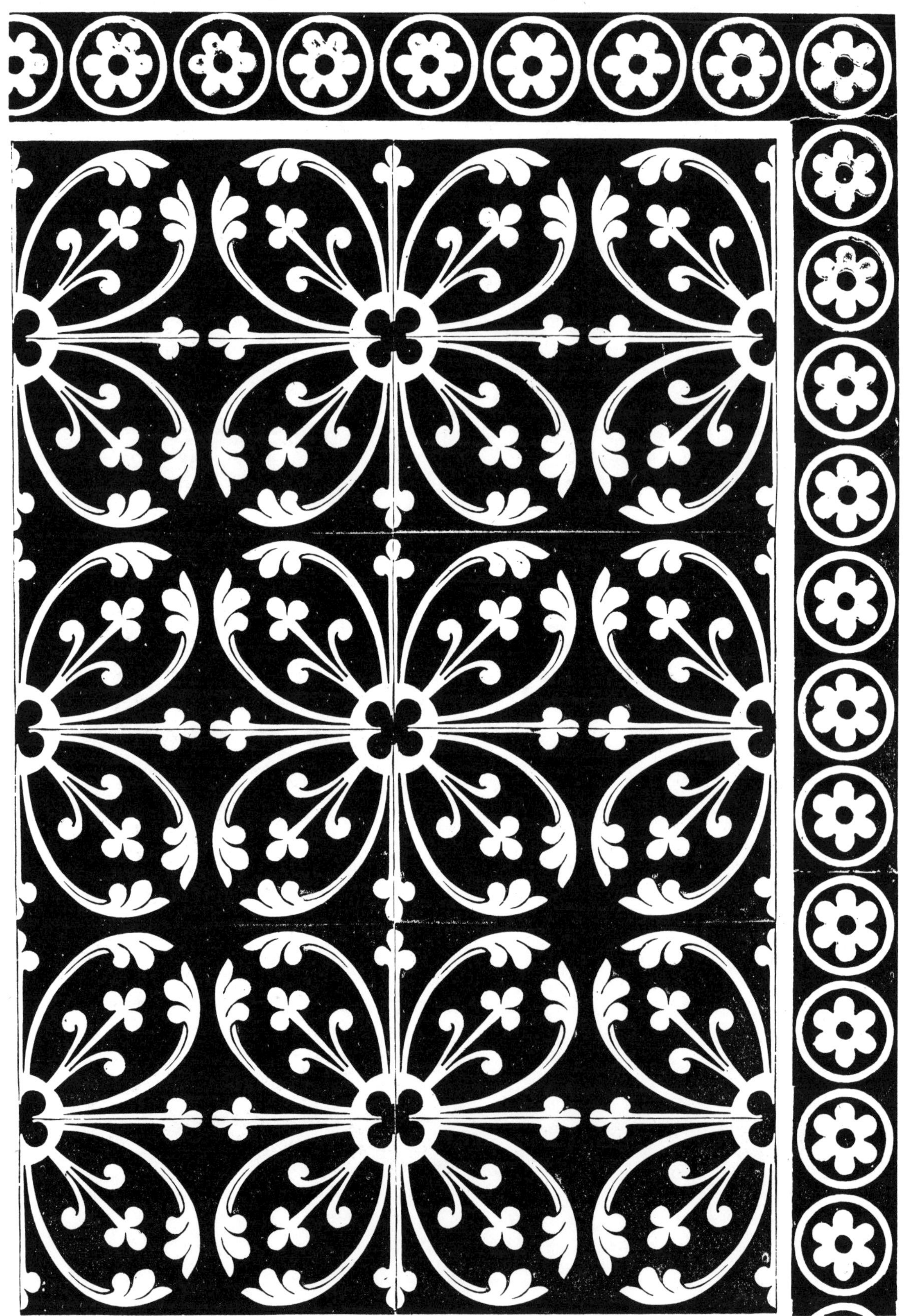

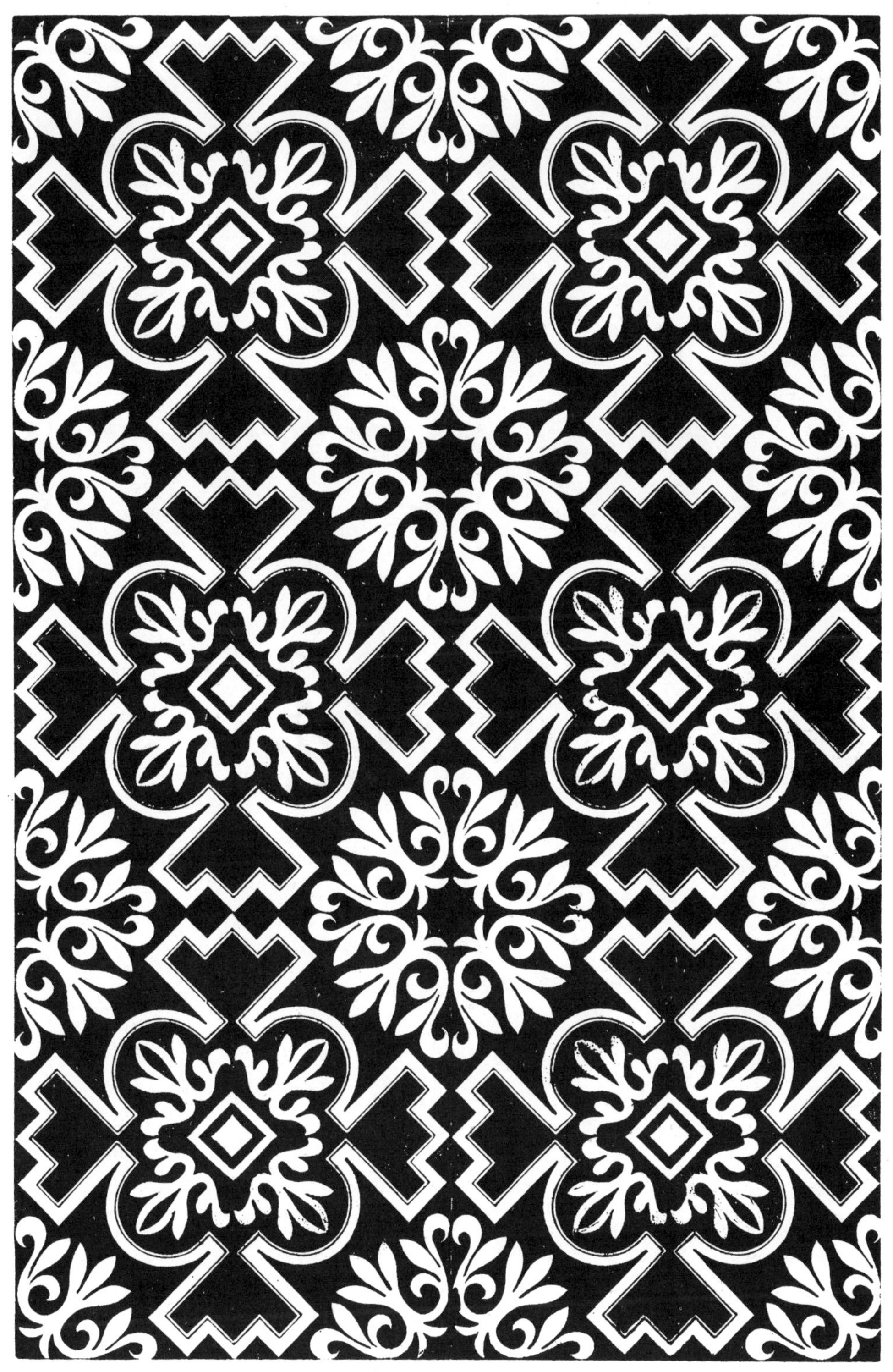

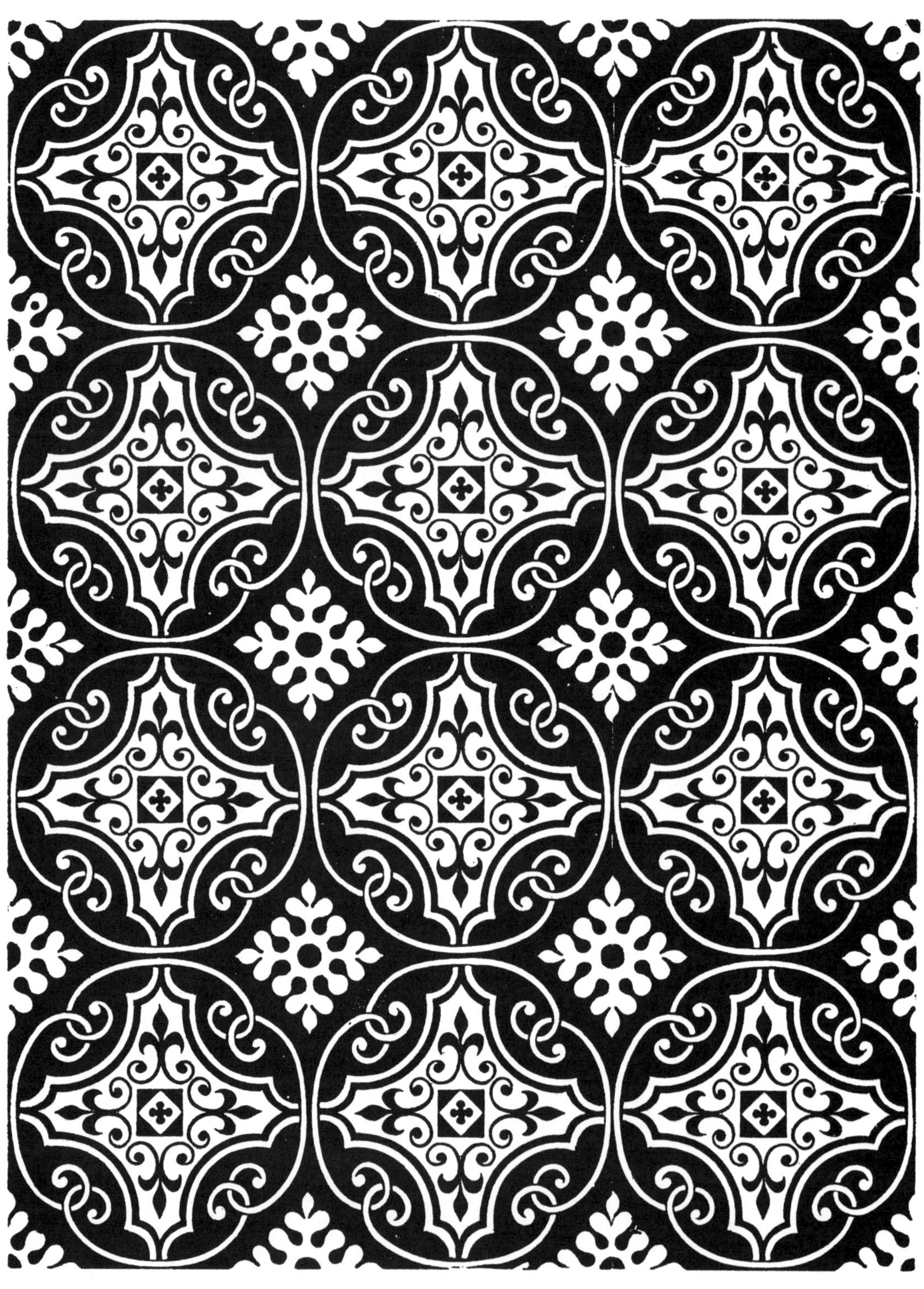

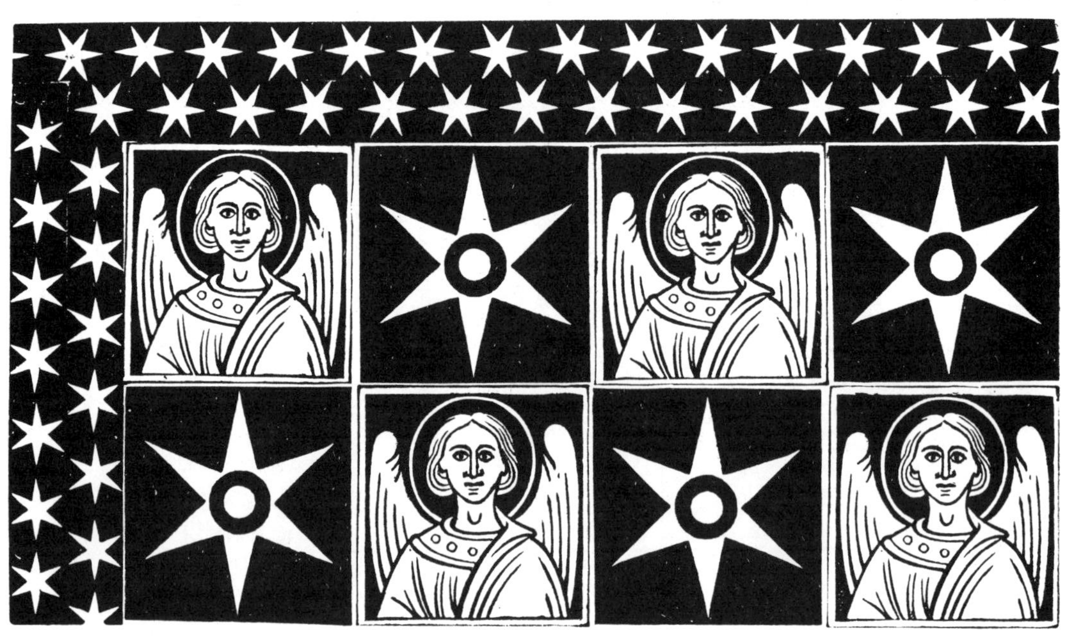

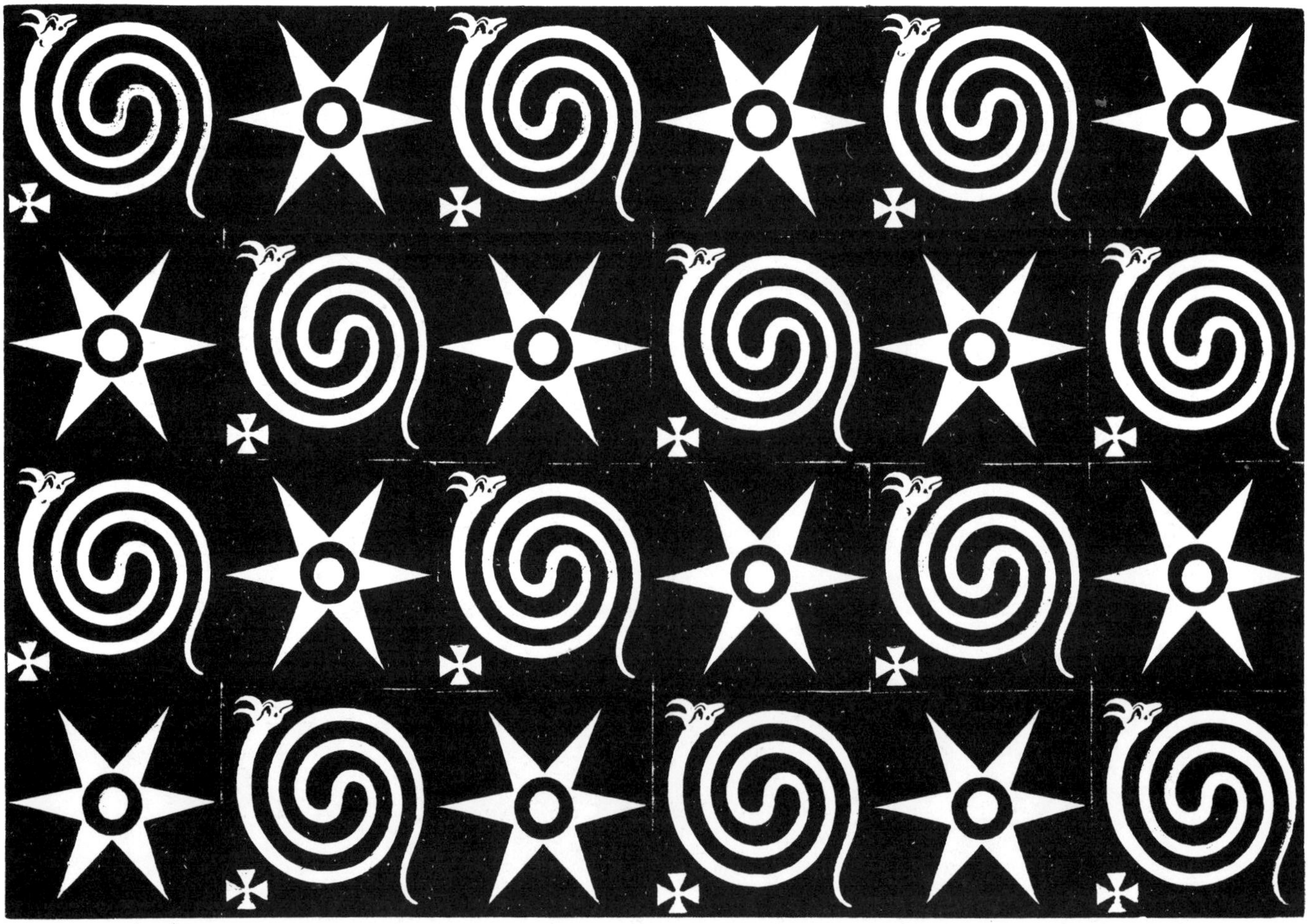

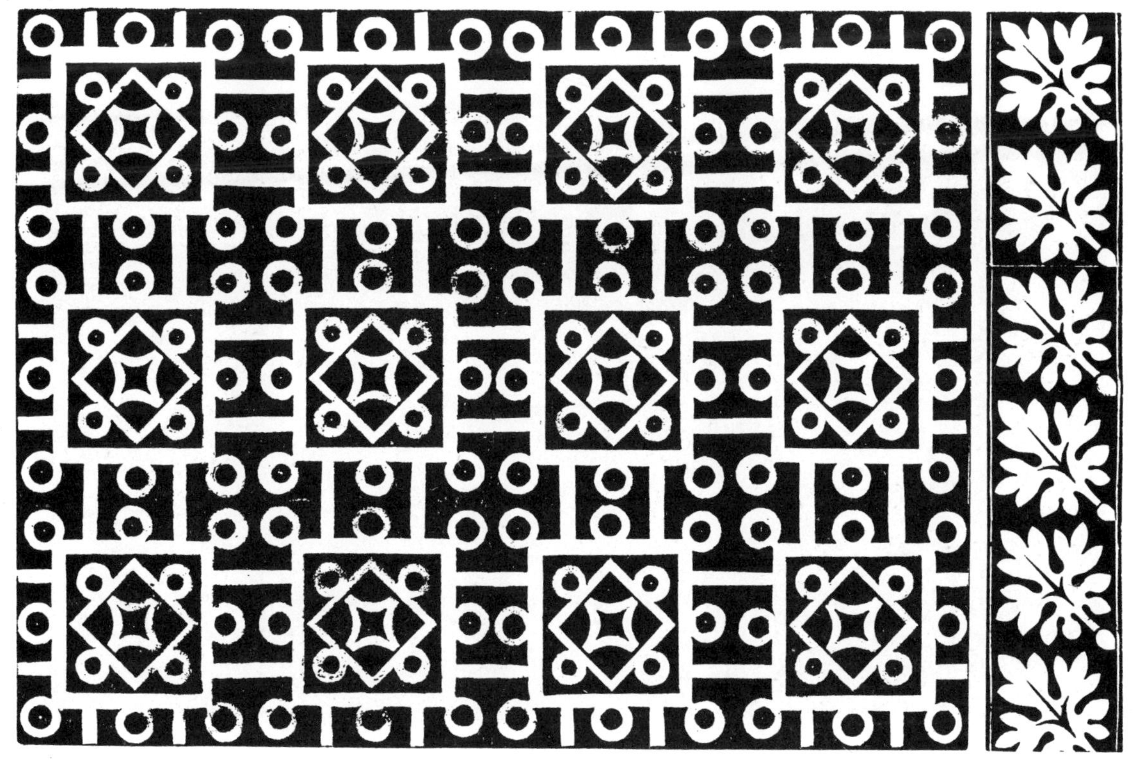

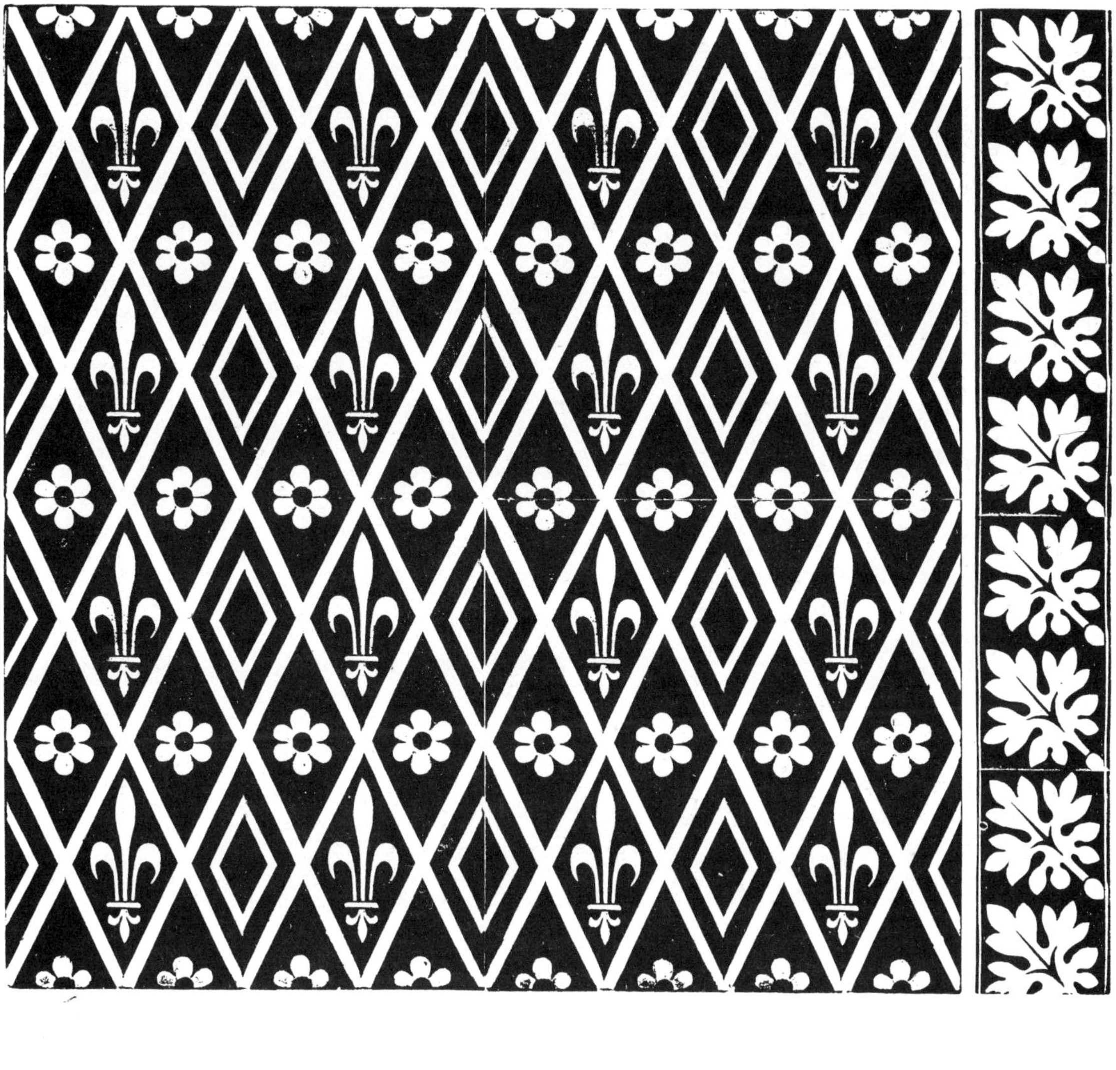

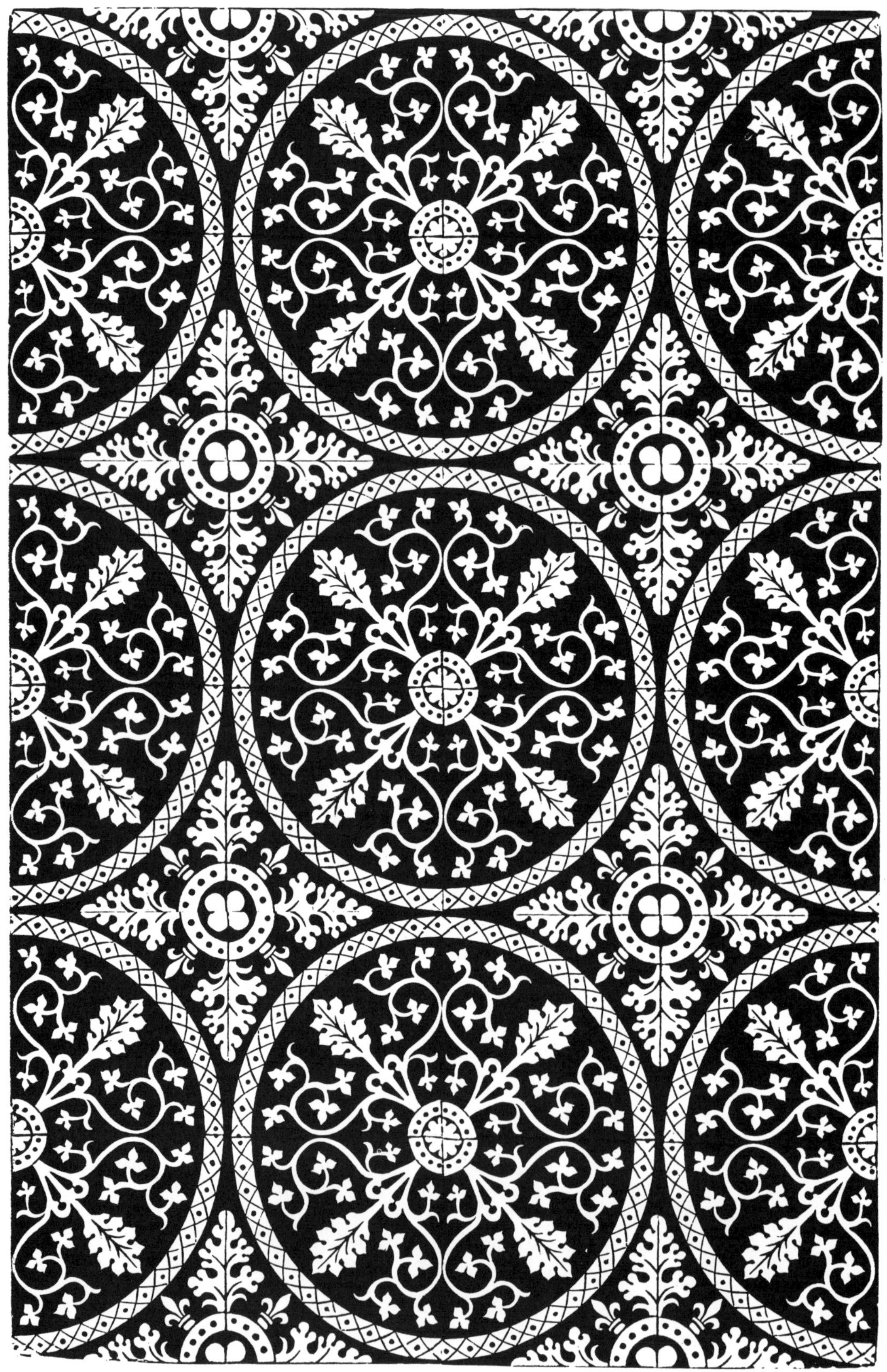

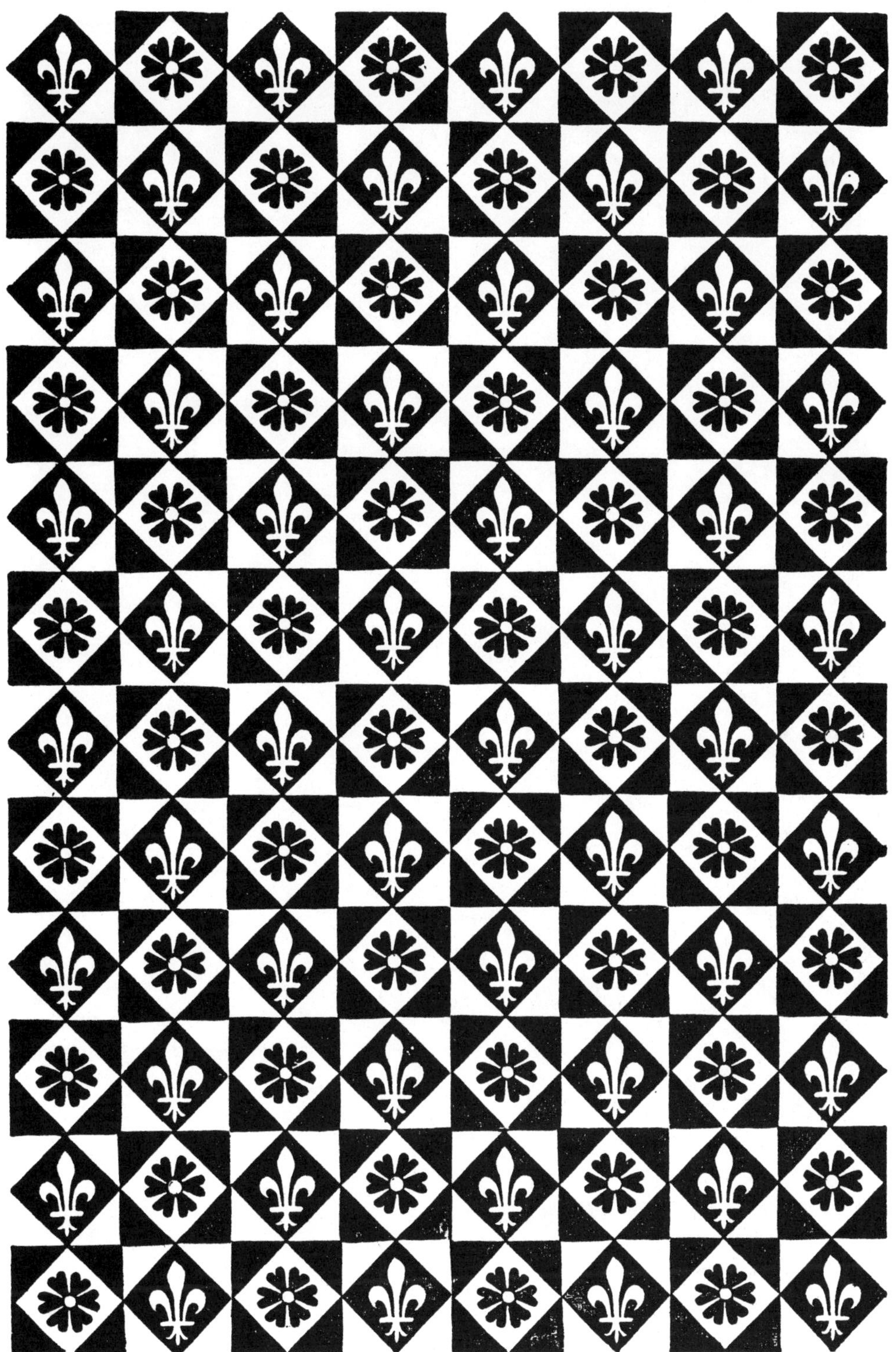

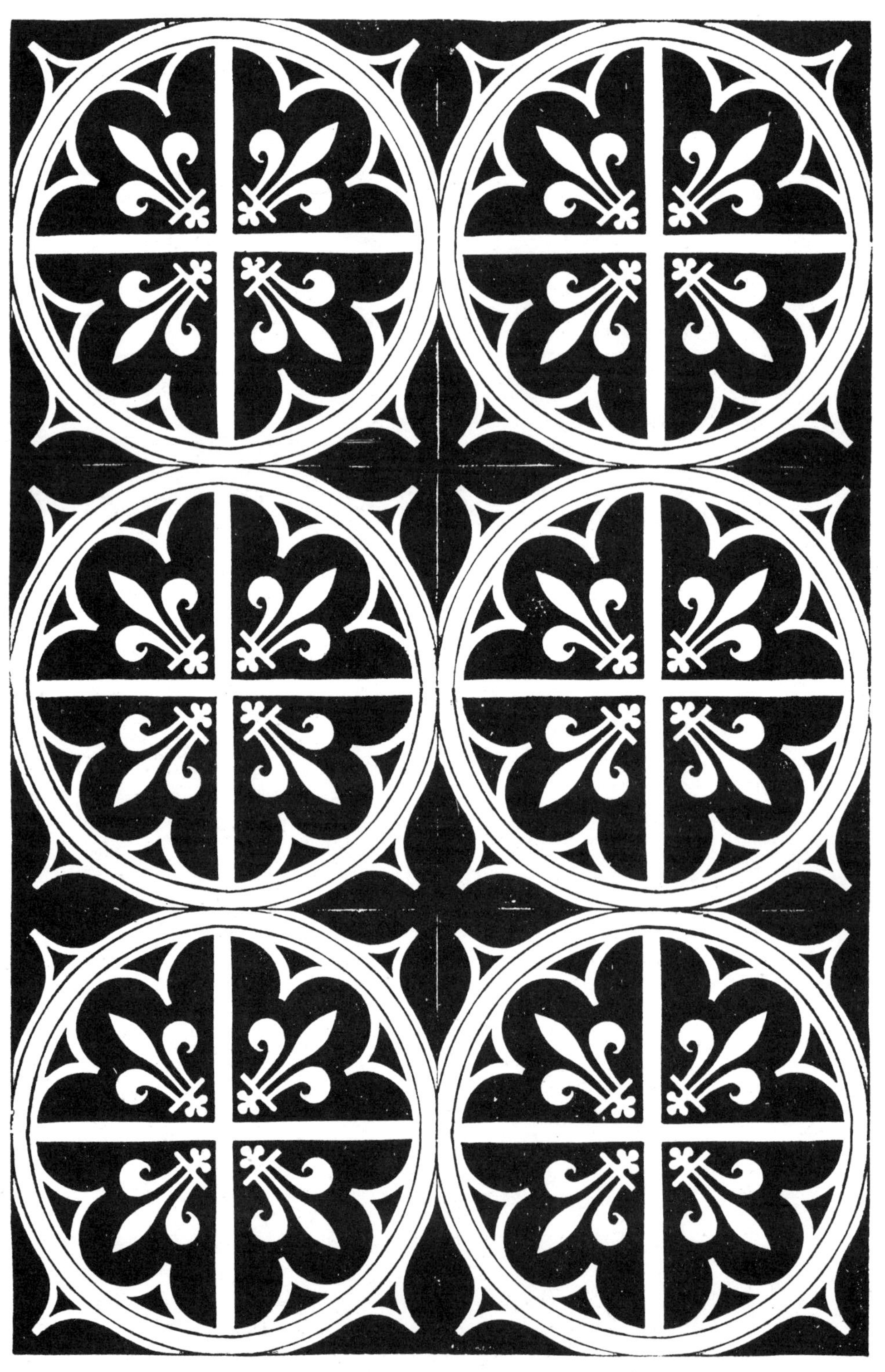

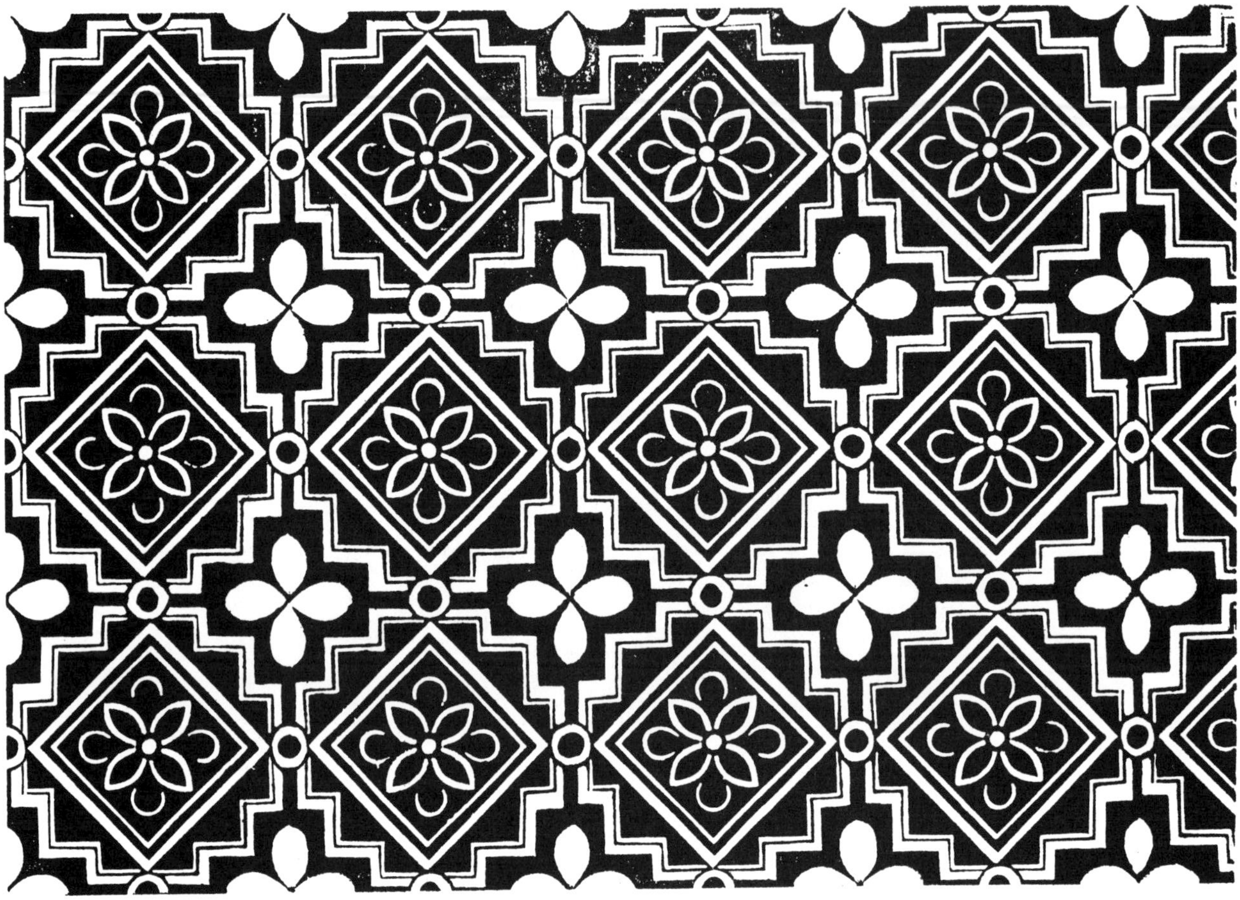

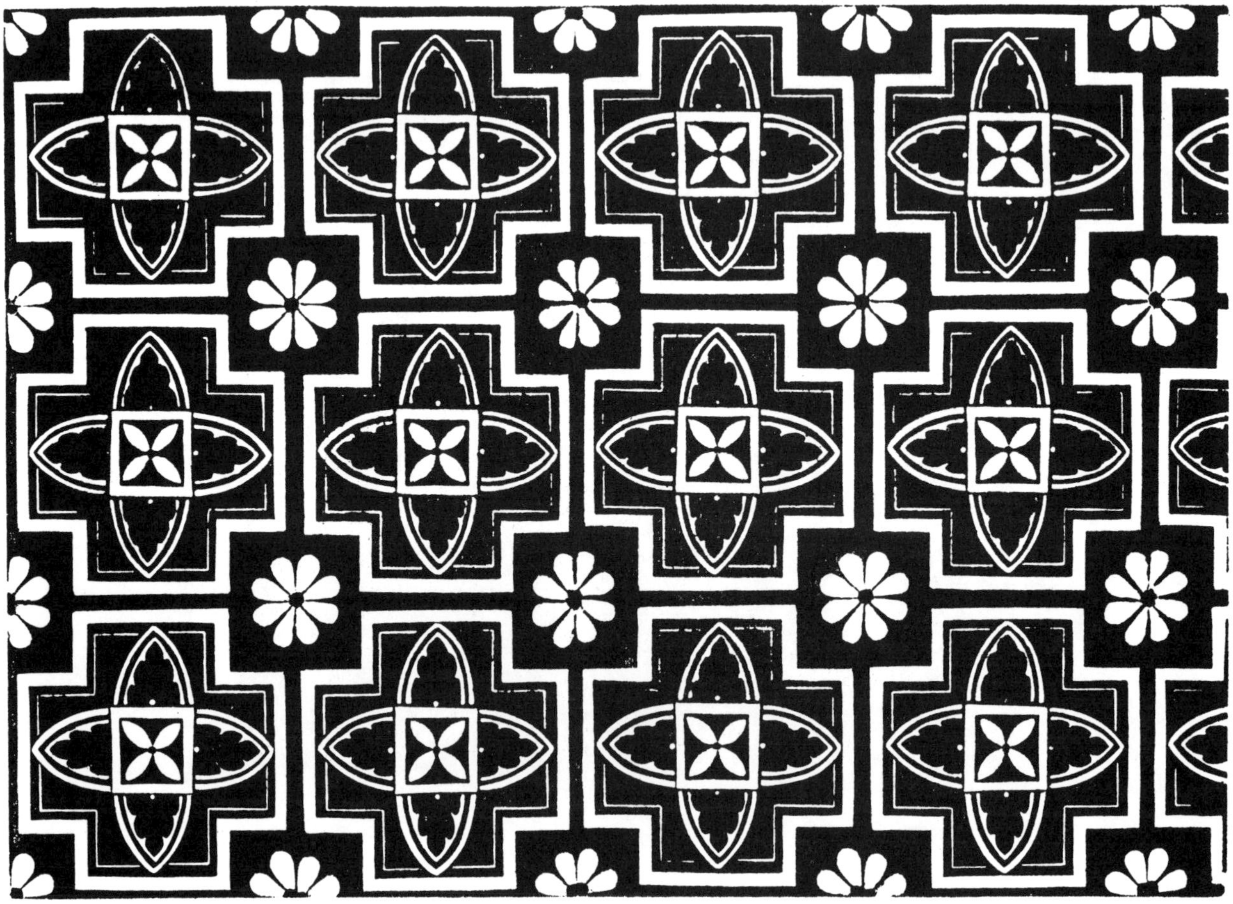

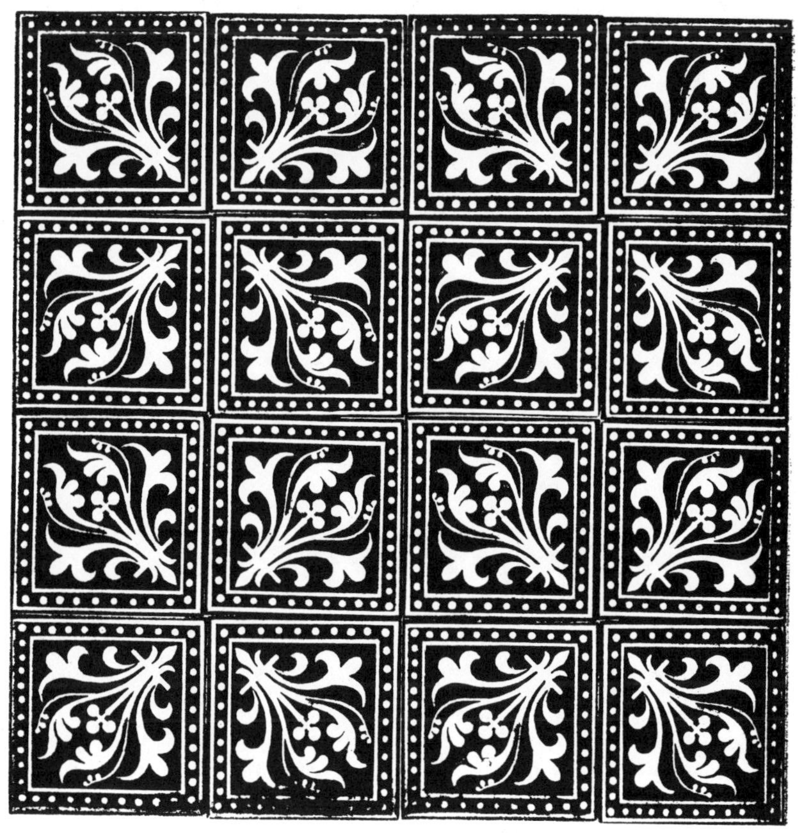

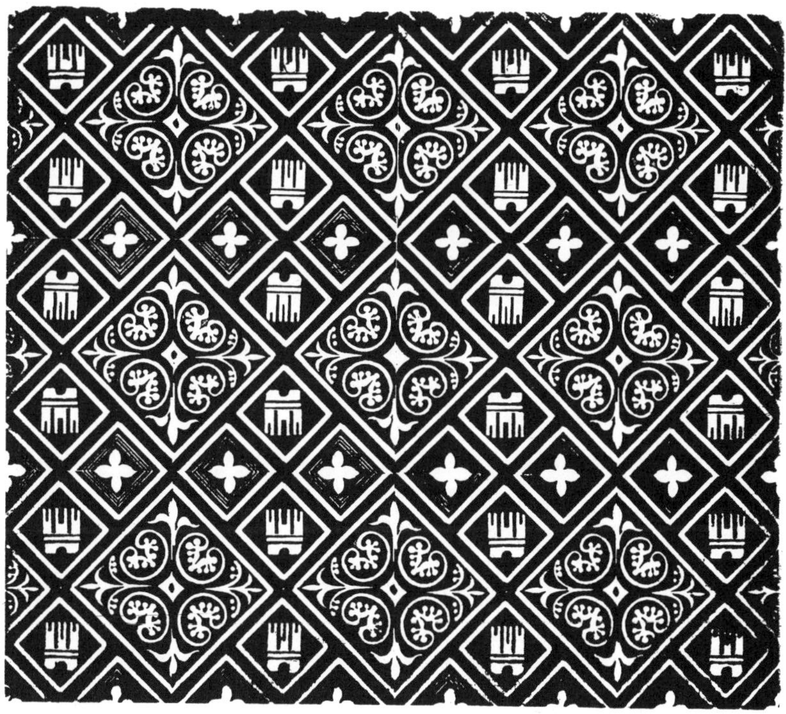

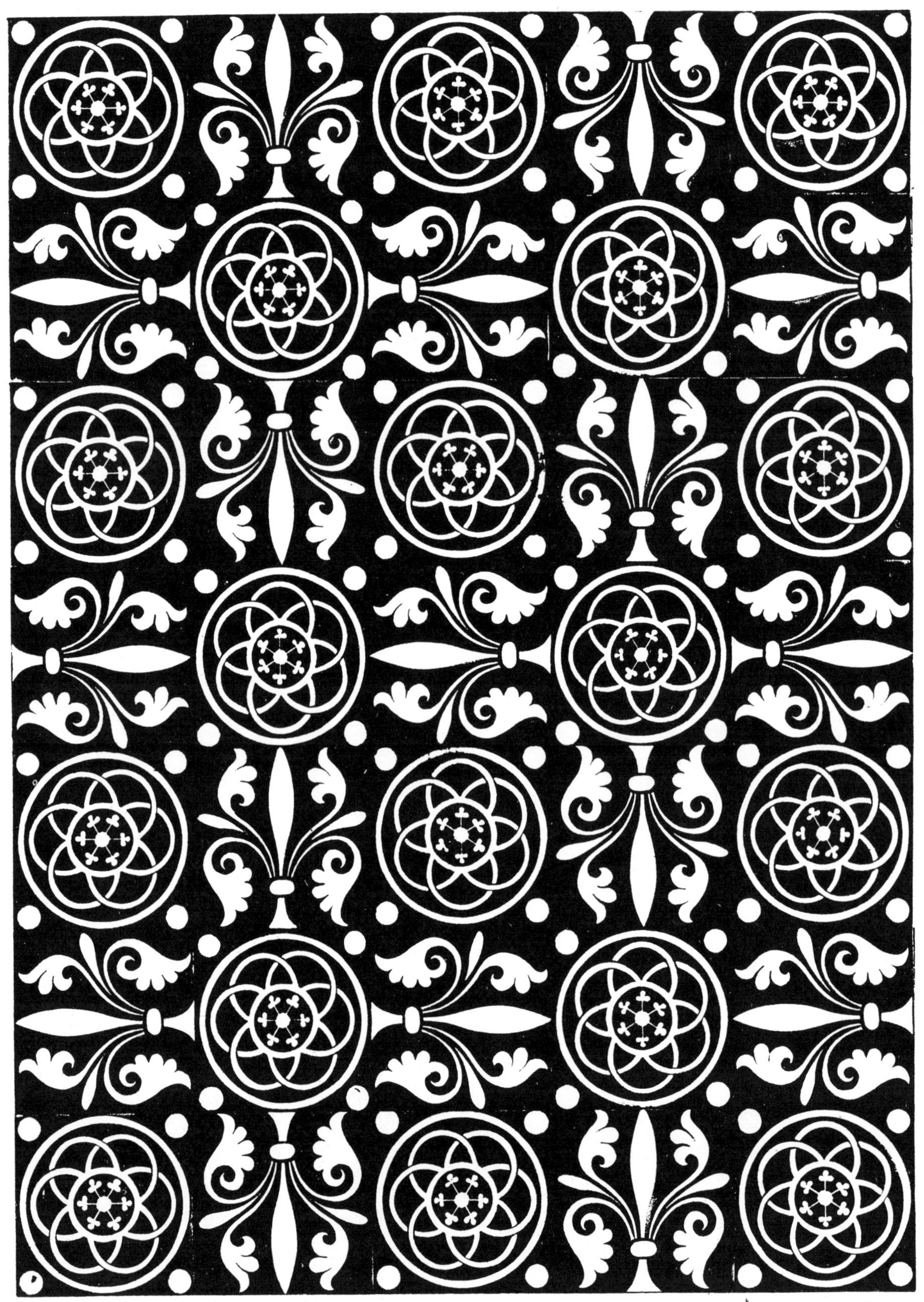

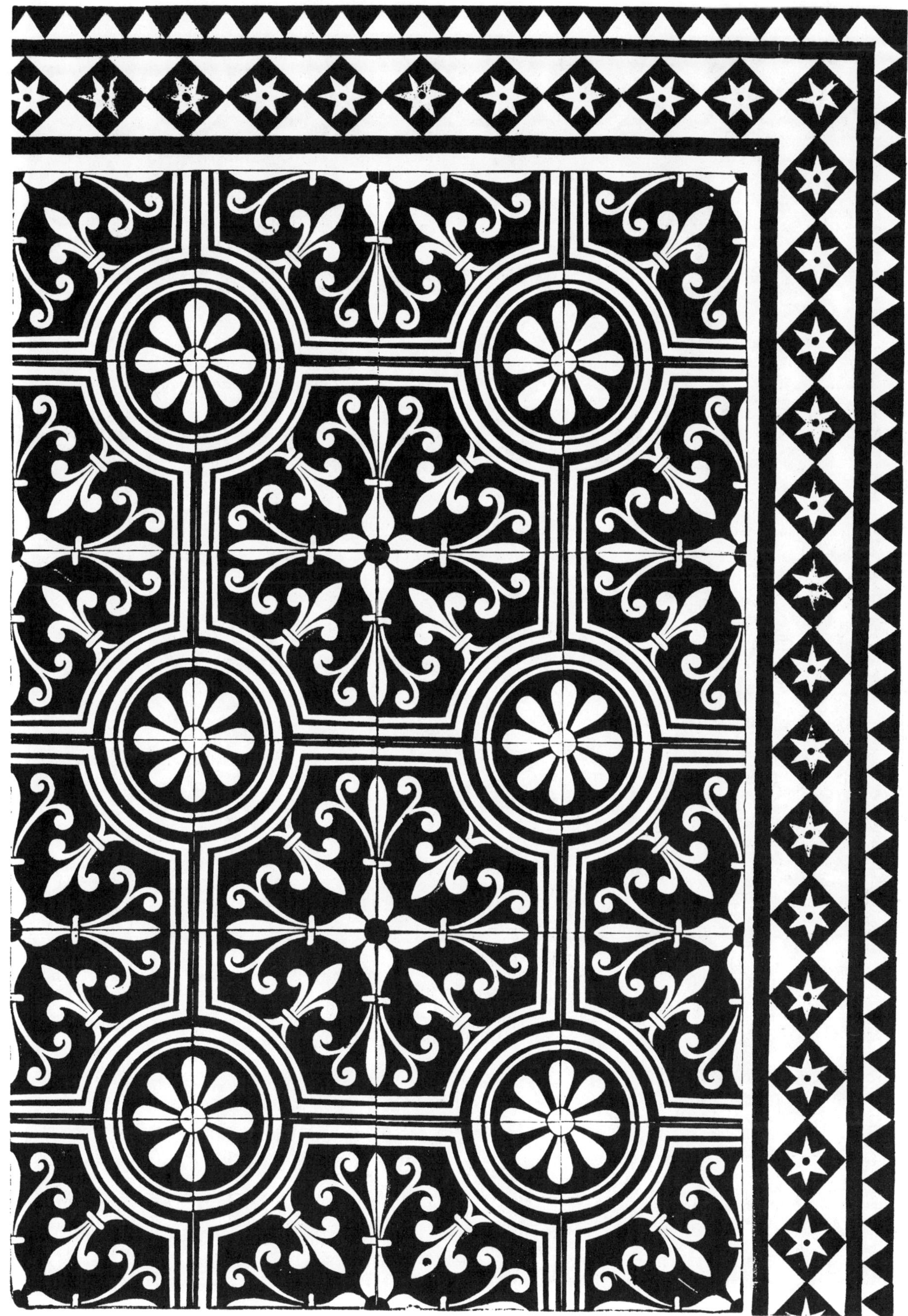

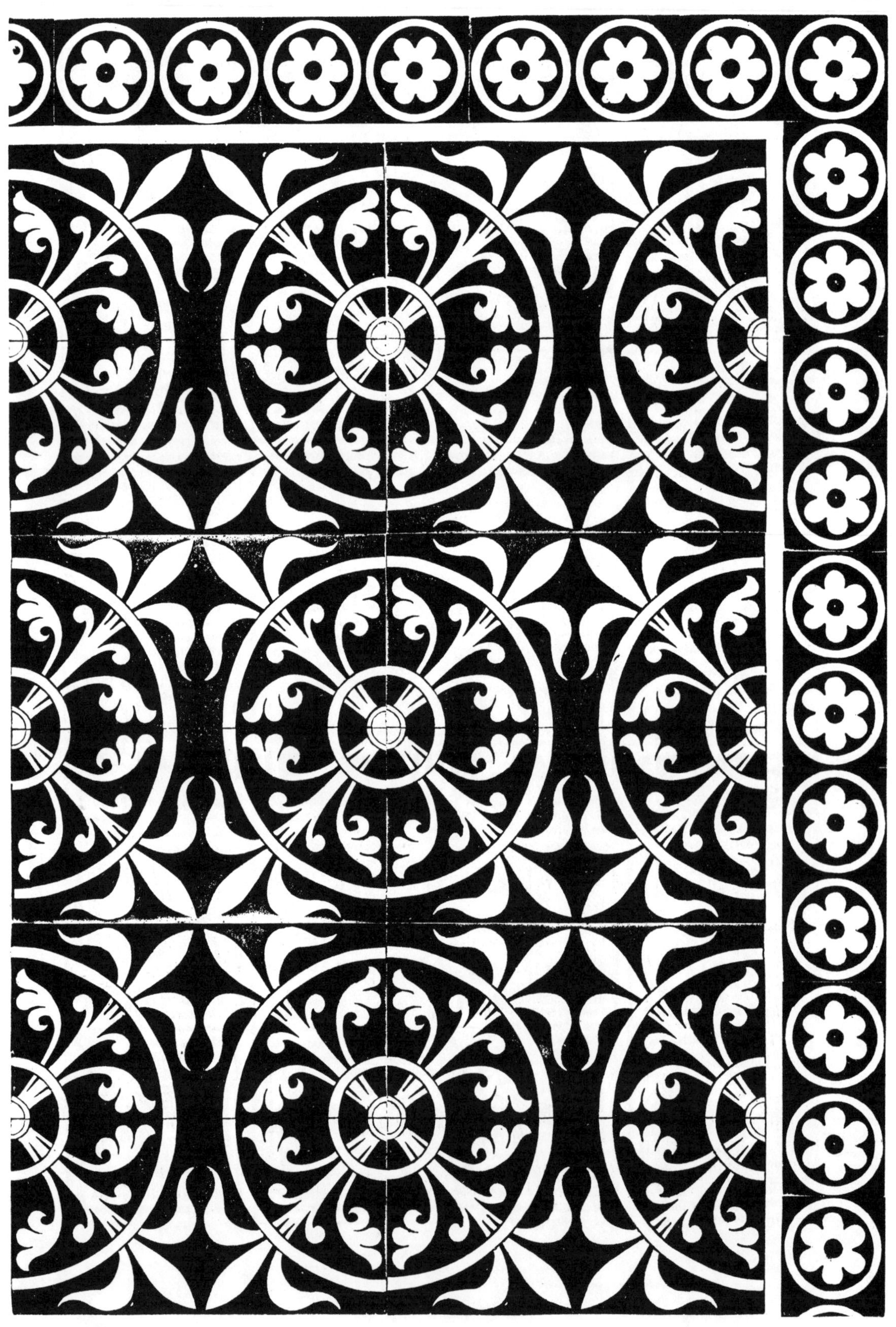

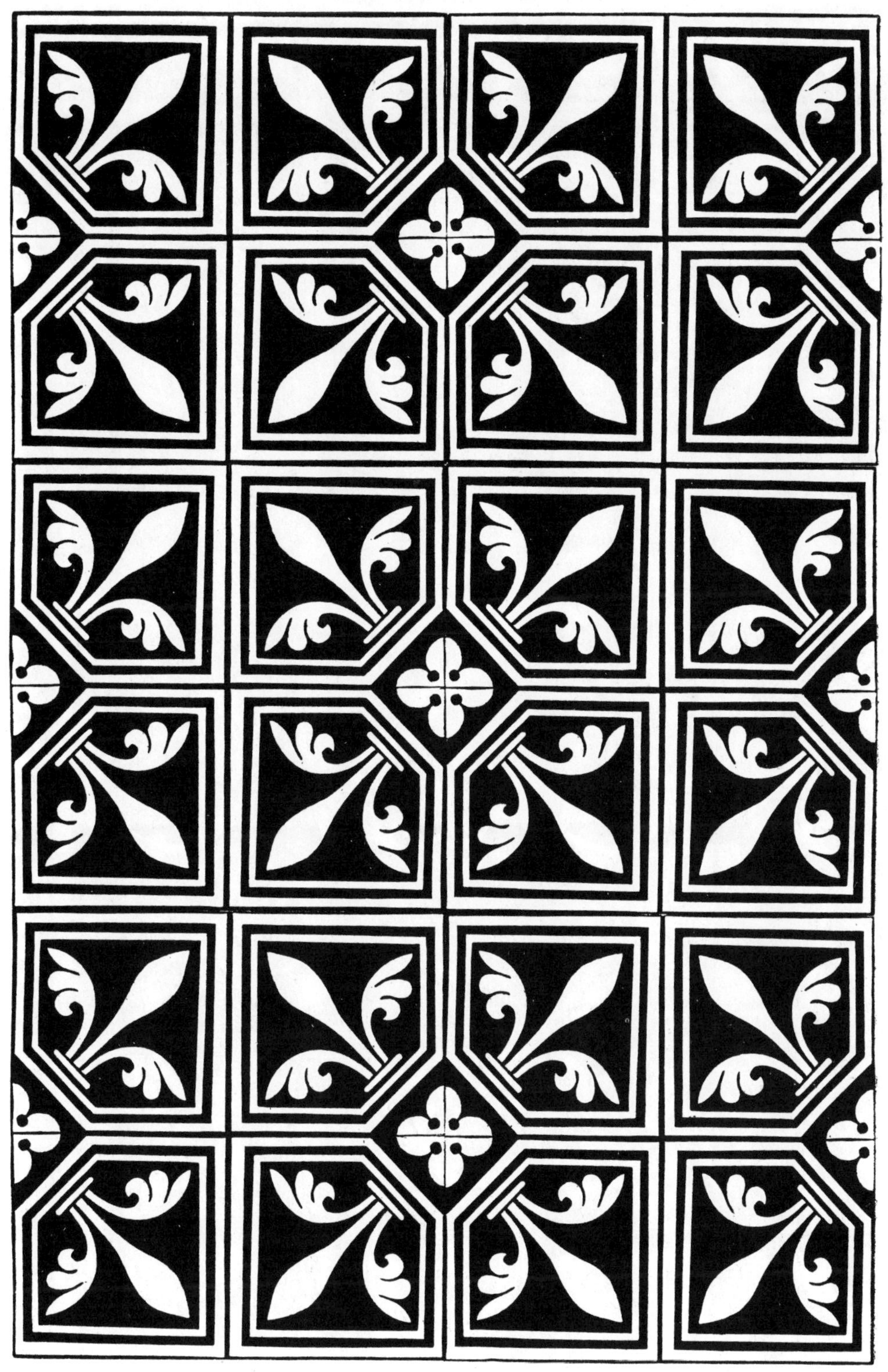

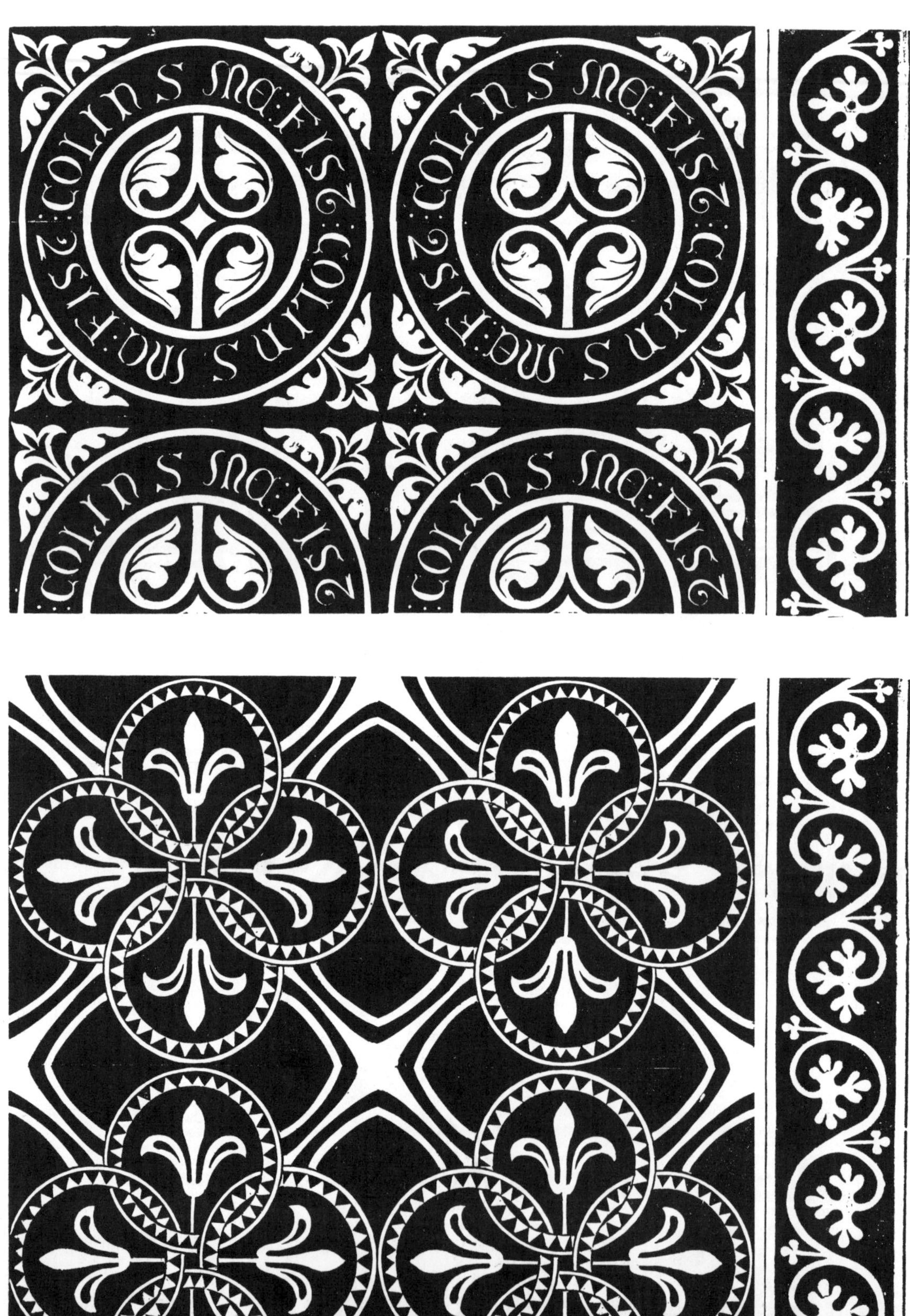
COLIN S MA:FIS

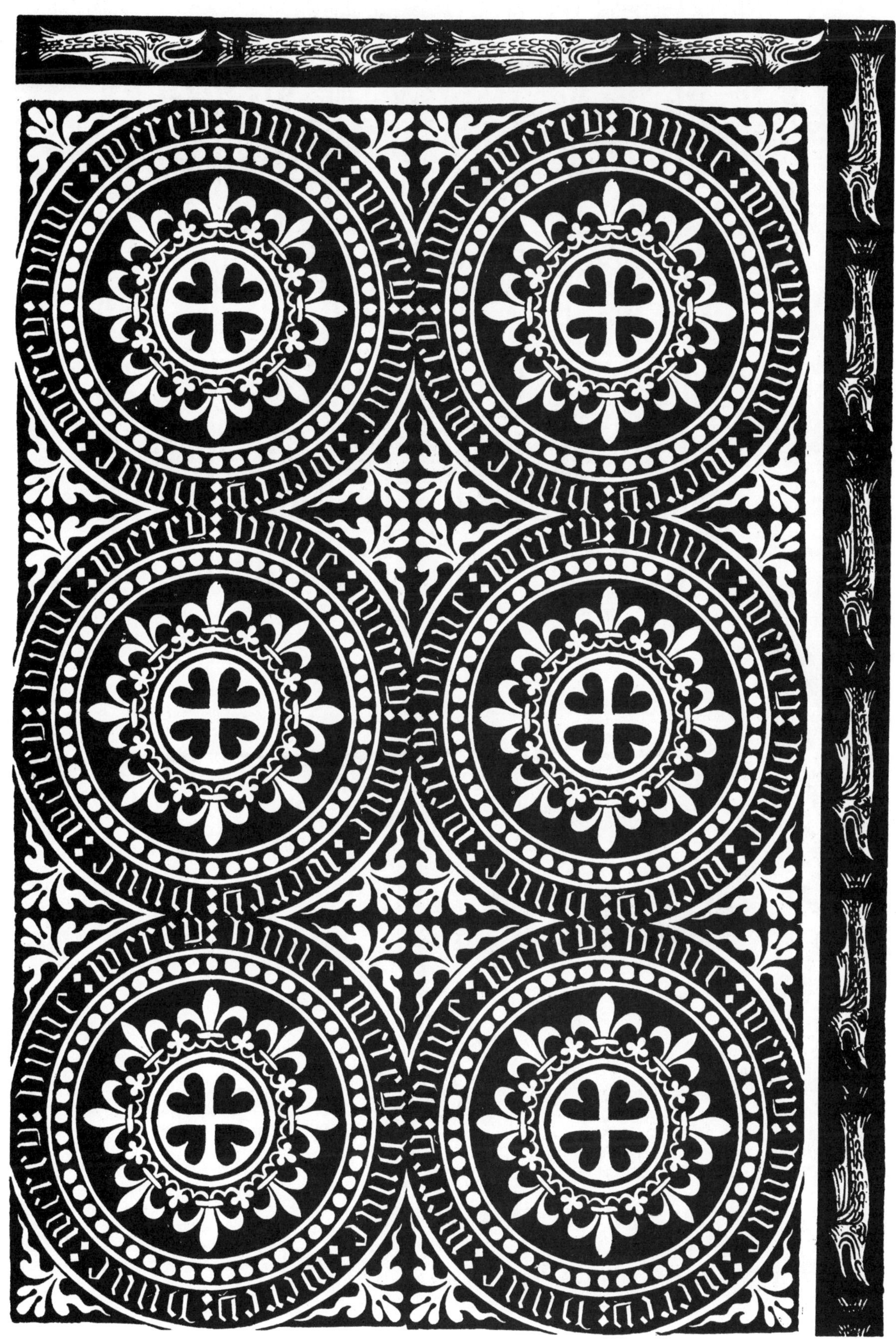

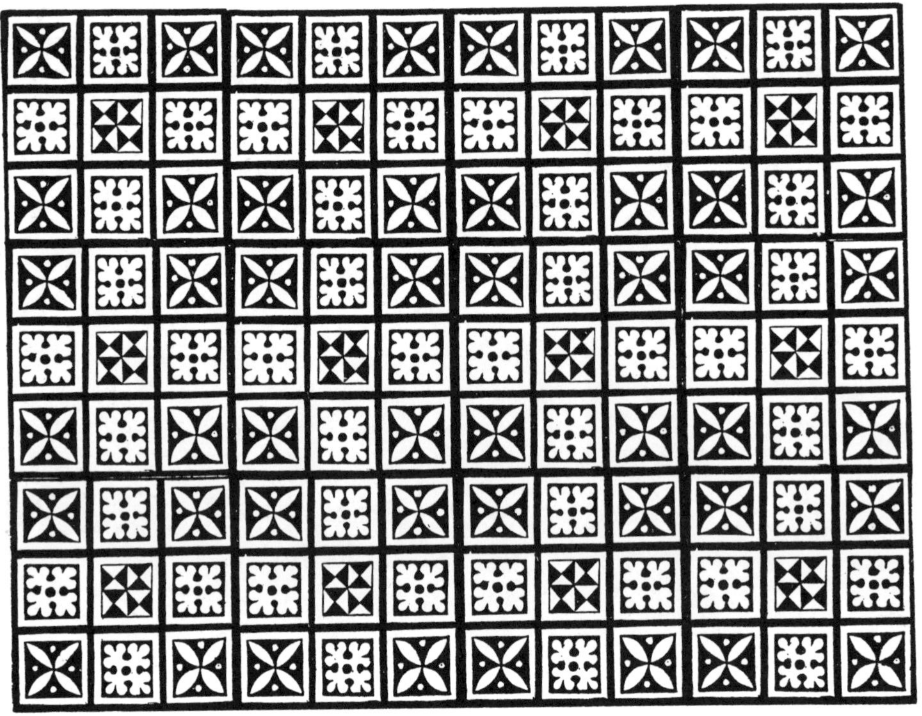

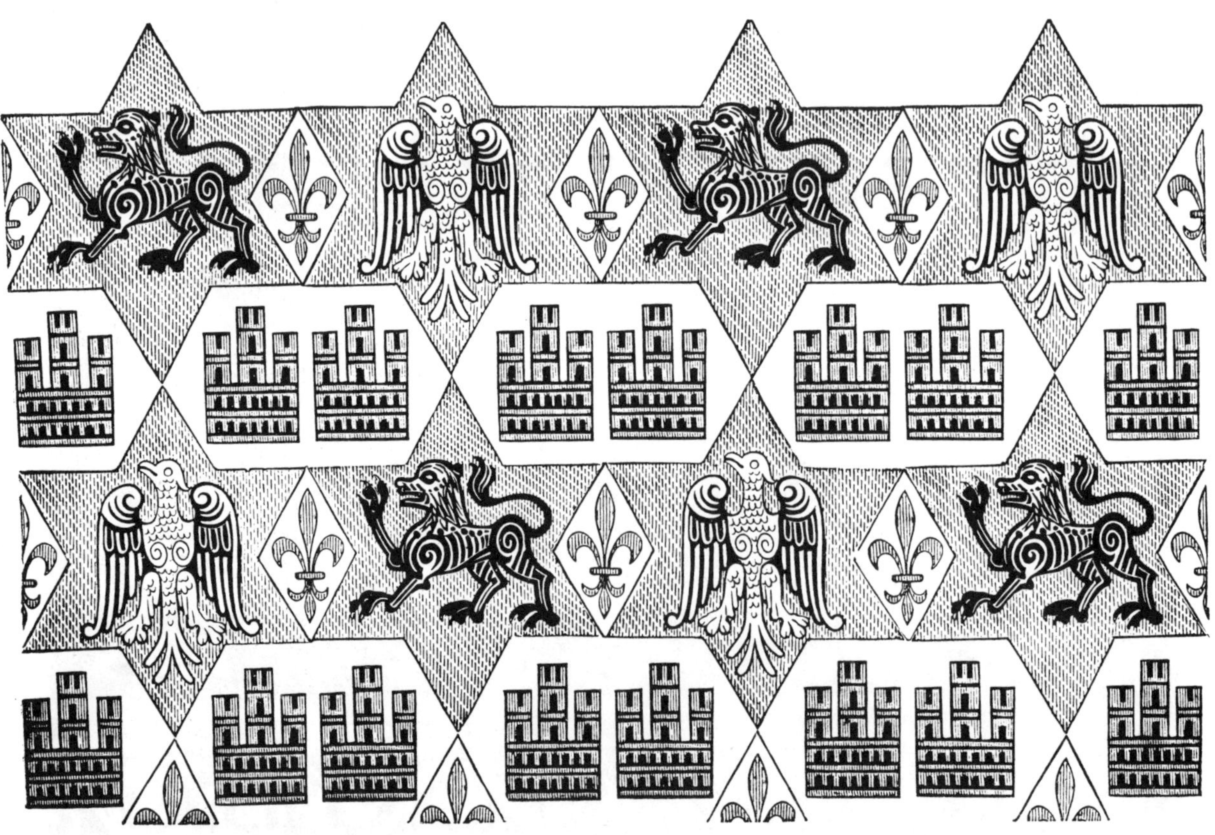

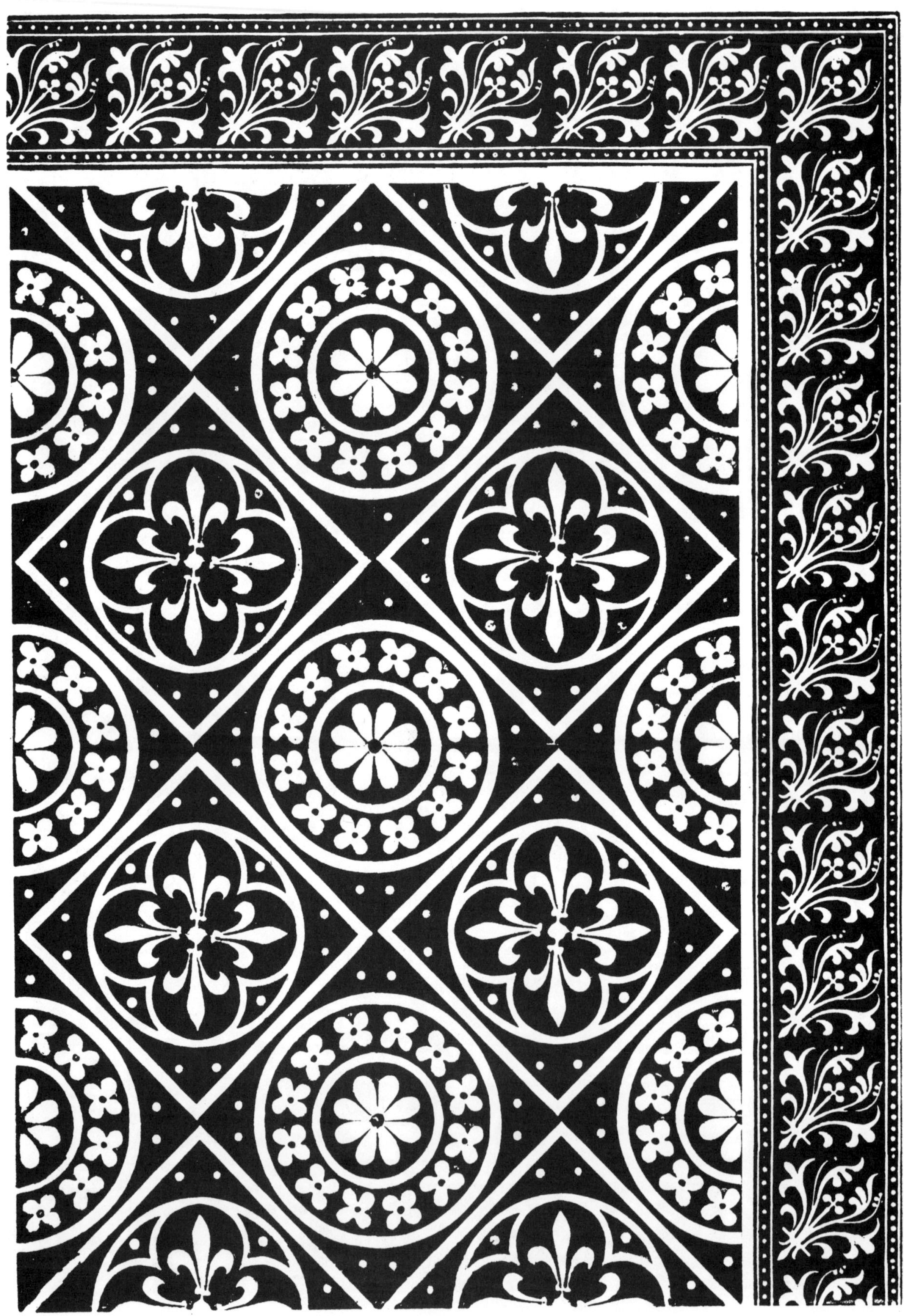

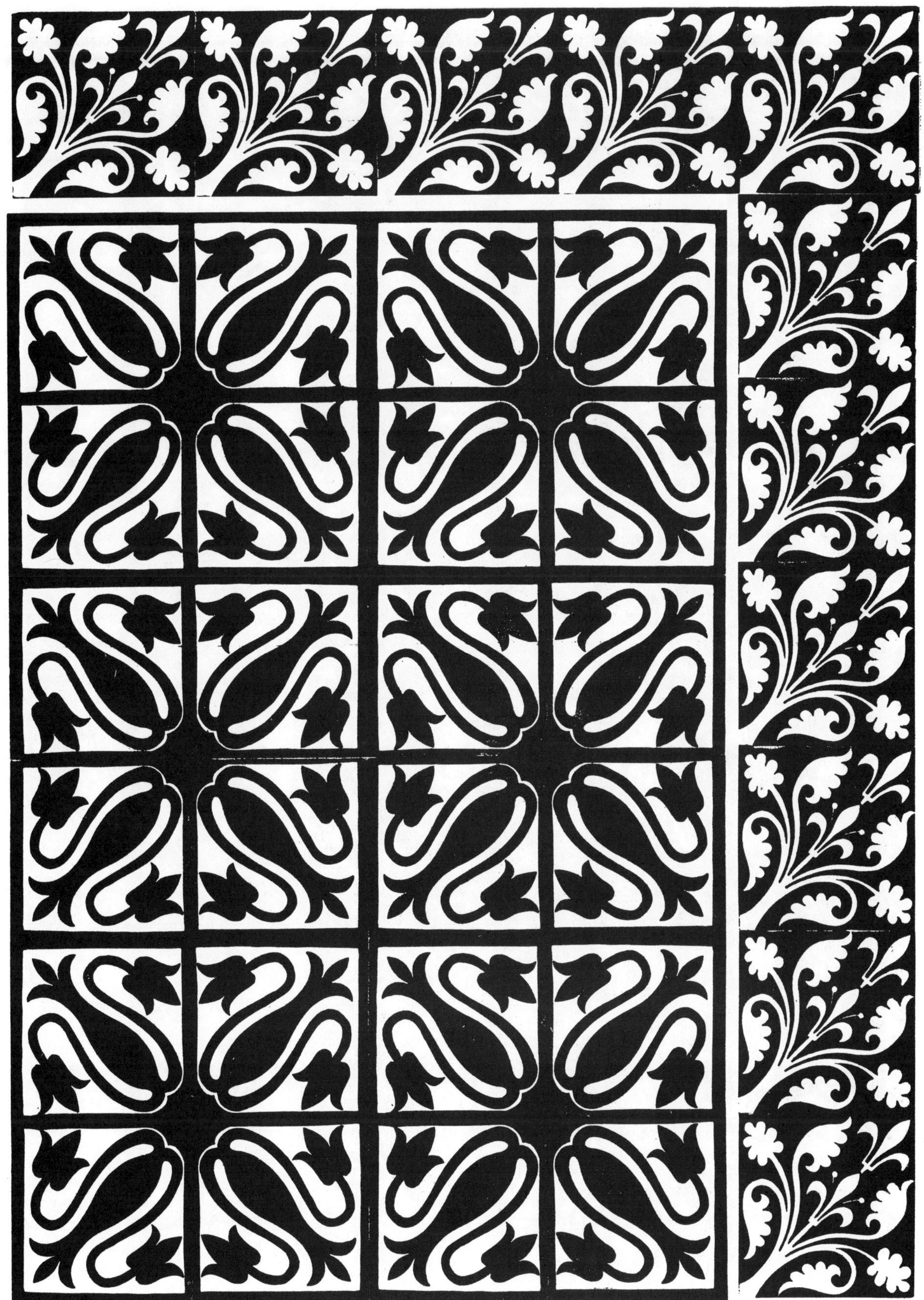

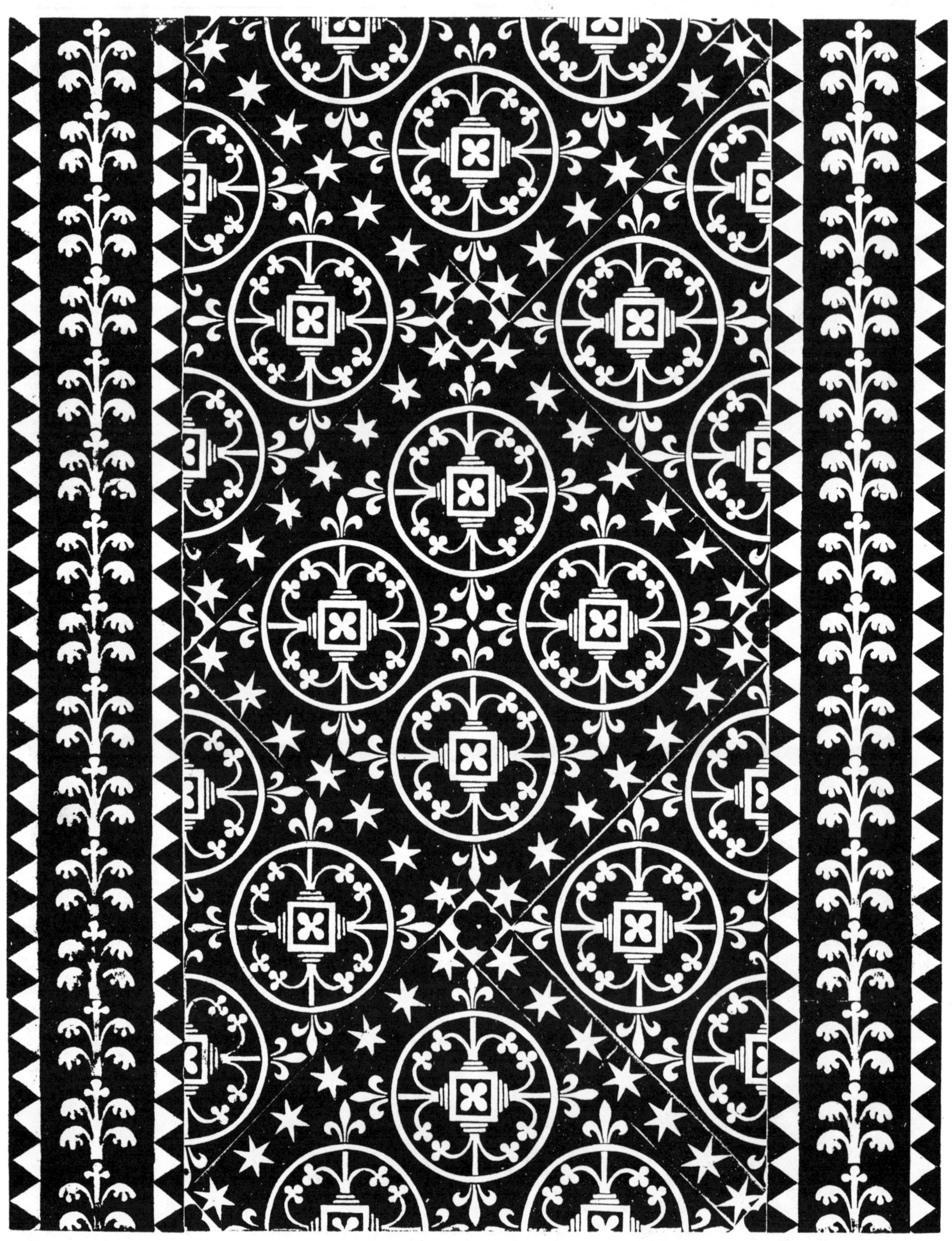

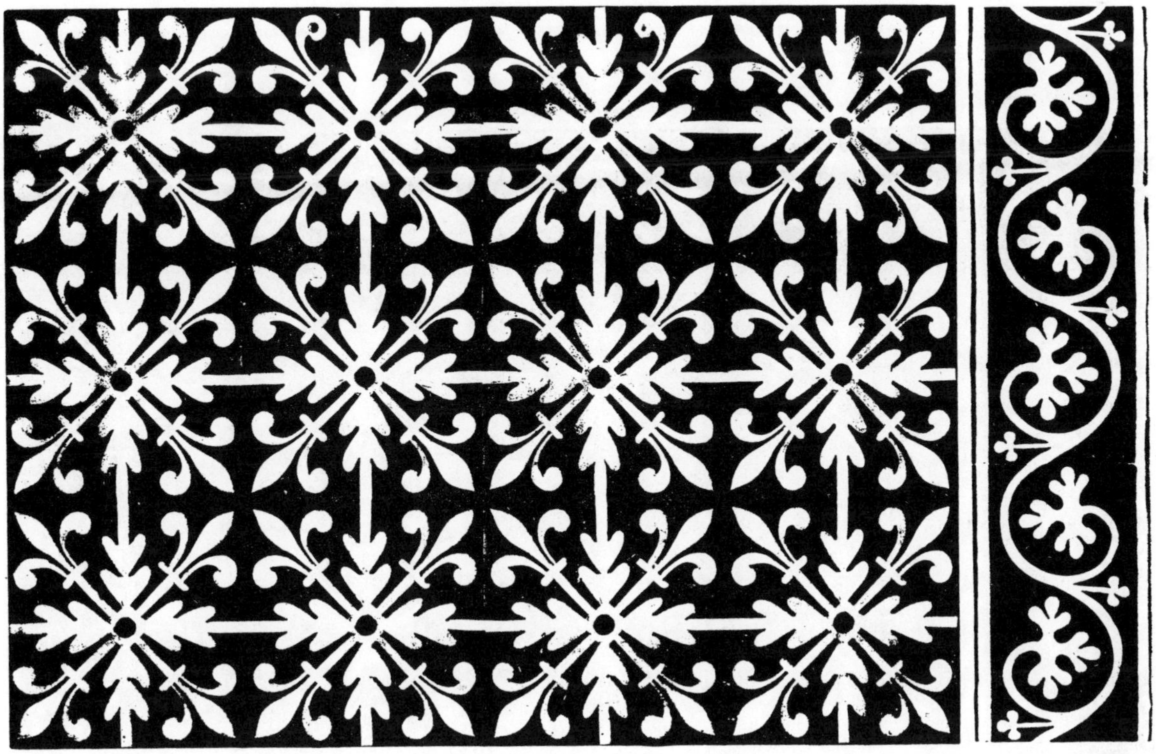

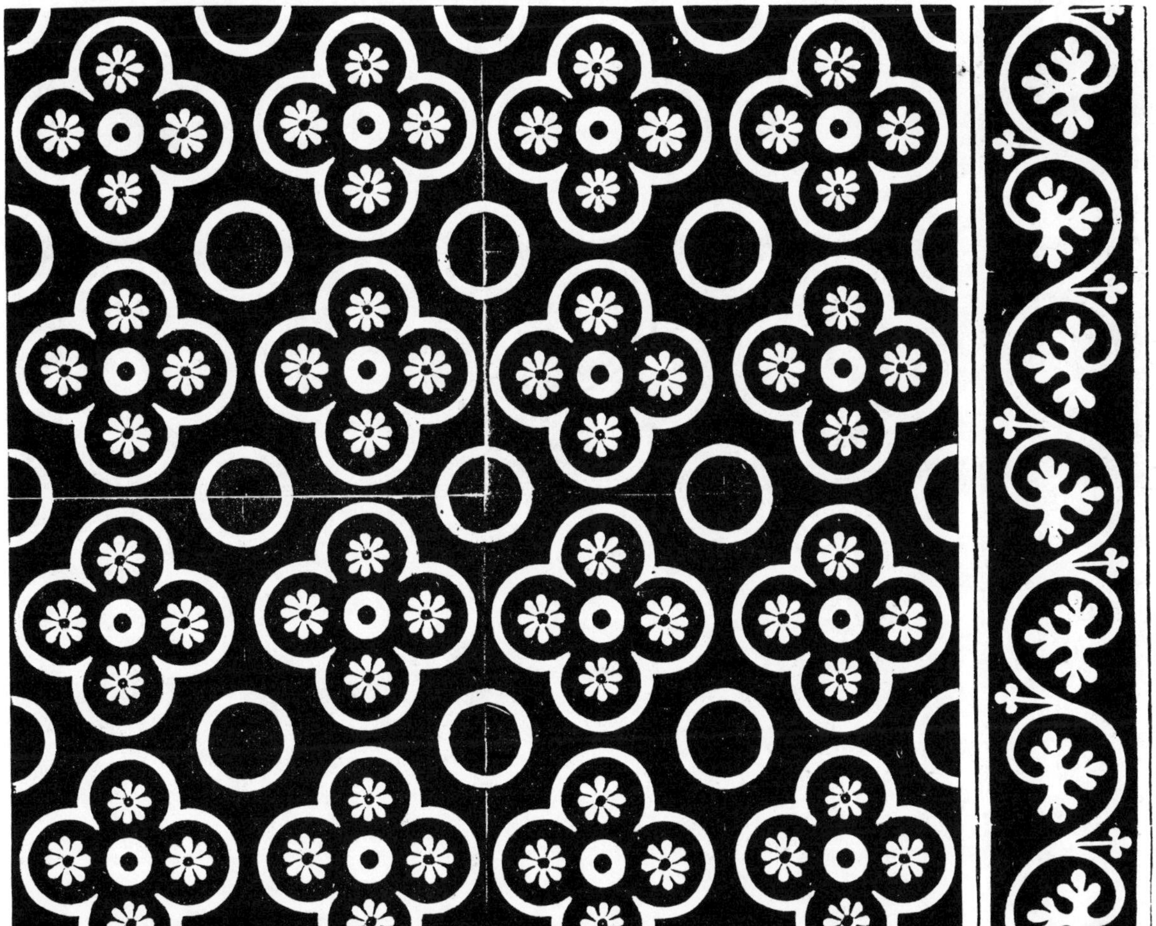

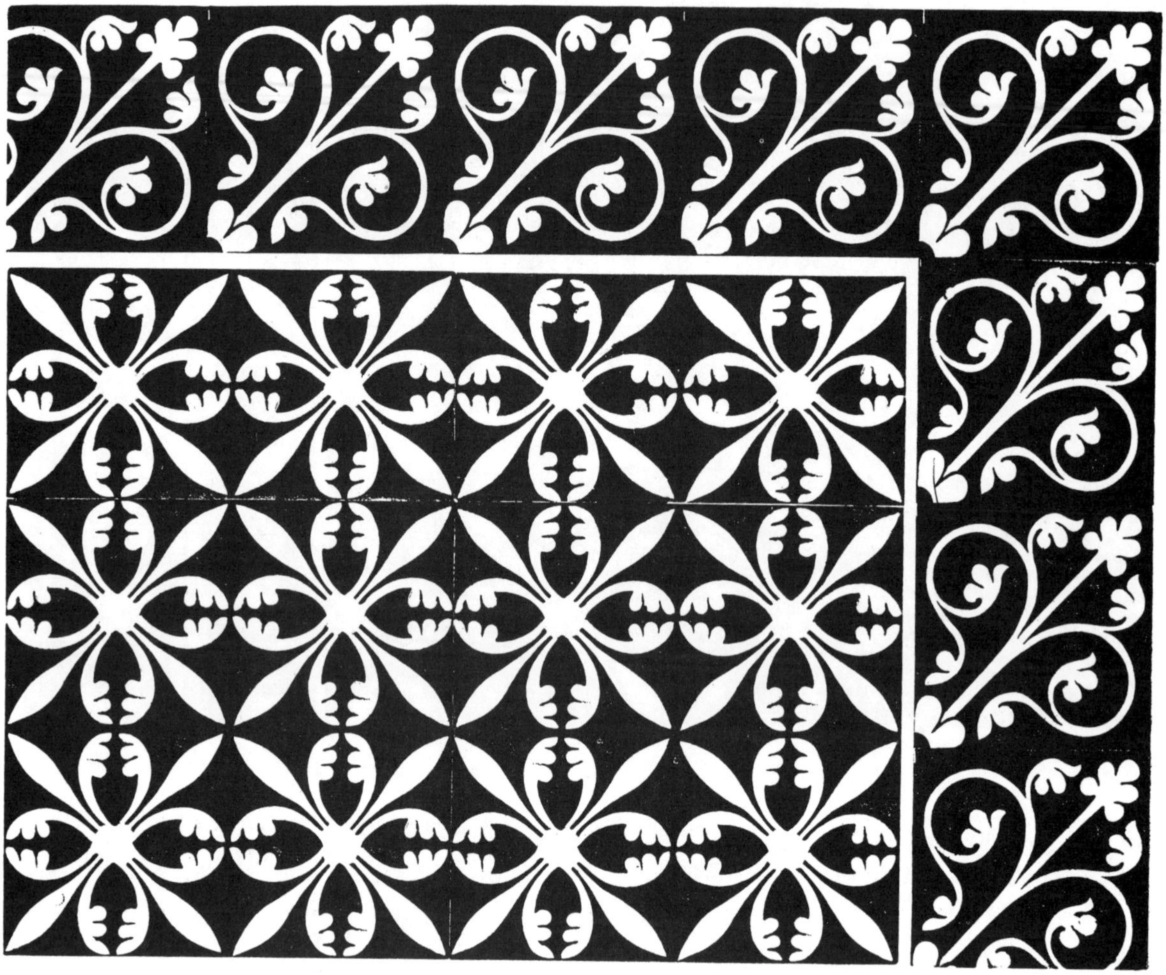

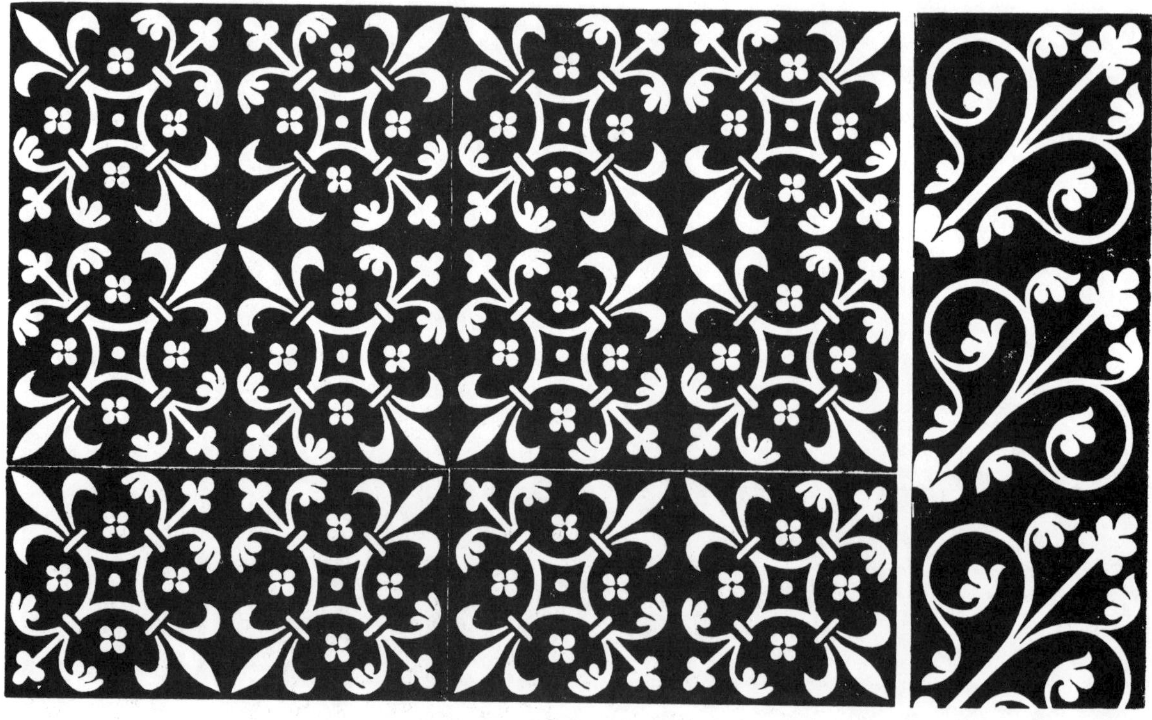

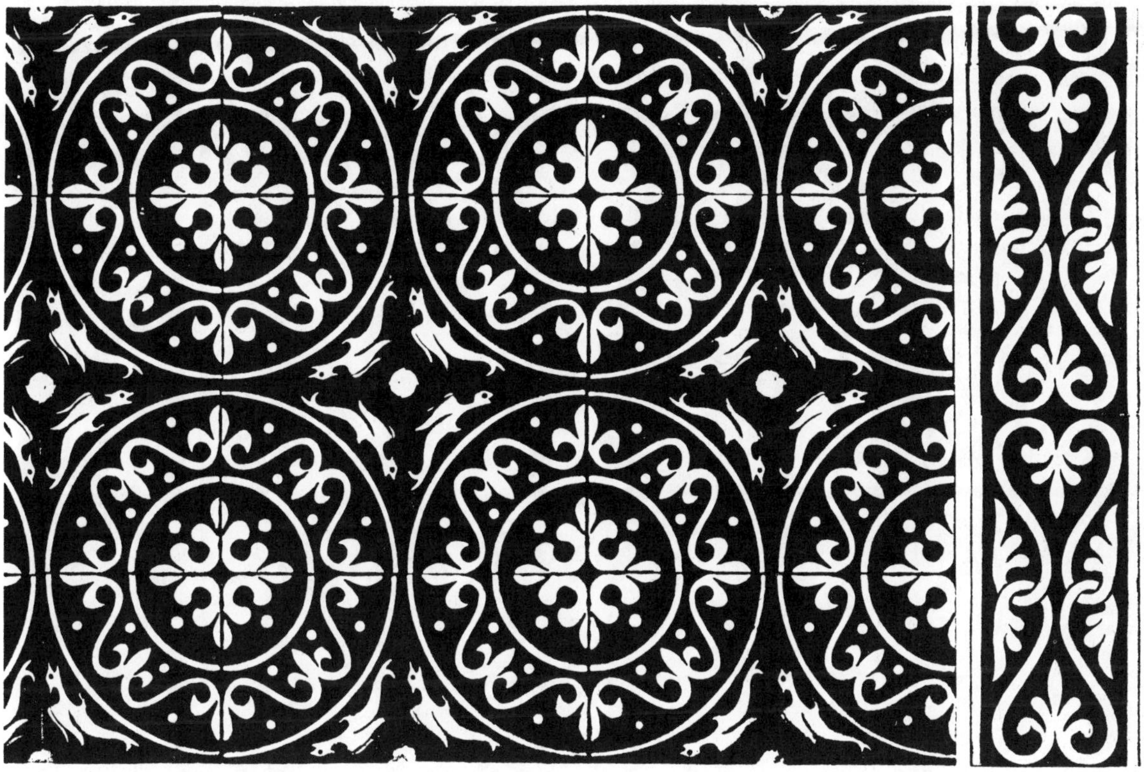

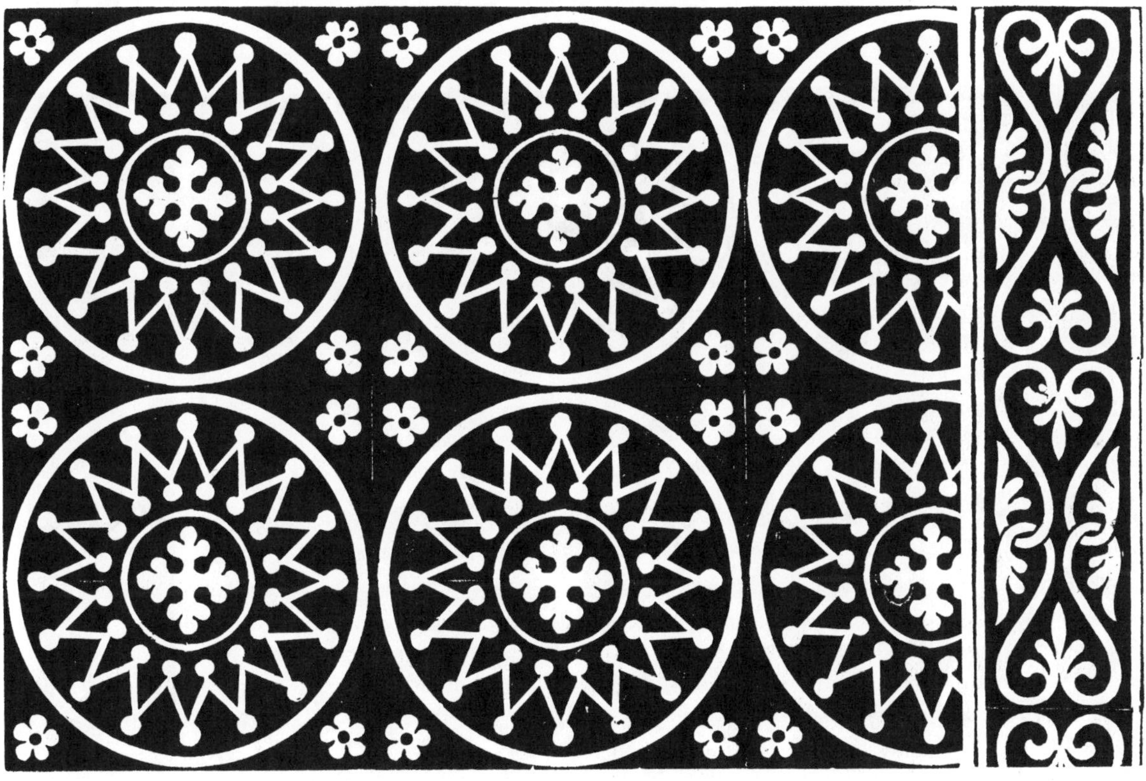

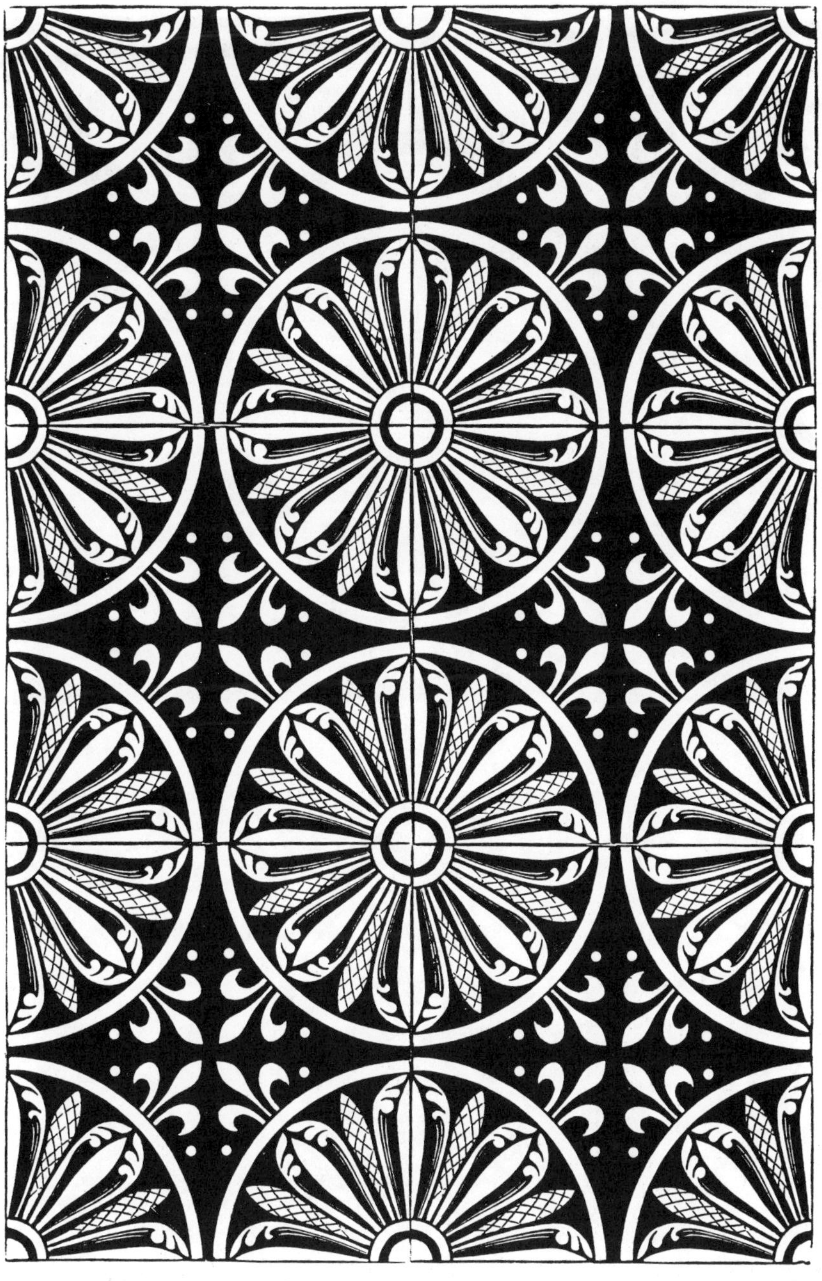

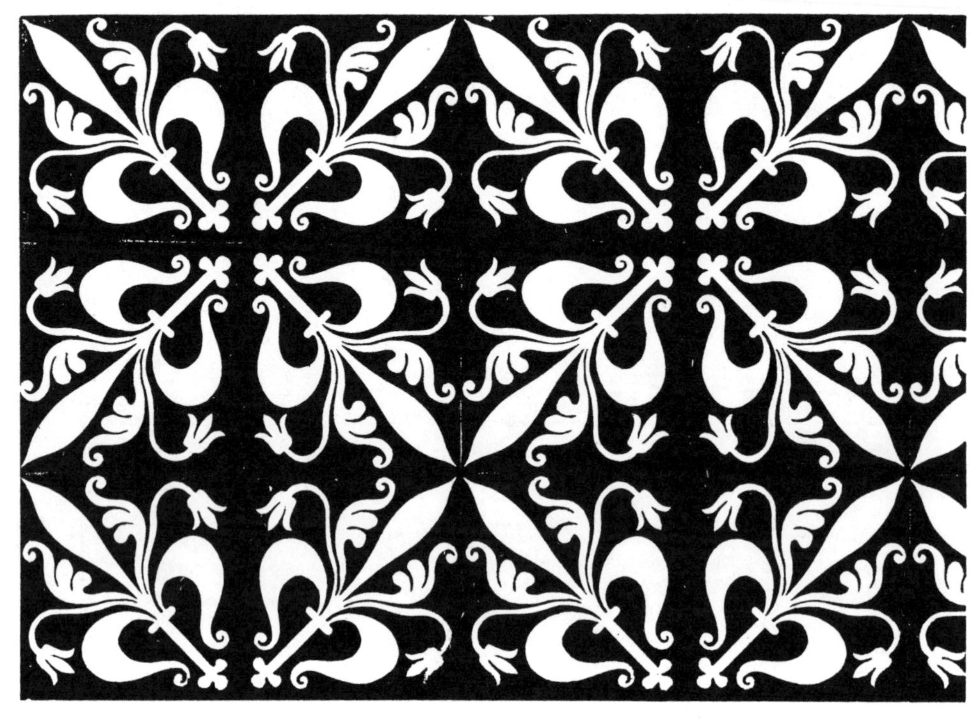

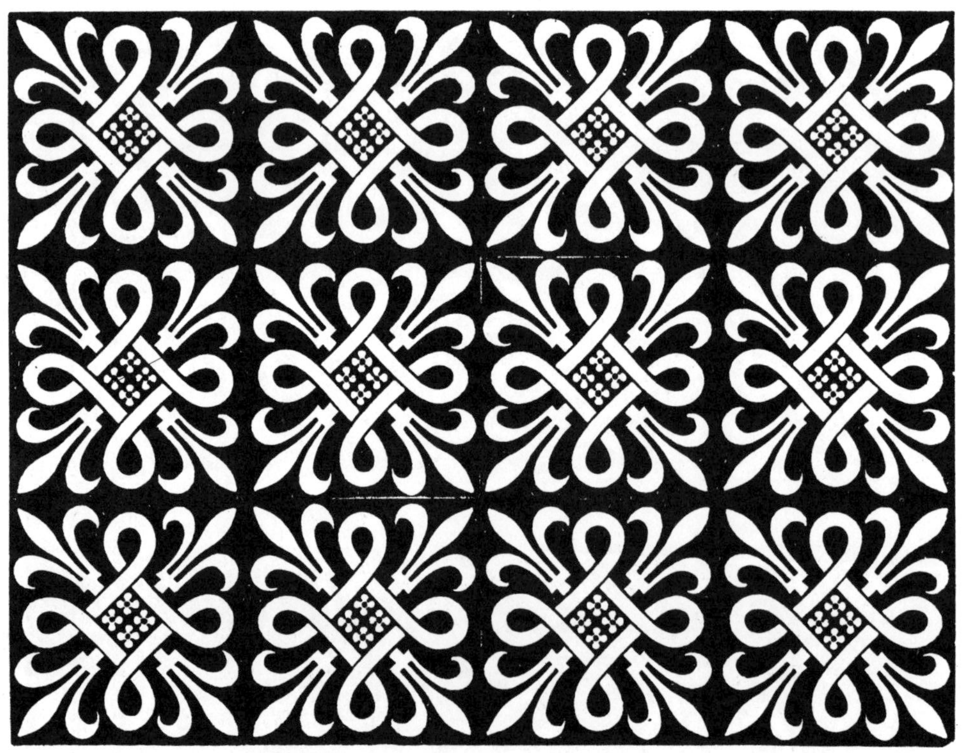

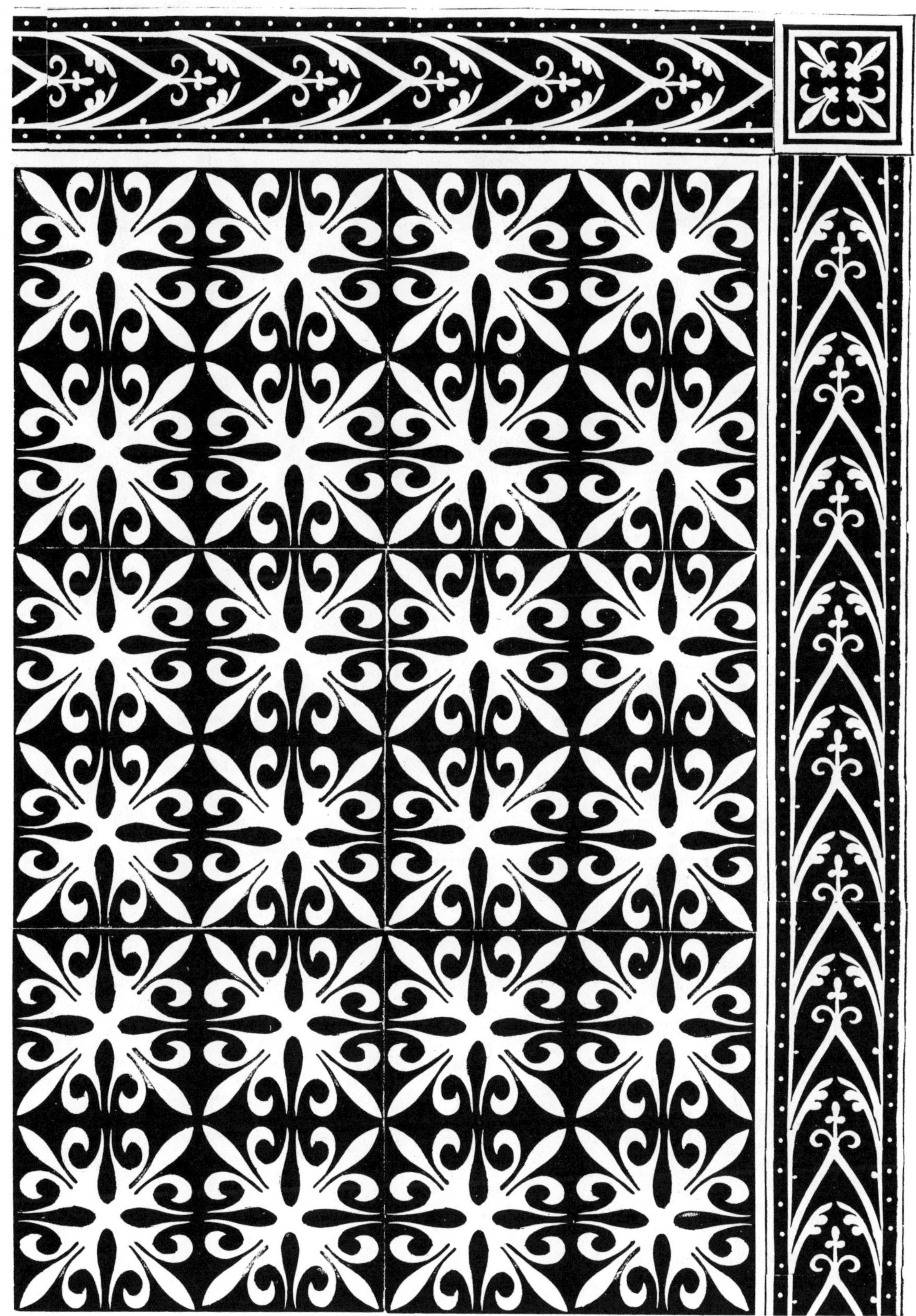

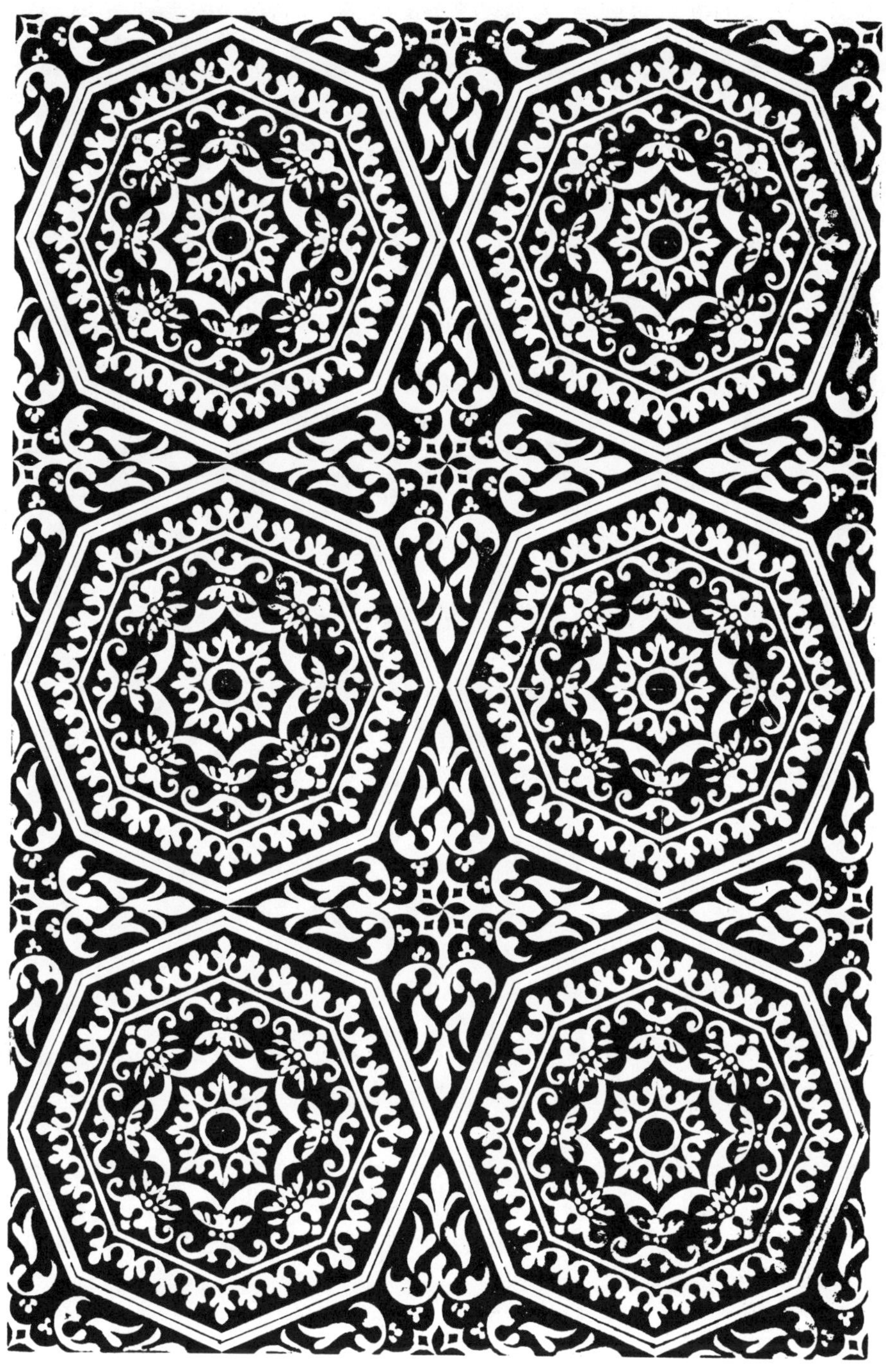

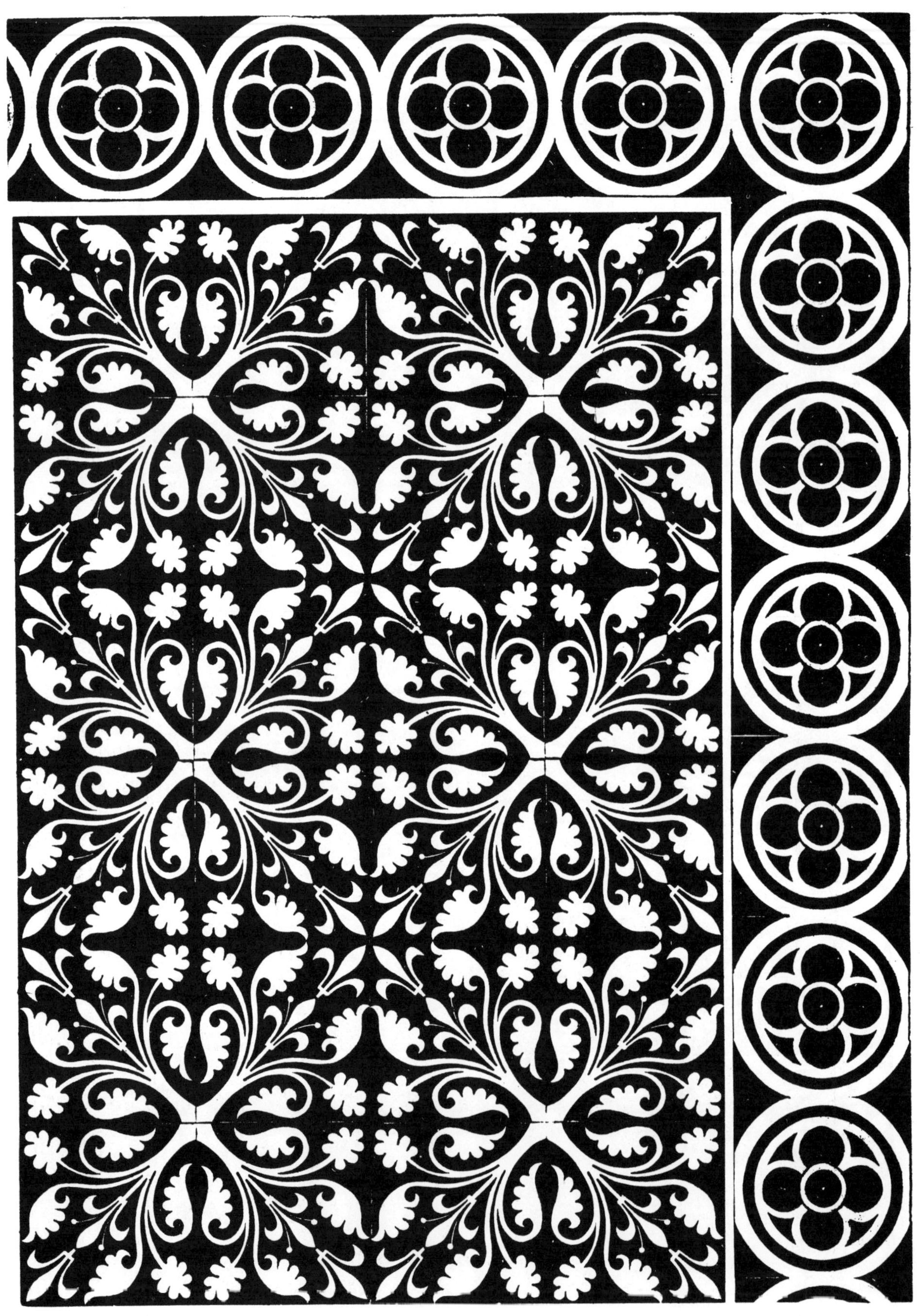

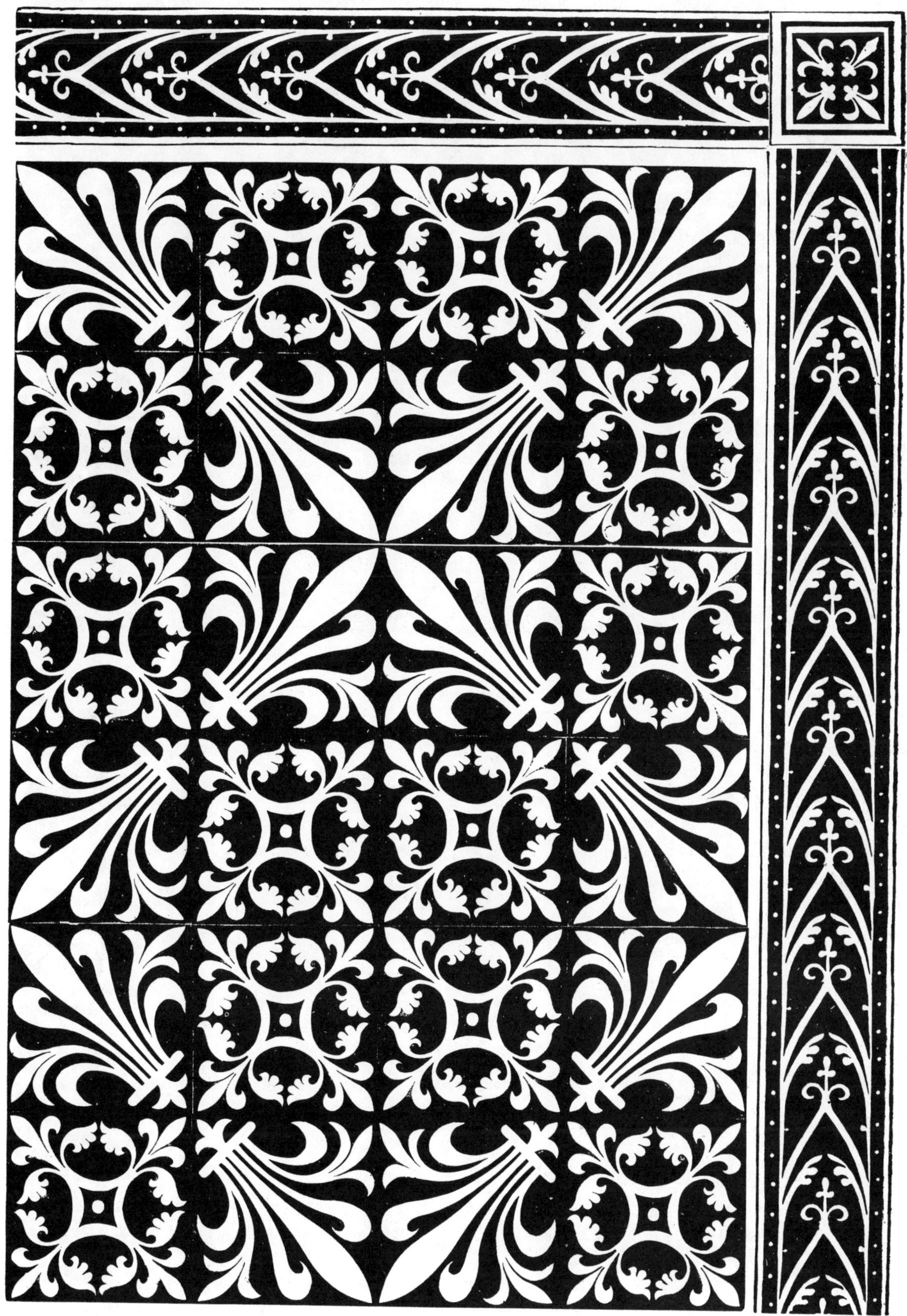

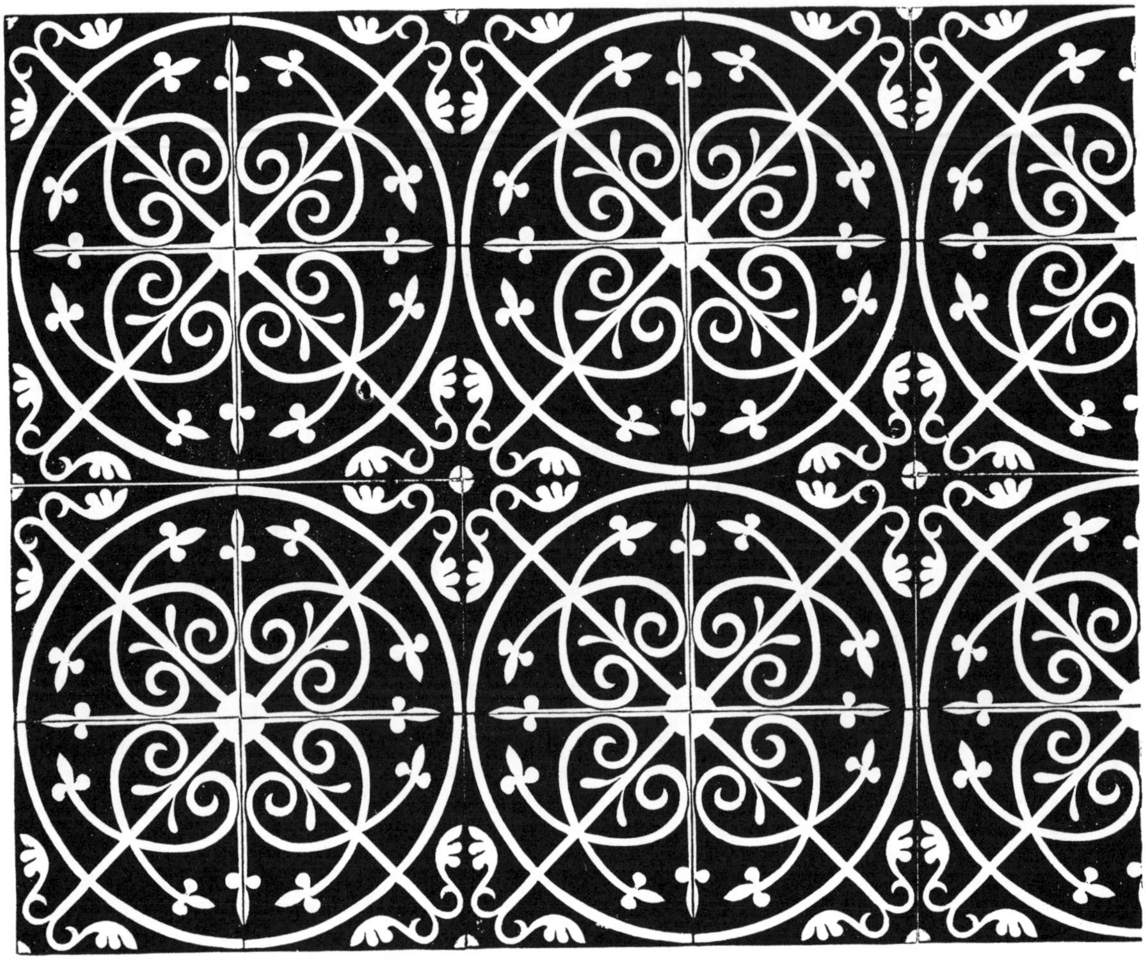

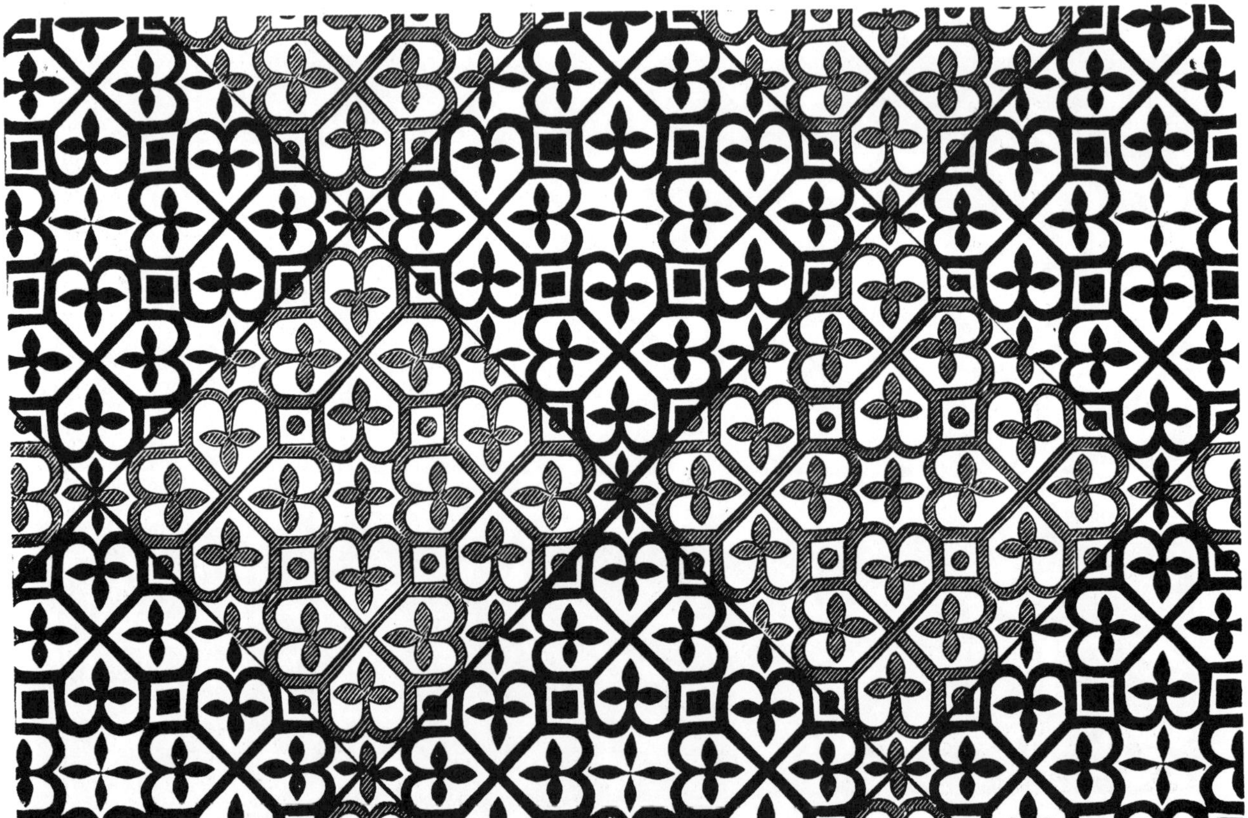

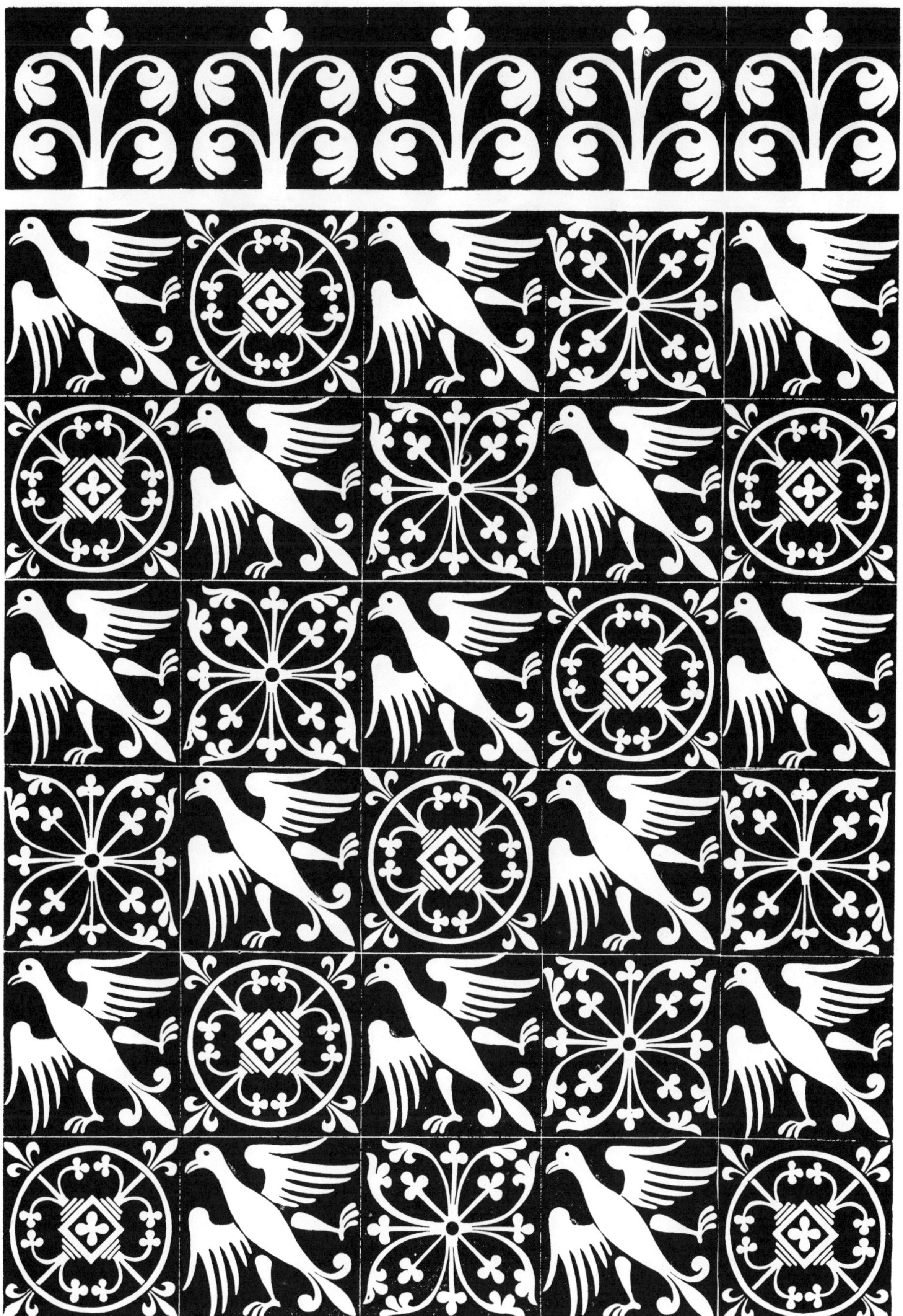

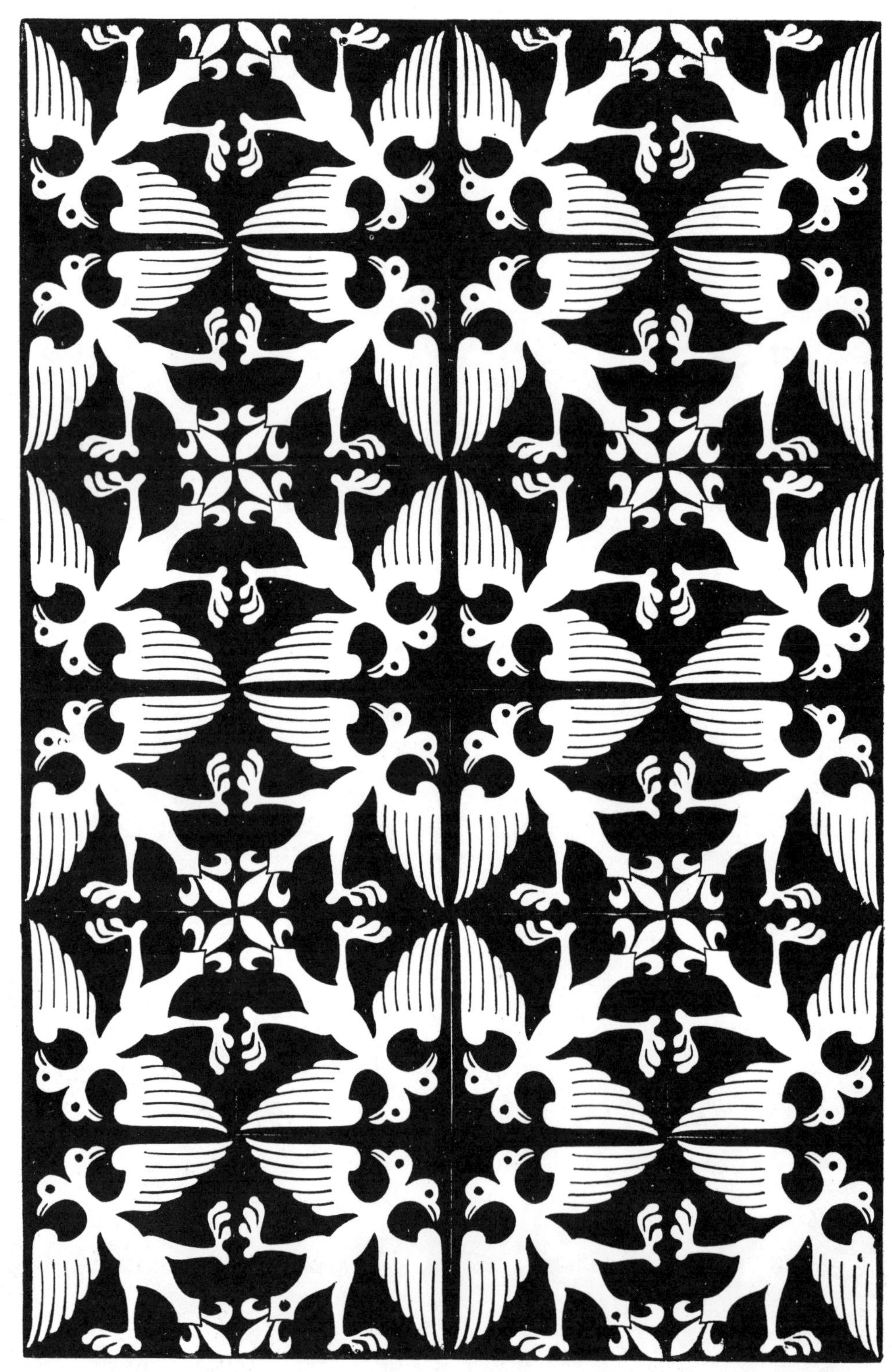

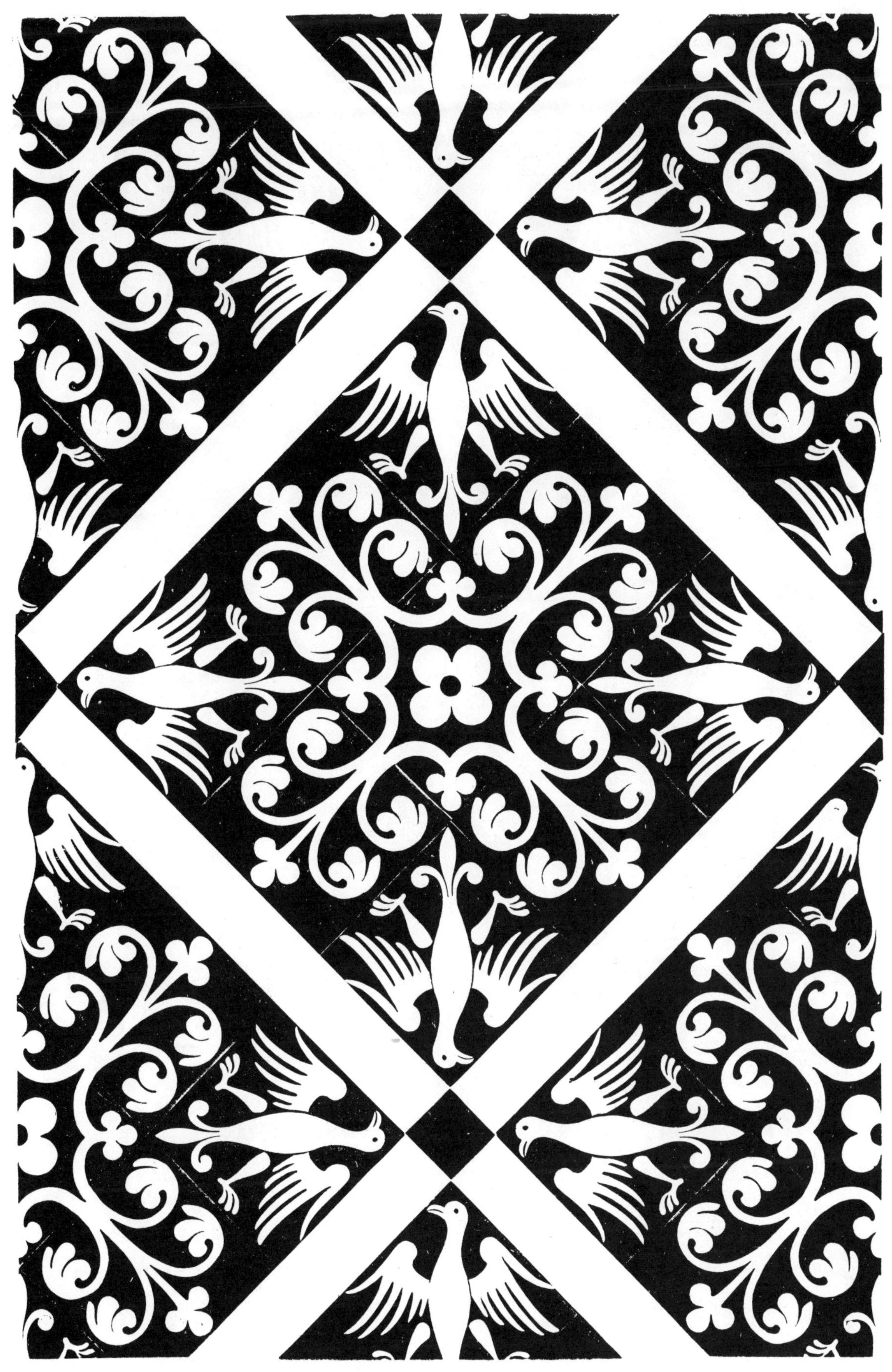

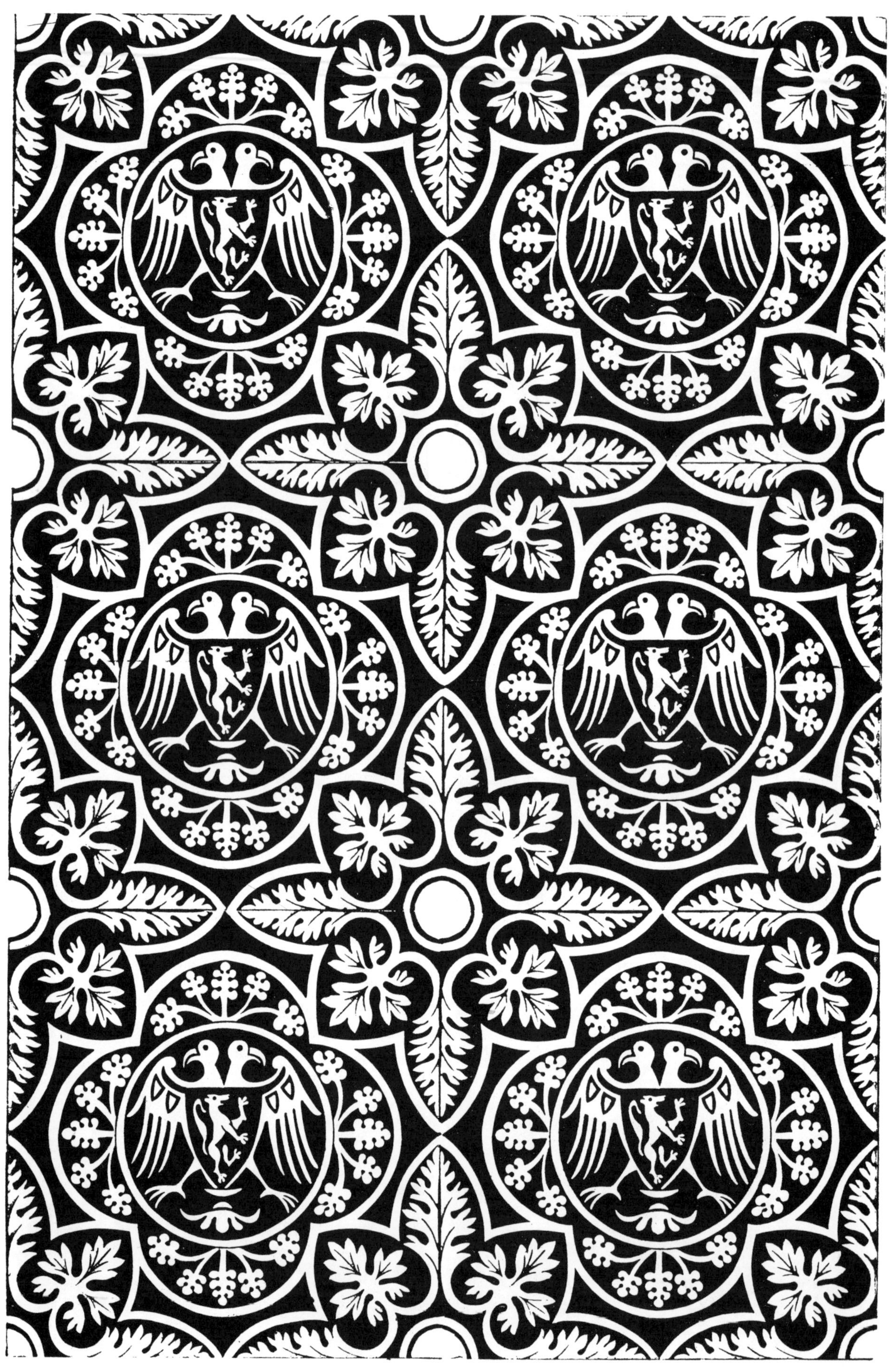

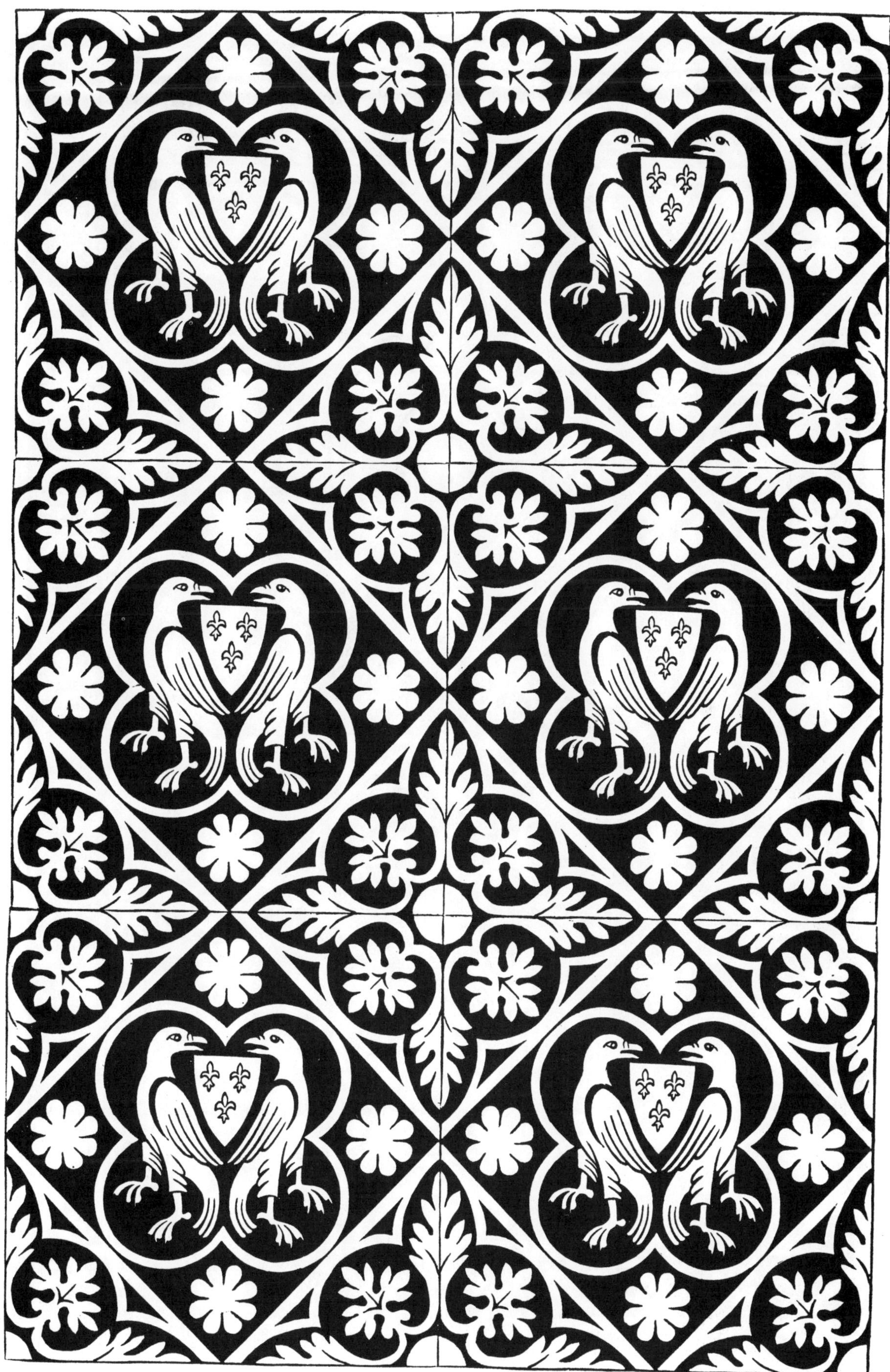

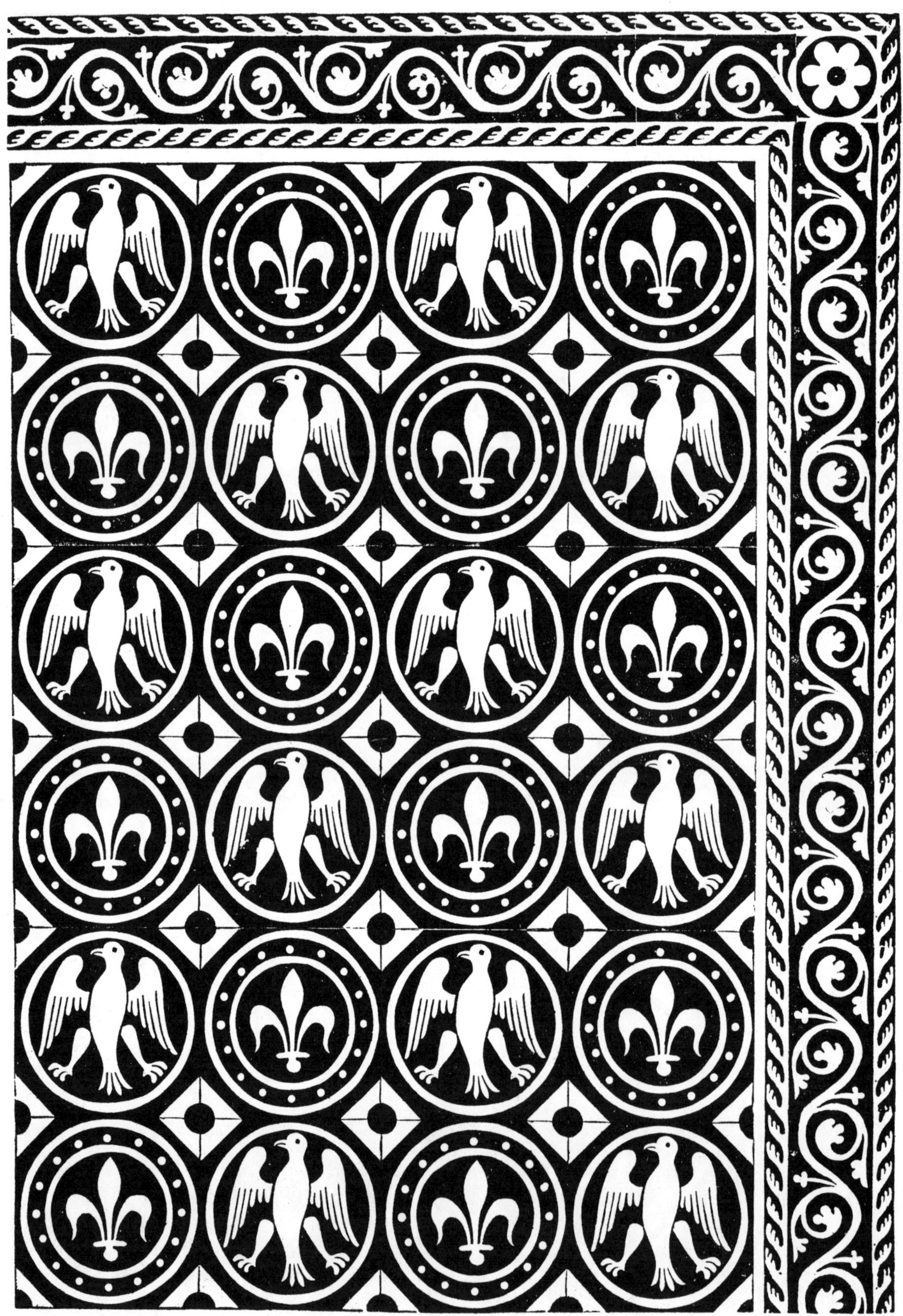

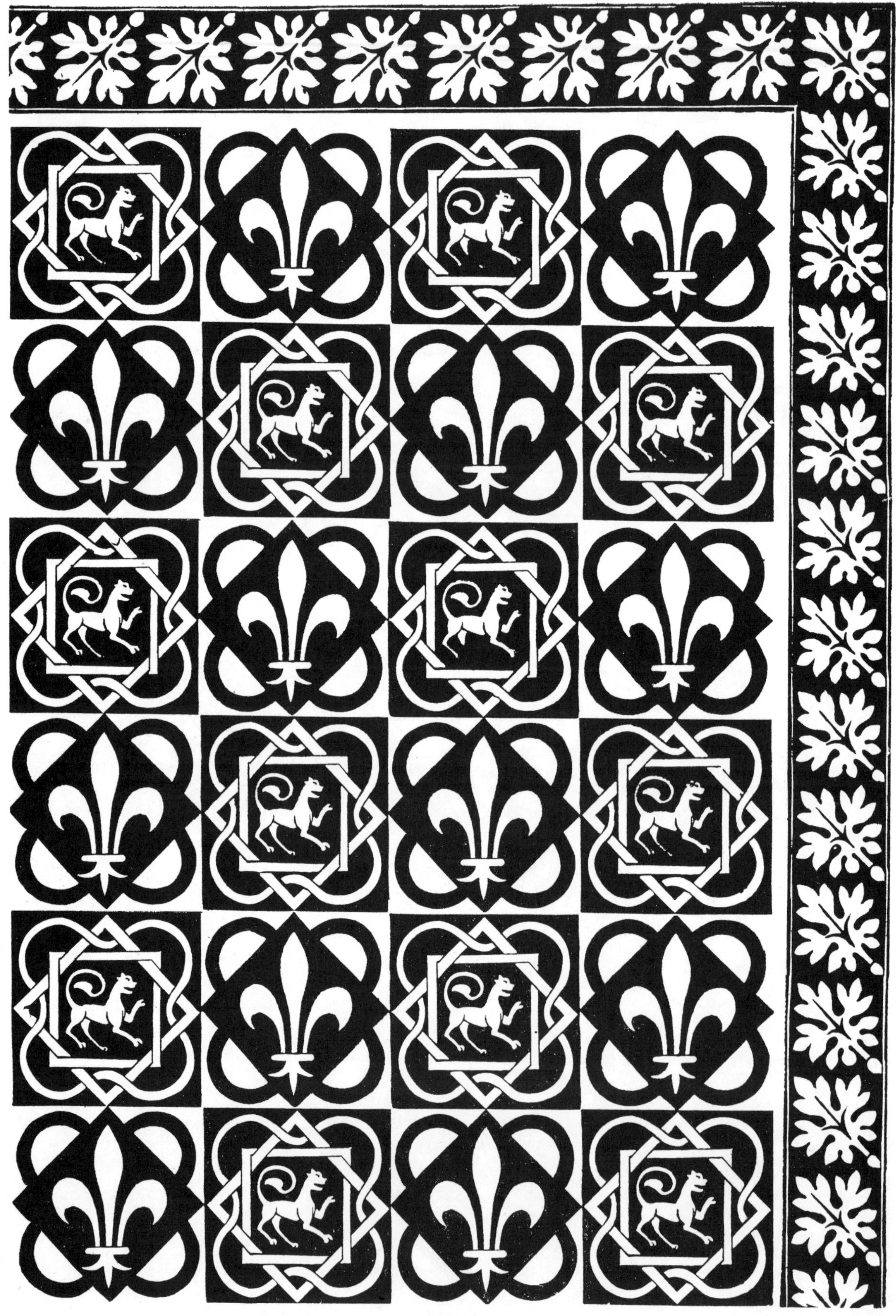

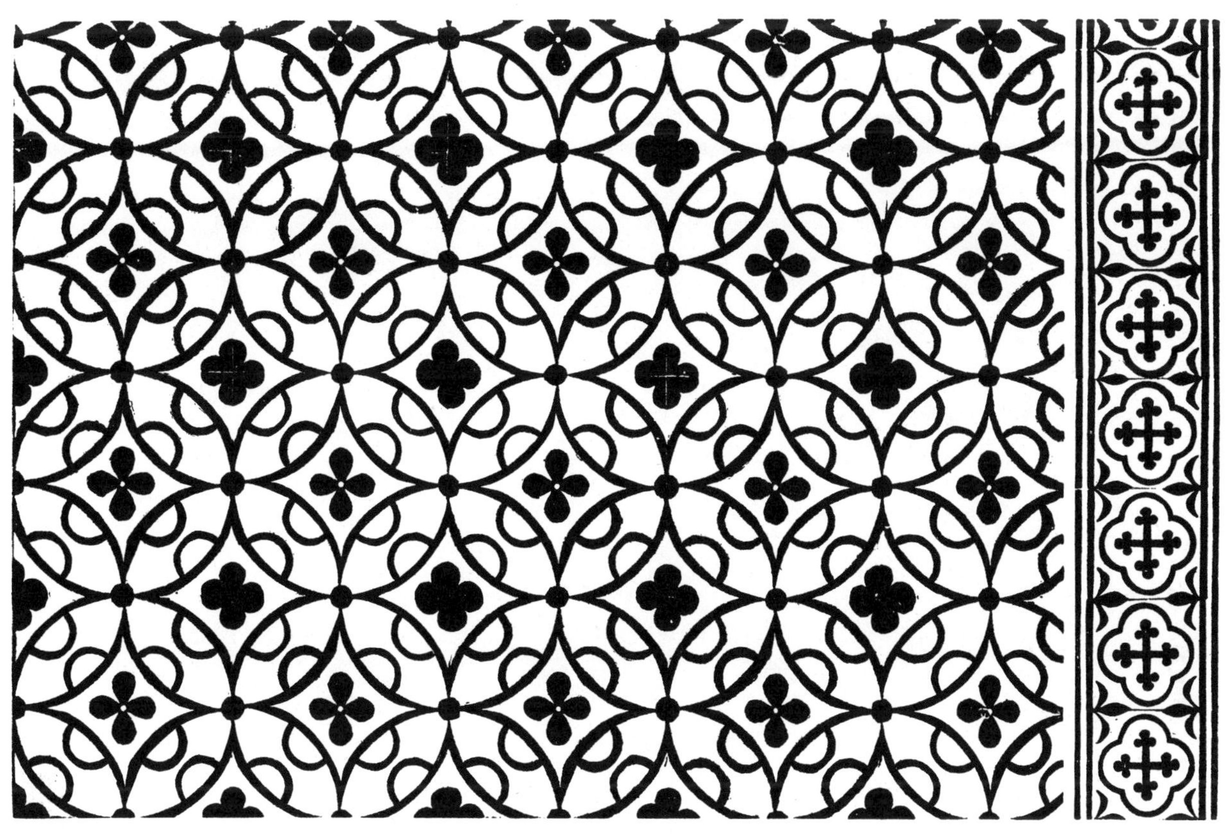

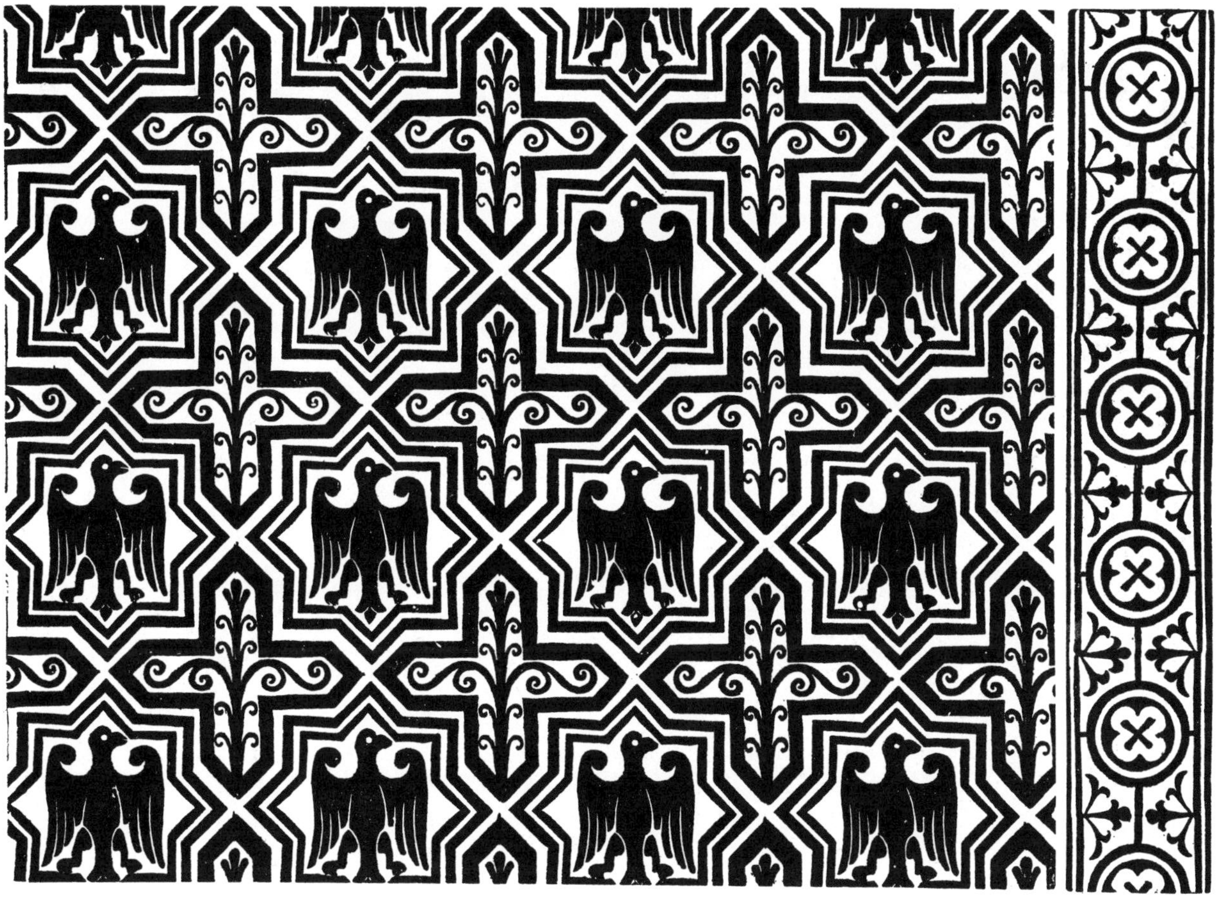

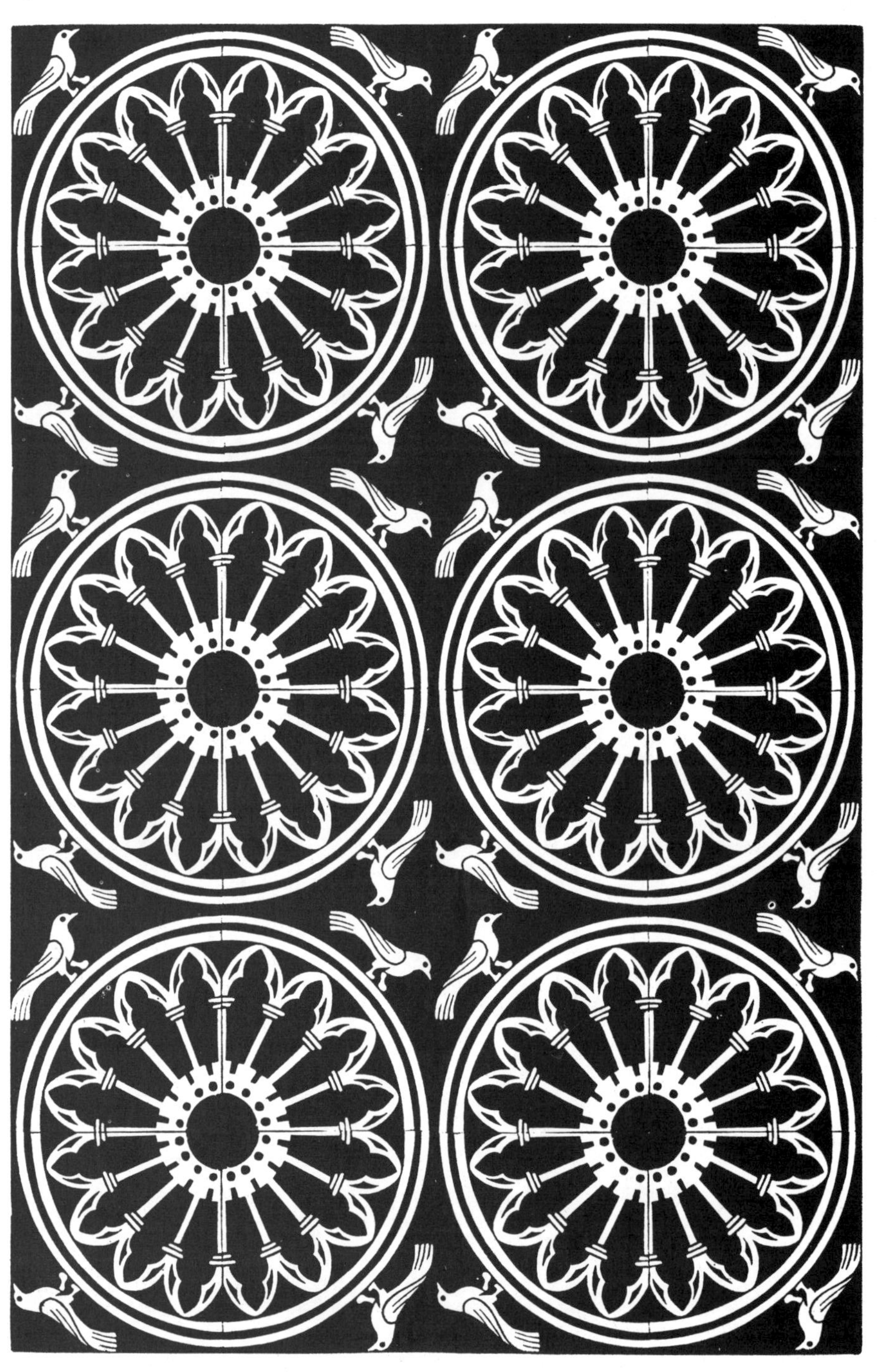

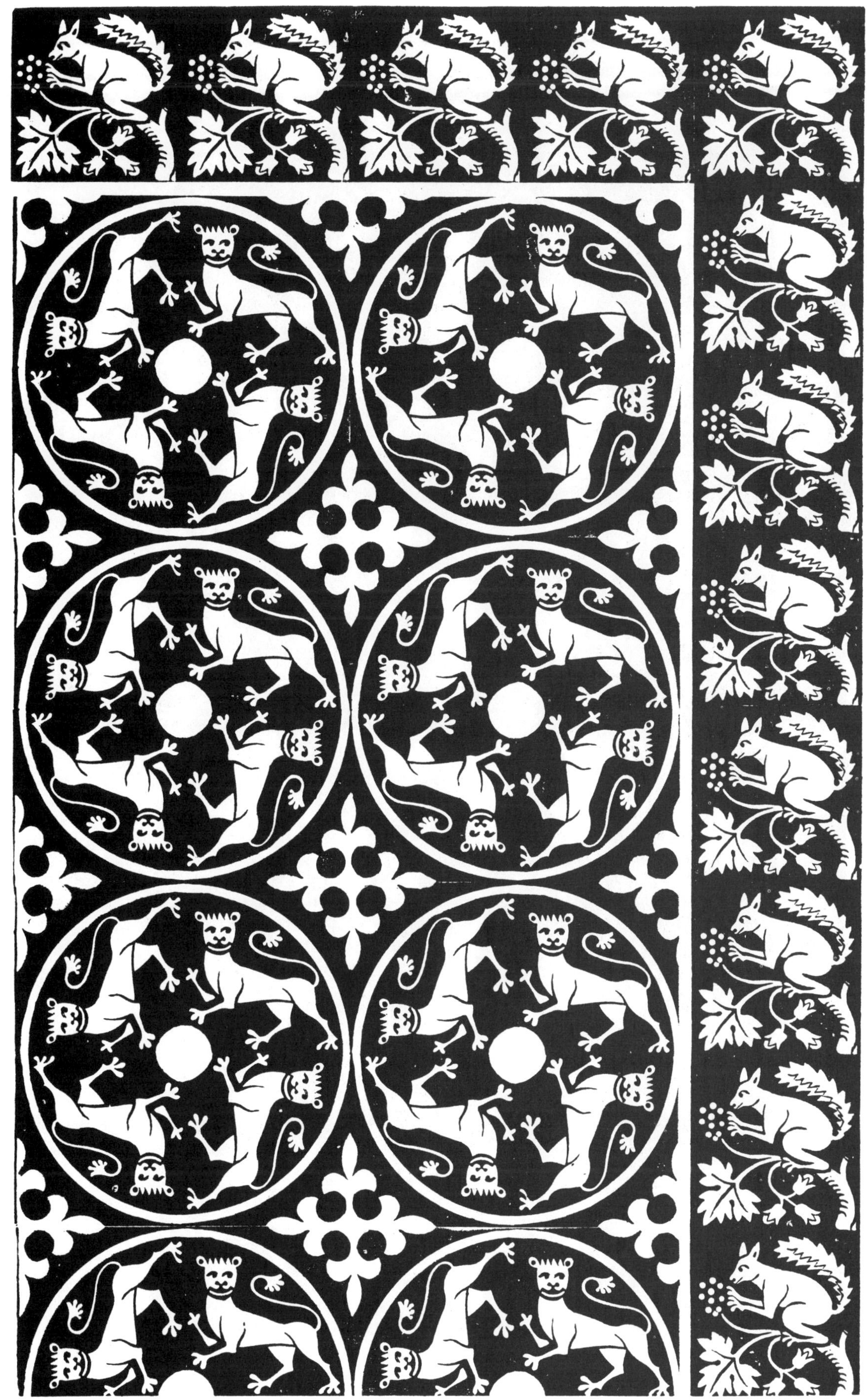

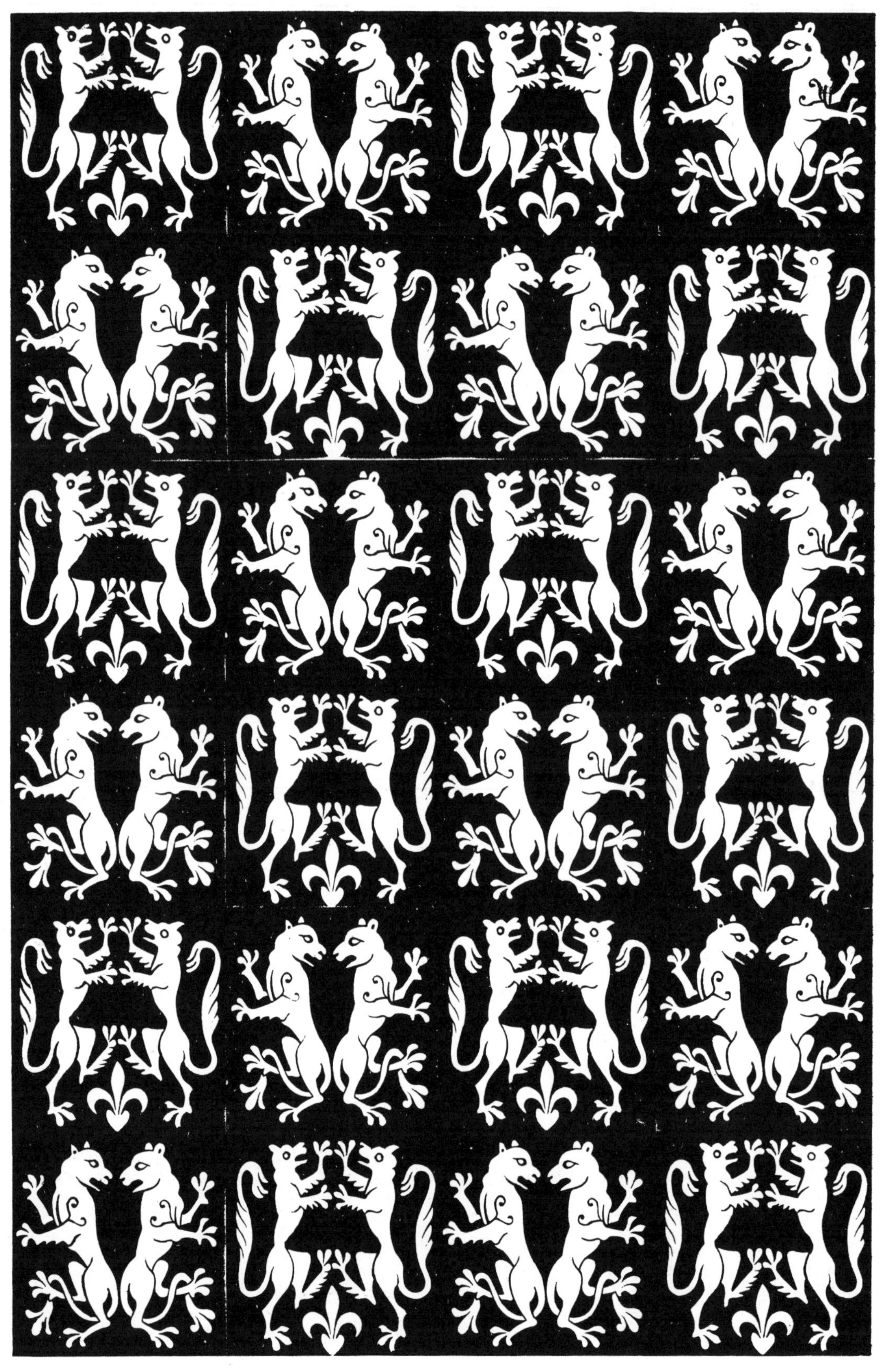

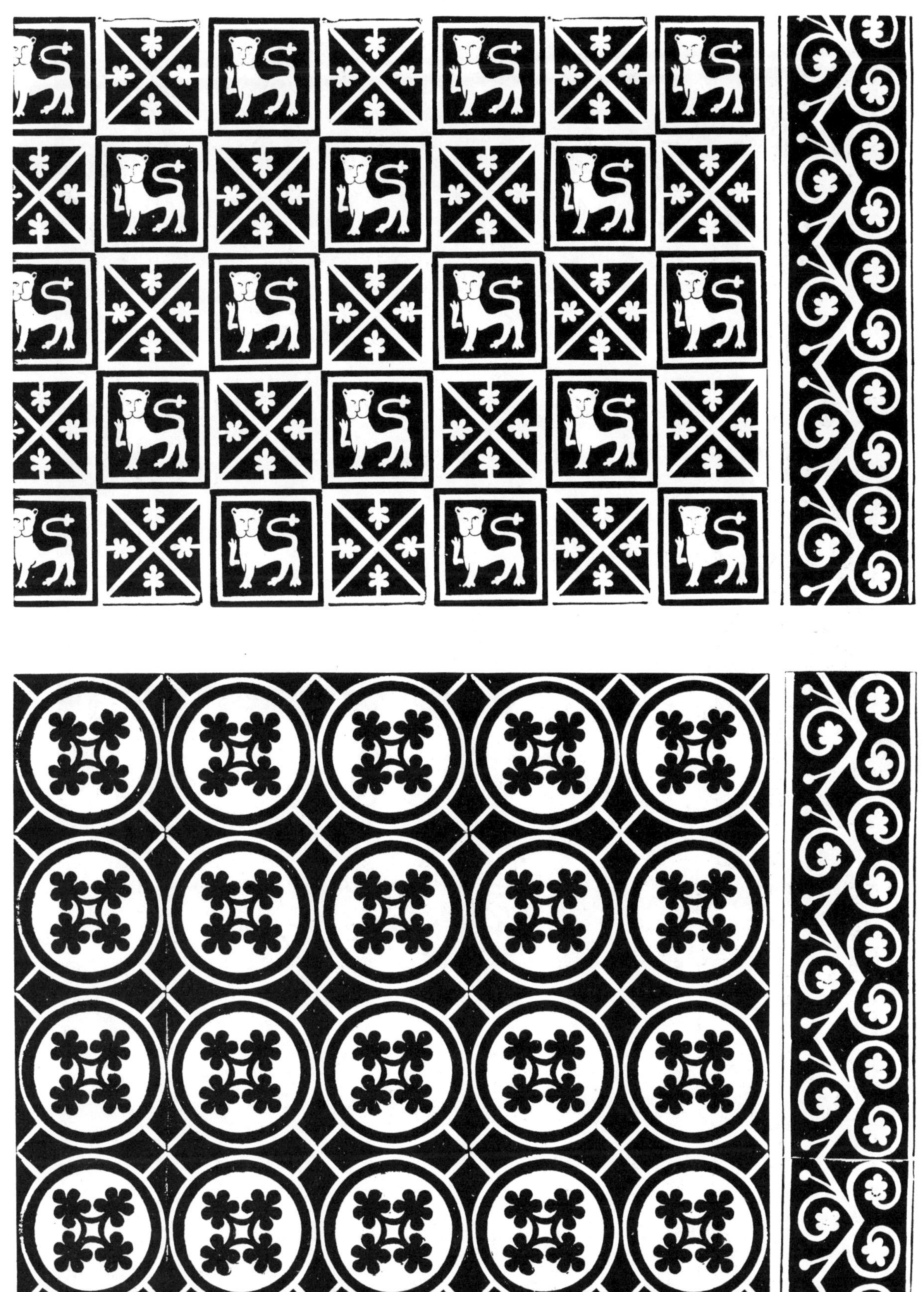

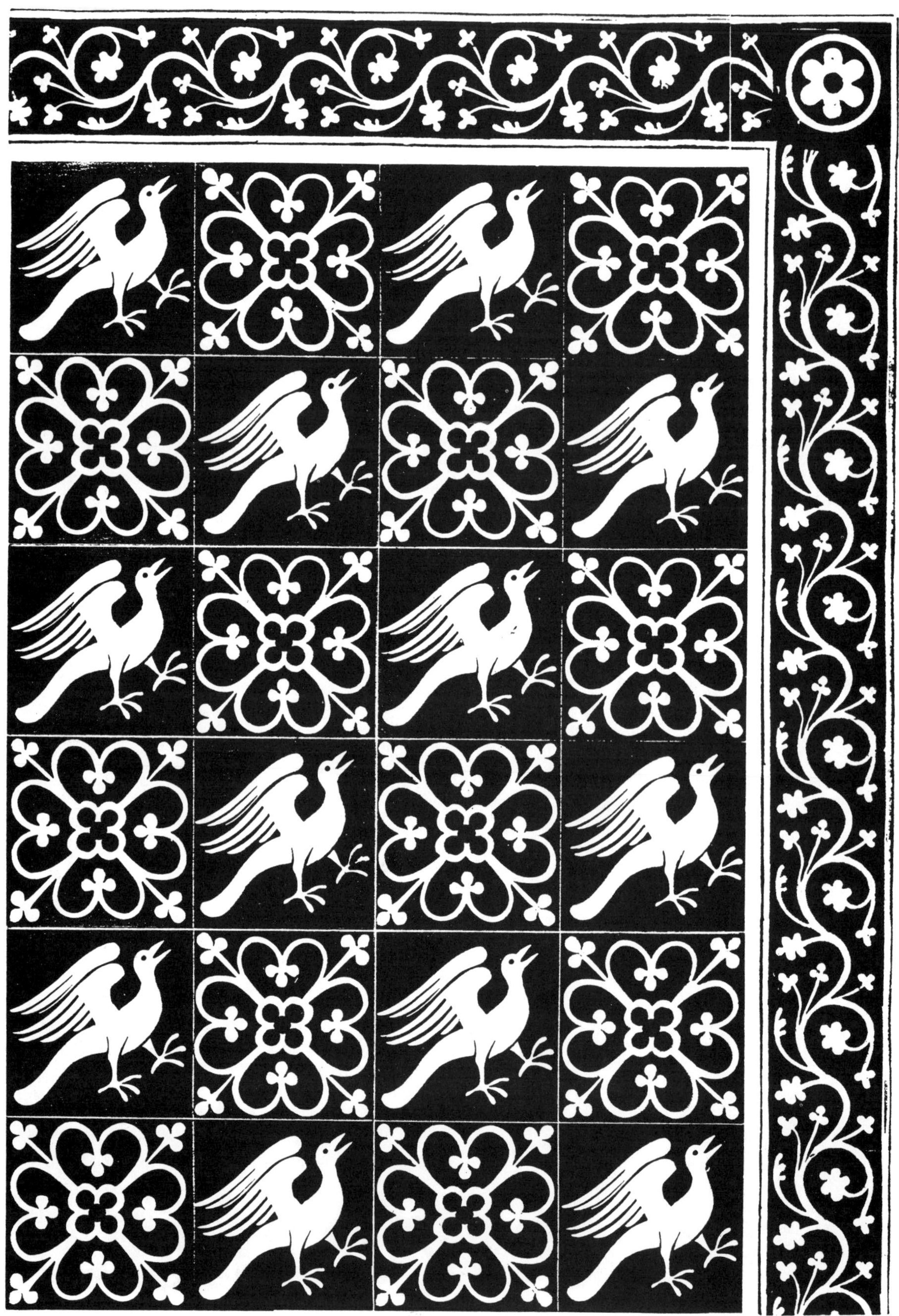

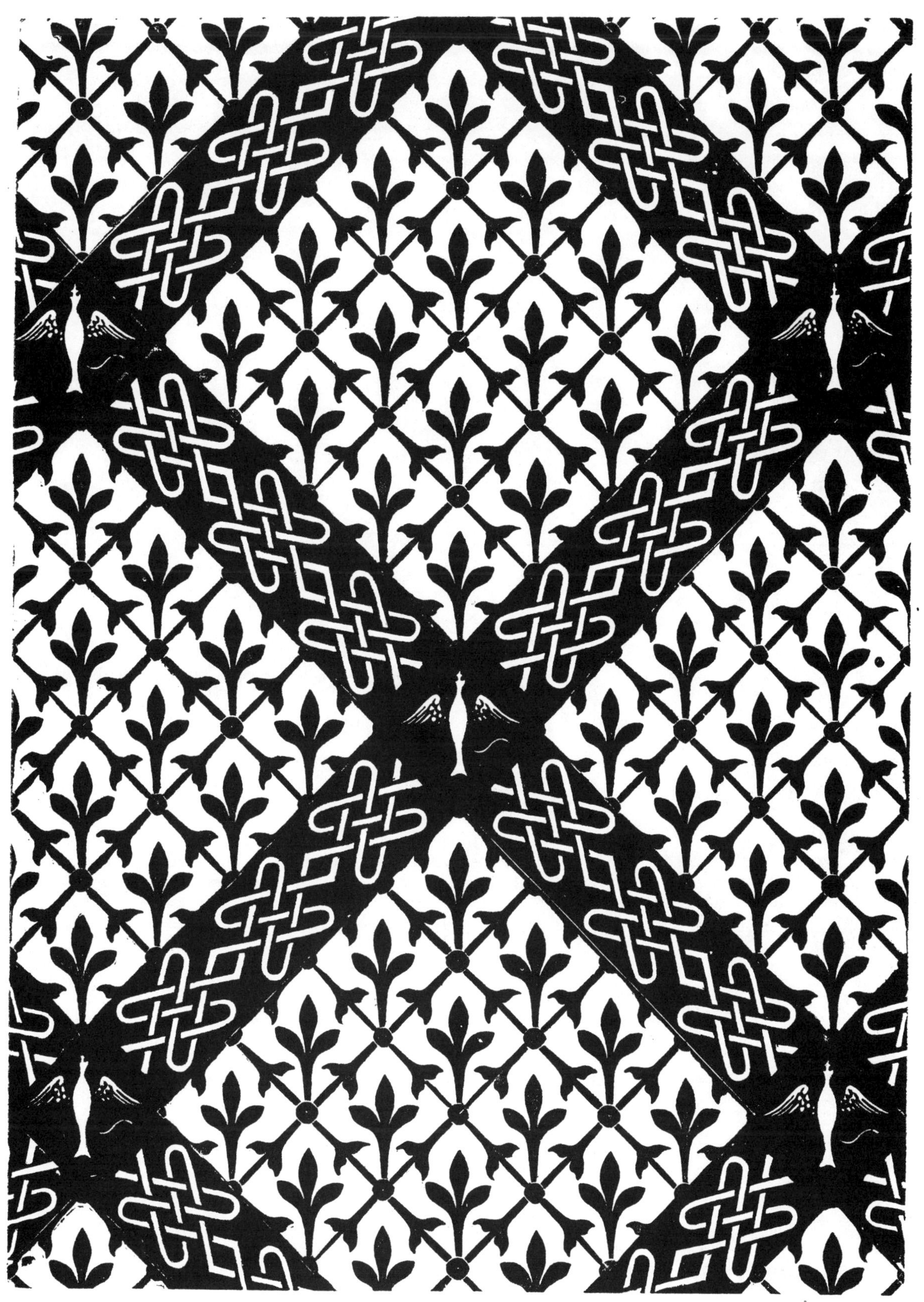

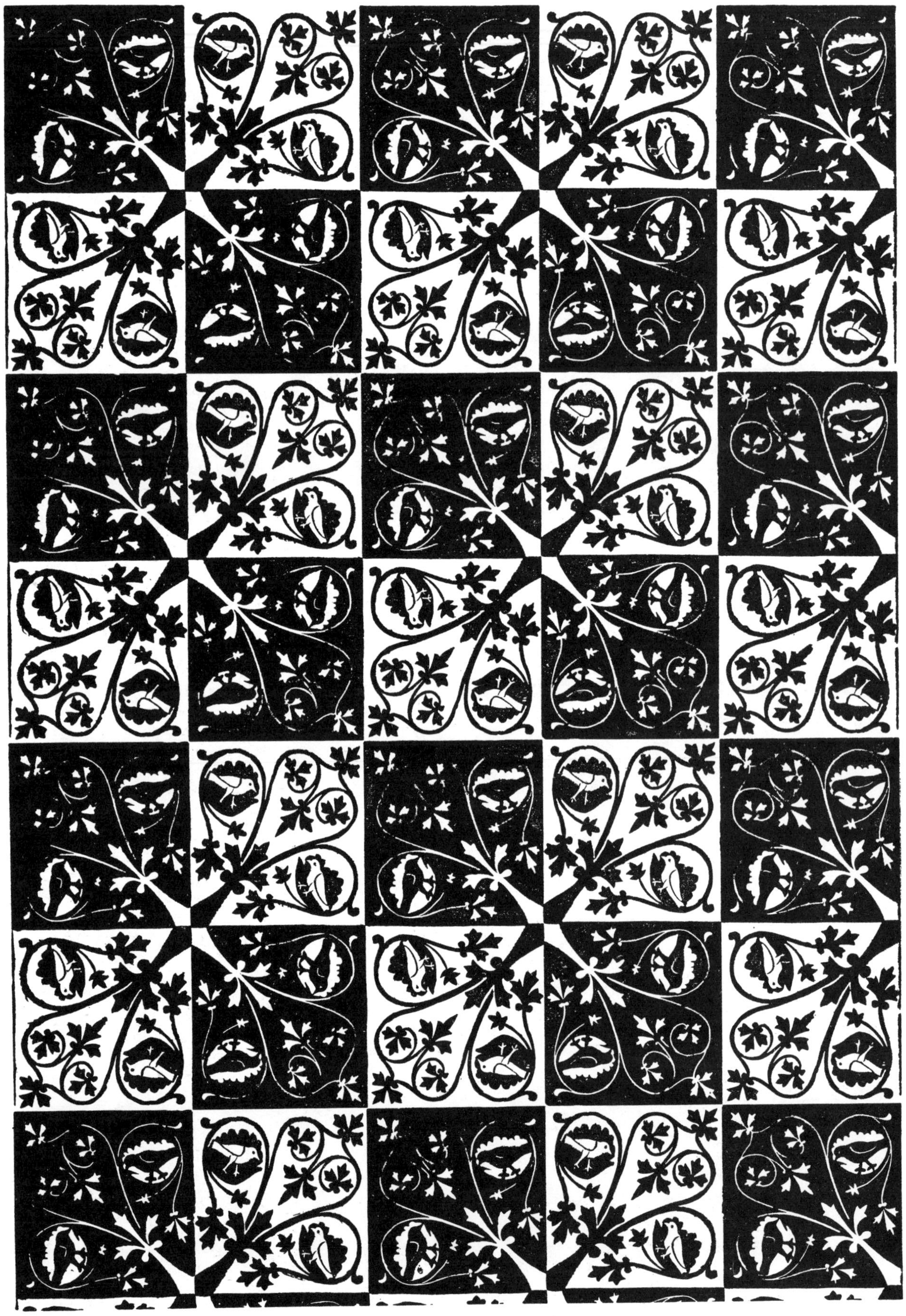

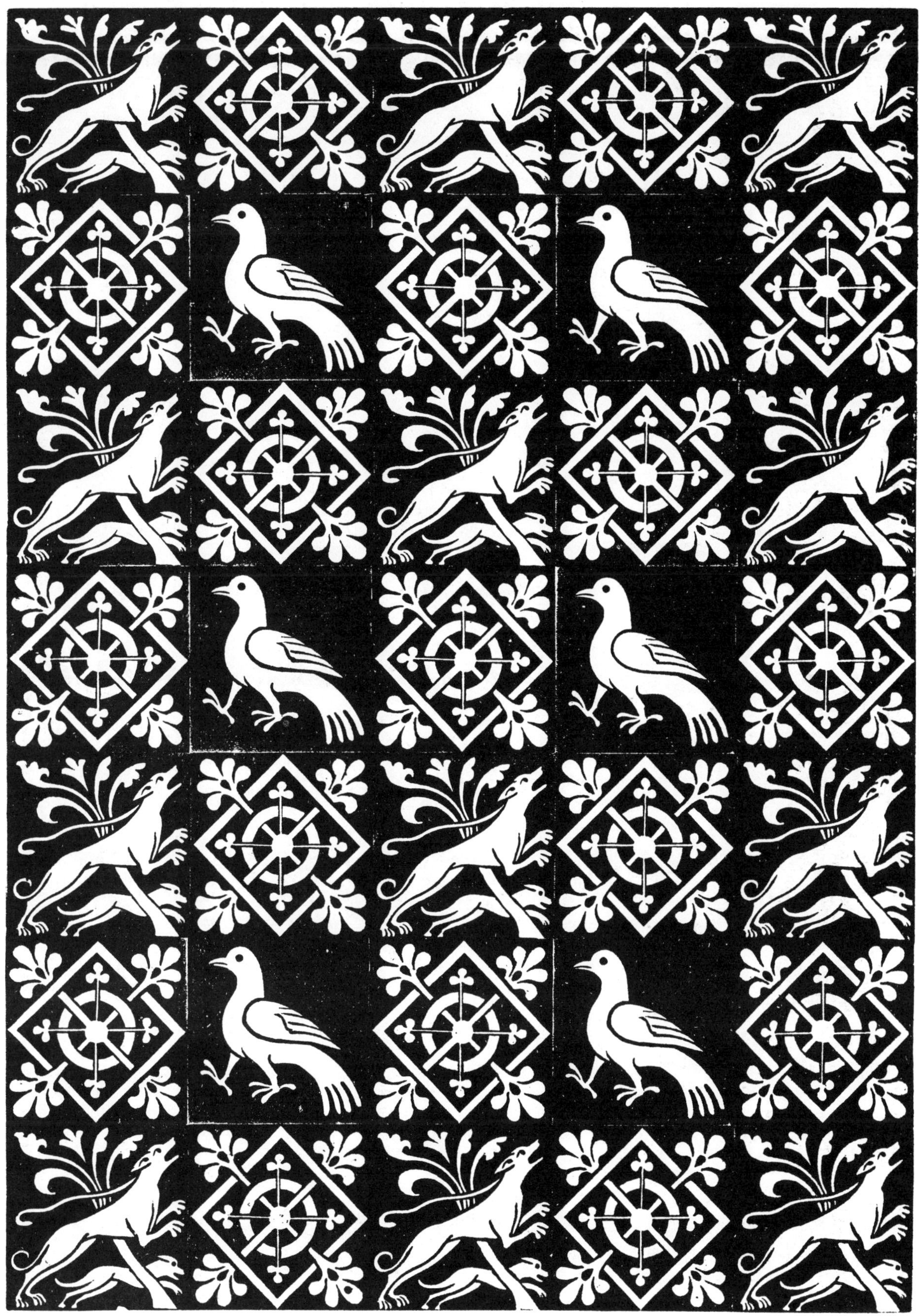

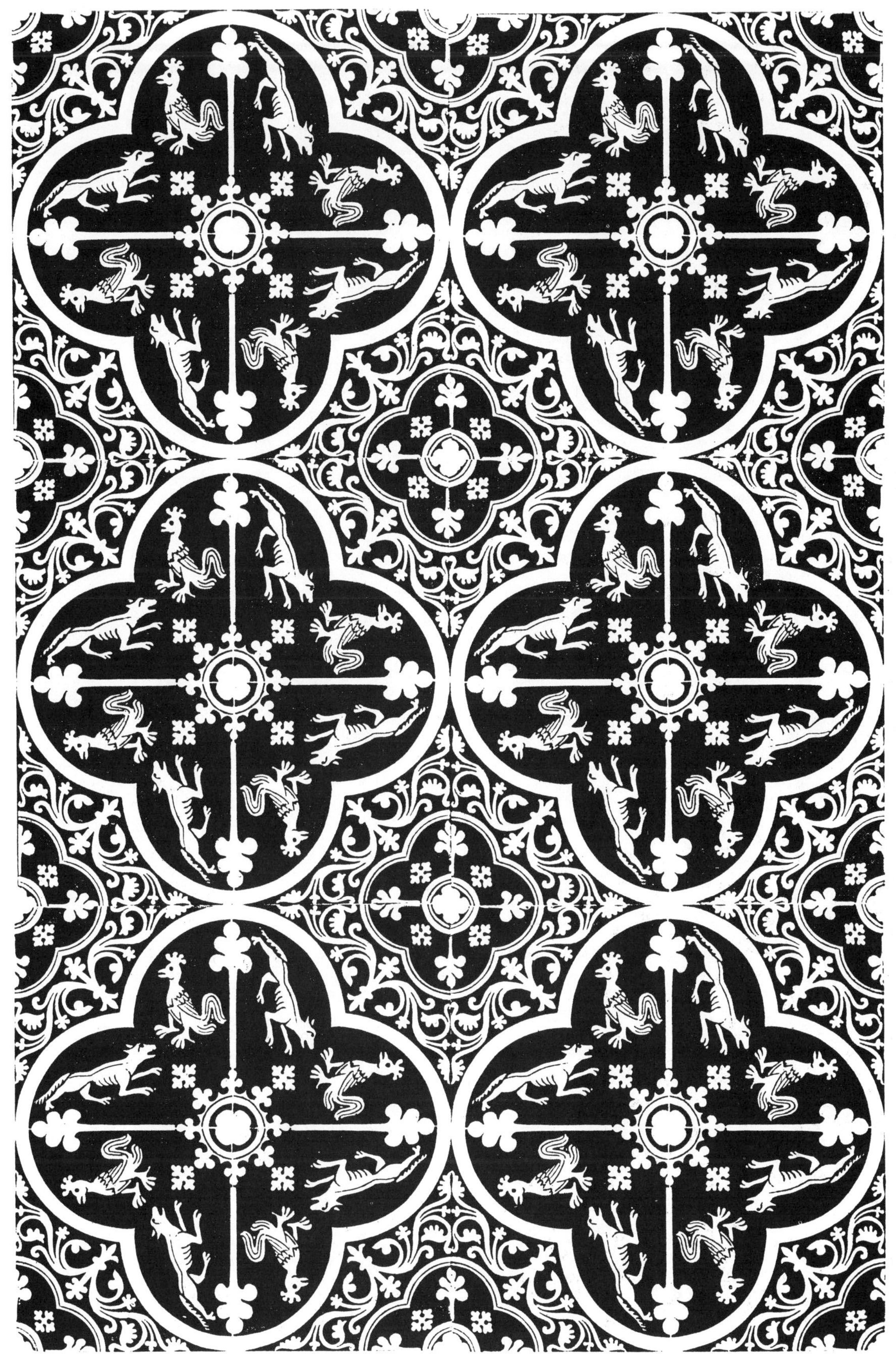

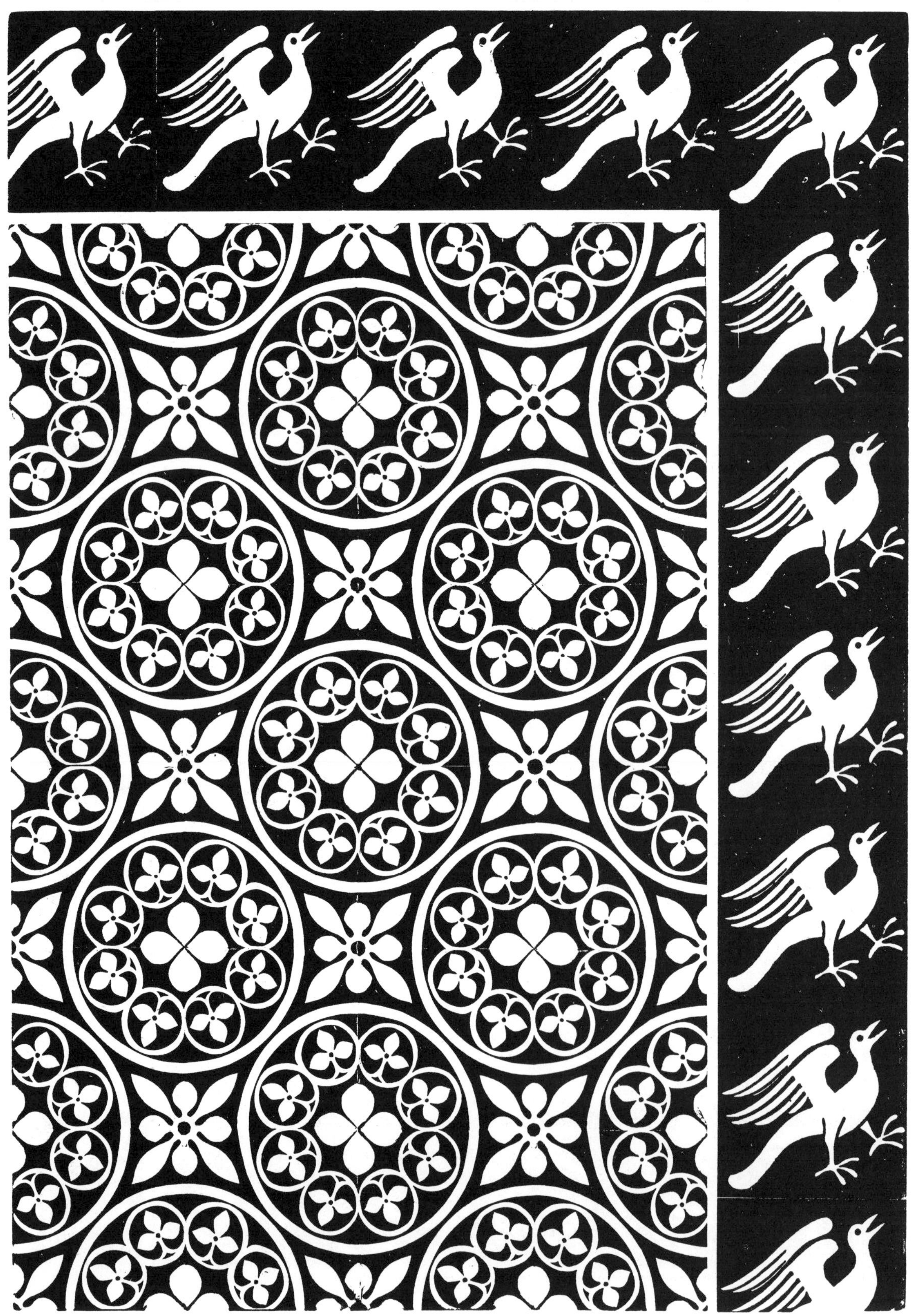

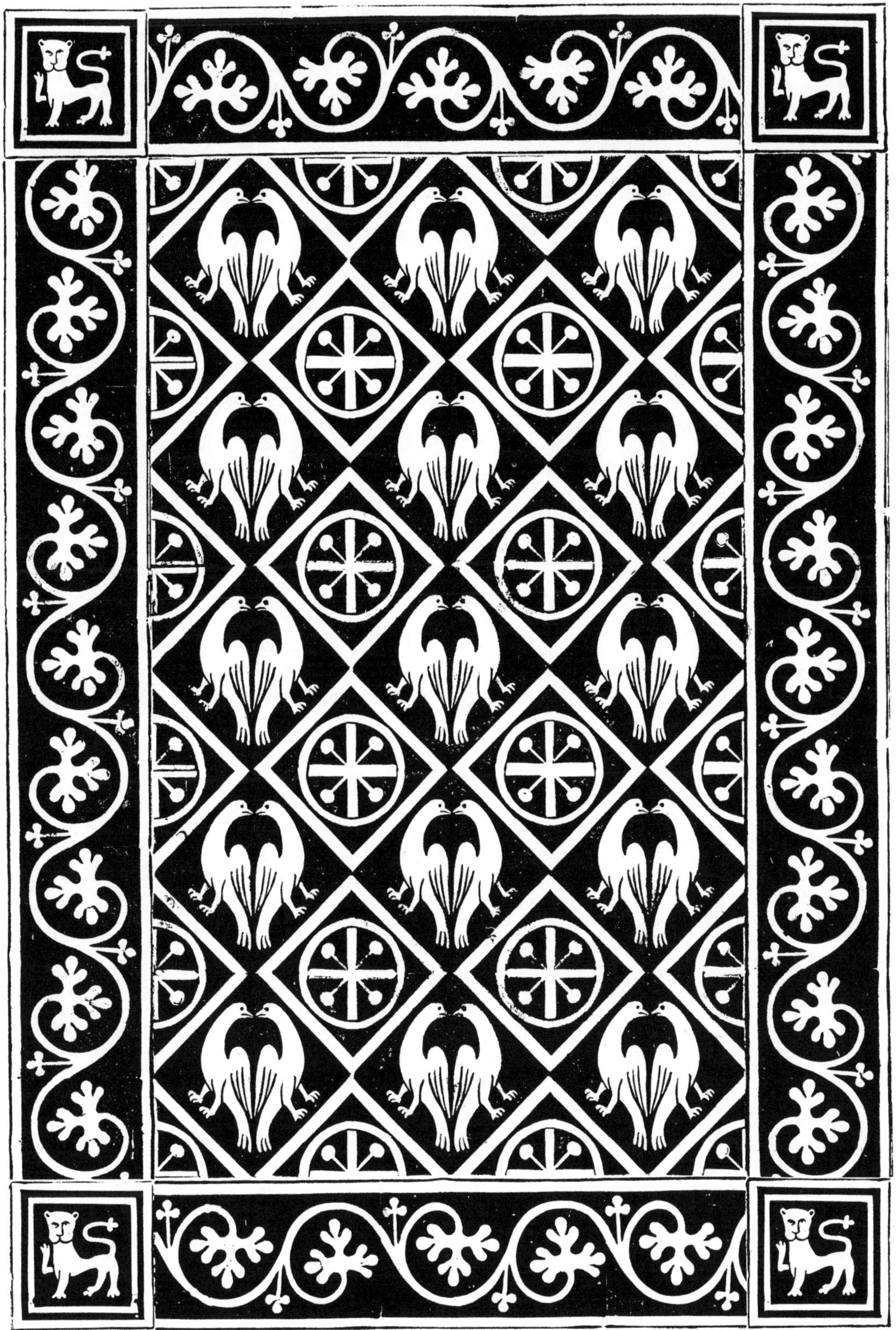

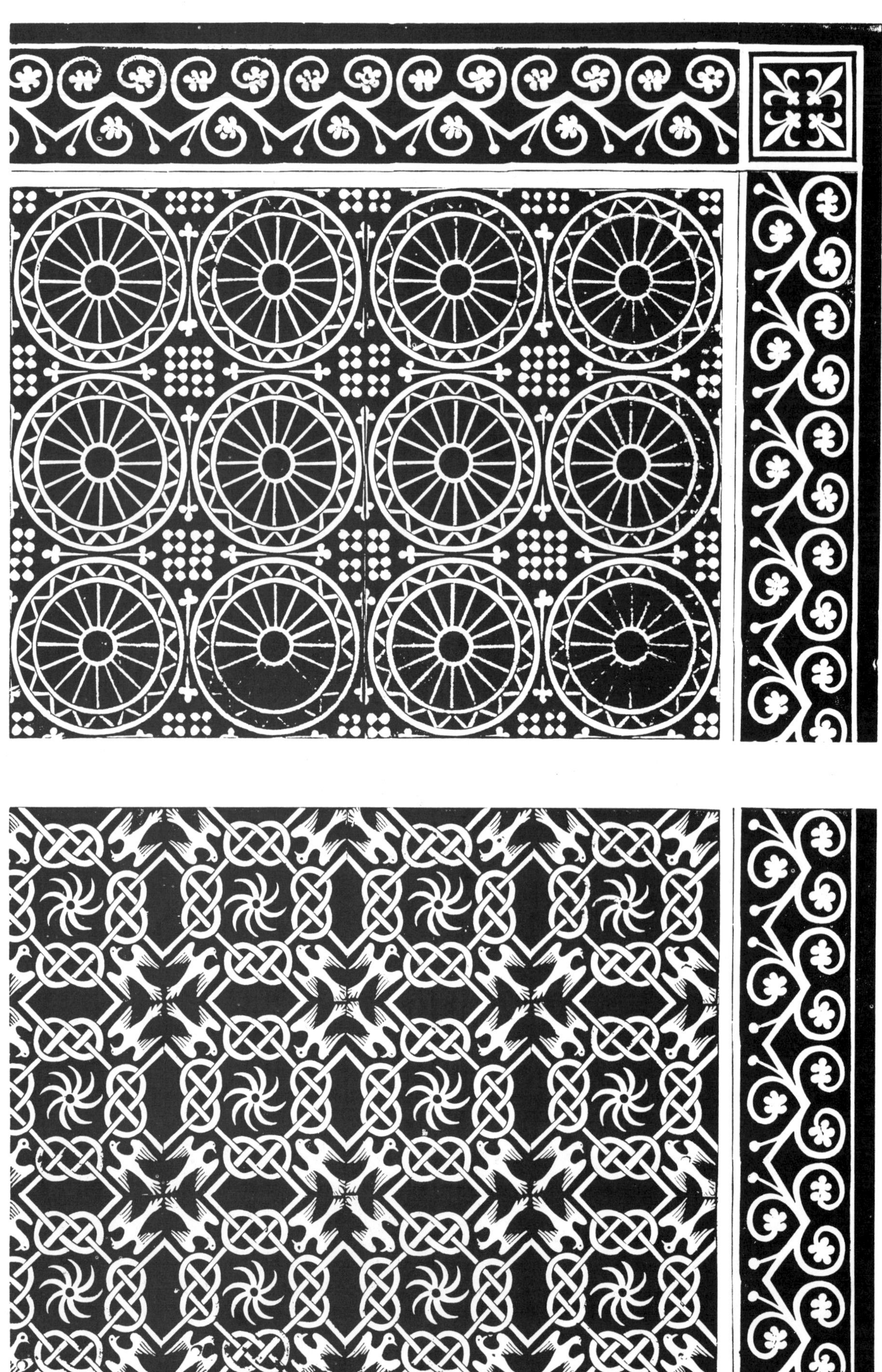

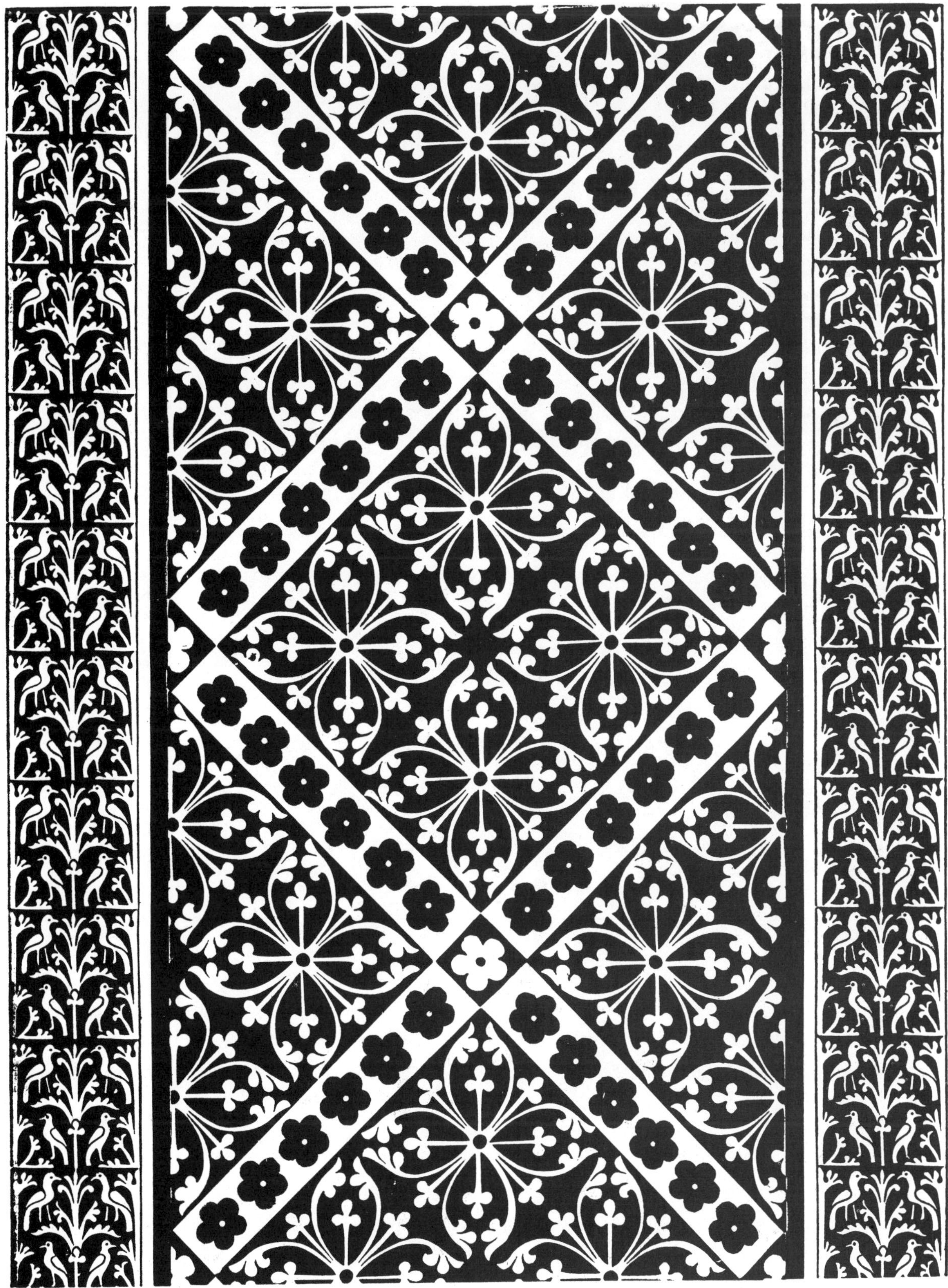

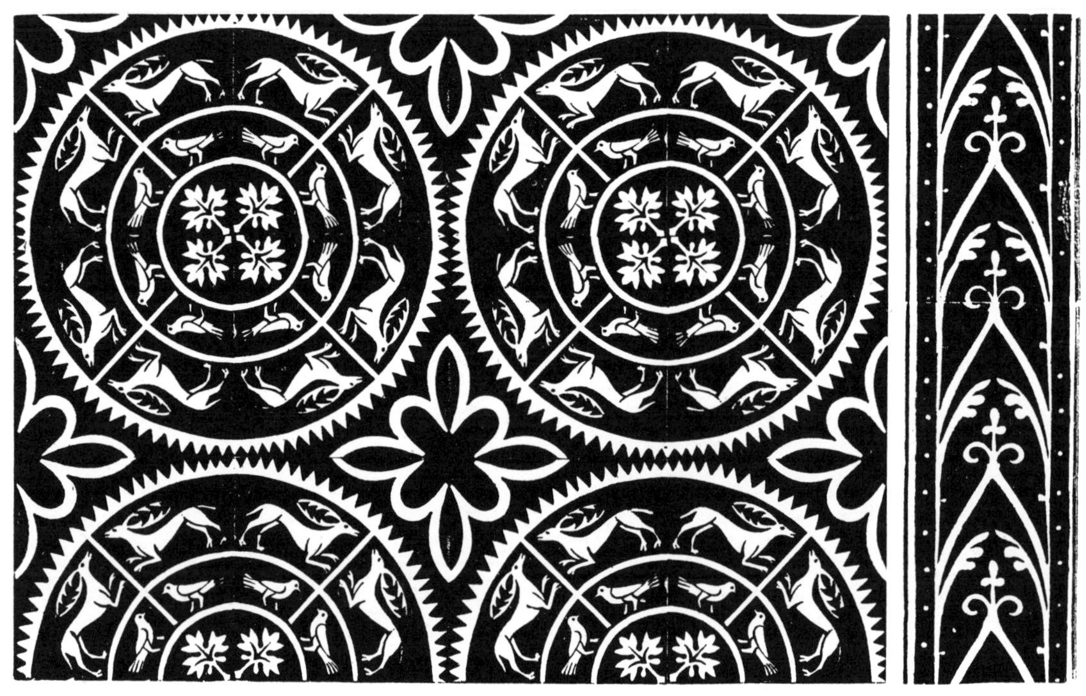

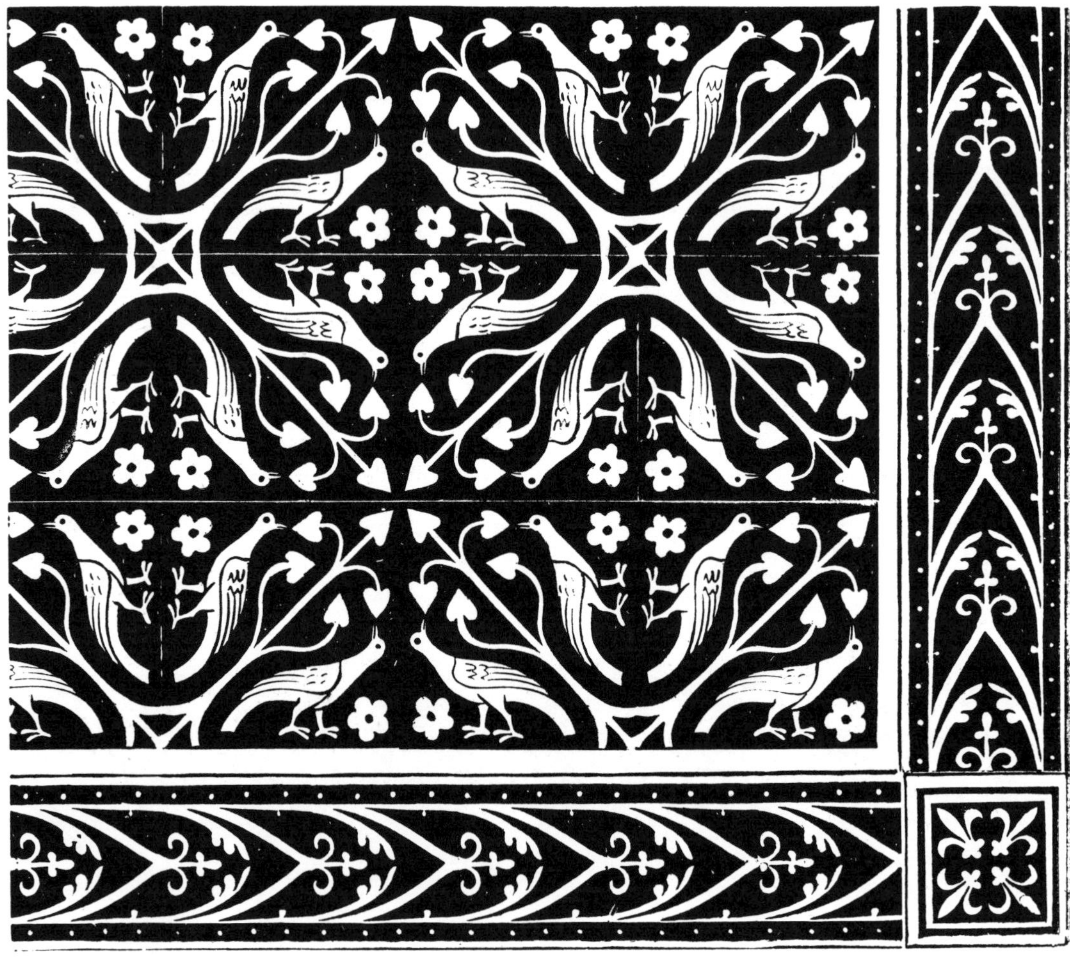

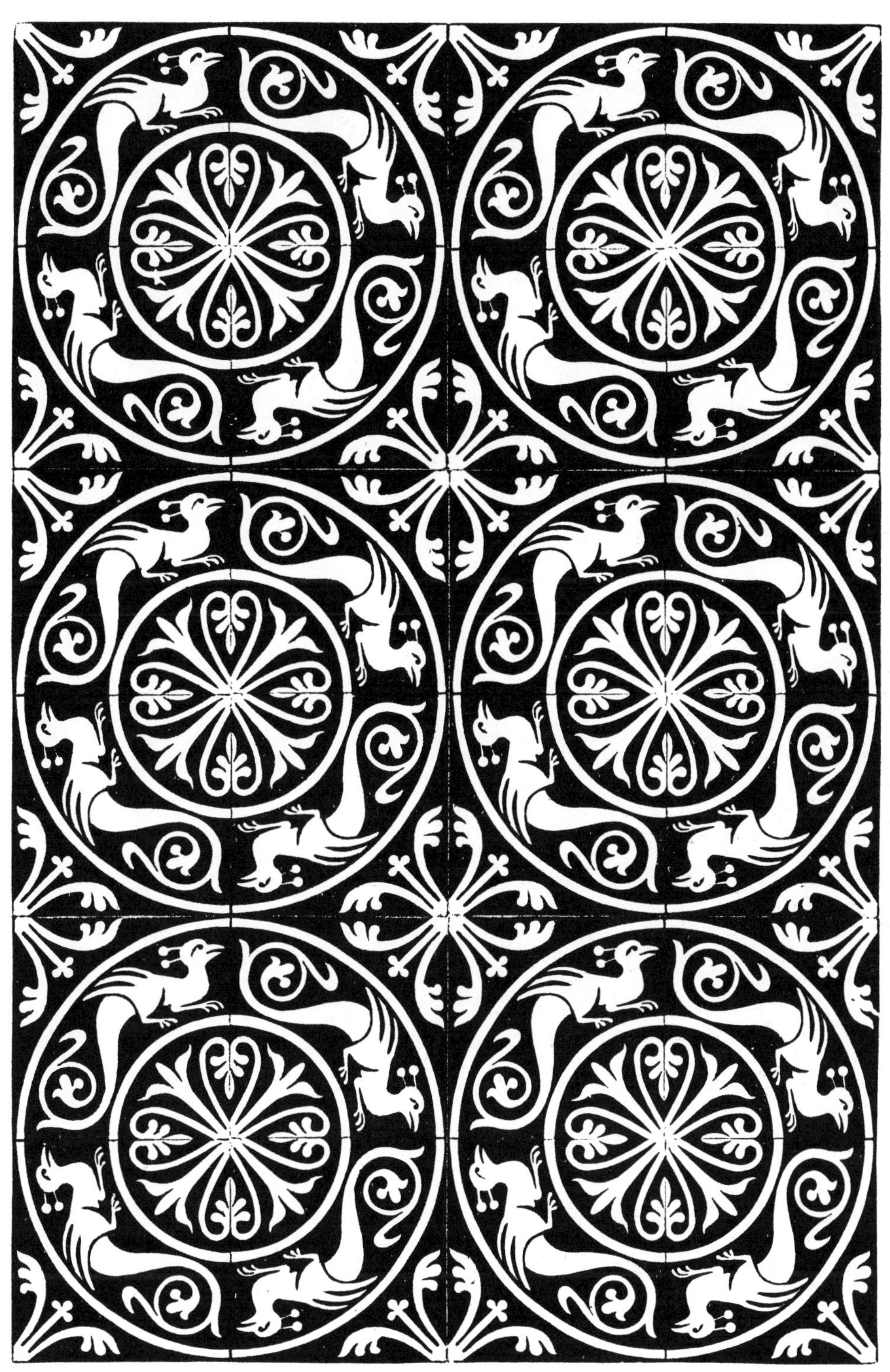

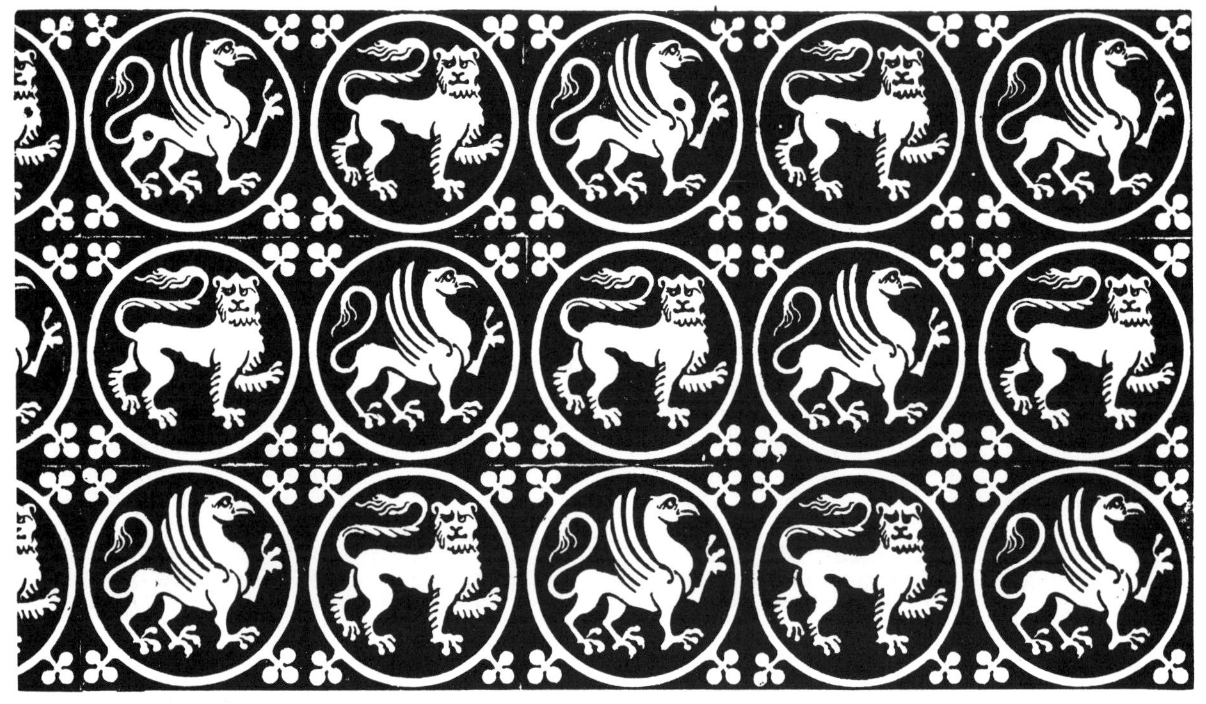

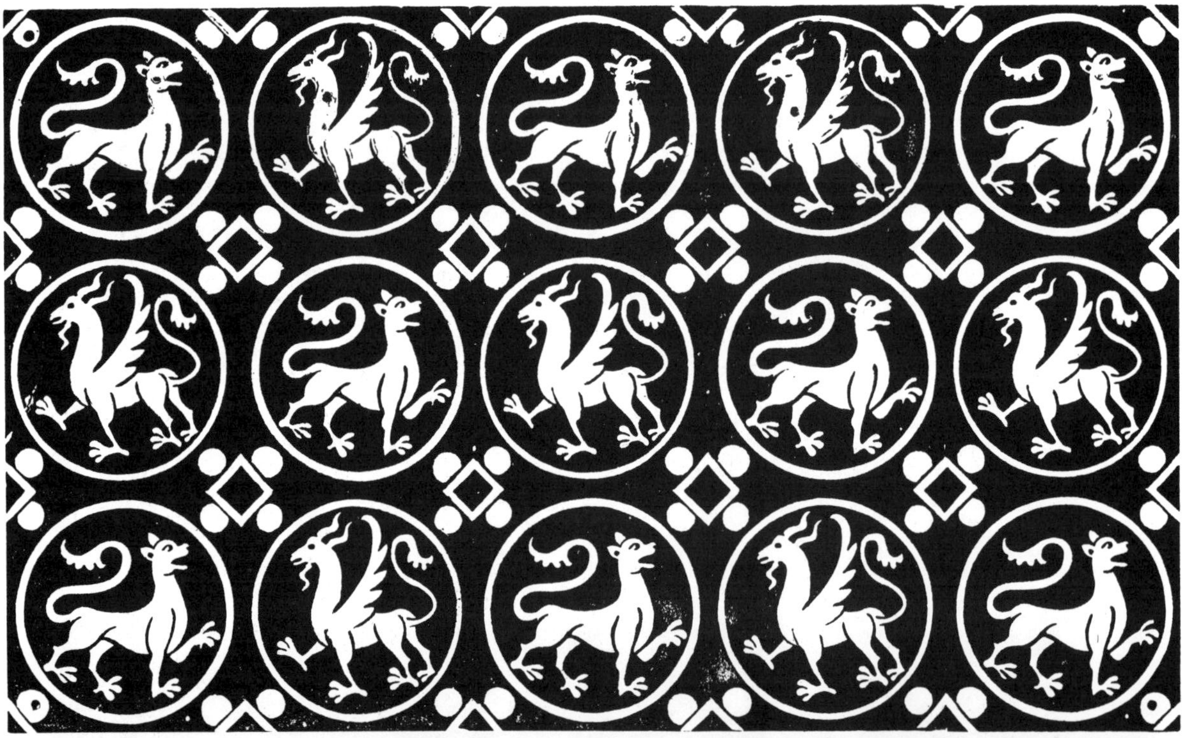

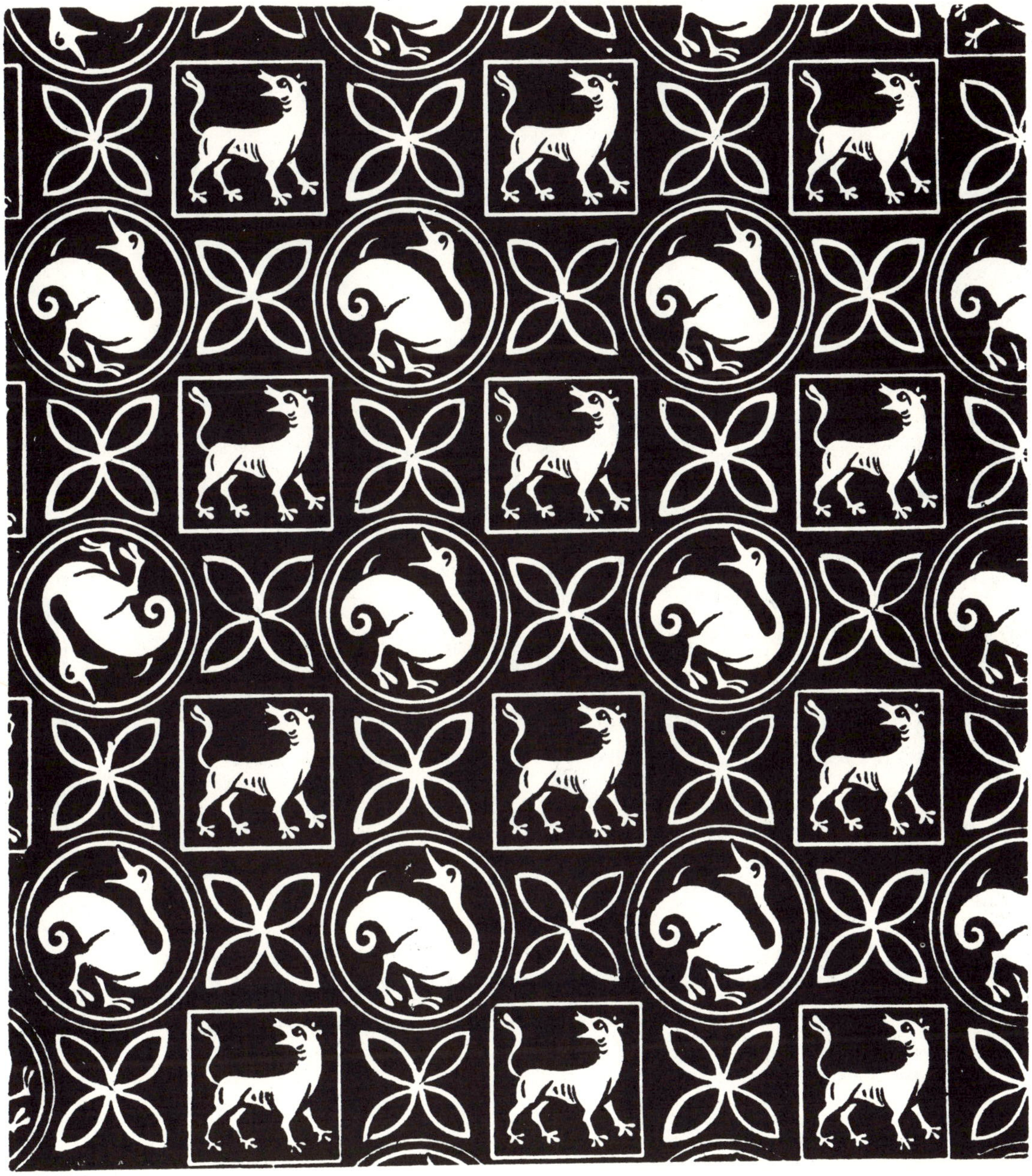

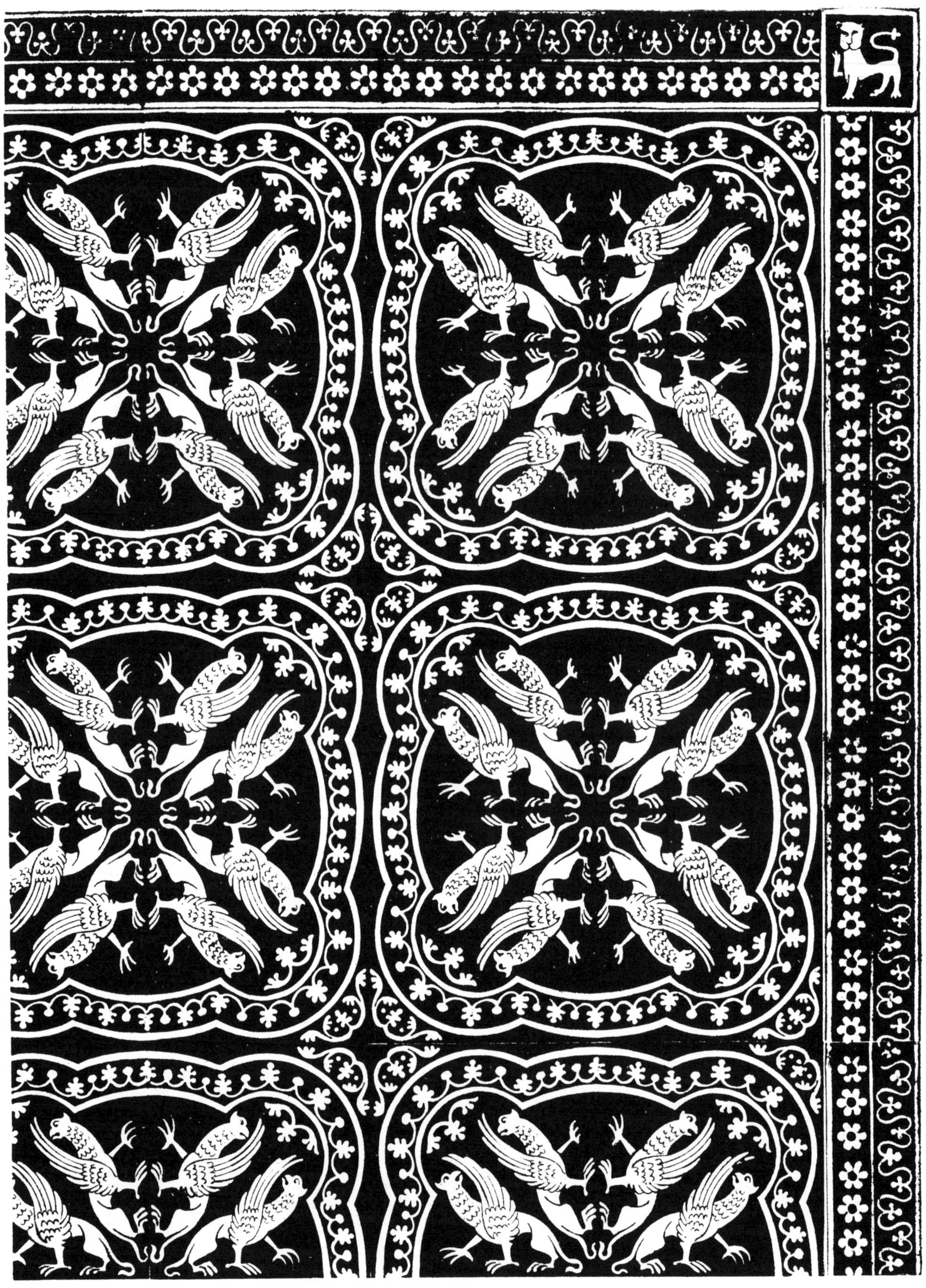

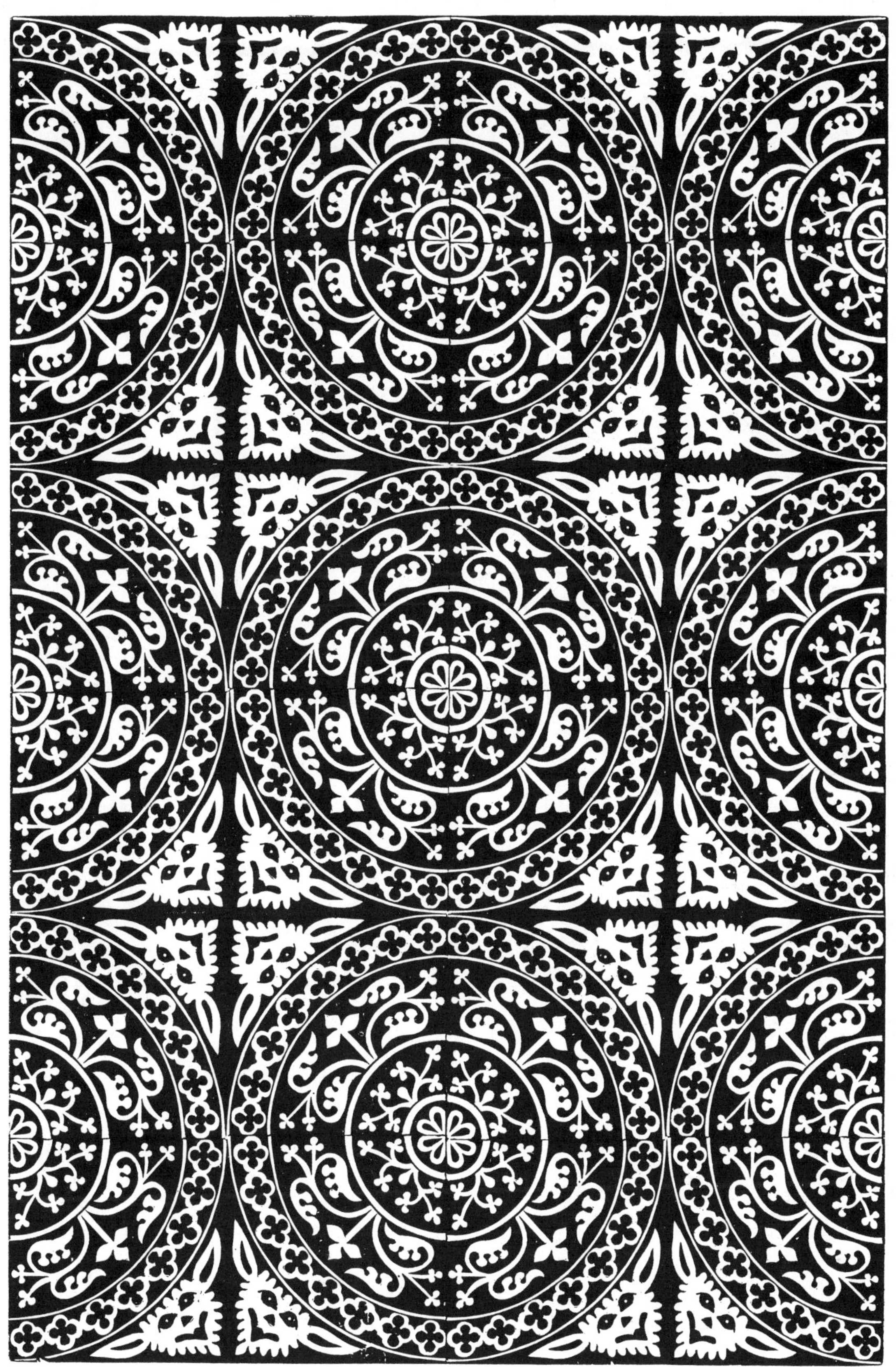

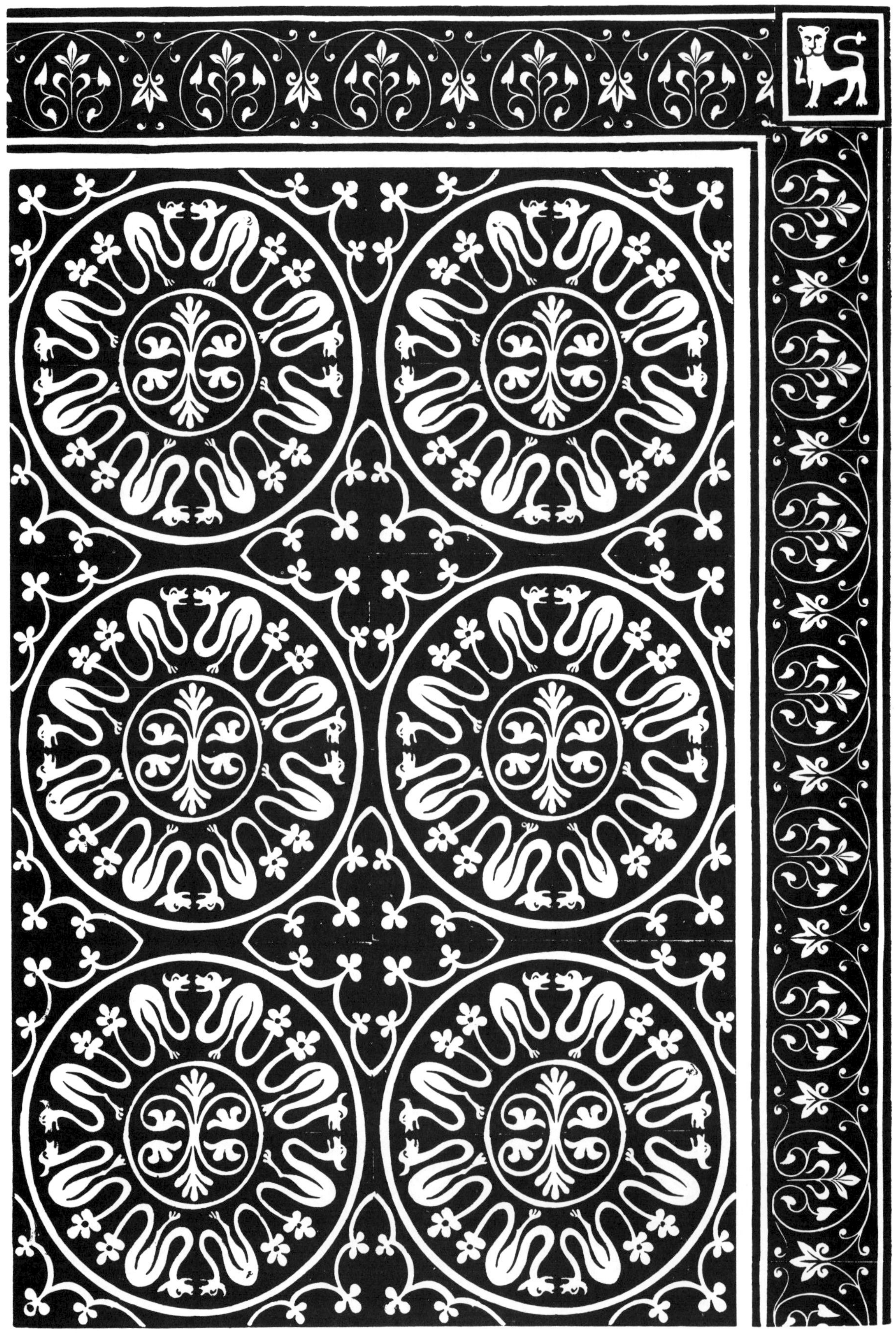

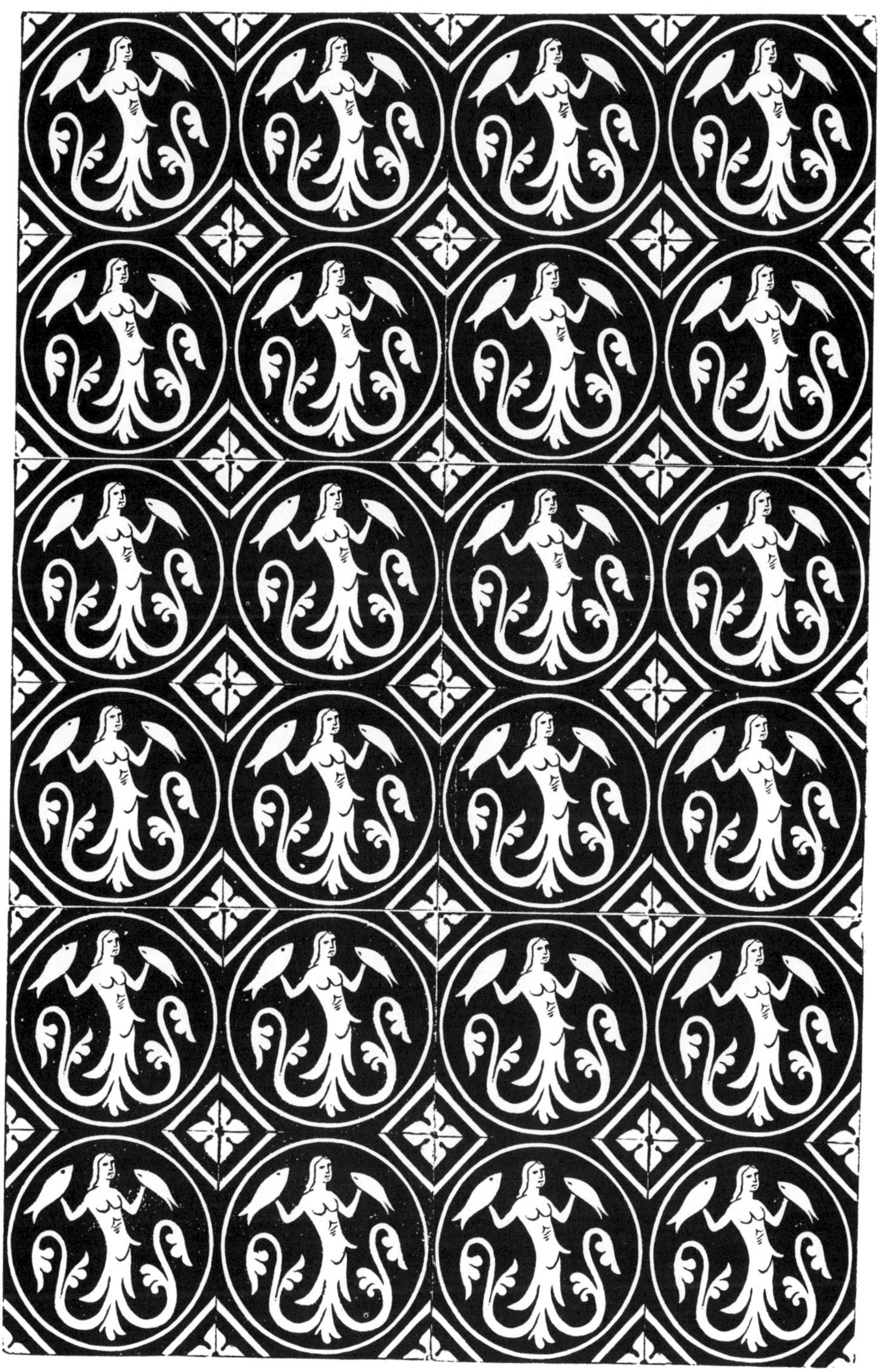

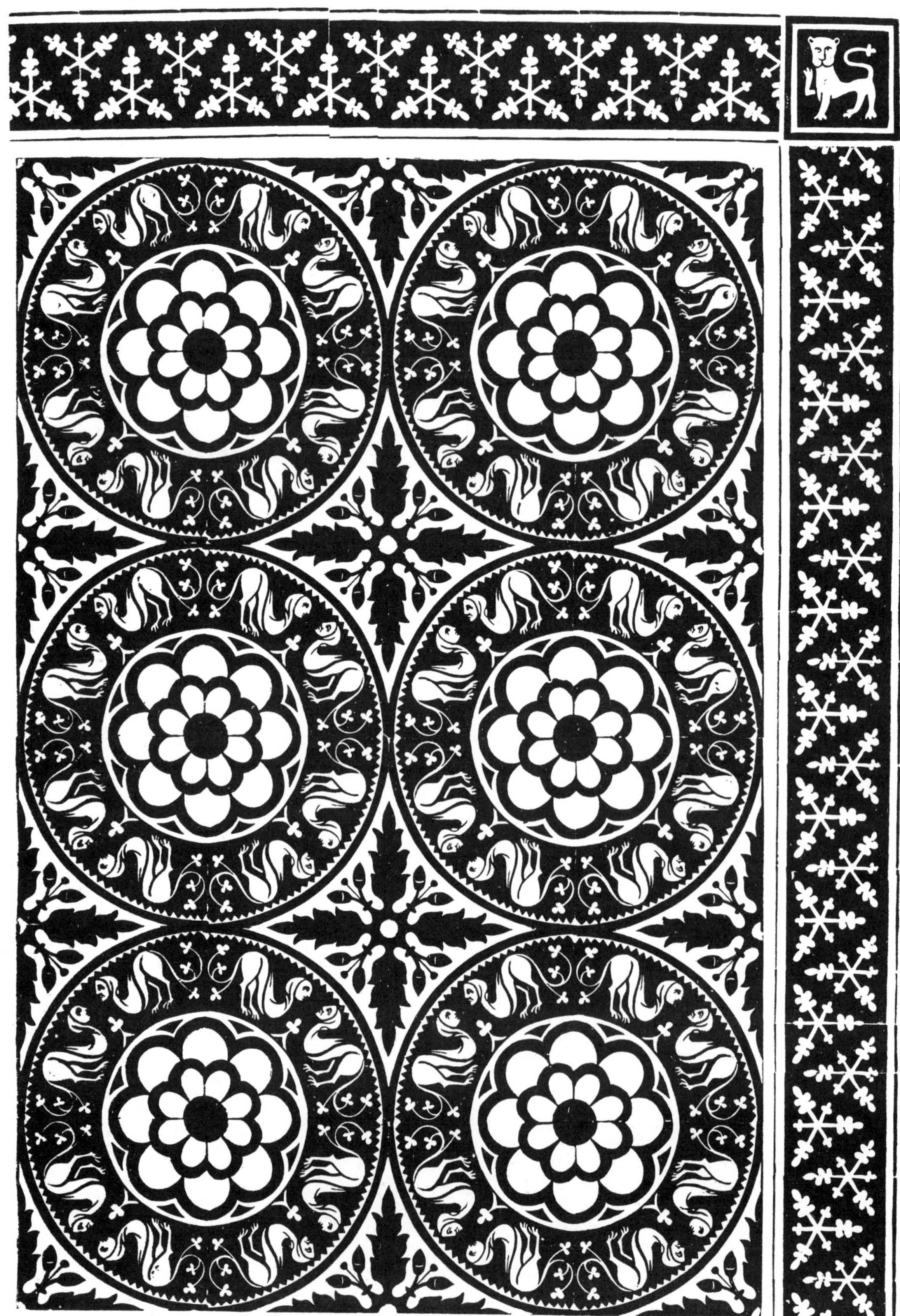

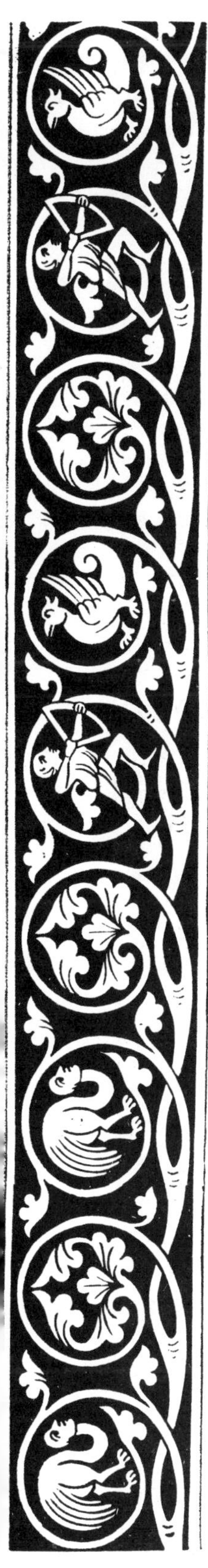

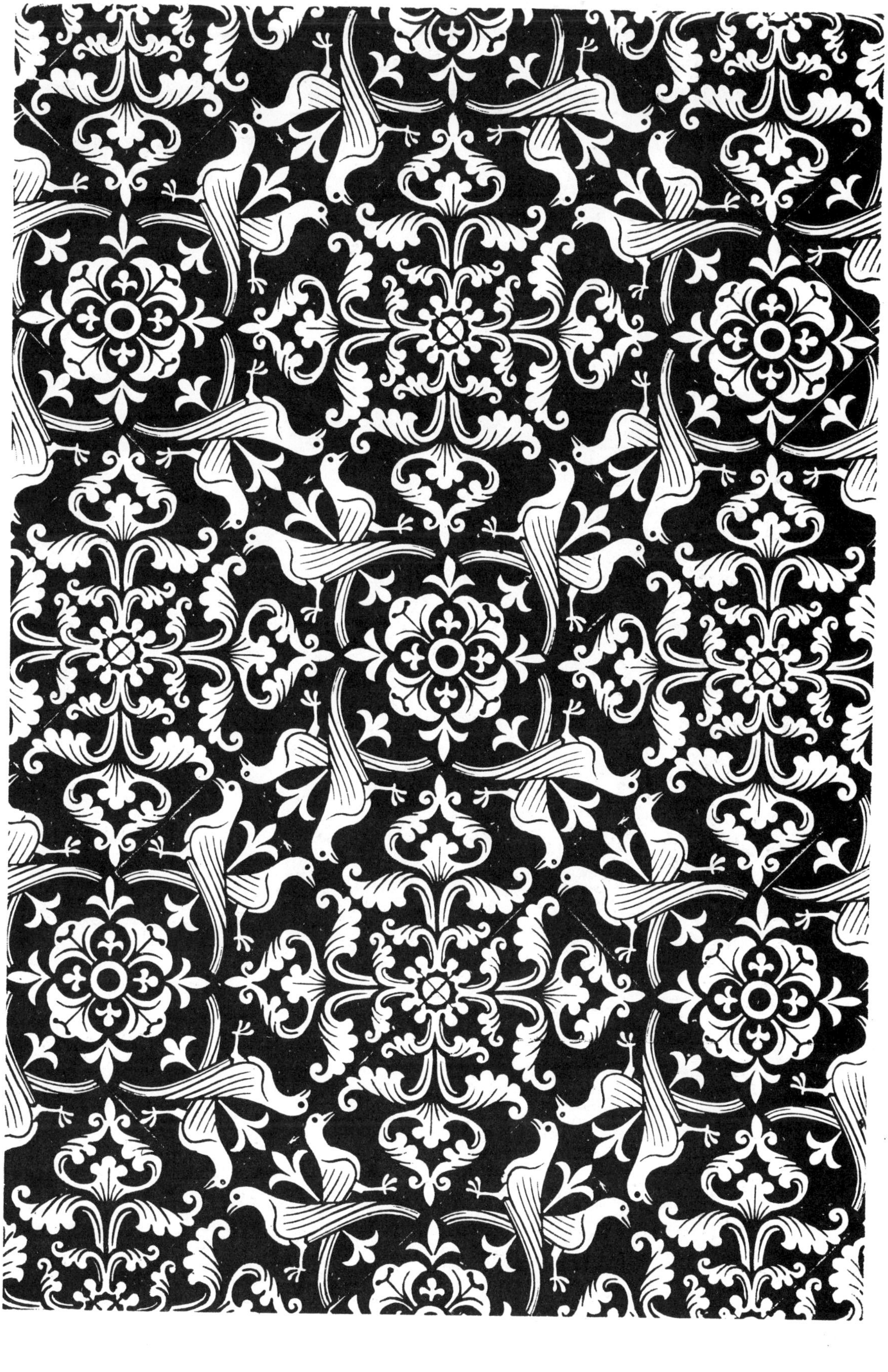

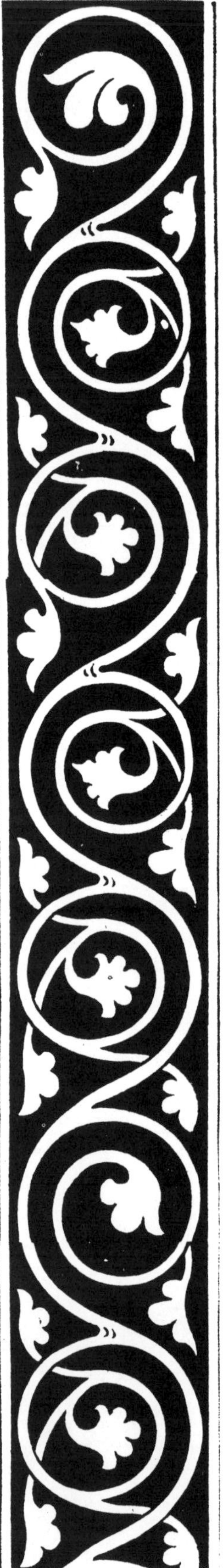

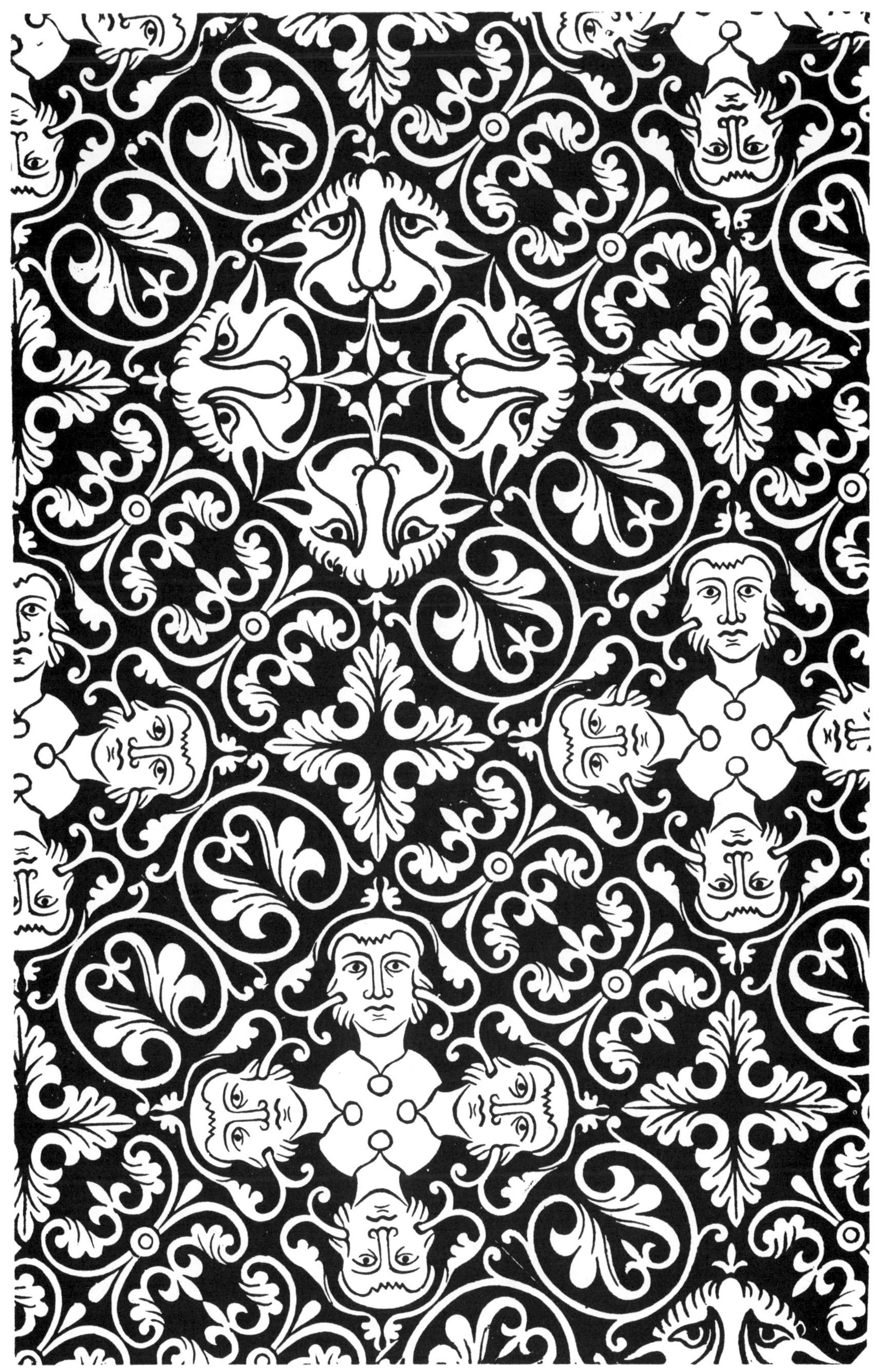

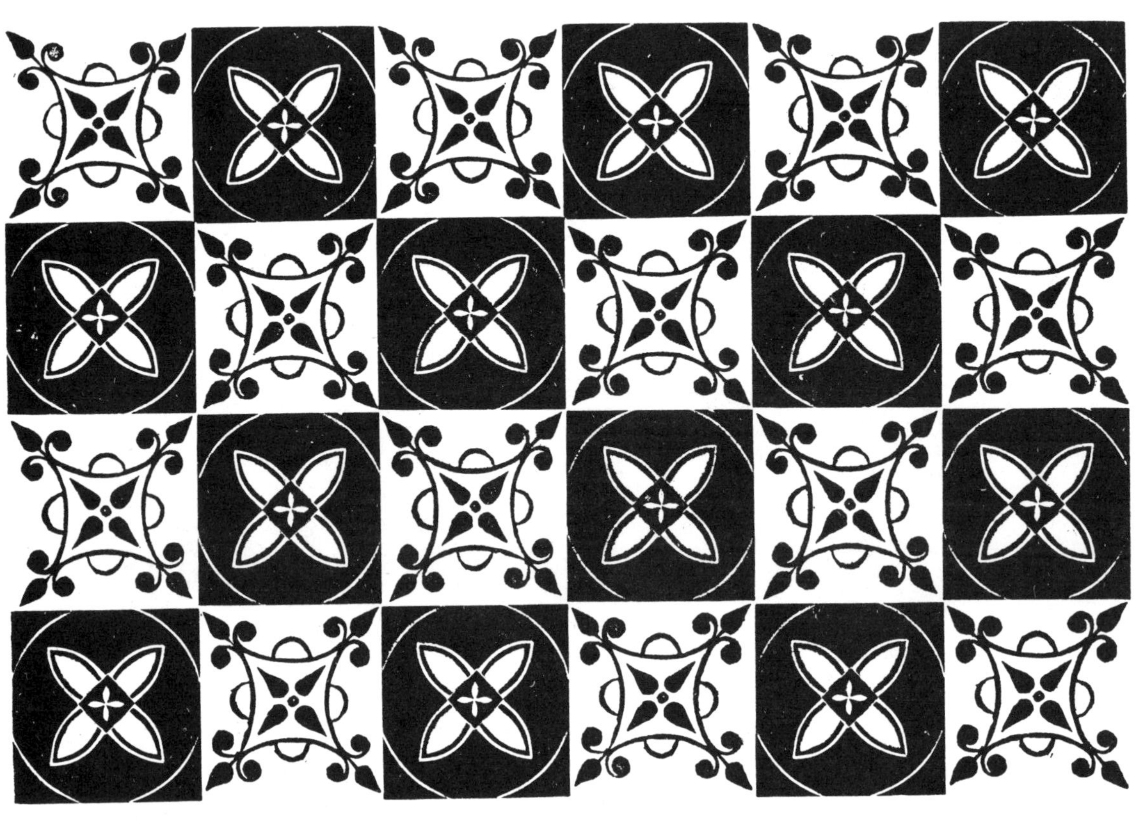

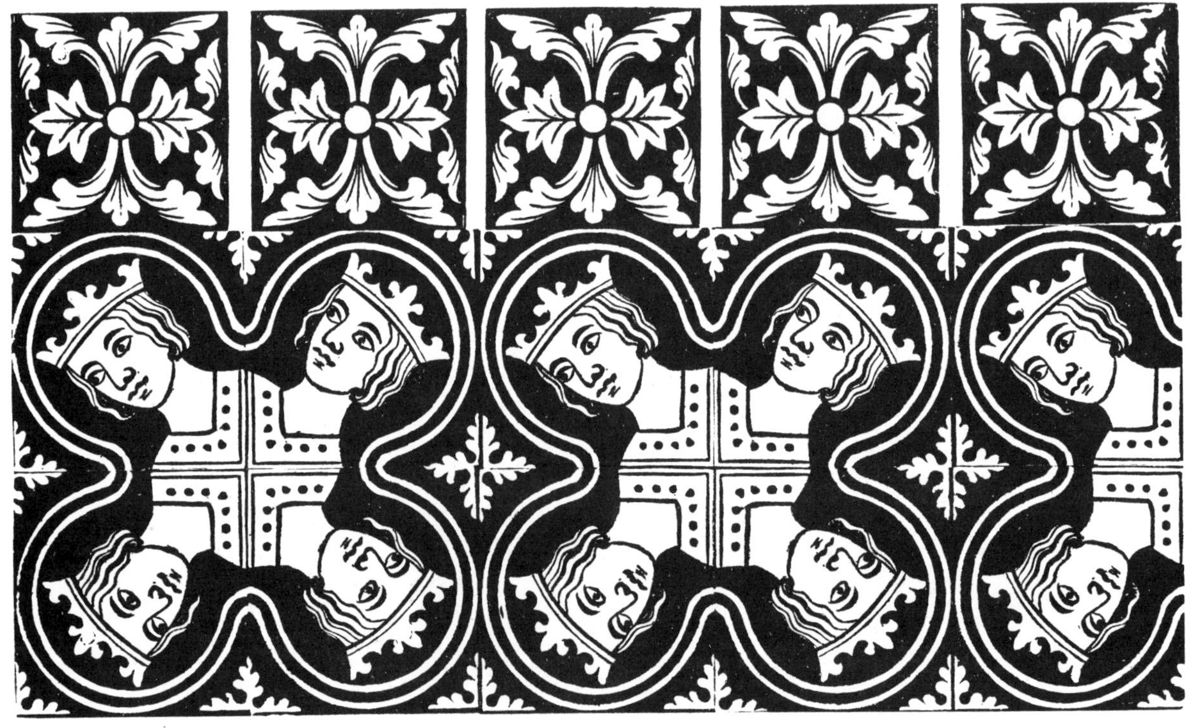

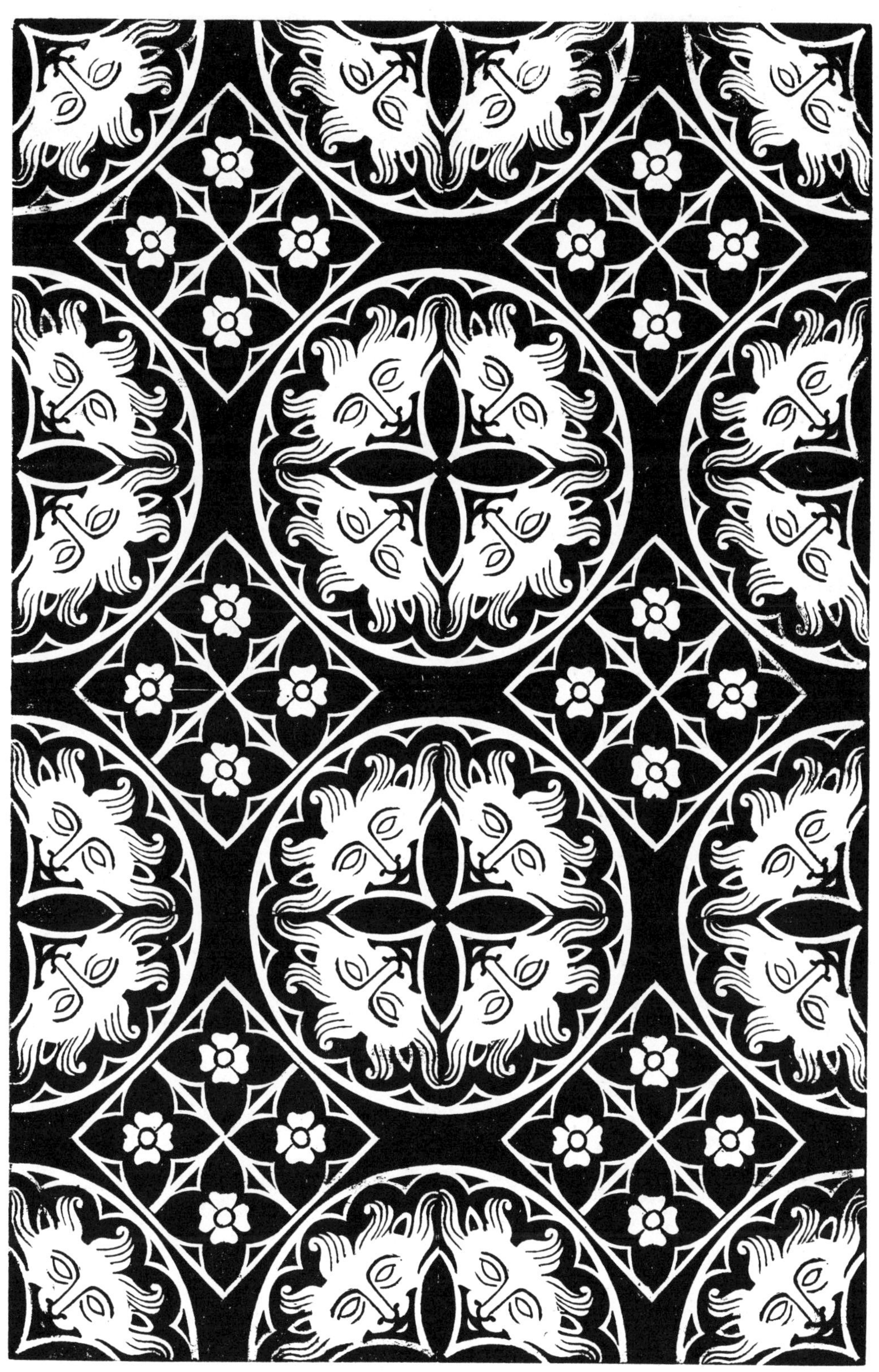

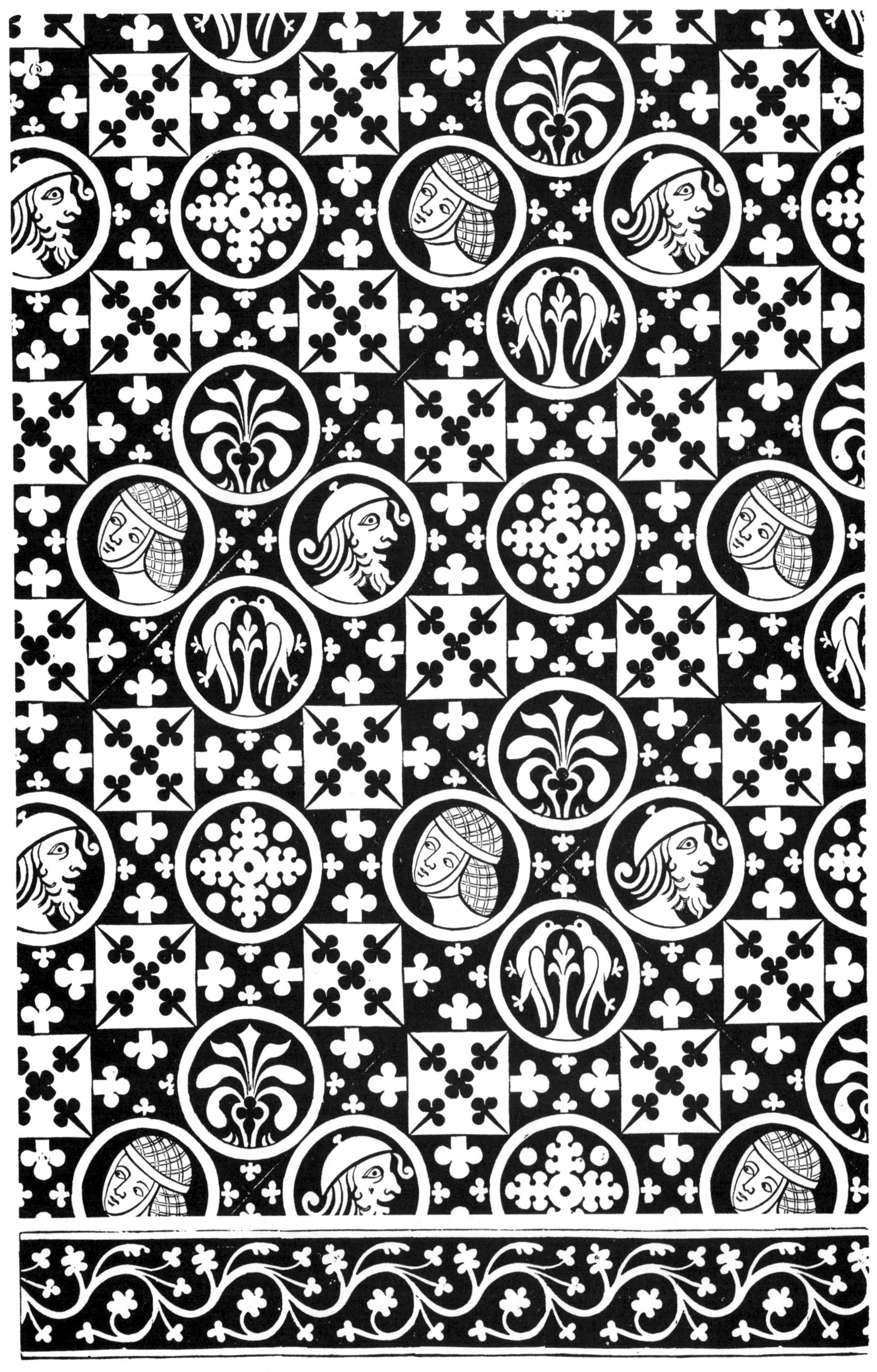

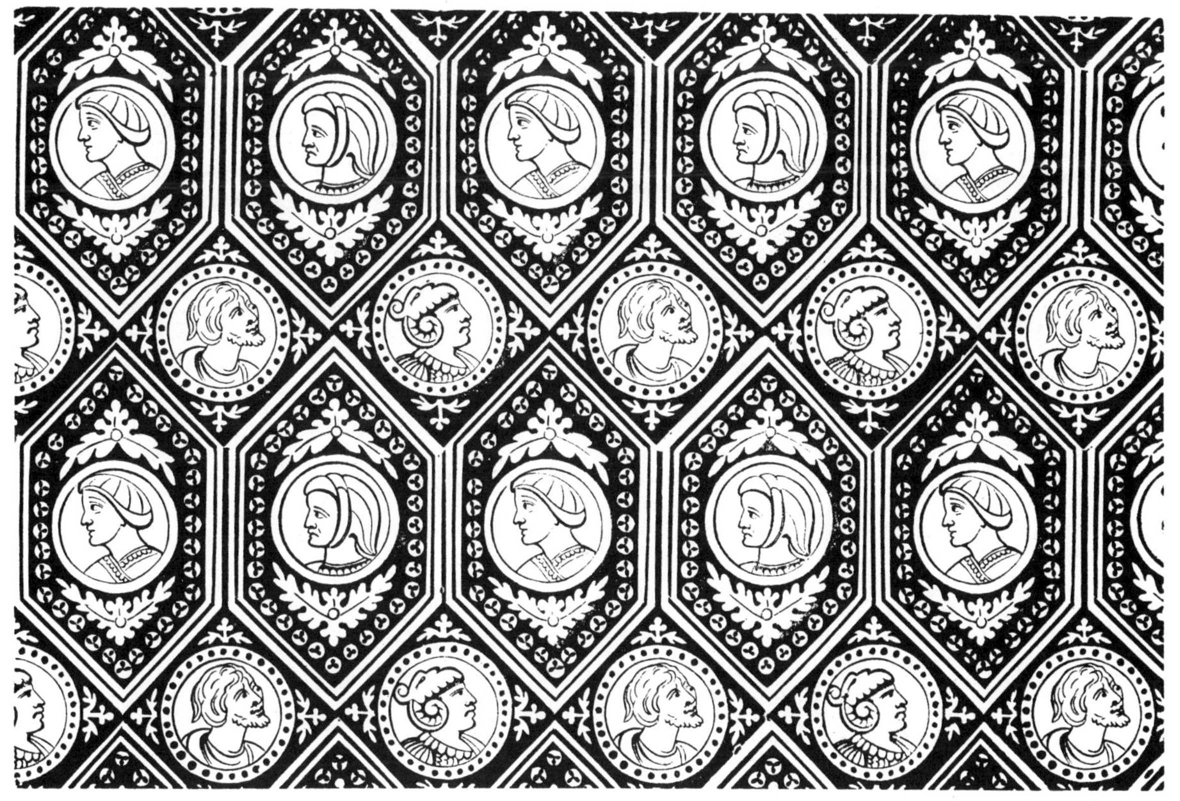

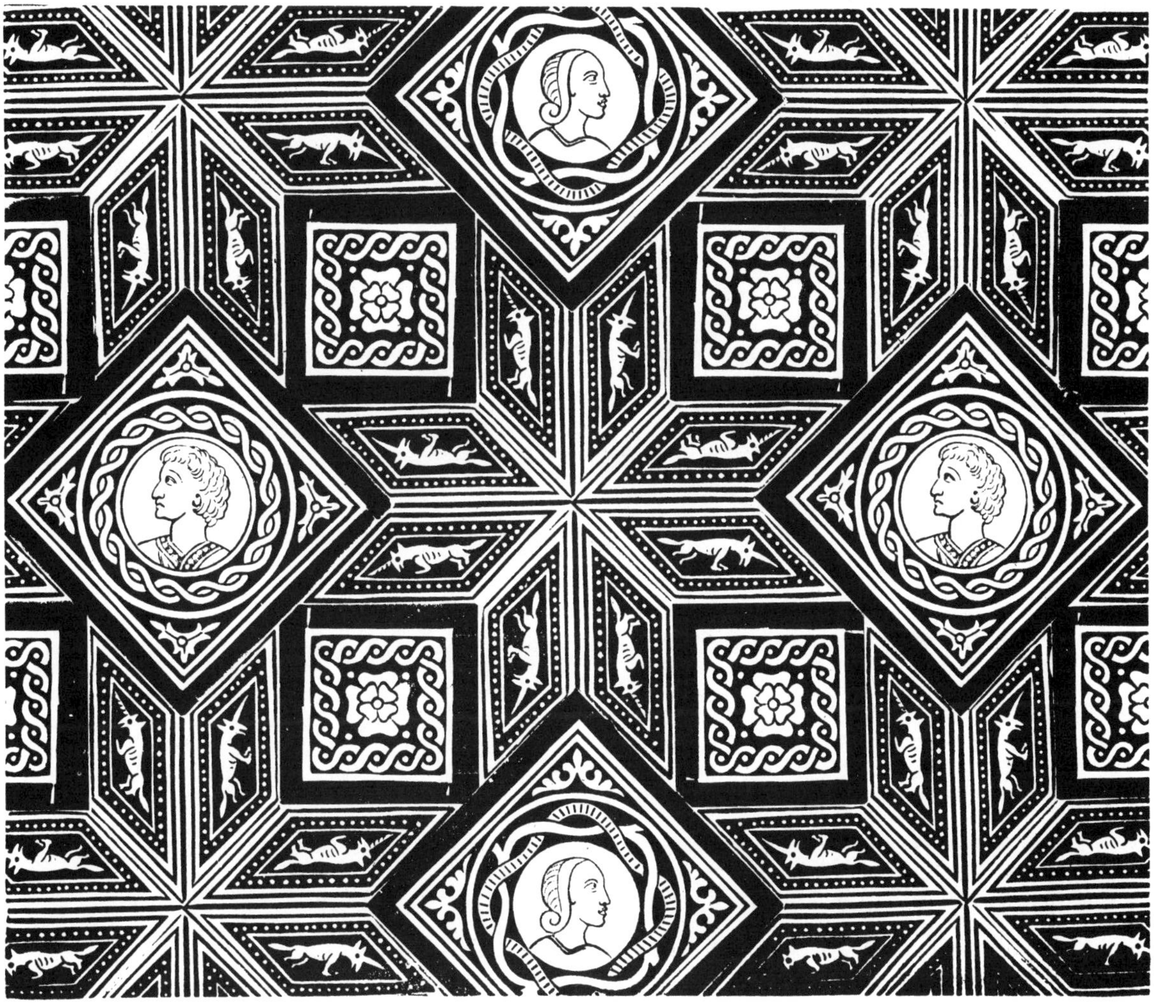

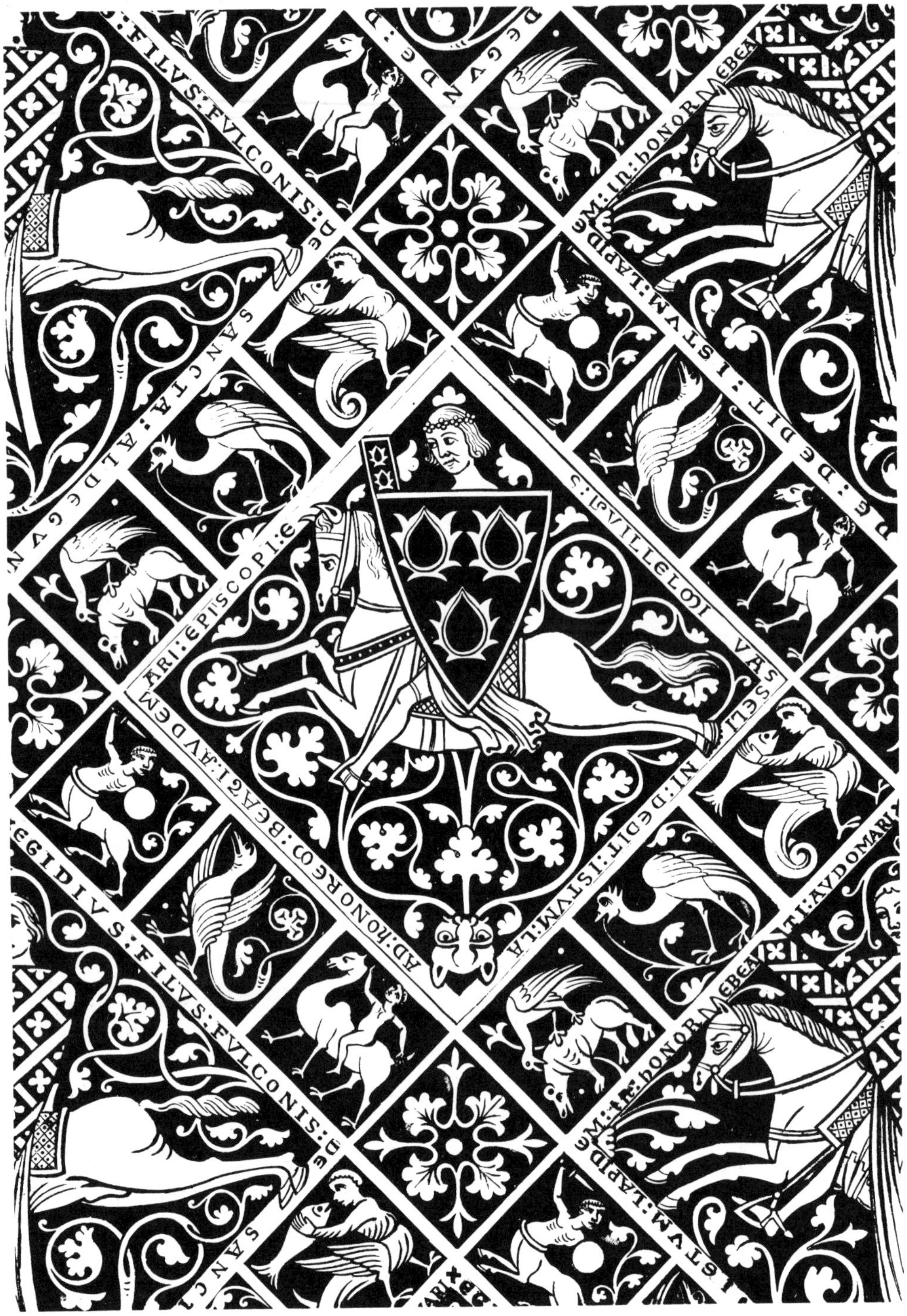

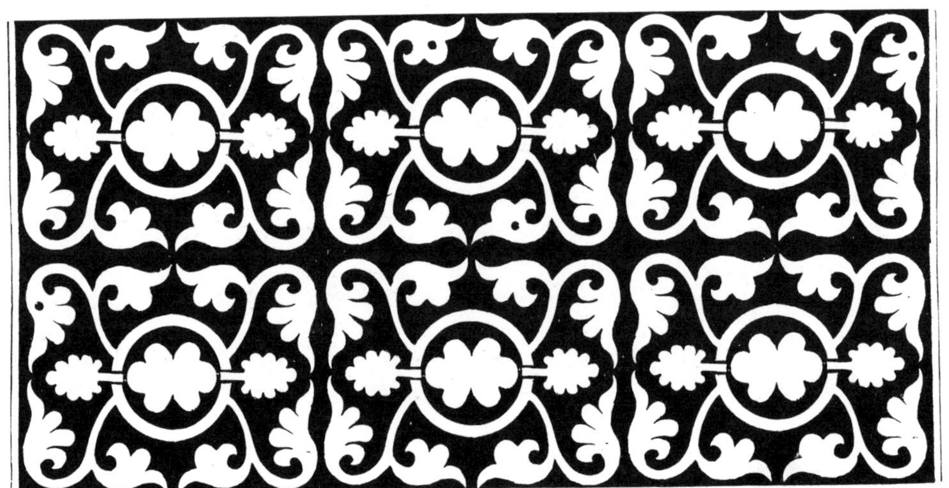

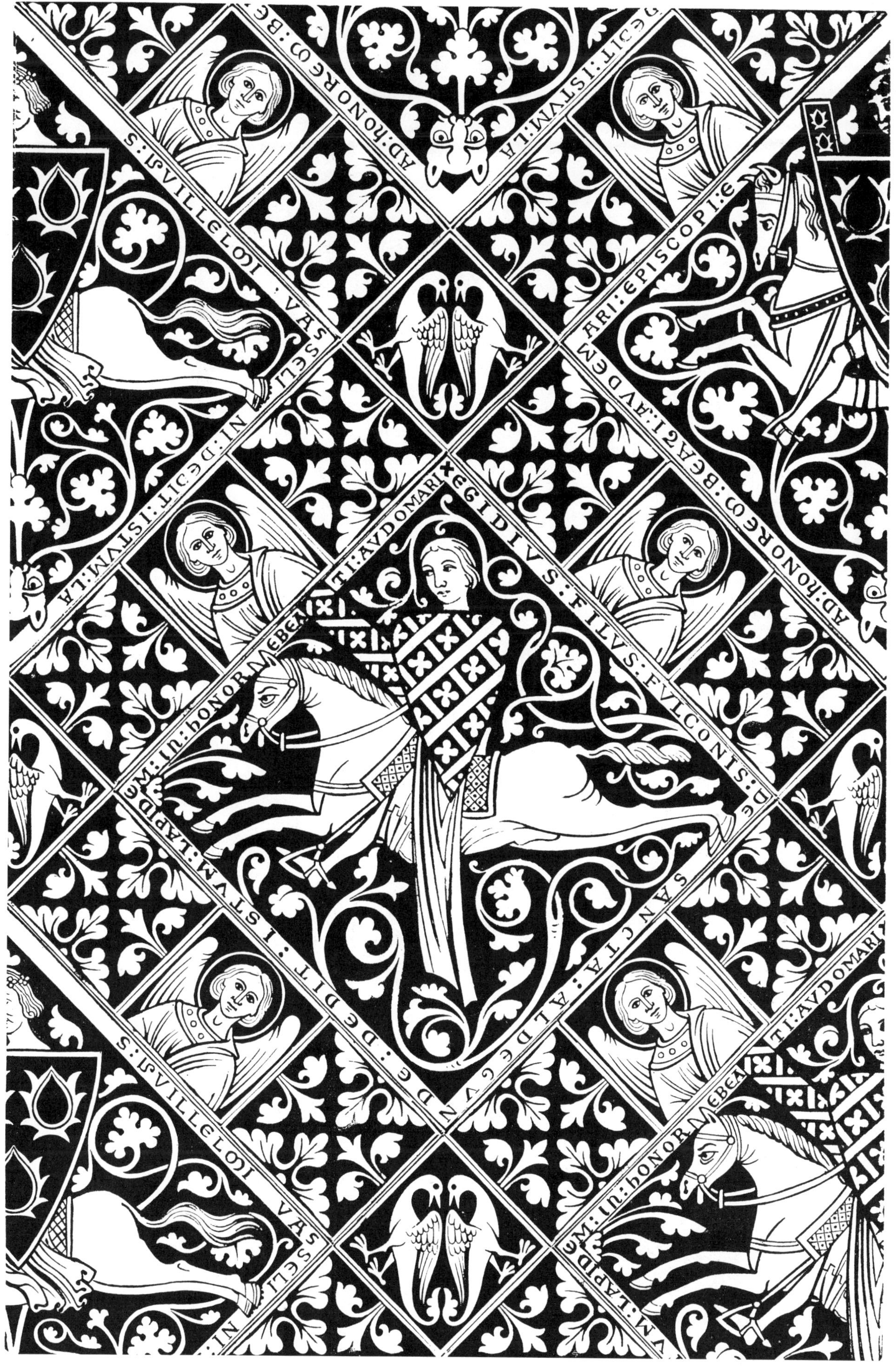
EGIDIVS: FILIVS: FVLCONIS: DE
SANCTA: ALDEGVNDE: DEDIT: ISTVM: LAPIDEM: IN: HONOREM: BEATI: AVDOMARI

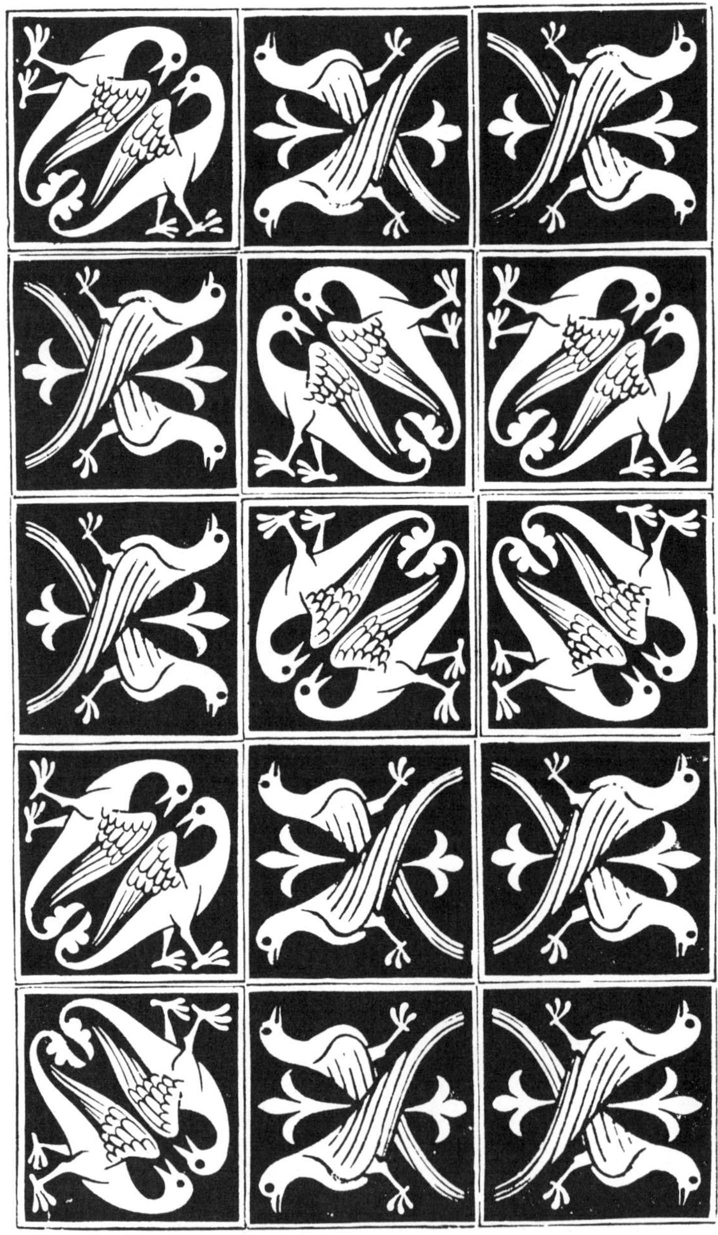

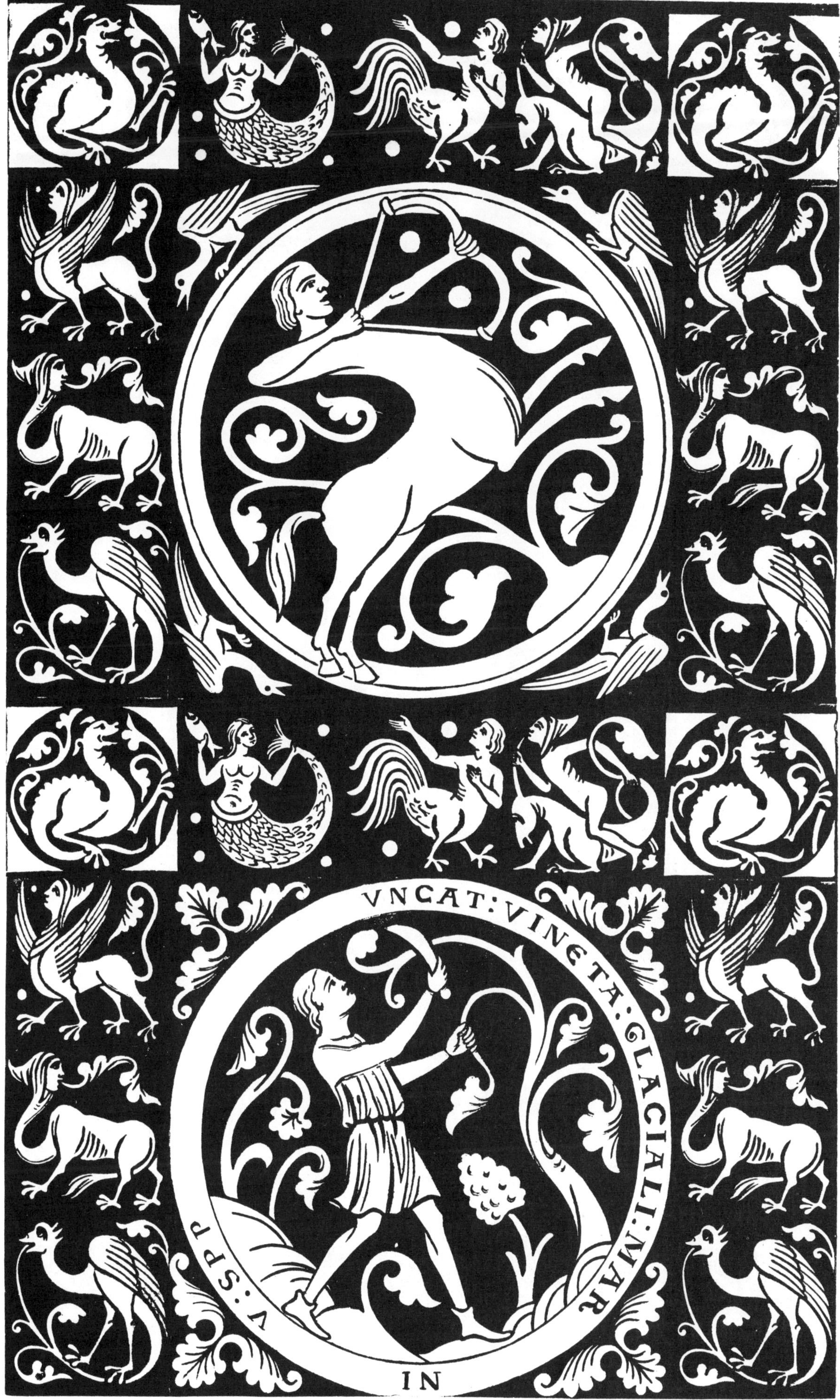
VNCAT: VINETA: GLACIALI: MAR
IN
V: SPP

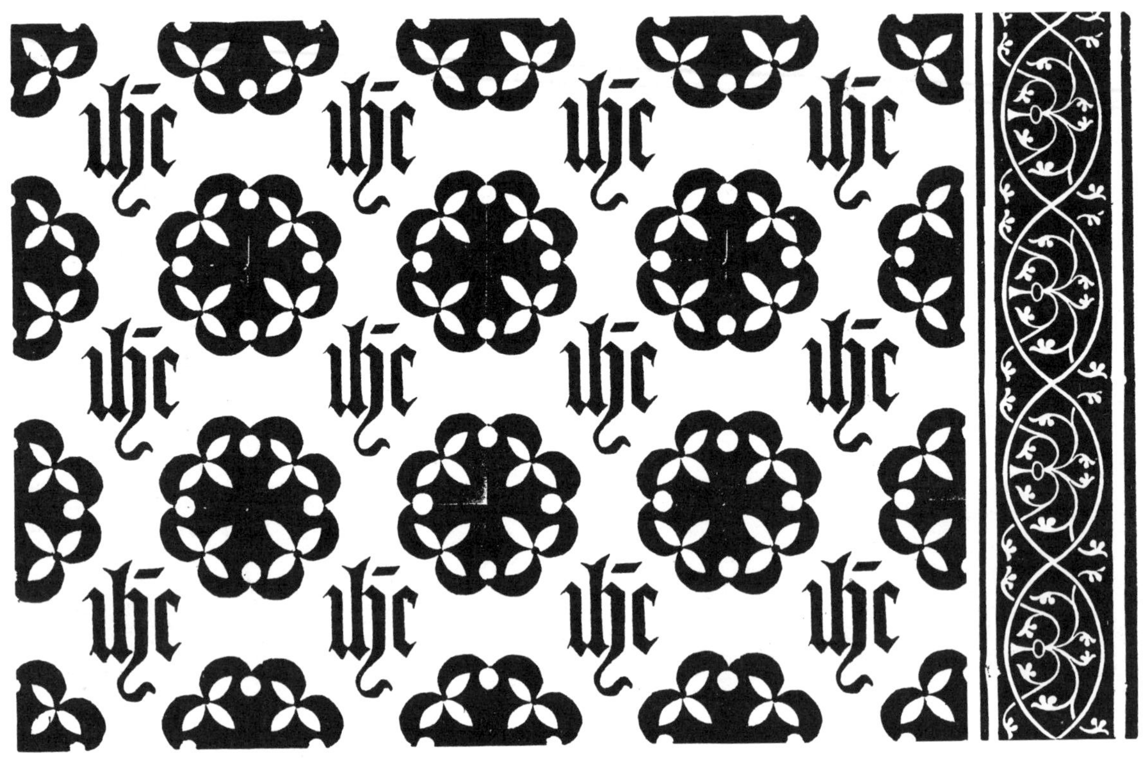

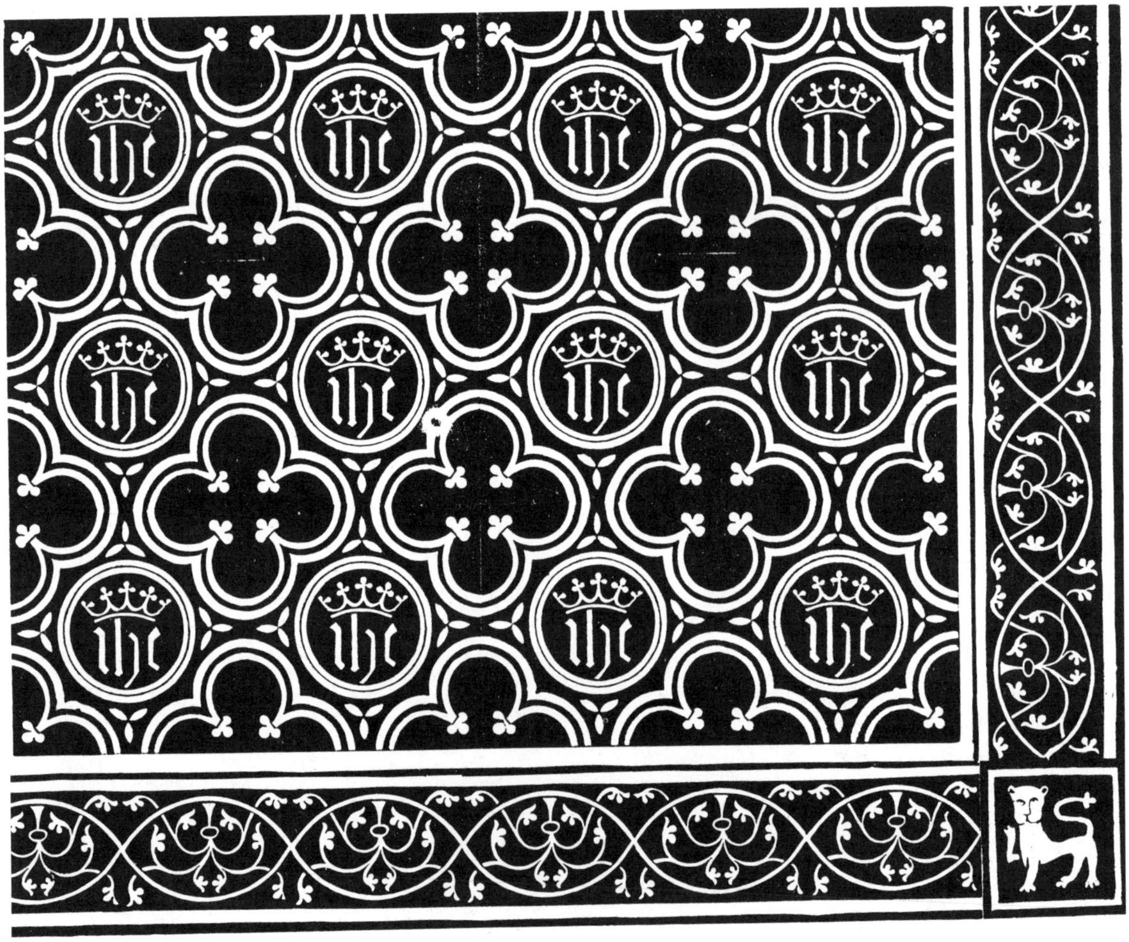

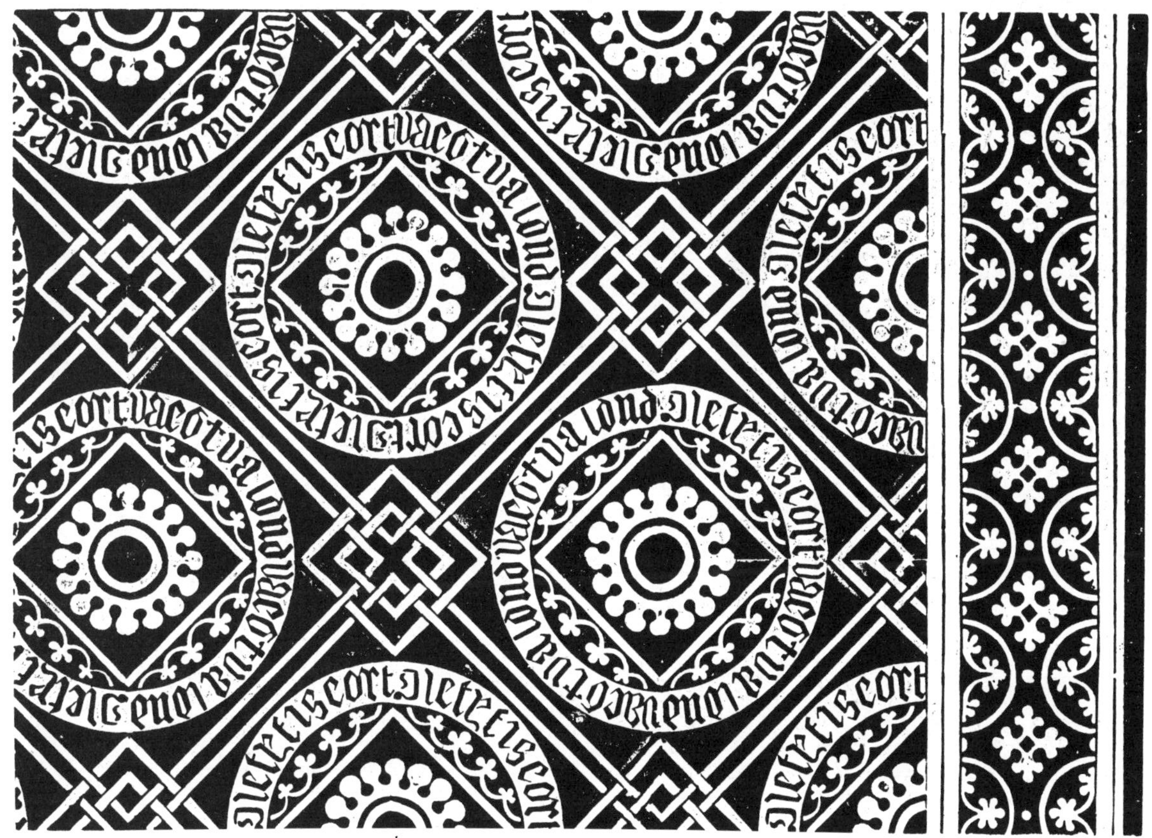

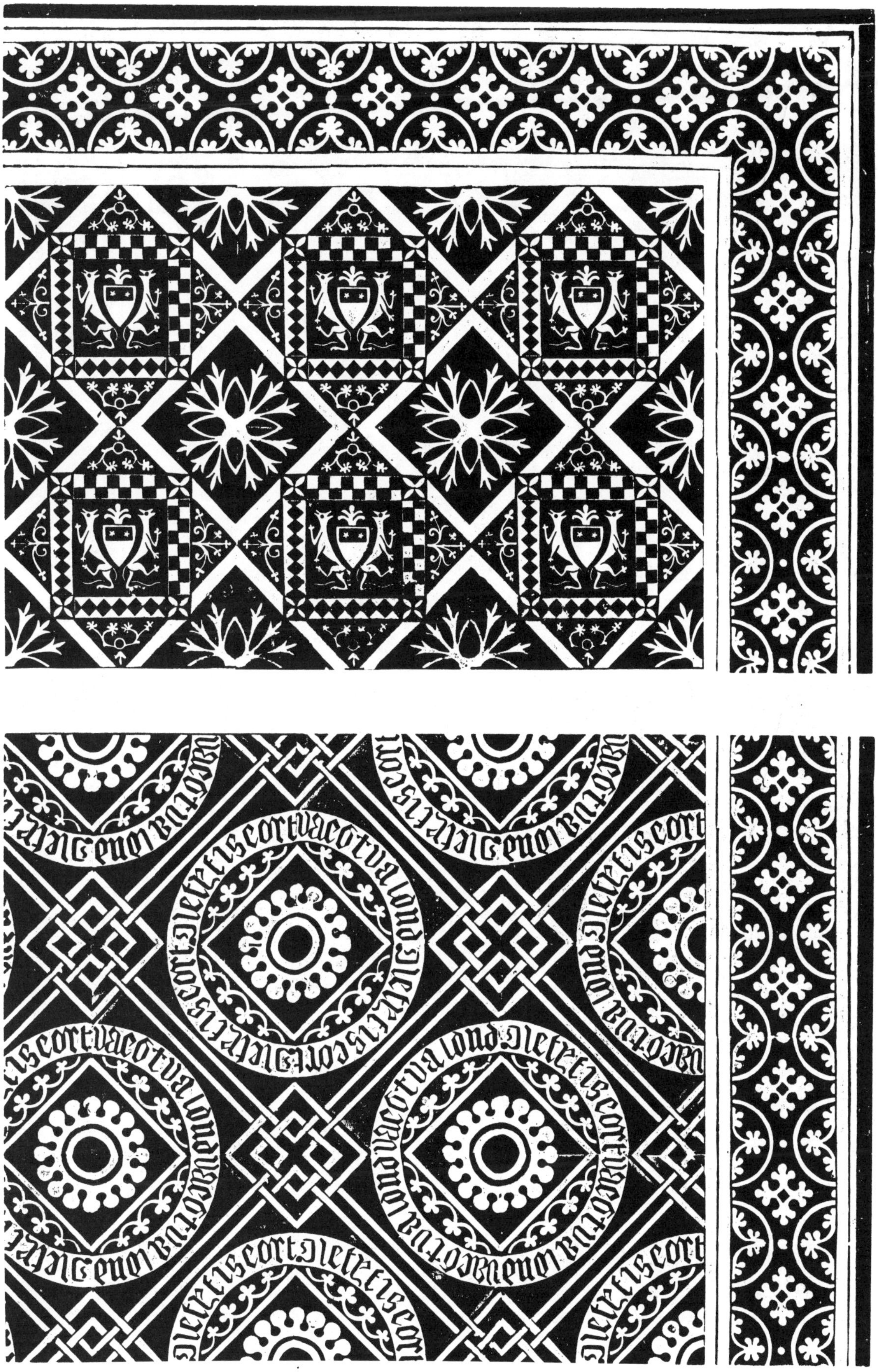

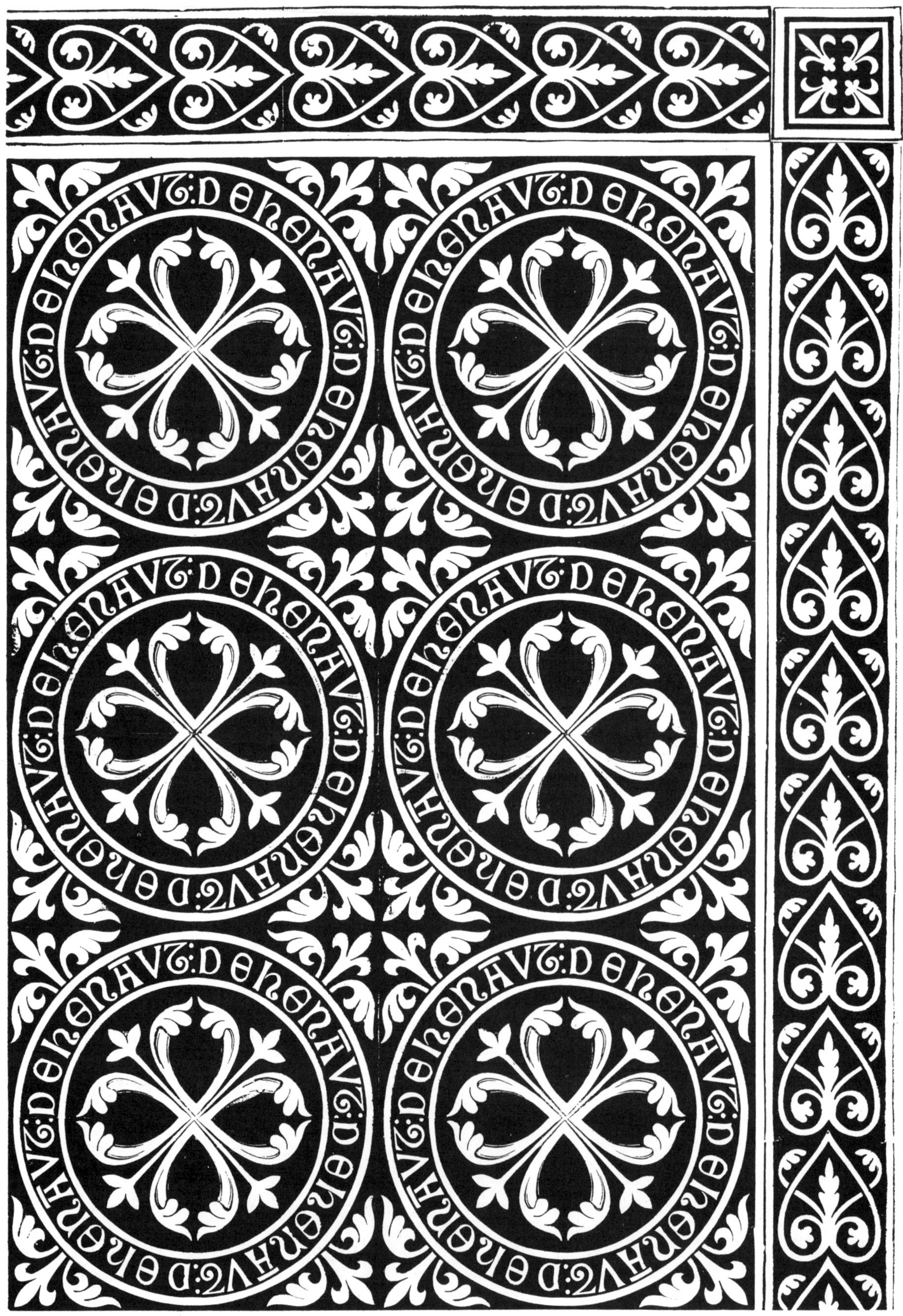

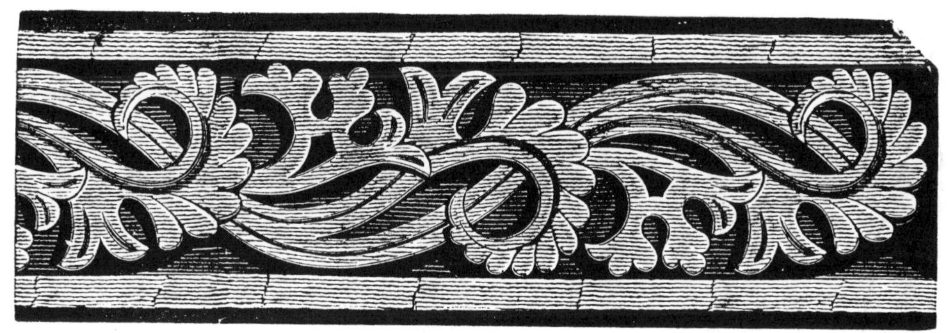

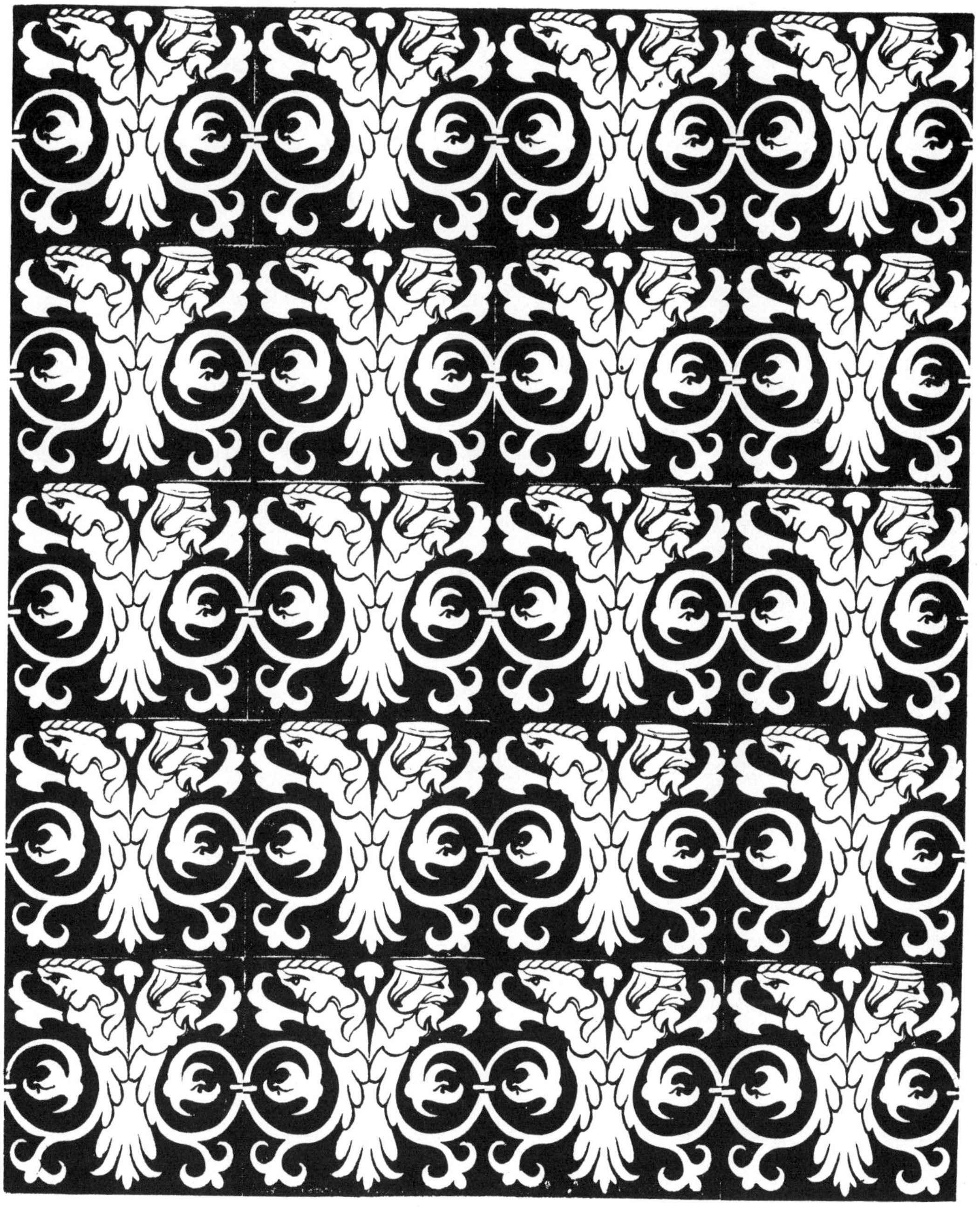

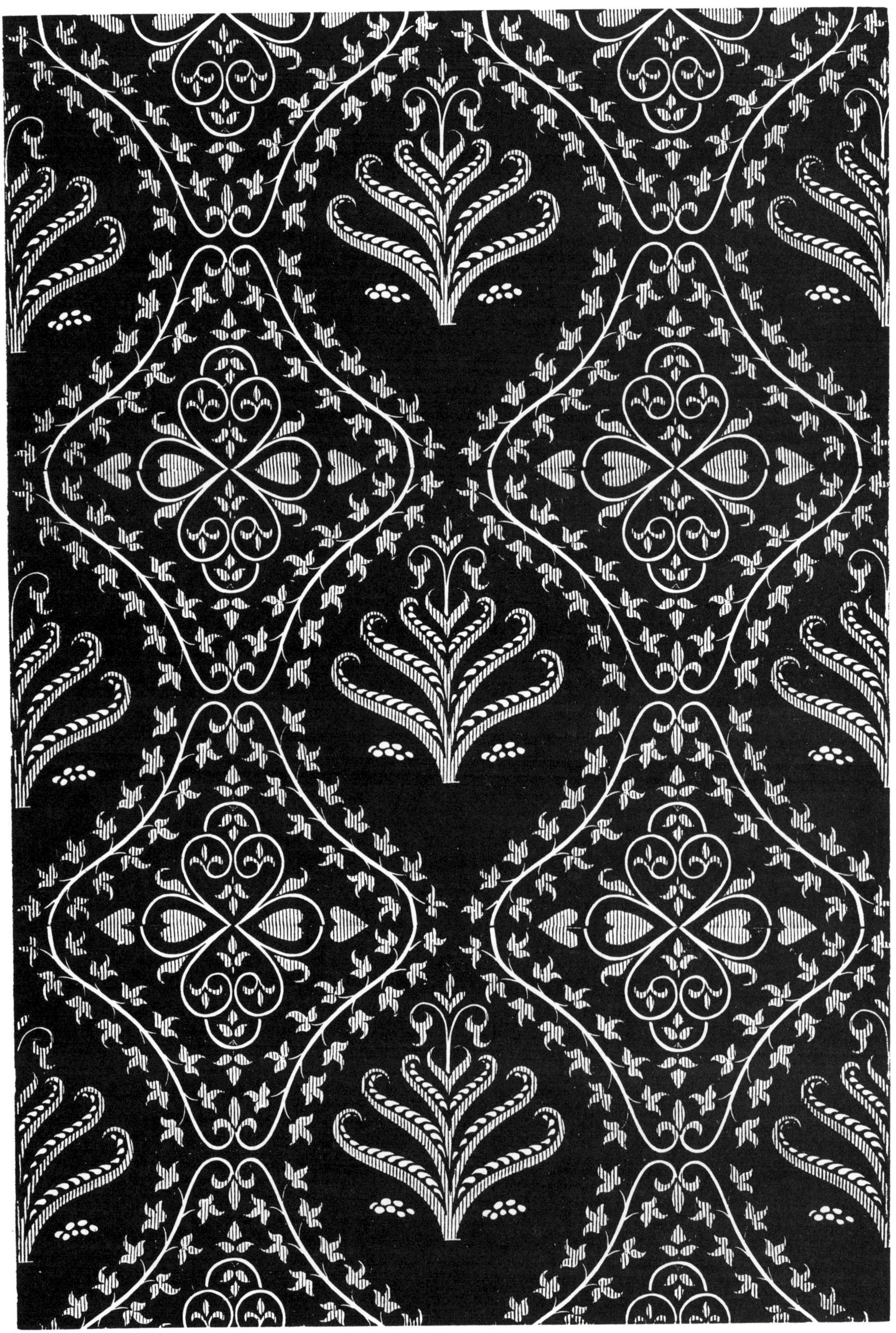

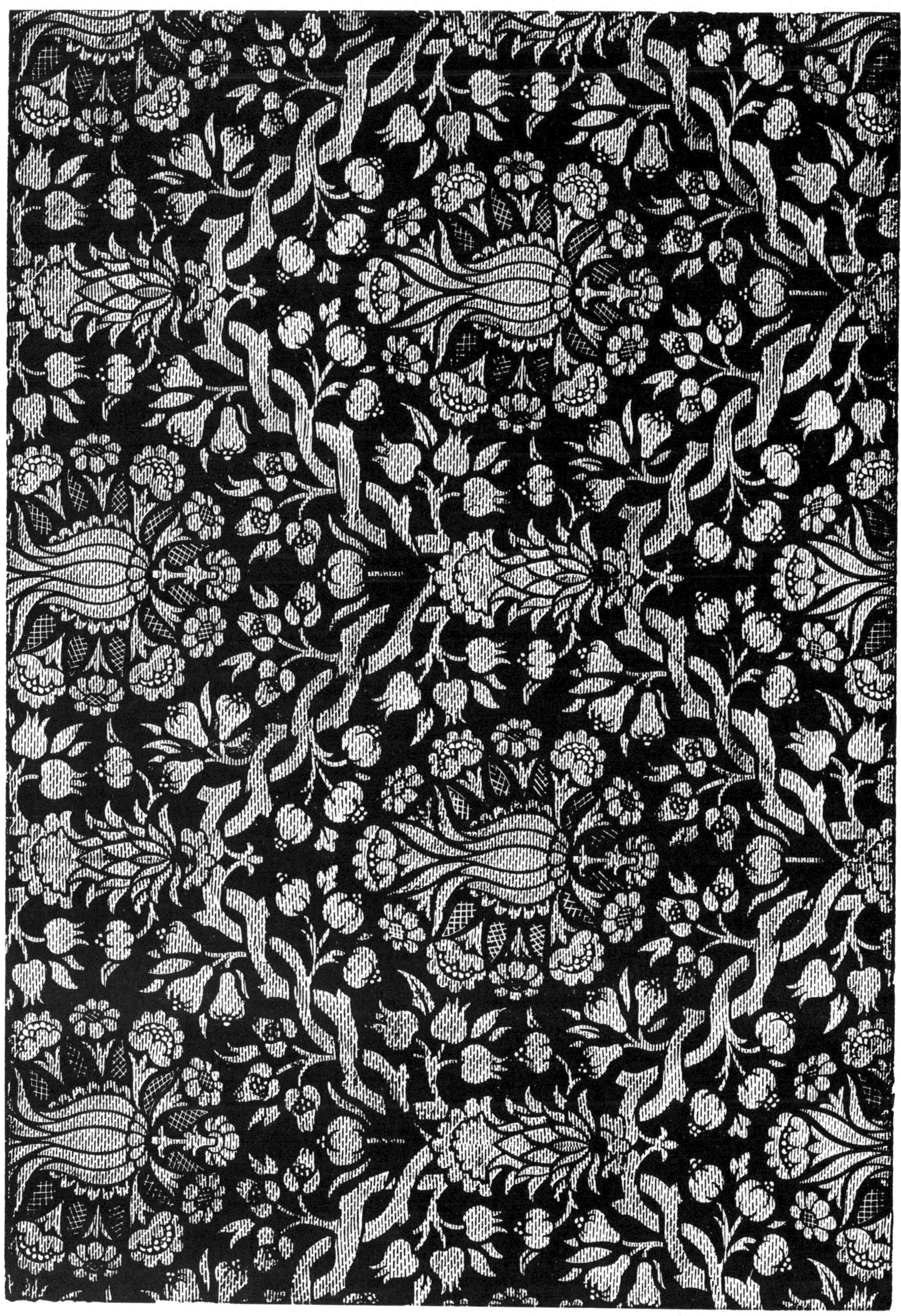

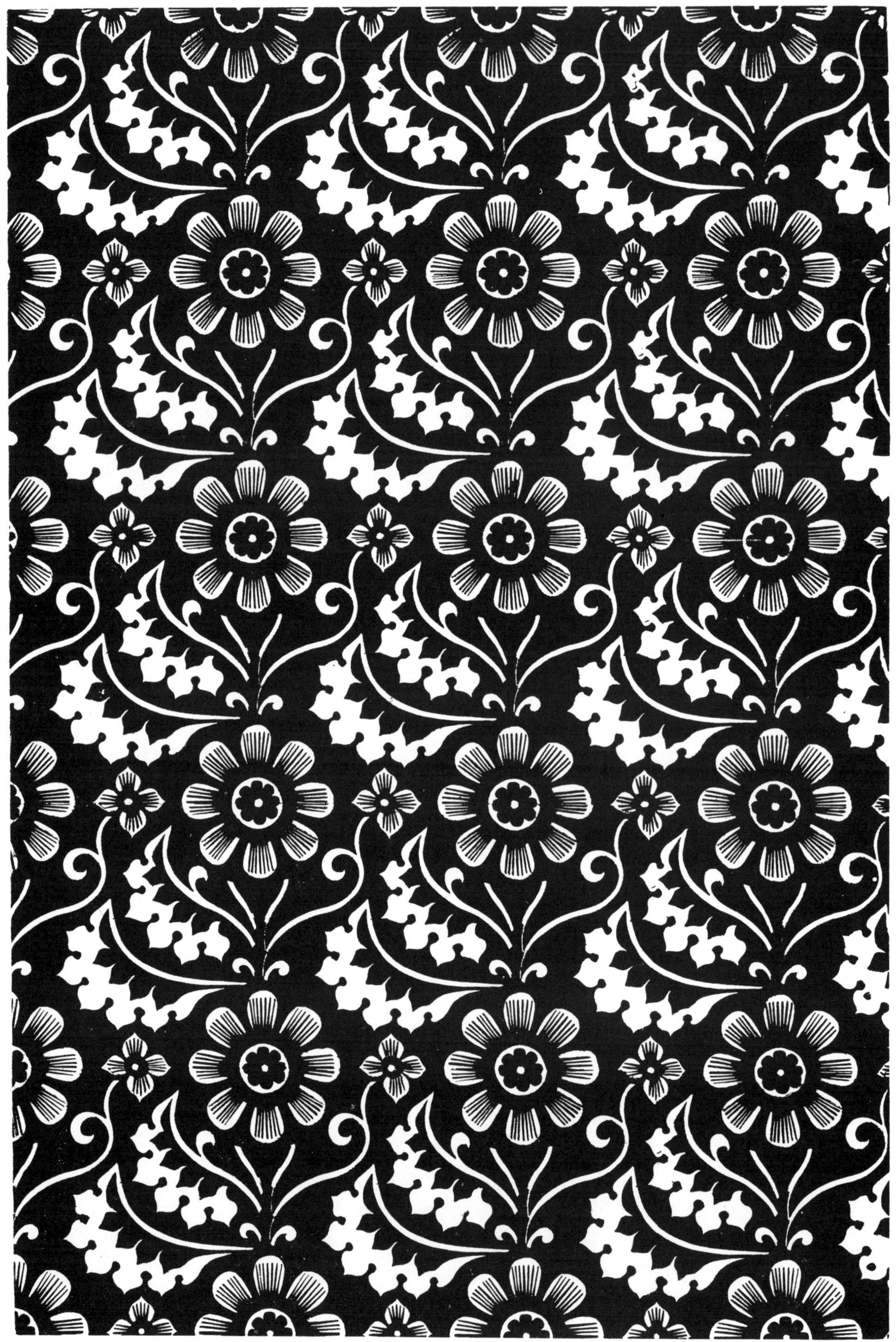

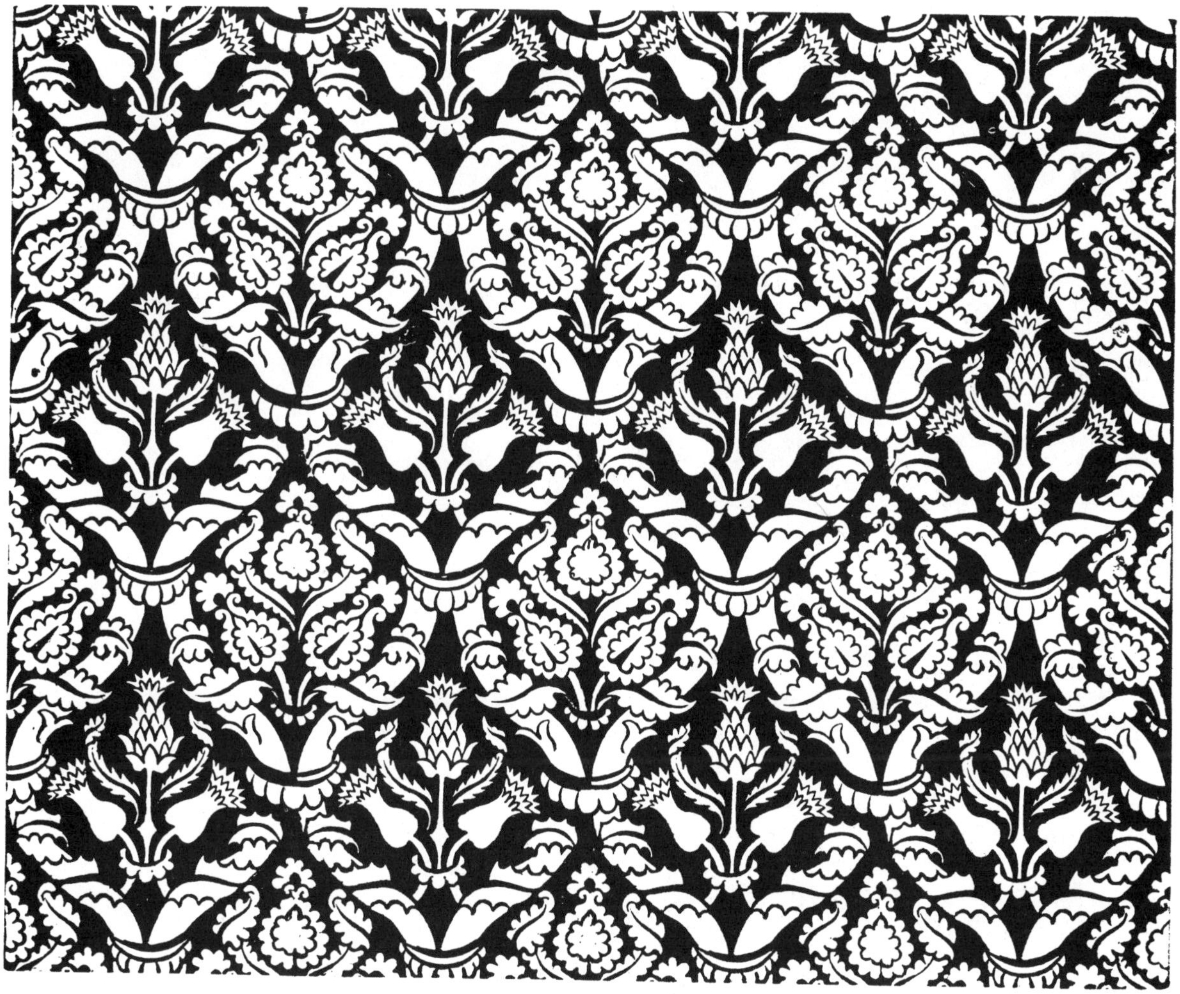

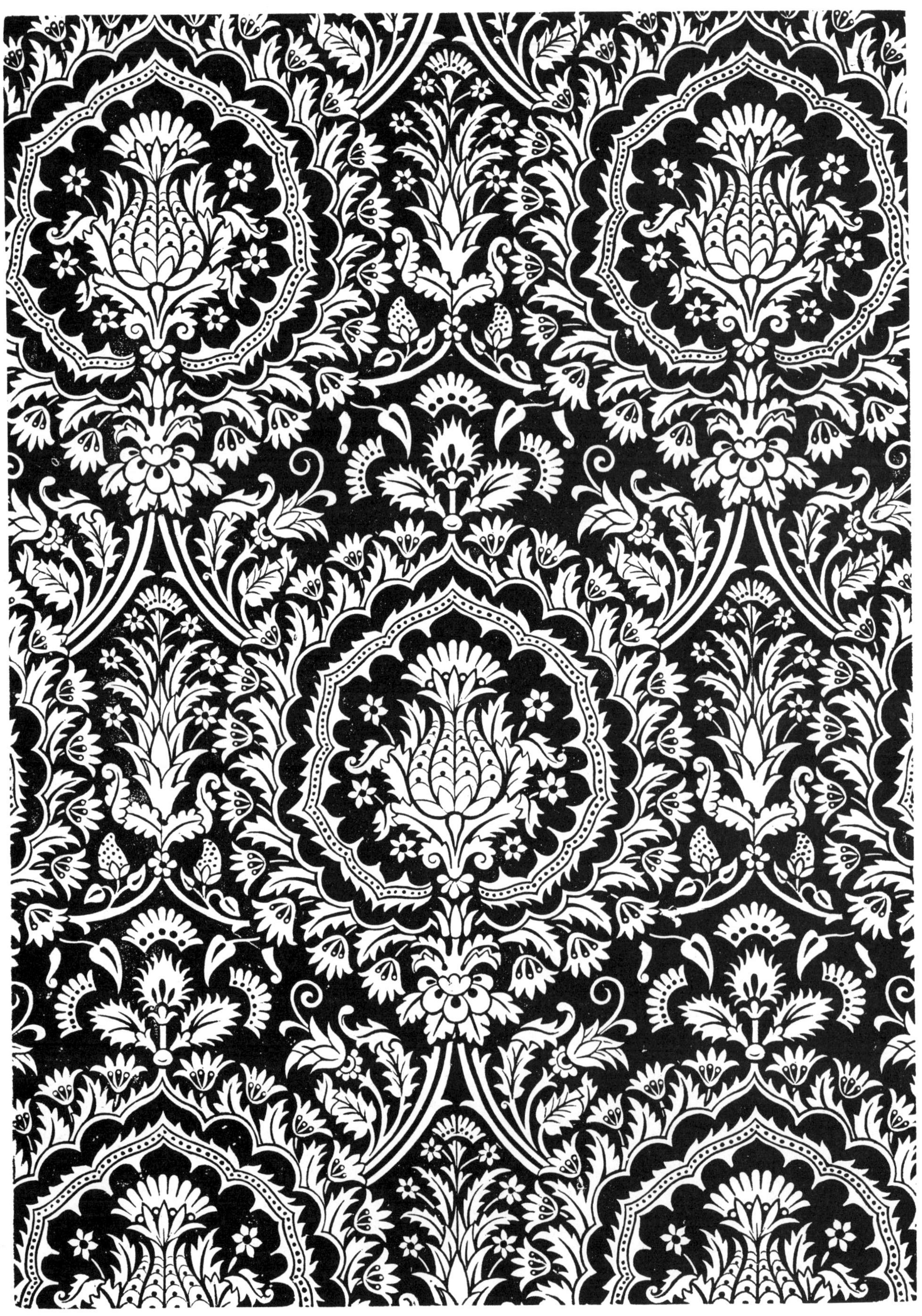

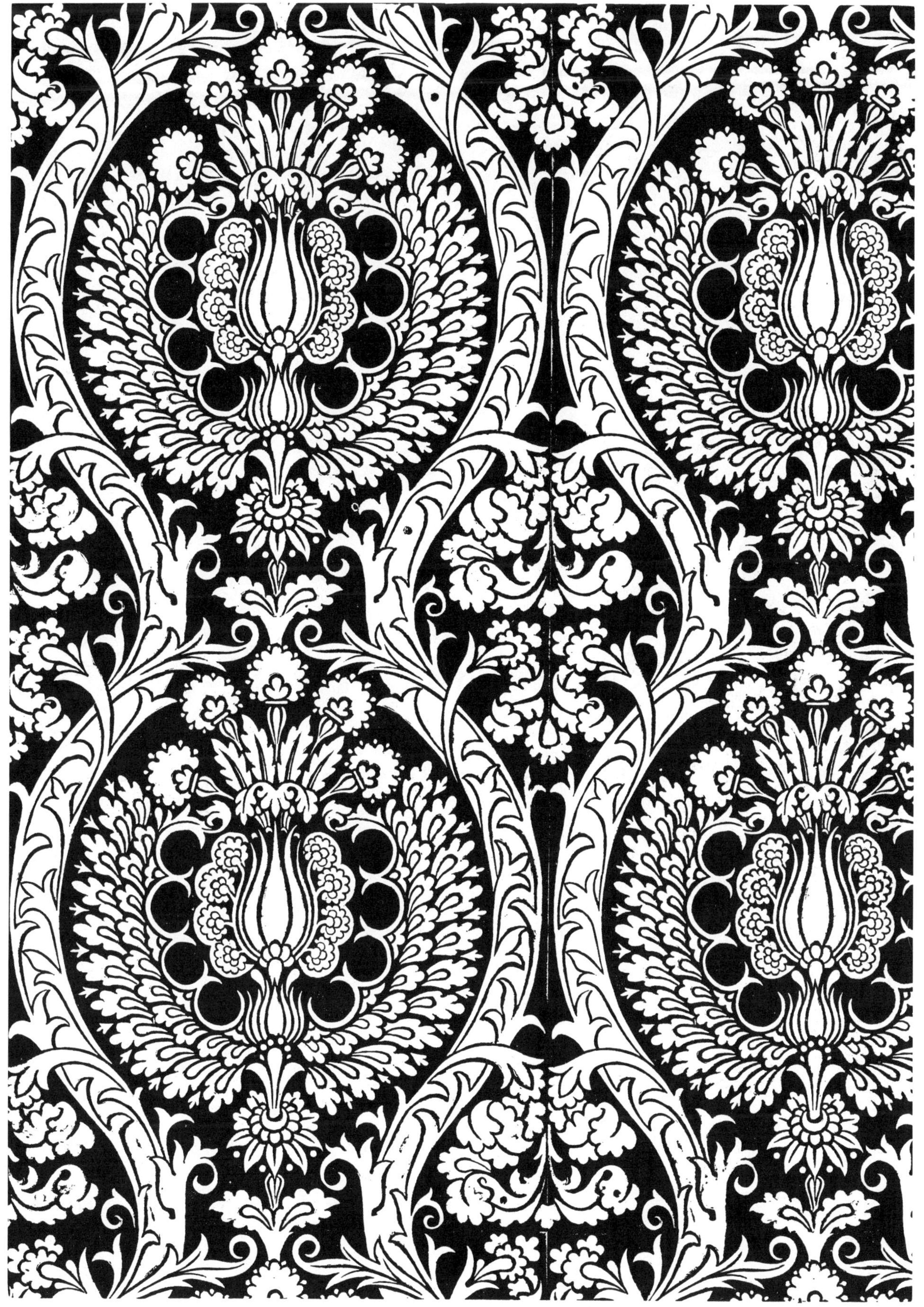

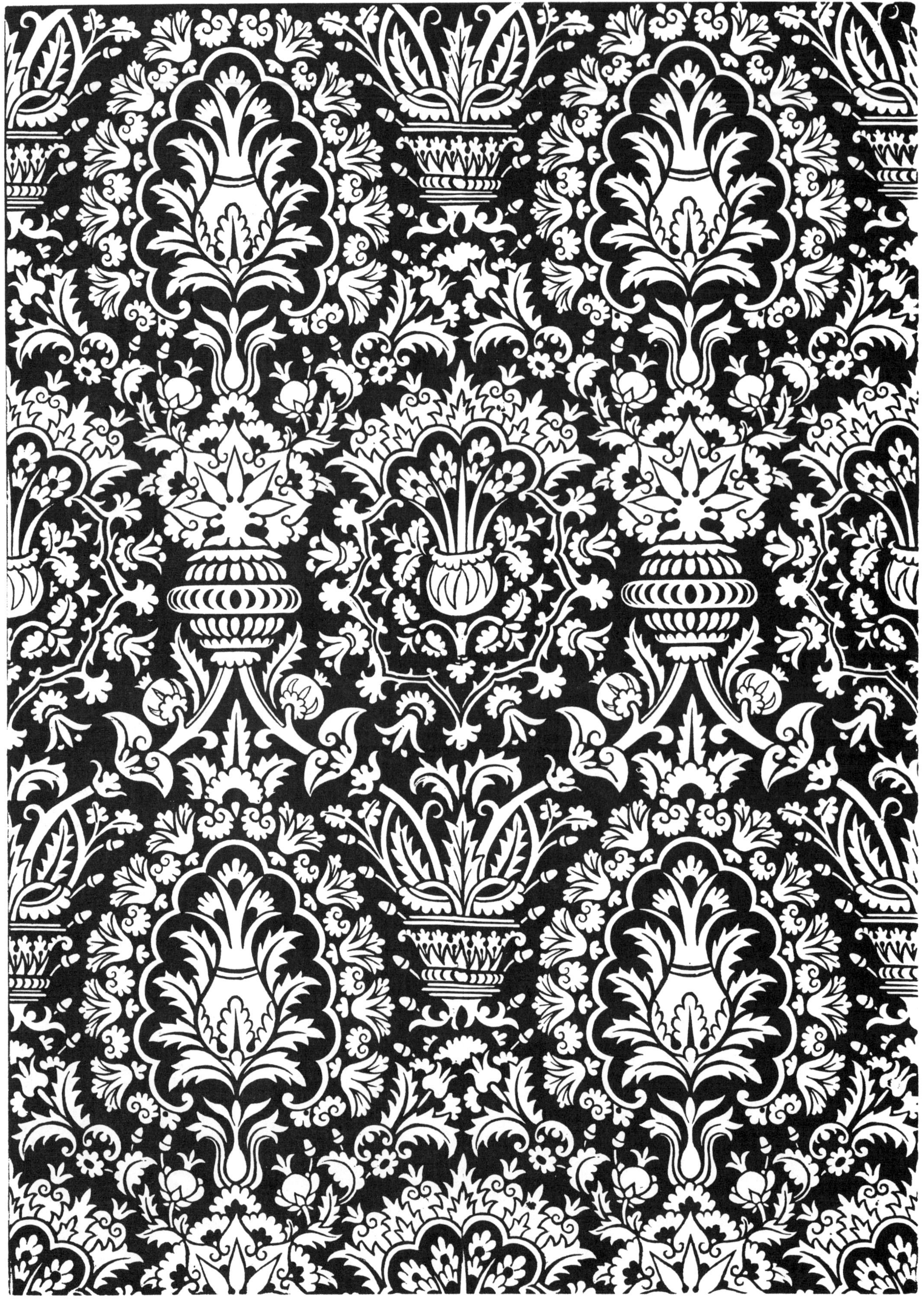

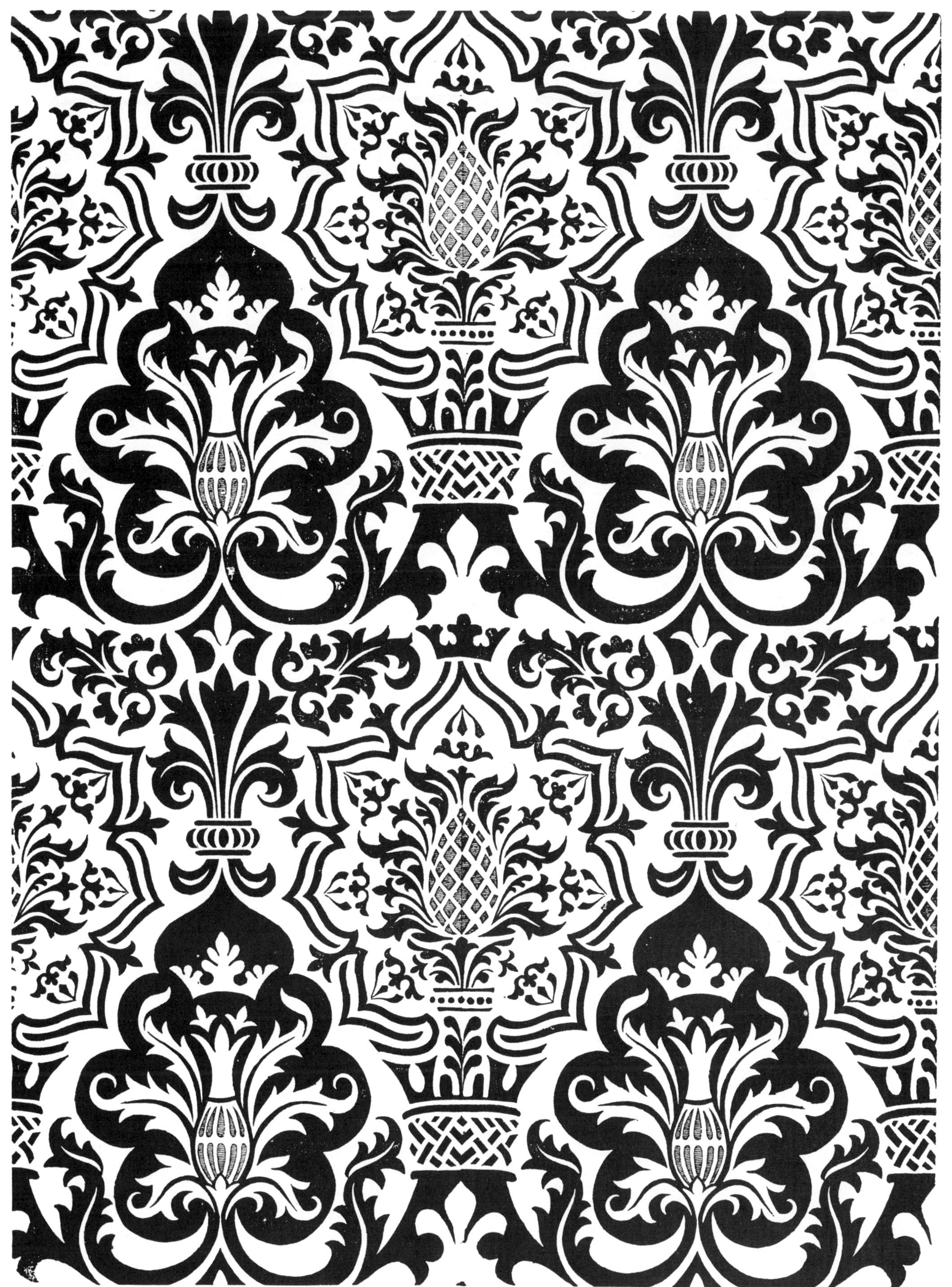

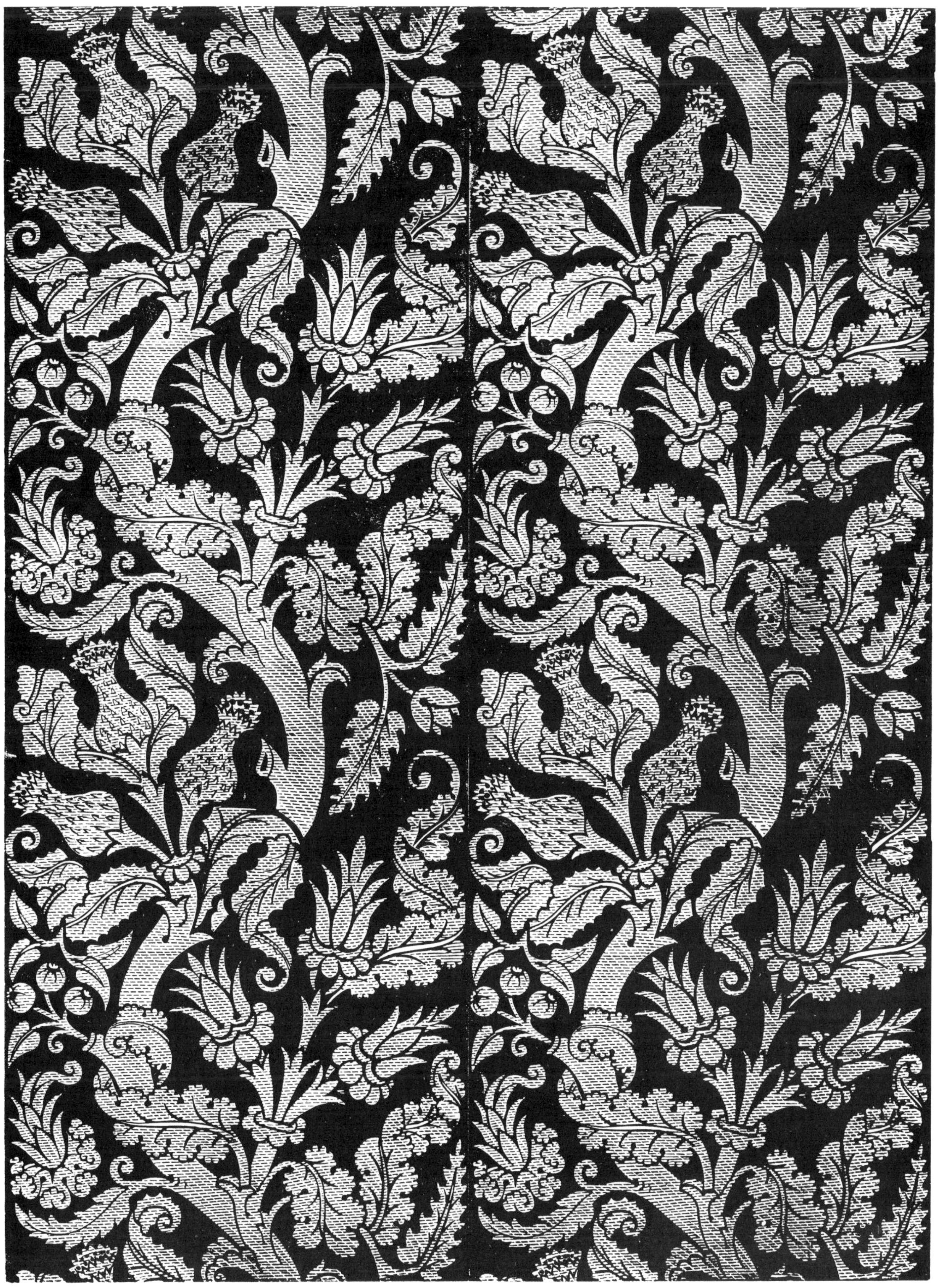

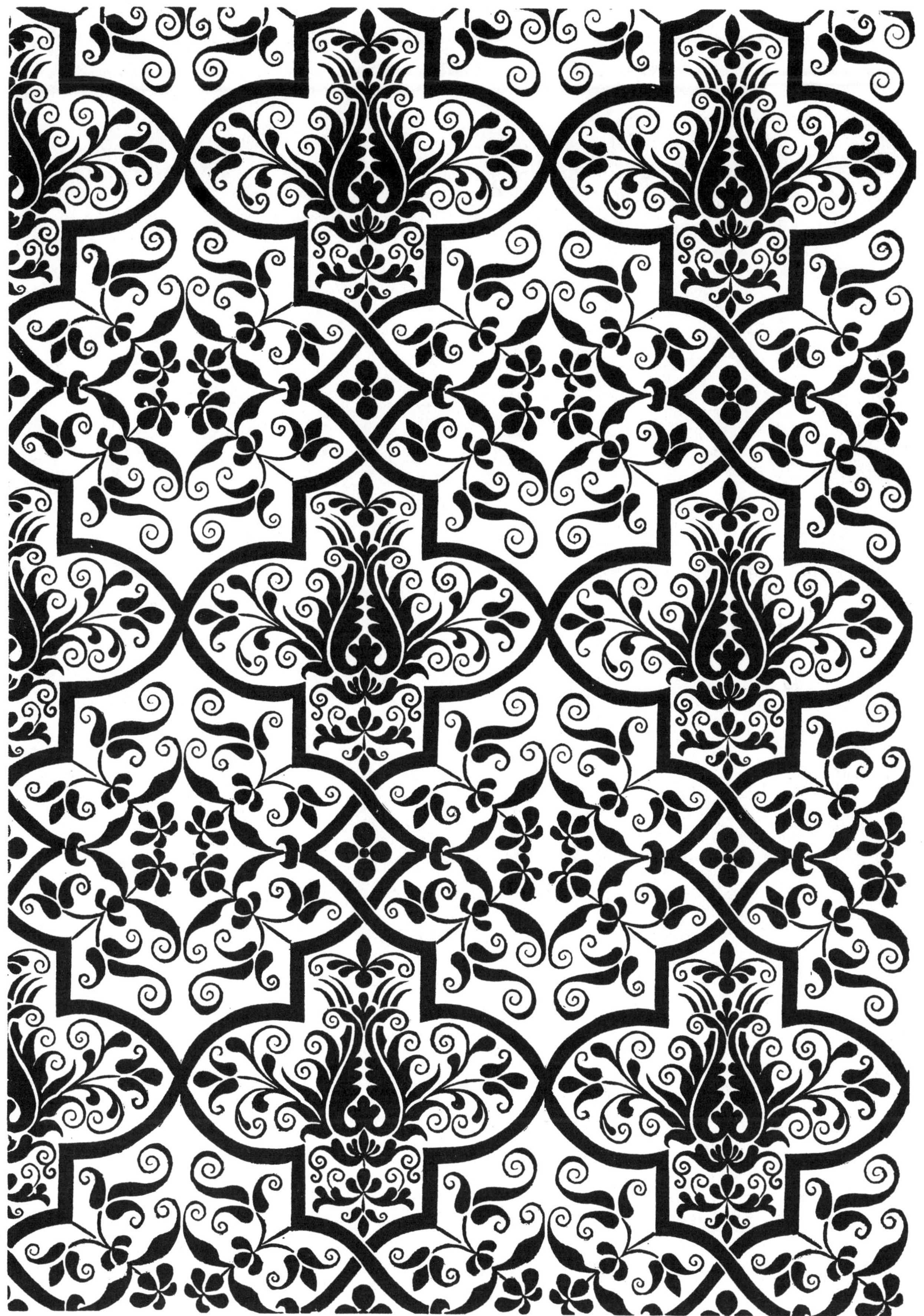

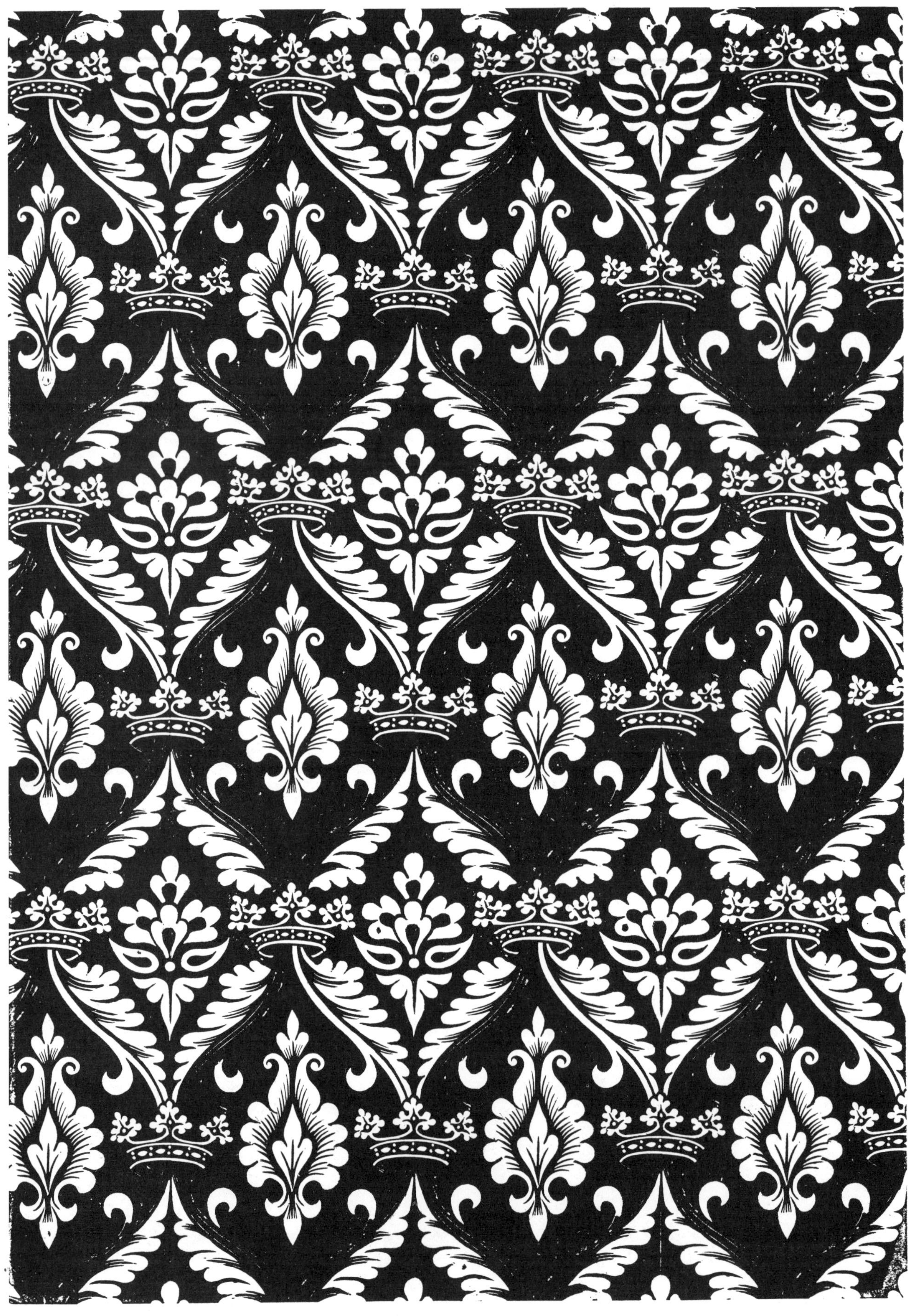

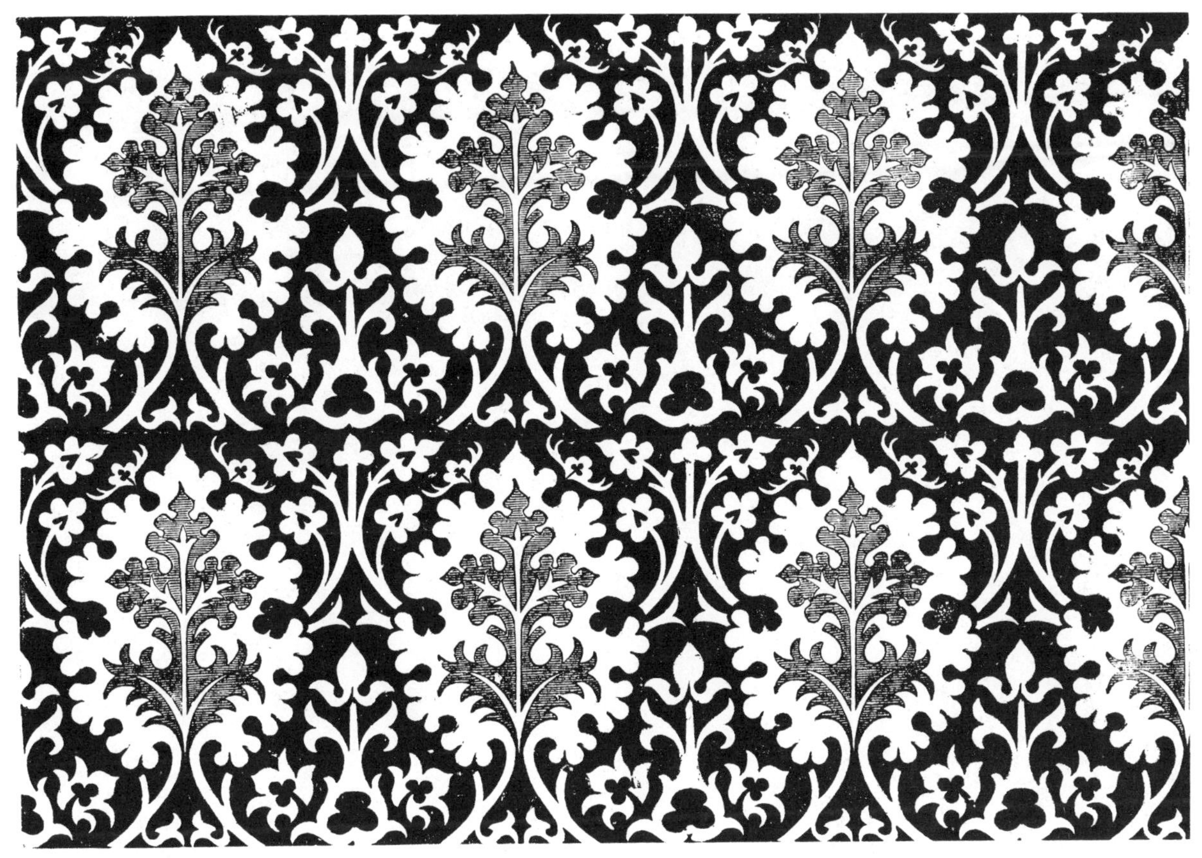

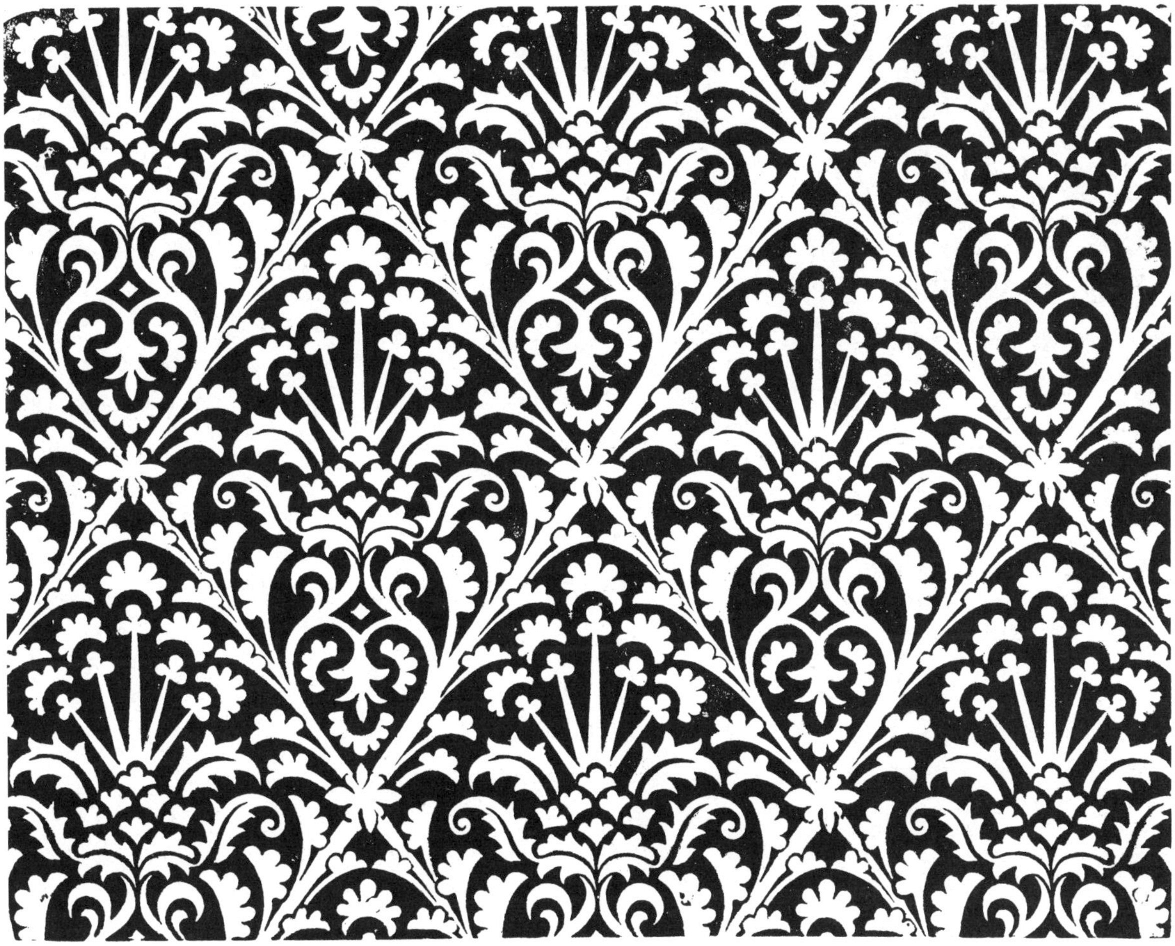

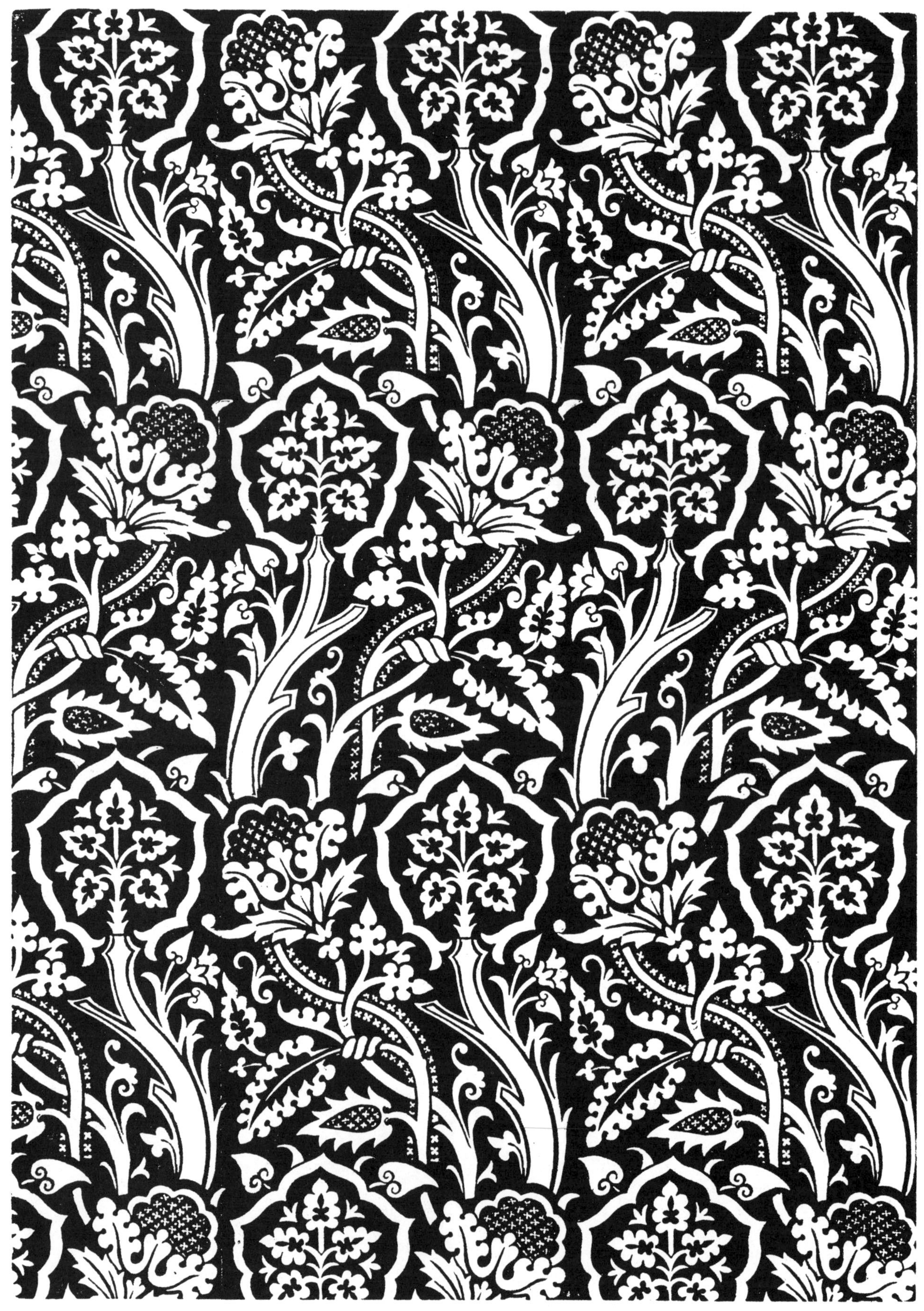

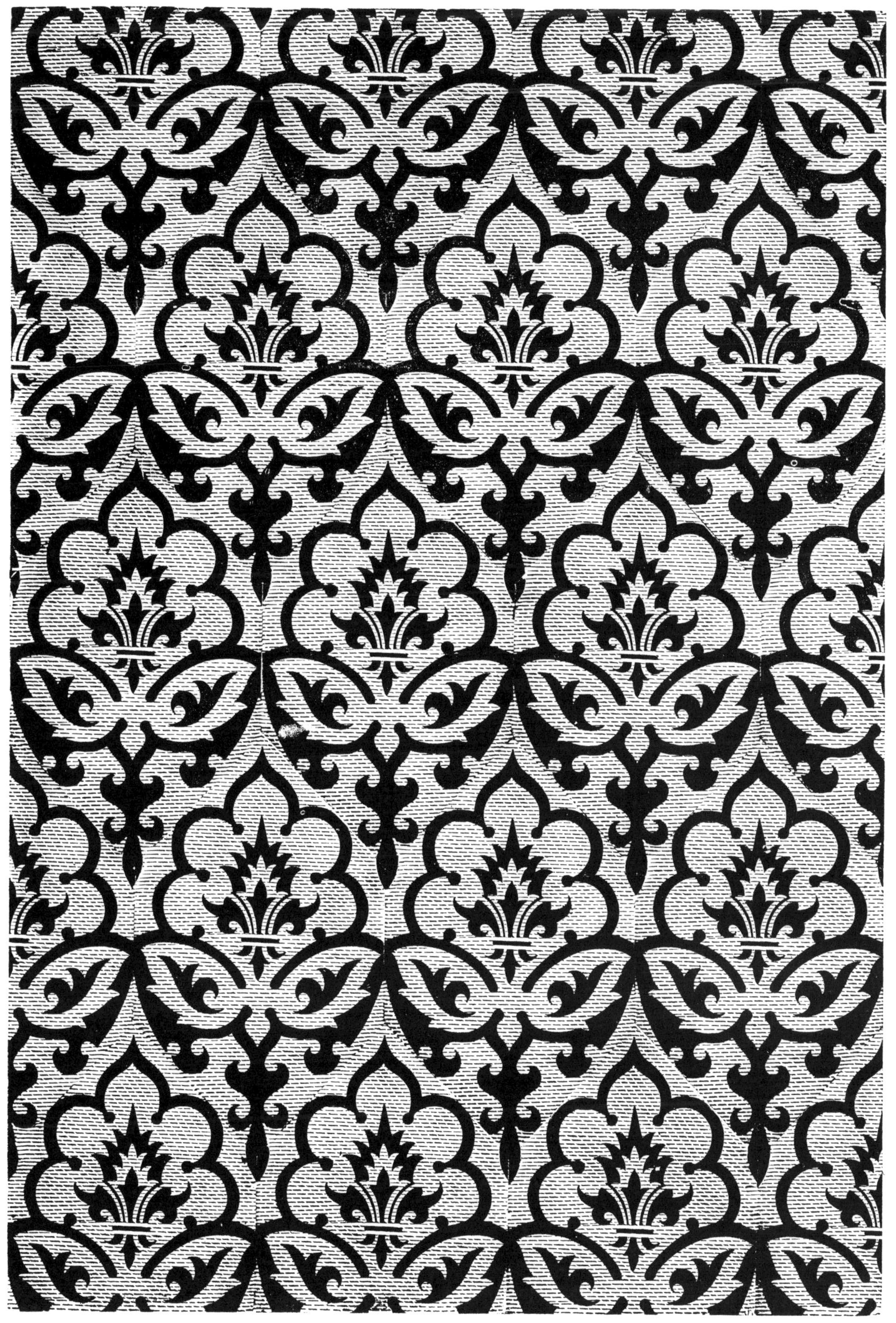

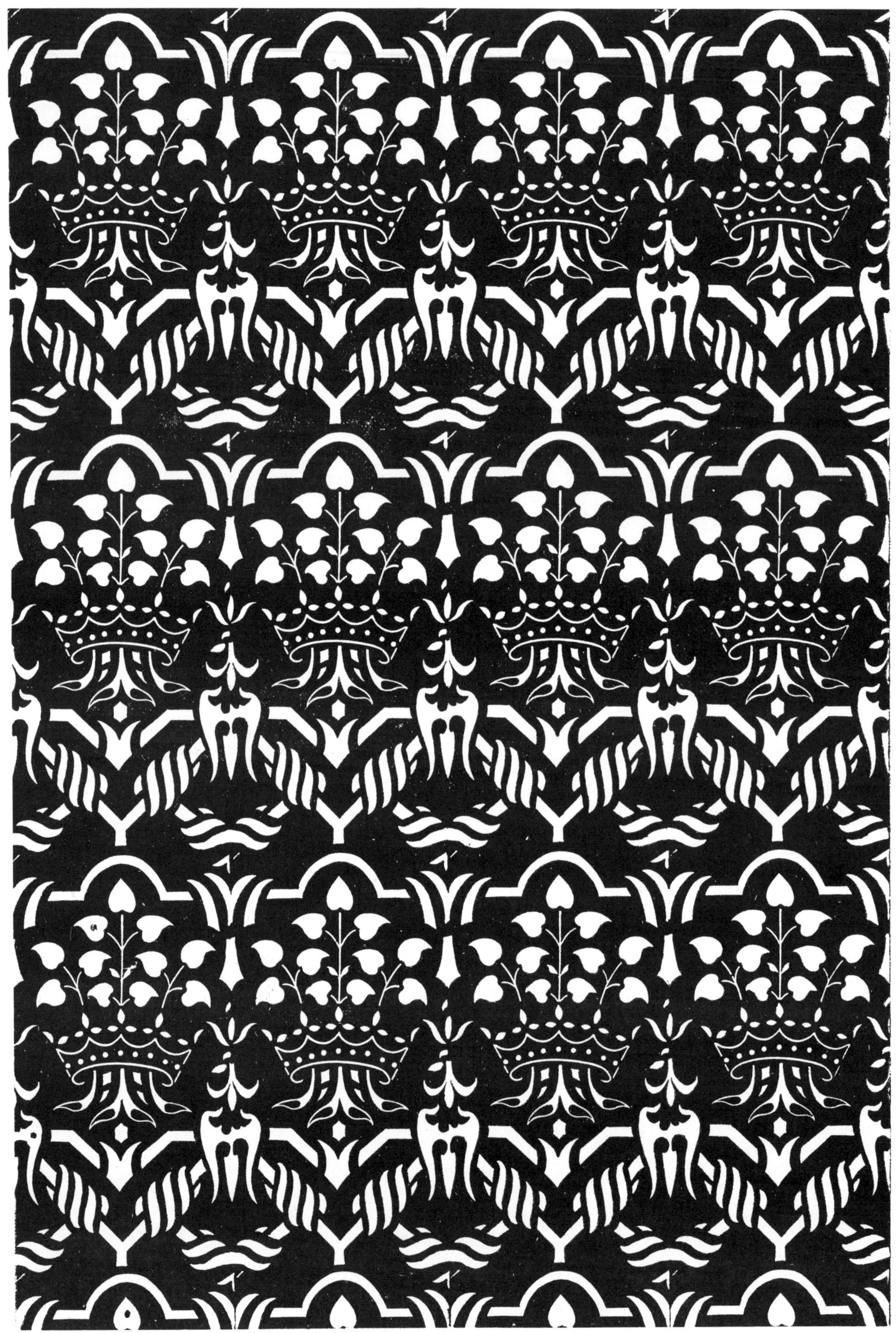

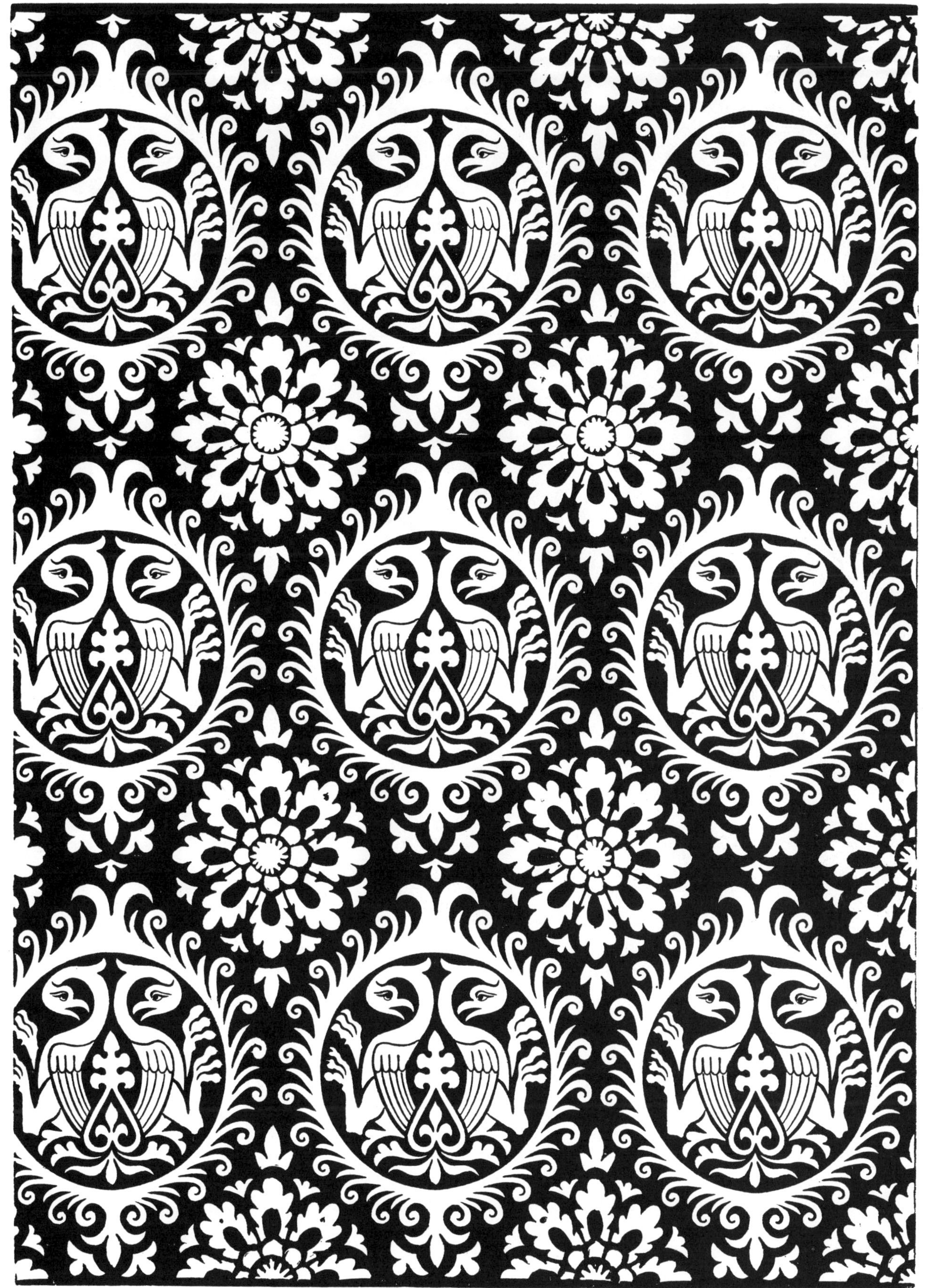

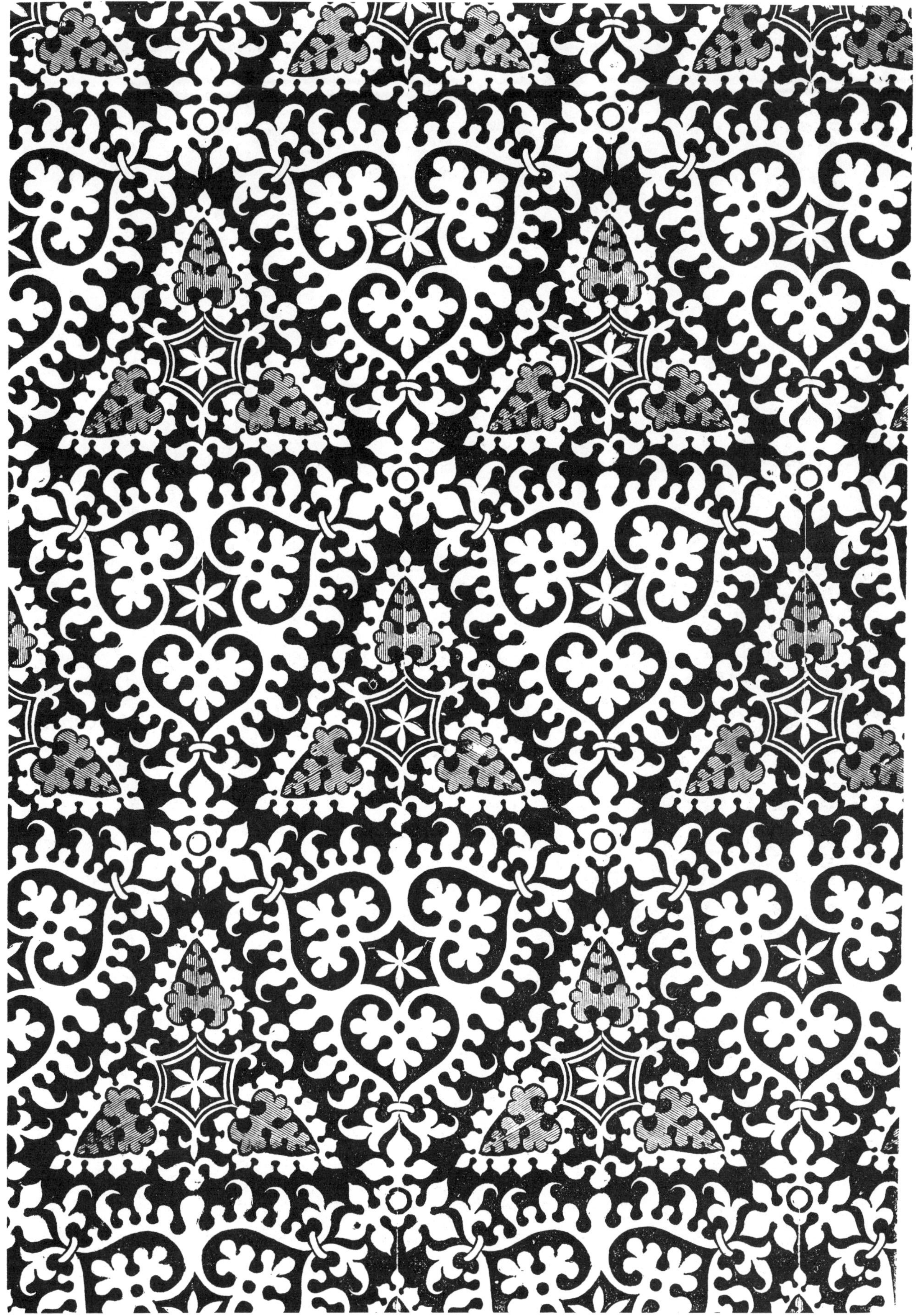

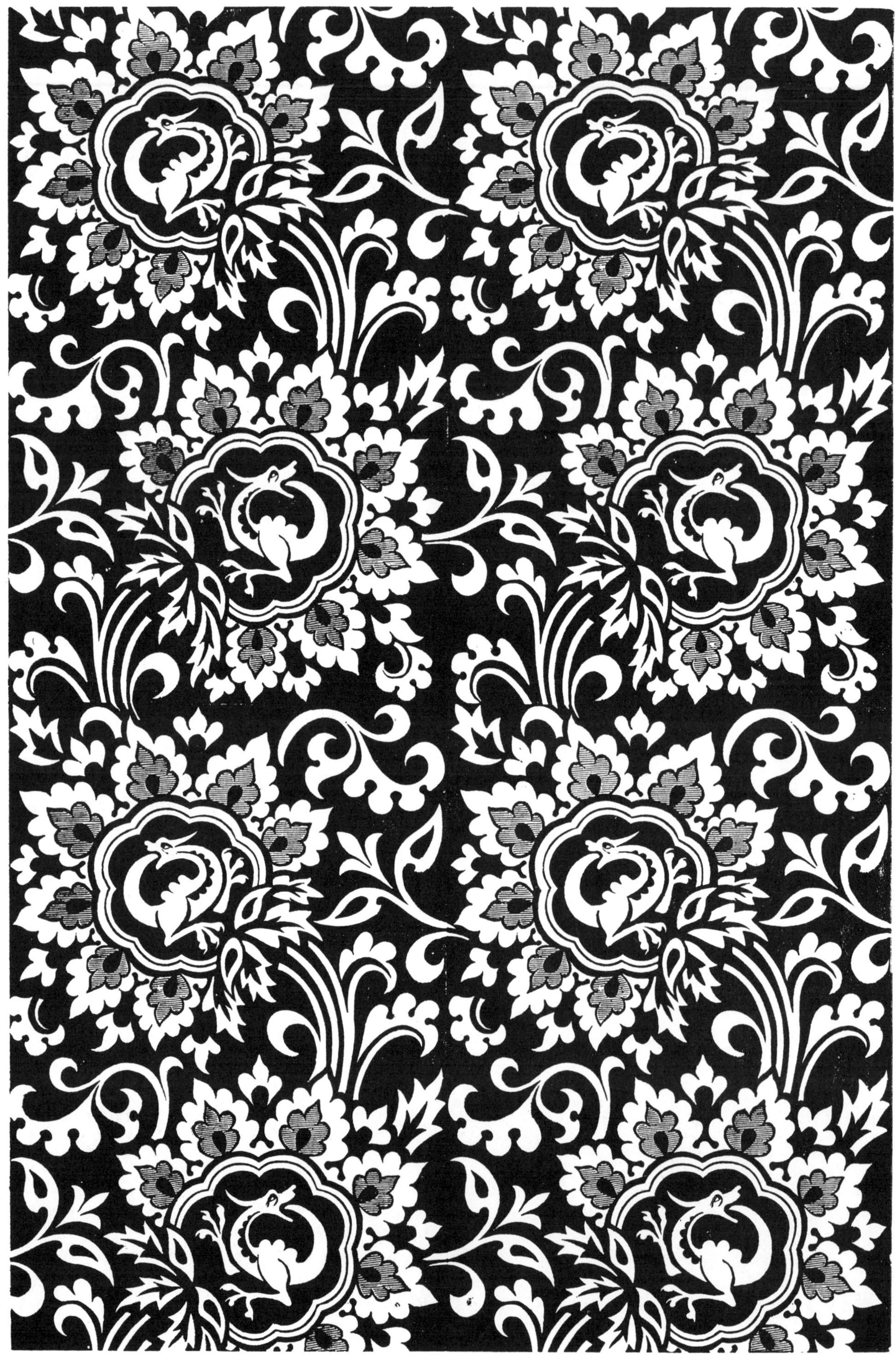

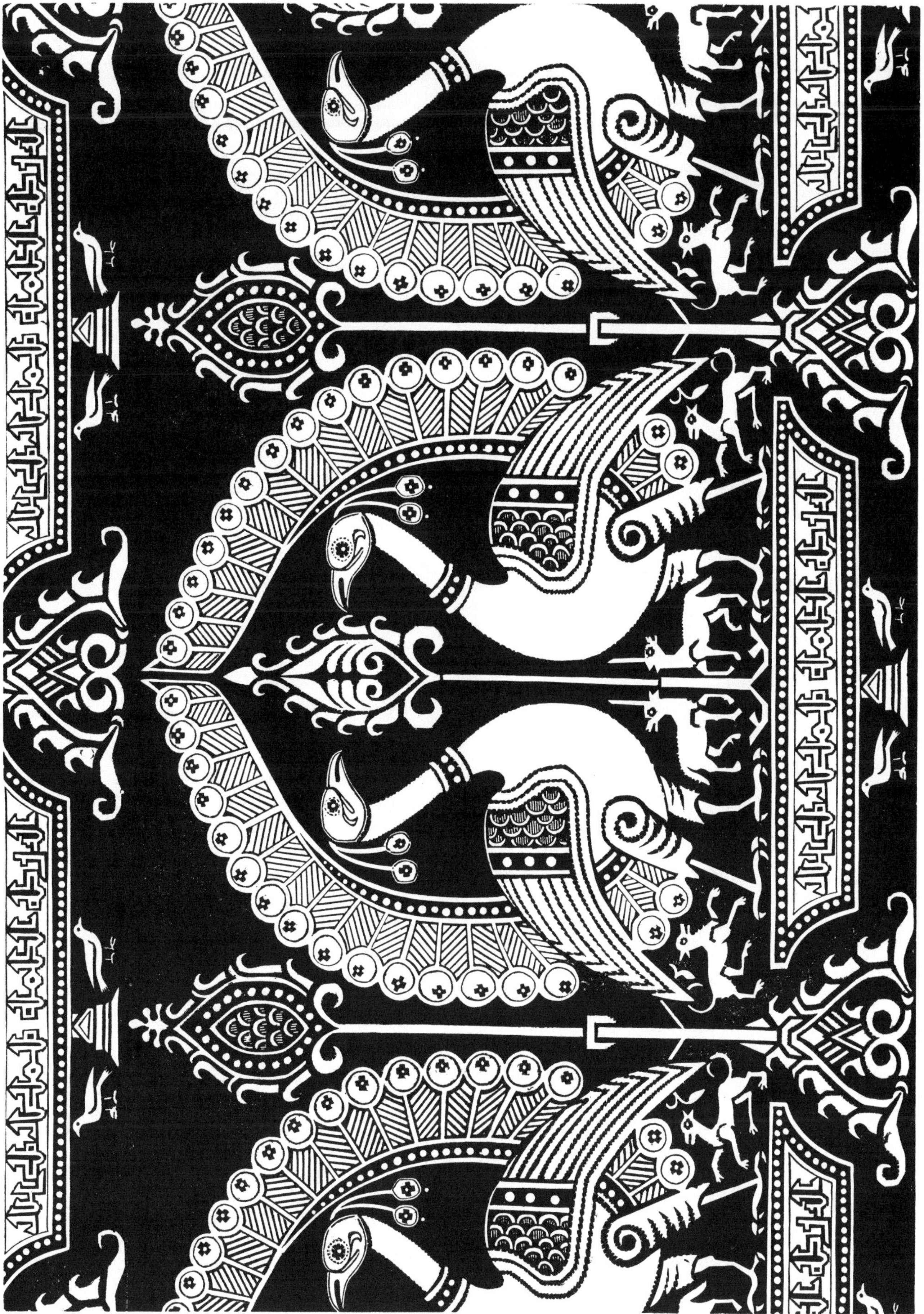

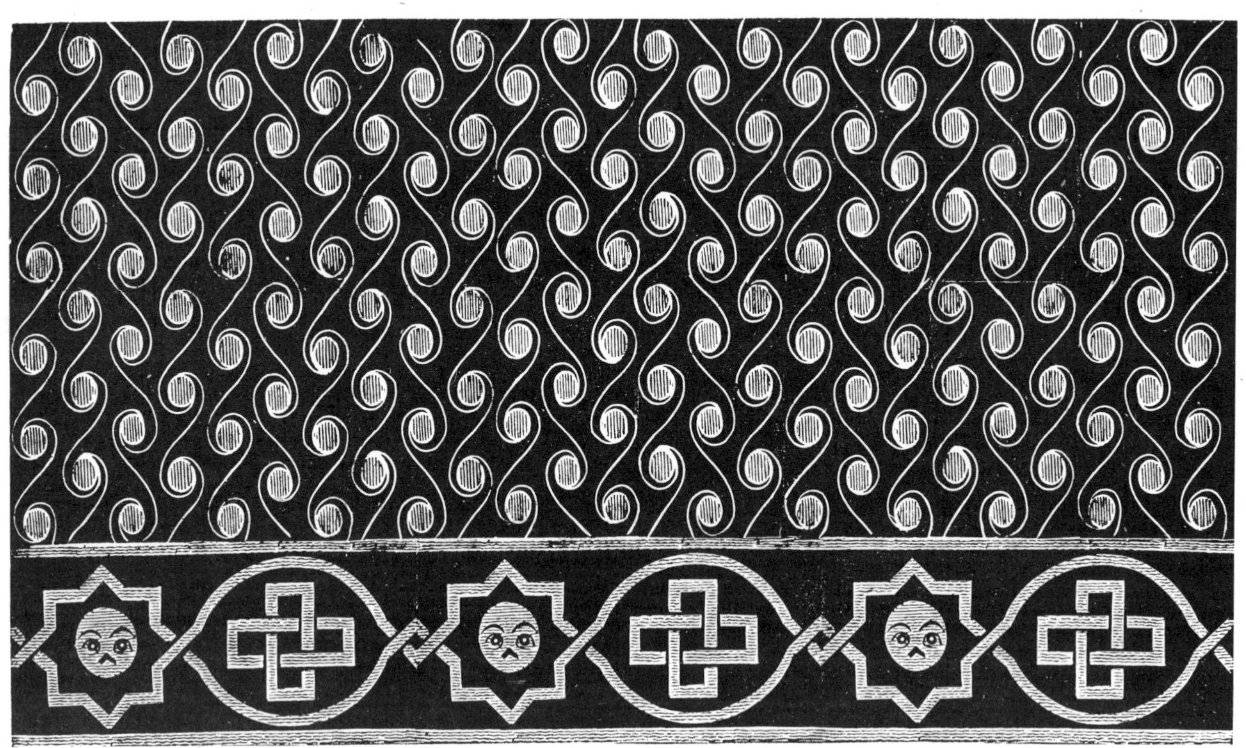

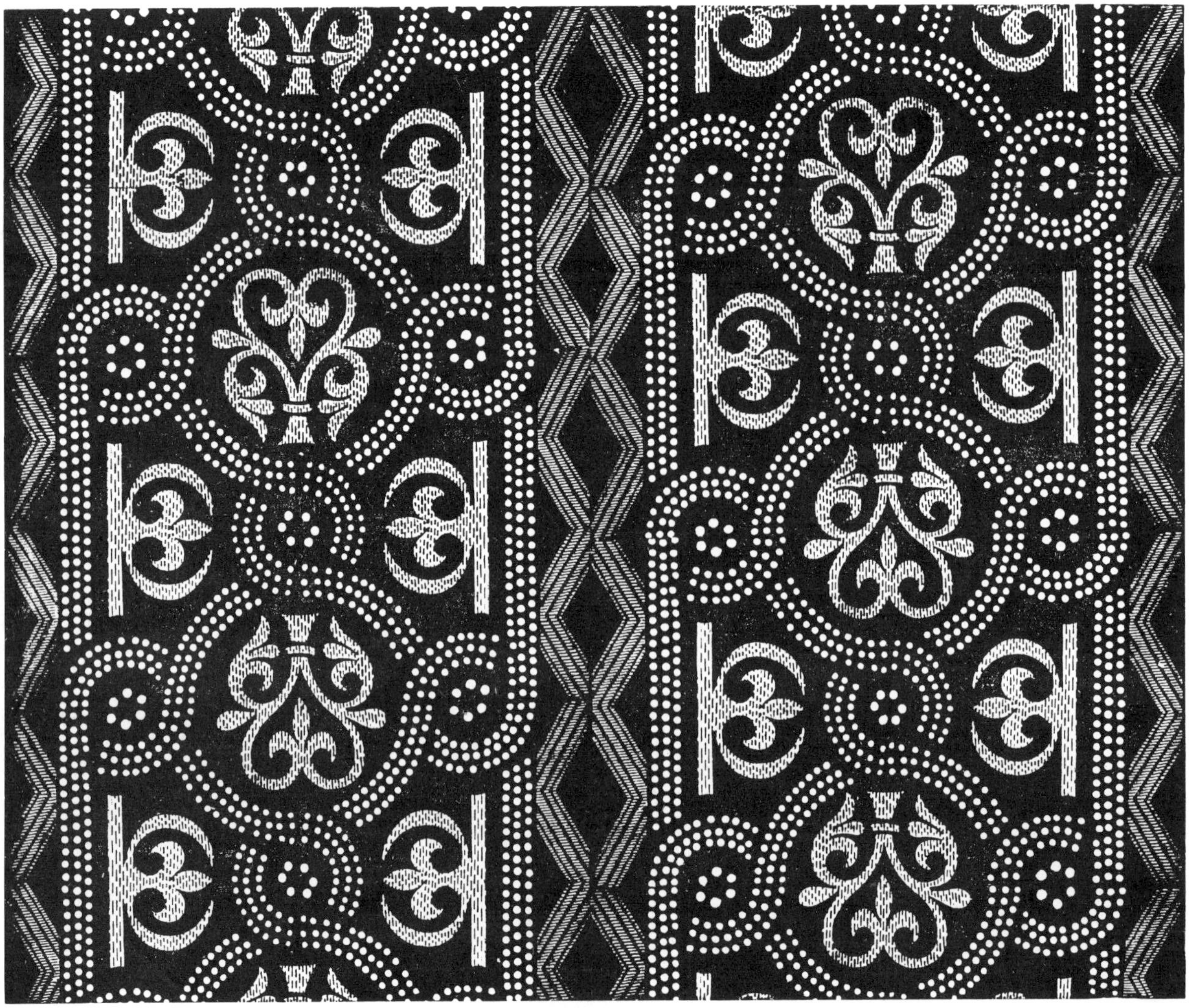